THE BATTLE FOR NORTH AFRICA

THE BATTLE FOR
NORTH AFRICA 1940–43

by
W. G. F. Jackson

with maps by Caroline Metcalfe-Gibson

*But it was in North Africa that a
really great opportunity was missed
owing to the failure of our highest
authorities to appreciate the strategic
possibilities of the African theatre.*
ROMMEL

MASON / CHARTER

To my son, Nigel Jackson, and his brother
officers in the Royal Green Jackets.

© W. G. F. Jackson 1975
ISBN 0 88405 131 5
First published in the U.S. by Mason/Charter
Publishers, Inc., 641 Lexington Ave., N.Y.C. in 1975.

Printed in Great Britain

Library of Congress Cataloging in Publication Data

Jackson, William Godfrey Fothergill, 1917-
 The battle for North Africa.

 1. World War, 1939-1945--Campaigns--Africa, North.
2. Africa, North--History--1882-   I. Title.
D766.82.J27   940.54'23   75-15807
ISBN 0-88405-131-5

CONTENTS

MAPS

SKETCH MAPS

LIST OF ILLUSTRATIONS

All the above photographs are reproduced by courtesy of the Imperial War Museum, London.

PREFACE

'The army (British and American) then in England lacked battle experience and had tended to become theoretical rather than practical. Officers did not understand those tricks of the battlefield which mean so much to junior officers and which save so many lives.'

Montgomery describing the armies in England
before 'Overlord' (Memoirs: page 217).

Military academies, staff colleges and students of war on both sides of the Atlantic will always be interested in Eisenhower's 'Overlord' invasion of Europe, but the North African Campaign, which made 'Overlord' possible, will receive less attention than it deserves because the connection between the two is not immediately obvious. The Allied sword, which Eisenhower wielded so successfully in June 1944, was forged and tempered in the long three year struggle in the deserts, mountains and jungles of Africa north and east of the Sahara. In these operations, British and American servicemen gained battle experience; staffs learnt their business; equipment was proved; and battle-winning tactics were evolved. The final phases of the North African fighting also provided the essential dress-rehearsal for 'Overlord' without which the American Chiefs of Staff, particularly General George Marshall, would not have appreciated how outclassed the American forces and their British colleagues would have been if they had tried to land in Northern France in late 1942 or early 1943 as Marshall advocated. And there is another and deeper reason for connecting the North African Campaign with 'Overlord'. Western-type democracies can rarely be ready for war. In the 1930s Britain and America were no exceptions and were forced to buy time in which to rebuild their neglected military establishments in the face of Nazi, Fascist and Japanese aggression. The narrowness of the English Channel compelled Britain to fight for time; the broad sweep of the Atlantic allowed America to buy time initially by diplomatic means. The 'Battle of Britain' fought in the air, the 'Battle of the Atlantic' fought at sea, and the 'Battle of North Africa' fought at sea, on land and in the air, were Britain's contribution to the Western World's strategic delaying action. It is just as important to study the failures – and there were more failures than successes – of British and American servicemen in Northern Africa, when they were fighting against odds, as it is to concentrate upon the halcyon days of 'Overlord' when experience and resources had been accumulated and victory was assured.

The 'North African Campaign' is the study of human endeavour as men fought with inadequate resources to make good British and American military neglect. The story falls into three distinct periods. In the first, entitled 'British Imperialism', the forces of the British Commonwealth and Empire clashed with Mussolini's 'Roman' legions and all but destroyed the Italian African Empire before the Germans could intervene. In the second period, 'German Professionalism', Rommel came almost as near to destroying the British position in the Middle East. And in the third period, 'American Materialism', American equipment and supplies and the eventual arrival of American forces in French North Africa brought the long campaign to an end with the surrender of quarter of a million Axis soldiers in Tunisia in May 1943.

Part 1

BRITISH IMPERIALISM

'In general therefore we should be ready to seize any opportunity of obtaining, without undue cost, successes against Italy which might reduce her will to fight.

Our subsequent policy should be directed to holding Germany and dealing decisively with Italy, while at the same time building up our military strength to a point at which we shall be in a position to undertake the offensive against Germany.'

Anglo-French statement of
strategic policy in September 1939.
(*Grand Strategy*: Vol II, page 10).

1

The Price of British Idealism

(1919 to 1940)

'It is to be assumed that the British Empire will not be engaged in any great war during the next ten years, and that no Expeditionary Force will be required.'

Basis of British Defence Estimates from 1919 to 1932.

The story of the North African Campaign begins with the 'No War for Ten Years' rule which was imposed by successive British Governments from 1919 to 1932. This policy was like the candy shop notice which says 'Free Sweets Tomorrow'. Tomorrow never comes; nor did the 10 year point draw any nearer as the assumption was renewed regularly each year despite changes of government. Such a financially attractive basis for military planning was hard to discredit in a democracy sickened by four years of apparently pointless slaughter during the First World War. Demands for precautionary increases in military expenditure fell on determinedly deaf ears.

The flood tide of British Imperialism reached its high water with the signature of the peace treaties at the end of the First World War. The dismemberment of the remains of the old Turkish Empire and the expulsion of German colonial administrators from Africa increased Britain's overseas commitments but gave her Empire greater security. She was able to dominate the Suez Canal bottleneck on her route to the East and ensure the safety of the Persian and Iraq oilfields on which her Navy and industries were becoming slavishly dependent. Moreover, she had become, by default, the paramount world power. The United States had returned to isolationism; France was exhausted; Germany was prostrate; and Russia was in revolutionary turmoil.

Success breeds success and also rivals. The Japanese were the first to challenge British hegemony. Their military pretensions in the Far East worried the British Chiefs of Staff, but made little impact on British politics which were more concerned with setting a good example at disarmament conferences. Britain's conversion from Victorian militarism to League of Nations' idealism was total. The shock of defeat in 1914 had made the British vow 'never again' would they be caught so unprepared. Then the grim casualty lists from 1915 to 1917 turned the struggle into 'the war to end war'. And by the time peace came in 1918, the 'never again' of unpreparedness had been translated into 'never again' another World War. It is hardly surprising that

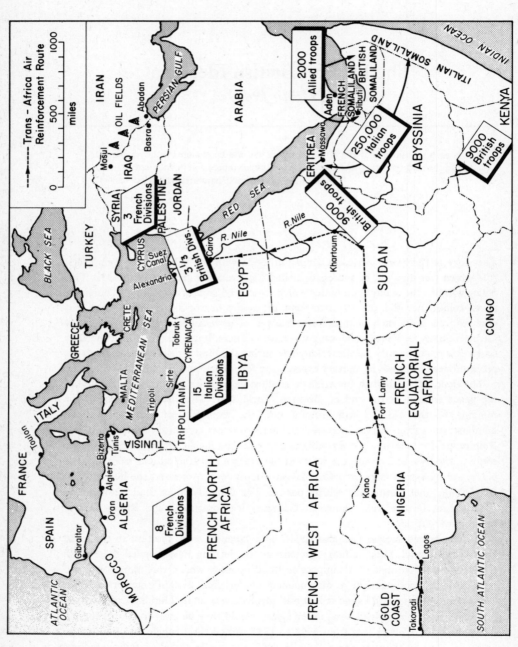

Map I: The North African Theatre

successive British Governments should mirror this deep-seated mood of the country by formulating and maintaining the 'Ten Year Rule'. Even Winston Churchill accepted its validity when he was Chancellor of the Exchequer:

It has been contended that the acceptance of this principle lulled the Fighting Departments into a false sense of security, that research was neglected and only short term views prevailed especially where expense was involved. Up till the time when I left office in 1929, I felt so hopeful that peace of the world would be maintained that I saw no reason to take any new decision; nor in the event was I proved wrong. War did not break out till the autumn of 1939.

(Churchill: Vol I, page 40).

But Churchill was wrong. Ten years were not long enough to wean the British people away from their idealism and, at the same time, to overhaul the Japanese and Germans with a major rearmament programme if they had been willing to authorise the appropriate expenditure, which, regrettably, they were not.

Germany did not join Japan as a potentially hostile power in the eyes of the British Chiefs of Staff until 1933 — only six years before the outbreak of war. In that year Hitler became Chancellor; the German delegation walked out of the Disarmament Conference; and Germany began her overt rearmament. 1933 to 1937 were what Churchill called the 'locust years' in which a half-hearted British rearmament programme was started; but, in reality, they were the years in which re-education of the British electorate was compelled by events rather than government conviction or policy. The depth of official misjudgment of the situation is illustrated by the government assessment of Mussolini's Italy at the end of 1933: 'She was friendly, in the sense that she need not be considered as an enemy; consequently no expenditure was to be incurred or any steps taken on her account'. (*British Official History*: Vol 1, page 2).

Military preparations were to be made against Germany only, but Mussolini was the first European leader to ape British Imperialism. Defying the League of Nations, he conquered Abyssinia and added Haile Selassie's backward realms to the Italian colonies of Eritrea, Somaliland and Libya to form his new 'Roman Empire'. It would have been possible for Britain to snuff out the whole enterprise by closing the Suez Canal. Britain did reinforce her Mediterranean Fleet; she did impose sanctions; and she was prepared to take extreme measures; but she found herself unsupported by the other members of the League. The long-term implications of the failure of the world's collective security organisation were as obvious in London as they were in Berlin, Rome and Tokio. The main prop of British idealism had been knocked away and replaced by the realisation that rearmament was unavoidable. At the end of 1935 the British Chiefs of Staff gave the first of their 'Three Power Enemy' warnings to their Government:

. . . the danger of the simultaneous hostility of Germany, Japan and Italy, they said, emphasised the need for allies, and especially for friendship with France. It was necessary, in their view, not to be estranged from any Mediterranean power

that lay athwart our main artery of communication with the east . . . The Cabinet
agreed: Germany and Japan constituted far likelier threats, and it was hoped that
relations with Italy could be improved by diplomatic means.

(Ibid: page 5).

The efforts of British diplomacy to win back Italian friendship were doomed from the
start. The Italian people would have welcomed a rapprochement with Britain.
Mussolini's dreams of imperial glory stood in the way. Each time the British Foreign
Office had some success Italy's Fascist government plunged into a new adventure
alien to British interests. The climax came in January 1937 when, in spite of Italy's
involvement in the Spanish civil war, the two Governments signed the Anglo-Italian
Joint Declaration, or 'Gentlemen's Agreement', pledging both countries to respect
each other's interests. The subsequent torpedoing of British ships off Spanish ports by
what could only have been Italian submarines; hostile references to Britain in the
Italian press by high ranking military officers; and derogatory broadcasts to Arab
countries under British protection, all led the British Government to conclude
regretfully 'that Italy could no longer be regarded as a reliable friend'. The ban on
financial expenditure on defensive measures against Italy was lifted just two years
from the outbreak of war with the militarily restrictive proviso that nothing was to be
done which could be construed by the Italians as provocative. Diplomacy was to
remain the principal means of meeting the Italian threat until British forces in the
Mediterranean could be strengthened.

Towards the end of 1937, two events made the British Chiefs of Staff renew their
'Three Power Enemy' warning. Italy joined Germany and Japan in the
Anti-Comintern Pact, and then left the League of Nations. The British Chiefs of Staff
added an ominous rider to their renewed warning:

> Without overlooking the help we should hope to receive from France and from
> other possible allies, they could not foresee the time when our defence forces would
> be strong enough to safeguard our territory, trade and vital interests against
> Germany, Italy and Japan simultaneously. They therefore emphasised the
> importance, from the point of view of Imperial Defence, of any diplomatic action
> that would reduce the number of our potential enemies and give us allies.

(Ibid: page 11).

Measures were being put in hand to reinforce British Naval, Army and Air Forces in
the Mediterranean when, quite unexpectedly, the chances of improving relations with
Italy brightened. Hitler invaded Austria without taking Mussolini into his confidence.
British diplomacy was quick to profit by Italian hostility to the arrival of German
troops on the Brenner Pass. The abortive 'Gentlemen's Agreement' of 1937 was
re-affirmed and a new 'Bon Voisinage' Agreement was signed to regulate
Anglo-Italian relations in Africa. These marginal diplomatic successes were soon lost
in the swirling currents of the Munich crisis when Britain was forced to swallow her
pride and accept that she was neither psychologically nor materially ready for war
with the dictatorships. By the turn of the year Chamberlain's scrap of paper, which

was 'to give us peace in our time', was seen to be worthless. The Cabinet authorised the Chiefs of Staff in February 1939 to approach their French colleagues to prepare plans:

> On the basis of war against Germany and Italy in combination – possibly joined by Japan – and the scope should include all likely fields of operations, especially in the Mediterranean and the Middle East.
>
> *(Ibid:* page 20–21).

Military planning for what was to become the 'Battle for Northern Africa' started with this directive.

*   *   *

When the Anglo-French military planners reviewed their combined resources and those of the hostile powers, they had little difficulty in agreeing that they must prepare for a long war. Germany, Italy and Japan had achieved a substantial lead in their military preparations. On the other hand, their assets were limited. Provided they did not succeed in enforcing a quick victory when war broke out, they would be overwhelmed in the long run by the weight of resources gathered in from the British and French Empires. The general strategy formulated by the Anglo-French planners envisaged:

> . . . a war in three phases. The first would be one of preserving as far as possible the integrity of Allied territory and of defending vital interests. The second would be one of holding Germany and dealing with Italy; meanwhile Allied military strength would be built up until such time as a major offensive strategy became possible. Command of the sea would enable economic pressure to be applied from the outset, and would later confer freedom of choice in striking at the enemy's most vulnerable points. Italy was so obviously the weaker partner that counter-offensive operations against her in North Africa were expected early in the war. The final phase of the war would be the defeat of Germany.
>
> *(British Official History: The Mediterranean and the Middle East:* Vol 1, page 23).

This strategic concept was to stand the test of time, although Britain lost her principal ally, France, and gained another, the United States, in the process. The British Cabinet gave their approval in 1939; and the US Government subsequently endorsed it in a modified form when the United States entered the war in 1941.

The high level Anglo-French talks were followed in May and June 1939 by regional talks held at Rabat, Aden and Jerusalem. The military situation in North Africa, the Levant and the Mediterranean is shown at Map I on page 2.

In general terms the French were politically dominant in the west, while the British exerted the greater influence in the east. France garrisoned her North African territories of Morocco, Algeria and Tunisia with eight colonial divisions; and had other lighter forces in her West-African and Equatorial territories. Her strong

Mediterranean Fleet controlled the western basin of the Mediterranean from Toulon, Mers-el-Kebir (Oran) and Bizerta, while the only British forces in the west were the small garrisons and dockyard facilities of Gibraltar and Malta.

In the Eastern Mediterranean and East Africa the Allied strengths were more equal but by mutual consent the British took the lead. The French had a substantial garrison equivalent to two infantry divisions in Syria and a small force holding Jibuti in French Somaliland. The centre of gravity of the British position lay in Egypt, astride the Suez Canal. Egypt had nominally become an independent sovereign state in 1922. While the Egyptians were keen to end certain reserved rights held by the British, they had no wish to exchange British for Italian or German occupation. In 1936 a new Anglo-Egyptian Treaty of Alliance was ratified by which the British forces were to be withdrawn to the immediate vicinity of the Canal, and Egypt for her part undertook to improve communications, ports and airfields for the joint defence of Egypt by British and Egyptian forces. There was no guarantee that Egypt would necessarily declare war unless she herself were attacked. British forces in Egypt consisted of the under-strength and partially equipped 7th Armoured Division in the Western Desert and an infantry brigade in Cairo. There were about two divisions worth of troops fighting Arab terrorists in Palestine and lightly equipped local forces in Trans-Jordan, Iraq, the Sudan, British Somaliland and Kenya. Cyprus, Aden and British stations in the Persian Gulf had small garrisons. Britain's main contribution to the military security of the eastern basin lay in her powerful Mediterranean Fleet which had moved its base from Malta to Alexandria for greater security in event of war with Italy. Both the British and French air forces were small, widely dispersed and generally equipped with obsolescent aircraft. They were not expected to influence the military balance in North Africa.

There were two potential areas for land operations against the Italians. Marshal Balbo had 15 Italian and locally raised Libyan divisions in Tripolitania and Cyrenaica where they were centrally placed to attack or be attacked by the numerically inferior French forces in Tunisia and British troops in the Western Desert of Egypt. The Duke of Aosta, the Italian Viceroy of Abyssinia, had 250,000 mixed Italian and colonial troops, consolidating Mussolini's recent East African conquests, which could invade the Sudan, British and French Somaliland or Kenya whose frontiers were garrisoned by a meagre 20,000 British and French colonial troops. The Italian position looked remarkably strong and its strength was artificially enhanced by the barrage of Italian propaganda which was made credible in the eyes of the local peoples by the obvious numerical superiority of the Italian forces, by their recent victories in Abyssinia, and by the weak appeasing attitudes of the British and French Governments. Nevertheless, the Anglo-French military planners were well aware of the cracks and weaknesses in the Fascist façade. Italy's economic position was shaky and growing more so as the heavy costs of her aggressive foreign policy accumulated. She had been on a war footing since 1935 and could not sustain the renewed rearmament effort which Mussolini was determined to thrust upon her. Her position at sea was as superficially impressive as it was on land. Her ships were well built, well armed and fast, and her large number of submarines constituted a real threat to shipping in the Mediterranean and Red Sea. Nevertheless, the Italian Navy was out-numbered by the Anglo-French fleets, and had neither the operational experience nor the naval tradition to present a significant challenge. The Italian Air Force also had its weaknesses. It did have numerical superiority, but it had reached its peak of readiness for war in 1936. Most of its aircraft were out-of-date by German standards, though ahead of the British and French types in service in the Mediterranean, and its reserves were known to be low. Bearing all these factors in mind, the Anglo-French planners recommended an offensive strategy at sea to isolate and eventually starve the numerically superior Italian armies and air forces ashore in Africa.

While the Anglo-French staff talks had been in progress the slide to war had gained momentum. At the end of March 1939 Britain and France guaranteed the integrity of Poland. A week later Mussolini invaded Albania without warning Hitler. Britain and France responded with guarantees for Rumania and Greece. Germany and Italy allied themselves officially in the 'Pact of Steel', bringing the Rome-Berlin Axis into being. And on 21 August the world was startled by the announcement of the Soviet-German Non-Aggression Pact. War was certain, and in a much wider arena than had been contemplated so far. A new dimension had been added to the North African Theatre. A German approach was now possible, with Russian agreement, through the Balkans and Turkey to the Suez Canal and the Iraq and Persian oilfields; and a complementary Soviet thrust could sweep through Persia and Afghanistan to the north-west frontier of India.

The British Chiefs of Staff had appreciated for some time that their command structure in the Middle East was inadequate to meet a threat of this magnitude. The man they selected to take over as Commander-in-Chief Middle East was General Sir Archibald Wavell, who was to be responsible for all British land operations from the Balkans in the North to Kenya in the South, and from the Western Desert of Egypt in the West to the Persian Gulf in the East – a vast command. He was to co-operate closely with Admiral Sir Andrew Cunningham, Commander-in-Chief of the British Mediterranean Fleet, and with Air Marshal Sir Arthur Longmore, Air Officer Commanding-in-Chief of the British Middle East Air Forces. Wavell, Cunningham and Longmore were to constitute the Commanders-in-Chief Committee, Middle East, and were, in effect, the British High Command responsible for military policy in the coming North African Campaign. In theory they were co-equal; none was even *primus inter pares*. They were jointly responsible to the Chiefs of Staff in London, who were themselves responsible to the War Cabinet. There was no supreme commander, but Wavell acted as permanent chairman and so wielded greatest influence. Wavell and Longmore had their headquarters in Cairo to be near the Ambassador and Egyptian Government, but Cunningham was forced to keep his headquarters at Alexandria so that he could go to sea with his fleet as British naval tradition demanded when a major fleet action seemed likely. Co-ordination was achieved through a small joint planning staff and a joint intelligence centre. Unsatisfactory though this organisation may appear to be today, it was a great advance on anything seen in the First World War.

Wavell took up his appointment in Cairo on 2 August 1939, just a month before the outbreak of war with Germany. He had extensive operational experience in the First World War, first in France and then under Allenby in the Palestine campaign against the Turks. He was a man of paradox. On the one hand, he was a Winchester scholar, a lover and writer of poetry and an author of repute; while on the other, he was a tough regimental soldier, an excellent staff officer and a man who knew his own mind. Surprisingly, in spite of his clear brain and lucidity on paper, he found himself at a disadvantage in debate; and, although he had a light-hearted approach to life, he could be taciturn and uncommunicative. It is a tragedy that he and Churchill never found common ground upon which their great intellects could meet because their strategic policies were in harmony. They were both 'Easterners' at heart, and believed in the traditional British peripheral strategy in dealing with continental powers. Before he took over command he set out his thoughts in a short appreciation concluding:

> The last war was won in the West ... The next war will be won or lost in the Mediterranean; and the longer it takes us to secure effective control of the Mediterranean, the harder will the winning of the war be.
>
> (J. Connell: *Wavell*, page 211).

Admiral Cunningham, another confirmed 'Easterner', believed in the strategic importance of the Mediterranean. He had, like Wavell, a distinguished record in the First World War, winning three DSOs while taking part in naval operations in the Mediterranean, including supporting the Army at Gallipoli and Salonika. He was a fine seaman, steeped in the traditions of the Royal Navy, and a firm believer in offensive action, but he was a man who depended more upon military judgement based on an accumulation of battle experience than upon intellectual ability. In his autobiography he records his view of the policy to be pursued:

> My considered opinion ... was that, if Libya was completely cut off and the Italians there were kept fighting, it was most likely that Libya, Eritrea, Abyssinia and Italian Somaliland would be out of the war in six months. I further believed that the surrender of the Italian Army in Libya, coupled with naval attacks on the Italian coast in places where material damage could be done, would have a great moral effect and might well cause the Italians to lose heart and think that they had had enough.
>
> (*Sailor's Odyssey*, page 210).

Air Marshal Longmore had started his service as an aviator in the Royal Navy and was also dedicated to offensive action. He was a less complex character than Wavell and Cunningham and saw his aim in simpler terms: 'to reduce this (the Italian Air Force's) potential superiority at the outset by an immediate offensive against aircraft, fuel, supplies, air bases and maintenance facilities'. (British Official History: Vol 1, page 41).

The triumvirate met for the first time on board HMS *Warspite*, Admiral Cunningham's flagship, in Alexandria Harbour on 18 August. They recorded that they felt a lack of a comprehensive plan to govern the action of the three Services, and decided to examine the possibilities of taking offensive action against the Italians in Libya and of improving the security of shipping in the Red Sea. Their ideas met with an immediate rebuff from the Chiefs of Staff in London, who reiterated the Government's view that 'Italy's neutrality would be decidedly preferable to her active hostility, and urged that no attempt should be made to compel her to declare her position if this would be likely to bring her in against us'. (*Ibid*: page 39).

Wavell seems to have been remarkably badly briefed by the Foreign Service representatives in Cairo about British diplomatic efforts in Italy, and of the delicate balance in Italian foreign policy. Count Ciano, Mussolini's Foreign Minister and son-in-law, led a strong anti-war and anti-German faction in the Fascist hierarchy which had the support of the King. The erratic nature of Italy's relations with Britain was caused primarily by Mussolini's personal inconsistencies. He had no wish to play second fiddle to Hitler, and yet he could not bring himself to break with his fellow dictator. Ciano's diary of 13 August 1939 records:

> I return to Rome completely disgusted with the Germans, with their leader, with their way of doing things. They have betrayed us and lied to us. Now they are dragging us into an adventure which we do not want and which may compromise the regime and the country as a whole . . . The Duce's reactions are varied. At first he agrees with me. Then he says that honour compels him to march with Germany . . .
>
> (*Ciano*: page 125).

Italy's unpreparedness for war is clearly put by Ciano in a further entry dated 24 August. 'The Army is in a pitiful state. The military review and manoeuvres have fully revealed the unhappy state of unpreparedness of all our major formations . . .' (*Ibid*: page 133).

The British Ambassador, Sir Percy Loraine, had established a close understanding with Ciano and was well aware of Italy's desire to avoid war with her former ally, Great Britain. Knowing that Italy's actions depended upon Mussolini's whims rather than closely debated political decisions, he appreciated the need to avoid provocation more clearly than Wavell. It is to Loraine's credit that Italy remained neutral when Britain declared war on Germany. In the last week of August Mussolini struggled with the conflict of conscience and ambition. On 26 August, he presented a long list of his requirements to Hitler: 17,000 vehicles and a total of 17,000,000 tons of supplies – coal, iron, timber, oil and cereals. When Hitler explained that these could not be met and said that he proposed to annihilate Poland and beat France and England without Italian help, Mussolini decided to 'stand looking out of the window'. (*Ciano*: page 135–136).

Much strategic uncertainty was removed when Chamberlain's ultimatum to Germany expired and Britain declared war on 3 September 1939. Italy adopted a policy of non-belligerency favourable to Nazi Germany; and the United States took up a similar stance favourable to the Allies. The British and French forces in the Mediterranean were given valuable breathing space of which they made better use than the Italians. And in America, President Roosevelt began his long and difficult struggle to persuade isolationist elements that their country's best interests lay in helping the British and the French democracies to resist Nazi aggression. In his first speech he said: 'This nation will remain a neutral nation, but I cannot ask that every American remain neutral in thought as well. Even a neutral cannot be asked to close his mind or his conscience . . .' (Robert E. Sherbrook: *White House Papers*, Vol 1, page 127).

Other uncertainties were removed. The Dominions of the British Commonwealth, although politically independent in every way, entered the war in quick succession of their own accord. Australia and New Zealand declared war on the same day as Great Britain; South Africa followed suit on 6 September with the proviso that her forces were only to be used within 'South Africa' – a term which General Smuts later stretched to include Kenya and eventually the Western Desert of Egypt by sending only volunteers to serve there. Canada entered the war on 10 September, her Expeditionary Force being directed towards Europe rather than the Mediterranean.

Encouraging though this response had been, it highlighted the greatest weakness in Britain's preparation for war. She found that she could not equip all the men coming forward from her own shires, let alone from the Commonwealth and Empire as well. In March 1939 she had doubled her Territorial Army to create an Expeditionary Force to support the French on the Western Front – a measure which the planning assumptions of the 'Ten Year Rule' had specifically stated was unnecessary. It was decided to ship contingents from India, Australia, New Zealand and South Africa to Wavell's command as they became available so that they could train and acclimatise themselves in desert and tropical conditions while their equipment was being manufactured in the United Kingdom and shipped to the Middle East. Scarcity of equipment remained one of the limiting factors in the North African Campaign until the Autumn of 1942 when US equipment began to arrive in adequate quantities.

The German and Soviet partition of Poland in the Autumn of 1939 seemed to point to German aggression being aimed towards south-eastern Europe. Wavell and his French colleague in Syria – General Weygand – spent many discouraging weeks trying to reach a satisfactory arrangement with the Turks to help counter the German threat through the Balkans if it materialised in the spring. Shortage of equipment was again a stumbling block. However much the British and French Governments might wish to bring the Turks into the war on their side, no way could be found for doing so without meeting the Turkish demand for the re-equipment of their forces with modern weapons. The Turks would, quite understandably, go no further than signing new treaties of mutual assistance until such time as the Allies could meet their equipment demands, particularly anti-aircraft guns.

During December the British Chiefs of Staff took stock of the strategic situation. Wavell went back to London to put the Middle East point of view. He was not too successful. The Chiefs of Staff acknowledged the weakness of the forces at his disposal, and the fact that his theatre had no indigenous resources other than oil. They made it clear that in their view the Western Front and Singapore must be given priority over the Middle East, but they acknowledged that no major offensive operations could be mounted by Wavell until an adequate logistic base had been established in Egypt. They directed that no more reinforcing formations should be sent to the Middle East until a base capable of supporting nine divisions had been built up. A similar policy was to be followed by the Royal Air Force which would concentrate on improving the logistic mobility of its existing air squadrons before any more were sent to Egypt. The Royal Navy would fare no better. Most of Admiral Cunningham's ships, including his flagship, HMS *Warspite,* would be withdrawn for service elsewhere as circumstances demanded.

Wavell returned to Cairo very depressed. He wrote at the time:

> I thought the policy of doing nothing whatever that could annoy the Italians – in appeasement, in fact – quite misguided. I was allowed to send no agents into Italian territory, though all our territories were full of Italian agents, to do nothing to get in touch with the Abyssinian rebels, and so on. Meanwhile stores continued to pass through the Suez Canal to Italian East Africa, and we even continued under a pre-war agreement to inform the Italians of our reinforcements to Middle East . . .

(J. Connell: *Wavell,* page 220).

Britain was still only half-heartedly at war. The well-meaning Chamberlain had not yet been replaced by Churchill. At the beginning of March new and hostile winds began to blow. Hitler and Mussolini met on the Brenner Pass. The tone of Italian propaganda sharpened. New age groups of Italian reservists were called up and the Italian garrison of Libya was strengthened. The Chiefs of Staff began to consider what measures should be taken to frighten Mussolini back into neutrality. They concluded that not much could be done on land or in the air where the Italians held the advantage. Naval pressure might be effective.

Orders had just been given to reinforce Cunningham when the ice of the Phoney War was suddenly broken by the German invasion of Norway. On 21 April Mussolini delivered a raucous anti-Allied speech with the theme 'Work and Weapons'. On 23 April the Allied Governments re-affirmed that it was still their policy not to provoke Italy but to be ready if she became an aggressor. The British instituted precautionary measures including the move of the 7th Armoured Division to its war stations in the Western Desert of Egypt. The French took similar action. On 14 May HMS *Warspite* returned from Norway and rejoined the Mediterranean Fleet. Cunningham hoisted his flag in her again and made ready for war.

The final steps in the slow approach to the North African Campaign were being taken by both sides. In May 1940 no-one – not even the Germans – knew how grossly the military balance of power had been upset by the lead won by Germany in her rearmament programme and by the blind determination of the governments of the idealistic Western Democracies to show that the First World War had been the 'war to end all wars'.

2

The Hollowness of the Italian Challenge
(May to September 1940)

'On the 10th day of June the hand that held the dagger has plunged it into the back of his neighbour.'

Roosevelt's Charlottesville Speech on 10 June 1940.

No general is worthy of his steel until he has experienced the bitterness of defeat; and no democracy can be true to itself until it has closed its ranks in the face of national disaster. The British and French democracies were tried by fire in the Spring of 1940. The British found a leader, closed their ranks and fought on; the French did not. The unexpected success of the German 'Blitzkrieg' on the Western Front brought reality to an unreal world. It showed with brutal clarity the changes which had been taking place in the political and military balances of power during the inter-war years. No one had been able to gauge the true state of post-Versailles Europe until military operations tore away the veils of propaganda and wishful thinking. When the clash of arms occurred in May 1940, German power became obvious to the world, and, with some surprise, to the Germans themselves. It paralysed the French; hurried the Italians, who feared they might miss their share of the spoils; worried the Americans, who felt powerless to intervene; and it made the British realise the peril of their position. The time which the British would now have to buy before they could re-establish their national security seemed infinite. The added threat of an Italian declaration of war could not make their position much worse.

Wavell, in Cairo, wrote a personal appreciation in his own handwriting on 24 May as the news of disasters in France began to reach the Middle East. In a paragraph headed 'Worst Possible Case' he postulated:

. . . UK in a state of siege and subject to heavy bombing attacks.

Middle East cut off and attacked by Italy, supported perhaps by German air or troops.

Egyptians and other people of the Middle East frightened, unfriendly and hostile.

We have to maintain our position in Egypt by force, i.e. by declaring martial law and taking over the country.

We might have anti-British rising in Iraq. Should we try and maintain position there or evacuate temporarily?

Should we try to hold Basra, or ask India to do so?

We might possibly evacuate Somaliland.

Aden must be held . . .

(J. Connell: *Wavell*, pages 229–230).

Mussolini took a political decision to go to war in the first week of May, just before the Germans opened their attack in the West. His meeting with Hitler at the Brenner Pass persuaded him that he could prevaricate no longer if he was to have any voice in the eventual reorganisation of Europe.

On 10 June, as the German Armies reached the Seine west of Paris and the French Government left its capital for Tours, Mussolini announced the coming declaration of war from the balcony of the Palazzo Venezia. At 4.45 pm that afternoon Ciano informed the British Ambassador that the King of Italy would consider himself at war with the United Kingdom at a minute past midnight. The Ambassador asked if this was a declaration of war. Ciano replied that it was. When midnight came nothing happened. No Italian Armies sprang forward; no Italian battle fleet left port; and no Italian bombers sought out vital British or French targets. There were no Italian war plans worthy of the name.

The British Cs-in-C in Cairo had been watching events in Europe with growing anxiety. They had suspected since early May that Italy was on the verge of intervention. As the German offensive in France gathered momentum, so the chances of Italy deciding to profit by Germany's successes grew, and their own hopes of receiving reinforcements diminished. They were, however, far from dismayed at the prospect of the Italian entry into the war. Wavell wrote another short appreciation:

THE POSITION – MAY 1940

1. Oil, shipping, air power, sea power are the keys to this war and they are interdependent.

    Air power and naval power cannot function without oil.

    Oil, except in very limited quantities, cannot be brought to its destination without shipping.

    Shipping requires the protection of naval power and air power.

2. We have access to practically all the world's supplies of oil.

    We have most of the shipping.

    We have naval power.

    We have potentially the greatest air power, when fully developed.

    Therefore we are bound to win the war.

3. Germany is very short of oil and has access only to very limited quantities.

    Germany's shipping is practically confined to the Baltic.

    Germany's naval power is small.

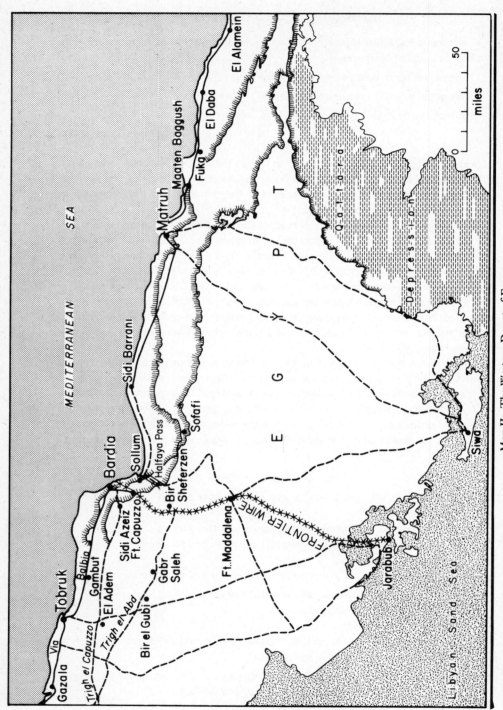

Map II: The Western Desert of Egypt

Germany's air power is great, but is a diminishing asset.
Therefore Germany is bound to lose the war.

(J. Connell: *Wavell*, page 232).

By modern standards Wavell's view had a simple naivety about it, but it highlighted the importance which he and his successors placed upon the security of the Iraqi and Persian oilfields and upon the need to deny Rumanian and Caucasian oil to the Axis. The North African Campaign was to be part of the great strategic struggle for oil – the key commodity which ranked with shipping, as the two most important strategic items in the Second World War.

The British Chiefs of Staff, faced with more pressing problems nearer home, had sent warning signals to each C-in-C, reminding him that, although the Mediterranean forces must, at first, be strategically on the defensive, it was important, in view of the grave situation in the West, that local offensive action should be taken against the Italians whenever possible.

The Royal Navy were the first to demonstrate the emptiness of the Italian challenge. Admiral Cunningham took the Mediterranean Fleet to sea an hour after the midnight dead-line. He swept westwards along the Libyan coast and then north-west to within 120 miles of the Heel of Italy without meeting any Italian surface forces. Other French and British warships bombarded shore targets, and naval aircraft bombed oil storage tanks as far north as Venice. Only the large force of Italian submarines showed any sign of offensive spirit, one boat torpedoing and sinking the British cruiser *Calypso*. Cunningham was disappointed with the lack of Italian reaction in the Mediterranean. In the Red Sea his colleagues dealt with four of the eight Italian submarines based there, but the six large Italian fleet destroyers at Massawa did not put to sea. And throughout the world Italy lost 130,000 tons of merchant shipping by capture, scuttling or internment in neutral ports.

In the air, Air Marshal Longmore's bombers attacked ports and airfields in Libya and Eritrea soon after midnight. He avenged the loss of *Calypso* by setting fire to the Italian Cruiser *San Giorgio* in Tobruk harbour. Unfortunately shortage of spares and reserve aircraft soon forced Longmore to reduce the intensity of his operations. Moreover, he found that his primitive early-warning system and the slowness of his Gladiator fighters made interception of the more modern Italian Savoia bombers difficult. Appreciating that he might have to face a greatly reinforced Italian Air Force before long, which might include a German contingent, Longmore decided to conserve his air effort.

On land, the British caught General Berti's Tenth Italian Army just as unprepared in Libya. The British Western Desert Force under Lieutenant-General Sir Richard O'Connor had grown since the outbreak of war with Germany to two partially equipped divisions: Major-General Creagh's 7th Armoured Division with two armoured brigades, each with only two instead of three tank regiments, and 7th Support Group with two motor infantry battalions and a field and an anti-tank regiment, Royal Artillery; and Major-General Beresford-Peirse's 4th Indian Division with two instead of three Indian Infantry Brigades. O'Connor quickly dominated the frontier area with this small force, which breached the frontier wire – a barbed wire fence some 12 foot deep and 16 foot high, built by the Italians along the Egyptian frontier from the coast near Sollum to the oasis of Jarabub 150 miles to the south – and raided Cyrenaica at will. At the end of the first week of war Mussolini confessed to the King: 'Affairs on the Egyptian frontier did not turn out too brilliantly . . . I believe Balbo will restore the situation'. (*British Official History*: Vol 1, page 118 footnote).

The erosion of Italian morale continued. In the first three months of the war the Italians acknowledged the loss of 3,500 men in frontier skirmishing while the British lost 150. Balbo was not to be allowed to restore the situation. He was shot down over Tobruk by his own anti-aircraft guns. In his place came Marshal Graziani – an Italian 'hero' of the Abyssinian campaign and a faithful Fascist henchman of Mussolini's. It was to prove an unfortunate appointment. Marshal Balbo had been genuinely respected by both sides who felt the loss of this internationally famous airman. Had he lived, the course of the early battles in the Western Desert might have been less disastrous for the Italians.

A greater tragedy was being enacted at Bordeaux which was to have far reaching effects upon the opening and closing phases of the North African Campaign. The French Prime Minister, Paul Reynaud, had intended to withdraw his French Government to Algiers to continue the war from French North Africa, relying upon the combined resources of the French and British Empires, on the naval superiority of the Anglo-French fleets, and on American aid. At the decisive Cabinet meeting on 13 June, Marshal Pétain expressed the French attitude which the British and Americans found difficult to understand in 1940 and more difficult still in the closing phases of the North African Campaign, three years later:

> It is the duty of the Government, whatever may happen, to remain in the country . . . The renewal of France must be expected from the soul of the country itself, which we will preserve by staying where we are rather than from a re-conquest of our territory by Allied guns under conditions and a lapse of time which we cannot foresee . . .
>
> An armistice is, in my view, the necessary condition for the survival of France.
>
> (Langer: *Our Vichy Gamble*, page 26).

The British and American ambassadors strove to keep the French Empire and Fleet out of German hands. The most they could do was to extract a promise from Pétain when he succeeded Reynaud that the French Empire and Fleet would not be allowed to fall intact into German hands. In the armistice negotiations Mussolini made substantial demands on French colonial territory but Hitler refused him. He needed French support in his continued struggle with Great Britain with whom he hoped to come to terms without further fighting. He realised that he must avoid antagonising the French who might easily revert to their British connection in desperation. Leniency seemed to be the most profitable policy. In the Armistice terms he demanded only the occupation of the north-east of France and the Atlantic coast. The French Empire was to remain unscathed and the French Fleet was to be demobilized. The

German Government solemnly declared that 'it did not intend to use the French War Fleet'. This declaration did not impress the British Government.

When the Franco-German Armistice came into effect on 24 June 1940, the British commanders in Cairo found it hard to believe that their erstwhile colleagues would not fight on. They misunderstood the intensity of Frenchmen's attachment to France herself, and did not appreciate the depth of anti-British feeling which had arisen in French minds. General de Gaulle's rallying cry of 'Free France' found few echoes. A British military mission to Algiers was rebuffed by General Nogues, who led Morocco, Algeria and Tunisia into the Vichy camp. General Mittelhauser in Syria followed suit, in spite of Wavell's efforts to dissuade him. General Legentilhomme, in French Somaliland, held out for over a month in Jibuti but was eventually replaced by a Vichy nominee. Only French Equatorial Africa declared for de Gaulle. Cunningham was successful in persuading Admiral Godfrey to immobilise the French ships in Alexandria. Admiral Somerville, who had just begun to form his famous Force 'H' at Gibraltar to replace the French naval presence in the Western Mediterranean, was less fortunate. Admiral Gensoul refused the British ultimatum to fight on or demobilize his French warships in the naval base at Mers-el-Kebir near Oran. In the ensuing action 1,297 French sailors lost their lives. Only the new battle-cruiser *Strasbourg* managed to escape. French bitterness was increased; her fleet was neutralised and of no further help to the British; and French North Africa became vulnerable to German infiltration in the wake of French resentment. Henceforth only American diplomats could deal with the French without acrimony.

On 3 July, the day on which Admiral Somerville was forced to open fire at Mers-el-Kebir, the Chiefs of Staff sent their views to the Cs-in-C in Cairo.

Their policy was to concentrate initially on the defence of the United Kingdom and start the release equipment for the Middle East when the situation following the impending trial of strength could be more closely judged. This might not be for two months; meanwhile, everything that could be spared would be sent, including, if possible, modern fighters to re-arm the squadrons in Egypt, and bombers to replace wastage. The situation in Syria was having disturbing effects in Iraq and even Persia; subject, therefore, to the consent of the Iraqi Government, it was proposed to send a division (5th Indian Division) from India to secure the Anglo-Iranian oilfields.

(*British Official History*: Vol 1, page 129).

Reinforcing the Middle East was no longer an easy matter. The Mediterranean was closed to all but fast and heavily escorted ships. The long haul round the Cape of Good Hope took a month longer for fast convoys and over two months more for the slow. Aircraft could not be flown out over France and French North Africa. Fortunately French Equatorial Africa's allegiance to de Gaulle made it practicable to establish a trans-African air reinforcement route between Takoradi on the Gold Coast through Lagos, Kano, Fort Lamy to Khartoum and finally Cairo.* The creation of

* See Map I, page 2.

this route is a saga of its own. Suffice it to say here that 5,000 British fighters and bombers were flown to the Middle East Air Force along this route during the North African Campaign in addition to large numbers of American planes. The passage of important convoys through the Mediterranean created other epics. Most of the major naval actions fought by the opposing battle fleets were brought on by the British covering and the Axis trying to attack convoys bound for Egypt and Malta the strategic importance of which grew as the months passed. The role of the island fortress changed from being the main base of the British Mediterranean Fleet before the war to that of an unsinkable aircraft carrier anchored in the Sicilian Channel astride the Axis lines of communication to Libya.

July and August 1940 were months in which both sides rethought their strategies in the light of the sudden and surprising collapse of France. On the German side Hitler accepted the necessity for Göring's Operation 'Eagle' (The Battle of Britain) and Operation 'Sea Lion' (the still-born invasion of England). His Operations Staff were the first to be appraised of the reason for his half-heartedness. General Warlimont records what happened when General Jodl visited his section of OKW* which dealt with forward plans: 'Jodl went round ensuring that all the doors and windows were closed and then, without any preamble, disclosed to us that Hitler had decided to rid the world "once and for all" of the danger of Bolshevism by a surprise attack on Soviet Russia to be carried out at the earliest possible moment, i.e. in May 1941.' (*Warlimont:* page 111).

Many of the German strategic decisions taken in the summer and autumn of 1940 are inexplicable unless Hitler's emotional absorption with his intuitive decision to attack Russia in the Spring of 1941 are thoroughly understood. The defeat of Russia was to Hitler the surest way of bringing Britain to her knees without risking a cross-channel operation. He did not believe that it would take him more than one summer's campaign to finish off the Soviet Union. He could then destroy the British Empire, if necessary, before turning again upon the British Isles.

Hitler's military staff were horrified at this turn of events. The bitterest lessons of German history made wars on two fronts anathema to them. The Führer was about to commit the cardinal error by turning eastwards before he had settled affairs in the west. All they could hope was that some unforeseen event or a further flash of intuition would divert his mind to a more realistic strategy before it was too late. The German naval and army staffs came together in proposing other attractive alternatives, one of which was the destruction of the British position in the Mediterranean. There were three practicable ways of doing this: bringing pressure to bear on Franco for a joint operation to close the Straits of Gibraltar; reinforce the Italians in Libya with German panzer divisions to attack Egypt and the Suez Canal from the west; and advance through the Balkans and Turkey to threaten the Canal and the Iraqi and Persian oilfields from the north. Hitler refused to contemplate the last of these routes because its use would open the Eastern Front prematurely. He

---

* 'Ober Kommando der Wehrmacht', the German Supreme Military Headquarters, controlling the three fighting services.

1. The British High Command responsible for North African affairs in 1940:
Anthony Eden, Secretary of State for War; General Sir John Dill, Chief of
Imperial General Staff; Admiral Sir Andrew Cunningham, C-in-C Mediterranean
Fleet; Air Marshal Sir Arthur Longmore, AOC-in-C Middle East Air Force;
General Sir Archibald Wavell, GOC-in-C Middle East.

2. The Victors of the first round in the Western Desert: Lieutenant General Sir
Richard O'Connor talking to General Sir Archibald Wavell in the desert at the
time of the "Compass" offensive.

3. Matilda tanks of 7th Royal Tank Regiment, which led all the attacks on Italian fortified positions during the "Compass" offensive.

4. Heavily laden Australian Infantry with a Matilda tank attacking at Bardia.

accepted the other two as possibilities but was rebuffed by Franco and Mussolini. The former demanded an exorbitant price in terms of annexations of French North African territories; and the latter refused German reinforcements for Libya, telling Badoglio: 'If they get a footing in this country we shall never get rid of them.' (*Badoglio:* page 32).

For the moment there was no point in pressing these plans because nothing could be spared for operations in the Mediterranean until the outcome of the Battle of Britain and the need for 'Sea Lion' were known.

*   *   *

While Hitler was reshaping his strategy, Cunningham and Somerville were showing that, despite the loss of French naval support, the Royal Navy could still dominate the Mediterranean. In the first week of July, British light naval forces, working in close co-operation with RAF and Fleet Air Arm squadrons, destroyed four Italian submarines and three destroyers. In the second week of July, the first clash occurred between the heavier ships of the opposing fleets, revealing the strengths and weaknesses of the two sides. The British regretted the slowness of their ships and the weakness in their air reconnaissance, but were delighted to find how ineffective the Italian Air Force's high level bombing proved to be and how poorly the Italian air and naval forces co-operated. The Italian sailors, for their part, were worried by the thinness of the armour on their ships and by the haphazardness of the support given

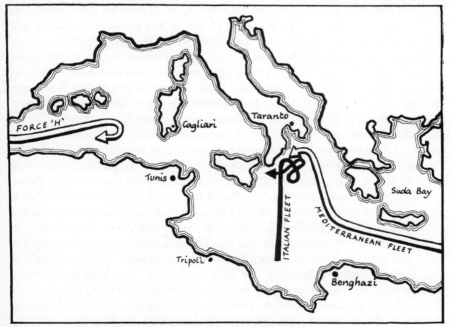

Fig 1 The Fleet Engagement off Calabria: 8th and 9th July 1940

by their airmen. As the 'Action off Calabria' was typical of several of such operations it is worth looking at it in outline.

Two convoys were due to sail from Malta to Alexandria with important naval reinforcements and stores. It was expected that the Italians would try to intercept them, and so it was decided to cover the movement with a fleet operation from both ends of the Mediterranean. Somerville with Force 'H' was to draw the Italians' attention westwards by sailing from Gibraltar to attack the Italian air base at Cagliari in southern Sardinia, while Cunningham's Fleet sailed westward from Alexandria covering the convoys. British submarines were deployed to report Italian movements from their home ports. Early on 8 July, one of these submarines, *Phoenix*, reported two Italian battleships and four destroyers steaming south towards Benghazi. *Phoenix* herself did not return, while four Italian submarines suffered similar fates at the hands of British destroyers and aircraft covering the fleet. All the British ships came under heavy and sustained Italian high-level bombing, Cunningham's Flagship *Warspite* having some 300 bombs aimed at her in 22 attacks. The carrier *Ark Royal* with Somerville was given similar treatment. As Force H's operations were only diversionary, Somerville did not press home his attack on Cagliari and withdrew to Gibraltar to avoid unnecessary damage to his capital ships.

Continual heavy air attacks and further air-reconnaissance reports of the Italian Fleet, which was found to contain six cruisers as well as the two battleships reported earlier, convinced Cunningham, rightly as it proved later, that the Italians were at sea to cover an important convoy of their own, making for Tripoli. He cancelled the sailing of his own Malta convoys and made best speed to place his fleet between the Italians and their base at Taranto. By 2.15 pm he was between the Italians and Taranto. Half an hour later Vice-Admiral Tovey's cruisers sighted the Italian ships. *Neptune* was the first British warship in the Mediterranean since Nelson's day to signal 'Enemy battle fleet in sight', but Tovey's situation could have been serious. His four 6-inch gun cruisers were advancing upon a larger force of Italian 8-inch gun cruisers supported by battleships. Furthermore, his ships carried only half their correct outfit of ammunition due to shortage of naval shell at Alexandria. Tovey engaged although heavily outgunned and outranged. Fortunately *Warspite* came up in time to discourage the Italian cruisers with her 15-inch salvoes, and hit the Italian Flagship *Giulio Cesare* from which unciphered radio messages were intercepted ordering all ships to make smoke and reporting that Admiral Campioni, the Italian C-in-C, was constrained to retire. The Italian battleships turned away and in some confusion made for the Straits of Messina behind a thick pall of smoke which proved most effective. Air strikes launched from the carrier *Eagle* were unsuccessful. In destroyer actions one Italian cruiser and several Italian destroyers were damaged but none were sunk. By 5 pm not a single enemy ship was in sight. The British suffered four hours of high-level bombing and were delighted to hear from further radio interceptions that Campioni's ships were being attacked by Italian aircraft!

The effect of the action off Calabria and other lesser engagements became apparent at the end of July. Another fleet operation was organised to fly Hurricanes to Malta off the carrier *Argus* which sailed from Gibraltar on 31 July. This time Somerville's

Force H reached and attacked Cagliari air base, and Cunningham swept the eastern basin. Apart from high-level bombing of both fleets, there was no Italian naval reaction. The Italian Fleet stayed in harbour, and Malta was successfully reinforced.

On land, the Italians were superficially more successful. In East Africa the Duke of Aosta mounted a number of limited offensives against British-held frontier posts which he attacked with gross numerical superiority. On the Sudan border, two Italian colonial brigades just managed to dislodge three companies of the Sudan Defence Force from Kassala at the cost of 117 Italian casualties to 10 British. A similar story could be told at Karora on the Red Sea and at Gallabat and Kurmak further inland.* The Italians did not follow up and the frontier areas remained friendly to the British. On the Kenyan border, one company of the King's African Rifles was forced to abandon the frontier post at Moyale by four Italian colonial battalions. Italian commentators talked about great victories. All that Aosta had done was to take a few untenable outposts.

In British Somaliland, Aosta could claim more substantial success. Until 1939 the British had intended to abandon this territory without a fight as it had no strategic value. Wavell recommended that, for reasons of prestige, British Somaliland should be held. The collapse of the French in Jibuti undermined this decision because it released more Italian troops than were originally expected and opened up an additional line of advance to Berbera, the capital of British Somaliland. Wisdom after the event shows that Wavell was wrong to continue recommending resistance, but in war nothing is certain. In his judgment the risks in this case were worth taking. A Corps of 3 Italian and 23 colonial battalions supported by 21 batteries of artillery proved to be too much for Brigadier Chater's mixed force of five Indian, British, Rhodesian and East African battalions with only one artillery battery. The campaign lasted just sixteen days and ended with the British naval evacuation of Berbera on 19 August. Mussolini made great play of his conquest of this small inhospitable portion of the British Empire.

In the Western Desert of Egypt the two opposing Cs-in-C were both out of sympathy with their Governments at home. Graziani had no wish to attack, but was under pressure from Mussolini to do so. Wavell was willing to match Churchill's desire for an early offensive, but found it difficult to prove to his impetuous political master that he and Longmore lacked essential resources to make offensive operations practicable. Action in the Western Desert stagnated until September while policy decisions were taken in Rome and London.

When Graziani succeeded Balbo there had been no plans for an Italian invasion of Egypt. The disappearance of the French threat to Tripoli from Tunisia emboldened Mussolini who ordered Graziani to invade Egypt. Graziani lost no time in complaining that his forces were neither adequate nor ready for a 350-mile advance across a waterless desert to the Nile Delta. Mussolini might have visions of entering Cairo as the 'Protector of Islam' riding a grey horse at the head of his legions, but this could only happen if careful logistic preparations were made and his army was

* See Map III, page 48.

reinforced with modern tanks, guns and aircraft. Mussolini accepted that more time was needed, but insisted that Graziani must attack, whether ready or not, when the first German soldier set foot on England. Graziani bowed to the logic of Mussolini's direction without enthusiam.

Wavell's predicament was of a different kind. With the invasion of Britain imminent he could not expect reinforcement from home. His tanks and trucks, and Longmore's aircraft, could not operate indefinitely without replacement or overhaul. Replacement being impossible, overhaul had to be adopted. Towards the end of July he authorised 7th Armoured Division to withdraw its two armoured brigades to refit, leaving the motor battalions and the artillery of 7th Support Group under Brigadier 'Strafer' Gott to act as a covering force on the frontier. Longmore had to place further flying restrictions on his aircraft sortie rate, confining his attacks in support of the Army to major targets which could not be hit by any other means. In London, Wavell's and Longmore's shortages were fully appreciated by the Cabinet Committee set up under Anthony Eden, Secretary of State for War, to advise on the affairs of the Middle East. At the end of July this Committee recommended that Wavell should come home to discuss his requirements in detail with them and the Chiefs of Staff. Churchill agreed. He had been fretting for some time about Wavell not using his resources to best advantage. He had never met 'my commander in the field' as he called Wavell. 'I felt an acute need' Churchill wrote, 'of talking over the serious events impending in the Libyan desert with General Wavell himself. I had not met this distinguished officer, on whom so much was resting . . .' (*Churchill*: Vol II, page 376).

Wavell flew home with a representative from Longmore's staff in the first week of August, arriving in London as the Battle of Britain opened. He presented his views to the Chiefs of Staff and War Cabinet. He intended, he said, to fall back from the Libyan frontier, if Graziani advanced in strength; and to check him decisively at Mersa Matruh, about one-third of the way from the frontier to the Nile. He had adequate water there; logistic stocks had been built up; and he could be supplied by rail as well as road. Graziani, on the other hand, would be grappling with the problems of supplying his troops over 150 miles of particularly arid desert with a poor road and no railway behind him. Wavell did not believe that he would advance with much enthusiasm under these conditions; and suggested, with some prescience, that the real danger to Egypt lay in the arrival of German armoured and mechanised reinforcements for Berti's Army. He stressed the paucity of the British Intelligence Service in Italian colonial territories caused by the 'don't provoke Italy' policy. The Germans could land undetected in Tripoli or even Benghazi. Egypt would not be secure until the RAF squadrons had been rearmed with modern aircraft; the 7th Armoured and 4th Indian Divisions had been brought up to strength in men, modern tanks, anti-tank guns and field artillery; the Australian and New Zealand Divisions, training in Palestine, had been similarly equipped; the theatre had been provided with a higher scale of heavy and light anti-aircraft guns; and there was an adequate supply of ammunition of all types for intense operations.

Wavell's equipment demands were not easy to meet. For the first nine months of the war all British war production had been used to arm the British Expeditionary Force in France. Most of this equipment had been lost at Dunkirk. Throughout June and July every tank, gun and rifle that emerged from British factories, or from the shiploads of US equipment sent over to England in Roosevelt's generous gesture after the fall of France, went towards re-equipping the disarmed divisions as they re-assembled in England to meet the German invasion. Eden's Committee and the War Cabinet agreed that risks should be taken to strengthen Wavell's and Longmore's forces in spite of the threatened invasion. A shipping list, including three tank battalions (one of which was to be equipped with the new heavy 'Infantry' tanks, nicknamed 'Matildas'), guns of all calibres and ammunition to match, was drawn up and agreed. The decision remained to be taken as to whether these precious weapons should be risked in the Mediterranean or sent by the safer route round the Cape of Good Hope. Churchill had no doubt about the correct policy. In a minute to the First Sea Lord on 13 August he said:

> It seems . . . extremely likely that if the Germans are frustrated in an invasion of Great Britain, or do not choose to attempt it, they will have a great need to press and aid the Italians to attack Egypt. The month of September must be regarded as critical in the extreme.
>
> In these circumstances, it is very wrong that we should attempt to send one armoured brigade round the Cape, thus making sure that during September it can play no part either in the defence of England or Egypt.
>
> (*Ibid*: page 397).

Cunningham felt that if the tanks were vital to the defence of Egypt then the risk of naval losses should be accepted to get them there in time. Wavell took a more balanced view and did not endear himself to Churchill by so doing. He maintained that the risk of losing valuable equipment, which would take many months to replace, did not justify the time saved by going through the Mediterranean. If the Italians did attack in the Western Desert before the reinforcements arrived, he could use his existing tanks more boldly, knowing that replacements were on their way. A compromise was struck. The tank convoy, code-named 'Apology', would sail to Gibraltar where it was to arrive in time to join a naval reinforcement operation code-named 'Hats' in which the carrier *Illustrious*, the battleship *Valiant* and two new anti-aircraft cruisers were to be sailed through the central Mediterranean to join Cunningham. If, when the 'Apology' convoy reached Gibraltar, the Cs-in-C Middle East decided that an Italian invasion was imminent, it would be risked in the Mediterranean with 'Hats'; if not, it would go round the Cape. Churchill approved this plan on 15 August, the critical day of the Battle of Britain when every RAF fighter squadron was engaged. Churchill commented: 'The decision to give this blood transfusion while we braced ourselves to meet a mortal danger was at once awful and right. No-one faltered'. (*Ibid:* page 379).

Wavell's visit to London had won him all the immediate reinforcements he could reasonably expect. It also gave him promises of further formations, including a second armoured division, later in the year. The Air Ministry had been helpful too, and had promised a more generous flow of new aircraft to Longmore, whose persistent demands for reinforcement had been irritating Churchill. The most welcome reinforcements agreed by the Air Ministry were a number of American built Glen-Martin reconnaissance planes which had been destined for the French and had been diverted to Britain. In other respects Wavell's visit was a disaster. He failed to win Churchill's confidence. The two men were complete opposites in personality and style. Churchill thrusting, prying, criticising and cajoling until he got his way, met the taciturnity of Wavell who saw no reason to make a special effort to please a politician. They were also opposed in experience. Kitchener's campaign in the Sudan, service in India and work as a war correspondent in the Boer War had made a vivid impression on Churchill's young mind. Such minor wars were 'war' to him. Wavell had served in India too, but his principal experience lay in major war on the Western Front and with Allenby in Palestine. Churchill could not, or maybe would not, master the problems of logistic support for modern fighting forces. All delay for the build up of the vast tonnages of ammunition and supplies needed by armies and air forces operating at high intensity irked him. He was suspicious of manpower absorbed by base organisations; critical of time required for training and rehearsal of troops; and convinced that he and he alone had the imagination and drive to seize and hold the initiative. Wavell, like other professional soldiers of his generation, had studied the Middle East disasters of the First World War such as Townsend's surrender at Kut, the failure of the first Battle of Gaza, and of Churchill's own brainchild, Gallipoli, all of which had been brought about by inadequate preparation. Wavell was a man who enjoyed taking risks and using novel methods when great prizes were at stake, but he was no gambler. He knew what was practicable and what was foolhardy. He was not prepared to let his military judgment be swayed by any politician, however brilliant, and he certainly saw no reason to credit Churchill with superior military judgment.

The principle bone of contention between the two men at this time was the use Wavell was making of the Rhodesian, South African, and East and West African troops assembling in Kenya. None of them was adequately acclimatised, trained or equipped; the logistic preparations for a 200 miles advance across the waterless bush country of Northern Kenya could not be completed overnight; and the season was wrong for major military operations. Wavell commented to the CIGS when rebutting a goading minute from Churchill: 'I am sure you will keep considerations of geography, climate, desert, distances, etc., constantly in the minds of the Middle East Committee. It all looks so simple to them and others on a small scale map.' (J. Connell: page 249).

After one particularly gruelling night's discussion with Churchill which lasted from 10 pm until 2 am, Wavell considered resigning. Eden recorded in his diary: '*August 13th*. Found Wavell waiting for me at 9 a.m. He was clearly upset at last night's proceedings and said that he thought he should have made it plain that if the Prime Minister could not approve his dispositions and had no confidence in him he should appoint someone else. (Eden: *The Reckoning*, page 131).

Talking to Eden, Churchill described Wavell as 'a good average Colonel . . . and would make a good Chairman of a Tory Association'. Matters were settled two days later. Eden's diary relates:

> *August 15th*. More Wavell talks, when Winston told me he must stay another day. I was against this, for Wavell is doing no good here and should either return or be replaced. Winston asked me who was a possible alternative. I said Auchinleck, he agreed. But we both felt that he had not sufficient evidence to compel a change which at the moment might have a very bad effect on morale throughout Middle East. At a further meeting of the four of us in the afternoon, Winston suddenly agreed that Wavell should leave tonight.

Churchill himself has written: 'While I was not in full agreement with General Wavell's use of the resources at his disposal, I thought it best to leave him in command'. (Churchill: Vol II, page 376).

Wavell's subsequent victories never eradicated these doubts from Churchill's mind. Wavell's feelings about Churchill were confirmed by a detailed draft directive from the Prime Minister which arrived in Cairo for his comment as soon as he arrived back from London. In this document Churchill spelt out in unnecessary detail how Wavell was to manage his theatre of operations. Wavell noted: 'It showed clearly that Winston did not trust me to run my own show and was set on his own ideas'. (J. Connell: page 266).

On 25 August the British Cs-in-C reported that they could discern no obvious signs of Graziani taking the offensive at an early date. The tank convoy was, therefore, despatched round the Cape. Operation 'Hats' proved an anti-climax. The Italians failed to challenge the British capital ships as they passed through the central Mediterranean. Churchill could not resist crowing, 'I told you so'. (Churchill: Vol II, page 399).

Graziani's reluctant invasion of Egypt eventually began early on 13 September. The British covering force identified two Italian columns advancing: one along the coast through Sollum and the other through the desert south of the escarpment which runs parallel to the coastal strip.* A spectacular artillery display heralded the coastal column's advance. The airfield and empty barracks at Sollum were heavily shelled and when the dust and smoke cleared away 'the enemy was disclosed to the westwards with his motor-cycles, light tanks, and other vehicles drawn up as if on parade waiting the order to advance . . . The enemy's close formation presented excellent targets to the artillery and the air . . .' (*British Official History:* Vol I, page 210).

The small British covering force from Gott's Support Group fell back as planned enjoying the 'Gunner's dream' of lush targets of close packed vehicles. The Italians' desert column soon gave up its exposed route and descended through the Halfaya Pass onto the coastal strip. The British fought an unhurried withdrawal battle for four days against five out of the seven Italian divisions – two divisions were left in reserve at Tobruk – which composed Berti's Italian Tenth Army. On 16 September the Italians reached and occupied Sidi Barrani – a little more than a village with a mosque, police station and a few white mud-brick buildings – to the acclaim of the

---

* See Map II: page 14.

Italian Radio which announced 'the trams were still running in Sidi Barrani'! (Wilson: page 44). This was as far as Graziani deemed it wise to advance without a pause for a logistic build up and the construction of a fully metalled road and water pipeline to supply him from the frontier.

For several days the British expected Graziani to push on to the first natural objective on the road to the Nile – Mersa Matruh. The Royal Navy made the Italians' pause uncomfortable by bombarding their camps from the sea, and the Royal Air Force joined in doing their best to discourage a further advance. They need not have worried. Graziani was in no hurry; the Italian challenge to the British Empire was already spent. Mussolini had won cheap victories at the frontier posts of Kassala, Gallabat and Moyale; he had conquered the worthless deserts of British Somaliland; and he had advanced 60 miles into Egypt. But his battle fleet had been driven into harbour and had refused three chances of a fleet action; his air force, despite its numbers, had been ineffectual; and his Army was more intent on digging in at Sidi Barrani than advancing on Cairo. The British reply was taking shape in the minds of the British Cs-in-C Middle East. Even Churchill was unaware of Wavell's real intentions.

3

The British Commonwealth's Reply
(October to December 1940)

'We could not foresee when a landing in Europe would be practicable again, but our sea power, using exterior lines, made it possible to build up our strength in Egypt and in the Western Desert. This was the theatre where the Army must prove itself'.

Anthony Eden: *The Reckoning*, page 124.

The British Commonwealth's reply to the Italian challenge exemplified Napoleon's maxim that the moral is to the physical as three is to one. British military dynamic overawed the Italians despite their numerical superiority in Northern Africa. The old adage 'two is company, three is none', was also borne out. British and German strategic affairs reached major turning points in September and October 1940. Both high commands changed course, but had their plans disrupted by Italian military incompetence and by Mussolini's ill-advised politico-military adventures. Had it not been for Mussolini's failures in the Mediterranean sphere of interest allotted to him by Hitler, the Anglo-German contest in North Africa might never have taken place. The British unwittingly defeated the Italians too soon. If they had waited six months, Hitler would have been irrevocably committed to his Russian campaign and unable to divert forces to help his hapless ally.

In British strategic planning a consensus is always necessary before a major change of direction can be effected. More often than not those responsible for policy are unaware that a radical alteration has taken place until they look back in retrospect. The diversion of resources from the defence of the United Kingdom to the Middle East had started during Wavell's visit to London in August. His long and tiring debates with Churchill were part of a typical British decision-making process. The initial reinforcements sent out in the 'Apology' convoy were for the defence of the British position in the Middle East. During September the British appreciated instinctively that successes in the Battle of Britain and the approach of autumn weather were restoring to them their traditional security from invasion. Decisions to meet Wavell's and Longmore's continuing demands for reinforcements became easier to take, and more minds began to accept the credibility of an offensive policy against Italy in the Mediterranean.

British planning for the destruction of the Italian position in Africa started when Wavell arrived back in Cairo. It too was a developing process. The first reference to offensive planning comes in a note to his Chief of Staff, Arthur Smith, dated 11 September 1940 – two days before Graziani advanced cautiously into Egypt. In this note he said: 'What preparations can we make now? At any rate the sooner we can make an outline plan, calculate our requirements and submit them to the War Office, the more likely we are to have what we want when the time comes'. (J. Connell: page 274).

Ten days later Wavell sent his first directive to Lieutenant-General 'Jumbo' Wilson,* who commanded all British Troops in Egypt, outlining his ideas for a counter-stroke against Graziani's force when it resumed its advance from Sidi Barrani. In it he said: 'I wish every possible precaution that our military training can suggest to be made to ensure that if the enemy attacks Matruh, the greater part of his force shall never return from it'. (*Ibid*: page 275).

There matters rested for a month with the British planning and training for their counter-offensive on the assumption that Graziani would press on towards the Nile. No-one on the British side knew what a reluctant general they had in front of them. An entry in Ciano's diary dated 2 October showed the Italian side of the picture: 'Graziani feels that we must still wait for some time, at least all of November, to complete our logistic preparations . . . If our supply line should not function well we would have to retreat. And in the desert a retreat is equivalent to a rout'. (Ciano: page 295).

In the meantime the first major Allied offensive in the North African Campaign had been launched and had failed. De Gaulle tried to secure a foothold at Dakar in French West Africa and was repulsed. Superficially British and French relations were not improved, but the continued resistance of Britain was beginning to have its effect in France. Weygand, who is credited with saying in June 'In three weeks England will have her head twisted off like a chicken's' resigned from Pétain's Cabinet in disgust at Prime Minister Laval's collaborationist policies and was appointed Delegate General to North Africa. His new feelings were expressed in another apocryphal remark made at about the time of de Gaulle's failure at Dakar: 'If they come to North Africa with four divisions I will fire on them; if they come with twenty divisions I will welcome them'. (Langer: page 86).

Even four divisions would have over-stretched British resources at that time. Early in October intelligence reports began to suggest to Wavell that the possibility of German intervention in Libya was hardening into probability. Anthony Eden accepted a plea from Wavell for further reinforcements, but found it difficult to carry conviction when arguing Wavell's case in Whitehall, particularly with the Air Ministry who believed that Battle of Britain losses should be made good before substantial reinforcements could be diverted to Longmore in the Middle East. Moreover, Chuchill was still unconvinced of Wavell's competence. Since the end of August a cycle of six-weekly convoys from the United Kingdom to the Middle East had been started, which, together with convoys from India and Australasia, would be

---

* Later Field Marshal Sir Maitland Wilson.

bringing to Egypt an average of 1,000 men per day with a matching tonnage of equipment, vehicles and stores. Amongst these convoys Wavell would receive the balance of 2nd Armoured Division, units to make up deficiencies in his existing divisions, and Australian and New Zealand Brigades to complete the 6th and 7th Australian and 2nd New Zealand Divisions. The 1st South African Division would be arriving in Kenya and the 5th Indian Division in the Sudan. Churchill felt that Wavell's command was becoming a bottomless pit which devoured precious resources without giving anything in return. He agreed readily to Eden's request to fly out to Cairo to review the situation on the spot with the C-in-C.

Eden's arrival in Egypt on 15 October coincided with further development of Wavell's plans. The three responsible generals – Wavell, Wilson and O'Connor – had been impressed with the performance of the 7th Royal Tank Regiments 'Matilda' 'I' tanks which had arrived on the 'Apology' convoy. The significance of the arrival of these tanks and much that happened in the desert thereafter lies in British pre-war tank philosophy and tank design which has received more adverse criticism than any other aspect of British military policy in the inter-World War years. There is no doubt that there was muddled thinking and some deep-seated prejudice amongst senior officers at the time, but far less than the armoured enthusiasts would have us believe. Too little has been said in defence of the War Office directors who were honest men struggling to visualise the shape of future war with the imprint of their personal and very recent experiences in the First World War indelibly etched on their minds. It is remarkable that they made so few mistakes in spite of the limited resources at their disposal. They visualised three classes of tank; the Light Tanks armed only with machine guns and used primarily for reconnaissance; the fast Cruiser Tanks which were classed as medium tanks, carrying the standard British 2-pounder anti-tank gun and designed for general purpose tank action in armoured divisions; and the slow, heavily armoured 'Infantry' medium tanks, 'Matildas', built specifically for the support of infantry.

This was a logical family, bearing in mind British experience in the First World War. There was no controversy about the light tank which was produced to much the same specification by most armies for reconnaissance. The decision to have two types of medium or main battle tank stemmed from a realistic appraisal of power-weight ratios. The Cruiser sacrificed protection for speed; and the 'I' tank did the opposite, sacrificing speed for protection so that it could survive more readily when supporting the slower moving infantry. With hindsight it is easy to see that the British were over-concerned with speed and armour, and paid too little attention to ensuring superiority of their tank guns. For this the tank enthusiasts, like Martel, Liddell Hart, Fuller and Hobart, must bear some responsibility; but, here again, their attitude was sensible in the light of their experience which made men of their generation give pride of place to the machine gun for attack and defence. It is noteworthy that in Liddell Hart's works there are very few references to the importance of tank guns. He records General Hobart, the commander of the first British tank brigade, and later the first commander of 7th Armoured Division when it was formed in Egypt just before the war, as considering:

the new 2-pounder would suffice, but hoped that it might be developed to an even higher velocity, as that was the factor important for penetrating the armour of enemy tanks. He did not want a larger calibre gun as it would mean that 'fewer projectiles' could be carried . . .

(Liddell Hart: *Memoirs*, Vol 1, page 392).

This was again a logical view to take before the war, but the Battle of France in May 1940 had shown that British tanks had four weaknesses:

   (i)   Mechanical reliability must be improved;
  (ii)   More armour thickness would be required;
 (iii)   A better armour piercing weapon than the 2-pr would be required;
 (iv)   A weapon firing a high explosive shell of not less than 3″ calibre would be of great value.

(Unpublished official report on Tank design dated Sept 1943; page 2).

Desirable though it was to correct these faults immediately the losses sustained in France made this impracticable. Neither the Chiefs of Staff nor Churchill could countenance any change of design that would slow down production of new tanks needed for the immediate defence of the British Isles. Furthermore, it was believed that 'I' tanks would be needed in greater numbers than the Cruisers and so production was geared to give them priority. A larger 6-pounder gun had been called for by the General Staff in 1938 and was almost fully developed by the summer of 1940, but it could not be fitted into the turrets of the existing designs of British tanks. The 1943 report quoted above remarked: 'After some argument the War Office were persuaded, rightly or wrongly, that it would take longer to provide a special gun and install it into the existing tanks, than to design and develop new tanks to take the all but existing 6-pr gun . . .' (*Ibid:* page 9). No-one seems to have thought of providing the artillery anti-tank batteries with a towed 6-pounder instead of the 2-pounder. There would have been no difficulty in doing so. This error was to prove a costly mistake.

    The attribute of the 'Matilda' which attracted Wavell and his generals' attention was its thickness of armour, making it impervious to any of the anti-tank weapons known to be in the hands of Italian troops. The three of them began, in their different spheres, to consider what action they should take if Graziani did not leave his defended camps around Sidi Barrani in the near future. It was Wavell who brought matters to a head by telling Wilson that he thought it was time to launch a counter-offensive. Wilson records:

He (Wavell) stressed that the most important factor for success was surprise, to achieve which secrecy in preparation was paramount. We discussed the question of security at some length because it was evident that the Italian Legation had left behind agents to report our activities and there were others under diplomatic cover who were prepared to help the Nazi regime . . . The question of leave parties from the Western Desert had to be considered; one remembered the precautions taken for the offensive in front of Amiens on 8 August 1918, and the consternation caused when a certain corps recalled its officers from leave, thereby giving notice that something was about to happen . . . It was decided that only the Commanders and certain senior Staff Officers whose work was essential to give effect to the plan should be in the know. Nothing would be put on paper . . .

(Maitland Wilson: page 46).

Memories of 1918 had other repercussions. Politico-military in-fighting of the First World War still cast shadows upon soldiers' attitudes to politicians in 1940. Wavell decided not to reveal his full intentions to Eden. Instead he allowed Wilson to brief him only on British contingency plans for harassing and finally destroying the Italians as they lunged towards Mersa Matruh. Eden seems to have been satisfied and cabled Churchill asking for a further battalion of 'I' tanks, saying that it was hoped to launch offensive operations on a serious scale in January. He knew nothing of a directive being drafted by Wavell to Wilson and O'Connor, which was sent off on 20 October, instructing them to work out a plan for a two-pronged attack upon the Italians where they stood: Beresford-Peirse's 4th Indian Division was to advance along the coast to Sidi Barrani, while Creagh's 7th Armoured Division drove through the desert south of the escarpment to attack the Italian flank and rear. Wavell wrote:

The operation I have in mind is a short and swift one, lasting four to five days at the most, and taking every advantage of the element of surprise. I should not propose to attempt to retain a large force in the Sidi Barrani area, if the attack were successful, but to withdraw the bulk of the forces again to railhead, leaving only light covering forces in the forward area.

(J. Connell: page 278).

In other words, Wavell envisaged, at this stage, a major raid, and no more. The combination of Churchill's restiveness, Wilson's and O'Connor's enthusiasm, and Mussolini's misguided reactions to Hitler's political moves, were to transform these early ideas into a much more ambitious plan code-named 'Compass'.

While Wilson and O'Connor developed their speculative ideas into concrete military proposals, Wavell and Eden flew to Khartoum to meet General Smuts, the Prime Minister of the Union of South Africa, to discuss operations against the Duke of Aosta's forces in the Italian East African Empire. As the party flew southwards, Mussolini's troops crossed the Albanian frontier into Greece on 28 October. A new strategic situation had been created.

*   *   *

No consensus was needed on the Axis side to change strategic direction. The German High Command was little more than an instrument which translated the Führer's intuitive decisions into military action. Hitler's personal enthusiasm for his attack on Russia grew with Göring's failure to win the Battle of Britain, and as the approach of the equinoctial gales decreased his prospects of launching 'Sea Lion' in 1940. His mind turned without prompting away from the inhospitable waters of the English

Channel to the more exciting prospect of planning the greatest armoured 'blitzkrieg' the world had ever seen, for the spring of 1941. He did, however, accept the arguments of the German Naval Staff that full use should be made of the intervening months to cripple the British in the Mediterranean so as to secure his southern flank, and as a first step he had discussed Mediterranean policy with Mussolini at the Brenner Pass on 4 October. He did not reveal his Russian plans; nor that references he made to an invasion of England in the Spring of 1941 were only part of a deception plan designed to throw his allies as well as his enemies off the true scent. Mussolini again turned down Hitler's offers of German air crew to deal with the Royal Navy and of German panzer formations to support Graziani in Egypt. The German High Command had previously ordered the 3rd Panzer Division to prepare for desert operations and had sent General von Thoma to examine conditions at Sidi Barrani. Von Thoma's report did not flatter the Italians, but it did confirm the Italian staff's objections to the dispatch of German troops because their arrival would have over-burdened Graziani's tenuous supply lines. 3rd Panzer Division was nominated instead for Plan 'Felix', the capture of Gibraltar.

Hitler next turned his attention to France and Spain, preparing the way for 'Felix'. He met Laval at Montoire on 22 October on his way to meet Franco at Hendaye on the Franco/Spanish frontier. His talk with Laval made him feel that Franco-German collaboration against Britain was a possibility, but his meetings with Franco were disappointing. Franco maintained his claim to French North African territory, which Hitler could not concede without jeopardising the progress he had made with the French. The deciding factor, however, was Franco's own appreciation of the outcome of the war. As long as America remained in support of the British, he could not see how Germany could win in the longer term. Spain was dependent on Britain and the US for food and supplies of all kinds. She could not discard her neutrality unless Britain collapsed, which now seemed unlikely, or the Axis could supply her needs, which he knew was impracticable. Credit for this turn of events must be given to American diplomatic effort which effectively blocked Hitler's route to Gibraltar. Mussolini's reluctance to accept German help in Libya barred the central route across the Mediterranean to Suez. Quite unexpectedly the Balkan route began to open up in spite of Hitler's earlier reluctance to use it.

When France fell in June the weaker of her allies slipped quickly over onto the winning side of the fence. Rumania sought salvation by joining the Axis, but this did not endear her to her neighbours, most of whom considered that she had acquired far too much territory at their expense in the Treaty of Versailles. In their view, she should be forced to pay a price for the defeat of her French patrons. Hitler and Mussolini offered their 'good offices' to settle these claims. Russia demanded and took back Bessarabia and most of Bukovina. At a series of conferences in Vienna Hitler awarded a large slice of Transylvania to Hungary and the southern Dubrodjia to Bulgaria. Germany and Italy then jointly guaranteed the rump of Rumania. At the beginning of September the Government of King Carol collapsed and was replaced with the pro-Axis administration of General Antonescu who invited a German military mission to enter the country. Hitler accepted, overtly 'to aid Rumania, our friend', but covertly to protect the Rumanian oil-fields and to prepare for the Russian campaign. True to form he authorised the German 'demonstration troops' to enter Rumania 'to help train the Rumanian Army', without informing Mussolini, who decided to seize his own share of the Balkans by attacking Greece without informing Hitler. The Führer heard of Mussolini's intentions on his way back from Montoire and hurriedly diverted his train to Italy in the hope of dissuading him before it was too late. His train arrived in Florence on 28 October. Mussolini greeted him with the words, 'Führer, we are on the march'. The defeat, which awaited the Italian army advancing into Greece, was to upset Hitler's plans and almost ruined Wavell's 'Compass'.

Churchill responded to Greek appeals for help with his characteristic zeal for honouring obligations. General Metaxas, the Greek Prime Minister, invoked the British Guarantee given by Neville Chamberlain in 1939. Churchill replied: 'We will give you all the help in our power. We will fight a common foe and we will share a united victory'. (Churchill: Vol II, page 472).

At the same time he cabled to Eden:

> I recognise importance of your conference with Smuts but hope first Wavell, and thereafter you, will return to Cairo.
> We here are all convinced an effort should be made to establish ourselves in Crete, and that risks should be run for this valuable prize . . .
>
> *(Ibid:* page 473).

Help for Greece and forces to occupy Crete could only come from one place – the Middle East. The British Cs-in-C acted with vigour. Crete was occupied by an infantry brigade; Suda Bay* was established as an advance refuelling base for the Navy; and Longmore gained unusually high praise from Churchill for despatching air squadrons immediately to Greece. Wavell, however, was faced with a difficult decision.

> All this meant a considerable drain on my resources, and led to my disclosing to Eden my plans for an early attack on the Italians. I had not intended to do so until the plans were further advanced . . . But Eden was proposing to sap my strength in aircraft, AA guns, transport etc., in favour of Greece, thinking I had only a defensive policy in mind, to such an extent that I had to tell him what was in my mind to prevent my being skinned to an extent that would make an offensive impossible.
>
> (J. Connell: page 277).

Eden was acting under Churchill's direction which was set out in a cable dated 2 November 1940.

Prime Minister to Mr Eden
    Greek situation must be held to dominate all others now. We are well aware of

* See Map I on page 2.

our slender resources. Aid to Greece must be attentively studied lest the whole Turkish position is lost through proof that England never tries to keep her guarantees . . .

(Churchill: Vol II, page 474).

Eden was so impressed with Wavell's exposition of his real but secret plans that he scribbled across Churchill's signal: 'Egypt more important than Greece. Enemy air in Libya unaltered'. (Eden: Vol II, page 169)

Meanwhile Wavell's plans for 'Compass' had advanced through one more stage in their gestation. Wilson and O'Connor disliked Wavell's idea of a two-pronged attack and proposed an alternative plan of penetrating with both divisions a 15-mile gap,* which had been found at the south-eastern corner of the arc of Italian fortified camps around Sidi Barrani. The 4th Indian Division supported by the 'I' tanks would attack the camps in succession from their rear while the 7th Armoured Division protected it from counter-attacks launched by Italian reserves. This was a plan after Wavell's own heart. It was daring, original and, if successfully executed, would undoubtedly achieve surprise. It would need a standard of training and staff work which Wilson and O'Connor were confident could be reached by their desert-hardened regular troops. On 2 November, the day Eden and Churchill were arguing about the relative priorities of Greece and the Western Desert, Wavell accepted the new 'Compass' plan and issued his only directive to Wilson to start executive planning and preparation.

Eden reached London on 8 November and was at last able to brief Churchill on Wavell's plans. Churchill wrote: 'Here then was the deadly secret which the Generals had talked over with the Secretary of State. This was what they had not wished to telegraph. We were all delighted. I purred like six cats. Here was something worth doing'. (Churchill: Vol II, page 480).

Churchill had other things to purr about. In spite of Mussolini's urging the Italian admirals had failed to find a suitable opportunity to challenge the Royal Navy. They had put to sea at the end of September to intercept a Malta-bound convoy from Alexandria with a substantial superiority in all classes of ship over Cunningham's covering force. An engagement could have been forced by the Italians but they turned away and sought shelter in Messina and Taranto. A week later they refused to be drawn by another 'coat trailing' convoy for Malta. Even the British occupation of Crete brought no serious Italian naval reaction. Cunningham decided, like Wavell, that it was time to attack the Italians in harbour. An ideal opportunity was presented when air reconnaissance showed the Italian Battle Fleet berthed in Taranto apparently safe from surface attack and protected by anti-torpedo booms and an anti-aircraft balloon barrage.

The Royal Naval aircraft then in service could only mount an effective attack on the Italian battleships by dropping torpedoes at low level and at very close range within the anti-torpedo booms. An attack on the Italian ships in harbour would have to be by night to lessen the effect of the ships' anti-aircraft fire and to give some

---

* See Fig 3 on page 38.

chance of surprise. The barrage balloons would be a hazard to low flying torpedo bombers but, on balance, were considered a lesser hazard. Rear Admiral Lyster, commanding the Fleet Air Arm in the Mediterranean, devised the plan which Cunningham accepted. Operation 'Judgment' should have taken place on 21 October – Trafalgar Day. Unfortunately the carrier *Illustrious* suffered an accidental fire on her hangar deck. 11 November was then proposed but the carrier *Eagle* developed a defect in her fuel system, probably caused by the large number of near misses she had suffered recently from Italian high level bombing. Cunningham decided to go ahead with 'Judgment' using *Illustrious* only, but with some of *Eagle's* specially trained air-crews embarked in her.

Illustrious approached her target as part of a naval force ostensibly covering convoys to Malta and Suda Bay. At 9 pm she reached her flying-off position for 'Judgment', 170 miles south-east of Taranto. Last minute air photos, taken by RAF crews flying American Glen Martins from Malta, showed five battleships in the outer harbour with a sixth entering. There were a number of cruisers and destroyers with them, and a further group was in the inner harbour. *Illustrious* launched two waves of Swordfish; the first of 12 and the second of eight aircraft. As they approached Taranto two flare-dropping aircraft from each wave wheeled right to drop a line of flares east of the harbour against which the battleships would be silhouetted for the torpedo aircraft attacking from the west. The flare-droppers flew on to divert the Italian anti-aircraft defences by attacking the ships in the inner harbour. The official account recorded:

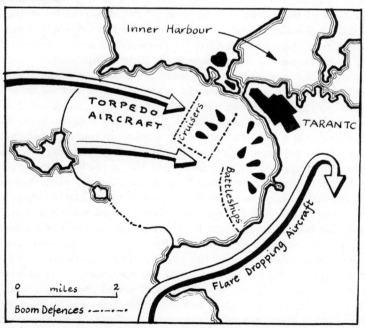

Fig 2 The Fleet Air Arm Attack on Taranto: 11th November 1940

The leader attacked the southernmost battleship, the *Cavour*, and his torpedo struck home under the fo'c'sle as the aircraft, badly damaged, crashed near the floating dock. One minute later the *Littorio* was struck under the starboard bow by a torpedo dropped by the second sub-flight, and a few moments afterwards she was hit again on the port quarter. The other torpedoes either missed, exploded prematurely, or failed to go off, though they were all dropped from close range . . .

The second wave . . . one torpedo struck the *Duilio* on the starboard side and another hit the damaged *Littorio* which was then hit by a fourth torpedo which failed to explode . . . Half the Italian Battlefleet had been put out of action at least temporarily, by the expenditure of 11 torpedoes and for the loss of two aircraft . . .

(British Official History: Vol I, pages 237-238).

While the Fleet Air Arm was dealing with the Italian battlefleet, three of Cunningham's cruisers sailed into the Straits of Otranto to interfere with Italian sea communications with Albania. They surprised and sank a convoy of four merchantmen before rejoining the fleet. *Illustrious* hoped to repeat the operation the following night, but bad weather prevented a repetition.

The effect of the night's work was far-reaching. The damage inflicted on the Italians was greater than that suffered by the Germans in the fleet action off Jutland in the First World War. Unfortunately the operation was closely studied by the Japanese who copied it on a much larger scale at Pearl Harbour a year later.

Taranto delighted the British people and helped them to withstand the growing German blitz on their cities and the onset of the second winter of the war. It depressed the Italians and added to the indignities of defeat suffered by their troops in the mountains of Greece. It infuriated the Germans. Ciano was summoned to the Berghof where he was left in no doubt about Hitler's displeasure. Two days later Hitler spelt out his views in a personal letter to Mussolini, castigating him for the diplomatic consequence of his premature attack on Greece and the failures of his naval forces in the Mediterranean and his troops in Egypt. He informed Mussolini that German divisions would move through Rumania and Bulgaria to end the Greek campaign for him as soon as the weather permitted which would not be before March 1941. He still did not mention his plans to attack Russia, but he did indicate that he would need his troops back by the beginning of May at the latest. In the diplomatic field he had three objectives: to induce Spain to enter the war on the Axis side, thus blocking the western entrance to the Mediterranean; to reach an understanding with Yugo-Slavia and Turkey; and to encourage Russia to look eastwards. The principal military action before March would be in the air: the bombing of England would continue and he proposed to attack the British Fleet in the Mediterranean. A *Geschwader* of German bombers (100 aircraft) with fighters and reconnaissance aircraft in support would be made available for operations in the Mediterranean. Finally, he emphasised the need for the Italians to take Mersa Matruh as soon as possible so that Alexandria could be attacked. Surprisingly no new offer of German panzer units was made. Mussolini commented to Ciano, 'He really smacked my fingers', but in his reply he accepted Hitler's proposals including the dispatch of the

Luftwaffe *Geschwader* to challenge British naval supremacy in the Mediterranean – Operation 'Mittelmeer'.

Taranto had one irritating effect as far as Wavell was concerned. On 14 November he received a meddling signal from the Prime Minister which did not improve their relations. It said:

> Chiefs of Staff, Service Ministers and I have examined general situation in light of recent events. Italian check on Greek front, British naval success against battle fleet at Taranto, poor showing of Italian airmen have made over here (in Battle of Britain), encouraging reports received of low morale in Italy ... above all the general political situation, make it very desirable to undertake operation of which you spoke to Secretary of State for War. It is unlikely that Germany will leave her flagging ally unsupported indefinitely.
>
> Consequently it seems that now is the time to take risks and strike the Italians by land, sea and air. You should act accordingly in concert with other Cs-in-C. We should be prepared to postpone reinforcement of Malta in order to give you more aircraft for your operations if this can be done in time. Telegraph latest date by which these should arrive in Egypt in order to be of use.
>
> (Churchill: Vol II, page 483).

Wavell refused to be hurried. He appreciated as much as anyone else that he was faced with a race against time – a race to destroy Graziani and Aosta before the Germans intervened – but he was also confronted with the physical problems of the rate of replacement of Longmore's air squadrons, which had gone to Greece; of the rate of logistic build-up which he could achieve in the Western Desert with the limited transport resources at his disposal; and, most important of all, of the time needed for training and rehearsal of the troops which were to carry out in the attack. He did not reply direct to Churchill. Instead he cabled to Eden on 16 November:

> Operation is in preparation but not possible to execute this month as originally planned. Now working to date about end of first week December unless enemy moves meanwhile when earlier counter-stroke may be possible.
>
> Am discussing possibilities of air support with A.O. C-in-C. Desirable that four fighter squadrons should be available. Please keep intentions entirely secret; premature disclosure is chief danger to plan.
>
> (J. Connell: page 281).

Churchill was forced to contain his impatience, though this did not last for long.

In the Western Desert detailed planning, reconnaissance and training were being pushed ahead in the greatest secrecy. Preparations for 'Compass' had really started in the mid-1930s when a handful of Englishmen led by Major R. A. Bagnold had experimented with and mastered the techniques of operating in the desert. They developed such things as desert-navigation by sun compass; 'unsticking' devices like the ubiquitous sand-channel to extricate vehicles from soft sand; simple radiator condensors to conserve water; special low pressure tyres and reinforced suspensions for vehicles; and a way of life for men working in the desert. In short, they acquired and handed on to the British units in Egypt that indefinable quality known as 'desert sense' — the ability to live, move and fight by day and by night in the strange lunar-like surroundings. The British made the desert their ally; it always remained an enemy to the Italians.

The operational area of the Western Desert is shown on Map II. There are four important topographical features: the sandy coastal strip; the easily crossed pebble and boulder strewn Libyan plateau; the difficult salt marshes of the Qattara Depression and sand dunes of the Libyan sand sea; and the escarpments, which divide the coastal strip from the desert plateau. The coastal strip varies in width and the escarpment in height from an easily traversable shelf east of Sofafi to difficult 500-ft cliffs to the west which cannot be climbed by vehicles except at recognised places. The only habitations of any size or permanency are on the coast. The most important were: Gazala in the west just before the desert gives way to the more fertile country of the Djebel Akhdar in Cyrenaica; Tobruk, the small port with naval replenishment facilities; Bardia, much smaller with rudimentary port facilities; Sollum on the Egyptian side of the frontier with just a small jetty; Sidi Barrani where Graziani was halted; Mersa Matruh where Antony and Cleopatra enjoyed each other and where O'Connor had his advanced logistic installations; and finally Maaten Baggush where Wilson had his advanced headquarters alongside Air Commodore Collishaw's RAF Group Headquarters responsible for supporting the Western Desert Force. On the British side, a railway, water pipe-line and tarmac road reached as far west as Mersa Matruh. The road continued in reasonable condition as far as Sidi Barrani and then

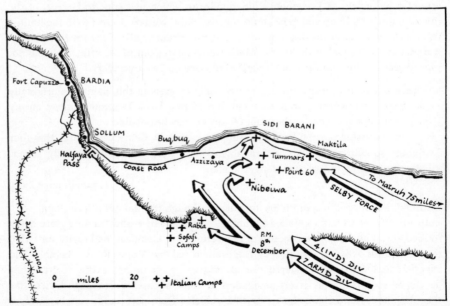

Fig 3 The Italian Forts and O'Connor's Plan of Attack at Sidi Barrani: November 1940

became an unsurfaced track. On the Italian side Graziani was in the process of building a metalled road and pipe-line forward from the well built via Balbia on the Libyan side of the frontier. Inland to the south there was nothing but desert tracks and ancient Roman underground water cisterns, called 'birs', many of which were dry but some containing brackish water.

Air photography, covert intelligence sources and patient patrol work in the desert gave O'Connor an accurate picture of Graziani's dispositions. General Berti's Tenth Italian Army had increased in strength to nine divisions. The 1st and 2nd Libyan Divisions held the coastal sector with fortified camps at Maktila, Tummar East, Tummar West, and Point 90. The 4th Blackshirt Division was in reserve behind them in Sidi Barrani. The Maletti Armoured Group was at Nibeiwa, and the 63rd (Cirene) Division held a group of camps on the escarpment at Rabi and Sofafi. They were supported by the 62nd (Marmarica) Division on the escarpment between Sofafi and the Halfaya Pass and the 64th (Catanzaro) Division on the coast at Buq Buq. The 1st and 2nd Blackshirt Divisions were left guarding the frontier. The 15-mile gap in the Italian circle of forts, which O'Connor was bent on exploiting, lay between Rabia and Nibeiwa. O'Connor considered two alternative directions of attack after penetrating the 15-mile gap. He could either destroy the Rabia – Sofafi group; or turn north and take Nibeiwa and then the Tummars. He discarded the Sofafi group because they were sited in difficult broken ground in which the 'I' tanks would be at a disadvantage. The route from Sofafi down to the coast was also difficult which would make exploitation to cut off the Italian retreat too slow. He chose Nibeiwa as the first objective for Beresford-Peirse's 4th Indian Division, supported by the 'I' tanks of 7th Royal Tank Regiment. Once Nibeiwa had fallen, the two Tummar camps and then Sidi Barrani would be attacked in succession. Creagh's 7th Armoured Division would mask the Sofafi/Rabia group of camps and attempt to cut the coast road at Buq Buq to prevent any interference by Italian reinforcements from the west. The Matruh garrison under Brigadier Selby, with the support of the monitors and gun boats of the Royal Navy would divert the Italian attention to the coast road while operations were developing in the desert.

There were difficult organisational and logistic problems to solve. Some units would have to cross as much as 75 miles of open desert to reach the final assembly areas for the attack. The 'I' tanks could not make more than about eight miles in the hour at the best. The final assembly and advance through the Rabia – Nibeiwa gap into the Italian rear would have to be made by night to avoid detection. O'Connor decided to carry out his initial concentration in the desert 40 miles south-west of Matruh on the night D-2/D-1. He would then risk a daylight advance during D-1 to his assembly area some 15 miles south-east of Nibeiwa where he would lie up until the time came to move into the forming-up positions for the assault on Nibeiwa which would take place soon after dawn on D-day. As moonlight would be needed for the final forming up, the attack would have to take place in the last quarter of the moon, around the end of the first week of November or December. November was far too early, so the target date became 9 December. Wavell did not report this date to Churchill. He knew that politicians seized upon target dates, and gave them a finality which was not intended. Vagueness at this juncture was essential. There were too many variables still to be resolved.

The success of O'Connor's approach march would depend upon the completeness of the air-cover, and upon enough transport to carry the infantry of 4th Indian Division forward in one lift as well as supplying the force in action. Longmore planned to strike all Italian airfields as well as providing fighter cover over the desert while the approach march was taking place. There were doubts as to whether the RAF would be successful, if replacements for the squadrons sent to Greece did not arrive in time. There were also doubts about the transport situation, and so risks were taken in establishing dumps of ammunition and supplies in the desert half-way between Matruh and Nibeiwa long before the operation was due to take place. These dumps were set up on the pretext of supporting the counter-attack on Graziani if he advanced on Matruh, but could well have given the game away if the Italians or talkative gentlemen in the British supply services had appreciated their true significance.

The most difficult problem of all was how to train and rehearse the troops without them realising that an attack was imminent. This was done by organising a series of training exercises designed to study the attack on fortified camps. A replica of Nibeiwa was set up in the desert. 'Training Exercise No. 1' was carried out on 26 November and 'Training Exercise No. 2' was quite openly scheduled for the second week of December. The 'post-mortem' on the first exercise would make significant changes in the tactics which would be tried out again, as far as the troops were concerned, in Training Exercise No. 2. Nothing appeared unusual, but the few staff officers 'in the know' had to work feverishly to modify the actual plans and timings as a result of the disguised rehearsal. Wilson went as far as taking the American military attaché, Colonel Bonner Fellers, with him to see 'the training'.

'Training Exercise No. 1', mounted by Beresford-Peirse, used the orthodox methods set out in the pre-war official pamphlet 'The Division in the Attack', based upon First World War experience. In O'Connor's view and that of his principal commanders it took too long and was too cumbersome. Moreover, air photos taken more recently of the real target showed minefields round most of the perimeter except at the entrance in the north-east corner of the camp which seemed to be used as a point of entry by Italian supply columns. The difficulty would be to reach this point without disturbing the Italians as it would mean moving the assault force right through the Nibeiwa-Rabia gap into the heart of the Italian position to attack from the north-west, instead of south-west, as originally intended. There would, however, be a bonus in this. Once inside the ring of Italian camps the assault forces would be immune from Italian air attack.

O'Connor accepted the difficulties and risks. His final plan envisaged a diversionary attack by one battalion on the eastern face of Nibeiwa in the early hours of 9 December to divert the Italians' attention from the passage of the attacking units into their final assault positions. Bomber aircraft were to keep up harassing attacks all night drowning the noise of the 'I' tanks as they churned forward. At 7 am the artillery would carry out a quick 15-minute registration of targets and at 7.15 am would start a general bombardment of the camp as the 'I' tanks approached the north-west entrance. The supporting infantry would be carried to within a few hundred yards of the camp in trucks, driven by New Zealanders. There they would dismount and follow the tanks into the camp. The process was to be repeated by the same tanks and artillery but with fresh infantry at the two Tummar Camps as soon as the tanks could be reassembled.

O'Connor's tactical planning went more smoothly than Wavell's at strategic level. Churchill was becoming intolerably impatient. On 22 November he sent a vindictive minute to Eden and the CIGS.

> General Wavell's telegram to CIGS does not answer the question I put ... I expected to hear either that the reinforcements of aircraft were insufficient, or that when they arrived he would act. It is not clear that he has made up his mind ...
>
> A British victory in Libya would probably turn the scale, and then we could shift our forces to the new theatre (Greece). How long would it be before the Germans could strike at Greece through Bulgaria? There might just be time for Wavell to act in Libya before the pressure becomes decisive.
>
> Anyhow all his troops, except the barest defensive minimum, will be drawn out of him before long ...
>
> (J. Connell: page 283 – not recorded by Churchill).

Four days later he addressed himself to Wavell personally, stressing the far-reaching repercussions of a successful 'Compass' and then demanding:

> If success is achieved, presume you have plans for exploiting it to the full. I am having a staff study made of possibilities open to us, if all goes well, for moving fighting troops and also reserves forward by sea in long hops along the coast, and setting up new supply bases to which pursuing armoured vehicles and units might resort. Without wishing to be informed on details, I should like to be assured that all this has been weighed, explored, and as far as possible prepared ...
>
> (Churchill: Vol II, page 483).

More generously he added: 'As we told you the other day, we shall stand by you and Wilson in any well-conceived action irrespective of result, because no one can guarantee success in war, but only deserve it'. (*Ibid:* page 484).

It was too late to do anything to increase the administrative backing for exploitation. O'Connor would have to improvise as best he could if the Italians collapsed. Neither Wavell nor Wilson told him of another development because they thought it would worry him. Beresford-Peirse's 4th Indian Division would be withdrawn at the end of the battle to go to the Sudan where it was to take part in the destruction of the Duke of Aosta's Empire. Timings were tight because the ships of a convoy returning from Suez to Britain via the Cape would have to be used, otherwise there would be a six weeks' delay before any other shipping would be available. Wavell intended to replace the Indians with Major-General Mackay's 6th Australian Division. Such were the pressures to do everything in Africa before the Germans could intervene in the Balkans that this plan was accepted as realistic. It hardly suggested rapid exploitation after a victory at Sidi Barrani.

On 5 December Wavell send Wilson the executive order to attack on 9 December. Churchill was not informed. His impatience frothed over late on 5 December. The CIGS sent a hastener to which the curt reply was: 'Actual date dependent on weather conditions. Will cable when firmly fixed'. (J. Connell: page 288).

Later on 6 December Wavell sent a fuller signal:

1. If weather permits preliminary move night 7/8 December, approach march 8/9 December, attack morning 9 December.
2. Feel undue hopes being placed on this operation which was designed as raid only. We are greatly outnumbered on the ground and in air, have to move over 75 miles of desert and attack enemy who has fortified himself for three months. Please do not encourage optimism . . .

Churchill exploded! The CIGS tried to soothe him by suggesting that Wavell was writing down the operation to avoid disappointment. Churchill was not mollified. He minuted:

Naturally I am shocked at paragraph 2, and I trust that your explanation of it will be realised. If, with the situation as it is, General Wavell is only playing small, and is not hurling on his whole available force with furious energy, he will have failed to rise to the height of the circumstances. I never 'worry' about action, but only about inaction.

(*Ibid*: page 289 – not recorded by Churchill).

During 7 and 8 December Wavell was seen with his family around Cairo, taking part in the normal social routine. He gave a dinner party for 15 on the evening of 8 December. No-one noticed anything unusual.

*   *   *

'Compass' was one of those rare battles which did go according to plan. It was fought with professional standards which were never again achieved by the British in the Western Desert until Montgomery won El Alamein. The expansion of the British Army in the Middle East was to bring with it an over-dilution of experienced officers and men which lowered standards and led to a break up of the close co-operation between infantry, tanks and guns upon which so much depends in battle. 'Compass' was a battle fought by a regular army.

The preliminary moves went smoothly. On 7 December the RAF opened its offensive, catching the Italians off-balance and destroying substantial numbers of their aircraft on their airfields. Fighter patrols kept the Italian reconnaissance aircraft away from O'Connor's force as it moved through the desert to its concentration area just south of its line of supply dumps. During 8 December attacks on the Italian airfields and RAF fighter cover kept the skies clear for the second and most risky leg of O'Connor's advance. A ground haze lasted until mid-morning and then the weather became overcast. One Italian reconnaissance aircraft was seen but as no air attacks developed the British concluded that they had not been seen. By dusk all units had reached their allotted assembly areas 15 miles south-east of the Rabia–Nibeiwa Gap. On the coast, Selby's Matruh garrison had advanced to a position south-east of Maktila ready to take advantage of the naval bombardment of the coastal camps. Selby also deployed a large number of dummy tanks in a harmless stretch of desert to attract the Italian airmen and to suggest a major threat was developing along the coast road.

The essence of the final phase of the approach march was accurate navigation by the assault force and its supporting artillery to bring them through the Italian line into their correct positions for attack. The night was bitterly cold. The Italians in Nibeiwa seemed alert in the first half of the night. Flares went up over the desert and occasionally their forward posts opened fire. By midnight all was quiet except for the drone of lone bombers and the occasional crunch of bombs dropped in the routine harassing of the Italian camps. Away to the north the hour-and-a-half's bombardment of Maktila and Sidi Barrani by the 15-inch guns of the monitor *Terror* and the smaller pieces of the gunboats *Aphis* and *Ladybird* could just be heard. The advance through the gap started as the moon rose after midnight. No Italian patrols were met. The Maletti Group in Nibeiwa were good troops but even the best can lose their inquisitiveness and alertness if left too long in a defensive position in which nothing ever seems to happen. It should not have been possible for Brigadier Savory's 11th Indian Brigade, supported by Lieutenant-Colonel R. M. Jerram's 7th Royal Tank Regiment with 48 'I' tanks and the whole of the 4th Indian Divisional Artillery with 72 guns, to slip undetected into its forming up positions around Nibeiwa; but this is what happened.

At 5 am the diversionary attack on the eastern face of Nibeiwa launched by 4th/7th Rajput Regiment, woke the Italians up, diverting their attention from the final moves of the assault force. By 6 am all was quiet again. The Italians relaxed and started the early morning routine of any military camp. As daylight grew a slight haze covered the desert. At 7 am the artillery registered the camp and at 7.15 am drenched it with high explosive as the 'I' tanks approached the north-west entrance. About 20 Italian medium M13 tanks were caught unmanned and destroyed outside the perimeter. As the 'I' tanks burst into the camp the 2nd Queen's Own Cameron Highlanders and 1st/6th Rajputana Rifles debussed from their New Zealand-driven trucks about 700 yards from the entrance and followed in the tanks' wake. Some of the Italian garrison, particularly the artillery, fought well, others were caught in their dug-outs. The gradual realisation that the heavy armour of the 'I' tanks was impervious to their anti-tank weapons had a decisive effect on the Italians. General Maletti was killed by a burst of machine gun fire from one of the 'I' tanks as he emerged from the mouth of his dug-out. By 10.40 am all was over. 2,000 prisoners and 35 tanks had fallen into Savory's hands for the loss of eight officers and 48 men. Alan Moorehead described the scene in the camp when he reached it some time after the attack:

Sand was blowing now out of the immense ruts cut by the tanks, and, walking through it, we went from one tent to another, from one dug-out by subterranean passage into the next. Extraordinary things met us wherever we turned. Officers' beds laid out with clean sheets, chests of drawers filled with linen and abundance of fine clothes ... uniforms heavy with gold lace and bedecked with medals ... dressing tables in the officers' tents strewn with scents and silver mounted brushes ... and never did an army write or receive letters as this one did. For five miles around the landscape was strewn with their letters ... I read one letter which contained a piece of doggerel that, roughly translated, runs like this:

'Long live the Duce and the King.
The British will pay for everything.
On land and sea and in the air
They'll compensate us everywhere'.

But there was much hard common sense besides. One letter-writer insisted: 'We are trying to fight this war as though it is a colonial war in Africa. But it is a European war in Africa fought with European weapons against a European enemy. We take too little account of this in building our stone forts and equipping ourselves with such luxury. We are not fighting the Abyssinians now!'

There was the whole thing; the explanation of this broken, savaged camp ... The British brigadier in this action had not for many weeks or even months lived as the Italian non-commissioned officer was living ...

(Moorehead, *Desert War*, pages 24–27).

The tank crews of 7th Royal Tank Regiment had no time to view the havoc they had wrought. They wheeled north and with the divisional artillery came into immediate support of Brigadier Lloyd's 5th Indian Infantry Brigade for its attack on Tummar West. Six tanks were unfortunately damaged on a minefield during re-assembly. The attack itself was almost a complete replica of the Nibeiwa attack and equally successful. Surpise, however, had been lost. The weather deteriorated with a sand-storm rising, making target recognition difficult. Again the Italian gunners fought the hardest, but were demoralised by their inability to stop the 'I' tanks. The attack started in the early afternoon and was as good as over by 4 pm. Darkness came before it was possible to press home the attack on Tummar East. The tanks managed to break in but the camp was not cleared until the following day.

Meanwhile 7th Armoured Division under Brigadier Caunter, deputising for Creagh who was unfortunately in hospital, had moved successfully into the Italian rear areas. Its 4th Armoured Brigade had been directed to destroy an Italian tank concentration believed to be near Azziziya but finding nothing continued northwards to cut the coast road between Sidi Barrani and Buq Buq by evening; its Support Group had blocked any movement eastward out of the Sofia-Rabia group of camps; and its 7th Armoured Brigade had remained in reserve in the Sofia-Rabia Gap providing a firm base and ready to cover a withdrawal if things went wrong. On the coast Selby tried to cut off the garrison of Maktila but started too late because news of the fall of Nibeiwa did not reach him until 3.20 pm. The 1st Libyan Division made good its escape towards Sidi Barrani during the night.

Operations on 10 December were less precisely mounted. The enemy's dispositions were not so accurately known; surprise had gone; and the weather had deteriorated further, bringing with it worse sand-storms. Beresford-Peirse's 4th Indian Division undertook two tasks: clearing Tummar East with 5th Indian Brigade; and isolating Sidi Barrani with Brigadier Lomax's 16th British Brigade, which thrust north to cut the coast road west of the village while 11th Indian Brigade closed the exits from the south. He relied on Selby's force to drive the Libyans and Blackshirt troops into the net from the east. Fighting was more of a dog-fight than on the previous day, but by evening Sidi Barrani itself had fallen and the trapped Italian units in the coastal sector were hemmed in a pocket east of the village. The 4th Armoured Brigade helped 4th Indian Division with tank support and so was unable to exploit with more than light forces towards Buq Buq.

11 December proved to be the end of the battle. 4th Indian Division and Selby Force crushed all resistance east of Sidi Barrani. 7th Armoured Brigade came out of reserve during the night and cut off most of the 64th Catanzaro Division around Buq Buq. 4th Armoured Brigade was first ordered into reserve and then told to cut off the 63 (Cirene) Division which was reported withdrawing from Sofafi. The order for some unexplained reason arrived too late. The Support Group pursued the Cirene Division as it withdrew but failed to catch it. By nightfall all resistance had ceased east of the Buq Buq – Sofafi line. Twenty-four hours later all Italians in Egypt except for the rearguard at Sollum were either dead or prisoners in British hands. The total capture was 38,300 prisoners with 237 guns and 73 tanks. British losses totalled 624 killed, wounded and missing. It was difficult to comprehend the scale of the Italian disaster until the dejected columns of prisoners were seen trudging eastwards away from the battlefield.

Why did the Battle of Sidi Barrani, as 'Compass' is now called, go so well? First of all, hard training over months under General Wilson's firm and realistic direction. Staffs, regimental officers and soldiers knew the desert and had gained an enthusiasm for their task which the Italians never achieved. Secondly, imaginative and original planning, aimed at achieving surprise, paid off. Wavell, Wilson and O'Connor were all brought up on studies of the campaigns of Lee and Jackson in Virginia and knew that numerical superiority was not necessarily a pre-requisite to success in war. The Confederate actions appealed to British soldiers, as they usually had to fight like the Confederacy under conditions of numerical inferiority. They were also inspired by Allenby's successes at Gaza and Megiddo against the Turks in 1918. They were well aware of the dangers of the 'Compass' operation, but they overcame the risks by meticulous staff work and extreme secrecy. And thirdly, the personalities of the senior commanders blended harmoniously to form a cohesive team. Wavell's unshakable determination prevented Churchill hurrying the command into an ill-prepared action. Wilson's organisational ability and knack of inspiring realism in training provided the standard of professionalism needed for the ambitious plan proposed. And O'Connor's quiet genuineness provided the tactical leadership in the field. It was a tragedy that this team was not to survive. Wavell eventually succumbed to Churchill's impatience; Wilson was promoted; and O'Connor was captured. But this is anticipating events.

Mussolini's wry comment on hearing that five Italian generals had been captured and one killed was: 'This is the ratio of Italians who have military qualities and those who have none'. (Ciano: page 317).

Churchill was unstinting in his praise, and yet his congratulatory signal contained the seeds of his next strategic tussle with Wavell.

> The Army of the Nile has rendered glorious service to the Empire and to our cause, and we are already reaping the rewards in every quarter ... Your first objective now must be to maul the Italian Army and rip them off the African shore to the utmost extent ... I feel convinced that it is only after you have made sure that you can get no further that you will relinquish the main hope in favour of secondary action in the Sudan or Dodecanese. The Sudan is of prime importance and eminently desirable and it may be that the two Indian Brigades (i.e. the 4th British Indian Division) can be spared without prejudice to the Libyan pursuit battle ...
>
> (Churchill: Vol II, page 542).

Wavell had already ordered O'Connor to release 4th Indian Division and Wilson was making the detailed arrangements to ship it south to Port Sudan in the empty ships of the returning UK convoy. He was also moving Mackay's 6th Australian Division forward to replace Beresford-Peirse's men. Churchill failed to appreciate the nicety with which Wavell was having to juggle his resources.

4

The British Fashion of War
(December 1940 to February 1941) .

'It was in fact an improvisation after the British fashion of war rather than a setpiece in the German manner . . .'

Wavell: Despatches 10 July 1946 page 3530.

The British always feel their way; they never have the preponderance of resources to do otherwise. The Germans, and for that matter the Americans, do things on a grander scale, basing their actions upon closely argued policies and sweeping concepts. British foreign policy can be defined as the pragmatic pursuit of their own enlightened self-interest; and their military planning follows a similar pattern. It would be nice to suggest that the Cs-in-C, Middle East, were pursuing a far-sighted strategy which led inexorably to the destruction of the Italian Empire in Africa; but, as Wavell confessed in his Despatches, this was not so. In retrospect, step seemed to follow step in logical sequence. In fact, no-one could guess, at the time, what would happen next. Operations developed as growing confidence, increasing resources and the random coincidence of events led from one British success to another. If genius was displayed, it lay in brilliance of improvisation rather than concept.

The autumn of 1940 had brought to the British a quickly changing sequence of emotions: first the relief that the British Isles had been spared invasion, although their people were suffering the rigours of the Luftwaffe's winter blitz; secondly, the exhilaration of dispatching precious troops and supplies eastwards in the traditional Imperial manner; thirdly, the warm realisation that the Italians were not the 'Romans' of Fascist propaganda; and finally, the full return of national confidence which came with the victories at Taranto and Sidi Barrani. Regrettably this laudable escalation of spirit was only psychological. The hard material facts of the situation remained unchanged. Britain was still alone and, though not held up to so much international ridicule as she had been in the summer, her resources of trained and equipped men were absurdly inadequate to resist the Axis forces which were at the height of their mobilised strength. Time had still to be bought. The struggle would begin again when the spring weather uncovered the shores of the British Isles and opened the Balkan passes.

There are two sides to the coin of buying time: 'heads' you build up your own

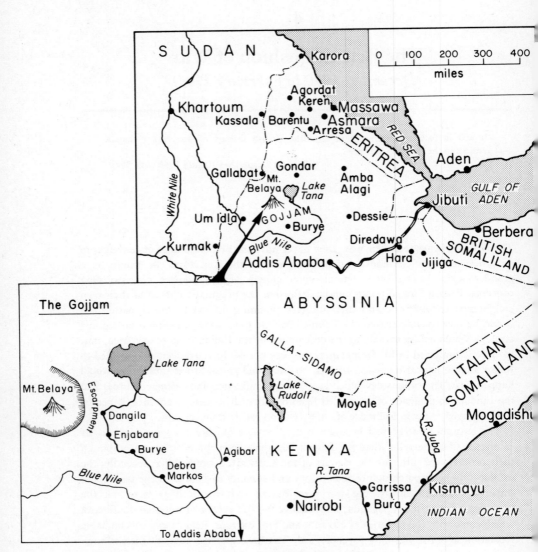

Map III: The East African Theatre

resources; and 'tails' you try to reduce those of your enemy. Both sides are equally important. The Battles of Taranto and Sidi Barrani were welcome beginnings in the process of weakening the less virile of the two Axis partners. An event of greater significance had taken place in the United States. President Roosevelt had been elected for his third term at the beginning of November. Churchill had written to congratulate him and, at the same time, to place before him a full and frank exposition of Britain's situation as he saw it. The letter reached the President on his post-election vacation in the Caribbean. It made a deep impression on his mind. Churchill left the heart of the matter until the end of his letter:

> Last of all, I come to the question of Finance. The more rapid and abundant the flow of munitions which you are able to send us, the sooner will our dollar credits be exhausted . . . The moment approaches when we shall no longer be able to pay cash . . .
>
> . . . I do not believe that the Government and people of the United States would find it in accordance with the principles which guide them to confine the help which they have so generously promised only to such munitions of war and commodities as could be immediately paid for. You may be certain that we shall prove ourselves ready to suffer and sacrifice to the utmost for the Cause, and that we glory in being its champions. The rest we leave with confidence to you and to your people, being sure that ways and means will be found which future generations on both sides of the Atlantic will approve and admire.
>
> (Churchill: Vol II, pages 500–501).

The idea of Lend-Lease had been germinating in many American minds, but it was Roosevelt who gave expression to it with his homely analogy:

> Suppose my neighbour's house catches fire and I have a length of garden hose four or five hundred feet away. If he can take my garden hose and connect it up with his hydrant I may help him to put out the fire. Now what do I do? I don't say to him before that operation 'Neighbour, my garden hose cost me 15 dollars; you have to pay me 15 dollars for it.' No! what is the transaction that goes on? I don't want 15 dollars – I want my hose back after the fire is over.
>
> (White House Papers, Vol I)

Roosevelt's determination and persuasive powers drove the Lend-Lease Bill through Congress until it became law in March 1941. His magnanimous response to Churchill's plea for help secured the obverse of the coin of buying time. It was up to the British to secure the reverse by their own efforts.

Taranto and Sidi Barrani had given them the tactical advantage in the Mediterranean and Northern Africa, but the British High Command was living on borrowed time. Hitler still held the strategic initiative. There were too many imponderables in the situation to permit the development of a clear-cut British military plan. How quickly would the stream of reinforcements arrive at Suez? In what state would they arrive? How long would they take to acclimatise and settle down in the strange desert environment? What would they be able to achieve when they were ready for operations? And when and where would Hitler strike next – across the English Channel, at Gibraltar, into Libya, through the Balkans or, as few dared hope, at his ally, Russia? The answer given to all these questions depended upon the personal view point of each member of the British High Command amongst whom there were honest differences of opinion. Churchill, working in Whitehall, viewed the situation through rose-tinted spectacles: reinforcements, once sent, were in action; British tanks, guns and aircraft were a match for anyone; resolution not material won battles; delay for whatever cause was criminal. Wavell, surrounded by the cares of an operational theatre, took a more practical and hence less optimistic view: new units could not be thrown piecemeal into battle; equipment had to be overhauled and modified for desert conditions on arrival; supplies of all kinds had to be stockpiled; distances were immense and could not be ignored; lack of indigenous resources, particularly of water, had to be overcome; everything took time : the one commodity Churchill would never allow. It is surprising that a greater antagonism did not grow between the men in Whitehall led by the Prime Minister and the commanders in the Middle East led by Wavell. Churchill became more than ever convinced that Wavell was misusing the precious resources sent to him at such risk and cost. Wavell, for his part, had every right to resent Churchill's meddling in the military affairs of his theatre of war, and in his stubborn, honest way refused to allow Churchill's 'barracking', as he called it, to affect his judgment or decision. Every British move in North Africa became the occasion for a stream of signals between Prime Minister and C-in-C. Two races developed: a strategic race between the British attempting to do as much damage to the Italians as possible before the Germans could intervene; and a personal race between Churchill's growing disillusion with Wavell and Wavell's ability to throw victories in his face. The British and Wavell lost both races in the end, but relationships between politicians and service chiefs never sank to the abysmal level of the First World War. Both sides respected the others' integrity, though not necessarily judgment which was quite a different matter.

The core of the disagreement between the men in Whitehall and those in Africa lay in the policy to be pursued in Abyssinia. Churchill believed that the Duke of Aosta's Empire could be reduced by the slow blight of internal revolt sponsored by the British clandestine operations and by economic and military blockade imposed by the Royal Navy. Only small defensive detachments need to be left to cover Sudan and Kenya; the rest of the British forces, particularly the South African Division arriving in Kenya, should be moved north to form a central reserve in Egypt for use in emergencies in the Balkans, Turkey, Syria or Iraq. Wavell could not agree. Aosta's 250,000 men in Abyssinia were a serious threat to the Sudan and Kenya, and would not wither away very quickly. He did agree that the principal weapon against the Italians should be the 'Patriot Revolt', but the frontiers had to be held securely by regular troops and there were not, as yet, enough of these to protect the Sudan and Kenya properly.

The whole policy for East Africa had been thrashed out at Khartoum at the end of October during Anthony Eden's visit. Wavell had instructed his commanders in the Sudan and Kenya to adopt an aggressive defensive posture and to submit plans for

5. Italian artillery captured after Beda Fomm.

6. Prisoners from the Italian Tenth Army.

7. Colonel Wingate inspecting "Patriot" troops.

8. "Patriot" bands awaiting the Emperor Haile Selassie's arrival at Debra Marcos.

future offensive operations. These plans were presented at the Khartoum conference in the presence of General Smuts and the Emperor Haile Selassie who was awaiting the opportunity to return to his country. Smuts supported Wavell in his anxiety about Kenya and was prepared to send more South African troops and transport to Mombasa to help Wavell liquidate the Italian threat to Kenya more quickly. He supported Churchill as well in that he wished to move his South Africans up to the main Egyptian theatre as soon as Kenya was secure. The upshot of the conference was that: General Platt, commanding in the Sudan, was to attack Gallabat in November and Kassala in January, using the 5th Indian Division which was arriving from India; General Alan Cunningham, who had just taken over in Kenya, and, who, incidentally, was the soldier-brother of the naval C-in-C, would study the possibility of carrying out Smuts' plan by attacking Kismayu in Italian Somaliland in January; and Haile Selassie would receive greater material support to re-enter his country as soon as an area of 'free territory' could be dominated for him by the Abyssinian 'patriots'.

Until the Khartoum conference 'Patriot' affairs had been taking shape very slowly. 101 Mission led by an ex-settler, Colonel D.A. Sandford, who had been expelled from Abyssinia by the Italians in 1933, had crossed the frontier in early August to contact and advise the supporters of Haile Selassie's cause in the Cojjam region south of Lake Tana. In Khartoum itself the British had been raising four battalions of Abyssinian exiles under British officers and NCOs to support Sandford at the appropriate moment. Eden appreciated that the Emperor would need an energetic military adviser at his side. Both he and Wavell had met and been impressed by a young major called Orde Wingate, who was also known to other important political figures in Whitehall. At Wavell's request Wingate was sent out from England to take over as the Emperor's adviser and commander of the local forces being raised to support him.

General Platt's November attack at Gallabat, which was mounted by a brigade of 5th Indian Division, failed. It was led by Brigadier J. W. Slim*, who later won fame as the commander of the British XIV Army in Burma. His vivid description of his Indian Brigade's action paints the scene in the Sudan before the Battle of Sidi Barrani had had its demoralising effect on Italian troops.

> My orders were to capture Gallabat-Metemma with the object of opening one of the main routes into Abyssinia . . With the preponderance of force probably on the side of the well-entrenched enemy, my only hope of success rested on surprise and speed. I guessed that the arrival of Indian infantry before Gallabat must have been observed, but I did not think the Italians would expect us to be so rash as to attack though their obstacles and wire without the support of artillery. It was therefore above all essential that I should hide from them the fact that I had a regiment of field artillery and, still more, the presence of what I hoped would be my secret weapon — a squadron of six light and six cruiser tanks . . .

Surprise was achieved and Gallabat was taken by Slim's two Indian battalions. The

* Field Marshal Lord Slim.

British battalion – the third battalion of his brigade – was sent through to seize Gallabat Hill.

Slim continues:

> . . . a distant drone of aircraft approaching from the east grew louder . . . I stepped out, looked towards Metemma and saw a sight, none the less disturbing because we had been expecting it . . . the bombers shook out of line ahead and flew unhurriedly across Gallabat. At once, machine by machine, they began to drop their heavy bombs. The whole of Gallabat Hill spouted with great gouts of smoke and flame . . .

Slim went forward to see what had happened on Gallabat Hill:

> Just where the track from Gallabat passed below us was a traffic control post manned by Baluchis. I was surprised a few minutes later to see the Indian officer in charge hurrying up the hill. He arrived excited and breathless from running.
>
> 'The British soldiers from Gallabat,' he panted, 'are driving through my post, shouting that the enemy are coming and that the order is to retire. We cannot stop them. They drive fast at anybody who tries! . . .
>
> I walked on to the shoulder of the hill. Two trucks about a hundred yards apart were coming very fast down the track; a couple of sepoys stood waving their arms to them to stop. The trucks filling with gesticulating soldiers crashed on . . . ignoring my frantic signals . . . yelling 'The enemy are coming!' I had seen panic before and I recognised it.

(Slim: Unofficial History, pages 129 – 140)

There was no excuse for a regular battalion to succumb in this way, but this minor affair was symptomatic of the real situation – not the situation as seen in Whitehall or even Cairo. There were too many new and untried units coming into action for the first time. Unless they were handled with great care – as Wavell and his generation knew from their experiences in the First World War – disasters could happen through lack of 'battle sense' amongst the officers and NCOs. Two fears stalked men's minds in the early years of the Second World War: 'Panzer fear' – the horror of being over-run by tanks when troops had no effective anti-tank weapons to defend themselves; and fear of unimpeded air attack. The Italians succumbed to the former at Sidi Barrani; and the British suffered the latter at Gallabat. The Italians were still masters of the air over Abyssinia. Their military strength would dwindle, but in November 1940 Aosta's forces could not be ignored as Churchill supposed.

General Cunningham was no more successful in Kenya but for different reasons. His examination of the problems of attacking Kismayu led him to report that the operation should be delayed until after the rains in May. He would not have enough transport to move an adequate force forward through the northern bush country of Kenya unless adequate supplies of water were found on the route. So far little had been discovered. Wavell forwarded Cunningham's assessment to London. Churchill took strong exception to the suggested delay, and demanded earlier action, forcing

Wavell to review the situation again with Platt and Cunningham in Cairo. He concluded, in spite of Churchill's nagging, that conditions were not yet propitious for major offensive operations. Practical difficulties forced him to put back timings rather than bring them forward as Churchill wanted. Platt's offensive at Kassala was to be delayed until February when 4th Indian Division would have completed its move from the Western Desert; and Cunningham's offensive towards Kismayu was set for late May or possibly June. Wavell had summed up his policy just before the 'Compass' offensive began:

> The ruling idea in my mind in the decisions taken at this conference was that the fomentation of the patriot movement in Abyssinia offered with the resources available the best prospect of making the Italian position impossible and eventually reconquering the country. I did not intend a large scale invasion either from Kassala towards Asmara and Massawa, or from Kismayu to the north. The two operations to Kassala and Kismayu were designed to secure our flanks and I intended that our main effort should be devoted to furthering and supporting the rebellion by irregular action.

(Wavell Dispatches: page 3528)

*　　*　　*

The Battle of Sidi Barrani upset the calculations of the British, Italian and German High Commands, and made December another month of decision. It showed the British how little they need fear Mussolini's legions; it depressed the Italian people still further; and it irritated the Germans more than ever, bringing to a head decisions which were pending within OKW. On 10 December Hitler ordered 'Mittelmeer' (Luftwaffe intervention in the Mediterranean). Next day he cancelled 'Felix' (attack on Gibraltar). A few days later he issued three OKW Operational Directives in quick succession: Directive No. 19, 'Plan Anton', a contingency plan for the occupation of Vichy France; No. 20, 'Operation Marita', the invasion of Greece; and the fatal No. 21, 'Operation Barbarossa', the invasion of Russia. 'Marita' and 'Barbarossa' were to be carefully synchronised and put into active preparation forthwith. General List's Twelfth Army of 18 divisions was nominated for 'Marita'.The German General Staff calculated it would take 78 days to assemble List's troops in Rumania, and, at the last possible moment, to bridge the Danube and pass them rapidly across Bulgaria to the Greek frontier which they they would cross at the end of March. The Greek campaign was expected to last three to four weeks. Four more weeks were allowed for List's divisions to refit and move back northwards to take their place on the Russian frontier in time for the opening of 'Barbarossa' in the middle of May. It was confidently assumed that Russia would collapse before the autumn. Renewed preparations for 'Sea Lion' would be used in the spring as a cover plan for 'Barbarossa'. Once Russia had capitulated, Hitler would turn on England, executing 'Sea Lion' as the 'coup de grace'. This was a grand design in the traditional German manner.

The British had nothing comparable with which to oppose such a concept; only their traditional skill at improvisation which enabled them to accelerate their operations as Italian weakness grew and unexpected events created new situations. In the Western Desert, O'Connor found himself embarrassed by the milling mass of Italian prisoners, which threatened to absorb all his slender logistic resources needed to exploit his success, as Churchill demanded, with a rapid advance westwards into Cyrenaica. He was aghast when he heard that 4th Indian Division was to be sent to the Sudan and replaced by Major-General MacKay's 6th Australian Division whose training and equipment were barely complete. The infantry cutting-edge of his force was being taken from him. From his parochial point of view this seemed a disastrous decision, but Wavell was like a juggler, trying to keep three balls in the air at the same time – operations in the Western Desert, in the Sudan and in Kenya. He could not hesitate because the availability of shipping and the irascibility of his trainer, Churchill, would not let him pause.

The Italians evacuated Sollum and all their posts on the Egyptian frontier on 16 December, falling back into the security of the fortified perimeter of Bardia. Creagh's 7th Armoured Division, supported by the 16th British Brigade, which had been left behind by the 4th Indian Division as unsuitable for operations in the Sudan, followed them up, encircling the fortress and cutting the Tobruk – Bardia road to prevent the Italians reinforcing the garrison. The morale of the Italian troops had recovered slightly, but Marshal Graziani was not in a psychologically fit state to give them the resolute leadership they needed.

First, he ordered the Tenth Army to hold Bardia and Tobruk; then he had second thoughts about his decision and suggested to Mussolini that Bardia should be evacuated so that Tenth Army could concentrate on holding the more important port of Tobruk. Mussolini refused on the grounds that the British must be delayed as far east as possible to allow time for reinforcements to arrive from Italy. General Bergonzoli – 'Electric Whiskers' to both the Italians and the British – was ordered to hold Bardia with his XXIII Italian Corps, consisting of the 1st and 2nd Blackshirt Divisions, the 62nd (Marmarica) and the 63rd (Cirene) Divisions – a total force of 45,000 troops with 400 guns.

British Intelligence grossly underestimated the Bardia Garrison, assessing it as about 20,000 demoralised troops. On 16 December Wavell cabled General Sir John Dill, who was now CIGS, that he had three courses open to him. He could try to induce the garrison to surrender, and to this end he was having a proclamation printed which would be dropped from the air over Bardia. If this failed, he could lay siege to the fortress; or he could leave an escape route open to the garrison so that he could attack them in the open desert as they tried to withdraw. He preferred the last course and proposed to encourage it by heavy naval and air bombardments. He brought forward MacKay's Australians to invest the southern half of the perimeter, while Creagh's 7th Armoured Division covered the northern half with a light screen of reconnaissance troops, keeping his main force ready to attack any attempted Italian break-out.

Italian actions soon showed that the British had temporarily misjudged their opponents. Bergonzoli showed no signs of giving up; nor of breaking out. Mussolini had sent him a personal signal, to which he had replied: '. . . I have today repeated to my troops your message – simple and unequivocal. In Bardia we are and here we stay'. (*Australian Official History*: Vol I, page 201).

Bergonzoli had good reason to believe he could defeat the British if they attacked. The defences of Bardia were new and complete. A well sited anti-tank ditch some 12 feet wide by 4 feet deep covered the whole perimeter. This was backed by dense wire entanglements and minefields which were covered by fire from two lines of mutually supporting reinforced-concrete and steel-shuttered pill-boxes, and from concealed artillery positions deep inside the fortress. Bardia was well stocked with ammunition and supplies, whereas the British would have to move everything they needed over 200 miles of desert track. Bardia's weakness lay, like that of most other fortresses, in the length of its perimeter. An attacker could always concentrate overwhelming strength at the point chosen for his breach. It was difficult for the defender to hold large enough reserves for counter-attack while at the same time manning all his perimeter posts. Moreover, as was shown at Nibeiwa, it was easy to surprise defenders who were holding fixed defences. Boredom made observation lax and the security of concrete made men less prepared to expose themselves to find out what was going on outside. Bergonzoli placed his faith in mines, wire, concrete and anti-tank ditches; O'Connor, whose Western Desert Force was renamed the XIII Corps, placed his, perforce, in the fighting spirit of MacKay's Australians.

It may seem surprising that Australian troops had not been used earlier. Their leading brigade had arrived in the Middle East almost a year earlier. Two difficulties arose: lack of equipment, and Australian political determination not to operate piecemeal as separate units within a British force. In July 1940, Wavell had proposed the formation of a composite '6th Australasian Division' consisting of the 16th Australian and 4th New Zealand Brigades which were the only formations ready at that time. Neither General Freyberg, commanding the New Zealand contingent, nor General Blamey, commanding the Australians, would countenance this. Freyberg spoke for them both. Writing to Wavell, he said:

Have just received your proposal for reorganisation with its repercussions on the New Zealand Expeditionary Force . . . I do not wish to disclose to the New Zealand Government the proposals as outlined by you to break up the New Zealand Forces, as they would make a most unfavourable impression in New Zealand official circles with repercussions you have probably not foreseen. The answer to any such proposal would, I am sure, be an uncompromising refusal.

(*Ibid:* page 103).

Freyberg's letter was a timely reminder that forces from Commonwealth countries could not be treated as 'British' troops; they were allies of the British with contingent commanders who were responsible to their own home governments and not to the British War Cabinet in London. The Australians and New Zealanders were no less keen to beat the Axis forces than their British colleagues, but they were determined to do so in their own way under their own commanders within the overall British plan.

Men of the Australian and New Zealand expeditionary forces were also conscious of the great fighting traditions of their forebears in the First World War and were keen to emulate their prowess as soon as they were adequately equipped. It was not until the middle of November that MacKay was able to hold his first 6th Australian Division exercise and even then his troops lacked some essential equipment, particularly transport. He could not be ready for 'Compass' but could be soon afterwards.

The feeling that the Italian Defence of Bardia would collapse without siege or assault persisted amongst the British for some days. The 16th Australian Brigade reached the perimeter on 19 December and came into the line on the south-western face. For a week Brigader A. S. Allen, commanding the brigade, probed the Italian defences with splendidly robust patrolling. O'Connor suggested to MacKay that his Australians should make a series of raids under cover of artillery bombardment, any one of which might result in a bridgehead being established within the defences. Things were not to be hurried, and yet time was not to be wasted. The Australians soon found, however, that Italian resistance was far from demoralised, particularly in the southern sectors held by their 62nd and 63rd Divisions. By 24 December MacKay advised O'Connor that a set piece 'Operation approaching those in France during 1916–18' would be needed. O'Connor agreed and suggested:

> Some plan would have to be made which would ensure that the few remaining 'I'
> tanks (only 18 were left after Sidi Barrani) succeeded in getting safely across the

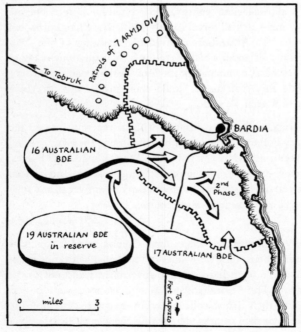

Fig 4 Operations
at Bardia:
January 1940

anti-tank ditch and minefields, and that this could only be done by an infantry attack on a narrow front against the enemy front line preceding the advance of the tanks. If successful, a bridge could be made over the anti-tank ditch and a path through the minefield cleared. I instructed him (MacKay) to think something out on these lines.

(*Ibid:* page 154).

On 27 December Brigadier S. Savige's 17th Australian Brigade reached the perimeter and relieved the 16th British Brigade in the southern sector which was then withdrawn into reserve, leaving the Australians covering the whole of the southern half of the defences while 7th Armoured Division watched the northern half. Brigadier H. C. H. Robertson's 19th Australian Brigade was held back in the Nile Delta ready to embark for an amphibious landing in Bardia Harbour if a sudden collapse occurred. Next day MacKay decided that he had enough information on which to base his plan. He chose to break-in with Allen's 16th Australian Brigade at a point mid-way between the Tobruk-Bardia and Fort Capuzzo-Bardia roads. Here the ground was slightly higher, which would give better artillery observation and would allow the slow and ponderous 'I' tanks a downhill run within the perimeter. Intelligence reports had also suggested that the point selected lay on the boundary of two Italian divisional sectors. After Allen's break-in, Savige's 17th Australian Brigade with two battalions would pass through the breach and roll up the Italian defences in a south-easterly drive. His third battalion would mount a diversionary attack on the southern face of the perimeter. It was also agreed that Robertson's 19th Australian Brigade would be brought up from the Delta to act as divisional reserve, but O'Connor stressed that he did not want it used unless it was essential, because he wanted it for his attack on Tobruk which would be mounted as soon as Bardia fell.

'D' Day for MacKay's attack was set for 2 January but was later postponed to 3 January to give more time for preparation. O'Connor arranged for him to be supported by all available artillery, though this only amounted to 120 of the 154 guns belonging to XIII Corps. Some of the disparity between the Italian and British artillery would be made up by British naval and air bombardment. 7th Armoured Division would help by harassing the northern half of the perimeter, and all the 7th Royal Tank Regiment's 'I' tanks, which had been raised by repair to 20 would be under MacKay's command. O'Connor's greatest difficulty lay, as Bergonzoli predicted, in bringing forward water, ammunition and other supplies. The Italians had taken two and a half months to stock Sidi Barrani for their advance on Mersa Matruh. O'Connor was using no more than two and a half weeks to do the reverse. It was a hand to mouth affair in which every available British and captured Italian truck was pressed into service.

'H' hour was set for 0530 am. As in the First World War, the men were over-loaded with equipment. It was still very cold in the desert at night. The description of their dress is worth recording:

The men were heavily laden; each wore his woollen uniform with a sleeveless leather jerkin over or under the tunic, and most had also a greatcoat with skirts

turned back to allow freedom of movement. They wore steel helmets, with
respirators hanging on their chests; some carried sandbags wrapped round their
legs; and, in pouches, pockets and haversacks, 150 rounds of ammunition, one or
two grenades and three days' rations of tinned beef and biscuits. They set out
carrying picks and shovels but the combined load was too heavy and most of the
tools were abandoned.

(Ibid: pages 163-164).

This was the last time that Australians would advance into battle so heavily laden.
Distances were too great in the Second World War. Lightness of equipment became
the order of the day in subsequent attacks. Experience was being bought as well as
time.

The 2/1* Australian Battalion led the assault behind an artillery barrage, carrying
bangalore torpedoes with which they breached the wire fences. Accompanying
sappers cleared the mines and broke down the faces of the anti-tank ditch to open
paths for the 'I' tanks. It was still dark while this work was going on. The Italian
reaction proved sporadic and ineffective. By 0635 am the 2/2 and 2/3 Australian
Battalions were advancing through the breach supported by the 'I' tanks and were
fanning out in a great arc to form a bridge-head for the 17th Australian Brigade's
attack south-eastwards which was due to start at 11.30 am. All along the expanding
arc of the Australian advance small actions developed between platoons of
Australians, one or two 'I' tanks and individual Italian strong-points. Some Italian
posts fought well; others gave up without a fight. The depressing effect of seeing the
tracers of their anti-tank shells striking the 'I' tanks' hulls and ricocheting high in the
sky reduced their resolution. As at Nibeiwa, the Italian artillerymen fought hardest
and the most effectively. A local counter-attack was launched by six Italian medium
tanks, but this was stopped by Australian 2-pounder anti-tank guns which easily
penetrated their thin armour. By 8.30 am Allen's Brigade was firm on their objective
with 8,000 prisoners streaming to the rear behind them. They had suffered
comparatively few casualties themselves, but the 'I' tanks had been battered by
artillery firing over open-sights and took some time to rally for refuelling and
re-arming to support Savige's 17th Australian Brigade attack.

In the interval between the two brigade attacks, the battleships *Barham, Valiant*
and *Warspite* with seven destroyers tore up the rear of the Italian position with
45 minutes' bombardment by 15-inch guns. The monitor *Terror* with her faithful
gunboat supporters then took over and continued a sporadic naval bombardment
throughout the day. The RAF concentrated upon the Italian airfields and was so
successful that the Italian Air Force failed to intervene in Bergonzoli's support.

Savige's operation was not as successful as Allen's. His men had started their
march to their assembly area at 12.30 pm the previous day. The plan was
over-complex and arrangements went awry. When they did reach their forming up
positions in the bridgehead, their 'I' tanks were late in arriving and fewer in number
than they had hoped due to losses in the first phase. Fighting was much more severe

* The 2 in front of all Australian battalion titles signified battalions raised for the Second World War.

than earlier in the day. As Savige's men pushed along the line of Italian defences taking them in the flank and rear, the 62nd and 63rd Divisions fought back stubbornly, their artillery putting up a very creditable resistance. By dusk, however, MacKay's division was poised to crush all further resistance the following day.

During the afternoon MacKay had given out his orders for the second day. He had obtained O'Connor's approval to use Robertson's 19th Australian Brigade to reinforce the final attack which began at 11.30 am next day. Allen's 16th Australian Brigade swept forward towards Bardia town while 17th and 19th Brigades cleared up the southern sectors of the perimeter. There were very few 'I' tanks left in running order, but they had done their work the previous day. Italian morale gave way and their resistance decreased as the Australian infantry pushed into the soft core of the fortress which was full of technical and logistic troops who were over-willing to surrender in embarrassing numbers. At 4 pm 16th Australian Brigade entered Bardia. Its advance had been too quick for the Italians to blow up the logistic installations. The water supply – the most important prize – was intact. The harbour, however, was obstructed by ships sunk by British air attacks and was almost unusable. It was only next day that the true size of the garrison was revealed. Bergonzoli had escaped on foot to Tobruk, but his four divisional commanders and 40,000 of their men marched eastwards into captivity. Australian losses amounted to 456 men. Only six 'I' tanks remained to advance westwards with Creagh's 7th Armoured Division and Robertson's 19th Australian Brigade toward Tobruk.

While the loss of Bardia and its garrison was a further blow to Italian morale, it had a greater effect on the German and British High Commands. On 11 January Hitler issued OKW Directive No. 22 (Assistance in the Mediterranean). Two specific measures were to be taken: first a 'Special Blocking Detachment' strong in German anti-tank, anti-aircraft and tank units was to be sent to Africa to help the Italians defend Tripoli by neutralising British tank and air superiority; and, secondly, Fliegerkorps X, which was assembling in Sicily for Operation 'Mittelmeer', would extend its area of operations to support the Italian army in the Western Desert. In the subsequent negotiations between the German and Italian Staffs on the implementation of this directive, the Italians agreed to send their Ariete Armoured and Trento Mechanised Divisions to Tripoli early in February: and the Germans informed the Italians that a specially constituted 5th Light Motorised Division was being prepared for dispatch to Africa in mid-February to undertake the 'blocking detachment' role ordered by Hitler in Directive No. 22. The codeword for the dispatch of 5th Light Division was 'Sonnenblume' (Sunflower).

'Sonnenblume' would not affect affairs in the Mediterranean for over a month, but the repercussions of 'Mittelmeer' were to be felt by the Royal Navy a few days after the fall of Bardia. By the middle of January Fliegerkorps X had 186 bombers, fighters and reconnaissance aircraft on airfields in Sicily. The German pilots soon showed their skill. Admirals Cunningham and Somerville set out from Alexandria and Gibraltar at the end of the first week of January to pass the 'Excess' convoy of five fast merchantmen through the Mediterranean. Somerville's Force 'H' with the carrier *Ark Royal* handed over the convoy to Cunningham's main fleet, comprising the battleships *Warspite* and *Valiant* and the carrier *Illustrious,* for the passage through the Sicilian Channel. The British ships had been attacked ineffectively by Italian bombers during 10 January. The Fulmar fighters from *Illustrious* were intercepting one of these Italian raids, when her radars detected a large force of aircraft approaching from the north. She recalled her Fulmars and turned into wind to launch more fighters. She had only just resumed her course when she was attacked with great determination and accuracy by 30 to 40 German Junker 88s and 87s (dive bombers) before her fighters could intervene. She was hit six times. For three hours she circled out of control; then she managed to head for Malta, steering with her engines. She was attacked again on two occasions as she limped towards the island, receiving one more direct hit. In Malta her troubles began all over again. For the next fortnight the Luftwaffe pounded the dockyard to prevent her ever sailing again. The dogged efforts of the British and Maltese dockyard engineers and workers were rewarded when she slipped away to Alexandria at dusk on 23 January, eventually reaching the United States for repair via the Suez Canal. The balance of naval power, which she had helped to swing in favour of the Royal Navy at Taranto, now swung back to the Axis. A new and uncomfortable era had started for the British Fleet in the Mediterranean. The dominance achieved by the Luftwaffe came just at the right time for the Axis, making it practical to ship Italian and German reinforcements to Tripoli to shore up Graziani's tottering position in Libya. It could hardly have come at a worse time for the British. Two more months' freedom from German intervention would have seen the final expulsion of the Italians from Africa and the end of the North African Campaign. Instead the bombing of *Illustrious* heralded the opening of the real battle for Northern Africa, fought by two races of equal fighting quality – the British and the Germans.

The arrival of the Luftwaffe had another damaging effect on the British position in the Middle East. Over the next few months German mine-laying aircraft began operations from the Dodecanese Islands against the Suez Canal. They were highly successful, using both magnetic and acoustic mines. Some ships were sunk in the fairway blocking the canal for several days on end, but the main delay was caused by the need to sweep for mines after each raid. Thousands of troops were used each night along the canal to observe the points at which the mines were dropped. In very vulnerable areas nets were stretched across the canal, not, as was rumoured at the time, to catch the mines, but as a method of pin-pointing accurately the position of the mines from the holes made in the nets. The uncomfortable truth emerged that one Fliegerkorps had achieved what neither Hitler's diplomacy nor the whole of Mussolini's armed forces could accomplish. The Mediterranean was closed to British convoys and the capacity of the Suez Canal was seriously reduced.

While the fall of Bardia may have depressed Mussolini and annoyed Hitler, it made Churchill almost unmanageable. There was an element of gleeful 'I told you so' in his dealings with the Chiefs of Staff and Wavell at this time. One of many clashes occurred over an offer by Prime Minister Smuts to supply an extra South African division to accelerate operations in East Africa. Churchill wished to accept the offer but Wavell was lukewarm. He did not need more fighting formations. What he wanted was reinforcements to replace casualties, replacement equipment to keep his experienced units in action, and the logistic units to give them increased endurance over greater distances. Churchill's logistic 'blind spot' remained. Even in his congratulatory signal to Wavell on the fall of Bardia, he criticised the number of base troops in Egypt. But it was Anthony Eden – now Foreign Secretary – who created the most jarring note in Middle East affairs. He minuted the Prime Minister on 6 January:

Saluations and congratulations upon the victory of Bardia! If I may debase a golden phrase, 'Never has so much been surrendered by so many to so few'.

The object of this minute, however, is to call attention to a less satisfactory sector of the international horizon, the Balkans. A mass of information has come to us over the last few days from divers sources, all of which tends to show that Germany is pressing forward her preparations in the Balkans with a view to an ultimate descent on Greece. The date usually mentioned for such a descent is the beginning of March, but I feel confident that the Germans must be making every effort to antedate their move . . .

(Churchill: Vol III, page 13).

On 10 January the Cs-in-C Middle East were warned that they might have to divert tank, anti-tank, anti-air and field artillery units to help the Greeks, who were short of these specialists, as well as RAF Squadrons. Wavell felt sceptical about Eden's intelligence and cabled to Dill:

. . . Our appreciation here is that German concentration is more a war of nerves designed with object of helping Italy by upsetting Greek nerves, inducing us to disperse our forces in the Middle East and to stop our advance in Libya. Nothing we can do from here is likely to be in time to stop German advance if really intended, it will lead to most dangerous dispersion of force and is playing the enemy's game . . .

(J. Connell: page 310).

Churchill reacted venomously:

Our information contradicts idea that German concentration in Rumania is merely 'move in war of nerves' or 'bluff to cause dispersion of force' . . .

2. . . . Destruction of Greece would eclipse victories you have gained in Libya and might effect decisively Turkish attitude, especially if we had shown ourselves callous of fate of allies. You must now therefore conform your plans to larger interests at stake.

3. Nothing must hamper capture of Tobruk but thereafter all operations in Libya are subordinate to aiding Greece . . .

4. We expect and require prompt and active compliance with our decisions for which we bear full responsibility . . .

(Churchill: Vol III, page 16 and J. Connell: page 313).

In the Western Desert, O'Connor had already surrounded Tobruk after an unopposed advance from Bardia. MacKay was again given the task of breaking into the fortress, which British Intelligence, this time correctly, estimated was held by 25,000 men and 200 guns of General Mannella's XXII Corps : half the size of the garrison of Bardia to man defences of similar construction but with twice the length of perimeter. The 61st (Serti) Division was the principal fighting formation in the garrison. The nearest reinforcements were the 60th (Sabratha) Division at Derna and an armoured group of unknown strength under General Babini at Mechili.* It was thought that Graziani intended to delay O'Connor as long as possible at Tobruk while he built up a new defensive line between Derna and Mechili, covering the great fertile Djebel Akhdar bulge of Cyrenaica.

The port of Tobruk was logistically essential to O'Connor for a further advance westwards by his XIII Corps. MacKay's attack, once launched, had to be quick and deep enough to forestall any plans Mannella might have made to blow up the installations and block the harbour. O'Connor's operational staff estimated that MacKay would need about 1000 tons of artillery ammunition for a successful assault; and his logistic staff calculated that this could not be dumped at the guns much before 21 January because the port of Bardia was still blocked and every ton of supplies had to be ferried overland by trucks from Mersa Matruh.

While MacKay's Australians prepared for their assault on Tobruk with their characteristic determination to dominate their opponents, Wavell and Longmore flew to Athens to discuss with the Greeks the German threat and what should be done to counter it. General Metaxas, the Greek Prime Minister, viewed the situation in the Balkans with greater realism and less emotion than Churchill. He was prepared to accept logistic help which Wavell offered, but not fighting units. In his view, the arrival of the few British tank and artillery regiments available would provide Hitler with the pretext he needed for attack without giving Greece enough help to repel a German invasion. He was not refusing British help; only postponing it until a larger force could be released from North Africa or elsewhere to sway the military balance. Wavell agreed with his diagnosis and reported to London:

> Present proposal is a dangerous half-measure. I do not believe that troops it is proposed to send are sufficient to enable the equivalent of three Greek divisions to hold Salonika if the Germans are really determined to advance on it.
>
> We shall almost inevitably be compelled to send further troops in haste or shall become involved in retreat or defeat. Meanwhile advance in Libya will be halted and Italians given time to recover . . .
>
> (J. Connell: page 315)

It is a pity that he did not maintain this view as events, which are described in the next chapter, unfolded.

Metaxas had temporarily saved Wavell's Western Desert campaign. Churchill and the Chiefs of Staff were forced to accept his verdict. Quite unexpectedly, the Duke of Aosta saved Wavell's East African plans as well. The defeat at Sidi Barrani and the

* See Map IV, page 92.

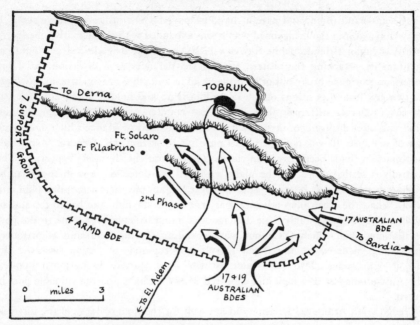

Fig 5 The Capture of Tobruk: 21st to 22nd January 1941

loss of Bardia undermined Italian morale in East Africa. The British became military giants overnight in Italian eyes. The activities of British patrols and raiding forces on the frontiers were grossly exaggerated. The Viceroy himself became openly pessimistic and asked Mussolini, on 11 January, for permission to abandon the Sudan frontier because he considered it too flat and open for him to resist British mechanised forces. Mussolini agreed that he should withdraw to the hill country around Agordat and Barentu, blocking the main approaches to Asmara and Massawa.* On 18 January, Platt was embarrassed to hear that the Italian garrisons of Kassala and Gallabat had slipped away from their positions. He was forced to open his offensive next day, three weeks earlier than he had intended. 4th Indian Division was still in the process of arriving in the Sudan. Nevertheless, Beresford-Peirse set off in pursuit, improvising in true British style. Coincidentally, the Emperor Haile Selassie was flown into a small air-strip prepared for him at Um Idla, 30 miles inside Abyssinia in the valley of the Blue Nile, by Sandford and Wingate. The 'Patriot Revolt' was gaining a satisfactory momentum, encouraged by the news of the Italian defeats in Libya.

Around Tobruk preparations for the Australian assault were going ahead. At 05.40 am on 21 January MacKay attacked, using a similar but improved version of his Bardia operation. The Australian infantry advanced, this time without jerkins or greatcoats and with minimum equipment. Allen's 16th Australian Brigade broke in at a point due south of Tobruk, using bangalore torpedoes for the wire, pick and shovel

* See Map III, page 48.

for the anti-tank ditch, and careful hand-probing for the mines. 18 serviceable 'I' tanks churned into the bridgehead which was expanded with the help of Robertson's 19th Australian Brigade, while Savige's 17th Australian Brigade distracted Italian attention by attacking the eastern face of the defences as a diversion. At 2 pm Robertson's brigade broke out of its bridgehead in a north-westerly direction towards the two key Italian positions of the Forts Pilastrino and Solaro. Their advance was not easy and met stiff resistance. They were counter-attacked by Italian medium tanks and after disposing of these, they pressed on against resistance which showed no sign of collapse. It was not until 9.30 pm that Pilastrino fell. General Mannella's headquarters had been over-run near Solaro and he himself captured. The Australians settled down for the night with half the defended area in their hands. Explosions were clearly heard in Tobruk as the Italians put their demolition plan into effect. When the Australian advance was renewed at daylight the hoped-for Italian collapse began. Surprisingly little damage was found to have been done to the port installations upon which O'Connor was depending. As the thousands of prisoners were being garnered in, the Royal Navy's inshore squadron began sweeping the harbour for mines. Two days later British ships started discharging supplies. The Australians lost 355 men and captured 25,000 Italians and the valuable port in return.

Creagh's 7th Armoured Division did not wait for the final collapse of the fortress. 7th Armoured Brigade advanced along the coast road, but found the deep wadis and broken ground increasingly unsuitable for its tanks. Robertson's 19th Australian Brigade was, therefore, ferried forward to take over the advance on Derna, so that Creagh could concentrate on an advance across the desert further south, heading for Mechili to cut off the Italians on the coast road. There were rumours that German generals had been seen at the front and that Italian commanders were encouraging resistance by telling their troops that German help was on the way. Whether this was so or not, the Italians appeared to be fighting back and to be plentifully supplied with ammunition and mines with which to delay the British advance.

On 24 January 4th Armoured Brigade fought a successful tank versus tank action with Babini's Group near Mechili in which nine Italian medium tanks were destroyed in exchange for one British cruiser and six light tanks. O'Connor saw an opportunity to trap Babini, whose force was out of supporting distance of the 60th (Sabratha) Division which was resisting the Australian advance on Derna, and of the 17th (Pavia) and 27th (Brescia) Divisions which were thought to be further west in the Djebel Akdar. O'Connor was out of luck. A combination of inaccurate maps, some misunderstandings, and the reluctance of the British tank units to operate at night led to Babini escaping north-westwards to join the Sabratha Division during the night. O'Connor had had a greater success than he realised at the time. The loss of nine Italian medium tanks made a deep psychological impression on Babini and his officers, the effects of which were to emerge later.

On the same day Wavell arrived at O'Connor's headquarters to discuss the practicability of the immediate advance on Benghazi required by Churchill and the Chiefs of Staff after the Greek refusal of British operational troops. The C–in–C and his desert commander found themselves in a dilemma of a type which was to recur on a number of occasions during the North African Campaign. The requirements of Whitehall appeared to the men on the spot to demand unjustifiable risks, particularly in logistics. The factors demanding a rapid advance on Benghazi were obvious. The Italians must be kept on the run; the quicker Italian airfields were captured in the 'bulge' of Cyrenaica the safer would Malta and convoys through the Mediterranean become; and the quicker Benghazi was taken and organised as an advanced base, the sooner troops could be pulled into reserve for possible future commitment in Greece. The factors arguing for a pause before plunging ahead with another westward leap were just as pressing. O'Connor's advance had started as a raid. Wavell's logistic staffs had worked miracles in improvisation to enable him to reach Mechili. Time was needed to increase the capacity of the port of Tobruk so that transport could be released to support O'Connor's further advance. Time was also needed to dump stocks of fuel, ammunition and supplies at Mechili to sustain that advance. And there was a third factor, which was possibly the most important. 2nd British Armoured Division had reached Suez. Its regiments were being sent forward one by one as they were made ready to relieve those of 7th Armoured Division which were mechanically on their last legs. Creagh had only about 50 Cruiser and light tanks left and most of these were at the limit of their track and engine life. The first two regiments of 2nd Armoured Division would reach Mechili on the 7 and 9 February. O'Connor recommended that for logistic and organisational reasons 10 February was the earliest date by which he could sensibly resume his advance. Wavell agreed, noting that the Italians were fighting hard to retain Cyrenaica so that a fortnight's delay would not invalidate the tactical plan O'Connor was contemplating.

O'Connor's plan, which had been maturing in his mind since the fall of Bardia, was to send 7th Armoured Division across the desert south of the Djebel Akhdar* to cut the main coast road south of Benghazi, while 6th Australian Division forced the Italian main body back through djebel country to the north. The surprise appearance of British tanks south of Benghazi should be fatal to the Italian command in Cyrenaica. It was a plan which Wavell supported with enthusiasm. Whether he could contain Churchill's impatience long enough for O'Connor to make adequate preparations and whether the situation in Greece would allow the fortnight's pause, were both problematical.

Neither Churchill nor Greece was responsible for the sudden and unexpected change in the situation which occurred during 1 and 2 February. Air reconnaissance showed unmistakable signs of an Italian evacuation of Cyrenaica. If the Italians were to be intercepted south of Benghazi, there could be no waiting for the two new tank regiments, nor for further supplies from Tobruk. Creagh would have to advance with what he had, but was it really practical to cross another 150 miles of unreconnoitred desert tracks to reach the Gulf of Sirte with his tanks and vehicles in their present state? Would he be able to do much with the few tanks which would survive the journey? And could he be supplied when he reached the coast? O'Connor's staff

* See Map IV; page 92

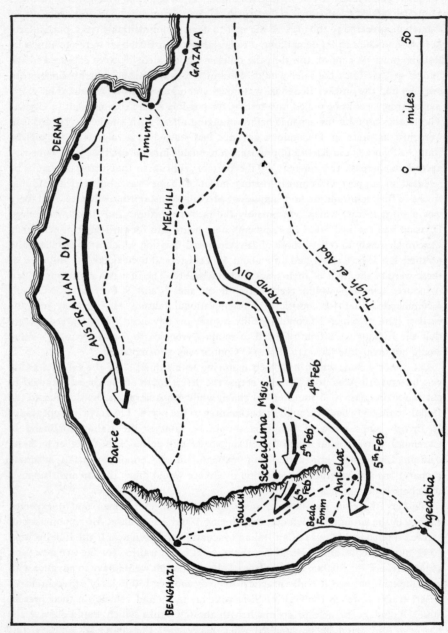

Fig 6 O'Connor's March to Beda Fomm: 4th to 6th February 1941

reported that it was just possible logistically. After consulting Wavell, O'Connor ordered an advance to begin at first light on 4 February. 7th Armoured Division was to advance to Msus and then to push on to the coast if it seemed sensible to do so. 6th Australian Division was to give the Italian rear-guards no respite as they withdrew through the djebel.

What had happened to cause this sudden Italian withdrawal when they seemed to be recovering and their front was stabilizing satisfactorily? The short answer is that Graziani lost heart when he heard of Babini's withdrawal from Mechili and of his complaints about the inferiority of the Italian medium tanks in battle with the British cruisers. The action at Mechili, which was to the British an annoyingly bungled affair, made a decisive impact on Graziani's mind. Mussolini contributed to his depression by warning him of reports of possible British landings in French North Africa. And the activities of the British Long Range Desert Group, coupled with those of Colonel Leclerc's Free French Forces from French Equatorial Africa, added to his worries by causing unrest amongst the Senussi tribes in Southern Libya. He decided on 1 February that he must abandon Cyrenaica. He reported to Mussolini that he proposed to cover Tripoli from Sirte while awaiting the arrival of the Ariete Armoured and Trieste Mechanised Divisions from Italy and any help that might be forthcoming from the Germans. When he left Benghazi on 3 February, the Italian withdrawal was in full swing.

Creagh appreciated the need for speed and so headed his advance with a wheeled column of all arms under Lieut-Colonel J. F. B. Combe of the 11th Hussars who provided the armoured cars in the column. Brigadier Caunter's 4th Armoured Brigade came next with the majority of the fit medium tanks, followed by the Support Group. 7th Armoured Brigade brought up the rear with very few operational tanks.

The first 50 miles of the advance was agonizingly slow. Rocks and steep wadis caused delay and damage, particularly to the light tanks. The wheeled column made slower progress, at first, than the tanks and tended to delay the main column. O'Connor was travelling with Caunter's brigade in a staff car accompanied by Brigadier Dorman-Smith who records O'Connor saying as he passed brokendown tanks and vehicles – 'My God, do you think it's going to be all right!' (C. Barnett: page 33).

Later the going improved enabling the wheeled column to make quicker progress. Combe's armoured cars reached Msus by mid-afternoon. The small Italian garrison fled, and some of the British armoured cars had pushed on to Antelat within 20 miles of the coast road by dusk. The main body struggled on through a clear, moonlit night to reach the Msus area by daybreak. Air reconnaissance reports of the speed and completeness of the Italian withdrawal persuaded Creagh, with O'Connor's subsequent approval, to drive south-west to Beda Fomm. Combe's force was to block the coast road and subsidiary tracks running south, while the rest of the division came up on the eastern or desert flank of any Italian force trying to escape southwards from Benghazi. By midday, the British armoured cars were across the main road at Beda Fomm when the first Italian column came in sight. It was thrown into confusion and stopped by artillery fire. During the afternoon the block was strengthened by the arrival of Lieut-Colonel J. W. L. Renton's 2nd Battalion, the Rifle Brigade and 4th Armoured Brigade's tanks came into action on the flank. By dusk, when the fight was broken off, 1000 prisoners had been taken and the road was strewn with burning vehicles. Further air reports showed that much larger Italian forces were moving south from Benghazi. The British block was absurdly weak to contain the withdrawal of the Tenth Italian Army which still had four unbroken divisions.

At 7.30 am next day, 6 February, the battle reopened with a series of attempts by small parties of Italians to slip through. The weather deteriorated making observation difficult in repeated rain squalls. Sir Basil Liddell Hart describes the scene:

> . . . the enemy's main columns began to appear on the scene, escorted by tanks. There were over a hundred M13 medium tanks in all, whereas Caunter had only twenty-nine cruiser tanks. Fortunately, the Italian tanks came along in packets, instead of in a concentrated body, and kept near the road, whereas the British tanks skilfully manoeuvred to gain fire positions where their hulls were concealed and protected by folds in the ground. A series of these tank battles went on all day, the brunt being borne by the nineteen cruisers of 2nd Royal Tank Regiment . . .

> (Liddell Hart: *The Tanks:* Vol II pages 58–59).

By nightfall the small British force was still holding firm in its blocking position. Signs of demoralization were apparent in the Italians' apathetic inability to co-ordinate an effective attack. At day-break on 7 February about 30 Italian medium tanks made what was to prove the Tenth Army's last effort. The British artillery asked for and was authorised to engage targets within the Rifle Brigade's position. Its fire and that of the Royal Artillery anti-tank guns supporting the battalion checked and finally destroyed the last of the Italian tanks almost within reach of the battalion officers' mess truck. White flags began to appear along the coast road. The Battle of Beda Fomm was over. Liddell Hart sums up:

> Everywhere the Italian infantry and other troops surrendered in crowds when they had lost the protection of their tanks. Altogether 101 tanks were found on the battlefield, mostly in the area where 2nd Royal Tank Regiment had fought the previous day. Of the total, forty-eight had been hit by 2-pounder shells, eight by other guns, six were uncertain, while thirty-nine had been abandoned intact. Only four tanks were lost by the 4th Armoured Brigade in the fight . . .

> The achievement of the tanks owed much to the efforts of those who kept them supplied with petrol and ammunition under great difficulties . . .

> (*Ibid:* pages 61–62).

O'Connor's XIII Corps with two under-strength British Commonwealth divisions had destroyed the nine divisions of the Italian Tenth Army, demonstrating, if demonstration was needed, the superiority of the British military dynamic over the Italian. It had done something more which is important to the story of the North African Campaign. It had won its success by sound tactical methods. It had achieved close and intimate co-operation between tanks, artillery and infantry; and the tanks fought, whenever possible, hull down, using the 2-pounder guns with lethal effect.

This was the last time for many long months that such methods could be used. Many extraneous factors intervened to warp British tactics, but, as the story unfolds, it should be remembered that the British did know what was needed and demonstrated it at Beda Fomm. Many myths and legends have arisen about British military prejudices which are said to have led to later disasters. These were less the fault of the officers and soldiers in the desert than of the unreliability and inadequate performance of their equipment and, regrettably, to the ineptness of some of the men who rose to higher command in the rapid expansion of the British Army which was already taking place. Beda Fomm was the last battle fought by Britain's pre-war professional army.

When the news of the Italian surrender reached O'Connor, he signalled Wavell, beginning – 'Fox killed in the open . . .'

Another Fox was already on his way to the desert. Lieutenant-General Erwin Rommel was about to leave Germany for Tripoli via Rome with the task of setting up the 'Sonnenblume' operation to save the Italians in Tripolitania.

5

British Strategic Misjudgment
(February and March 1941)

'I am still sure that my instinct, to fight as far forward as possible in defence of the Middle East, was correct. We did not know then that the Germans would attack Russia. I believed that they were more likely to concentrate on the Middle East, and that we must gain time; we could do this best by fighting well forward.'

(Wavell: March 1950, quoted by J. Connell, page 330)

December and January had been months of British victories in the Western Desert. In February and March these victories were reflected in the progressive collapse of Italian morale in East Africa. The British commanders there – Cunningham, Platt and Wingate – stepped into the limelight of world publicity as they dismembered the demoralised Italian Empire. Paradoxically their successes contributed to a cumulative spiral of British strategic misjudgments, which developed concurrently with their tactical triumphs. The impetus of their mistakes gathered momentum with each cycle of decision making until their rush to disaster became irresistible. There were four distinct cycles in this accelerating progression which came to its climax at the beginning of April when Wehrmacht re-opened its offensives with the return of European campaigning weather.

It will be recalled that there were three British forces operating around the Italian East African Empire. General Platt, in the north, had opened his offensive from the Sudan on 19 January when the Italians withdrew voluntarily from Kassala. Wingate, in the west, had crossed the Abyssinian frontier with the Emperor on 20 January and was making his way up to the isolated fortress-like feature of Mount Belaya which he had chosen as the initial base for the Patriot Revolt. And Cunningham, in the south, was raiding southern Abyssinia from Kenya with three Commonwealth brigades – 2nd and 5th South African and 25th East African – under command of Major-General Brink's 1st South African Division. The Duke of Aosta decided that he could discern a pattern of three British offensives and disposed his forces accordingly. He gave General Frusci the task of opposing Platt with the largest Italian force, consisting of three colonial divisions plus three colonial brigades to defend Eritrea, and three colonial brigades and five Blackshirt battalions to cover the Gallabat approach to Gondar. He made General Nasi responsible for opposing Wingate in the Gojjam with four colonial brigades. And he gave General De Simone 10 colonial brigades to defend southern Abyssinia and Italian Somaliland from

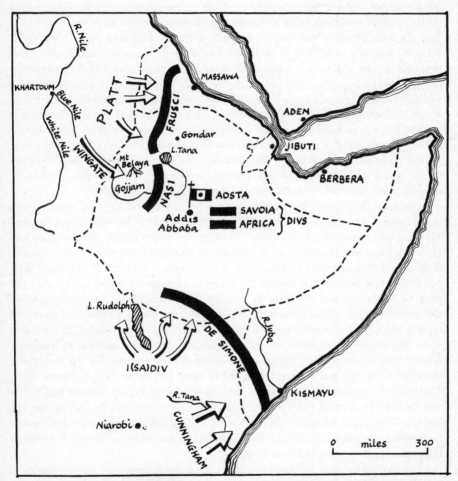

Fig 7 The Operational Situation in East Africa at the beginning of February 1941

General Cunningham. Each general was also allotted a variable number of irregular native 'bande'. In reserve at Addis Ababa and Harrar he held his two best divisions – the Savoia Division and the 'Africa' Division.

Platt's advance from Kassala in pursuit of Frusci's planned withdrawal went far faster than the British expected or the Duke of Aosta would have liked. 4th and 5th Indian Divisions advanced by parallel routes on Agordat and Barentu respectively. They overtook and mopped up a number of Italian units, which were withdrawing too slowly, and at one point were astonished to be attacked by native cavalry. By 25 January both divisions had reached the hills and were attacking Frusci's positions. With the help of a handful of 'I' tanks and by climbing the steepest hills in the Italian positions as only Indian troops can climb, Platt's sepoys manoeuvred the Italians out of their defences in five days' brisk fighting. Frusci was forced to abandon his line and fall back to the much more formidable mountain barrier of the Keren escarpment which blocked the only practicable road to Asmara and Massawa. By the afternoon of 1 February, 4th Indian Division was surveying the scene which was to confront it for the next six weeks. A wall of mountains reared up from the floor of the valley of the Ascidera and in that wall they could find only one narrow breach – the Dongolaas Gorge which carried the road and railway to Asmara* and this was blocked by demolition of the retaining walls of the road which hugged the cliff side.

In western Abyssinia, British affairs were not going smoothly for personal and topographical reasons. There was a clash of personality between Sandford and Wingate; and the approach to Mount Belaya proved more difficult than Wingate had expected. Sandford, the older, more experienced and level headed of the two, was not fired with the same impatient zeal as the young Zionist visionary. Platt defined their positions by appointing Sandford as the Emperor's personal political adviser with the rank of Brigadier, and Wingate as military force commander with the rank of Lieutenant-Colonel. This arrangement irked Wingate because all instructions and reports had to pass through Sandford. Wingate called his force 'Gideon'. It was based upon the Frontier Force Battalion of the Sudan Defence Force, manned by Sudanese regular troops, and the 2nd Ethiopian Battalion of Abyssinian exiles. He had also a number of 'Operational Centres' designed to raise and assist Patriot Forces. Each 'Operational Centre' was commanded and supervised by British officers and NCOs and manned by men of the 1st Ethiopian Battalion which was broken up for the purpose. His supply columns contained some 15,000 camels which were only suited for work in the plains. Sandford had hoped to obtain mules at Belaya but Italian requisitioning prevented him from doing so.

Wingate decided that he could not risk taking the Emperor by known tracks to Belaya and so set off to reconnoitre a cross-country route using a direct compass bearing through the bush. At first the going seemed adequate so he advised the Emperor to start off behind him. As he approached Belaya he ran into a difficult lava belt not shown on the poor maps available. By the time he had retraced his steps he found the Emperor's party:

* See Fig 9, page 80.

in the thick of the chasmous lava region west of Belaya. They had lost animals and trucks, and endeavouring to preserve the Emperor's own truck had often meant manhandling it down gorges . . . The scene through which they passed was fearful in its natural desolation and to this was added the spectacle of dead and dying camels in great numbers, wretched beasts of burden unused to this kind of ground, and hurried through by men who in most cases were ignorant of camel-management . . . The reeking corpses with the occasional abandoned truck lay like markers along the path. On the 6 February, mounted on one of the few mules which Wingate could bring to his succour, the Emperor rode into the headquarters camp at the foot of Mount Belaya.

(Sykes: pages 261-262).

In Kenya, Cunningham, like Platt, began to realise that his earlier estimates of enemy resistance were being falsified by Italian loss of morale. Concurrently his engineers reported that they had found limited supplies of water on the tracks which they were pushing forward through the bush from the River Tana across the Somaliland frontier to the River Juba. He estimated that Italian demoralisation would enable him to reduce his attacking force from six to four brigades, and his logistic staff calculated that, with the water found en route, there was just enough transport to keep the reduced force supplied during an advance to the Juba, provided the port facilities of Kismayu could be captured within 10 days of the start of the operation.

While Cunningham was making his final preparations to take full advantage of the changed circumstances, General Smuts again offered Churchill a second South African Division. Wavell was loath to accept it because he still needed more transport and logistic units before he increased his fighting strength. Although he was heavily engaged with operations in the Western Desert and in delicate negotiations with the Greeks, he decided to fly down to Kenya to see for himself. Before he left he cabled Dill, the CIGS, asking for the decision on Smuts' offer to be deferred until he returned. Churchill saw the message and made it an occasion for another blistering attack on Wavell's generalship. In a cable dated 26 January he carped:

How can you expect me to face the tremendous strain upon our shipping, affecting as it does all our food and import of munitions in order to carry more divisions from this country to the Middle East, when you seem opposed to taking a South African division which would only have less than half the distance to come?

(Churchill: Vol III, page 74).

Wavell reached Nairobi on 28 January and was delighted when Cunningham proposed to bring his May offensive forward to 11 February. Churchill's suggestion in his Volume III (page 25) that it was his goading that produced this result is not true. Discovery of water and decline of Italian morale were the main causes. Wavell sanctioned Cunningham's offensive and two days later was with Platt in Eritrea. When he arrived back in Cairo on 1 February he heard of the capture of Agordat and Barentu and in a short signal to Platt on 3 February said: 'Now go on and take Keren and Asmara . . .' (*British Official History*: Vol I, page 402)

All Wavell's forces were on the move in East Africa. He could turn back to the affairs of the Mediterranean.

The first cycle of the spiral of British strategic misjudgment started with an act of God. General Metaxas died suddenly while Wavell was in Kenya. On 8 February, two days after the Battle of Beda Fomm, the new Greek Government asked to re-open talks to establish the size of the British Expeditionary Force which it might be practical to send if the Germans entered Bulgaria. This was not, as yet, a positive call for help but Churchill treated it as such. The vigour which he imparted to the staff studies of what could be done brooked only one answer. The opponents of the Greek enterprise were swept aside and rarely allowed to state their case. Wavell, himself, was in two minds about the best policy. On 10 February he cabled to the War Office:

> The extent of the Italian defeat at Benghazi seems to me to make it possible that Tripoli might yield to a small force if despatched without delay. I am working out the size of the force that would be required but hesitate to advance further in view of Balkan situation. But you may think the capture of Tripoli might have favourable effect on attitude of French North Africa ... I will make plans for capture of Sirte which must be first step. Please cable me your views as to effect on Weygand and war situation generally. Will probably go to Cyrenaica on 12th or 13th February to discuss with Wilson.
>
> (Kennedy: page 74).

In Rome the Italians and Germans faced a similar dilemma. Guzzoni, who had replaced Badoglio as Italian Chief of Staff, briefing Rommel on 11 February, said: 'If it becomes clear in the course of the next few days that Tripoli cannot be held, I will be the first to admit that it is not worth sending German units to Libya only to be captured by the enemy ...' (*Australian Official History:* Vol I, page 279).

Ironically on that same evening of 11 February the British Defence Committee, with Churchill in the chair, met to consider their policy at a special after-dinner meeting. The possibility of advancing on Tripoli was dismissed perfunctorily. Under Churchill's guidance the meeting agreed to give priority to Greece. Later that night two cables were despatched to Wavell: one from the Chiefs of Staff and the other from Churchill. The most important paragraph in Churchill's cable ran:

> 5. Our first thought must be for our ally Greece, who is actually fighting so well. If Greece is trampled down or forced to make a separate peace with Italy, yielding also air and naval strategic points against us to Germany, effect on Turkey will be very bad. But if Greece, with British aid, can hold up for some months German advance, chances of Turkish intervention will be favoured. Therefore it would seem that we should try to get in a position to offer the Greeks the transfer to Greece of the fighting portion of the Army which has hitherto defended Egypt, and make every plan for sending and reinforcing it to the limit with men and material ...
>
> (Churchill: Vol III, page 58).

Churchill then went on to say that he was sending out Eden and Dill to survey the whole position with the Cs-in-C in Cairo and possibly in Athens. He hoped that they would be able to offer the Greeks at least four divisions including one armoured division. All would depend on whether the Greeks could produce a viable military plan. He concluded:

> 10. In the event of its proving impossible to reach any good agreement with the Greeks and work out a practical military plan, then we must try to save as much from the wreck as possible. We must at all costs keep Crete . . . We could also reconsider the advance on Tripoli . . .
>
> *(Ibid:* page 59).

The first British strategic misjudgment had been made. While Churchill worked towards the establishment of a British foothold in Europe, Hitler was increasing the strength of the forces he was sending to shore up his ally in Libya and to establish a bridgehead for himself in Africa. The fundamental error was a misappreciation of relative resources. In order to establish a tenuous bridgehead in Southern Europe, Churchill was allowing the Axis to retain a secure foothold in North Africa from which they could attack the jugular vein of the British Imperial system – the Suez Canal. Hitler had enough resources to make full use of an African foothold; Churchill had neither the resources nor practicable objectives to make any use of a British lodgment in the Balkans. It was hard to see what good a four division expeditionary force could do in the face of Lists' Twelfth German Army with 18.

All the troops for Greece were to come from Egypt, Palestine and O'Connor's XIII Corps in Cyrenaica. Wavell knew he was taking risks in the desert but felt they were reasonable.

> Though unconfirmed reports had been received from time to time of the preparation of German troops for dispatch to Libya and of their progress via Italy and Sicily, no definite information to justify our expecting the presence of German troops in Africa had been received up to the middle of February . . .
>
> I estimated that it would be at least two months after the landing of German forces at Tripoli before they could undertake a serious offensive against Cyrenaica; and that, therefore, there was not likely to be any serious threat to our positions there before May at the earliest. I accordingly considered that a garrison of one armoured brigade and one division would be sufficient to have as flank guard in Cyrenaica and that it would be safe to have comparatively unequipped and untrained troops there so long as their training and equipment would be completed by May, by which time I hoped to have reinforcements available of at least one Indian Division from the Sudan.
>
> (Despatches: page 3425).

This was a reasonable enough judgment at the time, but it was being falsified while it was being made because German troops were already landing in Tripoli in a higher state of training than Wavell thought possible. While Churchill misjudged force levels, Wavell miscalculated time. In putting the Defence Committee's directive into operation Wavell made several unfortunate decisions. First of all, he broke up the successful and now experienced Headquarters XIII Corps. O'Connor was admittedly very tired and needed a rest. He was sent back to take over from Wilson as Commander British Troops, Egypt, in the Nile Delta, and Wilson came forward as Military Governor of Cyrenaica with a static administrative headquarters in Benghazi. Wavell had intended to replace HQ XIII Corps with HQ 1st Australian Corps but the latter was needed for Greece. There was thus no field force headquarters above divisional level with adequate mobile communications left in Cyrenaica. Secondly, he withdrew all his experienced troops from Cyrenaica. 6th Australian Division was replaced by the partially trained and inadequately equipped 9th Australian Division so that the former could get ready for Greece. 7th Armoured Division was at the end of its mechanical tether and had to be withdrawn to refit in the Delta, leaving the newly arrived tactically, and, as it proved, mechanically unreliable 2nd Armoured Division, one of whose armoured brigades was nominated for Greece, as the only armoured force in the desert. And thirdly, no troops were brought north from East Africa to replace those earmarked for Greece. Instead of letting the Duke of Aosta's forces waste from natural causes, as Churchill had advocated, Wavell continued to press on with their active dismemberment. The final order of battle resulting from these decisions was:

1. *Nominated for Greece*
   2nd New Zealand Division (untried)
   6th Australian Division (experienced)
   7th Australian Division (partially trained)
   1st Armoured Brigade of 2nd Armoured Division (untried)
   Polish Brigade (partially equipped)

2. *Cyrenaica Garrison*
   9th Australian Division (partially trained and equipped)
   2nd Armoured Division less one armoured brigade (Untried and mechanically in
      poor state)

3. *Eritrean Operations*
   4th Indian Division
   5th Indian Division   (both experienced)

4. *Kenyan Operations*
   1st South African Division
   11th African Division   (African troops not suited to operations
   12th African Division   north of Abyssinia)

5. *Gideon Force*
   1st Frontier Force Battalion (Sudanese)
   2nd Ethiopian Battalion (Abyssinians)

6. *Egypt and Palestine*
   6th Division (Ad hoc internal security division with no supporting arms)
   7th Armoured Division (refitting)
   1st Cavalry Division (still horsed)

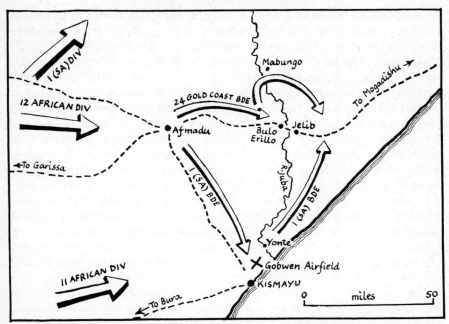

Fig 8 Cunningham's 'Canvas' Offensive: 11th to 14th February 1941

Cunningham opened his offensive, code-named 'Canvas', against Kismayu on 11 February while the strategic decisions on Greece were being taken in London. Like O'Connor's 'Compass', secrecy was paramount so no written orders were issued. The main striking force was provided by Major-General Godwin-Austen's 12th African Division with the 1st South African, 22nd East African and 24th Gold Coast Brigades under command and was concentrated on the upper reaches of the river Tana at Garissa, 250 miles east of the main railhead at Nairobi and another 250 miles from its objective, Kismayu near the mouth of the River Juba. Major-General Brink's 1st South African Division (2nd and 5th South African and 25th East African Brigades) was to support Godwin-Austen's western flank by pressing northward into southern Abyssinia between Lake Rudolf and Moyale And Major-General Wetherall's 11th African Division (21st East African and 23rd Nigerian Brigades) was to operate on his coastal flank from Bura on the Lower Tana towards Kismayu. Cunningham's plan was for Godwin-Austen to attack and capture Afmadu, the main Italian outpost in front of the Juba on 11 February. The 1st South African Brigade would then turn southwards to cut in behind Kismayu, taking Gobwen airfield and crossing the Juba in that area while the rest of the division advanced due east to force a crossing over the Juba and to clear the main road through Jelib to Mogadishu. Kismayu would be attacked frontally by Wetherall's division once the defenders had been unsettled by the South Africans behind them. So that surpise would be maintained Wetherall would leave the Tana four days later than Godwin-Austen. A specially organised naval force was to bombard coastal positions and to land supplies.

Since the Italians still enjoyed air superiority, as much land movement as possible would be by night. If Kismayu was not taken by 21 February, Cunningham would be forced to withdraw back into Kenya for want of supplies and water.

There proved to be no need to withdraw. South African Air Force Squadrons subdued the Italian airmen in preliminary air operations and softened up the Italian garrisons on the Juba, paying particular attention to Afmadu on 10 February. The bombing was too much for the Afmadu Garrison which melted away, allowing 22nd East African Brigade to occupy the place unopposed. 24th Gold Coast Brigade passed through and fought its way against stiffening resistance over the 60 miles to Bulo Erillo near the Juba, taking it on 13 February in a brisk action in which the attacking battalion lost nearly all its white officers and NCOs. 1st South African Brigade turned south as planned and lay up in the bush during 13 February within ten miles of Gobwen waiting for nightfall before trying to rush the airfield. Its Commander, Brigadier Dan Pienaar, had strict instructions not to break radio silence or to patrol forward in daylight so as not to alarm the Italians too soon. He heard explosions coming from the direction of Kismayu and suspected that an Italian withdrawal was in progress but could do nothing about it. He moved off again at dusk, secured Gobwen, and though he brushed with a few Italian parties withdrawing from Kismayu, he was too late to intercept their retreat. He was also too late to stop them destroying the pontoon bridge over the Juba between Gobwen and Jumbo. Kismayu was occupied on the evening of 14 February, six days ahead of the critical supply date.

General De Simone, Aosta's commander in the south, was holding all obvious crossings of the Juba but rivers act as a cloak as well as a shield. The defender finds it difficult to discover what the attacker is doing once he has been forced to withdraw his outposts from the attacker's bank. Cunningham instructed Godwin-Austen to tap along the whole front to find the weak spots in the Italian river defences. The Juba was 600 feet wide at Gobwen, and, although wadeable in places near Bulo Erillo, it was still a difficult obstacle for vehicles due to a wide belt of swampy tropical jungle on either bank. During the night 17/18 February, the South Africans established a bridgehead at Yonte, 10 miles upstream of Gobwen. And two days later the Gold Coast Brigade forced a crossing 30 miles upstream of the main road at Mabungo. The dual pressure directed northwards and southwards along the Italian bank of the Juba from the two bridgeheads combined with frontal pressure at Bulo Erillo caused the disintegration of De Simone's force. On 22 February Jelib was cleared by Godwin-Austen's men, and the southern door to Abyssinia swung open for Wetherall's 11th African Division to exploit towards Mogadishu.

Cunningham was now faced with a race against the rains rather than the demands of Whitehall. The wet season usually started in eastern Abyssinia later than at Kismayu. If he advanced as soon as his supply situation allowed, he might just keep ahead of the monsoon. His staff calculated that they could support up to three brigades on an 800-mile advance past Mogadishu to Harar, provided the brigades left behind were robbed of most of their transport. The supply situation would be eased if the Garrison of Aden could retake Berbera in British Somaliland and thus reduce the length of Cunningham's communications before the rains started to disrupt the rough Mogadishu-Harar road. Cunningham sought Wavell's authority to press on and asked for an attack on Berbera. Both requests were granted. Wetherall's 11th African Division crossed the Juba on 23 February and started its epic march on Harar with the 23rd Nigerian Brigade leading.

In western Abyssinia another march had started. The Emperor's arrival at Belaya fanned the flames of the 'Patriot' revolt as rumour enlarged the size of Wingate's force. A growing number of Chiefs in the area, through which Wingate hoped to operate, joined the Emperor. The local Italian commanders misread the size of the threat to their position and decided to abandon most of their isolated posts in the Gojjam and to concentrate near Lake Tana, and at Burye and Debra Markos on the main road to Addis Ababa. They tried to neutralise the Emperor's influence by handing over rule in the Gojjam to Ras Halu, the principal Chieftain of the traditional Gojjam dynasty and a known rival of Haile Selassie. This did not stop Wingate gathering further support. He was lucky to rediscover a little known route up the Abyssinian escarpment near Metakal which made the ascent easier for his long-suffering camels. He set out with Gideon Force on 15 February and by the 20th was established on the escarpment. One of his patrols frightened the Italians in Danghila into a panic evacuation and news reached him that the important fort at Engiabara was being evacuated as well. He reached it just in time to stop the Italian stores being looted and thereby provided his force with a month's supply of food. He was no longer so dependent on his camels, and could consider more ambitious operations against the Italian communications. His target became the Italian force which had withdrawn to the fortified area of Burye. Its commander, Colonel Natale, had some 7,000 men supported by artillery at his disposal; Wingate had 450. Nothing daunted he started his approach march to cut the road between Burye and Debra Markos on 25 February.

General Platt had not found things so easy in Eritrea. There was no sign of Italian panic at Keren. General Frusci's position grew less and less attractive as 4th Indian Division tried to find a way through or around it. From a distance it looked like a solid wall stretching as far as the eye could see. On closer examination the wall consisted of a jumble of precipitous rock-strewn mountains whose peaks rose 2,000 feet above the floor of the valley which itself was bare and open with only an occasional tebeldi tree breaking the monotony. No-one could move in daylight without being seen by the Italian observation posts dug in amongst the boulders. Apart from the road and railway, which disappeared into the Dongolaas Gorge, there were no obvious tracks up the escarpments; and reconnaissance reports revealed no way round. The walls of Frusci's fortress seemed, and were, solid. Provided he had enough troops with sufficient determination he was in an impregnable position.

Brigadier Savory's 11th Indian Infantry Brigade was the first to tackle the Dongolaas Gorge, which was overlooked by Fort Dologorodoc on the right and Mount Sanchil on the left. For three days Savory struggled with increasing artillery support to seize commanding positions from which deeper attacks could be mounted. He found no way of tackling Dologorodoc, but 2nd Cameron Highlanders secured a

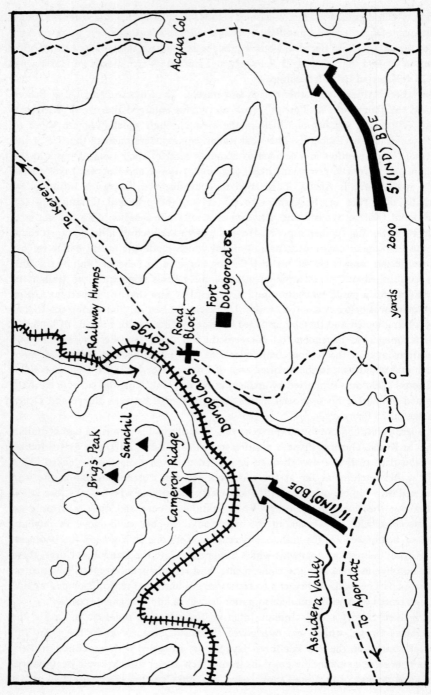

Fig 9 The Opening Battle of Keren: 3rd to 13th February 1941

lodgment on a spur of Sanchil which became known as Cameron Ridge. With this partial success, Savory developed his brigade attack next night and succeeded in reaching the top of Sanchil and its neighbouring peak, nicknamed Brigs Peak, but his men were too depleted in numbers and too exhausted to hold their gains and resist the violent counter-attacks launched against them next day. His line eventually solidified around Cameron Ridge, with the Italians overlooking them from Brigs Peak and Sanchil.

Brigadier Lloyd's 5th Indian Infantry Brigade was the next to take up the challenge. There appeared to be a possible approach to the rear of the Fort Dologorodoc group of features via Acqua Col on the extreme right at the eastern end of the Ascidera Valley. Lloyd decided to try it but his attack was no more successful than Savory's. His leading battalion, 4/6 Rajputana Rifles, reached the Col after severe hand to hand fighting in the dark, but again found that there were too few men left to hold their gains when daylight came. The battalion was withdrawn to a less exposed position.

Three tactical problems bedevilled 4th Indian Division's attempts to hustle General Frusci out of the Keren position. The first was how to bring artillery fire to bear effectively on the Italian positions which could never be seen on the reverse slopes of the numerous false crests in that jumble of crests. Whereas the British artillery observers could not see into the Italian positions, every British move could be watched by the Italians from above. Secondly, the features were so large, so rough and so steep, that attacking infantry found their numbers so depleted and the men who reached the top so exhausted, that they were always vulnerable to quickly mounted counter-attacks by fresh troops hidden near-by. Without artillery observation the infantry could not be properly supported; and without a successful infantry assault no observation could be won. The viciousness of this circle was heightened by the third tactical problem. The Indian Divisons were experts in mountain warfare but they had left their fine pack-mules behind in India. In consequence, water, food and ammunition had to be carried up to the forward troops on men's backs. Clambering up boulder-strewn mountain sides, plodding across loose shale, and pushing through thorn scrub and spear grass, was tiring work at any time. In the growing heat of Keren, even Indian troops, used to such conditions, found life to be a grim and never-ending fatigue in which more men carried and acted as mules than held the front.

In spite of Savory's and Lloyd's initial failures, Beresford-Peirse saw no reason to think that his division would not be able to reach Keren. The Italians had often resisted fiercely at first, then suddenly collapsed when enough pressure was brought to bear. He decided to launch a co-ordinated divisional attack with Savory taking Brigs Peak on the Sanchil feature first so that observed artillery fire could be brought to bear on the Italians defending Acqua Col. Lloyd would then attack and if he was successful, 29th Indian Infantry Brigade from 5th Indian Division would pass through to take Keren.

Neither Savory nor Lloyd succeeded. Savory took and lost Brigs Peak twice. Lloyd's attack on Acqua Col went well at first but was beaten in the end by Italian mortar and machine gun posts which the British artillery could not neutralise. Losses were mounting too fast to be sustained for much longer. Savory's brigade had lost two battalion commanders, three company commanders and 280 men; and Lloyd's had lost 223 all ranks. A way round had to be found or the attack would have to be supported with a much greater weight of fire. Platt directed Beresford-Peirse to call off the attempt to break through while further efforts were made to find alternative routes and to build up supplies of ammunition in case another frontal attack had to be undertaken. The First Battle of Keren had ended in Frusci's favour. What had happened to the Italians? Why were they fighting so well at Keren and nowhere else?

In the Duke of Aosta's appreciation of the situation, the security of Eritrea was fundamental. The colony was Italy's oldest East African possession. Massawa was his principal naval port and it contained the most important of his army and air force base installations. If Massawa fell, he would have little chance of holding out until a German victory in Europe unseated the British. Frusci's failure to hold Agordat and Barentu forced him to deploy the best troops of his central reserve. By the time 4th Indian Division reached Keren, the Savoia Division had arrived to reinforce Frusci. It was this fine division, together with Bersaglieri units already under Frusci's command, who were beginning to turn Keren into Aosta's 'Cassino'.

The second cycle of British strategic misjudgment began a week after 4th Indian Division had paused for breath at Keren. Eden and Dill arrived in Cairo on 19 February after a hazardous flight through the Mediterranean which had taken a week due to bad weather and aircraft unserviceability. While awaiting their arrival, Wavell had cleared his mind by writing a new appreciation of the situation. His reasoning led him to reverse his previous position on the Greek adventure. He summed up:

> . . . we have a difficult choice, but I think we are more likely to be playing the enemy's game by remaining inactive than by taking action in the Balkans. *Provided that conversations with the Greeks show that there is a good chance of establishing a front against the Germans with our assistance, I think we should take it.* (The italics are the author's.)
>
> (J. Connell: page 336).

In that sentence lay the key to all that followed. If the British had enforced this proviso on themselves and the Greeks, they might have arrested their slide to disaster on the second or third cycles of their spiral of misjudgment. Surprisingly Churchill began to have doubts of his own. In a cable to Eden, dated 20 February, he gave the British delegation a wide escape clause if they wished to use it:

> Do not consider yourselves obligated to a Greek enterprise if in your hearts you feel it will only be another Norwegian fiasco. If no good plan can be made please say so. But, of course, you know how valuable success would be.
>
> (Churchill: Vol III, page 63).

Eden and Dill, accompanied by the three Cs-in-C Middle East, flew to Athens secretly on 22 February to see whether a practicable plan could be devised for the military

9. Indian troops sheltering in part of Fort Dologorodoc which they had captured.

10. The leading British armoured car emerging from the Dongolaas Gorge after it had been cleared by the Indian Sappers and Miners.

11. The South African pontoon bridge over the River Juba.

12. The end in East Africa: the Duke of Aosta (second from left) leaving Amba Alagi after his surrender.

defence of Greece. Their discussions at the Tatoi Palace convinced them that Greece could be defended provided three things were done; first, the British provided four divisions; secondly, the Greek Government abandoned Thrace and Eastern Macedonia, withdrawing the garrisons to reinforce the 'Aliakmon Line' protecting Salonika and Central Greece; and thirdly, that both measures – despatch of British troops and evacuation of Eastern Greece – were put in hand at once. The Greek Government accepted these conclusions, and Wavell supported Eden in recommending them to Whitehall. The British Defence Committee had serious doubts about the plan's validity, but, as the men on the spot seemed confident, they did not feel justified in taking counsel of their fears. Churchill cabled on 24 February: 'Therefore, while being under no illusions we all send you the order "Full Steam Ahead" '. (Ibid, page 69).

The downward plunge accelerated. Only the limitations of available shipping placed any brake on the momentum which had been imparted to the Greek adventure. Fifty ships had to be withdrawn from convoys as they reached Suez and passed through the Suez Canal as and when German mining allowed. This was done at the expense of the import of supplies to the United Kingdom and to the flow of reinforcements to the Middle East. The expeditionary force was to be ferried to Greece in three contingents: first, the New Zealand Division and the 1st Armoured Brigade; then 6th Australian Division and the Polish Brigade; and finally 7th Australian Division and possibly the balance of an armoured division. The whole force was about 100,000 strong. The first ships would sail about 4 March with three week intervals between contingents. In these circumstances, there seemed little point in curtailing operations in East Africa because few troops could be shipped north to Egypt while the movement to Greece was in progress. Wavell found no difficulty, therefore, in authorising Cunningham's advance on Harar which was put to him in Athens.

No sooner had the fatal decision to intervene in Greece been taken than the third cycle of strategic misjudgment began. On 1 March, Bulgaria joined the Axis and the following day the German forces, concentrated in Rumania, crossed the Danube and started their approach march to assembly areas near the Greek frontier. Eden and Dill, who had been conferring with the Turks in Ankara, arrived back in Athens on 2 March and were astonished to learn that no order had been issued for the withdrawal of Greek troops from Thrace and Eastern Macedonia to man the Aliakmon Line. It was now too late for such a withdrawal to be made – militarily, they might be caught on the move by a German attack, and politically, such a withdrawal in the face of the German threat would cause consternation amongst the people of Eastern Greece. Although the moment had come for the British to withdraw from the whole enterprise and allow the Greeks to make what peace they could with the Axis, there was no-one with sufficient foresight, conviction or coolness of judgment to take such a decision. Too many people had committed themselves to the practicability of the operation to retract at this late hour. The British Ambassador was alarmed at the suggestion that the Greeks should be sacrificed. Eden and the Cs-in-C, though worried, felt that something could be saved from the wreck. Wavell put the risks squarely to Generals Blamey and Freyberg, the Australian and New Zealand Commanders, who agreed to accept them. The misjudgment was finally clinched by the intervention of General Smuts who summed up:

> There remain the Greeks – and ourselves. The Greeks have done better than anyone could have expected. The public opinion of the world is strongly on their side. If we do not stand by them, we shall be held up to public ignominy . . . It may be said that a German victory in the Balkans will result in a great setback to our cause; but the setback will probably be greater if we stand aside and don't help.
>
> (J. Connell: page 532).

Churchill cabled the War cabinet's decision to Eden on 7 March:

> . . . Chiefs of Staff advised that in view of steadfastly expressed opinion of Commanders-in-Chief on the spot, of the Chief of the Imperial General Staff, and Commanders of the forces to be employed, it would be right to go on. Cabinet decided to authorise you to proceed with the operation, and by so doing accepts for itself the fullest responsibility. We will communicate with Australian and New Zealand Governments accordingly.
>
> (Churchill: Vol III, page 94).

In a personal signal to Eden, he added:

> Do not overlook those parts of my instruction dealing with the economy of the Middle East armies. Am relying on you to clean this up, and to make sure every man pulls his weight.
>
> (*Ibid*: page 95).

It would have been better if Churchill had been making a closer study of the German order of battle instead of worrying about Wavell's logistic units. He and the Chiefs of Staff did not know then that Hitler was bent on invading Russia, so there is no excuse for their gross under-estimate of the German ability to over-run Greece. Four British divisions, even properly equipped and trained, had no chance of swaying the issue once the Wehrmacht was ordered to launch 'Marita'. The British closed their minds to the scale of the impending operations and went blindly ahead, repeating, as Churchill himself had warned, the Norwegian fiasco. No amount of sea power could offset the British weakness on land. It was far too early to challenge the Axis on the European mainland.

★   ★   ★

The momentum acquired by the Greek operation was matched by the snowballing effect of British successes in East Africa which swept the British along to their fourth and final cycle of misjudgment. At the beginning of March Rommel started his advance from Tripoli to El Agheila on the eastern frontier of Tripolitania.* British

---

* See Map IV; page 92.

and German armoured cars were already in contact around the Gulf of Sirte, but Wavell held steadfastly to his view that the Germans were unlikely to be strong enough to attempt to regain Cyrenaica before May. It would be wrong to blame him for this because the German General Staff held a similar view. No special measures were taken to accelerate the move of troops from East Africa to Egypt. The fruits of success in Abyssinia and Eritrea were to be gathered first. They were too attractive to be left ripening on the tree; and the picking seemed so easy.

The attack on Burye by Wingate's 'Gideon' Force was in the true tradition of its Biblical namesake. A mixture of audacity, endurance and deception combined to outwit Colonel Natale's Italian garrison. A fortuitous accident helped Wingate. His camel train of about 700 beasts, instead of keeping closed up during his march to outflank and then attack Burye from the east, straggled over four miles, giving Italian observers the impression of a much larger force. The attacks Wingate mounted on the Burye forts and on other strong points on Natale's line of retreat to Debra Markos, were small, repeated and, although ill-co-ordinated at times, remarkably effective in lowering Italian morale. The novel use of loud-speakers by a special propaganda section set up by Wingate led to a growing stream of desertions from among the locally enlisted troops in Natale's garrisons. The RAF contributed with spasmodic bombing of the Italian forts, and Wingate's strength grew with the arrival of more 'patriot' bands whose leaders had decided that loyalty to the Emperor was politic. On 3 March Wingate heard that Natale intended to withdraw to Debra Markos and made his dispositions accordingly. Next day the withdrawal began covered by Italian fighter aircraft. Wingate's harassing tactics were not entirely successful but did result in the loss of 2,000 Italian troops together with useful captures of guns, vehicles and supplies. The Italian 'elephant' was running from a British 'mouse' into the temporary safety of the Debra Markos forts. Here General Nasi took charge, sacking Colonel Natale and replacing him with Colonel Maraventano, but he failed to put new life into the Italian cause in the Gojjam. The Emperor had arrived in Burye on 14 March, while Wingate continued a series of well-prepared raids on isolated Italian positions. At one moment there was a danger that Gideon Force would be trapped between Ras Hailu's followers and the Italians. Wingate brazenly demanded Ras Hailu's surrender. Ras Hailu refused, and withdrew into Debra Markos to join his Italian protectors. Between 19 March and 3 April Gideon Force, with not much more than 300 regular troops supporting loosely knit 'patriot' bands surrounded and harassed 12,000 well-equipped soldiers in the Debra Markos defences. Deserters came over to Wingate's side at a rate of about 100 per day.

On 1 April the Italians abandoned their out-post line to the west of their main forts, and on 4 April Colonel Maraventano abandoned Debra Markos and withdrew up the Valley of the Blue Nile, hoping to reach other Italian forces at Dessie. Two days later Haile Selassie entered Debra Markos where Ras Hailu surrendered and did homage to him as Emperor.

Maraventano's withdrawal had not been an unpremeditated or unauthorised action. The Duke of Aosta had left Addis Ababa and was heading for Dessie as well. Wetherall's 11th African Division had reached and taken the Imperial Capital on

5 April. The snowballing of success on Cunningham's front had been even more pronounced than in Wingate's operations. Supply was Wetherall's main problem. Until he reached the hill country around Jijiga his armoured cars managed to manoeuvre De Simone's rear-guards out of every delaying position which they tried to hold in the flat bush country. The Nigerian Brigade entered Jijiga on 17 March after a 750-mile advance with its leading troops averaging 65 miles per day. The Italians continued to fall back until they reached the Marda Pass which looked quite as formidable as the Keren position. Wetherall decided to await the arrival of 1st South African Brigade before attacking. Early on 21 March reports reached him that the Italians were not intent on staying. The Nigerians attacked at mid-day and secured a foothold by dusk. Next morning the Italians had gone and were next found holding the equally difficult Babile Pass. The Nigerians frightened them out of this on 26 March and entered Harar the same day. By this time two Indian battalions had landed from Aden to reoccupy Berbera, thus shortening Cunningham's communications by 600 miles. It was now easier to supply the whole of Wetherall's division for an advance on Addis Ababa.

The complexion of Cunningham's advance changed in two respects. Wavell had begun to feel increasing concern about the Western Desert and had warned Cunningham that the 1st South African Division was to move to Egypt as soon as he could release it. Wavell doubted if it was worth-while advancing beyond Diredawa on the Addis Ababa–Jibuti railway but was prepared to consider Cunningham's views. The latter reported that there was not much to stop him taking Addis Ababa and, although the fall of the capital would not necessarily mean the Duke of Aosta's capitulation, success in Eritrea as well might end the campaign. He could release HQ 1st South African Division and 5th South African Brigade straight away, and the availability of the Jibuti railway would enable him to release some transport as well. Wavell accepted this view and authorised Cunningham to advance on Addis Ababa.

The second change in Cunningham's campaign occurred on the Italian side. All the Italian commanders were showing a growing concern about the safety of Italian civilians and women and children as their grip upon internal security weakened. Appeals to the British for help began to come in as Wetherall's troops puched north-westwards towards the capital. On 30 March Wavell, at Cunningham's instigation, sent the Duke of Aosta a message which was dropped on Addis Ababa saying that he was prepared to help in safeguarding the lives of Italian women and children. Wavell's terms were neither accepted by the Italians nor by London; the latter misconstruing the limited nature of Wavell's proposals and insisting on 'unconditional surrender'. Nothing came of this first approach. The problem of civilians became more acute as British successes could no longer be disguised. Wetherall was making steady progress in his advance on the capital, impeded primarily by demolition; and to the north, in Eritrea, Platt's Indian Divisions had at last broken through.

We left 4th and 5th Indian Divisions baffled in front of Keren. Further attempts to find a way round were not successful. On 1 March Platt decided on two divisional assaults to clear the way through the Dongolaas Gorge. 4th Indian Division would open the attack by seizing Sanchil and the supporting peaks on the left of the Gorge. 5th Indian Division would then storm Fort Dologorodoc. The offensive would be supported by carefully co-ordinated RAF bombing and all available artillery with 300 rounds per gun at the gun positions and a further 450 per gun in reserve.

Early on 15 March the Italian positions and gun areas were attacked by the RAF. At 7 am 4th Division's attack started with a heavy artillery bombardment. Sanchil and Brigs Peak were taken and lost. Peaks further west were taken and held. At 10.30 am 5th Division attacked Fort Dologorodoc and failed. The attack by both divisions was halted until darkness would give some cover from Italian observers on Sanchil. During the night 4th Division tried Brigs Peak and Sanchil again and failed. 5th Division was more successful and by first light had captured and held Fort Dologorodoc. Unfortunately this success did not clear Italian observation off the road block in the Dongolaas Gorge.

On the second night General Platt used his two remaining reserve battalions in another attempt to take Brigs Peak and Sanchil, again without success. 5th Division tried to exploit from Dologorodoc but were beaten back. It looked as it stalemate was inevitable. The night attacks had, however, covered a reconnaissance of the Dongolaas block by the Indian Sappers and Miners. They found the obstruction less complete than had been thought and reported that, provided a low north-easterly spur from Sanchil, called the 'Railway Bumps' could be captured, the block could be cleared in 48 hours. Platt decided to pause while careful preparations were made for the capture of the 'Railway Bumps' and the opening of the road. He fixed 25 March for the renewal of the offensive and gave the task to 5th Indian Division.

Between 18 and 22 March the Italians launched a succession of counter-attacks on Fort Dologorodoc. Seven times the Italians came forward and were repulsed on each occasion with damaging losses. General Lorenzini, who had made a reputation for himself with both sides as a great leader, was killed. General Frusci became increasingly anxious about the waning strength of his force which was suffering severely from the RAF's attacks, from British artillery fire and from its own attempts to drive the Indians off the mountain sides. When the 5th Indian Division's attack went in early on 25 March Italian resistance started to crumble. The 'Railway Bumps' were taken and the Sappers and Miners of both divisions, working by reliefs under mortar and artillery fire, started clearing the block. They worked non-stop until a negotiable passage was ready at 5.30 am on 27 March. The 'I' tanks crawled through in support of the 29th Indian Infantry Brigade which entered Keren later that morning against negligible resistance. Frusci had realised during the 26 March that he was powerless to stop the Gorge being cleared and had decided to withdraw while there was still time to do so. The Battles of Keren were over. In the final offensive the British had fired 100,000 shells borne by 1,000 trucks from the railhead 150 miles away over the poorest of tracks. They had lost 500 killed and 3,000 wounded but the fate of Eritrea was sealed. Asmara fell on 1 April. Part of Frusci's force marched sought to join Aosta at Dessie and the rest withdrew on Massawa which fell on 8 April. The most important prize gained by the British with the capture of Massawa was President Roosevelt's declaration, made on 11 April, that the

Red Sea and the Gulf of Aden were no longer 'Combat Zones'. US ships could sail direct to Suez, thus lifting off British shipping some of the burden of supplying the Middle East. Moreover, the Lend Lease Bill had been finally passed by Congress and signed by the President on 11 March so that these ships could carry far more American weapons and supplies than Britain could ever afford to buy. Time was being bought successfully. It would be many more months before the British would be fighting with material superiority, but a start had been made to supply their needs.

The loss of Keren was decisive in another respect. The Duke of Aosta appreciated that only a very quick victory in Europe could save him. He too had to buy time, although his chances of doing so had become very slender indeed. He chose three areas remote from the British thrusts: the mountainous region of Amba Alagi between Asmara and Dessie to which he withdrew himself with the 'Africa' Division when he abandoned his capital on 3 April and to which the remnants of Frusci's forces had also withdrawn; Gondar where General Nasi was concentrating such forces as had evaded Wingate; and Galla-Sidamo in Southern Abyssinia where General Gazzera collected the remnants of the forces which had opposed Brink's 1st South African Division.

Wavell was by now hard pressed in the Western Desert and was keen to speed up the return of troops to Egypt. The quickest way to do so was to open up the road from Addis Ababa through Dessie to Massawa whence troops could be lifted by sea to Suez. Platt and Cunningham were ordered to advance from north and south to clear the road and, in so doing, destroy the Duke of Aosta's personal refuge. Caught between these two forces, Aosta had little chance, but managed to delay the final decision until 16 May, always hoping for a reprieve. Fearing that if he held out much longer he, his officers and men, and his wounded would fall into the hands of Abyssinian irregulars, he asked for an armistice which was granted on 19 May. The campaign straggled on for another two months as each Italian force was mopped up in the remote regions to which its commander had withdrawn rather than surrender. The last to ask for an armistice was General Gazzera who gave up on 3 July.

The limelight of world interest had long since lifted off East Africa. On 6 April 1941, the Wehrmacht opened its simultaneous onslaught on Yugoslavia and Greece. The Anglo-Italian war was over. The British had achieved much by their pragmatism. Success had truly bred success, but it had also led to strategic over-confidence. British Imperialism now faced German professionalism. Unfortunately for the British, Wavell had been guilty of a fourth major strategic misjudgment in the first week of March which will be described in the next chapter.

Part 2

GERMAN PROFESSIONALISM

'National Socialism, moreover, gave the 'avant garde' in the General Staff the upper hand in many questions of principle. Elsewhere in Europe, in France and England, for example, where military development was neither interrupted or revolutionised by internal upheaval, this was not the case and there grew up a tremendous rigidity and adherence to system which could in no way meet the requirements of modern warfare. We, on our side, would have had very little advantage over the French and British even with our up to date tank and air arms, if these arms had not been matched by equally up-to-date organisation, training and tactical doctrine.'

Rommel's conclusions on Modern Military Leadership.
(Papers: page 516).

6

Gathering the Fruits of British Strategic Misjudgments

(April 1941)

'The all-night unloading of this 6,000 ton transport was a record for the port of Tripoli. The men received their tropical kit early next morning, and by eleven o'clock were fallen in on the square in front of Government House. They radiated complete assurance of victory, and the change of atmosphere did not pass unnoticed in Tripoli. After a short march past, Baron von Wechmar (commanding the 3rd Reconnaissance Unit) moved off to Sirte and arrived at the front 26 hours later. On the 16th (February) German reconnaissance troops . . . made their first move against the enemy. I now took over command of the front'.

(Rommel: *The Rommel Papers*, page 102).

April 1941 was almost as disastrous for the British as June 1940. All their apparently logical decisions, taken since O'Connor opened his 'Compass' offensive, turned sour from February onwards. By the end of April they were almost back where they started with a German instead of Italian enemy threatening Egypt. The Anglo-German desert drama had started, unbeknown to the British, when O'Connor's victory at Beda Fomm forced Hitler to order 'Sonnenblume'. It is interesting to compare the timings of O'Connor's plan for his advance on Tripoli with Rommel's action to defend it. O'Connor's armoured cars passed through El Agheila on 8 February and, if they had not been stopped, would have been in Sirte on 12 February, two days before von Wechmar's 3rd Reconnaissance Unit – the leading element of Rommel's Afrika Korps and of Major-General Streich's 5th Light Division – landed in Tripoli. O'Connor planned to advance from Sirte on 20 February and, with the help of Cunningham's Fleet and Longmore's Air Forces and the landing of a brigade group near Tripoli, expected to enter the city without much difficulty by the end of the month. Rommel himself agreed that there was nothing to stop him: 'If Wavell had continued his advance into Tripolitania no resistance worthy of the name could have been mounted against him'. (Rommel: page 95).

The actual course of events was very different. Rommel decided that he must impose caution on the British by showing a German presence in the forward area, and by attacking their logistic system. He rushed von Wechmar's 3rd Reconnaissance Unit forward to Sirte which was entered by German instead of British armoured cars on 16 February. Simultaneously he persuaded General Gariboldi, the new Italian C-in-C who had replaced Graziani, that Sirte could be held now that German troops were arriving. Gariboldi authorised the advance of the newly arrived Italian Ariete

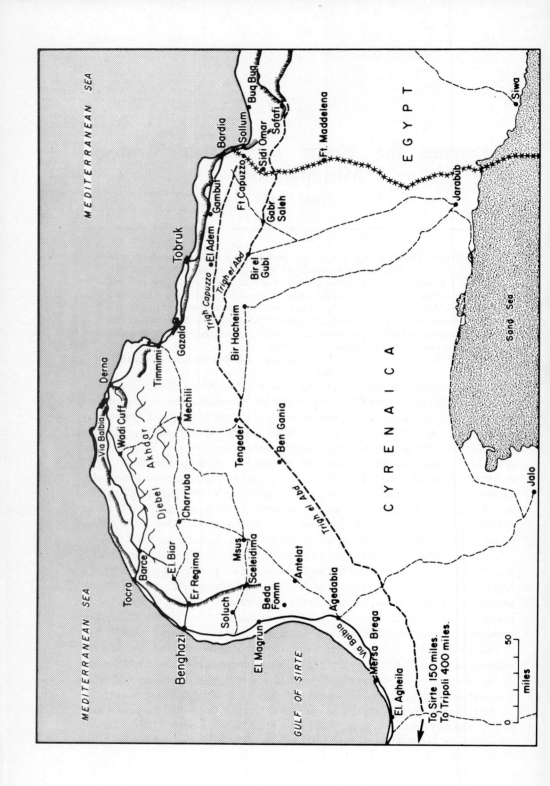

Armoured Division to support von Wechmar in a further advance to El Agheila, and the use of the Pavia and Bologna Infantry Divisions to build up a defensive base at Sirte. Rommel's most successful measure, however, was to cajole the Italians into agreeing that the Luftwaffe should neutralise the port of Benghazi in spite of the danger to Italian life and property in the city. On 18 February, Fliegerkorps X started a series of concentrated attacks on the port which forced the British to abandon it as a supply base. This German success was to have dire consequences for the British later.

The British obtained their first positive identification of German troops on 21 February when a pilot flying west of El Agheila spotted an eight-wheeled armoured car which only the Germans possessed at that time. Three days later the first clash occurred between reconnaissance troops. At much the same time radio intercepts began to suggest the presence of a German headquarters in Africa. Thus, the British knew by 24 February, when Wavell accepted the Greek plan to hold the Aliakmon Line as practical, that there were German troops facing them on the Tripolitanian frontier.

By 1 March, when Bulgaria joined the Axis and German troops crossed the Danube on their approach march to the Greek frontier, Rommel was satisfied that Tripolitania was secure because he had enough German troops of Streich's 5th Light Division ashore to stiffen the five available Italian divisions (Ariete, Brescia, Bologna, Pavia and Savona). He was further reassured by his intelligence sources and air reconnaissance reports which pointed to British withdrawal from, rather than reinforcement of, Libya.

Intelligence reports reaching London of the arrival of German troops at Tripoli prompted Churchill to ask Wavell for a short appreciation. Wavell's reply, dated 2 March, was sanguine and was the first clear indication of the beginning of the fourth cycle of British strategic misjudgments which were to accumulate over the next five weeks.

> Latest information indicates recent reinforcements to Tripolitania comprise two Italian infantry divisions, two Italian motorised artillery regiments and German armoured troops estimated at a maximum of one armoured brigade group. No evidence of additional mechanical transport landed, and enemy must still be short of transport . . .
>
> 2. Tripoli to Agheila is 471 miles and to Benghazi 646 miles. There is only one road, and water is inadequate over 400 miles of the distance; these factors, together with lack of transport, limit present enemy threat. He can probably maintain up to one infantry division and an armoured brigade along the coast road in about three weeks . . .
>
> 3. He may test us at Agheila by offensive patrolling, and if he finds us weak push on to Agedabia in order to move up his advanced landing grounds. I do not think that with this force he will attempt to recover Benghazi . . .
>
> (Churchill: Vol III, pages 174–175).

This comforting appreciation coincided with the views of Hitler and the German

High Command, but took no account of Rommel's personality. As yet no one on the British side knew who was commanding the German troops in Tripoli; and in Berlin no plans were being made for an offensive in Africa until Major-General von Prittwitz 15th Panzer Division had been landed safely in Tripoli in about mid-May. The accuracy of Wavell's assessment of the intentions of the German High Command was unfortunate because it removed the German threat to Cyrenaica from the debate on Greece. Had this threat been amplified, it might have swayed the balance of argument as to whether the Aliakmon Line could still be held in view of the Greek failure to withdraw their troops from Thrace. It is just possible that had Wavell become more alarmed about his desert flank, the Greek Expedition might never have sailed.

During the second week of March evidence of the German threat grew apace. Wavell's Director of Intelligence, Brigadier John Shearer, sent to the Commander-in-Chief an appreciation, dated 5 March, written from the German point of view. He suggested that the unidentified German Commander would operate more quickly than Wavell's logistic staff believed possible. Shearer suggested that he would plan his operations in three phases: measures to secure Tripolitania against British attack; re-occupation of Cyrenaica; and finally invasion of Egypt. The first phase was complete; the second might start by 1 April. Shearer was very near the mark but he could not bring convincing evidence to bear which would disprove the calculations of the British logisticians who still held to their view that lack of transport over the 650 miles from Tripoli to Benghazi would prevent a major German offensive developing much before mid-May. Wavell accepted the logistic instead of the intelligence staff view.

Rommel was identified as the commander of the DAK – Deutsches Afrika Korps – on 8 March. His reputation was known through his pre-war book on infantry tactics and the aggressive part played by his 7th Panzer Division in France in 1940. In the next few days British Intelligence gained a better picture of Rommel's force, concluding that there was in Tripolitania a panzer brigade with one panzer regiment supported by mechanised infantry and artillery, and that troops to make up a fully established armoured division were on their way to Tripoli. Sustained operations were still considered unlikely for logistic reasons.

Wavell took the opportunity to fly to Cyrenaica with Dill before the latter left for England with Eden after their negotiations in Athens. General Wilson, who was Military Governor of Cyrenaica, had been given command of the British Expeditionary Force to Greece and had been replaced by Lieutenant-General Philip Neame, VC, from Palestine. Wavell found Neame worried and rather depressed. He also disliked what he saw of Neame's dispositions and said so, adding:

> I told Neame that if his advanced troops were driven back he was not to attempt the direct defence of Benghazi, but to pull his Armoured Brigade back on to the left of the Australians on the escarpment above Benghazi . . .

But the really alarming picture was the state of Cruiser tanks of the 2nd Armoured Division, which were the core of the whole force. Out of fifty-two tanks, half were already in workshops, and the remainder kept breaking down at intervals. I was also appalled at the size and unwieldiness of the 2nd Armoured Division's Headquarters. Gambier-Parry, though he had only one brigade to handle, had brought forward the whole of the headquarters, with the idea of getting them exercised in the field . . .

I came back anxious and depressed from this visit, but there was nothing much I could do about it. The movement to Greece was in full swing and I had nothing left in the bag. But I had forebodings and my confidence in Neame was shaken".

(J. Connell: pages 385-386).

Neame had a right to complain about the state of the Cyrenaica Garrison. In the first place it was established as a Garrison, and not as a fighting force. His headquarters was not mobile, had too few radio sets, and was dependent on the local telephone service boosted by his own signallers. Gambier-Parry's force was a division only in name. It had its large and cumbersome headquarters, designed for war in Europe and not the desert; one instead of two armoured brigades; and half a support group with only one motor infantry battalion, one field artillery regiment, an anti-tank battery and a machine gun company. His second armoured brigade and the bulk of the support group were on their way to Greece. He had hardly any organic logistic transport because this had been taken from him to operate the long haul from Tobruk to Agheila when Benghazi was abandoned as a base. He was forced to rely on stocks dumped at Msus for the armoured brigade, which was to operate on the desert flank, and at El Magrun, south of Benghazi, for his support group, which would operate astride the main coast road — the via Balbia. The three tank regiments of his 3rd Armoured Brigade under Brigadier Rimington were equipped with a motley collection of tanks: one had over-mileage and unreliable British Cruisers; another light tanks which were numerically well below strength; and the third captured Italian M 13 medium tanks. His reconnaissance regiment had only converted from horses to armoured cars in January!

Major-General Morshead's 9th Australian Division was stronger but had major deficiencies as well. Two of its brigades had been transferred to 7th Australian Division for Greece, and in exchange Morshead had received two brigades which were less advanced in their training and equipment. His divisional staff was not complete and he was short of basic needs such as anti-tank weapons, light automatics and, like Gambier-Parry, transport. But worst of all, the transport available in Cyrenaica could not support all his division in the Benghazi area. One brigade had to be left in Tobruk, while the other two held the escarpment east of Benghazi.

There was certainly little Wavell could do about the physical condition of Neame's garrison in the time that was left to him. It is surprising, however, that he did not replace Neame with O'Connor and Gambier-Parry with a more experienced desert commander from 7th Armoured Division which was back in the Delta refitting. Neither Neame nor Gambier-Parry was up to his job; nor had either the experience or personality to face up to a man like Rommel under such adverse circumstances.

Rommel's worries were of a different kind. Africa presented him a challenge of a type rarely experienced by German soldiers, who are more accustomed to fighting in Europe. His worst and longest lasting problem, which plagued him throughout his campaign and eventually defeated him was the insecurity of his extended lines of communication from Germany, which were controlled by the Italian Army through Italy and Libya, and by the Italian Navy across the Mediterranean. Rommel's fortunes waxed and waned with the degree of success achieved by British naval and air forces attacking the weaker links in this chain, which might have snapped altogether on several occasions had it not been for the extraordinary powers of improvisation of the German logistic staff.

Rommel's second worry was the inexperience of his troops in desert conditions. They had not been artificially acclimatised as was popularly supposed in England. Their clothing was found unsuitable; the importance of fresh rations was under-estimated; the amount of water needed was over-estimated; and the majority of the men suffered from homesickness once the novelty of their arrival in North Africa had worn off. But this natural unfamiliarity of a 'Continental' European Army in a strange overseas theatre was amply counter-balanced by battle experience gained in the German campaigns in Poland and France. German battle drills, which had been fully developed and proven in these campaigns, gave the Afrika Korps a tactical superiority which the British, after their easier operations against the Italians, found hard to match.

And Rommel's third worry lay in the equipment field. German technical staffs too had no experience of desert conditions. They avoided sending out diesel vehicles because they believed they would over-heat. They failed to fit adequate air and oil filters to the tank engines; they fitted double tyres to their wheeled vehicles which proved unsatisfactory; and they had devised no practical way of extricating vehicles from soft sand. But these relatively minor errors were offset by the basically high reliability and rugged design of German equipment which had been developed in the open-handed financial climate of the German rearmament programme in the 1930s and was in marked contrast to British equipment whose development had been starved of funds during the same period. The German workshop commander supporting the panzer regiment of Streich's division was pleasantly surprised by the performance of the tanks on their march eastwards from Tripoli. They gave little trouble, provided they moved by night, or in the cooler hours of the day, and at a fairly low speed. Even these precautions proved to be unnecessary later.

Rommel's greatest personal difficulties lay in his relationship with both the Italian and the German High Commands. He was, in theory, subordinate to General Gariboldi and, through him, to the Italian 'Commando Supremo' in Rome, which was responsible for all Axis operations in Libya. Like any other partner in a military alliance, he did have the right of appeal to the German High Command. In practice, it was Hitler and Field Marshal von Brauchitsch, C-in-C of the German Army, who gave him his real direction through OKH, the Army's General Staff, and OKW, Hitler's Supreme HQ. He was on excellent terms with Hitler, but his relations with von Brauchitsch were cool at all times and frigid on occasions. He did not belong to the General Staff and so his organisational abilities were suspect. His General Staff critics were to find plenty of evidence in the coming months to support their critical view of his abilities.

While Wavell was visiting Cyrenaica with Dill, Rommel was flying back to Berlin to explain his future plans personally to Hitler and von Brauchitsch. Before leaving Tripoli Rommel had persuaded Gariboldi that it might be possible to mount an offensive to regain Cyrenaica in May before the hot weather. If all went well, they would drive on into Egypt and finally to the Suez Canal. He hoped to win Hitler's approval and the agreement for the despatch of various reinforcements which he would need to make this plan practicable. In anticipation of Hitler's support he ordered Streich to be ready to attack El Agheila as soon as he returned from Berlin.

Rommel found it difficult to persuade von Brauchitsch that his ideas of an early offensive were sound because he was not aware of 'Marita' or 'Barbarossa' which would absorb all German resources in the Spring and Summer of 1941. Rommel describes the coolness of his meeting:

> The C-in-C of the Army informed me that there was no intention of striking a decisive blow in Africa in the near future, and that for the present I could expect no reinforcements. After the arrival of 15th Panzer Division at the end of May, I was to attack and destroy the enemy around Agedabia. Benghazi might perhaps be taken. I pointed out that we could not just take Benghazi, but would have to occupy the whole of Cyrenaica, as the Benghazi area could not be held by itself.
>
> (Rommel: page 105).

His interviews with Hitler were more amicable as the latter decorated him with 'Oakleaves' to his Knight's Cross for services in the Battle for France. How much Hitler encouraged Rommel to disregard the conservativism of OKH is not known, but it seems probable that Rommel was more prepared to take the risks he did knowing that he had the Führer's support. As soon as he arrived back in Africa, he ordered Streich to launch his attack on El Agheila. Next day von Wechmar's 3rd Reconnaissance Unit had little difficulty in driving out the light British covering force which retired to the defile of Mersa Brega. Churchill's sixth sense warned him something was wrong. On 26 March he cabled:

> We are naturally concerned at rapid German advances to Agheila. It is their habit to push on whenever they are not resisted. I presume you are only waiting for the tortoise to stick his head out far enough before chopping it off. It seems extremely important to give them an early taste of our quality. What is the state and location of 7th Armoured Division? Pray give me your appreciation.
>
> (Churchill: Vol III, page 178).

Wavell saw no reason to change his previous assessment of German intentions but he did confess that the quality which Churchill wanted to show was no longer available in Cyrenaica. In his reply he said:

> I have to admit to having taken considerable risk in Cyrenaica after capture of Benghazi in order to provide maximum support for Greece . . . I, therefore, made

arrangements to leave only small armoured force and only partly trained Australian division in Cyrenaica ... Next month or two will be anxious, but enemy has extremely difficulty problem and am sure his numbers have been much exaggerated ... Steps to reinforce Cyrenaica are in hand ... my own chief difficulty is transport.

(Ibid: page 179).

Wavell often stressed that shortage of trucks hampered him more than anything else during his campaigns. He was promised by the War Office that 3,000 trucks a month would be shipped to him from the United States. The figures for arrivals were 2,341 in January, 2,094 in February, 725 in March and 705 in April. The forces sent to Greece were fully equipped and so Cyrenaica went short and the shortage was accentuated by the neutralisation of Benghazi.

Wavell was equally disappointed in the Royal Navy's and Royal Air Force's efforts to stop the flow of Axis ships to Tripoli. Convoys of about four ships sailed every two or three days from the Italian west coast ports. By the end of March 15 convoys of German ships had landed 25,000 men, 8,500 vehicles and 26,000 tons of ammunition and other stores for the Afrika Korps. The convoys hugged the north coast of Sicily, slipping across to the Tunisian coast during darkness and sailed down to Tripoli inside French territorial waters. Until the beginning of February the British naval rules of engagement forbade attacks on single ships or small unescorted convoys unless they were within 30 miles of the Libyan coast. As it became more important to stop Axis traffic from Europe to North Africa than to assuage neutral opinion, the rules were relaxed to allow attacks on sight anywhere south of the latitude of Malta; and in March the French were warned that British warships would enter French North African territorial waters to deal with Axis shipping. In spite of these relaxations only nine German ships were sunk and nine damaged, totalling 86,000 tons, from February to May. The Italians lost a further 31 ships, (102,000 tons). This was not enough to stop the Axis building up their forces in Libya. Three words spell out the reasons for this failure: Luftwaffe, Malta and Greece. Fliegerkorps X's air bombing of Malta, which started in January with the arrival of the damaged *Illustrious,* subdued the British air reconnaissance force on the Island without which Axis convoys could not be located. Fliegerkorps X's presence in Sicily also closed the Central Mediterranean to British cruisers and made the operations of light naval craft and submarines from Malta hazardous. And the diversion of British naval and air effort to protect convoys from Egypt to Greece meant that the Axis convoys to Libya enjoyed a corresponding immunity, but encouraged the Italian Navy to put to sea with disastrous results.

On the 24 March, when Rommel attacked at El Agheila, Cunningham detected preparations for some major naval enterprise by the Italian Fleet which he thought might be connected with the expected German invasion of Greece. Timings of British convoys to and from Greece were altered in such a way as to clear the sea area south of Greece and Crete of all British shipping without alarming the Italians. Cunningham sailed with his Battle Fleet on 27 March on hearing that the Italians had been sighted, as expected, steering for Crete. In the ensuing surprise night engagement off Cape Matapan Admiral Iachino's Flagship *Vittorio Veneto* was torpedoed by naval aircraft, and three of his 8-inch cruisers and two destroyers were sunk by naval gun fire with the loss of 2,400 officers and men. Cunningham returned to Alexandria with his Fleet intact.

March ended with high hopes on the British side. Keren had fallen the day before Matapan; British columns were approaching Asmara, Massawa and Addis Ababa; and a British Expeditionary Force was taking up its positions in the Aliakmon Line in northern Greece – but British euphoria was to be short lived. Strategic mistakes made in February and March were to be compounded by tactical errors on the battlefield. Wavell, standing in the eye of the storm, was forced to look to the four points of the compass – north to Greece, south to Abyssinia, west to Cyrenaica and, by the end of the month, east to Iraq and Syria. Rarely has a military commander had to direct so many divergent operations simultaneously. And few men, other than Churchill, could have borne the responsibilities thrust upon him. It is a tragedy that he and Churchill finally lost faith in each other during this bitter period. Failure, like success, has its own disagreeable rewards.

Rommel paused for a week after taking El Agheila while he reconnoitred the new British position at Mersa Brega, and while he moved his troops and supplies forward for what he conceived as a reconnaissance in force into Cyrenaica to test British reactions and to prevent them building up too strong a defensive position. Gariboldi accepted his plan with the proviso that he must not advance round the corner into

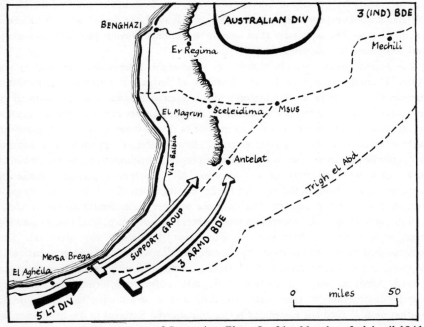

Fig 10 Rommel's Reconquest of Cyrenaica: Phase I – 31st March to 3rd April 1941

Cyrenaica without his express authority. OKH, in Berlin, enjoined similar caution. There is no evidence that Rommel himself intended, at that moment, to exceed his authority. The 'Raid into Cyrenaica' as Rommel called his first offensive can be divided into two phases: before and after his decision on 3 April to disobey Gariboldi and OKH.

Rommel started his operation with marked numerical and qualitative superiority on land and in the air. Streich's 5th Light Division was superior to Gambier-Parry's 2nd Armoured Division in everything but artillery. The 5th Panzer Regiment with two tank battalions could deploy 150 new and reliable medium and light tanks to deal with 3rd Armoured Brigade's 70 cruisers, light tanks and captured Italian M13 tanks. Streich's infantry consisted of 2nd and 8th Machine Gun Battalions and two Panzerjäger (anti-tank) battalions equipped with 50mm anti-tank guns and a few of the ubiquitous dual-purpose 88mm anti-air/anti-tank guns which were to make such a reputation for themselves in the desert. Gambier-Parry's infantry amounted to the Tower Hamlets Motor Battalion (a Territorial Army unit) supported by one 2-pounder anti-tank battery and one 40mm Bofors anti-aircraft battery. In artillery 5th Light Division had only one 12-gun field battery to 2nd Armoured Division's 24-gun field regiment. Rommel could oppose Morshead's 9th Australian Division with up to five Italian divisions, one of which (the Ariete) was armoured. And in the air, Fleigerkorps X had sent 50 dive-bombers and 20 twin-engined fighters to Libya for close support of the Afrika Korps against which the RAF could present no more than 30 bombers and fighters. Moreover, whereas Fliegerkorps X could send reinforcements from Sicily to Libya, Group Captain Brown, the RAF Commander in Cyrenaica, could expect little help from Egypt. All available British aircraft had been sent to Greece. The odds were thus heavily in Rommel's favour provided his logistic staff could keep him supplied.

The Mersa Brega position, which was some eight miles wide, was held by the Tower Hamlets, supported by the artillery of Brigadier Latham's emasculated Support Group. Brigadier Rimington's 3rd Armoured Brigade was concentrated on his desert flank ready to counter-attack at the appropriate moment. Streich opened his attack at 10 am on 31 March, and in spite of dive-bomber support, was repulsed. Latham asked Rimington to counter-attack, but Gambier-Parry intervened because he did not believe there was enough time for proper co-ordination of the attack before dusk. This was the first of a succession of unfortunate decisions made by Gambier-Parry which, in the end, led to the disintegration of 3rd Armoured Brigade without a serious engagement. Streich made another unsuccessful attack at about 5.30 pm behind more dive-bombing, but by then Latham appreciated that he had too much against him to hold such a wide front throughout the night. He had accomplished his mission of imposing maximum delay without becoming inextricably involved, and was authorised by Cyrenaica Command to withdraw during the night towards Agedabia with 3rd Armoured Brigade conforming. Neame was following Wavell's instructions to trade space for time, but in abandoning the Mersa Brega position he uncorked the Cyrenaica bottle and allowed Rommel to use his numerical superiority once he was through the defile.

Little happened on 1 April because Rommel was still following up relatively cautiously. Gambier-Parry pulled his division back northwards through a series of delaying positions with the Support Group on the via Balbia and the armoured brigade on the desert flank. Neame's broad intention was to delay the German advance on Benghazi, while at the same time being ready to oppose a move across the desert towards Mechili and Timimi, if one should develop. On 2 April German pressure increased and things began to go wrong on the British side. The Tower Hamlets had difficulty in extricating themselves from one position and lost a company in the process. 5th Royal Tank Regiment, equipped with cruisers, checked the German advance, destroying three German tanks at the cost of five of their own. By evening it was clear to Gambier-Parry that his chances of holding Agedabia were dwindling; and it would be unwise to let the support group and armoured brigade drift apart which was likely to happen if he kept the Support Group on the via Balbia while the 3rd Armoured Brigade withdrew through Antelat. He sought Neame's permission to abandon the main road so that he could keep his division concentrated upon the German's open flank. He gave a depressing picture of his force; only 22 cruisers and 25 light tanks still running and he was losing an average of one tank every 10 miles of his withdrawal through mechanical breakdowns.

Neame would have agreed to Gambier-Parry's proposal, which the latter was putting into effect while awaiting a reply, if the decision had not been taken out of his hands by the arrival of Wavell who had flown up from Cairo. In spite of his earlier direction to Neame that he was to abandon Benghazi rather than lose part of his force, he ordered Neame to refuse Gambier-Parry's request and insisted that Benghazi should be covered because he still believed that the German effort would die away after they reached Agedabia. The instructions to Gambier-Parry did not go out until 9 pm and such was the state of Neame's communications that they did not reach the armoured division until 2.25 am the following morning.

Meanwhile Wavell sent off a signal to Cairo summoning O'Connor to take over command – a thing he should have done a fortnight earlier; and then caused greater confusion by not carrying out his intention to replace Neame. O'Connor explained what happened when he reached Cyrenaica:

> It seems to me the situation was definitely more serious than the Chief believed, and that one of the most important things to do was to get our defences organised much further east than the Benghazi area. And I felt that I should be employed on this task, as soon as possible. I felt also that changing horses in mid-stream would not really help matters ... I therefore decided that I would ask the Chief to reconsider my replacing Neame, and to consider, as an alternative, my remaining with him for a few days, but ultimately returning to organise the defence of Egypt.
>
> (J. Connell: page 393–394).

Wavell agreed and left Neame in charge with O'Connor as his adviser. In military affairs duality in command never works. It did nothing to improve matters in Cyrenaica, and as the days went by made things very much worse. Order-counter-order multiplied, and there was no-one organising a secure base in rear

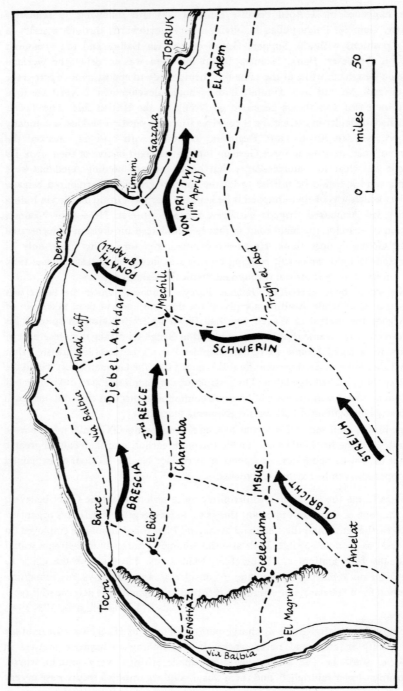

Fig 11 Rommel's Reconquest of Cyrenaica: Phase II – 3rd to 11th April 1941

to which the British could withdraw. On the 'other side of the hill' there was only one commander, but he had his difficulties too.

Rommel's experienced eye noted all the tell-tale signs that things were not well on the British side. They were falling back too easily, doing too little fighting and leaving too much equipment behind. The Luftwaffe reports showed a general withdrawal northwards and eastwards which made him conclude that the British were abandoning Cyrenaica. He saw his opportunity to turn the tables on the British by emulating O'Connor's march to Beda Fomm in reverse. His target would be Timimi, enabling him to cut off all British forces in the bulge of Cyrenaica. Wavell had hesitated before authorising O'Connor's dash to Beda Fomm because of the possibility of having to send troops to Greece: Rommel found Gariboldi and OKH equally reluctant to allow him to make for Timimi because 'Marita' was about to start. Ignoring his superiors and his supply position, which was growing precarious, Rommel decided to copy O'Connor, improvising as well, if not better, than the British.

At this early stage in the Afrika Korps' existence Rommel was not receiving the whole-hearted co-operation from his own officers to which he grew accustomed later on. Streich complained that he would need four days to refuel and refit. Rommel lost patience and ordered him to dump his equipment and use all his trucks to replenish his division in 24 hours. While waiting for Streich, Rommel set about organising 'ad hoc' columns from units which were ready. He placed these under whatever German commanders happened to be available and whom he could trust to follow his own tireless example. Major-General Kirchheim, who was visiting the theatre at the time, was pressed into commanding a composite force of the 3rd Reconnaissance Unit and the Brescia Division and ordered to advance on Benghazi. Colonel Count Schwerin was put in charge of part of the Ariete Division, reinforced with German reconnaissance and anti-tank detachments, and told to push north-eastwards to Mechili, using the ancient desert caravan trail to Egypt – the Trigh-el-Abd. Streich, with the lighter elements of his 5th Light Division, was to follow Count Schwerin as soon as refuelling would allow; and Colonel Olbrich, commander 5th Panzer Regiment, was to lead his two panzer battalions and the heavier elements of Streich's division over O'Connor's old route in reverse from Antelat via Msus to Mechili. Rommel supervised everything himself, flying from column to column in his small Storch aircraft, determined to prove that he was right and his masters were wrong.

3 April was a disastrous day for the British, their discomfiture being caused by their own doing rather than by German action. Gambier-Parry was not able to reverse his decision to withdraw the whole division through Antelat. Neame was thus forced to order the evacuation of Benghazi and the demolition of all stores accumulated there. It was fortunate that the Support Group did not withdraw on Benghazi, because its supply depot at El Magrun had been destroyed in the general confusion. The whole division became dependent on supplies at Msus. At about midday it arrived at the Sceleidima Pass and was ordered to extend the Australian flank southwards by taking up positions to deny all routes up the escarpment. Orders had just been given when a report from the RAF suggested that German

reconnaissance vehicles were approaching Msus. New orders were issued which did not reach some of the units concerned. Gambier-Parry had, in the meantime, complained to Neame that it was impractical to hold his sector of the escarpment because the units could not be supplied. Cyrenaica Command accepted his pleas and authorised the further withdrawal of the whole division to El Biar in direct support of the Australians. Some units heard this order, others did not; some reacted, others including the 3rd Armoured Brigade, stayed where they were. The divisional headquarters lost touch with its subordinate formations, and, in consequence, several reports of enemy advances were, in fact, moves by its own units. 3rd Armoured Brigade, on its own initiative, moved on Msus, arriving early on 4 April to find no Germans in the place but no supplies of fuel either because the local garrison had heard the RAF reports about the German advances and had destroyed the dumps. The rest of the division eventually assembled tired and frustrated at El Biar.

Bad luck, which always pursues forces in defeat, continued unabated. Information reaching Neame suggested that Msus was in German hands and so about midnight on 3/4 April he ordered a general withdrawal to a line running from Wadi Cuff to Mechili. 3rd Indian Motor Brigade, which had just arrived in Cyrenaica, was ordered to garrison Mechili where it would be joined by Gambier-Parry's division – or what was left of it. Morshead's Australians would withdraw by stages through the djebel. About midday Neame decided that he had acted too precipitately. The old feeling that the Germans would be content, for logistic reasons, with limited gains – particularly of Benghazi – returned. He decided to delay the Australian withdrawal, causing them the frustration of counter-marching. Almost as soon as Neame's new orders had been issued, the Australians holding the Er Regima Pass east of Benghazi were heavily attacked by 3rd Reconnaissance Unit, which though stopped, caused the Australians almost 100 casualties and made Neame accept the need to restart the withdrawal. Order-counter-order began to plague the Australians as much as the British units of 2nd Armoured Division which continued to expend itself to no avail. Three convoys of fuel sent to its armoured brigade were destroyed by the Luftwaffe. It struggled on, abandoning tanks as they ran out and filling up the better machines from the older before destroying them. Availability of fuel rather than the orders of the divisional headquarters dictated its withdrawal route and so it was drawn northwards towards the via Balbia where stocks were more plentiful and away from the desert flank which it should have been protecting.

Rommel meanwhile was driving his men forward with relentless energy across the desert tracks. Air reconnaissance confirmed the continuation of the British withdrawal and showed activity around Mechili, which Rommel designated as the focus for the advance of 5th Light Division before it made a decisive thrust to cut the coast road at Timimi. On 4 April things went as badly for the Germans as the British. Count Schwerin ran out of petrol and water half way to Mechili; Streich's column made heavy weather of the Trigh-el-Abd and was strung out over 25 miles of crumbling desert track; Olbrich had not left Antelat with his panzer battalions; and in the north, Kirchheim's mixed German and Italian columns were being checked by the Australians as they tried to push eastwards from Benghazi. Some Axis troops had no rations; many vehicles were over-heating due to too much low gear work; and several important detachments simply lost their way. Towards evening on 5 April Rommel could stand the lack of progress no longer. Leaving Kircheim to drive the Italians on through the Djebel Akhdar against the Australians, he took over the lead of the principally German columns in the desert. He collected Lieutenant-Colonel Ponath's 8th MG Battalion from the head of Streich's group and drove through the night with headlights blazing, making for Mechili. He was attacked by British aircraft and had to drive on without lights much more slowly, reaching Mechili with Count Schwerin's force and 15 trucks of Ponath's battalion early on 6 April. Positioning Count Schwerin's men to cut the British Garrison's withdrawal routes to the east, he ordered Ponath to push on towards Derna to interfere with the British withdrawal on the via Balbia, while he himself dashed back to urge more units forward to Mechili, partcularly Olbrich's two panzer battalions whose advance had been mismanaged by inexperienced staffs. They ran out of fuel on 6 April and lost their way on several occasions.

Brigadier Vaughan's lightly equipped 3rd Indian Motor Brigade refused to be over-awed by the arrival of Rommel's leading troops at Mechili. His reports to Neame and O'Connor alerted them to the danger in their rear. The German cross-desert stroke, which Neame had always feared was obviously well advanced. At 4 pm on 6 April orders were issued for the immediate continuation of the British withdrawal without waiting for darkness and to Gazala instead of Derna. In spite of shortages of transport and the usual muddles that occur when orders are changed at the last moment the Australian withdrawal went relatively smoothly and by 7 am the following morning the leading Australian brigade was in a defensive position at Timimi to cover the withdrawal of the rest of the Cyrenaica Garrison. Credit must be given to Morshead and his staff for this feat of organisation which included an extensive demolition and mining programme as well as the extrication of the troops without loss. The Australian account describes the men's feeelings:

> The troops started out tired and unshaven and unwashed. They seemed to be abandoning an ideal position for a stand and running away once more – contrary to everyone's wish to 'have a go'. They piled into overcrowded vehicles, amid rifles, Bren guns and equipment where no position offered comfort yet no move was possible. The sleep they needed was unattainable . . .
>
> *(Australian Official History*: page 87).

Less credit is deserved by 2nd Armoured Division's staff which allowed its division to disintegrate. The Headquarters reached Mechili with few fighting troops and were more of an embarrassment to Vaughan than a reinforcement. The Support Group should have followed, but a muddle in orders diverted it northwards to the Australian withdrawal routes and it went back with them to Gazela. The 3rd Armoured Brigade could not reach Mechili for lack of fuel and had to turn north again to find supplies on the via Balbia. It, too, joined the Australian withdrawal, with only seven cruisers left. Three failed to negotiate the steep track out of Derna and were destroyed. The last four were instrumental in helping the rear-guard to keep Ponath off the withdrawal route. They were all knocked out during the action leaving the brigade tankless – a sad end to an abortive campaign in which the desire of the higher command to preserve the available armour resulted in its destruction through mechanical and logistic failure rather than enemy action.

Colonel Ponath had only embarrassed the Australian withdrawal when he reached the Derna area the previous evening. He was lucky, however, to carry off a coup which probably affected the whole pattern of the Desert War. After seeing the final withdrawal was well under way, Neame and O'Connor had set off in a staff car for Timimi where their next headquarters was to be established. The driver lost the way while the two generals snatched what sleep they could in the back of the car. He veered too far north towards Derna, and ran into one of Ponath's patrols. There was no escape. Both O'Connor and Neame were captured before they were fully awake. The loss of O'Connor was a serious blow to the British. He was one of the few men who might have been able to destroy the Rommel myth, which grew up in the succeeding months. Wavell felt so strongly about his loss that he suggested to London that any six Italian generals should be exchanged for him. Whitehall turned the request down: 'We cannot discriminate in favour of generals'. (J. Connell: page 410).

Gambier-Parry and Morshead were the only British generals left in the field. The former was surrounded at Mechili; and the latter was making his way back to Tobruk. Rommel demanded Mechili's surrender twice during 7 April and was refused. During the night plans were made to break out. The attempt started at dawn on 8 April. Some of the Indian units broke through successfully, but the Headquarters 2nd Armoured Division was too late in moving and was forced to surrender, Gambier-Parry being captured in his command vehicle. The *Indian Official History* (page 163) can rightly claim that Vaughan's three-day stand at Mechili stopped Rommel's Beda Fomm. 5th Light Division was held up just long enough to allow the bulk of Morshead's Australian Division to slip back to Gazala.

During 9 and 10 April, Morshead withdrew by stages towards Tobruk. He was surprised to find not one but two Australian brigades organising its defences – his own 24th Australian Brigade, which had never left Tobruk, and the 18th Australian Brigade which should have gone to Greece. On 4 April the British Chiefs of Staff had agreed, in view of the situation in Libya, to stop the 7th Australian Division sailing for Greece. Its 18th Australian Brigade had been shipped straight to Tobruk instead.

Rommel did not halt as he might have done on the Derna – Mechili line to reorganise and bring up supplies. General Kirchheim had been wounded, but another visitor – General Prittwitz, commander of 15th Panzer Division, who arrived on reconnaissance ahead of his troops – was immediately given a strong group of all arms to reconnoitre Tobruk. Prittwitz was killed in the first attempt to probe the Australian defences. Count Schwerin took his place and continued to look for a weak spot on the southern face of the fortress with units of 5th Panzer Regiment and the Ariete Division. Streich's 5th Light Division was pushed round to the far side to prevent any attempt by the garrison to escape eastwards; and the Brescia Division came up on the western side. The investment of Tobruk was complete by the end of 11 April. Von Wechmar's hard working 3rd Reconnaissance Unit was directed on

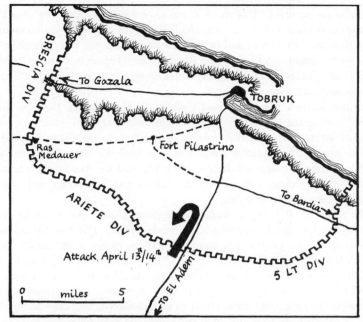

Fig 12 Rommel's First Assault on Tobruk – 13th/14th April 1941

Bardia; and a new battle group under Lieutenant-Colonel Knabe formed from newly arrived motorcycle and motorised infantry belonging to 15th Panzer Division, which had been flown to Libya by the Luftwaffe, was given Sollum as its immediate objective and permission to go on to Mersa Matruh if all went well. Rommel announced with confidence that in his view the British were collapsing as the French had done in the Battle of France and must be pursued to the Suez Canal . . . They must not be allowed to settle down in the Tobruk defences.

Rommel and his subordinate commanders in the Afrika Korps misjudged their opponents, as Wavell had misjudged the Afrika Korps before its offensive began. Rommel thought that the shipping lying off Tobruk was there to extricate the garrison, whereas it was in fact reinforcing it. Morshead made it quite clear to his men that there would be no further withdrawal by land or sea. The defence would be thoroughly aggressive. And so it was. Morale rose steeply as the first German probing attacks by Count Schwerin's group on 11 and 12 April were defeated.

Outside the fortress, Rommel's flying columns took Bardia which was unoccupied and went on to drive the light British covering forces out of Fort Capuzzo and Sollum. They got no further. A new force under command of Brigadier Gott, based upon 22nd Guards Brigade and other units hastily sent forward from the Nile Delta, barred the way into Egypt.

Rommel realised that he must eliminate the threat posed to his rear by Tobruk before he could press on towards the Suez Canal. He ordered Streich, in whom he was losing confidence, to lead his division personally in an attack up the El Adem –

Tobruk road on the night 13/14 April. It was to be a typical 'blitzkreig' attack which had crumpled so many Polish, French, and British positions in 1939/40. Ponath's 8th MG Battalion would break in during darkness and breach the anti-tank ditch so that the two panzer battalions of 5th Panzer Regiment could crash through by the shortest route to Tobruk harbour, throwing the whole defence into confusion. Such methods had always worked before.

Inside the fortress Morshead had given strict instructions that the infantry battalions holding the old Italian perimeter defences were to concentrate on dealing with enemy infantry, leaving the tanks to the artillery in their rear. Not only were there four British 25-pounder regiments close behind the Australians, but also an assorted collection of captured Italian guns, manned by Australian infantry and called the 'Bush Artillery', backed up the British and Australian anti-tank units, covering the main tank approaches.

On the morning of 13 April, leaflets were dropped on Tobruk calling upon the Australians to surrender by showing white handkerchiefs. The Australian comments are unprintable. The politest was that the need to ration water meant no white hankerchiefs were available!

Either the standard of German training left much to be desired or they were over-confident. Forming up in the afternoon was clumsy and offered the British gunners useful targets. After dark, Ponath's men managed, with considerable loss, to clear a way through the anti-tank ditch and mine-field to let Olbrich's tanks enter the perimeter defences carrying infantry on their backs to widen the breach for the following echelons. Few of the infantry survived the tanks' passage. At daylight the tanks found themselves alone as they started their advance into the heart of the fortress. Past experience in Europe suggested that Tobruk should have capitulated when the garrison saw the two panzer battalions advancing remorselessly into its vitals. The opposite happened. Field gunners, anti-tank gunners, 'Bush Artillery' and a handful of British cruiser tanks met the attack, and stopped it. The Germans lost 17 tanks; 150 German dead were counted inside the perimeter and 250 Germans were captured. Rommel wrote later: 'I was furious, particularly as the tanks had left the infantry in the lurch'.

Thinking some of Ponath's battalion were still holding out he tried to extricate them next day with the Ariete Division but 'they received a few rounds of artillery fire from Tobruk. The confusion was indescribable. The division broke up in complete disorder, turned tail and streamed back . . .' (Rommel: pages 125–126).

Rommel tried again on 16 and 17 April using the Ariete Division reinforced by units of the Italian Trento Division which had reached the front. Although he directed the operation personally, he could not make a breach in the Australian defences. Both German and Italian morale began to slump with lack of success. After some brisk raiding by the Australians had resulted in the capture of two complete Italian infantry battalions, which surrendered voluntarily, Rommel was forced to conclude that: 'It was now finally clear that there was no hope of doing anything against the enemy defences with the forces we had, largely because of the poor state of training and useless equipment of the Italian troops. I decided to break off the attack until the arrival of more troops'. (Rommel: page 128).

Rommel had picked all the fruits ripened by British strategic misjudgments in February and March. The British were a match for the Germans provided conditions were reasonable. In Western Cyrenaica in April 1941 they were not, and the British were forced to withdraw in indecent haste and confusion. From now on, the side which could built up its resources quickest and whose equipment proved the most reliable would hold the advantage. It was to be an evenly matched contest, in which events outside North Africa were to have a decisive effect on the outcome. Within North Africa a 'gentleman's war' was to be fought in which tactical skill, courage and endurance were to be the hallmarks of both sides.

While Rommel had been making a name for himself with his rapid reconquest of Cyrenaica, the centre of gravity of the war, which had stood in Africa during the winter months, swung northwards, first to the Balkans and then to Russia. The Yugo-Slav Government of Prince Paul had tried to join the Axis on 25 March and had been overthrown two days later by a pro-Allied coup d'etat. This was more than Hitler could tolerate. Before the day was out, Operational Directive No. 25 had been issued by OKW modifying Plan 'Marita' to include the invasion of Yugo-Slavia as well as Greece. In one of the most brilliant pieces of staff work, the German General Staff re-deployed their forces assembled for 'Marita' and 'Barbarossa' and launched them within 10 days of Hitler's decision. On 6 April, Belgrade was bombed and General von Weich's Second Army and General List's Twelfth Army invaded the two countries. The Yugo-Slav armies collapsed, enabling the Germans to outflank the Aliakmon Line. After a short three-week campaign the British Expeditionary Force, which had been sent to Greece instead of ending the North African Campaign, was being withdrawn without its equipment back to Crete and Alexandria. The whole process of buying time to build up resources had been set back many months. Few mistaken strategic decisions can ever have been penalised more severely and more quickly than the decision to aid Greece without adequate resources.

And in the east of Wavell's wide-spread command more trouble was brewing. The pro-British Regent of Iraq was toppled by the Axis-backed clique of Rashid Ali. Although the new Iraqi Government took no overtly hostile action against the British in Iraq, it was clear that Anglo-Iraqi relations were deteriorating rapidly. The British Imperial position in the Middle East seemed to local observers to be on the point of collapse. The temptation to reinsure with the Axis agents was becoming a matter of understandable prudence.

7

British Tactical Mistakes
(May and June 1941)

'It was certainly not realised by the British, as it was by the Germans, that the 88-mm gun, and perhaps the new 50-mm anti-tank gun also, had been the principal cause of their defeat . . . Had the real menace been detected . . . thought might have been given, as it certainly was not by anyone, to the need for greater concentration of our own artillery resources to defeat them.'

Field-Marshal Sir Michael Carver: *Tobruk*, page 28.

'The Shadow of Barbarossa' might have been an appropriate title for this chapter had it not been for Rommel's refusal to fight his campaign within the strict dictates of German grand strategy. What mattered in the North African Campaign in May and June 1941 was not the hidden effects of the coming German invasion of Russia, but the first clashes of German and British tactical method and weapon philosophy which emerged as the British recovered from their shock defeat in Cyrenaica in April. The British were to make a series of tactical mistakes during this period of the desert war which were to have consequences almost as serious as their strategic misjudgments earlier in the year.

Rommel's sweeping advance to the Egyptian frontier did not cause an equal and opposite reaction in the two high commands. Instead of applauding Rommel, Berlin found his victory embarrassing. He had been sent to help an ailing ally and not to open a new offensive front at the very moment when all available German forces were moving secretly to their concentration areas in eastern Europe. Rommel's demands for reinforcements with which to exploit success were coldly received in Berlin. General Halder, Chief of Staff at OKH, recorded in his diary on 23 April 1941:

Rommel has not sent in a single clear report, and I have a feeling that things are in a mess . . . All day long he rushes about between his widely scattered units and stages reconnaissance raids in which he fritters away his strength . . . His motor vehicles are in poor condition and many of the tank engines need replacing . . . Air transport cannot meet his senseless demands, primarily because of lack of fuel . . . It is essential to have the situation cleared up without delay . . .'

(Quoted in *British Official History:* Vol II, page 41).

In London Britain's worst fears seemed to be confirmed. The three pronged concentric attack on their position in the Middle East – Rommel across the desert, List from Greece through Turkey and Syria, and an unknown German personality behind Rashid Ali in Iraq – was turning the grand German strategic design, against which Wavell had prepared his 'worst possible case' in 1940, into reality. The feeling in London at the time is illustrated by the Churchillian outburst which occurred at a dinner party when General John Kennedy, Director of Military Operations, suggested that the Germans could make the British position in the Middle East untenable:

> Churchill flushed at this, and lost his temper . . . 'Wavell has 400,000 men. If they lose Egypt, blood will flow. I will have firing parties to shoot the Generals'.
>
> 'You need not be afraid they will not fight' I replied. 'Of course they will fight. I am only arguing that we should decide the price we are prepared to pay and can afford to pay, for the defence of the Middle East' . . . I added that surely he was aware that Wavell had a plan for withdrawal from Egypt should it be forced upon him . . .
>
> At this he fairly exploded. 'This comes as a flash of lightning to me', he exclaimed. 'I never heard such ideas. War is a contest of wills. It is pure defeatism to speak as you have done'.
>
> (Kennedy: pages 105–106).

Churchill practised what he preached. British strategy in the North African Campaign developed along three lines: firstly, cutting the Axis supply lines across the Mediterranean to starve Rommel; secondly, reinforcing the Middle East with as many men, tanks guns and aircraft as limited shipping capacity would allow; and thirdly, hammering the life blood out of the Germans in the Western Desert. Churchill could bring naval and air power to bear on supply lines; and he could force the reluctant War Office to send more than they thought prudent to the Middle East; but he could not affect the actual fighting in the desert as much as he would have liked.

The first specific ideas for cutting Rommel's supply lines had been considered in the British Admiralty in the first week of April. The idea was to block Tripoli harbour in Zeebrugge style, sinking the old battleship *Centurion* in the entrance. The technical problems of sailing her from Gibraltar to Tripoli under German air attack killed this proposal. The Cs-in-C Middle East would have preferred an allocation of heavy bombers to keep Axis ports under heavy air attack, but this would have diverted aircraft from the British bomber offensive against Germany upon which Churchill pinned great hopes in 1941. The Cs-in-C had to content themselves with basing six of their own small force of Wellington bombers on Malta and building up a destroyer raiding force under Captain Mack to intercept Axis convoys off the Tunisian Coast. Churchill was far from content with these measures. On 14 April he issued a directive in Whitehall which read:

> . . . It becomes the prime duty of the British Mediterranean Fleet under Admiral Cunningham to stop all sea-borne traffic between Italy and Africa by the fullest use of surface craft, aided so far as is possible by aircraft and submarines . . . Every convoy which gets through must be considered a serious naval failure. The repuation of the Royal Navy is engaged in stopping this traffic.
>
> (Churchill: Vol III, page 187).

Churchill went on to suggest that it would be worth sacrificing one of Cunningham's battleships to block Tripoli harbour as *Centurion* could not reach her target. The Admiralty proposed that his oldest battleship, HMS *Barham,* and one of his 'C' Class cruisers should be used. The Admiral objected as forcefully as Churchill might have done in his place. He believed quite rightly that the operation would destroy the British sailors' confidence in their high command. Secrecy would preclude calling for volunteers; and there was scant hope of getting the men away after sinking their ships. Churchill accepted his alternative which was to bombard the port at night with his main battle fleet. The operation was disguised as the usual convoy running. The Fleet arrived off Tripoli in the early hours of 21 April, achieving complete surprise. The shore defences did not reply during the first 20 minutes of the bombardment and then only with haphazard fire. The Italian anti-aircraft batteries never did realise that they were being bombarded by ships and continued to pump ammunition skywards. Nearly 500 rounds of 15-inch shell and 1,500 of lesser calibres were fired in 40 minutes while Tripoli was illuminated with flares dropped by *Formidable's* aircraft. Smoke from burning fuel tanks and dust thrown up by bursting shell obscured targets badly and made fire-correction difficult. When the damage was assessed later it was found to be disappointing. Axis shipping was not inconvenienced for more than a day. More damage had been done by Captain Mack's destroyers which intercepted a large Axis convoy, reported by air reconnaissance, off the Tunisian coast. In a brisk night action Mack's ships destroyed the five merchantmen in the convoy and three of its escorting destroyers for the loss of one of his own ships. Churchill would have liked a repeat bombardment of Tripoli; Cunningham would have preferred more reconnaissance aircraft with which to increase the chances of Mack repeating his successful interception; neither was to have his wish granted because the evacuation of the British Expeditionary Force from Greece drew all naval and air effort away from Tripoli, allowing the Axis convoys carrying 15th Panzer Division to reach Africa almost unscathed. Wavell cabled Churchill:

> I have just received disquieting intelligence. I was expecting another German Colonial division . . . I have just been informed that latest evidence indicates this is not Colonial but armoured repeat armoured division . . . I will cable again when I have digested this unwelcome news.
>
> (Churchill: Vol III, page 217).

Wavell went on to spell out the tank problem. He had one weak regiment of 30 mixed cruisers and 'I' tanks in Tobruk and a squadron of 18 cruisers watching the frontier area. None of his tanks in Greece was likely to come back. The output of reconditioned tanks from his workshops in the Nile Delta would not put more than another 30 to 40 tanks into this field in the next six weeks. The Germans had about 90 medium tanks already in Libya with 5th Light Division. 15th Panzer Division would bring another 138 into action if it turned out to be a fully established panzer division. Rommel would take a lot of stopping with such a force at his disposal, provided he could supply it as he advanced.

Churchill reacted with his characteristic pugnacity, determined to force the

Admiralty to repeat the 'Apology' operation of the previous autumn by sending tanks to Wavell through the Mediterranean. The Admiralty were not the only objectors. General Sir Alan Brooke, Commander-in-Chief Home Forces, had misgivings as well. Charged with the defence of the United Kingdom, which still lay, as far as the British could tell, under threat of German invasion, he could hardly be expected to support the withdrawal of tanks from his new armoured divisions which were just beginning to feel that, at last, they had some equipment with which to hit back for the first time since Dunkirk. The War Office technical staff were equally unhappy because the time available for them to prepare the tanks for shipment was much too short. Churchill shrugged off all objections and won his way. The Defence Committee agreed to ship tanks and Hurricane fighters in five fast merchant ships through the Mediterranean as soon as they could be assembled and loaded. The convoy was code-named 'Tiger', and Churchill began to refer to the 300 tanks in it as his 'Tiger Cubs'. His whole being was engaged in the fate of these precious machines: their passage through the Mediterranean; their unloading in Egypt; their manning by the regiments of Creagh's 7th Armoured Division which had been tankless since Beda Fomm; and their advance into battle against Rommel whom he was already building up in his mind as a personal foe. Wavell's next offensive, which was to be called 'Battleaxe', must rival 'Compass' and avenge the loss of the 'Compass' gains.

In Berlin, Hitler's being was equally deeply engaged with the final diplomatic and military preparations for 'Barbarossa'. The Yugo-Slav and Greek campaigns, though overwhelmingly successful from the German point of view, had delayed the German

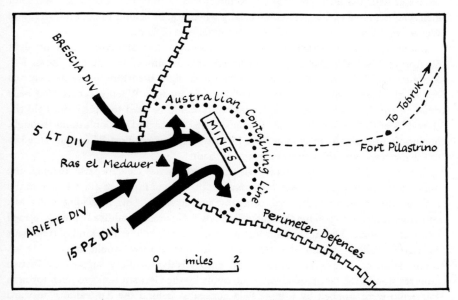

Fig 13 Rommel's Last Attempt to take Tobruk in 1941: 30th April to 2nd May

General Staff's strategic timetable by six weeks and has used up precious resources. The prospect of further dispersion of effort to help the African side-show appealed to neither Hitler nor OKH. Hitler agreed to Field-Marshal von Brauchitsch's proposal that his Deputy Chief of Staff, General von Paulus, who a year and a half later was to surrender his 6th German Army at Stalingrad, should fly to Libya to assess Rommel's handling of the African situation. General Halder recorded in his diary that von Paulus was 'perhaps the only man with enough influence to head off this soldier gone stark mad' (quoted by *British Official History:* Vol II, page 153). Thus, while Churchill was bending every muscle to reinforce Wavell, Hitler was allowing the German General Staff to hamstring Rommel.

Von Paulus arrived at the Afrika Korps HQ on 26 April to find Rommel in the midst of preparations for what he intended should be his decisive attack on Tobruk. He refused to sanction Rommel's plan until he had examined the situation for himself. General Gariboldi visited the front while von Paulus was there, and the two reluctantly accepted Rommel's view that it would be fatal to wait until 5th Light Division had carried out more training, and the panzer elements of 15th Panzer Division had arrived by sea. The longer they waited, the stronger Tobruk would become. Rommel had been short of infantry and sappers for an assault on fixed defences. The arrival of 15th Panzer Division's infantry and engineer units by air had alleviated this shortage and he was now confident of success. He was, in fact, about to commit, through his own impatience, the very mistake, which Wavell was to be forced into a few weeks later by Churchill's desire to use his 'Tiger Cubs'. He attacked too soon and with too little preparation. Rommel was to find that Australians were not men who could be easily shaken, especially when dug in behind mines and wire; and Wavell was to find the Germans just as formidable in defence.

Rommel planned to attack the western sector of the Tobruk perimeter on the night 30 April/1 May. His chosen point of attack was dominated by the low rise of Ras Medauar which he decided should be taken in a night breaching operation, carried out by the two German divisions attacking side by side. When a breach had been made in the Australian defences, Italian units would be used to widen and hold the shoulders of the breach while the Germans passed 5th Light Division's tanks through, hoping to upset the Australian defence by thrusting towards Fort Pilastrino — the key to the fortress — and then on towards the harbour.

Rommel did have some success. His breaching parties cleared paths through the mines and wire in the dark; Ras Medauar was taken; and his tanks did debauch in the rear of the Australian forward company positions; but his attacking units lost cohesion in trying to subdue the Australian posts. No amount of dive bombing seemed to affect the issue. The Australians just did not surrender under this kind of treatment as other soldiers, whom the Germans had met before, would have done. A combination of Australian stubbornness and effective artillery support by British gunners slowed the German advance; attempts by the German tanks to push towards Pilastrino were stopped by a mine-field concealed behind the Australians' forward companies; and the Italians, who should have been widening the breach, refused to face British artillery fire. The Germans tried to widen the breach themselves, but it

13. Rommel with his Afrika Korps staff in 1941.

14. The decisive weapon of 1941: a German 88 mm dual purpose anti-air and anti-tank gun in action at Mersa Brega in April 1941.

15. Air Marshal Sir Arthur Tedder, AOC-in-C Middle East Air Forces and General Claude Auchinleck, GOC-in-C Middle East.

16. Lieutenant-General Willoughby, and Norrie, Commander XXX Corps with Lieutenant-General Neil Ritchie, Commander Eighth Army.

17. Brigadier Jock Campbell, VC, driving Lieutenant-General "Strafer" Gott, Commander XIII Corps.

was a slow and unrewarding process in which the Australians gained the upper hand. By the end of the day the Germans held about three miles of the original perimeter including Ras Medauar, but Morshead had sealed off the breach with his reserves. Only 35 out of the 81 German tanks engaged were still in action and the German infantry and sappers had lost heavily. Von Paulus persuaded Rommel that the attack should not be pressed any further. The battle was allowed to subside into a series of limited attacks by both sides as the opposing commanders fought to secure tenable defensive positions in the area of the breach. Sandstorms made conditions increasingly difficult, and forced the two sides to settle down to a regular siege. Churchill glowed:

To General Morshead from the Prime Minister of England.
The whole Empire is watching your steadfast and spirited defence of this important outpost of Egypt with gratitude and admiration.

(*Australian Official History*: Vol III, page 235)

Rommel complained: 'The high casualties suffered by my assault forces were primarily caused by their lack of training . . .' (Rommel: page 133).

Von Paulus cabled his view of the African situation to Berlin. Rommel was in tactical and logistic difficulties. The attacks on Tobruk should not be renewed. The Afrika Korps' principal task should be to hold the bulge of Cyrenaica irrespective of who held the Egyptian frontier positions at Sollum and Bardia or even Tobruk. A defence line should be established on the eastern edge of the Djebel Akhdar, running southwards from Gazala on the coast into the desert, to which Rommel could fall back if he was forced to do so by a British offensive. Von Paulus also stressed the need for greatly improved protection of Axis shipping in the Mediterranean and of its terminal ports at Tripoli and Benghazi. Rommel was short of ammunition, petrol, food and vehicles. Until these shortages could be made good, no more fighting troops should be sent to him. The first priority would be extra medium artillery and anti-tank units as soon as the logistic position allowed. General Halder approved Von Paulus' report commenting: 'By over-stepping his orders, Rommel has brought about a situation for which our present supply capabilities are insufficient.' (Quoted in *British Official History*: Vol II, page 157).

Von Paulus' cable to Berlin had wider repercussions than he could have anticipated. It was intercepted and decoded by the British; and provided Churchill with just enough evidence to goad Wavell into premature action in the Western Desert at a time when events in other parts of his huge theatre were beginning to crowd in upon him.

Prime Minister to A. P. Wavell   5 May 1941.
Have you read my telegram of 4th inst? Presume you realise the highly secret and authoritative character of this information? Actual text is more impressive than paraphrase showing enemy 'thoroughly exhausted' unable pending arrival of 15th Panzer Division and of reinforcements to do more than hold ground gained at Tobruk . . .

(J. Connell: page 427).

Wavell replied at once:

> I saw the secret message yesterday and at once ordered Creagh to visit Beresford-Peirse and discuss possibility of using all available tanks for offensive operations . . .
>
> I have already issued orders for offensive in Western Desert at earliest possible date to be prepared on assumption 'Tiger' successful.
>
> Iraq commitment is worrying me more than anything at present and I have gravest doubts about this and about its effect on Egypt and Palestine. Crete, Cyprus and Syria are also potential dangers.
>
> My numbers may be impressive on paper but equipment still very short, particularly AFVs, AA Guns and transport . . .
>
> (J. Connell: page 428).

General Beresford-Peirse, who had commanded 4th Indian Division at Sidi Barrani and Keren, had been brought back to command a new Western Desert Force on the Egyptian frontier. It was based upon 7th Armoured Division's Support Group under Brigadier Gott, reinforced by 22nd Guards Brigade and a medley of units scraped together to protect Egypt.

While Beresford-Peirse was preparing to take advantage of Rommel's assumed weakness, Wavell had to turn his back on the Western Desert to deal with the deteriorating situation in Iraq and Syria. Wavell had always tried to avoid becoming embroiled in the affairs of Iraq which he believed should be handled by C-in-C India, who was responsible for furnishing troops and supplies, if intervention in Iraq became necessary at any time to protect British interests. Rashid Ali's coup d'etat in April made such intervention imperative. Both Wavell and Auchinleck (C-in-C India) were asked by Churchill what forces they could provide for operations in Iraq. Auchinleck offered an Indian brigade group immediately, followed by the balance, of the 10th Indian Division as soon as shipping could be assembled. Wavell said he could spare nothing and advised strong diplomatic action, possibly backed by a show of strength by the RAF, instead of military intervention. His reluctance to respond was noted by Churchill with some disfavour. In spite of his protests, he was ordered to take command of any British military operations in Iraq which might be needed if Rashid Ali became openly hostile. In the British Chiefs of Staff view, India was too far away to give immediate and effective assistance to British communities in Iraq.

Under the Anglo-Iraqi Treaty the British were entitled to use the port of Basra at the head of the Persian Gulf for the passage of troops from India to Palestine and Egypt. In the middle of April, the British Ambassador in Baghdad had precipitated affairs by announcing the passage of the leading brigade of 10th Indian Division. Rashid Ali had no legal reason to object and the brigade had landed without trouble on 17 April, in the midst of secretly conducted negotiations between Rashid Ali and the Germans. For once the Germans had been too slow. It was no part of their strategic plan to raise revolts in Iraq and Syria until much later in the year when their troops might be advancing through the Caucasus into Northern Iraq. Rashid Ali's premature dependence upon them for military support was embarrassing. The arrival at the end of April of a second convoy at Basra carrying more of 10th Indian Division, forced Rashid Ali to challlenge the British before they became too strong. Unfortunately for his cause, his German backers were not ready to supply him. The form of challenge, which he chose, was to attack the British Flying Training School at Habbanyia on the Euphrates west of Baghdad. Iraqi troops started moving on to the plateau overlooking the air base during 29 April.

At 6 am on 30 April an Iraqi officer arrived at the RAF Station and demanded that Air Vice-Marshal Smart, commanding RAF Habbayia, should stop all flying and confine British personnel to the cantonment. Smart replied that any interference with flying would be treated as an act of war. Five hours later a second emissary arrived, this time accusing the British of violating the Anglo-Iraqi Treaty. Smart referred him

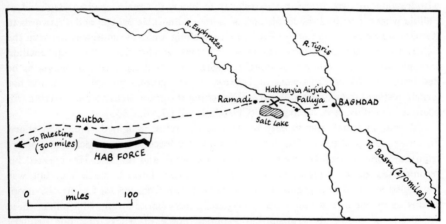

Fig 14   British Operations in Iraq: 30th April to 30th May 1941

to the British Ambassador in Baghdad as this was a political matter. Smart knew that the cantonment was well nigh indefensible but he had taken the precaution of fitting his 33 miscellaneous training aircraft with bomb racks; and had organised a rudimentary defence plan, using his 1,000 British airmen, 1,200 locally raised Iraqi and Assyrian Levies, and as many as possible of the 9,000 civilians on the station who could and were willing to take part in the defence of the seven mile perimeter.

The brigade's-worth of Iraqi troops sent to overawe Habbanyia contented themselves on 1 May with digging in on the plateau while great diplomatic activity went on in Baghdad. About 300 men from the 1st King's Own Royal Regiment were flown into Habbanyia from the Indian Brigade at Basra, accompanied by Colonel Ouvry Roberts from the staff of the 10th Indian Division who took over the army side of the defence. Eight Wellington bombers were flown from Egypt to Shaibah, near Basra, ready to support Habbanyia. The British Ambassador demanded the withdrawal of Iraqi troops, and when Rashid Ali showed no signs of complying, Smart was authorised to attack his besiegers.

Before dawn on 2 May all 33 available aircraft took off and with the eight Wellingtons from Shaibah bombed the Iraqi positions. The Iraqis replied with artillery fire, doing much less damage than expected to the station which was dependent on one power station and one very prominent water tower, neither of which the Iraqis managed to hit. The pilots of the flying school, many of them partially trained, flew 200 sorties that day. Five aircraft were lost, mainly to Iraqi Air Force fighters of types superior to Habbanyia's training aircraft; and the station suffered 13 killed and 29 wounded including nine civilians. This intense flying effort was kept up for four days. On 6 May, a patrol from the King's Own Royal Regiment found that the Iraqis had abandoned their positions during the night, apparently withdrawing in two directions: eastwards to block the main road to Baghdad at Falluja where it crossed the Euphrates on a long vulnerable bridge; and westwards to Ramadi where the main road to Rutbah passes along a narrow causeway between the Salt Lakes and the Euphrates. The close siege had been lifted, but the Iraqi rebellion was not over. Churchill was as delighted with Smart's defence of Habbanyia as he had been with Morshead's work at Tobruk: 'Your vigorous and splendid action has largely restored the situation. We are all watching the grand fight you are making. All possible aid will be sent. Keep it up'. (Churchill: Vol III, page 330).

Aid was, as usual, not so easy to send as Churchill imagined. Time was short, distances great and troops few. Churchill wanted a force to be sent across the desert from Palestine. Wavell believed it would be too weak and too late. He repeated his recommendation of diplomatic action and proposed Turkish mediation, but was over-ruled and told to despatch a scratch force drawn from the 1st Cavalry Division, consisting of one mechanised cavalry brigade, a lorry-borne infantry battalion, three squadrons of the Arab Transjordan Frontier Force in trucks and one artillery regiment. There were no tanks or armoured cars, and no anti-tank and anti-aircraft guns available for the force which was christened 'Habforce'.

Habforce, led by a flying column in the faster vehicles of the force, crossed the Iraq frontier on 13 May. Ominously, it was attacked after leaving Rutbah on 15 May by German aircraft, flying from French bases in Syria. The physical difficulties of moving the force across the Iraqi desert in temperatures of 120°F in the shade were matched by finding the approaches to Habbanyia cut by flood waters from the Euphrates. As the force approached Habbanyia on 18 May it was again attacked by German aircraft. German intervention seemed to be growing.

But the Germans had their difficulties too. They appreciated that they must support Rashid Ali or forfeit all the Arab goodwill which they had been fostering so carefully over the early months of 1941. On the other hand, they had few ways of bringing units and warlike stores into Iraq except by air. German agents worked with a will; nevertheless Iraqi political opinion began to swing away from Rashid Ali. News from Habbanyia was discouraging; the RAF was bombing strategic targets all over

Iraq; and then the Iraqis themselves shot down Major Axel von Blomberg, son of the German Field Marshal, by mistake as he was landing at Baghdad airfield. The small force of 14 German fighters and seven bombers operating in Iraq were not enough to hold Arab opinion in German favour.

At Habbanyia the Iraqi forces, blocking the main roads east and west of the station, protected themselves with more flooding. After careful and ingenious preparation, Colonel Ouvry Roberts launched a series of attacks by the garrison to open both blocks. Supported by 57 RAF aircraft, which bombed the Iraqi positions, he seized the Falluja bridge intact on 19 May, thus opening the road to Baghdad for Habforce which started its advance on the capital on 27 May. Resistance was sporadic, rumour doing most of the damage to Rashid Ali's cause. Greatly exaggerated reports of British strength, including non-existent tanks, persuaded him to flee to Persia and on 30 May the pro-British Regent returned to Baghdad. Wavell had been proved wrong. Firm action by improvised forces had succeeded. Usually all's well that ends well but not in Wavell's case — worse was to come.

The Royal Navy passed the 'Tiger' convoy successfully through the Mediterranean while the Iraqi revolt was in progress. It arrived in Egyptian ports on 12 May. One fast merchant ship, carrying 60 tanks and 100 Hurricane fighters, was lost. 240 'Tiger Cubs' arrived safely. Wavell decided, as he had done in 1940, that with this reserve behind him, he could risk his available tanks by ordering Beresford-Peirse to take advantage of Rommel's supposed weakness revealed in von Paulus' intercepted signal. On 15 May Brigadier Gott advanced with little more than a reinforced brigade

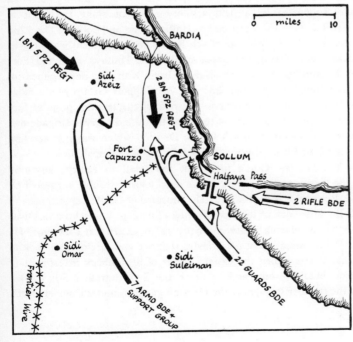

Fig 15
Operation
'Brevity': 15th
to 16th May
1941

group to challenge the Germans in the frontier area. His offensive was to live up to its code-name, Operation 'Brevity'.

'Brevity' was the first of several Anglo-German operations fought out around the Halfaya–Sollum–Capuzzo–Bardia area. The significance of this piece of desert lay not only in it being the extreme northern and seaward end of the Libyan frontier through which the only metalled road ran from Egypt into Libya, but also in the defensible defile created by the coastal escarpment which squeezed the coastal plain into a narrow funnel with just two passable westerly exists; north-west up the winding main road from Sollum harbour to Sollum barracks on top of the escarpment; and westwards up the steep desert track through Halfaya Pass. In general there were only four approaches for a British force attacking westwards across the Libyan frontier: first, along the coastal plain opening up the Halfaya and Sollum passes from below; secondly along the top of the escarpment towards Fort Capuzzo, clearing Halfaya from above and cutting the main road west of Sollum barracks; thirdly, along any one of a number of increasingly wide arcs through the desert to the south-west, crossing the frontier wire wherever the commander of the desert outflanking force considered appropriate; and fourthly, the Long Range Desert Group's route 150 miles southward across the desert to the oasis of Siwa and from there westwards to Jarabub and Jalo, skirting the northern edge of the Libyan Sand Sea.* The last of these routes was often contemplated, but was never used by major forces because of obvious logistic difficulties.

Gott chose to use the first three routes in a pattern of attack which was imposed on all subsequent commanders by the force of geography. He sent one infantry battalion (2nd Rifle Brigade) supported by a field artillery regiment along the coast to neutralise and, if possible, take the lower end of Halfaya Pass and Sollum. The 22nd Guards Brigade supported by 24 'I' tanks of 4th Royal Tank Regiment was to clear the top of the escarpment, taking the upper end of the Halfaya Pass and Fort Capuzzo. And the skeleton 7th Armoured Brigade Group with only one regiment of 29 cruiser tanks (2nd Royal Tank Regiment) and 7th Support Group would move round the German's open flank to appear in the rear of the frontier posts at Sidi Azeiz. Such was the paucity of transport at this time that 22nd Guards Brigade had to be given given trucks belonging to 4th Indian Division which was just arriving back in the Delta from East Africa after its successful Eritrean Campaign.

'Brevity' was not a success. Gott's force was too small to achieve anything significant unless the Germans really were in the deep logistic trouble suggested by von Paulus's signal. Rommel was kept adequately informed of Gott's dispositions and intentions through the efficiency of his German radio intercept unit whose task was made all the easier by the glaring laxity of British radio security at that time. He concluded that the British were intent on relieving Tobruk and forcing him back to Gazala. He had time to strengthen the eastern sector of his Tobruk investment to prevent the garrison breaking out, and to move the 2nd Battalion 5th Panzer Regiment towards the frontier to support the German garrison under Colonel Herff,

* See Map II, page 14.

whose defences were still under-developed and rudimentary compared with later standards. When Gott's attack started Herff had real cause for anxiety. The Guards Brigade over-ran the upper defences of Halfaya, Capuzzo and Sollum. 7th Armoured Brigade forced back the German reconnaissance units' screen on the desert flank towards Sidi Azeiz. Only on the coast road did the British suffer a temporary setback when they were checked trying to take the lower end of the Halfaya Pass. As the day wore on fortunes began to change. The Germans lost the lower end of Halfaya, but the Guards Brigade found itself too dispersed to be able to exploit towards Bardia as had been intended. Nine 'I' tanks had been lost and there was some lack of co-operation between tanks and infantry at Capuzzo which had unfortunate results when Colonel Herff launched a tank counter-attack. The unsupported British infantry lost heavily, but Colonel Herff was far from satisfied with the situation when night fell and was making preparations for a fighting withdrawal to Tobruk when Rommel intervened, ordering him to counter-attack again next day with the 1st Battalion 5th Panzer Regiment which should reach him by dawn. Rommel's personal 'feel of the battle', helped by his air reconnaissance and radio intercept, had enabled him to gauge the situation more accurately than Herff.

Gott was just as anxious as Herff. The German counter-attack at Capuzzo had demonstrated the exposed position of 22nd Guards Brigade on top of the escarpment. At 9 pm he signalled Beresford-Peirse recommending a withdrawal to Halfaya. British radio communications let him down. Receiving no reply by 2 am, he ordered the withdrawal to start. Three quarters of an hour later Beresford-Peirse's reply arrived telling him to hold on. It was too late.

The Germans had their troubles too. Rommel had intended Herff to concentrate the tanks of both panzer battalions for a dawn counter-attack. The tanks from Tobruk ran out of fuel, and then the two panzer battalions missed each other in the dark. The Guards Brigade slipped away unmolested, and 7th Armoured Brigade withdrew suffering more from mechanical breakdown amongst its cruisers than from enemy action. By dusk on 16 May 'Brevity' was over. Losses were not heavy in men or tanks on either side, but Gott's offensive was to have an unfortunate effect on future operations in the desert. When he withdrew from Capuzzo and Sollum he held on to Halfaya on a spring-board for Wavell's main offensive – Operation 'Battleaxe' – which would come when the 'Tiger Cubs' were ready. Ten days later, Colonel Herff retook Halfaya, using a strong panzer force and then set to with a will to create a line of strongly fortified posts stretching from Halfaya in a wide arc north-westwards into the desert through Point 206 and Point 208 on the Hafid Ridge to Sidi Azeiz. Rommel describes this work, which in all probability would never have been undertaken if Gott had not demonstrated the weakness of the German frontier positions:

> In constructing our positions at Halfaya and on Hill 208 great skill was shown in building in batteries of 88 mm guns for anti-tank work, so that with the barrels horizontal there was practically nothing seen above ground. I had great hopes of the effectiveness of this arrangement.
>
> (Rommel: pages 137–138).

He was not to be disappointed! The British were. Wavell ends his summing up on 'Brevity' with the words: 'The enemy tanks showed a disinclination to engage closely and we were able to withdraw with little loss'. (Despatches: page 3441).

In these two quotations lie the seeds of what happened during 'Battleaxe'. It did not occur to anyone on the British side that German reluctance to pit tank against tank was a deliberate act of tactical policy. It was interpreted as a healthy respect for British tanks, as indeed it was in part, but only in part.

Churchill was not unduly upset by Gott's failure to achieve anything substantial. He was pinning his hopes on his 'Tiger Cubs' entering battle almost as soon as they were unloaded at Port Said. Three inter-connected factors frustrated his hopes: events in Crete and Syria; technical problems in unloading and making his 'Tiger Cubs' ready for desert warfare; and the arrival of the balance of 15th Panzer Division in Africa, bringing Rommel's tank strength up to some 200 medium tanks.

After the British evacuation of Greece, the Luftwaffe High Command recommended to Hitler that Crete should be captured to protect Axis shipping in the Aegean; to keep British bombers away from the Rumanian oil-fields; and to threaten the British naval control of the Eastern Mediterranean. Malta was considered as an alternative target, but was discarded because Crete could serve as a stepping stone to Cyprus and then into Syria and Iraq at the appropriate moment. German losses sustained in wresting Crete from Freyberg's mixed New Zealand, Australian and British garrison were so heavy that Crete neither acted as a German stepping stone into the Levant nor as a blue-print for an attack on Malta. Hitler concluded that further airborne attacks of the Crete type were neither desirable nor practicable. Both Malta and Cyprus were spared such treatment.

The German failure in Iraq and their near failure in Crete did not stop their attempts to subvert the Vichy regime in Syria; nor did they lessen British anxiety about the German threat to the back door of their position in the Middle East. The British Chiefs of Staff began to doubt the ability, indeed the willingness, of General Dentz, the French High Commissioner in Syria, to abide by the letter as well as the spirit of the Franco-German armistice agreement; and they came under intense pressure from de Gaulle and other Free French leaders to occupy Syria before the Germans could do so. The Cs-in-C Middle East appreciated London's anxiety, but could not meet Churchill's incessant demands for decisive operations in the Western Desert and a campaign in Syria at the same time. Not only had Wavell used his last uncommitted reserves to form 'Habforce', but the Royal Air Force was equally short of aircraft and could not provide air cover for two such widely divergent campaigns simultaneously.

In the latter half of May signals between London and Cairo grew in acrimony, reflecting the sense of frustration felt by the Cs-in-C in Cairo at the ambivalent attitude of the Chiefs of Staff in London who appeared to want everything at once without calculating the resources required. The Free French aggravated the situation by supplying inaccurate and over-optimistic assessments of pro-Allied feeling in Syria, and by demanding the use of the Free French units which were forming in Palestine, in spite of the danger that their appearance in Syria would be more provocative to the

Vichy troops than an invasion by the British. Matters came to a head on 17 May, when Wavell cabled Dill:

> Hope I shall not be landed with Syria commitment unless absolutely essential. Any force I could send now would be painfully reminiscent of the Jamison Raid and might suffer similar fate . . .
>
> (J. Connell: page 460).

This cable was not well received in London. Two days later Churchill summoned the CIGS to Downing Street to tell him that he had decided to get rid of Wavell, sending him to replace Auchinleck in India. A few days afterwards, Wavell, unconscious of Churchill's decision, was stung by what he believed to be Free French politico-military intrigue in London into offering his resignation. In a cable to Dill he said:

> . . . All reports from trustworthy sources including Arab and Syrian agree that effect of action by Free French alone likely to be failure . . . You must trust my judgment in this matter or relieve me of my command. I am not willing to accept that Catroux, de Gaulle, or Spears should dictate action that is bound seriously to affect military situation in the Middle East.
>
> (*Ibid*: page 462).

Churchill responded angrily, but did not put his avowed intention of relieving Wavell into effect. His political instincts told him to bide his time for a more suitable moment. Wavell was too great a public figure to be dismissed without good and obvious cause. Churchill's reply was couched in terms which forced Wavell to milk the forces he was assembling for 'Battleaxe' to give life to 'Exporter' – the invasion of Syria timed for 8 June. General Wilson, back from Greece, was made responsible for mounting the 'Exporter' force which was to consist of Major-General Laverack's 7th Australian Division less its brigade in Tobruk and the 5th Indian Brigade of 4th Indian Division, just arriving back from Eritrea. There were no tanks available, and very few armoured cars. A motorised cavalry brigade and a horsed cavalry regiment were taken from the Palestine garrison to give the force a mobile element. The Free French force under General Legentilhomme consisted of a scratch division of two brigades. And the Royal Navy provided a British cruiser squadron to bombard the main coast road from Palestine to Beirut, and a fast 'Glen' ship suitable for landing commandos on the coast to help the northward advance.

'Exporter' and 'Battleaxe' became inextricably entwined by the second and third factors which were frustrating Churchill's hopes – the technical problems of making his 'Tiger Cubs' serviceable and the completion of 15th Panzer Divisions on the German side. Some of 15th Panzer Division's tanks had been identified during 'Brevity' making it important to ensure that the 'Tiger Cubs' were fully battle worthy before they were committed. As they were unloaded it transpired that they were quite unfit for desert operations.

> . . . the Crusader tanks arrived in the country (Egypt) in an extremely bad

condition, and all had to be sent to base workshops for rectification before they were fit for issue. The reason for this was partly damage caused on the voyage by sea water, careless stowage and partly slipshod workmanship and inspection at the factories in England . . . In some cases, there were evidences indicative of sabotage.

(Unpublished Official Report: page 4).

The failure to deliver tanks in battle-worthy condition was one of the by-products of the British unreadiness for war. Her peacetime logistic staffs and organisations were woefully inadequate and had no experience of handling the vast quantities of equipment her newly raised armies would require. There had been a necessary but over-rapid expansion of depot and workshop staffs, resulting in a gross dilution of skilled workers. Most of the newcomers were the proverbial 'butchers, bakers, candlestick makers' pitched into uniform. It took time to train them and give them experience. And, sad to relate, the dockers in English ports were not as loyal as they might have been. Pilfering was rife, and slipshod stowing went uncorrected until sufficient military supervisory personnel had been trained.

The exasperating delays in making the 'Tiger Cubs' serviceable forced Wavell to incur Churchill's further displeasure by postponing 'Battleaxe' until 15 June. This was too soon for the soldiers; wrongly timed for the airmen; and too late for Churchill. It did not give Creagh's 7th Armoured Division enough time to master the new and unfamiliar 'Crusader' tanks which had arrived amongst the 'Tiger Cubs', nor to carry out divisional training with these new equipments. Regimental commanders had barely enough time to train their own units, let alone train with their supporting infantry and artillery. The airmen's problem was even worse. They were expected to support both operations which were almost simultaneous. Churchill's dissatisfaction with the number of operational aircraft available led to the recall of Air Marshal Longmore for consultation. He never returned to his command and was replaced as Air C-in-C by his deputy, Air Marshal Tedder. Longmore's criticism of Whitehall's decisions over many months had been more outspoken than Wavell's. He was less in the public eye and so could be dispensed with more easily.

Emboldened by their success in driving Wavell, against his will, into forceful action in Iraq, the British Defence Committee showed scant sympathy over his or Tedder's fears about the closeness of 'Exporter' and 'Battleaxe'. Both operations were pushed forward despite the misgiving of the men on the spot; and despite the obvious change in German dispositions in Europe that had revealed to the Chiefs of Staff the possibility of an early German attack on Russia. One or other operation should and could have been delayed, but neither was because Whitehall under-estimated both Dentz and Rommel.

'Exporter' opened on 8 June with a proclamation broadcast by General Catroux, promising the ending of the French Mandate of Syria and the granting of independence. The British Ambassador issued a corroborative statement. Soon afterwards Laverack's Australians crossed the frontier using two thrust lines: up the coast road aiming for Beirut; and up the Litani Valley making for Rayak.* Further

* See Fig 19 on page 137.

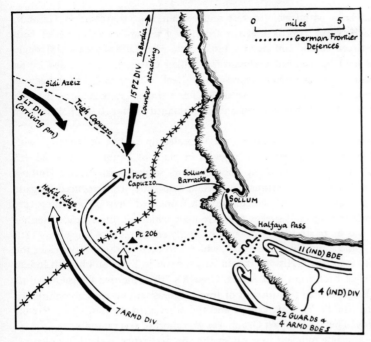

Fig 16
'Battleaxe'
1st Day: 15th
June 1941

inland, on the desert flank, 5th Indian Brigade advanced ahead of Legentilhomme's Free French Force towards Damascus. This time Wavell was proved right. The Vichy French fought well and showed particular bitterness towards their compatriots in the Free French units. The British forces were not large enough to enable Dentz to plead 'force majeur'. Instead he reacted as if the whole honour of France was at stake.

The Syrian Campaign lasted five weeks and fell into three phases, only two of which were to occur in the last few weeks of Wavell's command in the Middle East. Each phase was marked by the British finding it necessary to divert more resources to Syria at the expense of the Western Desert. Resistance met in the initial advance from 8 – 13 June forced Wavell to reinforce Wilson with two brigades of the 6th British Division which was responsible for securing his main base in the Nile Delta. Damascus was taken by the Indians and Free French in the second phase from 14 – 22 June which coincided with 'Battleaxe'. The third phase could not start until more troops and aircraft could be released by the success or failure of 'Battleaxe'.

Wavell's 'Battleaxe' directive to Beresford-Peirse also envisaged three phases: defeat of the Axis forces on the frontier and the securing of the Halfaya–Sollum–Capuzzo–Bardia area; defeat of the troops investing Tobruk; and, finally, exploitation to the Derna-Mechili area. British intelligence of German dispositions was reasonably accurate. The investment of Tobruk was in the hands of the Italians, 'corsetted' by German detachments. 15th Panzer Division, under Major-General Neumann-Silkow, had taken over responsibility for the frontier area from Colonel Herff's 'ad hoc' force; and 5th Light Division, now under Major-General von

Ravenstein, had been withdrawn to rest and retrain near the coast at Gambut, centrally placed between Tobruk and the frontier. The panzer regiments of both divisions had between 90 and 100 medium tanks each. The Halfaya area was strongly entrenched and held by a mixed German and Italian Garrison commanded by an ex-Lutheran pastor, turned soldier, called Major Bach who seems to have been as expert at inspiring men militarily as spiritually. The string of posts running through Points 206 and the Hafid Ridge were an unknown quantity as far as the British were concerned.

Beresford-Peirse's plan for 'Battleaxe' was a scaled-up replica of 'Brevity' with divisons in the place of brigades, and brigades in place of battalions. His old 4th Indian Division under Major-General Messervy was to deal with Bach's Halfaya defences, Sollum, Capuzzo and ultimately Bardia, helped by 4th Armoured Brigade equipped with 'I' tanks. Creagh's re-equipped 7th Armoured Division would operate on the desert flank to protect Messervy from German armoured interference. Neither British division was up to strength. Messervy had only one of his own brigades – 11th Indian Brigade – and 22nd Guards Brigade, which had been on the frontier since the Germans reached it in April. His 5th Indian Brigade was in Syria and his 7th Indian Brigade was not yet back from East Africa. Creagh's 7th Armoured Division had its 7th Armoured Brigade with two instead of three regiments: one with reconditioned cruisers from the Middle East workshops and the other with the new Crusaders off the 'Tiger' convoy. The 7th Support Group was also short of several units.

This is an appropriate moment to consider the characteristics of the Afrika Korps' tanks in mid-1941. German tank philosophy called for three types of tank, like the British, but for different reasons. They too had a light tank for reconnaissance, but, instead of dividing their medium tanks into cruiser and infantry versions, they gave their Pzkw IIIa 50mm anti-tank gun and their Pxkw IVa 75mm close-support gun to deliver high explosive shell or smoke.

There was little to choose between light tanks and between the British cruisers and the German mediums as far as weight, armour and speed were concerned. The main difference lay in mechanical reliability and armament. The German machines had their mechanical faults, but they did prove themselves more reliable than the British. In gun power, the Pzkw II with its 20mm cannon could outmatch the British light tanks and armoured cars. The British (40mm) 2 pounder was found to be marginally superior to the 50mm (short) anti-tank gun in the Pzkw III, but they had nothing to match the 75mm (short) close-support gun in the Pzkw IV which could inflict damage on tanks with its high explosive shell at 3000 yards, and was lethal against unprotected anti-tank guns at ranges far beyond their own effective reach.

There is a temptation in all desert battles to compare opposing tank strengths to the exclusion of other factors. It is a useful short hand because the tank was the principal weapon in desert fighting, but it did depend on support by the other arms – artillery, infantry, engineers and logistic services – which were co-ordinated within the divisional structure of both armies. For 'Battleaxe' two British divisions – 7th Armoured and 4th Indian – were opposing two German mobile divisions – 5th Light and 15th Panzer - manoeuvring around the Axis frontier defences manned by

German and Italian static garrisons. The numbers of tanks (200 on each side), men and guns were about equal, but 5th Light Division was 50 miles away and would not be able to intervene on the first day. The outcome of 'Battleaxe' would depend on the amount of damage the two British divisions could inflict on 15th Panzer Division before 5th Light Division arrived on the battlefield. Wavell appreciated how fine the timings and how narrow his margin of superiority over Rommel would turn out to be. He could not, however, convince Churchill who was sure that the 'Tiger Cubs' had given him all he needed for success. In truth, the two sides were so closely matched that generalship, tactics and training would be the deciding factors in 'Battleaxe'.

The RAF's pre-'Battleaxe' air operations subdued the Axis Air Forces and gave Beresford-Peirse a measure of local air superiority during the battle. On the ground fortunes were very mixed in the early stages. Messervy's attack went well except where he had to contend with Bach's Halfaya defences. The main body of the Guards Brigade, supported by 4th Armoured Brigade which defeated one of 8th Panzer Regiment's battalions, took Point 206 and the Capuzzo area, ending the day with 500 Axis prisoners. At Halfaya, Bach defeated both British attacking forces. 11th Indian Brigade failed to take the lower defences, losing four out of six Matildas engaged on mines; and the Guards Brigade detachment, which attacked the upper defences, lost 11 out of 12 of its Matildas to guns which could not be positively identified.

Creagh's 7th Armoured Division made an equally uncertain start. 7th Armoured Brigade advanced somewhat blindly, not knowing quite what to expect and finding it difficult to identify features in the shimmering heat haze. 2nd Royal Tank Regiment led the advance in its old cruisers so the the 6th RTR's new Crusaders could be kept in reserve for decisive action at the right moment. There was not much opposition until the Hafid Ridge area was reached. The enemy fire seemed to be coming from three distinct crests. 7th Armoured Brigade attacked three times during the day with varying success. In the first, 2nd RTR failed to secure even a foothold on the first crest. Its second attack was more successful and over-ran the Axis gun positions on the first ridge. More enemy guns were spotted on the reverse slope of the second crest. The majority of the 2nd RTR's tanks wheeled out of range in time, but five did not hear the order to turn or notice the other tanks turning and were never seen again. This was caused by lack of radio sets in the Middle East which restricted issues to troop leaders' tanks. The third attack was not mounted until 5.30 pm when erroneous reports suggested that the Germans were withdrawing from Hafid. Two 6th RTR squadrons in the new Crusaders were committed and ran into a well-laid ambush baited with a leaguer of dummy vehicles. Eleven were lost and six damaged – an unfortunate debut for the Crusader.

Late in the evening the leading elements of 5th Panzer Regiment, at the head of von Ravenstein's 5th Light Division, were seen approaching from the north-west. After a long range engagement in the gathering dusk both sides disengaged, 7th Armoured Brigade leaguering on the frontier and 5th Panzer Regiment at Sidi Azeiz. 7th Armoured Brigade had been reduced by enemy action and mechanical break-down to 37 fit tanks, though by dawn next day the number had been increased to 48 fit tanks.

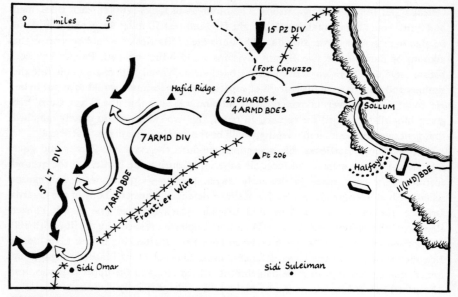

Fig 17 'Battleaxe' 2nd Day: 16th June 1941

At the end of the day Beresford-Peirse saw no reason to alter his basic plan for the morrow. He told Messervy to clear up Halfaya, consolidate the Capuzzo–Point 206 area and exploit to Bardia if opportunity arose. Messervy was to release 4th Armoured Brigade to Creagh to subdue the Hafid Ridge with its 'I' tanks. Creagh's principal task was to check 5th Light Divison which was expected to try to work its way round the open desert flank.

On the German side, Neumann-Silkow was as worried as Herff had been on the first evening of 'Brevity'. 15th Panzer Division's tanks had been severely mauled and the Axis defenders of the Capuzzo–Point 206 posts had suffered significant losses as well. It was with some relief that he welcomed von Ravenstein's leading tanks as they reached the Hafid area during the late afternoon. Rommel, however, was far from depressed. Continued laxness of British radio security enabled him to build up an accurate picture of what was happening on the British side. He decided to seize the initiative with the aim of relieving Bach's garrison at Halfaya. 15th Panzer was to attack due southwards, retaking Capuzzo and pushing on to Halfaya from the north, while 5th Light fought its way, as the British expected, round the open flank, striking eastwards to Halfaya at the appropriate moment.

16 June was a day of rapid movement and hard fighting in which the British could claim the advantage in the morning and the Germans the upper hand in the afternoon. Messervy again failed to take Halfaya, but secured Sollum and beat off 15th Panzer Division's attacks with the help of 4th Armoured Brigade which, in consequence, could not execute its attack on the Hafid Ridge. 8th Panzer Regiment was heard reporting its tank strength down to 30 fit tanks. Rommel's southward drive

by 15th Panzer Division had failed. On the desert flank 7th Armoured Brigade fought a running battle with 5th Light Division which zig-zagged down the frontier wire to Sidi Omar where darkness ended the contest. The British tanks had suffered severely. At the end of the day 7th Armoured Brigade had only 21 fit tanks left. 25 out of the 27 lost that day had been disabled, it was thought, by German tank guns. In these actions, the partially trained British units showed the tendency, to which they were to become prone, of attacking too soon without properly co-ordinated artillery support.

During the night 16/17 June, Beresford-Peirse again decided to persevere with his plan. Messervy seemed secure enough in the Capuzzo-Sollum area to allow 4th Armoured Brigade to reinforce Creagh on the desert flank. The German Staff were still worried. Halfaya could not hold out much longer without re-supply; 15th Panzer Division had suffered further losses and was in some disorder; little was known of 5th Light Division's progress; and British air attacks had been playing havoc with German supply columns. Rommel, again was far from discouraged. Piecing evidence together as it came in, he concluded that the British would re-open their offensive northwards from Capuzzo next morning and decided he would forestall them by launching a spoiling attack before dawn on 17 June aimed again at bringing his two panzer divisions together at Halfaya. 5th Light was to turn eastwards and head for Sidi Suleiman, while 15th Panzer skirted round Messervy's western flank to join 5th Light in a concentrated thrust to Halfaya. If they succeeded in getting there, they

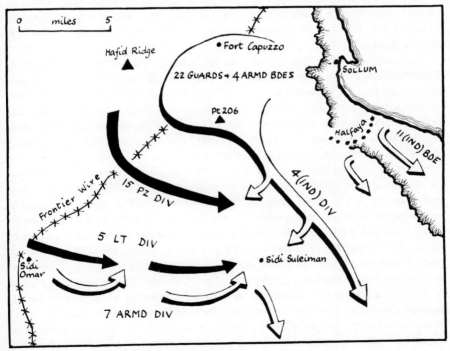

Fig 18 'Battleaxe' 3rd Day: 17th June 1941

were to turn north to attack Messervy's rear.

17 June was the day of decision. Wavell had sensed this in Cairo and had flown up to Beresford-Peirse's headquarters during the afternoon of 16 June to be readily available to take any major decisions which were needed. Rommel's attacks did forestall the British. Messervy fended off 15th Panzer Division with the help of 4th Armoured Brigade which was prevented once more from joining Creagh. 7th Armoured Brigade lost its battle with 5th Light Division which reached Sidi Suleiman by 8 am. Both British divisional commanders recognised the dangers of 5th Light's appearance in their rear. Creagh asked Beresford-Peirse to fly up to his headquarters to decide what should be done. Wavell accompanied him to assess whether to break off the battle or not. They arrived at 11.45 am but were too late. Messervy had been forced to extricate 22nd Guards Brigade, which was running short of ammunition. He had ordered a general withdrawal to begin at 11 am. Wavell saw it was useless to countermand Messervy's order. Instead he decided to break off the offensive and ordered Beresford-Peirse to withdraw the Western Desert Force back across the frontier to refit. Anxious but not dismayed he flew back to Cairo to deal with the crisis threatening in Syria.

Rommel's intercept unit had heard Creagh's request for a senior commander to visit his headquarters and had rightly concluded that the British were in trouble. He ordered both his panzer divisions to press on to Halfaya and was furious because he thought they had let Messervy escape through incompetence. In an angry mood he ordered them to turn north to sweep the Capuzzo area, but he was far too late. Messervy was already well south of the German thrust before the panzer divisions reached Bach at Halfaya.

'Battleaxe' was over. The British had not relieved Tobruk and had indirectly discredited von Paulus's appreciation. They had lost 1,000 men and half their tanks (27 cruisers and 64 'I' tanks); and had inflicted 700 casualties on the Germans, an unrecorded but substantial number on the Italians, and knocked out 50 German tanks. As the Germans held the battlefield they could recover most of their tanks together with a number of British 'I' tanks whch they repaired and manned themselves, causing some confusion in later battles.

Fortunately for the British, the Germans were in no position to exploit their success by advancing into Egypt. It would be several months before the inadequate tank workshops in Egypt could re-equip 7th Armoured Division with a reasonable establishment of tanks. In the meantime the frontier had to be held without many tanks. This task fell to Brigadier 'Jock' Campbell, who had taken over 7th Support Group when Gott was promoted to command 7th Armoured Division in Creagh's place. Under his dynamic leadership the 'Jock' columns came into being. These were small mixed forces of about a battery of field guns, a troop of anti-tank guns, a troop of anti-aircraft guns and a company of motorised infantry, whose task it was to provide a defensive screen in the vast no man's land of the Western Desert. 'Jock' columns had strict limitations. They could not hold ground against a determined attack and had to depend on their mobility to ride such blows; nor did they have the strength to do more than raid or ambush when required to act offensively. But they did appeal to the privateering instincts of British officers, who enjoyed commanding them. On each occasion when the British armoured forces suffered serious losses during the subsequent battles in North Africa, the 'Jock' column emerged as the momentary panacea in unhappy tactical situations of disorganisation following defeat.

The outcome of 'Battleaxe' was a great disappointment to Churchill, Wavell and the men of the Western Desert Force. There had been every excuse for the earlier British failure to hold Cyrenaica and for their discomfiture during 'Brevity', but everyone felt that 'Battleaxe' should have gone better. Lack of success, however, was less important than the failure to analyse correctly the causes of defeat. The British commanders knew that their troops lacked training due to Churchill's incessant demands for immediate action and they were rightly unhappy about the mechanical reliability of their tanks, but they ascribed their tank losses to a presumed superiority of German tank guns. This was incorrect. The damage was being done by easily concealed towed anti-tank guns handled by the panzer-jäger units. The villains of the piece were the new German 'long' 50mm towed anti-tank guns and the notorious 88mm of which Rommel had very few. During 'Battleaxe' he had only 12 88mms: four on the Hafid Ridge and four with each panzer division. The British 6-pounder gun would have redressed the balance but it was not in full production and would not reach the Western Desert for another year.

Towed anti-tank gun performance was not the whole cause for British failure. The German superiority lay in the tactical handling of tanks, anti-tank guns, artillery and infantry in a closely knit team. When their tanks met British tanks under unfavourable conditions they withdrew through their anti-tank guns, drawing the British tanks into their fire. On occasions, they used unarmoured supply columns to bait the trap as they did at the Hafid Ridge. Their fundamental philosophy was to use anti-tank guns to kill tanks; tanks to kill infantry, and artillery to kill anti-tank guns and infantry.

There was another psychological difficulty which made the British slower than the Germans to master the tactical problems of the Second World War. They have an inbred 'tribal' spirit which makes them take an inordinate pride in the capabilities of their own regiment or arm of the Service. This has great advantages which should never be under-estimated; nevertheless, it does make co-operation between 'tribes' more difficult. Each 'tribe' or arm tends to believe it can do the job best and would prefer to do so on its own. In the Middle East the co-operation between arms was made more difficult because all the tanks were manned by United Kingdom regiments. Commonwealth contingents had no tanks of their own. This worked when things went well, but led to unfortunate recrimination when they did not. Furthermore, the British prefer to run their affairs by committee, but war is a battle of wills, and the will of a committee is a flabby thing. As the story of the North African Campaign unfolds British amateurism stands out in harsh contrast to German professionalism in which Rommel's men showed an uncanny sense in devising new tactics in close co-operation with each other to meet the changing circumstances of the desert war; and Rommel himself demonstrated the advantages of single-minded personal command and was not to be stopped until the British found a military dictator of their own who knew how to quash the adverse effects of 'tribalism' while using its advantages to the full. This was not to happen until Montgomery reached the Western Desert in the fall of 1942.

Wavell was no dictator. Everyone liked and admired him. He was well suited to command a British major theatre at the outbreak of a great war. His calmness in adversity, his robust stability and his obvious honesty of purpose held men's loyalty however discouraging the outlook might be. His patient husbanding of resources, his careful allocation of those resources to the various commanders in his vast theatre, and his ability to improvise enabled him to achieve much while defeat and ruin faced Great Britain everywhere in the early years of the war. The conquest of Cyrenaica, Eritrea, Italian Somaliland and Abyssinia, and the reconquest of British Somaliland and Iraq were no mean feats.

When Wavell arrived back in Cairo after acquiescing to the abandonment of 'Battleaxe', he cabled Churchill:

> Am very sorry for failure of 'Battleaxe', and loss of so many Tiger Cubs, especially since I have realised from figures produced by liaison officer how short we are of requirements at home. Fear this failure must add much to your anxieties. I was over-optimistic and should have advised you that 7th Armoured Division required more training before going into battle. I should also have deferred 'Exporter' till we could have put in larger force, but in both places I was impressed by apparent need for immediate action.
>
> (J. Connell: page 523).

These confessions gave Churchill the opportunity he had been looking for over the last few weeks of getting rid of Wavell. He had probably been looking for it subconsciously ever since their first meeting the year before when Wavell was called home to discuss preparations for action in the Western Desert which led to his 'Compass' conquest of Cyrenaica. On 21 June Churchill cabled:

> I have come to the conclusion that public interest will best be served by the appointment of General Auchinleck to relieve you in command of the armies of the Middle East . . . the victories which are associated with your name will be famous in the story of the British Army, and are an important contribution to our final success in this obstinate war. I feel, however, that after the long strain you have borne, a new eye and a new hand are required in this most seriously menaced theatre . . .
>
> (Churchill: Vol III, page 310).

Wavell accepted the decision without rancour, but felt it unkind not to have allowed him a few weeks' leave at home before taking up his new post as C-in-C India which the Japanese were soon to make just as onerous by the end of the year. Churchill would not risk it; Wavell might talk.

Next day – 22 June 1941 – Hitler invaded Russia. When Auchinleck arrived to take over command on 1 July, he was faced with a new strategic situation.

8

The Shadows of Barbarossa and Lend-Lease
(July to October 1941)

'Prime Minister to Gneral Auchinleck   1 July 41.
You take up your great command at a period of crisis. After all the facts have been laid before you it will be for you to decide whether to renew the offensive in the Western Desert, and if so, when.'

(Churchill: Vol III, page 354).

When Auchinleck relieved Wavell, two events – Hitler's 'Barbarossa' and Roosevelt's Lend-Lease – were beginning to change the scenario against which the North African Campaign was being fought. London and Cairo viewed the probable impact of these developments in opposite ways. London jumped to the conclusion that the time would never be riper for the renewal of the British offensive in the Western Desert. Russia would almost certainly collapse before the autumn and the German Army would then arrive at the back door of Auchinleck's 'great command' as Churchill called it in his first cable to him – quoted above. Affairs in the Western Desert should be settled at once so that Auchinleck could turn all his resources north-eastwards to meet the German threat from the Caucasus when it came. Cairo was much more interested in the flow of tanks, trucks and equipment which Lend-Lease would provide, and looked upon Hitler's entanglement with Russia as a god-sent opportunity for a pause in which to rest, re-equip and retrain the British formations shattered by the strategic misjudgments of the spring. In brief, while Cairo craved time in which to refit its forces so that they could meet the Germans on more equal terms, London demanded immediate action to take advantage of 'Barbarossa'.

Auchinleck's first appreciation of the situation on assuming command was cabled to London on 4 July. The first seven paragraphs set out Auchinleck's views:

Fully realise critical nature situation. Subject to further investigation and consideration my views are as follows:
1. No further offensive in Western Desert should be contemplated until base is secure.
2. Security of base implies completion occupation and consolidation of Syria.
3. Consolidation Syria includes Cyprus secure against attack.
4. Immediate action required is therefore elimination Vichy French from Syria earliest possible moment and completion defence measures in Cyprus.

5. Offensive in Syria being prosecuted already with all vigour but hampered by shortage of mechanical transport. Iraqi force (Habforce) is giving all possible aid.

6. Reconnaissance shows at least one division required ensure reasonable possibility defence Cyprus and plans are being made accordingly.

7. Once Syria is secure, and this implies consolidation our position in Iraq, offensive in Western Desert can be considered but for this adequate and properly trained armoured forces, say, at least two and preferably three armoured divisions with a motor division, will be required to ensure success. This is first essential.

Churchill agreed that Syria must come first, but laid down —

Nevertheless Western Desert remains decisive theatre this autumn for defence of Nile Valley — only by reconquering the lost airfields in Eastern Cyrenaica can Fleet and Air Force resume effective action against enemy seaborne supplies.

(Churchill: Vol III, page 354).

Auchinleck, unlike Wavell, refused to be hustled into a premature offensive in the Western Desert. The problems of the defence of India were too fresh in his mind to allow him to ignore his northern front. In a well-argued cable to Churchill dated 15 July, he insisted upon time to re-equip and train his tank units in properly balanced formations. He demanded a fifty per cent reserve of tanks — 25 per cent to cover tanks in workshops and 25 per cent as immediate replacements for battle casualties — and estimated that these could not be made available before September at the earliest. This demand drew Churchill's famous quip: 'This was an almost prohibitive condition. Generals only enjoy such comforts in Heaven. And those who demand them do not always get there!' (Churchill: Vol III, page 356).

Further cables flowed to and fro between London and Cairo. The climax came when the Cs-in-C Middle East sent their considered views to the British Chiefs of Staff. They concluded:

5. *Conclusion*

A. Unless situation changes very greatly in our favour no land offensive is possible in September.

B. We still consider two, preferably three, armoured divisions necessary for offensive operations to retake whole Cyrenaica.

C. Provided:

   (i)   You send 150 cruisers by mid-September;

   (ii) We still retain air superiority;

   (iii) Enemy land forces are not seriously reinforced in the meantime;

   (iv) A serious enemy offensive is not threatening against Syria;

We should be able to undertake limited offensive to relieve Tobruk in November . . .

(J. Connell: page 265).

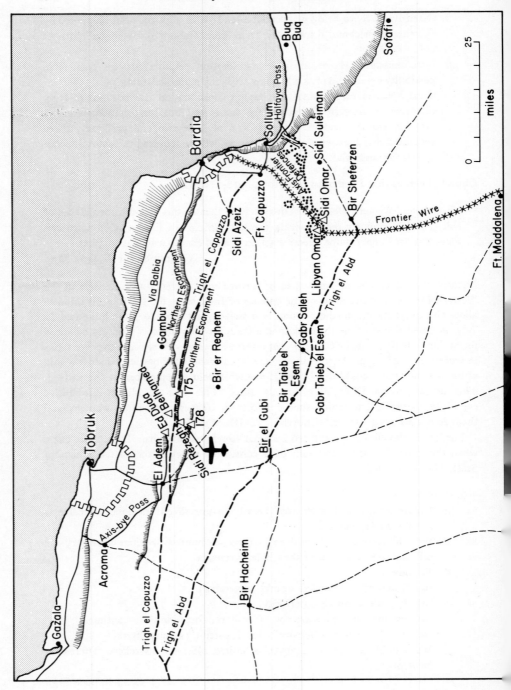

Churchill's heart sank. Had he exchanged a tired Wavell for an obstinate Auchinleck and an over-demanding Longmore for a cynical Tedder? He decided to summon Auchinleck home for consultation. Tedder went too at his own request and the two reached London at the beginning of August. Their meetings in Whitehall were in sharp contrast to Wavell's a year earlier. Auchinleck dominated the scene, putting his case lucidly and winning the debate. The two Cs-in-C arrived back in Cairo with three agreements reminiscent of Wavell's before 'Compass'. First, 'Crusader' would not be launched until the beginning of November. Secondly, risks would be taken again with the defence of the United Kingdom by despatching Major-General Norrie's 1st Armoured Division to the Middle East. Its 22nd Armoured Brigade would reach Egypt by mid-September, followed by the rest of the division in subsequent convoys. And thirdly, the RAF's order of battle would be raised from $34\frac{1}{2}$ to 52 squadrons by mid-October. In theory, they had a most profitable visit. In practice, everything would depend upon clearing up the unhappy situation in Syria, thus securing the northern front, and upon continuing success in the battle of supply.

While Auchinleck was taking over from Wavell, General Wilson pressed on with his distasteful operations in Syria. As soon as 'Battleaxe' was over, Tedder diverted air effort to Syria, neutralizing the Vichy Air Force which had been inflicting irritating losses on the invading Allied forces and upon Royal Naval ships supporting the advance along the Levant coast. Wilson summoned 'Habforce' from Iraq to advance on Palmyra from the east, and was authorised to use General Slim's 10th Indian Division from Basra for an advance up the Euphrates and the Baghdad–Aleppo

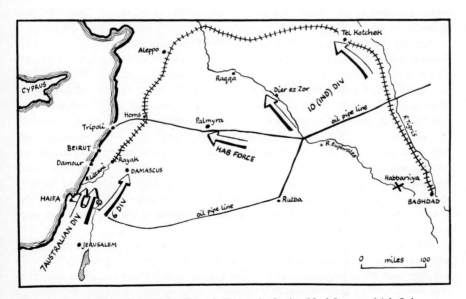

Fig 19　The Defeat of the Vichy French Forces in Syria: 23rd June to 14th July

railway into northern Syria. By 23 June, Wilson was in a position to change tactics to an all-out offensive to crush General Dentz with four converging forces: 7th Australian Division making the main thrust northwards up the coast with Naval support to capture Beirut; 6th British Division across the mountains from Damascus to threaten Beirut from the east; 'Habforce' from Palmyra to Homs; and 10th Indian Division to Aleppo.

6th Division's advance from Damascus made little progress against determined opposition in the ideally defensive hill country between Damascus and Beirut; 'Habforce' was resisted gallantly by the small Foreign Legion garrison of Palmyra which did not capitulate until 3 July; and Slim's 10th Indian Division was hampered more by logistic difficulties caused by lack of transport than French resistance. Slim took Deir-ez-Zor on the Euphrates and Tel Kotchak on the railway on 3 July, and then began to develop his threat to Aleppo, but before he could reach the city the Australians on the coast broke through Dentz's main defensive position on the Damour River covering Beirut. Their success was not easily won. It took five days' hard fighting with the support of 60 field guns on shore, five cruisers and eight destroyers off the coast and a number of heavy air attacks to persuade the French to accept the uselessness of further resistance. Dentz had been playing for time, hoping for reinforcements from France sent with German help – he was disappointed. On 11 July, he asked for an armistice. Peace negotiations were not easy, due to Vichy dislike of talking to Free French 'traitors to France' and their British collaborators. Dentz reluctantly agreed to sign the terms on 14 July. All Frenchmen were given the option of joining de Gaulle or being shipped back to Vichy France. French feelings were expressed in the choice they made. Only 5,700 out of 38,000 joined the Free French.

Syria settled down to an uneasy peace under British military occupation and Free French political control. Auchinleck's northern front was secure against further German infiltration, but not against attack if Russia collapsed, and the omens were not good. The German Northern Army Group was within 50 miles of Leningrad; their Central Army Group was annihilating large Russian forces surrounded at Smolensk on the road to Moscow; and their Southern Army Group was in the outskirts of Kiev. The French Colonial Army in Syria, upon which Allied strategy had been based in 1940, had disintegrated with the loss of its French officers and NCOs, and was no longer available to help support the Turks or block the routes southwards from the Caucasus; and Auchinleck could only muster three infantry divisions without tank support – 6th British, 7th Australian and 10th Indian – to garrison Syria, Iraq and Palestine. It is hardly surprising that he remained more worried about the North than the Western Desert.

The depressing news from the Russian front was tempered by more heartening news in the battle for supply. Both sides of the supply coin – the build up of British supplies and the strangulation of German supply lines – looked brighter than they had done for some time. Roosevelt's success in fighting the Lend-Lease Bill through Congress helped the former, while the diversion of Luftwaffe effort from the Mediterranean to Russia helped the latter. Neither, however, was decisive in its own right. A combination of several factors was, in the end, to give the British quantitative, though regrettably not qualitative, material superiority for 'Crusader'.

The effects of the passage of the Lend-Lease Bill through Congress were slow to develop. American industry needed time to increase production, but complex political constraints intervened as well. Roosevelt had exhausted much of his political credit in the Congressional debates, and had to advance more slowly. His argument that Lend-Lease was an alternative to direct American involvement in the war had been countered by isolationist contention that it was nothing more than a camouflaged step to war. Most Americans could see that their entry into the conflict was inevitable but few felt that the time was ripe when Roosevelt had signed the Lend-Lease Bill on 11 March. In consequence, its measures were not implemented as quickly as they might have been if there had been wholehearted political support for them in both parties. Hitler's invasion of Russia accelerated the ripening process, but weakened as well as strengthened the support the British hoped to gain from growing American involvement. The weakening came from the need to share American production with Russia; and the strengthening from Americans' greater willingness to change from a peace to a war economy. The situation was further complicated by America's own need to start expanding and equipping her own armed forces which were still on peace establishments. On the 9 August, Churchill and Roosevelt met off Newfoundland in HMS *Prince of Wales* and USS *Augusta*. The meeting is famous for the drafting of the 'Atlantic Charter'. The North African Campaign gained more from the less-publicised agreements on the sharing of American military aid.

The flow of Lend-Lease equipment to Africa was slow to start for two other and quite separate reasons. First, there were doubts in American minds about the validity of British strategy in the Middle East. Harry Hopkins summed up the feeling:

> No one in Britain appreciated the feeling which existed throughout the United States Military Command that the Middle East was a liability from which the British should withdraw ... It should be remembered that the problems of the Middle East, the interests of the Moslem World, and the inter-relationship of Egypt and India, were not well understood in the United States ...
>
> (Grand Strategy: Vol III, Part I, pages 125–126).

In spite of their misgivings the Americans began sending exploratory missions to Cairo to see what they could do to help. Some were friendly and co-operative; others were carping in their criticisms and irritated the men who had been struggling with so little for so long. The most important visitor was Averell Harriman, who visited Cairo to advise, at the highest political level, on the American aid programme. Thanks to his reports, the Trans-Africa air reinforcement route from Takoradi was expanded and an American air-supply route was established across the Southern Atlantic from the US via Brazil to Lagos and thence to Cairo along which the first US produced bombers reached Egypt in October. A programme was drawn up for American expansion of ports, roads, railways and airfields in Egypt, Palestine and Eritrea, together with workshops and servicing facilities for US equipment. The allocation of Lend-Lease funds for the purpose was made on 2 October. 'Crusader' would not benefit, but subsequent British operations would be helped.

The second reason for the slow start in improving the rate of supply of equipment to the Middle East was the lack of suitable weapons ready for shipment. By July 10,000 trucks had been landed with large consignments of non-warlike stores such as engineering machinery with which American contractors could establish a sound base infra-structure, but the two most important British requirements – medium tanks and anti-tank guns were not available. The US Army was developing tanks of its own as fast as it could and was making a better job of it than the British had done. They had, of course, profited by British and German experience, but their auto-motive industry with its advanced mass production techniques and its use of proven components in its tanks soon showed up the weaknesses in British design and production methods. In March only 16 medium tanks existed in the United States. In April the 'General Grant' medium tank was in prototype and production of the 'General Stuart' light tank was just starting. By May production of the 'Stuart' was in full swing and 84 reached Egypt in July – a remarkable achievement. They were not what the British really wanted, but they proved so handy and reliable in trials that their British crews dubbed them 'Honeys'. They were faster than the German tanks and better armoured than the Italian. Their weakness lay in their small 37 mm gun, which, though good for its calibre, could not hit hard enough, and in their short fuel endurance of 40 miles per fill. The British were glad to accept the 'Honeys' in default of 'Grants' which they hoped would reach them later. The real thing that the British needed – more powerful anti-tank guns (towed or tank-borne) – had not yet been developed in the USA.

Thus, in the latter half of 1941, the promised material plenty of US Lend-Lease still lay over the Middle East's horizon. Apart from trucks, the British remained dependent on their own resources and on the equipment which they had already bought from the USA. Churchill was far from satisfied that these resources, shipped at such expense in naval effort and at such great risk from the United Kingdom,which was still threatened with invasion, were being properly used. He noted that 239,000* men had been landed in Egypt between January and July; that the ration strength of the Army had risen to 530,000; and that the reported front line strength of RAF aircraft was far below what the experts in London believed it should be. His mind went back to his criticisms of Wavell's ration strength a year earlier and to a request made by Wavell for the establishment of a Minister of State in Cairo who could represent the views of the Cabinet to the Cs-in-C, and conversely the views of the Cs-in C to the Cabinet. Churchill extended this idea by sending out not only Mr Oliver Lyttleton to be Resident Minister in Cairo, but also General Sir Robert Haining to be Intendant General to oversee the theatre logistics, and Air Marshal Dawson to overhaul the aircraft servicing organisation. The appointment of the first

---

* The breakdown of the figure is interesting:

From UK	144,000
From Australia and New Zealand	60,000
From India	23,000
From South Africa	12,000

and third was a success; the second was not. Haining soon found that there was little wrong with the Army's administration. The unpalatable fact was that Egypt had few of the indigenous resources needed by a modern army and air force. Everything had to be imported and moved long distances to the various fronts. These things could not be done without a substantial logistic 'tail'. On his own recommendation his appointment was abolished within a few months.

The German High Command was equally dissatisfied with their command and logistic system in Africa. On von Paulus advice, Lieutenant-General Alfred Gause had been appointed German Liaison Officer to the Italian North African Command with a large German staff to improve Rommel's rudimentary supply organisation and to increase German influence in the Italian chain of command. Gause's appointment pleased neither Gariboldi nor Rommel. The former objected to the increase of German influence in Libya, and the latter to a rival German General in 'his' theatre. Arguments about Gause's position and responsibility went on for some weeks between Berlin, Rome, Tripoli and Gambut, where Rommel's Afrika Korps HQ was established. In the end Rommel won. The staff, which Gause had brought with him, was turned into Headquarters Panzer Group 'Afrika' with Rommel as C-in-C and Gause as his Chief of Staff. Rommel's principal Operations Officer was Lieutenant-Colonel Westphal and his Intelligence Officer was Major Freiherr von Mellenthin. The Afrika Korps was reduced to subordinate status and placed under Major-General Ludwig Crüwell with Lieut-Colonel Fritz Bayerlein as his Chief of Staff.

Such changes in organisation could only help to win the battle of supply. The obverse of the supply coin – the destruction of the enemy's lines of communication – was the task of the rival Navies and Air Forces. The British ships sailing round the Cape and aircraft flying across the Takoradi route were relatively secure compared with Rommel's supply lines across the Central Mediterrranean which depended upon the Luftwaffe for their security. The diversion of German air effort to Russia enabled the British to re-establish Malta as an offensive base. The island's garrison rose to 22,000 men; the average RAF strength reached 75 serviceable aircraft; and stocks of essential supplies rose to six months' duration. The effect of strengthening Malta was soon reflected in Axis shipping losses from air and naval action which rose from 16,000 tons in June to 64,000 tons in September. The RAF's effectiveness was improved by the introduction of search radars for its Wellington bombers, and homing devices on naval torpedo bombers with which to rendezvous when a target had been detected by the Wellingtons. At sea, Admiral Cunningham re-established a new convoy raiding force at Malta. Force 'K' (the cruisers 'Penelope' and 'Aurora' and two destroyers) under Captain Agnew emulated Captain Mack's feat by destroying the Axis 'Duisberg' convoy off the Calabrian coast on 8 November. Agnew sailed from Malta at dusk after an RAF 'Maryland' had located the convoy. He managed to manoeuvre his force unobserved until the enemy ships were silhouetted against a rising moon. In little over half an hour all seven merchant ships had been sunk together with one of the six escorting destroyers. It later transpired that the convoy had also been covered by a force of two Italian cruisers and four destroyers which did not engage. This success had a profound effect later upon 'Crusader'. The Italians were forced to reduce the size and frequency of their convoys to Libya during the vital preparatory period.

As long as success beckoned in Russia, OKW gave little thought to Mediterranean affairs. January 1942 was considered the earliest date for the Panzer Group Afrika to open its offensive to take Tobruk and advance to the Suez Canal. Ideas began to change when Hitler admitted in a secret memorandum, dated 28 August and issued only to a select few in the High Command, that his ambitious Russian campaign might not be over by winter. Absence of a German threat from the Caucasus Mountains would restore freedom of action to the British in the Middle East. If they concentrated against Rommel and drove him back to Tripoli, General Weygand, with American encouragement, might lead French North Africa into the Anglo-American camp. Sweeping aside German naval objections, Hitler ordered the restoration of Axis control of the Central Mediterrranean. German submarines were to be diverted from the Atlantic into the Mediterranean; motor torpedo boats were to be despatched from . the Baltic; and General Albert Kesselring, a German gunner turned aviator, was to move his HQ Luftflotte II (2nd German Air Force) from Russia to Italy where he would become German C-in-C South with authority to co-ordinate all German Naval and Air Operations in the Mediterranean. As soon as the Russian winter reduced Luftwaffe's operations, the aircraft of Luftflotte II would fly south to join Fliegerkorps X for a combined effort to re-establish German control of the Central Mediterranean.

Rommel was not slow to appreciate the change in the strategic climate within the German High Command. He had been travelling to and fro across the Mediterranean, attending conferences in Rome, Berlin and East Prussia throughout the summer. He stopped thinking about taking Tobruk in January and shortened his sights to October or November. Gause's Logistic Staff estimated that he would have enough ammunition and fuel, and his Intelligence Staff warned that the British were contemplating the relief of Tobruk themselves. An early attack on Tobruk seemed both feasible and desirable. Before taking a final decision Rommel decided to find out for himself what the British were doing on their side of the frontier.

Rommel's method of discovery was typical of his style. He decided to advance at the head of von Ravenstein's 5th Light Division, which had been renamed 21st Panzer Division, on a deep raid into Egypt with the twin objects of disrupting any British preparations for an offensive and gaining intelligence. He had a third purpose. In the lull in the desert war since 'Battleaxe' he had imposed a strict training programme on his troops to make good the weaknesses he had detected during his unsuccessful assaults on Tobruk and during 'Brevity' and 'Battleaxe'. New tactics were developed and practised which laid increased stress upon the close co-operation between tanks, anti-tank guns and artillery. A divisional-sized reconnaissance in force would provide an ideal opportunity to put theory into practice.

Rommel's 'Midsummer Night's Dream' as his raid was code-named, was not a great success and probably did more harm than good to the German cause because it gave Rommel a false impression of affairs behind the British lines. 21st Panzer

Division advanced in three columns intent on surrounding and capturing a large British supply dump which was thought to exist some 20 miles inside Egypt south-east of Sidi Omar. A column of empty supply vehicles accompanied the division to carry away the booty. The screen of South African armoured cars watching the frontier withdrew slowly, reporting the German advance. They were well supported by 'Jock' columns of 7th Support Group which fell back drawing the Germans on towards the British mine-fields and fixed defences based upon the old Italian forts around Sofafi. Captain Schmidt, Rommel's ADC, described the adventure:

> At dawn next morning we passed through a prepared gap in our mine-fields and drove east. Rommel, looking like a U-Boat Commander on his bridge . . . shouted out with an even more than unusual boisterousness: 'We're off to Egypt' . . . We sped on for some distance until we were not far west of Buq Buq . . . We saw no sign of a secret supply dump. There was nothing to see but a few empty bully-beef tins and a few ale bottles, also empty, unfortunately . . . I noticed suddenly that my mouth was parched.
>
> (Schmidt: page 93).

Schmidt was not the only person or thing parched that day. Von Ravenstein's tanks ran out of fuel and lay stranded in the desert, waiting for their supply echelons. The Support Group 25-pounder field guns did some damage, but the RAF did more with effective carpet bombing which the German soldiers referred to cynically as 'Party Congresses', equating the tight-packed well-disciplined formations of RAF bombers to the pre-war air displays at Hitler's Nazi Party rallies. Losses began to mount. With

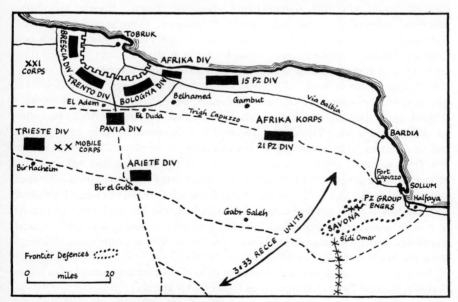

Fig 20 Axis Dispositions before 'Crusader'

the British showing every sign of gaining the measure of his raid, Rommel decided to abandon the operation and to withdraw while there was yet time.

'Midsummer Night's Dream' seemed to convince Rommel that the British were not ready for an offensive. He had found no dumps; he had disrupted no formations assembling in the desert; and documents captured in an abandoned South African office truck suggested that the British were more concerned with practising withdrawals from the frontier than attacks across it. There was ample evidence pointing to an opposite conclusion, but he chose to disregard it. Air photographs showed a railway and pipeline coming closer and closer to the frontier as the weeks went by. The Italian Intelligence staff issued a number of warnings culled from their agents in Cairo which were discounted as typical Italian jitters. Contemporary evidence suggests that Rommel became more and more obsessed with the problems of attacking Tobruk and refused to accept the possibility of the British forestalling him. Nevertheless his dispositions were well balanced and clearly designed to deal with any attempt by the British to save the fortress with a relieving attack from Egypt.

Since 'Battleaxe' Rommel had extended his frontier defences 20 miles inland to Sidi Omar to protect his rear while he dealt with Tobruk. He made extensive use of mine-fields, which were beginning to play an increasingly important part in desert warfare, replacing non-existent rivers as the obstacles upon which to base defensive positions. Rommel garrisoned the western or inland sector of the frontier defences with the Italian Savona Division, but kept the important coastal sector in German hands, using his Panzer Group's Engineer Headquarters to command a mixed Italo-German force which included Bach's successful Halfaya garrison. He made General Navarrini's XXI Italian Corps (Bologna, Trento, Brescia and Pavia Divisions) responsible for the investment of Tobruk; and gave the task of assaulting Tobruk from the south-east to Neumann-Silkow's 15th Panzer Division and a new German division – Major-General Summermann's 'Afrika' Division – formed from infantry units flown in during the summer as reinforcements for the siege of Tobruk. The Panzer Group artillery under General Böttcher would support the assault from gun positions between Ed Duda and Belhamed. Between these two fixed points – Tobruk in the West and the frontier defences in the east – Crüwell's Afrika Korps lay in mobile reserve with 21st Panzer Division and the reconnaissance units of both panzer divisions under command. Crüwell's HQ was at Gambut; 21st Panzer was on the Trigh Capuzzo midway between Tobruk and the frontier; and 3rd and 33rd Reconnaissance Units were covering the open desert flank westwards from Sidi Omar on the line of the Trigh el Abd. If the British did attack over the frontier, 15th Panzer Division was to rejoin Crüwell to give the Afrika Korps its full offensive potential. As a further measure of protection Rommel persuaded Bastico, who had replaced Gariboldi, to deploy General Gambarra's XX Italian Mobile Corps south of Tobruk with the Ariete Armoured Division at Bir el Gubi and the Trieste Motorised Division at Bir Hacheim to block any wide encircling move the British might attempt to relieve Tobruk. Rommel fixed 21 November as D-day for his assault.

Auchinleck's first problem in mounting 'Crusader' was the selection of commanders. The small Western Desert Force, which had fought 'Brevity' as an under-strength division and 'Battleaxe' as an improvised corps, was being expanded into the British Eighth Army, commanding two fully established corps each of two to three divisions with the full panoply of supporting and logistic troops. After the failure of 'Battleaxe' new commanders were needed. Churchill proposed 'Jumbo' Wilson for Eighth Army. Auchinleck argued that he needed a man with political as well as military talents to command Ninth Army which was forming in Syria and Iraq to protect the northern front. His choice for Eighth Army was General Sir Alan Cunningham, the victor of the Somali and Abyssinian campaigns. Churchill did not press his point, and so Cunningham took over Eighth Army and Wilson stayed in Syria forming Ninth Army. Unfortunately Auchinleck misjudged his man as he was to do on other occasions. Cunningham had all the external hall-marks of a successful army commander, but he lacked the depth of intellect to shape original policies suited to the novel environment of desert warfare.

Auchinleck's planners in Cairo gave Cunningham two alternative strategies to consider: Course 'A', to contain Rommel in the coastal sector while advancing on Benghazi, using the most southerly route, which ran along the northern edge of the Libyan Sand Sea through the oases of Siwa, Jarabub and Jalo;* and Course 'B', to use a shorter out-flanking route round the German frontier defences south of Sidi Omar, advancing on Tobruk astride the Trigh el Abd.† Cunningham rightly rejected Course 'A' as logistically impractical and strategically dangerous because it would split the British armoured and air forces between two widely divergent thrust lines which were not mutually supporting. When he studied Course 'B' in detail he found the geography forced him to adopt a scaled-up version of 'Brevity' and 'Battleaxe'. Corps would replace divisions, one corps masking the Axis frontier defences while the other swung wide round the desert flank to bring the German armour to battle somewhere between Tobruk and Sidi Omar. Cunningham, and most of the other senior British officers concerned with the operational planning, believed that the key to success lay in the destruction of the two German panzer divisions. He summarises his own tasks as follows:

(i)   The enemy armoured forces are the target.
(ii) They must be hemmed in and not allowed to escape.
(iii) The relief of Tobruk must be incidental.

(South African Official History, page 62).

The destruction of the German armour became as much an obsession with Cunningham as the assault on Tobruk was to Rommel. Whereas Rommel had a sound and balanced plan for storming Tobruk, and had been training his armoured forces all summer to fight a well co-ordinated action against any relieving British armoured forces, Cunningham was far from clear how the cliché 'destruction of the enemy armour' was to be achieved. He had no personal experience of armoured warfare and was in the hands of his advisers who belonged to one of two schools of

* See Map IV page 92.
† See Fig 22, page 155.

thought: the cavalry-type thinkers who equated the tank to the horse and believed in shock action in which speed and élan were all important; and the professional tank school who tended to naval analogies with epigrams like 'No tank commander will go far wrong if he places his gun within killing range of an enemy'. Both schools agreed that the enemy tank was the principal target, but neither gave enough thought to how the other arms could help in its destruction. Unhappily there is truth in the South African contention that Cunningham's formula for 'Crusader' was to win the great armoured battle in true Nelsonic style by 'engaging the enemy more closely', and depending upon superior British fighting qualities to win the day.

Cunningham decided to group his armoured forces under Lieutenant-General Pope's XXX Corps which was raised for the purpose. Pope had been the War Office's Director of Armoured Fighting Vehicles. He was killed in an air crash shortly after taking over and was replaced by Lieutenant-General Norrie from 1st Armoured Division which was arriving in Egypt. XXX Corps would advance on a wide front up the Trigh el Abd, outflanking the German frontier defences to engage the Afrika Korps somewhere around Gabr Saleh. Gott's 7th Armoured Division would lead with 7th and 22nd Armoured Brigades abreast and with 7th Support Group close behind. Major-General Brink's 1st South African Division with 1st and 5th South African Brigades would protect the open western flank by advancing on Bir el Gubi; and the 22nd Guards Brigade would protect the XXX Corps' Field Maintenance Centres which were to be established well west of the frontier early in the operation from which the fighting units could draw supplies.

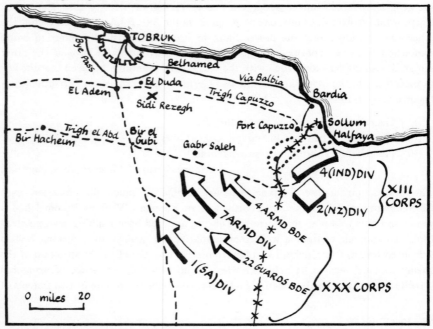

Fig 21 Cunningham's Plan for 'Crusader'

The Infantry divisions of Eighth Army were to be grouped under XIII Corps, which was reformed again from the Western Desert Force and given to Lieutenant-General Godwin-Austen who followed Cunningham from East Africa. XIII Corps was to keep the Axis troops in the frontier defences quiet until XXX Corps had won its armoured battle. When ordered to do so Major-General Messervy's 4th Indian Division would work its way round the Savona Division's positions to attack them from the rear, while Major-General Freyberg's 2nd New Zealand Division made a wider detour round Sidi Omar to cut the Trigh Capuzzo and via Balbia west of Bardia, thus encircling all Axis troops in the frontier area. 4th Indian and 2nd New Zealand Division would be supported by the 'I' tanks of 1st Army Tank Brigade.

Norrie was given two distinct tasks. Besides seeking out and destroying the Afrika Korps, he was to make sure that Crüwell did not manage to attack the desert flank of Godwin-Austen's infantry divisions as they carried out their task of containing the Axis frontier garrisons. Cunningham planned to help him by interposing Brigadier Gatehouse's 4th Armoured Brigade, mounted in new American 'Honeys' to act as a link between the inner flanks of the two British Corps. Gatehouse was to cover the flank of XIII Corps and, at the same time, be ready to assist XXX Corps in its armoured battle by appearing on the Afrika Korps' flank at a critical moment. His brigade was organised as a self-contained group of all arms with its own artillery, infantry, engineers and logistic troops. Cunningham further elaborated his plan by despatching Brigadier Reid's 29th Indian Brigade, supported by South African armoured cars, to simulate a Course 'A' advance along the oasis route to create a threat to Benghazi, drawing Axis attention southwards.

The simplicity of Cunningham's plan disguised the compromises inherent in it. Cunningham had been compelled to balance the forceful views of two sets of critics. On the one hand, the Infantry divisional commanders — Freyberg, Brink and to a lesser extent Messervy — believed it wrong to commit their divisions without close tank support. Field Marshal Carver, who was a GSO II in HQ XXX Corps at the time, has described this belief which persisted throughout the battle:

> The 'Crusader' operation was fought to an unending accompaniment of screams from one infantry division headquarters, or field maintenance centre, after another for tanks to come and protect them against the presence or threat of enemy tanks.
>
> (Carver: Royal Armoured Corps Journal, Oct 1948).

And on the other hand, the principal armoured commanders objected, with equal justification to the over-dispersion of their armoured forces and the indecisive nature of the plan. They appreciated that there must be concentration in time rather than space, but Cunningham's plan gave them neither. Norrie voiced their views:

> There were two main points in the plan over which I was not happy and had to express my disagreement.
> (a) I did not think the Gabr Saleh area was the best to go to in order to compel the enemy armour to fight.

(b) I considered the two tasks of destroying the enemy armour and protecting the
left flank of XIII Corps were conflicting.
(Norrie's Report quoted in *South African Official History:* page 110).

In Norrie's view there was no guarantee that Rommel would react to a thrust to Gabr
Saleh. It did not threaten anything particularly vital to the Germans. A violent
reaction was bound to occur if the British armoured force arrived in the Ed Duda –
Belhamed area, cutting the Axis by-pass road round Tobruk and coming near enough
to the fortress to allow the garrison to stage a break-out with a reasonable chance of
success. The Axis airfield of Sidi Rezegh, which lay just south of Ed Duda and
Belhamed, might provide a suitable objective, but to reach it and to fight a major
armoured battle with the Afrika Korps would require the concentration of all three
armoured brigades. Norrie asked to be given a free hand to destroy the German
armour unimpeded by his secondary role of protecting the open desert flank of
Godwin-Austen's infantry divisions which, in any case, had the support of 1st Army
Tank Brigade's 'I' tanks. The argument revolved round the employment of
Gatehouse's 4th Armoured Brigade Group, which Norrie wished to advance with him
to Sidi Rezegh, on the grounds that success in the armoured battle would give XIII
Corps greater protection than anything 4th Armoured Brigade Group could provide,
whereas its absence could jeopardise XXX Corps' chances of success in its battle with
Crüwell's Afrika Korps. Faced with these conflicting arguments Cunningham decided
to stick to his own plan, making one slight modification. 4th Armoured Brigade
Group would keep its dual role, but he would accompany Norrie in the early stages of
the advance so that he could give an immediate decision on its employment as soon as
the German reaction to XXX Corps' thrust to Gabr Saleh was revealed. This decision
had the merit of flexibility but was as dangerously indecisive as the use of Gabr Saleh
as an objective.

During October there were signs of 'first night nerves' in London, Sydney,
Wellington and Cairo. In London Churchill was demanding that Auchinleck should
start his offensive earlier than the target date of 11 November. In Sydney, the
Australian Government had become restive about their troops locked up in Tobruk.
In Wellington, the New Zealand Government was seeking assurances that Tedder
would be able to give their troops better protection from Luftwaffe attacks than it had
done in Greece and Crete. And in Cairo, Auchinleck was struggling with late arrivals
of reinforcements and delays in training programmes.

Auchinleck had opposed earlier Australian demands that their troops should be
relieved in Tobruk on the grounds that it was expensive enough in terms of naval and
air losses to keep the fortress supplied without adding the extra burden of a relief. The
Australian Government refused to relent, and so in the moonless periods of August,
September and October, Morshead's men were replaced by the 1st Polish Brigade and
the 6th British Division under General Scobie from Syria. Scobie's division was
renumbered 70th British Division to avoid confusion with 6th British Armoured
Division in England which might be sent to the Middle East. The August and
September reliefs were carried out without undue loss, but in October casualties

amongst ships and aircraft rose so steeply that Admiral Cunningham had to stop the operation, leaving one and a half Australian battalions in Tobruk for 'Crusader'.

The New Zealand Government's demands for assurances of adequate air support for Freyberg's men led inadvertently to an unfortunate clash between Tedder and Churchill in which Tedder almost lost his job. Quite by chance the New Zealand query reached London at about the same time as an appreciation of the air situation by Tedder arrived in the Air Ministry. Tedder had expressed doubts about his ability to maintain an adequate measure of air superiority because the Germans could reinforce quickly from Europe whenever they needed to do so. The Air Ministry used Tedder's appreciation in briefing the Prime Minister for his reply to the New Zealand Government. Churchill's reaction was characteristic. He refused to accept Tedder's figures and despatched the Vice-Chief of Air Staff to Cairo to examine the situation so that he could give the New Zealand Government the assurances it wanted. He wrote also to Auchinleck, giving him the chance to report unfavourably on Tedder: 'I thought it very wrong that such mis-statements should be made by the Air authorities in Cairo on the eve of a decisive battle, and I shall not conceal from you that such conduct has affected my confidence in their quality and judgment . . .' (J. Connell: page 316).

Auchinleck stood loyally – and with conviction – beside Tedder. On 23 October he cabled:

> I am not and have not been unduly anxious about the Air situation in spite of the way in which the relative strength of ourselves and the enemy may have been displayed . . . I have confidence in the ability of Tedder and his subordinates to do what we require of them . . .'
>
> *(Ibid:* page 322).

The conference between the Vice-Chief of Air Staff and the Air Staff in Cairo concluded that Tedder would be opposing 385 serviceable Axis aircraft with 528 serviceable aircraft of his own. With these figures Churchill reassured the New Zealand Government. Subsequent evidence shows they were not far wrong. Tedder's original view of Axis ability to reinforce was amply justified by later events.

Auchinleck did not go unscathed. He too had to withstand Churchillian attacks stemming from three causes: from the late arrival of 22nd Armoured Brigade, which did not reach Suez until early October instead of mid-September, and, as usual, was found to have tanks which needed workshop modification before they could be considered desert-worthy; from delays caused by the Australian relief in Tobruk; and from the slow progress made by Brink's South African Division with its desert training. He had to face a gale of objections from Churchill each time he asked for a postponement. Churchill was already working on plans to exploit 'Crusader' which he hoped would be as decisive as O'Connor's 'Compass'. His plans were premature but are interesting because they re-emerge later in the story of the North African Campaign. In the same letter of 16 October, in which he casts doubts on Tedder, Churchill wrote:

We have been considering how to help you exploit success, should it be granted to us . . . . Directions have been given here to prepare an expedition to Norway, and shipping for about four divisions, including an armoured division is being gathered. Winter clothing is being issued to the troops assigned. This forms a real cover. However, from about the middle of November, or perhaps even a little earlier I shall be holding a substantial force which can as easily steer south as north. Should your operation change the attitude of Weygand we could enter by Casablanca at his invitation; or alternatively action against Sicily in conjunction with your Army may be taken. . . . .

(Ibid: page 317)

Three operations of future significance were under active consideration in Whitehall. 'Acrobat' was the extension of 'Crusader' with a rapid advance to Tripoli and then on to Tunisia to link up, hopefully, with Weygand. 'Gymnast' was the invasion of French North Africa, possibly with American help. And 'Whipcord' was a landing in Sicily if it appeared that Mussolini's Fascist regime was on the point of collapse. All three were to be pushed off the planners' desks and into pigeon holes by the events in the desert and by Japanese treachery in the Far East, but this is anticipating events.

The atmosphere on the British side before 'Crusader' was one of renewed confidence; and on the German side of a continued sense of tactical superiority and hope that the Italians would react better with German support than they had done on their own. The quantitative figures for relative strengths, quoted in the British Official History (Vol III page 97) were:

	British	German	Italian	Axis Total
Men	118,000	65,000	54,000	119,000
Medium Tanks	610*	184	146	330
Serviceable Aircraft	530		342	342

* Including 173 'Honeys' but excluding 101 tanks inside Tobruk.

Thus the two sides were about equal in men, while the British had a 2 − 1 advantage in tanks and slightly less in aircraft. These figures do not give the full extent of British material superiority. There were another 180 tanks in reserve or in workshops, and a further 240 tanks were stowed in the hulls of ships coming round the Cape belonging to 1st Armoured Division and as replacements for battle casualties. The Germans had no such reserves or expectations. Rommel had been told to live on his own fat until January.

The British had every reason to feel confident. They appeared to have everything that they needed to make Churchill's dreams of exploiting 'Crusader' with 'Acrobat', 'Gymnast' or 'Whipcord' come true. In their insular way they were convinced that they possessed an inbred tactical flair; that their marksmanship and the speed of their tanks would enable them to outmanoeuvre the Germans in spite of the apparently lower performance of their tank guns; and that they had the stamina to outfight the Germans. They did not realise that their tactics were inadequate; that their marksmanship only passable; and that their higher commanders had not found the secret of bringing superior force to bear with decisive effect. They were to buy battle experience from the Germans during 'Crusader' in the hardest possible way – by coming very near to defeat.

9

Buying Battle Experience
(July to December 1941)

'Contrary to the generally accepted view, the German tanks did not have any advantage in quality over their opponents, and in numbers we were always inferior . . . To what then are we to ascribe the brilliant successes of the Afrika Korps? To my mind, our victories depended on three factors – the superiority of our anti-tank guns, our systematic practice of the principle of "Co-operation of All Arms", and – last but not least – our tactical methods.'

von Mellenthin: *Panzer Battles 1939–45;* pages 51–52.

'Crusader' was a very complex battle. It was fought to a finish in the great quadrilateral of open desert which lies between the Egyptian frontier and Tobruk. There was no clearly defined front line. British and Axis formations criss-crossed each other in bewildering patterns, each bent upon some purpose which might or might not have been based on valid intelligence of what was happening. The fog of war was so dense at times that the senior commanders on either side could do little to affect the issue, as formations, large and small, sought their own destiny in their own way. 'Crusader' was a series of battles within a battle, the outcome of any one of which was rarely known before another had begun. The opposing orders of battle were:

BRITISH	AXIS
ARMOURED FORCES	
XXX Corps (Norrie)	*Afrika Korps (Crüwell)*
7th Armoured Division (Gott)	15th Panzer Division (Neumann-Silkow)
7th Armoured Brigade	8th Panzer Regiment
22nd Armoured Brigade	115th Lorried Infantry Regiment
7th Support Group	21st Panzer Division (von Ravenstein)
4th Armoured Brigade Group	5th Panzer Regiment
22nd Guards Brigade Group	104th Lorried Infantry Regiment
1st South African Division (Brink)	*Italian Mobile Corps (Gambarra)*
1st South African Brigade	Ariete Armoured Division (Balotta)
5th South African Brigade	Trieste Motorised Division (Piazzoni)
INFANTRY FORMATIONS	
XIII Corps (Godwin-Austen)	*XXI Italian Corps (Navarini)*
2nd NZ Division (Freyberg)	Trento Division
4th, 5th and 6th NZ Brigades	Bologna Division

4th Indian Division (Messervy)	Brescia Division
5th, 7th, 11th Indian Brigades	Pavia Division
1st Army Tank Brigade	German 'Africa' Division
Tobruk Garrison (Scobie)	Böttcher Artillery Group
70th Division (Scobie)	*Frontier Garrisons*
32nd Army Tank Brigade	Savona Division
1st Polish Brigade	German Detachments under
Oasis Force (Reid)	Engineer HQ of Panzer Group
29th Indian Brigade Group	

RESERVES

2nd South African Division (de Villiers)	Italian Garrison Divisions in
3rd, 4th, 6th South African Brigades	Tripolitania & Western Cyrenaica

The battle-field* of 'Crusader' consisted, in the main, of vast stretches of gravelly desert over which tanks, guns and vehicles could be driven at will. There were areas of soft sand and difficult broken going, but these rarely affected tactical issues. The only topographic features of any significance were the desert tracks, the main coast road — the via Balbia — and the escarpments which rose in steps from the coastal strip to the desert plateau. There were two lines of escarpments in the battle area running parallel with the coast. The distance between them vaired as did their height and negotiability by vehicles and tanks. They were generally easier to cross than the major coastal escarpment running eastwards from Sollum into Egypt. Between the sea and the northern escarpment ran the via Balbia; between the northern and southern escarpments ran the Trigh Capuzzo; and south of the southern escarpment the Trigh-el-Abd ran diagonally across the desert from Bir Sheferzen on the Egyptian fronter to Bir-el-Gubi due south of Tobruk. The 'Axis Bypass' road, built by the Italians under German supervision to take Axis supply traffic round Tobruk, climbed the northern escarpment between the commanding features of Belhamed and Ed Duda where it met the Trigh Capuzzo. Just south of Belhamed the southern escarpment was fractured by a sloping plain some three miles wide which formed a natural 'tank run' from the desert plateau down to the Trigh Capuzzo, and in which lay the Axis airfield of Sidi Rezegh.

In November, the days could still be stiflingly hot and the nights unpleasantly cold. Dust storms were frequent and reduced visibility severely as long as they lasted, and yet heavy rain could suddenly turn the desert, and airfields in particular, into quagmires. It is easy to forget three other problems of desert warfare: the difficulty of establishing the identity of friend and foe at a distance; the unreliability of radio communications; and the hazards of desert navigation. Any action might start with the sighting of a few black blobs or a column of dust on the horizon. Even with powerful binoculars it was hard to tell what they were or to whom they belonged because both sides were using tanks and vehicles captured from the other. When a

* See map V page 136.

major force was approaching, clouds of dust obscured the scene. The British, whose earlier experience of operating in adverse air environment made them more sensitive to air attack, tended to move in loose swarms of widely dispersed vehicles to avoid presenting atrractive targets to Axis airmen. The Germans moved in tighter formations relying on concentrated anti-aircraft fire for protection. The airmen on both sides found identification of targets no easier than the soldiers on the ground. The vehicles of neither side carried adequate air recognition marking; and, if a pilot did identify a column he then had the problem of fixing and reporting its exact position. The consequential uncertainties were exacerbated by the inadequacies of the radio sets available in the 1940s. They were operated beyond their designed ranges; and their use of the lower frequency bands resulted in fading at dusk and dawn when staff traffic was at its highest, receiving reports of the days' or nights' events and issuing fresh orders. Electronic storms, which were as frequent as dust storms, blotted out communications for hours on end. And, as far as desert navigation was concerned, some men excelled, while others faltered. By day, dust and heat hazes made distance-judging difficult, and the grey-brown featurelessness of the landscape added to the inaccuracies of available maps. By night, the skill with which the commanders of the supply columns found their rendezvous with their fighting units was often little short of miraculous. The Germans tended to leaguer for the night where they stood at dusk and were thus able to recover damaged equipment on the battlefield. The British made a habit of withdrawing some miles to replenish, to repair and maintain equipment, and to sleep. The supply columns had to find the night leaguers from the sketchiest details given over the radio and were guided in by Verey light signals of varying colour and frequency which lit up the desert sky at night. The Germans fired illuminating flares as well to protect their leaguers. The British favoured silence, depending upon listening and watching for their protection.

In brief, the peculiarities of desert warfare created an all-pervading uncertainty of what was happening or had happened on the tactical battlefield. The dust thrown up by bursting shells, the black billowing oily smoke from burning vehicles and tanks, and the natural desert hazes made tactical control a matter of battle-instinct and personal judgment. Time and again units reported that they could not intervene because they were unable to discover what was happening within a pall of dust and smoke drifting across the battle-field. Nothing was ever clear-cut. The successful desert commanders acquired the 'feel of the battle'; the less successful did not.

'Crusader' lasted for three long weeks packed with the bewildering inter-action of events which are difficult to follow without an over-simplified theme to give shape to the narrative. There can be said to have been four phases. In the first, Cunningham sought a decisive armoured battle, which vanished Will-'o-the-wisp-like into the second phase as Rommel, after some initial hesitancy, seized the initiative and came close to defeating Eighth Army in spite of its numerical superiority. In the third phase Rommel over-played nis hand, thinking that he could deliver the 'coup de grâce' in the grandest manner. He failed and, though he fought back brilliantly, he was overwhelmed by British logistic superiority in the fourth and final phase, and was forced to abandon Cyrenaica.

CUNNINGHAM SEEKS HIS DECISIVE ARMOURED BATTLE
(18 to 20 November 1941)

Until the very last moment it was uncertain which side would attack first. Rommel's D-day was fixed for 21 November. Auchinleck's target date had been 11 November, giving him an ample margin, though neither he nor Rommel was aware of the other's date. The late arrival of 22nd Armoured Brigade caused the British date to slip to 15 November. Then at the very last moment Auchinleck was informed that Brink's South Africans could not complete their training on time because late issues of transport had prevented their practising brigade night marches in the desert. Brink demanded another week's training. Auchinleck considered the possibility of exchanging the roles of the South Africans with the 4th Indian or 2nd New Zealand Divisions, but discarded the idea as it was too late to change. Instead he risked Churchill's wrath by postponing 'D-day' three days to 18 November.

Surprisingly Churchill accepted the extra three-day postponement without rancour. Brink made the best of the decision to allow him three instead of six days by using the approach march to his assembly area to give his division more practice. The night march carried out during 16-17 November was discouraging. Vehicles suffered broken axles, transmissions and springs, and some units ran out of fuel. The *South African Official History* (page 121) quotes Brink as saying next morning in Afrikaans 'Nooit weer Nu' – 'Never Again'.

Eighth Army reached its assembly areas early on 17th November without alerting

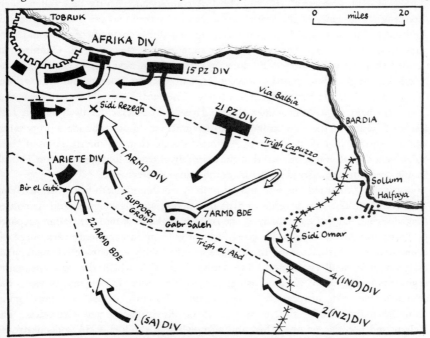

Fig 22 The Advance of XXX Corps: 18th and 19th November 1941

the Germans. Camouflage, radio discipline and deception measures had been greatly improved since 'Battleaxe'. Tanks came forward disguised as trucks with canopies on jettisonable frames. Radio silence was imposed and bogus traffic transmitted to simulate units in their old locations. The German intercept unit did detect a change in radio pattern, but its warning fell upon deaf ears in the Panzer Group HQ as the warnings of the Italian intelligence staffs had done earlier. Rommel had just returned from conferences in Rome with his mind concentrated upon the problems of his own assault on Tobruk. His units started to move to their assembly areas about the same time and with as much secrecy as the British. Both sides were tiptoeing on to the battlefield, facing in opposite directions intent on playing different games. The only German units lying in the path of Norrie's XXX Corps were the hard worked 3rd and 33rd Reconnaissance Units belonging to the two panzer divisions.

The secrecy of the British concentration was helped by several days of low cloud which reduced air reconnaissance. During the evening of 17th November these clouds turned into lowering thunder packs, and that night the desert was deluged with rain as thunder storms broke. The Axis air forces were worst hit. Their airfields were flooded more severely than the RAF's which missed the worst of the storm belt. At dawn Norrie's XXX Corps passed through the frontier wire near Fort Maddalena and advanced with the three armoured brigades in arrowhead formation towards Gabr Saleh. Cunningham accompanied Norrie, as planned. By dusk XXX Corps had reached all its objectives. Nothing had happened. There was no German reaction just as Norrie had predicted. 3rd and 33rd Reconnaissance Units had fallen back, reporting the advance of the British armoured car screen and the presence of about 200 tanks. This had caused von Ravenstein to despatch a company of tanks and some guns from 21st Panzer Division to their support, but that was all. Cunningham decided that the only thing to be done was to push on next day to Sidi Rezegh as Norrie had originally proposed to force a German reaction. Rommel, for his part, was unconvinced that the British were in earnest. The most he would concede was that they were bent on a 'Midsummer Night's Dream' in reverse. Crüwell alerted 15th Panzer Division on his own initiative, but Rommel would not sanction a proposal by von Ravenstein that his 5th Panzer Regiment should clear up the situation at Gabr Saleh next day. Rommel insisted that the assembly of troops for his assualt on Tobruk should continue unhindered by British activity in the desert.

Gott's 7th Armoured Division started probing north and north-westwards early on 19 November. The first brigade to drift into action was the novice 22nd Armoured Brigade which chased a company of the Ariete's tanks back into the Italian prepared positions around Bir-el-Gubi. In spite of warnings from the experienced armoured car commanders of 11th Hussars, the brigade attacked with inadequate reconnaissance and too little artillery support. The enthusiasm with which the new Yeomanry regiments went into action, using simple fire and movement tactics, was commendable but unsuccessful even against Italians, whose anti-tank guns, unhindered by artillery fire, destroyed 25 of the brigade's new Crusaders. The Italians did not emerge unscathed and acknowledged the loss of 34 tanks destroyed and 15 damaged. Had there been any infantry with the British tanks the Italian position might have collapsed. Many of the Italian garrison gave up early in the action, but finding no-one ready to accept their surrender re-manned their guns.

7th Armoured Brigade was more successful. Its tanks over-ran Sidi Rezegh airfield, destroying 19 Axis aircraft and thoroughly alarming the Pavia and 'Afrika' Divisions into whose rear areas they had suddenly burst in the early afternoon. Two infantry battalions of the 'Afrika' Division were rushed up to hold Ed Duda and to block a British advance down the Sidi Rezegh 'tank-run'. Failing light of the autumn evening ended 7th Armoured Brigade's advance. It leaguered on the airfield.

The main fighting of the day took place on Gatehouse's 4th Armoured Brigade Group's front at Gabr Saleh where it was carrying out its role of maintaining the link between the two British Corps. Gatehouse pushed his armoured cars northwards over the Trigh Capuzzo supported by one of his 'Honey' regiments to seek out the German armour. They had an exhilaratory time chasing the German reconnaisance detachments to within sight of Bardia but in doing so provided Crüwell with enough evidence to persuade Rommel to sanction von Ravenstein's operation towards Gabr Saleh. Towards evening Gatehouse found himself attacked by 21st Panzer Division's 5th Panzer Regiment. The British Official History described the action as indecisive but von Ravenstein leaguered on the battlefield while Gatehouse withdrew some miles south, leaving 23 of his Honeys behind – not a very good start to the great armoured battle which looked like occurring exactly where the British had hoped, but regrettably in the absence of 7th and 22nd Armoured Brigades.

During the second night of the battle neither Cunningham nor Rommel had enough information on which to recast their plans. Cunningham told Norrie to secure Sidi Rezegh with Gott's 7th Armoured Division, while Gatehouse covered his rear by holding firm at Gabr Saleh. He then flew back to Eighth Army Headquarters at Fort Maddalena where he was shown RAF reports of a general trend in German road movement westwards from Bardia and Gambut towards Tobruk. This was interpreted as a possible German withdrawal out of the frontier area caused by the arrival of strong British forces at Sidi Rezegh. 21st Panzer's attacks at Gabr Saleh seemed to be consistent with this interpretation as they could have been ordered to cover this withdrawal. British morale, which might have been slightly shaken by the tank losses at Bir-el-Gubi and Gabr Saleh, remained high; and confidence reigned at Cunningham's headquarters. Suggestions were made that it might be the right moment to order Scobie to break out from Tobruk. The British were succumbing to wishful thinking. The movements seen by the RAF were the assembly of Rommel's assault force for his attack on Tobruk. Withdrawal was the last thing any of the German commanders were considering.

Crüwell was the man of decision that night on the German side. He won Rommel's tacit agreement to the concentration of the Afrika Korps and its use in the piecemeal destruction of the widely scattered British armoured forces which lay spread out in a great arc from Sidi Rezegh to Sidi Omar. Mistakenly he chose to deal with a major British armoured force reported to be operating around Sidi Azeiz, and ordered 15th Panzer Division to attack eastwards along the Trigh Capuzzo while 21st Panzer Division disengaged at Gabr Saleh and moved eastwards as well to head off this

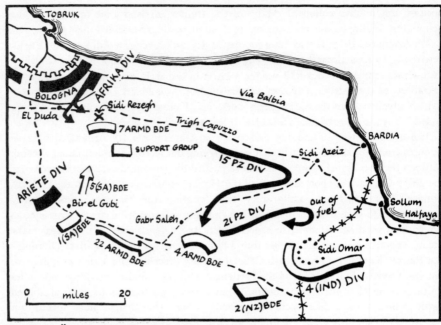

Fig 23 Crüwell's 'Wild Goose Chase' of 20th November

mythical British force if it tried to escape southwards around Sidi Omar. Crüwell's
target did not exist. The reports on which he was acting had been caused by
Gatehouse's reconnaissance towards Bardia.

During 20 November the British concentration at Sidi Rezegh went ahead and
Scobie started preparations to break out from Tobruk. 21st Panzer Division brushed
with 4th Armoured Brigade Group before disengaging for its move to Sidi Azeiz. 21st
Panzer's withdrawal increased the British impression of German discomfiture. They
were discomfited but not in the way the British thought. 21st Panzer Division ran out
of fuel and ammunition before it reached Sidi Azeiz; and 15th Panzer Division found
no British forces on the Trigh Capuzzo. Crüwell began to realise that the British axis
of advance must lie along the Trigh-el-Abd to Sidi Rezegh, and that the force at Gabr
Saleh was an isolated detachment covering their communications – an attractive
target for the Afrika Korps. Rommel, with uncharacteristic caution, directed Crüwell
to wait until he could concentrate his two panzer divisions before attacking.
Nevertheless, Crüwell decided to make contact with Gatehouse's 4th Armoured
Brigade Group by advancing on Gabr Saleh with 15th Panzer Division while 21st
Panzer Division refuelled.

The British radio intercept units were working well. Crüwell's orders were decoded
revealing the threat to Gabr Saleh. The British build up at Sidi Rezegh was prudently
slowed, and 22nd Armoured Brigade ordered to move as quickly as possible from
Bir-el-Gubi to support 4th Armoured Brigade Group. It looked as if the decisive
armoured battle would be fought after all at Gabr Saleh with the British still at a

tactical disadvantage. Two British armoured brigades with minimal artillery and infantry support would be opposing two complete panzer divisions well supported by their own artillery and infantry.

15th Panzer Division engaged 4th Armoured Brigade Group late in the day before 22nd Armoured Brigade had arrived. The RAF tried to provide bomber support but could not distinguish friend from foe and had to return without dropping their bombs. Before darkness intervened 26 more 'Honeys' had been destroyed; but Gatehouse was left with no feeling of defeat. Following normal British practice 4th Armoured Brigade Group withdrew, as it had done the night before and would do many times before 'Crusader' was over, to leaguer south of the battlefield, leaving 15th Panzer Division in possession and able to recover their own tank casualties and blow up any British tanks they found. After refuelling 21st Panzer set off on a night march to join its colleague.

At the other side of the battlefield the Support Group joined 7th Armoured Brigade at Sidi Rezegh bringing welcome artillery reinforcement and some badly needed infantry. The German 'Afrika' Division infantry had been working its way along the escarpment ridges which overlooked the airfield from north and south. The Sidi Rezegh ridge to the north was marked by the prominent white tomb of a moslem prophet with Trig Point 175 as its main tactical feature; and the escarpment to the south is best referred to as the Point 178 ridge after its most dominant feature.* By establishing themselves on these ridges the Germans were able to make life on the airfield very uncomfortable by directing the fire of Böttcher's artillery on to the British positions. 5th South African Brigade, which Gott had summoned northwards from Bir-el-Gubi, had halted for the night well short of Sidi Rezegh as Brink was not prepared to allow it to push on in the dark. Until it arrived Gott would have the equivalent of only one infantry battalion at Sidi Rezegh, but he was satisfied that the arrival of the South Africans next day would enable him to clear the Sidi Rezegh ridge and seize Ed Duda ready to link up with Scobie's breakout from Tobruk.

On the third day of the battle the British expected to be fighting two battles which they were confident of winning; the first at Sidi Rezegh where they hoped to link up with Scobie as he broke out from Tobruk; and the second at Gabr Saleh where 4th and 22nd Armoured Brigades were to deploy before dawn to battle positions ready to deal with the Afrika Korps and to pursue it relentlessly when it withdrew. The British felt very much on top, bottling the Germans up within the triangle Tobruk – Bardia – Sidi Omar.

On the German side Rommel's obsession with his assault on Tobruk was suddenly changed to an equally obstinate desire to prevent the British relieving the fortress. This change seems to have been caused by a British broadcast from Cairo which announced that a major British offensive had opened to drive the Axis forces out of Africa. Instead of allowing Crüwell to attack 4th and 22nd Armoured Brigades at Gabr Saleh next day, he ordered him to return with all speed to help destroy what appeared to be the largest and most dangerous British force threatening Tobruk from

* See Map V, page 136, and Fig 25, page 164.

Sidi Rezegh. Rommel's signal to Crüwell ran:

> The situation in this whole theatre is very critical. In addition to the strong enemy
> force south-east of Tobruk, 500 or 600 enemy vehicles are moving through the
> desert towards Benghazi from the south-east. On 21 November, Afrika Korps
> must begin moving in good time and follow the enemy tanks which have advanced
> towards Tobruk. Objective the airfield at Sidi Rezegh.
>
> (Quoted by *South African Official History,* page 173).

Reid's Oasis force was having some effect on German minds, but Cunningham's hope
of a decisive armoured battle began to fade with Rommel's decision to disengage from
Gabr Saleh and to make his primary objective the defence of his investment of
Tobruk.

Operations at the Sidi Rezegh side of the battlefield started on 21 November as the
British planned them. Scobie's men had lifted mines, cleared wire and bridged the
anti-tank ditch on the Tobruk perimeter during the night. His well-rehearsed break
out started around 8 am and met more German resistance than had been hoped.
Some of the Italian positions had been taken over by troops of the 'Afrika' Division
preparatory to Rommel's assault on Tobruk and gave a better account of themselves
than the Italian Bologna Division whose sector was attacked. By midday Scobie had
secured a 4,000 yard deep foothold in the Axis perimeter positions and had taken
1,000 prisoners, half of whom were German. News then reached him that 7th
Armoured Division would not be able to co-operate and so he cancelled the second
phase of his operation, which was to have been an advance to Ed Duda, realising that
he would be dangerously exposed unless he could join hands with Gott within 24
hours.

Sidi Rezegh and Gabr Saleh were too far apart for Gott to control both battles so
he made Brigadier Davy, commander of 7th Armoured Brigade, responsible for Sidi
Rezegh while he controlled 4th and 22nd Armoured Brigades at Gabr Saleh. He
instructed Davy to clear the Sidi Rezegh ridge with the infantry of Jock Campbell's
Support Group, preparatory to attacking Ed Duda and linking up with Scobie when
5th South African Brigade arrived. Soon after dawn Campbell's infantry, which
consisted of little more than 400 men from three companies of the King's Royal Rifle
Corps and one company of the Rifle Brigade, attacked and captured their objectives,
rounding up about twice their own number of German and Italian prisoners. The 6th
Royal Tank Regiment of Davy's brigade then drove over the escarpment past the
Prophet's tomb, aiming for Ed Duda. Rommel had been watching these events
personally and ordered von Wechmar's 3rd Reconnassance unit to intervene with a
detachment of 88 mm guns. As the British tanks crossed the Trigh Capuzzo they were
decimated by these guns and by guns of the Böttcher Artillery Group in positions
around Belhamed. 6th Royal Tank Regiment lost three-quarters of its tanks before it
managed to scramble back over the escarpment. Reports then began to reach Davy
that a large column of 150 tanks and 250 vehicles was approaching Sidi Rezegh from
the south-east. Handing over command of the operations on the northern side of the
airfield to Jock Campbell, he advanced with his two remaining tank regiments (7th

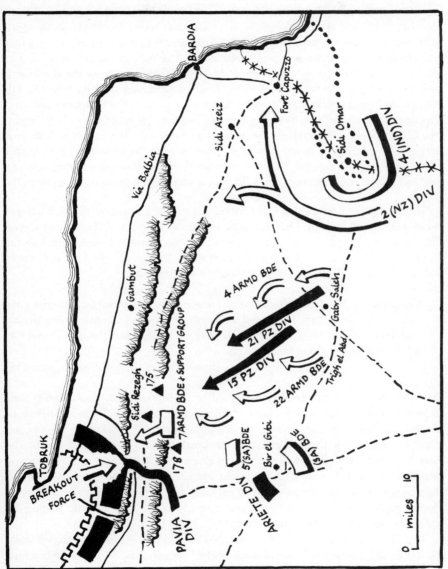

Fig 24 The Afrika Korps' disengagement from Gabr Saleh: 21st November

Hussars and 2nd Royal Tank Regiment) to meet this threat, little knowing that he was about to engage the whole Afrika Korps.

At Gabr Saleh the Germans had moved off early heading for Sidi Rezegh. 21st Panzer had disengaged without difficulty; but 15th Panzer was not so successful and started rather later. Both panzer divisions moved fast covered by rearguards equipped with 50mm and 88mm guns. 4th and 22nd Armoured Brigades pursued thinking that the Germans were withdrawing to avoid battle. The pursuit did not go well. The British attempts to cut in and engage the German columns from the flank were frustrated by the anti-tank gun screens. Both brigades ran short of fuel: the 4th Armoured Brigade because its 'Honeys' had such a short radius of action; and 22nd Armoured Brigade because its supply echelons had failed to reach it during the night. At Eighth Army Headquarters the impression grew that the Germans had been beaten and were trying to avoid being crushed between the three British Armoured Brigades – 7th in their path, 22nd on their southern flank and 4th in their rear. So perhaps they should have been if the British tactics and equipment had been up to the task.

It was at about 8.20 am that Davy sighted the leading elements of the Afrika Korps south-east of Sidi Rezegh. Unfortunately, the supply echelons of the Support Group had been leaguering in the area between his two armoured regiments and the approaching Germans. There was an immediate 'Sauve qui peut' as the supply vehicles scattered. Brigadier Davy described what happened:

> The enemy tanks were accompanied and in some cases preceded by anti-tank guns which were not at first recognised as hostile as they were mingled with British trucks and lorries. Some of these guns were very boldly handled and scored hits before their presence had been noticed . . .
>
> (*South African Official History*; page 178)

The 7th Hussars were virtually destroyed by 21st Panzer Division, losing their colonel and all but ten of their tanks which managed to join 4th Armoured Brigade Group later that day. 2nd Royal Tank Regiment attempted to maintain itself on the flank of 15th Panzer Division but could not break through its anti-tank screen. The way was open for Crüwell to force his way down the Sidi Rezegh 'tank-run', across Sidi Rezegh airfield, and on to Belhamed whither Rommel had summoned him to help deal with Scobie's break-out. The only obstacle in his way was the artillery of Jock Campbell's Support Group and one company of the Rifle Brigade holding the extreme eastern end of the Point 178 ridge.

The Germans reconnoitred the British positions at Sidi Rezegh thoroughly while their panzer battalions refuelled and replenished ammunition. A heavy dive-bombing attack heralded the resumption of the battle which became a duel between German tanks and British field and anti-tank gunners. The close co-operation of the German Pz III and Pz IV tanks soon demonstrated the soundness of German tank philosophy. The high explosive shell fired from the armoured protection of the Pz IV could kill the exposed British gun crews at a range of several thousand yards whereas the

25-pounder field gun could not stop the Pz IV at a much greater range than 600 yards. British tank regiments used the tactical formula of speed, manoeuvre and courage to close with their opponents; and the British gunners, for their part, sought salvation in cool disciplined shooting. When darkness fell Crüwell was still a long way from breaking through to Belhamed. Pressure of 22nd and 4th Armoured Brigades in his rear helped to delay him, and both panzer divisions ran short of ammunition, effectively bringing to an end the first of many hard Anglo-German slogging matches which were to be a continuing feature of 'Crusader'.

Neither of the opposing Army Commanders knew what had really happened during the day as they began to plan their operations for 22 November. Cunningham's picture was distorted by consistently over-optimistic reports from British units of the numbers of Axis tanks destroyed. Earlier in the day he he had concluded it was safe to start Goodwin-Austen's XIII Corps moving in the frontier area as the two panzer divisions had withdrawn from Gabr Saleh having, as he thought, 'taken a knock'. Freyberg's New Zealanders began their march round Sidi Omar towards the rear of Bardia, and Messervy's 4th Indian Division started its final moves to attack the Savona Division from the rear. By the time night fell Cunningham concluded that tank losses had been so heavy on both sides that the battle was bound to degenerate into an infantry contest. He decided to concentrate the bulk of Eighth Army around the 'beaten' Axis forces at Sidi Rezegh. He ordered XIII Corps to send Freyberg's New Zealanders with 'I' tank support westwards along the Trigh Capuzzo to intervene at Sidi Rezegh from the east, and ordered XXX corps to move the 5th South African Brigade to Sidi Rezegh from the south. He was somewhat querulous about the South African's failure to reach battle that day. He did not know that Gott had held them back when the armoured battle started and that they still lay 15 miles south of Sidi Rezegh.

On the German side there was little elation. Crüwell had failed to break through to Belhamed and did feel that he was surrounded by greatly superior British forces. On his own initiative he decided to withdraw the Afrika Korps north-eastwards to his administrative base at Gambut to refit and reorganise. Rommel knew little of Crüwell's battle of Sidi Rezegh and was only concerned with preventing Scobie and Gott linking hands at Ed Duda, thus raising the siege of Tobruk. He ordered Crüwell to bring the Afrika Korps round to Belhamed by a circuitous route and take charge of operations to keep the two British thrusts apart. His orders reached Crüwell too late. Crüwell had to let 15th Panzer Division continue its march to Gambut, but managed to change 21st Panzer Division's destination to Belhamed.

The two opposing commanders had one thing in common. They both appreciated that the first phase of 'Crusader' was over. Neither had achieved his initial objective. Cunningham had sought but had not found his decisive armoured battle. He was now bringing the whole weight of Eighth Army to bear on Sidi Rezegh to raise the siege of Tobruk. Rommel had been forced to abandon his cherished assault on Tobruk, and was acting defensively while he re-concentrated his Panzer Group, 'Afrika', to prevent Tobruk's relief. The course of future events would depend upon which commander took the most purposeful action in the next 24 hours.

ROMMEL'S REACTION The End of the First Battle of Sidi Rezegh and the Battle of Totensonntag
(22 and 23 November)

The morning of 22 November was strangely quiet. Some tanks from both panzer divisions were still standed on the plateau out of fuel and were chased over the escarpment by the two armoured brigades as they finished refuelling. The 5th South African Brigade arrived about midday and attacked the Point 178 Ridge on the southern escarpment at about 3 pm but were driven off by units of the 'Afrika' Division with over a hundred casualties. The brigade then took up defensive positions about two miles south-east of Point 178 with its supply vehicles stretching southwards away from trouble. The sound of heavy gun fire to the north instilled further caution into South African intentions and into movement northwards of the rest of the division from Bir-el-Gubi.

Crüwell and the Afrika Korps would have liked to use 22 November for rest, repair of tanks and reorganisation. Von Ravenstein established his infantry on Belhamed and allowed his panzer regiment to start its much needed tank maintenance. Crüwell, with the balance of the Afrika Korps at Gambut, did the same. At about midday Rommel decided that he must do more to interfere with the British build-up at Sidi Rezegh and drive their relieving force away from Tobruk. He drove to von Ravenstein's HQ at Belhamed and supervised the preparation of an attack by 21st Panzer Division which was to be launched to clear the British off the Sidi Rezegh

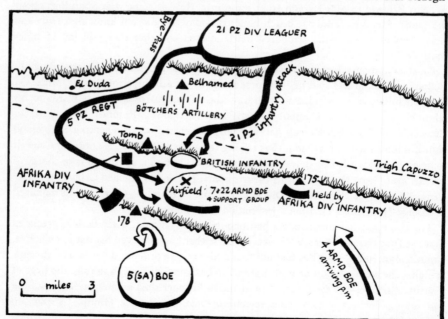

Fig 25 The Battle of Sidi Rezegh: 22nd November 1941

ridge and airfield during the afternoon. 21st Panzer's infantry would attack due south, supported by Böttcher's artillery, to wrest the Sidi Rezegh ridge from Campbell's Support Group, while its panzer regiment made a long detour via the 'Tobruk By-pass' to attack the airfield itself from the west, advancing up the 'tank run' with the sun behind it and in the eyes of the British gunners.

Tired though the Germans may have been, Rommel's presence created a renewed surge of energy. The violence of their attack came as a surprise to the British who believed another armoured clash to be unlikely and were in the midst of planning the final relief of Tobruk next day. The attack by the German infantry from the north was detected just in time and dispersed by artillery fire. 5th Panzer Regiment's onslaught up the 'tank run' from the west fell with no warning upon the remnants of 7th Armoured Brigade and the Support Group artillery. The long 50mm towed anti-tank guns with the panzer battalions destroyed the rest of 7th Armoured Brigade's few remaining tanks, leaving the British gunners to fight it out once more with the German tanks. 22nd Armoured Brigade tried to intervene. An eye witness described the scene:

> Suddenly through the gun positions came our tanks. The exhausted gunners relaxed . . . the relief was very short. With horrified eyes they saw tank after tank go up in flames, hopelessly outgunned. Sadly but with grim determination the gunners took up the battle again . . .
>
> (*Ibid:* page 211).

But it was not the enemy tanks that were the culprits. As usual it was the accompanying anti-tank guns. The tanks played a different role. The British infantry on the ridge by the Prophet's white tomb who had held the German infantry attack from the north, now found themselves with tanks in their rear. Unable to fight their way out, they were forced to surrender. 4th Armoured Brigade Group, which had been chasing the last stragglers of 15th Panzer Division over the escarpment away to the east was summoned back to Sidi Rezegh but could not reach the battlefield until late in the afternoon. By then most of the airfield had been over-run and a thick pall of dust and smoke hung over the valley making it difficult to find out what was happening. Brigadier 'Jock' Campbell, who won the VC for his outstanding leadership that day, did his best to head 4th Armoured Brigade's tanks into action. Gatehouse's intervention, although abortive in that his regiments were confused and disorganised in the mêlée, did have some effect. 5th Panzer Regiment was equally uncertain what was happening and had run out of tank ammunition. The appearance of the 'Honeys' tipped the scales and enabled Gott to withdraw the whole force from the airfield as the daylight faded, re-establishing his front facing north a few miles south of the Point 178 ridge, alongside the 5th South African Brigade. His tank strength had fallen to 144 – 10 with 7th, 34 with 22nd and 100 with 4th Armoured Brigades. The Germans reported 173 fit tanks with their two panzer divisions. Unknown to Eighth Army Headquarters the Germans had won numerical as well as qualitative superiority of tanks and anti-tank guns.

The loss of Sidi Rezegh was not the last disaster to befall Gott's division that day.

15th Panzer, answering a call for help from von Ravenstein, was approaching Sidi Rezegh along the top of the southern escarpment from the east after dark when it blundered into and over-ran the headquarter's leaguer of 4th Armoured Brigade Group. Gatehouse was away at Gott's headquarters at the time and so escaped capture. The strongest British armoured brigade had been effectively decapitated and was unable to operate coherently next day.

Elsewhere 22 November had been a better day for the British. Scobie had consolidated his salient outside the Tobruk perimeter. The New Zealanders took Fort Capuzzo, cut the via Balbia behind Bardia, severing the town's water supply as well as its links to the west. Freyberg started to advance westwards with his 4th and 6th NZ Brigades, supported by the 1st Army Tank Brigade, along the via Balbia and the Trigh Capuzzo respectively. 5th NZ Brigade stayed at Sidi Azeiz watching Bardia. 4th Indian Division had broken into the back of the Savona Division's defences at Sidi Omar and had occupied part of its defended positions.

At Eighth Army Headquarters confidence reigned. There was not much news from Sidi Rezegh, so Cunningham continued his policy of bringing up his infantry to take over the battle from the armour – the New Zealanders from the east and the rest of Brink's South Africans from Bir el Gubi where they were being replaced by 22nd Guards Brigade. Cunningham had no reason to believe that he had lost the initiative or that the balance of tank strength was no longer in his favour. A very different atmosphere, however, reigned at Panzer Group Headquarters. Rommel's obsession with Tobruk faded as he watched von Ravenstein's division storm Sidi Rezegh. Reports from his radio intercept unit and from Crüwell's headquarters, together with his intelligence staff's assessments and his own instincts, told him that the British must be in a bad way. At 10.30 pm he issued his orders for next day: 'On 23 November, Panzergruppe will force a decision in the area south-east of Tobruk by means of a concentric attack by D.A.K. and parts of Corps Gambarra . . .' (*Ibid:* page 233).

Rommel's intention was that the Afrika Korps should attack southwards from Sidi Rezegh while the Italian Mobile Corps advanced upon the rear of 7th Armoured Division and 5th South African Brigade from Bir el Gubi. These orders reached Crüwell, as usual, too late to be implemented. Crüwell had, however, anticipated Rommel's ideas and had given orders with the same aim but using a different method. He knew that von Ravenstein's infantry were exhausted, but Neumann-Silkow's 15th Panzer Division was fresh and ideally positioned to sweep round the British rear to join Gambarra for a combined attack northwards, driving the British into the waiting hands of von Ravenstein in the Sidi Rezegh area. It was a bold and imaginative plan. Von Ravenstein would reinforce the 'Afrika' Division's infantry on the Point 178 ridge with his own infantry, and would send his 5th Panzer Regiment, suitably reinforced with anti-tank and field artillery, to join Neumann-Silkow in his southward sweep. Crüwell hoped to meet Gambarra with the Ariete Armoured Division due south of the British position.

Sunday 23 November was the Lutheran 'All Saints Day' or Sunday of the Dead – 'Tottensonntag'. It could not have been more appropriately named in 1941. It was a

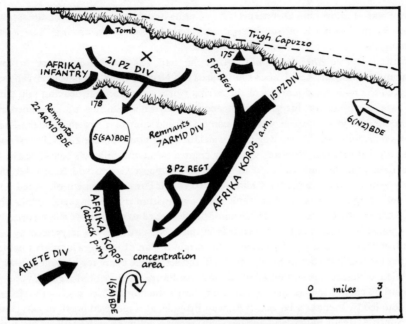

Fig 26   The Battle of Tottensonntag: 23rd November 1941

day of brilliant manoeuvre in true Teutonic style by Crüwell's Afrika Korps, culminating in the loss of the 5th South African Brigade, and heavy casualties on both sides. Though the Germans won the battle they probably lost 'Crusader' on Tottensonntag.

When dawn came on that fateful Sunday, Gott's division shook itself out from its night leaguers to form a front facing north while awaiting the New Zealanders' arrival from the east; and Brink's 1st South African Division started its advance northwards to join the 5th South African Brigade which formed the core of Gott's defensive position. Brigadier Armstrong, commanding 5th South African Brigade, had disposed his three battalions on the northern, eastern and western sides of a two-mile-wide box. His men had made some attempt to dig in, but the rock close under the surface of the desert made this difficult. The southern side of the box was undefended, and covered with a sprawl of logistic vehicles covering many square miles of desert, stretching southwards as far as the eye could see. A mile west of the South African box lay 22nd Armoured Brigade with about 30 operational tanks; and two miles eastward lay the Support Group which Gott had reinforced with the Scots Guards from 22nd Guards Brigade. Just south of the Support Group were the remnants of 7th Armoured Brigade with about 10 tanks and the Support Group's supply echelons. The remnants of 4th Armoured Brigade were trying to reorganise in the desert east of the main position with a total of about 100 tanks. Although the general direction of the front was northwards the fog of war was so dense that most units were peering in all directions not knowing what was happening. Operational control was at a low ebb. Disorganisation of units and disruption of communications caused by the lost battle of Sidi Rezegh could only be put right with time. There was to be no time.

Crüwell started the day badly. After he had left his headquarters to join Neumann-Silkow for the advance southwards 6th New Zealand Brigade over-ran and captured the main headquarters of the Afrika Korps near Gambut, leaving him with the bare essentials of his tactical headquarters. This did not upset immediate operations but was to affect German command and control a few days later. Then von Ravenstein's 5th Panzer Regiment was late in arriving, forcing Crüwell to set off with only 15th Panzer Division. Quite by chance Neumann-Silkow's course to Bir el Gubi took him through the area in which the Support Group and South African supply vehicles were leaguered. Chaos reigned as 8th Panzer Regiment ploughed into this soft target. Every British tank and gun within range engaged while the unprotected vehicles scattered. Neumann-Silkow wished to profit from the surprise he had created by attacking north-westards at once, but Crüwell was impressed by the British reaction and decided to keep to his original plan of joining Gambarra before starting his battle. Neuman-Silkow drew off and set course again for his junction with the Ariete which occurred soon after midday. 5th Panzer Regiment also caught up.

Again by chance the German advance cut across the bows of Brink's South African Division, led by Pienaar's 1st South African Brigade, as it motored north to join Gott. The South Africans halted and engaged the German columns with artillery but were too uncertain about what was happening to do more because they were without tank support. Thus, when Crüwell halted and turned north to organise his attack on Gott, he was sandwiched between the 5th South African and 22nd Armoured Brigades in the north, who were fully alert and taking measures to protect their rear, and 1st South African Division in the south, which was probing into the German assembly area. He was also plagued by small columns from 4th Armoured Brigade Group and the Support Group which Gott had improvised and which were biting at him from the east. As his units refuelled and re-armed ready for the assault they suffered considerable losses from British artillery fire. The two sides were too closely interlocked for effective intervention by the RAF.

It was not until 3 pm that Crüwell managed to assemble his long lines of tanks, guns and vehicles into the parade ground formation which he intended to use for what can best be described as a 'charge en masse'. The two panzer regiments and their supporting guns were to advance side by side, each in two waves with the infantry embussed close behind them. No-one was to halt or debuss unless further mounted advance proved impossible.The whole formation would roll forward until it came out the far side of the British position and joined hands with von Ravenstein's infantry which would be diverting British attention by attacking from the north. The Ariete would advance in the same way on the Afrika Korps' western flank.

Crüwell's charge succeeded but at great cost. The 5th South African Brigade was not easily over-run. The cohesion of the German formation was soon broken up and the fight developed into innumerable individual actions in which the South Africans fought back but suffered from the general British deficiency of a good anti-tank gun and felt deserted by the British armour. 22nd Armoured Brigade did what it could to help with its few remaining tanks. The fight went on until dark, but by then the South African position had disintegrated. Their Official History paints the final scene:

> The early winter's night descended rapidly, and all that was left of the 5th South African Brigade on the field of battle consisted of little groups of bewildered and disconsolate prisoners who huddled together neglected while German staff officers wrestled to discover what had happened . . .

> *(South African History; page 165)*

Crüwell had won a pyrrhic victory. Only 2,300 out of the origninal 5,700 South Africans engaged found their way back to the South African Division, which thereafter showed understandable reluctance to engage during the rest of 'Crusader'. Crüwell's panzer regiments, however, lost 72 out of the 162 tanks which went into action, and his losses in commanding officers and other key personnel was higher than any army could stand for long. In the 8th Panzer Regiment, for instance, 11 officers were killed and 8 wounded including its two panzer battalion commanders and five out of the six company commanders. The Afrika Korps had only 90 tanks left. Tottensonntag had lived up to its name on both sides.

Elsewhere on the battlefield the British were more successful. 4th NZ Brigade captured Gambut and 6th NZ Brigade, after fortuitously over-running Crüwell's headquarters went on to drive part of the 'Afrika' Division's infantry off Point 175 on the Sidi Rezegh ridge. 6th NZ Brigade's success was not easily bought and cost over 400 casualties. One of its battalions pushing on south-westwards managed to contact the South Africans before they were over-whelmed but was forced to withdraw back to Point 175 after dark. And away to the south, Oasis Force was approaching Jalo in spite of Luftwaffe attempts to stop it.

Tottensonntag had not been decisive at tactical level, but it was at Command level. That evening Rommel and Cunningham took the decisions which ultimately lost and won 'Crusader'. Rommel over-estimated the losses he had inflicted on the British and under-estimated their staying power. He appears to have become personally embroiled in the New Zealand attack on Point 175 and had only the sketchiest outline of Crüwell's battle when he got back to his headquarters at El Adem that night where he was in high spirits talking about a great victory. He has left no account of his thinking that night because the 'Crusader' period in his papers was written by Colonel Bayerlein at a later date. Four impulses seem to have led to the extraordinary decision he took that night. If it had succeeded, it would have been hailed as a stroke of genius; as it did not, it must be considered an error of judgment. The impulses perhaps were: the obvious need to pursue his supposedly beaten enemy; the pressing requirement to relieve his frontier garrisons before they were starved out; the fleeting attractions of raiding the British lines of communication to enjoy their discomfiture and use their supplies; and the ebullient desire to strike a spectacularly decisive blow to capture the headlines of the world press. His orders recorded in the Afrika Korps War Diary setting out the minutes of a conference with Crüwell said:

The Corps Commander (Crüwell) expressed the opinion that the beaten enemy should be pursued, the area between the Trigh el Abd and the Trigh Capuzzo cleared, and the vast amount of captured material salvaged.

The Commander in Chief (Rommel) issued orders as follows: Attack on Sidi Omar to relieve Sollum front. Infantry Regiment 155 and 'Afrika' Regiment (both of 'Afrika' Division) to salvage captured equipment and motorise themselves from it.

The divisions were to complete reorganisation of their formations and move off by 10.00 hours. 21st Panzer Division would lead the advance, accompanied by Afrika Korps Headquarters. 15th Panzer Divison in the rear.

(Quoted by the *South African Official History*: page 283)

At Fort Maddalena the truth about British tank losses began to dawn on the Eighth Army staff during 23 November. Cunningham consulted Godwin-Austen about the situation early on Tottensonntag morning and concluded that XIII Corps should take over all operations for the relief of Tobruk, using the Trigh Capuzzo as its centre line, so that XXX Corps could be withdrawn to a line running southwards from the New Zealand position on Point 175 to Bir el Gubi on which it could reorganise and absorb tank reinforcements. When Cunningham returned to his headquarters, he was given over-pessimistic reports which showed that he had about 44 tanks left in the three armoured brigades with which to oppose an estimated 120 on the German side. He repeated Beresford-Pierse's action during the similar crisis during 'Battleaxe' by asking Auchinleck to fly up to Maddalena at once to review the situation in case it was necessary to call off the battle and fall back to the frontier to defend Egypt. Auchinleck had been forewarned by senior staff officers that things were going wrong, and reached Eighth Army HQ by air that afternoon accompanied by Tedder. He was luckier than Wavell during 'Battleaxe' in that he arrived before any irreversible decision had been taken by Cunningham.

Auchinleck reviewed the situation carefully with the Eighth Army staff and decided to continue the offensive with no thought of retirement. Credit for this decision must go to Brigadier Galloway, the senior General Staff officer in Eighth Army HQ, who refused to reflect the depression of his commander – a difficult thing to do under such circumstances. The two British Corps commanders were consulted and were equally adamant that the offensive should go on. Even Norrie, who had borne the brunt of the fighting in the first five days, and had suffered the heaviest losses, saw no need to give up. Before returning to Cairo, Auchinleck gave Cunningham a written directive, paragraph 4 of which contained the executive order:

(i) Continue to attack the enemy relentlessly using all your resources even to the last tank.

(ii) Your main immediate object will be, as always, to destroy the enemy tank forces.

(iii) Your ultimate object remains the conquest of Cyrenaica and then advance on Tripoli.

(J.Connell; page 365)

Cunningham, his morale reinforced by his C-in-C, issued fresh instructions to his Corps commanders that night. He confirmed that Godwin-Austen would make the main effort with his XIII Corps while Norrie reorganised XXX Corps in the desert south-east of Sidi Rezegh.

ROMMEL'S ERROR OF JUDGMENT His dash for the Frontier wire and the Battle of the Trigh Capuzzo
(24 to 28 November)

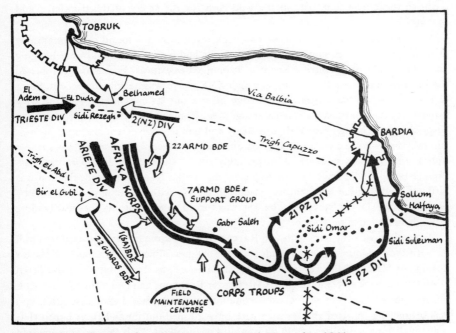

Fig 27 Rommel's Dash for the Wire: 24th to 26th November 1941

'Rommel's Dash for the Wire', or the 'Matruh Stakes' as it was more cynically referred to by the British who took part in it, started badly. The panzer divisions, not unnaturally, had some difficulty in getting ready by 10 am as Rommel demanded. It is surprising after their exertions in the last five days that they were able to move at all. Losing patience with the Afrika Korps Headquarters, he placed himself at the head of von Ravenstein's 21st Panzer Division, which was ready first, and set off impetuously at 10.40 am with Gause for the Trigh el Abd which he reached near Gabr Saleh.

Lieutenant-Colonel Westphal was left in charge of Panzer Group HQ while the three most senior German generals in Africa – Rommel, Gause and Crüwell – went charging off down the British lines of communication to win 'Crusader' and possibly start the invasion of Egypt. Rommel was full of confidence, telling Westphal before he left that the whole thing would be over in 24 to 36 hours at the most. Gause and Crüwell were not so sure.

Rommel's course led him between the South Africans and 7th Armoured Division. The former's artillery pounded his columns from the south and 7th Armoured Brigade and the Support Group columns had at him from the north. The 4th and 22nd Armoured Brigades were too far away to the north and were left unmolested to continue their reorganisation. There was nothing to block Rommel's progress down the Trigh el Abd along which most of the British headquarters and logistic units of XXX Corps were situated. The panic which ensued amongst the rear echelons did no credit to those who took part in the wild rush for the safety of the frontier – and Matruh!

When the dust settled and order had been restored it was found that remarkably little damage had been done. The fighting units had not panicked and were hanging on to the flanks of the Afrika Korps as it plunged eastwards. Fortunately, it missed the Field Maintenance Centres upon which XXX Corps was heavily dependent. Some German units did pass through the edge of one but its camouflage and the wide dispersal of its dumps saved it from recognition. Rommel had astonished rather than surprised the fighting units of Eighth Army and had to some extent alienated his own subordinates who knew that their tired units and worn equipment could not succeed unless the British collapsed. Surprisingly the RAF had a disappointing day. Fighter-bombers did their best to help slow the Afrika Korps, but identification was difficult, and the day bombers stayed on call all day without being given targets by Eighth Army. Towards evening the RAF was forced to evacuate its forward landing grounds by Rommel's advance.

Rommel crossed the wire with von Ravenstein's headquarters at 4 pm and sent him on with the headquarters escort unit to Sidi Suleiman almost within reach of Bach's position at Halfaya. The rest of 21st Panzer Division was strung out along the Trigh el Abd as far back as Gabr Saleh. Its 5th Panzer Regiment had had a rough time. At 6 pm it reported itself out of fuel and ammunition, having had heavy casualties, and was leaguering short of the frontier with only 20 medium tanks left. It hoped that some of its tank casualties would limp in during the night. 15th Panzer Division had had an easier time in its wake. It had also shed tanks and was down to 40 when it stopped for the night 12 miles short of the frontier. The Ariete was left a long way behind.

For the next two days German operations degenerated into a series of uncoordinated actions inspired by Rommel's presence at a particular spot rather than any master plan. Conditions were chaotic. Heavy losses of command vehicles when the New Zealanders had over-run the Afrika Korps HQ at Gambut, and the wide dispersion of subordinate headquarters made control well nigh impossible for the German staffs. Units were receiving orders from three sources – Rommel, Crüwell and Westphal away back at El Adem. Signals were being relayed by whichever headquarter's radio happened to pick up the messages. In the process they were corrupted and often misunderstood. To make matters worse Rommel was working on false information which made most of his plans impracticable. He thought

Godwin-Austen's XIII Corps was still disposed around the Axis frontier garrisons, and he planned to drive the British into the Axis frontier mine-fields. He did not know that 4th Indian Division was occupying most of the westerly half of his defences; nor had he any radio communications with the remnants of the Savona Division. By the end of the second day – 26 November – both panzer divisions withdrew on their own initiative into Bardia to refuel and replenish their ammunition. They had achieved nothing decisive and had sustained debilitating losses which they could ill afford, particularly from RAF attacks. The British airmen had had two good days. So critical was the British situation believed to be that risks of wrong identification were accepted enabling the RAF to develop the full potential of its fighter-bombers and day bombers. The Afrika Korps had a very uncomfortable time.

Meanwhile, the New Zealanders were making steady progress along the Trigh Capuzzo and were able to launch a series of night attacks, using stealth and the bayonet. 4th NZ Brigade took Belhamed from the 'Afrika' Division, but 6th NZ Brigade were not so successful in ousting the Bersaglieri from the Sidi Rezegh ridge and so could not exploit to Ed Duda. Scobie, nevertheless, decided to seize Ed Duda himself with 70th Division and succeeded. During the night 26–27 November, while the two panzer divisions were refuelling in Bardia, the New Zealanders attacked again and joined hands with the Tobruk garrison. The Italian commanders of the investing force started to show signs of growing nervousness. Colonel Westphal at El Adem also began to fear the worst and sent a stream of messages asking for the Afrika Korps' return to Tobruk. Late on 26 November Rommel accepted the urgency

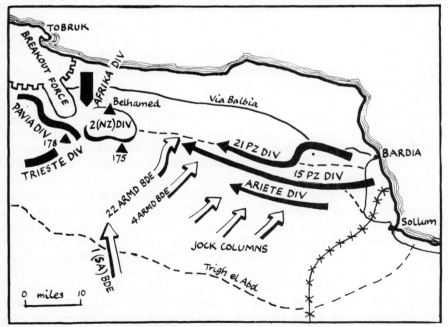

Fig 28 The Battle of the Trigh Capuzzo: 27th to 28th November 1941

of Westphal's appeals and ordered von Ravenstein to hurry back along the via Balbia to Tobruk next day, while Neumann-Silkow continued operations in the frontier area. Rommel was not yet prepared to abandon his frontier garrisons to their fate.

The two panzer divisions were delayed leaving Bardia on 27 November by poor traffic control which led to a number of irritating traffic jams. The German staffs were too tired to think. Neumann-Silkow set off south-westwards and over-ran the Headquarters of the 5th New Zealand Brigade which happened to lie in his path. Von Ravenstein headed west along the via Balbia intent on attacking Freyberg's rear. Rommel seems to have been influenced by more signals from Westphal and ordered Neumann-Silkow to give up his southward sweep and to head back to Tobruk along the Trigh Capuzzo. Rommel was unaware that there had been a change of Army Commander on the British side.

Auchinleck had returned to Cairo on 25 November overtly satisfied with Cunningham's handling of the battle and his own decision to fight on, but an inner disquiet remained. He discussed the situation in depth with Tedder, Oliver Lyttelton, Minister of State, and Arthur Smith, his Chief of Staff; and then decided in the calmer atmosphere of Cairo to replace Cunningham in whom he had lost confidence. A replacement was not easy to find. Norrie and Godwin-Austen were too deeply embroiled in the battle and, in any case, had not shown enough aptitude in higher command to attract favourable attention. There was only one man sufficiently in Auchinleck's mind and with a strong enough personality and that was his Deputy Chief of General Staff, Major-General Neil Ritchie, who was a comparatively junior major-general but had done most of the 'Crusader' planning at GHQ level. Rightly or wrongly Auchinleck chose to send him up to Fort Maddalena to take over Eighth Army temporarily. He had again misjudged him man though this was not to be revealed for another seven months. Cunningham accepted his dismissal with dignity and retired exhausted to hospital in Cairo, later returning to England to hold several important posts with distinction thereafter.

During the two days in which Rommel had been floundering around the frontier area, the British had been recovering in a remarkable way. Units had been re-united; equipment had been recovered; and replacement tanks and crews had been arriving. Their earlier optimism had also returned. Reports of the two panzer divisional columns moving westwards from Bardia were misinterpreted again – this time with more justification – as a German retreat. Godwin-Austen spent the day consolidating his hold on the Ed Duda – Belhamed – Sidi Rezegh area and managed to clear all except the southern escarpment around Point 178 which was held tenaciously by a mixed German and Italian force under General Böttcher. HQ XIII Corps was drawn into the New Zealand position and Freyberg pushed out rear guards to the east to block the approach of the Afrika Korps. Two things, however, worried Godwin-Austen: shortage of artillery ammunition which was down to 50 rounds per gun; and the German hold on the Point 178 ridge which enabled German gunners to bring effective fire to bear on the New Zealand positions. Godwin-Austen asked Eighth Army for 1st South African Brigade to clear the Point 178 ridge and for a strongly escorted convoy of ammunition, fuel and food. Both requests were accepted;

the latter was accomplished with a 200-vehicle convoy brilliantly led by XXX Corps' Chief Engineer, Brigadier Clifton – appropriately a New Zealander; but the former was not because the South Africans were still suffering over-caution instilled into them by the loss of their 5th Brigade. Norrie failed to induce Pienaar to commit his brigade under the conditions of uncertainty prevailing at Sidi Rezegh.

Norrie's reading of the battle was much the same as Godwin-Austen's. His armoured brigades spent the 26th salvaging tanks on the field of Totensonntag which Crüwell would have liked to have done instead of dashing off with Rommel to the frontier. 7th Armoured Brigade was withdrawn to the Delta to refit. 4th and 22nd Armoured Brigades mustered about 120 tanks between them in the desert south of the Trigh Capuzzo; and the artillery of the Support Group and infantry of 22nd Guards Brigade combined to form a number of strong 'Jock' columns to clear the desert of stray Axis units which were out of fuel or had lost their way. This dispersion of artillery was understandable in the circumstances but led once more to the British tanks operating without adequate all arms support.

About midday on 27 November heavy columns of German tanks, guns and transport were reported moving westwards on the Trigh Capuzzo within striking distance of 4th and 22nd Armoured Brigades. Gott ordered the 22nd to attack and stop the head of the column, while the 4th Armoured Brigade attacked its flank from the escarpment south of the Trigh. Neither brigade was entirely successful as they both lacked artillery with which to deal with the German anti-tank gun screen, which was thrown out to protect their columns.

22nd Armoured Brigade succeeded in checking 15th Panzer's advance, and 4th Armoured Brigade's attacks from the flank worried Crüwell who ordered 21st Panzer to cross from the via Balbia to the Trigh Capuzzo to help. For a time the Germans felt that there was a grave danger of final defeat. Darkness intervened in time to save them. True to their usual practice the two British armoured brigades pulled back into the desert to replenish and leaguer for the night. There was no Support Group to take over the block on the Trigh Capuzzo for the night with infantry and anti-tank guns. The British congratulated themselves on the damage their armour had done to the Germans that day; and on the 'good show' put up by the 'Jock' columns which harassed the Italian Ariete as it struggled westwards in the wake of the Germans. The Germans, though the losers by day, became the victors by night. Neumann-Silkow did not halt at dusk. As the British attacks slackened he accelerated his advance along the Trigh and then pushed on in the darkness up onto the the desert plateau to leaguer only a short distance away from the New Zealand position on Point 175. Next morning, when the British armour rolled forward to continue the battle, they found the Germans strongly posted behind a screen of anti-tank guns on the top of the southern escarpment. Lacking artillery, which was well to the east in the 'Jock' columns harassing retiring Italians, the British armoured brigades could not intervene effectively all day.

The 28 November became a day of consolidation. Both sides were back in much the same position as they had been a week earlier at the beginning of the First Battle of Sidi Rezegh. Rommel was trying to re-unite his Panzer Group to prevent the British finally destroying his investment of Tobruk; and Ritchie, instead of Cunningham, was building up the British concentration at Sidi Rezegh under the impression that the Germans were trying to withdraw. Rommel had no intention whatsoever of withdrawing and was determined to regain the upper hand. His target, this time, was Freyberg's New Zealand Division. He still had the tactical superiority to beat his British opponents; his ability to survive logistically was less certain.

VICTORY BY LOGISTICS The Second Battle of Sidi Rezegh and the Battle of Bir el Gubi
(29 November to 2 December)

Rommel and Crüwell had different ideas, as usual, of how to deal with the New Zealanders on Belhamed and the Sidi Rezegh Ridge. Rommel believed the attack should come from the north, using the 'Afrika' Division, which had just been renamed 90th Light Division, as the principal assault formation. His instructions arrived too late for Crüwell to change his plan which was a boldly conceived encirclement that should never have been allowed to succeed. 90th Light Division would exert pressure on the northern side of the New Zealand position; 21st Panzer Division would attack the eastern face; the Ariete would take Point 175 on the Sidi Rezegh Ridge; and General Böttcher would hold the Point 178 Ridge with his *ad hoc* infantry group to provide a firm base for 15th Panzer Division which was to be

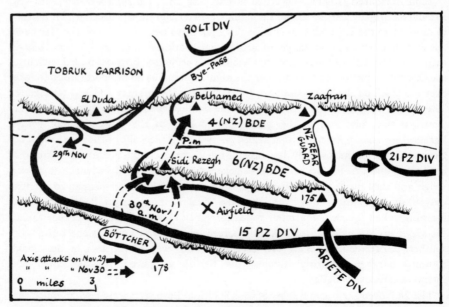

Fig 29 The Second Battle of Sidi Rezegh: 29th November to 1st December 1941

Crüwell's main striking force. Neumann-Silkow was to slip down the Sidi Rezegh 'tank run' covered by Böttcher to attack Scobie's men on Ed Duda, cutting off the New Zealanders from Tobruk and completing their encirclement to the west.

Crüwell had another bad start. Von Ravenstein lost his way and was captured in his staff car by the New Zealanders. His division had become the weaker of the two panzer divisions. The loss of its commander sapped its energy still further. 15th Panzer ran the gauntlet of New Zealand fire from the Sidi Rezegh Ridge as it made its way to its attacking position west of Ed Duda. Its attack on Ed Duda went in on schedule, but was stoutly resisted by the Tobruk garrison who threw the Germans off the foothold which they gained during their attack with a spirited night counter-attack using their 'I' tanks every effectively in the dark.

Surprisingly the Ariete had the most successful day. It succeeded in over-running Point 175 because the New Zealanders mistook it for the 1st South African Brigade whom they were expecting to arrive from the south at any moment. Before they realised their mistake the Italian tanks and infantry had entered and made the position untenable. Regrettably Pienaar's South Africans were still many miles away advancing hesitantly, shepherded by the two British armoured brigades, with the shadow of Tottensonntag falling heavily across their path.

Memories of Tottensonntag had the opposite effect on Rommel, who arrived at Crüwell's HQ early on Sunday 30 November — a week after the Afrika Korps victory. Crüwell was not optimistic about the future. 15th Panzer Division was shaken by its failure to hold its lodgement at Ed Duda; 21st Panzer, now under Böttcher's command, was suffering a steady attrition from the fire of the Support Group columns on the escarpment; and the Ariete had had a rough time fending off British counter-attacks from the south. Rommel, always at his best in adversity, was not prepared to give up and ordered Crüwell to smash his way into the New Zealand position using 15th Panzer Division, supported by all Axis artillery within range. Neumann-Silkow was to take the Sidi Rezegh Tomb area held by 6th NZ Brigade and then cross the Trigh Capuzzo to sieze Belhamed from 4th NZ Brigade, thus effectively severing Freyberg's links with Tobruk.

The British, by contrast, continued to act as though it was only a matter of time before the Germans were brought to the point of collapse by a policy of 'harassing and destroying the enemy as opportunity occurred'. They hoped to squeeze the Afrika Korps within their encirclement; but Rommel squeezed the New Zealanders within his own encirclement and cut into them as well. He provided the dynamic leadership which no-one on the British side seemed able to match.

Crüwell launched two brutally successful attacks on successive days and achieved Rommel's aim. In the afternoon of 29 November he over-ran 6th NZ Brigade on the Sidi Rezegh Ridge. It was a costly victory because the New Zealanders gave as good as they got but were forced off their positions by the weight of artillery brought to bear and the efficiency of the German attack. At dawn next morning he repeated the process at Belhamed, driving 4th NZ Brigade off the feature and finally cutting the British links with Tobruk.

The British woke up to Freyberg's danger too late. The South Africans did

eventually arrive on the evening of 30 November but failed to unseat the Ariete from
Point 175 which was their objective. Early on 1 December 4th Armoured Brigade
Group broke through to the rear of 15th Panzer Division on the Sidi Rezegh Airfield
and enabled the remnants of 6th NZ Brigade to disengage withdraw
north-westwards to Zaafran to which 4th NZ Brigade withdrew as well from
Belhamed. By 2 pm Freyberg was forced to conclude that he must give way and
extricate his division. Norrie, who was the only senior commander whom he could
contact, agreed and that night the New Zealanders evaded 21st Panzer Division and
withdrew to the frontier. Rommel had achieved his immediate aim of eliminating the
New Zealand Division. His encirclement had not been tight enough to prevent their
escape, but he had resealed Tobruk with Godwin-Austen's XIII Corps HQ inside it,
leaving him free to deal with Norrie. On paper it was a brilliant success, but like
Tottensonntag, it was another pyrrhic victory. A German officer, speaking to New
Zealand Brigadier Kippenberger, who was a prisoner at the time, summed up the
situation: 'We have taken Belhamed and our eastern and western groups have joined
hands . . . But it is no use . . . We have lost the battle . . . our losses are too heavy . . .'
(Kippenberger; page 103).

The Afrika Korps leaguered for the second time as victors on the battlefield of Sidi
Rezegh. Norrie's XXX Corps fell back into the desert to begin the tiresome business of
re-grouping, absorbing reinforcements and making new plans for the relief of
Tobruk. Rommel was satisfied with the tactical outcome. Tobruk had been
re-invested, but his conscience worried him about the frontier garrisons which he had
left behind. Strategic factors, however, were beginning to play an increasingly
important part in the struggle. Rommel discussed the progress of the battle with
Bastico and on 2 December sent a frank appreciation back to both Axis High
Commands, pointing out that, unless the flow of fuel, ammunition and replacement
equipment could be speeded up, the British would win the battle of attrition which
they had begun to wage in default of tactical skill. He admitted losing beyond repair:
142 tanks, 25 armoured cars and 42 anti-tank guns as well as 4,000 men, including a
divisional commander and 16 commanding officers. He still held his vital positions
around Tobruk and on the frontier. He had done immense damage to his opponents
and reduced their material superiority. His next step would be to re-open the via
Balbia to replenish his frontier garrisons and restore the situation to the
pre-'Crusader' position.

On the British side, Auchinleck was equally confident. He arrived at Eighth Army
HQ on 1 December and stayed with Ritchie for the next 10 days to be on hand if major
decisions were needed. Unlike Bastico, he could reinforce Ritchie and was doing so.
4th Indian Division and 5th NZ Brigade were relieved of their tasks on the frontier by
the 2nd South African Division, which had arrived from East Africa, and were sent
forward to join Norrie's XXX Corps which was sorting itself out in the desert east of
Bir el Gubi. Elements of the 1st Armoured Division had reached Egypt from England
and several units withdrawn from Syria were also being sent forward to Norrie.
Ritchie planned to use the reinforcements to reopen 'Crusader' as soon as possible
with two major thrusts. Norrie would attack north-westwards from Bir el Gubi and

18.   The billowing black smoke of a tank engagement.

19.   German tanks near Sidi Omar during the "Crusader" offensive.

20. British Crusader tanks moving into action.

21. A British anti-tank gun in action amongst burnt-out vehicles.

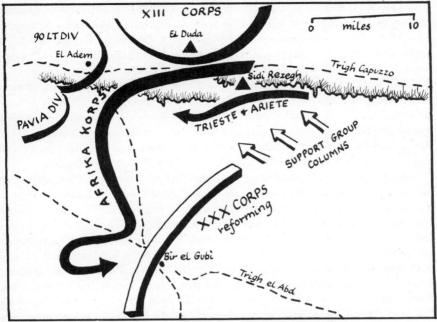

Fig 30 Operations around Bir El Gubi: 4th to 7th December 1941

Godwin-Austen would would break out south-westwards from Scobie's salient in the Tobruk perimeter, both aiming for El Adem to cut off all Axis troops east of Tobruk. Norrie told Ritchie that he hoped to be ready by 3 December then found his preparations did not go as quickly as he anticipated. Before a new date was fixed Rommel started his operations to relieve his frontier garrisons in a way which appeared to the British like another 'dash for the wire'.

On 2 December Rommel despatched two columns without tank support eastwards along the via Balbia and Trigh Capuzzo. 5th NZ Brigade ambushed and almost annihilated the former; and 4th Indian Division stopped the latter. Next day 21st Panzer supported an abortive assault on Ed Duda, while Crüwell set off with the 15th Panzer and Ariete for the frontier, hoping to rescue Major Bach's men and any of the Savona Division still holding out. By evening Ritchie and Rommel had taken equal and opposite decisions. Ritchie postponed Norrie's offensive *sine die* until he could be sure that he would not find Rommel floundering around in his rear areas; and Rommel recalled Crüwell to deal with the growing threat to his communications presented by Norrie's XXX Corps at Bir el Gubi. After a careful reassessment of his resources Rommel had concluded he could no longer maintain the investment of Tobruk and concentrate enough strength to defeat Eighth Army in mobile operations. He decided to attack southwards with Afrika Korps to keep Norrie quiet while disengaging all troops on the eastern perimeter of Tobruk to form a new line running southwards through El Adem to Bir Hacheim. His frontier garrisons would have to await another favourable turn of events.

Rommel's offensive was characterised by British caution and unusual German muddle, and was fought out against a background of growing crisis in the Axis camp. The Afrika Korps advanced southwards late on 5 December, leaving the Ariete temporarily at Sidi Rezegh to cover the disengagement of the infantry east of Tobruk. Crüwell made contact with the British north of Bir el Gubi and decided to carry out a complex night move to bring the Afrika Korps round to the west on a more favourable axis for attack. Little went right. The two panzer divisions became entangled and failed to sort themselves out until late on 6 December. They were heavily bombed and shelled. Neumann-Silkow was mortally wounded, and when the Afrika Korps advanced in the late afternoon after being joined by the Ariete, it failed to achieve anything decisive and leaguered short of Bir El Gubi, its objective.

While Crüwell was attempting to find some way of defeating XXX Corps which seemed to be growing like a many-headed hydra in the desert, Rommel was arguing with an uncongenial visitor. Colonel Montezemolo, emissary of the Italian Supreme Command, had arrived with the answer to his demands for replacement equipment and ammunition. He made it plain to Rommel that there could be no large imports before the end of December and then only if Kesselring's 2nd German Air Force re-established a measure of naval security in the Central Mediterranean. Rommel discussed this news with Bastico and decided that unless Crüwell could do something decisive in the next few days he would have to fall back to the Gazala position which had been prepared as a result of von Paulus' earlier visit. On 7 December he went forward to Crüwell's headquarters north-west of Bir el Gubi to assess the situation. Crüwell was adamant that nothing more could be done. The order to withdraw was given. That evening Bastico summoned Rommel to his headquarters to discuss future policy. Rommel refused to go on the grounds that he could not leave his operational headquarters. Bastico came to see him next morning. The meeting was stormy. The *Italian Official History* records:

> Bastico intervened excitedly to defend his officers against Rommel's charges of inefficiency . . . and Rommel like an overbearing and uncouth boar yelled that he had struggled for three weeks to win the victory and had now decided to take his divisions to Tripoli and have himself interned in Tunisia . . .
>
> (Quoted by *South African Official History*; page 468).

Rommel had been beaten, not by British military prowess but by lack of Axis logistic support, and he knew it. Withdrawal back to the Tripolitanian frontier was essential to embarrass the British with the long and uneconomic lines of communication which had been sapping Axis strength. He accepted Bastico's argument that the Gazala Line should be held as long as possible to allow for the evacuation of logistic installations from Cyrenaica and to give the Italian infantry divisions enough time to withdraw.

In the Axis evacuation of Cyrenaica, which started with Crüwell's disengagement at Bir el Gubi on 8 December, professional competence did not desert the Germans; nor did their newly acquired operational caution forsake the British. Rommel's rear guards fought methodical delaying actions which thwarted British efforts to create conditions for a second Beda Fomm. Rommel held the Gazala line from 12–17

December and slipped away at a time and pace of his own choosing. The British Oasis force had taken Jalo on 25 November, but it was not strong enough to worry Rommel unduly and was kept in check by the Luftwaffe. The British pursuit of Rommel's main body was co-ordinated by Godwin-Austen's XIII Corps. Norrie's XXX Corps, which was destined to move to Auchinleck's northern front, was given the task of reducing the German frontier garrisons on the way. Try as he would, Godwin-Austen failed to cut off any sizeable body of Axis troops in his pursuit. He reached the line Derna – Mechili on 18 December; Barce – Msus on 21 December; and entered Benghazi on Christmas Day just too late to stop the off-loading of a German supply ship which had run the British blockade with 22 new tanks on board. Another ship had reached Tripoli with a further 23, though two others had been lost on passage carrying 23 and 22 tanks respectively. Crüwell absorbed these welcome reinforcements quickly and gave battle on the 28 and 30 December to cover the final Axis withdrawal to El Agheila. He and his men had lost none of their old cunning. 22nd Armoured Brigade recoiled with the loss of 37 tanks in the first encounter and 23 in the second out of the 90 which had managed to reach Western Cyrenaica. Rommel started his final withdrawal on New Year's Day and his rear guards fell back over the frontier in a sandstorm on 6 January. Back on the Egyptian frontier, Norrie reduced the Axis garrisons one by one, using 2nd South African Division. Bardia surrendered on 2 January, and the remnants of Savona Division and Major Bach's garrison at Halfaya gave up on 17 January. 'Crusader' was over. The crude profit and loss account expressed in casualties on both sides speaks for itself:

The British lost 17,700 out of a force of 118,000 (15%)

The Germans lost 14,600 out of a force of 65,000 ($22\frac{1}{2}$%)
The Italians lost 23,700 out of a force of 54,000 (43%)

Total Axis losses 38,300 out of a force of 119,000 (32%)

When Rommel reached El Agheila, the two sides fell apart to rest and reorganise. The British were much wiser for their experience and, because they had won in the end, were just as confident of their own abilities. It was the first time that they had met the Germans on anything like equal terms. They had taken longer to clear Cyrenaica than they had hoped, and they had used up more resources than they could afford if they were to capture Tripoli without a long pause for a logistic build up. Whether they could have gone on was never put to the test. On the fateful night of 7–8 December, when Crüwell had started the Afrika Korps withdrawal from Bir el Gubi, the Japanese attacked Pearl Harbour. Resources which should have flowed into Egypt to support 'Acrobat' had to be diverted eastwards to stem the Japanese tide of conquest in the Far East. Tripoli faded as an objective as it had done the year before when the Greek crisis had intervened to stop O'Connor. History was shortly to repeat itself in a most disconcerting way as far as the British were concerned.

Looking back at 'Crusader', the most important thing the British had gained was not the great bulge of Cyrenaica with its airfields from which the RAF could help strangle Rommel's supply lines, important though these were. They had brought battle experience at every level of their rapidly expanding Army. The old desert hands had been lost in the deluge of newcomers most of whom had been called up and trained in England since war was declared. Cunningham's Eighth Army needed and gained the battle sense it had lacked on 15 November. Commanders and staffs had a clearer idea of the scale of the desert battlefield – what could and what could not be done with forces of a given size. Many myths and legends had been destroyed by the practical clash of battle. And amongst the junior officers, NCOs and men, the battle-hardening process had been going on apace turning enthusiastic amateurs into cynically cautious professionals. On the ground, the inadequacy of the British anti-tank guns was generally acknowledged, and in the air the superiority of the German Me 109F fighters was also proven. The urgency of shipping the new British 6-pounder anti-tank gun and flying the latest Spitfire to the Middle East needed no further emphasis in Whitehall where an awareness of erroneous tactical doctrine was acknowledged in training pamphlets issued to troops in England. The first paragraph on the pamphlet based on 'Crusader' said:

> The role of our armoured forces is usually the destruction of those of the enemy. This task can only be accomplished by direct attack if our tanks are better 'gunned' than the enemy's, or if we are greatly superior in numbers. At the moment we are neither better 'gunned', nor is it possible to be certain of adequate numerical superiority. It is only by obtaining the maximum support from the artillery for our armour that we can carry out this role.
>
> (*Notes from the Theatres of War*: No 2 Part 1, para 1, page 4).

It was easy enough to pontificate about tactical theory in the cool corridors of Cairo and Whitehall. It was quite another matter to win general acceptance of the necessary changes in tactics amongst hard-pressed units in the field. Armies are living organisms in which each man makes up his own mind about the best mode of operating, especially as his own life is at stake. Co-operation of all arms was easy to preach but day-to-day problems, shortage of time for unit training let alone combined training, and lack of insistence on all arms training by senior commanders led to the lessons of 'Crusader' being learnt only partially and less than partially applied. 'All Arms' training has to be enforced and carefully programmed from above. It will not grow on its own.

Co-operation in one respect was greatly improved. The Army and RAF were again on speaking terms. Even the New Zealanders acknowledged the greater freedom from Luftwaffe attack and the improved close support which the RAF had provided. Freyberg wrote generously to Tedder: 'I want to tell you I think your fellows are simply magnificent, and all my men say the same.' (Tedder: page 199).

But the greatest weakness on the British side lay in their inability to bring all their forces to bear to achieve their primary aim. They lacked sufficient 'big men' who had the battle instincts, organisational ability and will-power to overcome the British habit of command by consensus and treating all orders as an agenda for discussion. Such methods work in small wars where individual initiative is an immense asset, but they do not work when handling large complex forces of the type being created to drive the Axis forces out of Africa. Rommel made many mistakes, but there was no doubt who was master and who it was that appeared at the decisive moment. So far the British had not found their own type of Rommel. O'Connor might have been the man, but he was a prisoner. Cunningham, Ritchie, Godwin-Austen, Norrie, Gott, Messervy, Freyberg, Brink, all fell short in one respect or another.

Rommel summed up British generalship when talking to a captured British officer: 'What difference does it make if you have two tanks to my one, when you spread them out and let me smash them in detail? You presented me with three armoured brigades in succession.' (Chester Wilmot, *Tobruk*; page 300).

10

The Shadow of Pearl Harbour and the Spur of Malta

(January to May 1942)

'Every American Division which crossed the Atlantic gave us freedom to send one of our British divisions out of the country to the Middle East, or of course − and this was always in my mind − to North Africa. Though few, if any saw it in this light, this was in fact the first step towards an Allied descent on Morocco, Algeria or Tunis, on which my heart was set.'

(Churchill: Vol III, page 606).

New Year's Day 1942 saw Godwin-Austen's XIII Corps taking up its positions at the gateway to Tripolitania as O'Connor's XIII Corps had done just under a year before. It is tempting to talk about history repeating itself, but it is dangerous to draw too many parallels between O'Connor's and Godwin-Austen's positions because there were as many differences as there were superficial similarities. It is true that both failed to advance on Tripoli: O'Connor because his forces were diverted to Greece; and Godwin-Austen because similar diversions were needed to the Far East. Both were also brought to a standstill by difficulties of supply, and were driven back ignominiously by revitalised Axis forces at the very moment when they thought they were reasonably secure. Here the similarities end and the differences begin.

The first and most important difference stemmed from Ritchie's failure to inflict a Beda Fomm on Rommel's Panzer Group. Churchill appreciated what had happened quicker than the men on the spot. Cabling Auchinleck, he said:

I fear this means that the bulk of seven-and-a-half enemy divisions have got away round the corner . . . I note also that nine merchant ships of 10,000 tons are reported to have reached Tripoli safely . . . How does all this affect 'Acrobat'? I am sure you and your armies did all in human power, but we must face facts as they are . . .'

(J. Connell: page 423).

Auchinleck retorted on 12 January:

I do not think it can be said that the bulk of the enemy divisions have evaded us. It is true that he still speaks in terms of divisions but they are divisions only in name. For instance, we know that the strength of the 90th German Light Division originally 9,000, now 3,500 and has only one field gun left . . .

I am convinced we should press forward with 'Acrobat' for many reasons, not the least in order that Germany may continue to be attacked on two fronts, Russia and Libya ... We have very full and interesting records of daily conversations between our prisoners, Generals von Ravenstein and Schmidt. Making allowances for mental depression natural in prisoners of war, there is no doubt that German morale is beginning to feel the strain not only in Libya but in Germany. They speak freely also of great losses in recent fighting, mismanagement and disorganisation, and above all of dissatisfaction with Rommel's leadership. I am convinced the enemy is hard pressed more than we dared think perhaps.

(Ibid: pages 423–424).

But Churchill was to prove nearer the mark than Auchinleck. The effects of no Beda Fomm and the mauling of 22nd Armoured Brigade by Crüwell before he withdrew over the Tripolitanian frontier were factors which should not have been so under-estimated by the British High Command in the Middle East.

The second important difference was one of logistic scale. War damage had reduced the capacity of ports, roads and tracks since O'Connor's day, whereas the forces they would be required to support for an advance on Tripoli had quadrupled. Eighth Army's logistic staff estimated that XIII Corps would need 1,400 tons of supplies a day to sustain its advance. Barely 1,000 tons a day was reaching the forward area from Tobruk and from the railhead back on the Egyptian frontier. The port of Benghazi was little help. Ships sunk by RAF bombing blocked the quays and the navigable channels; German mines added to the hazards of navigation; and the harbour moles had been breached and could no longer provide a safe anchorage in the westerly and north-westerly gales which blew for weeks on end after the port fell into British hands for the second time. Eighth Army's logistic staff concluded reluctantly that XIII Corps would not be able to attack Rommel at El Agheila before mid-February. The British are often accused of logistic over-insurance, but in this case they were not guilty. XIII Corps had to remain on hard rations – bully-beef and biscuits – which they had been eating since the start of 'Crusader'!

The third important difference was political. In 1941 only the British and Greek Governments were involved in the strategic misjudgments which stopped O'Connor at El Agheila. At the beginning of 1942 the British had ceased to be the sole arbiters of Allied Mediterranean strategy. Churchill had crossed the Atlantic in the *Duke of York* to attend the 'Arcadia' Conference in Washington: the first of the series of Anglo-American strategic conferences which were to shape Allied policy for the rest of the Second World War. In preparation for 'Arcadia' Churchill drafted one of his masterly appreciations which did so much to invigorate Allied thinking during the most sombre moments of the war. In it he sketched how he saw the Allies turning from their strategic defensive to an all-out offensive to crush, first, Nazi Germany and then Japan. North Africa was to play a major part in the change from defensive to offensive operations because it was the only theatre in which Anglo-American armies could start the progressive erosion of Hitler's military power. The British Chiefs of Staff wrote a rather negative supporting paper, stressing all the practical difficulties but offering no valid alternative. The Americans were less well prepared and gave way in front of Churchill's advocacy for the traditional British peripheral strategy, although their instincts told them that they were accepting policies alien to their nature. Some American policy makers advocated standing back until the US had developed sufficient power to adopt her own strategy. They feared, quite rightly, that she would be foist with operations within the overall strategy more in keeping with her current than her potential strength. Her forces would be used up piecemeal, nibbling at Nazi outposts rather than concentrated in a decisive attack on the central source of German power. Roosevelt did not support this view and inclined, against the advice of his Chiefs of Staff, towards Churchill's policy which would bring American forces into action against Germany at the earliest date, albeit far from the heart of Germany. Operation 'Gymnast' – the British plan for the occupation of French North Africa – became 'Super Gymnast', incorporating British and American Task Forces, the former under General Sir Harold Alexander and the latter under General 'Vinegar Joe' Stilwell, and each comprising three divisions.

Churchill's concept for 'Super Gymnast' depended upon four elements: the readiness of trained troops; the availability of enough shipping; a favourable swing in French political opinion; and continued British success in Libya, represented by the execution of 'Acrobat'. General Alexander's force had been earmarked, trained and equipped some months earlier for alternative landings in Norway, the Azores or North Africa. There were more doubts about Stilwell's force. Part of the Marine Division, earmarked to lead his assault on the North African beaches, was in Iceland and would have to be replaced before it could be used; there was a shortage of specialist troops at that time in the US Army; and the fitness for battle of the new US Divisions, which were just mobilizing, was questionable. Availability of shipping was also critical, but enough could just be found by stopping all other military movements across the Atlantic while 'Super Gymnast' was in progress. On the political front, there were grave doubts about French opinion. It might just be possible to engineer an invitation from the Vichy authorities in Algiers for Allied intervention in French North Africa, but this depended upon the success of 'Acrobat'. Unfortunately Eighth Army's chances of advancing on Tripoli were already fading and with them went Churchill's first plan for the invasion of French North Africa.

Rommel's supply position had been improving far faster than the British realised. The gradual transfer of Kesselring's 2nd German Air Force from Russia, and the arrival of German submarines had begun to weaken the British naval hold on the Central Mediterranean. U-boats sank the famous carrier *Ark Royal* and the battleship *Barham*; and Italian frogmen penetrated Alexandria harbour damaging the battleships *Queen Elizabeth* and *Valiant* with underwater charges. Cunningham could not be reinforced with heavy ships because all available British warships had been diverted eastwards to oppose the Japanese in the Indian Ocean.

The build up of the 2nd German Air Force took effect more slowly. Bombing of Malta increased steadily, and by the end of January had reached the peak intensity of April 1941 when 700 tons of bombs had been dropped. These Luftwaffe attacks together with British naval losses made running convoys to Malta progressively more hazardous; and conversely, destroying Axis shipping much more difficult. On 5

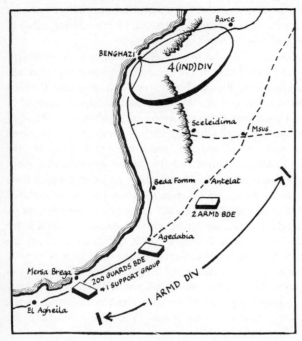

Fig 31　British Dispositions
in First Half of
January 1942

January, a large Axis convoy reached Tripoli bringing 54 new tanks and a large consignment of fuel for Rommel.

Rommel's Intelligence Staff were not slow to appreciate the change of circumstances. Von Mellenthin advised Rommel on 12 January that he would have temporary tactical superiority in western Cyrenaica if he struck straight away. Rommel queried his staff's calculations of available transport:

> When satisfied on this point he threw all his energy into the preparations, but insisted that the attack would not succeed unless it came as a complete surprise to the enemy. He decided not to report his intentions to the Italian Commando Superiore in North Africa (Bastico), nor did he inform the German High Command . . . The Commander of the Afrika Korps was not informed of the plan until the 16 January . . . Zero hour was to be 1830 on the 21st.
>
> (Von Mellenthin: pages 84-85).

Logistics rather than tactics dictated British deployment. There was only a weak covering force forward at Mersa Brega consisting of 200th Guards Brigade (the old 22nd re-numbered to avoid confusion with 22nd Armoured Brigade) and 1st Armoured Division's Support Group. The Guards Brigade had two instead of three battalions, one of which was split up into 'Jock' columns with batteries of the attached field artillery regiment, and the other was held back at Agedabia because there was no artillery to support it. The 1st Support Group had just arrived in the desert and was finding driving conditions in the 'hummocky' desert conditions around Mersa Brega very difficult for its inexperienced drivers and for its vehicles, many of which had not been properly modified for desert operations.

The nearest support for the screen on the frontier was the rest of 1st Armoured Division back at Antelat, and 4th Indian Division much further north in the Benghazi area. 1st Armoured Division, like Gambier-Parry's 2nd Armoured Division the previous year, was a division only in name. It had arrived in Egypt piecemeal in the wake of 'Crusader' to find itself sent across the desert, as partially trained as 2nd Armoured Division had been, to take over screening Eighth Army while it prepared for 'Acrobat'. It should have contained the 2nd and 22nd Armoured Brigades, but the latter had been withdrawn to refit at Tobruk and the former was down to about two-thirds of its tank strength due to mechanical breakdowns on its long march from Egypt. To add a final touch to 1st Armoured Division's inadequacy, its commander, Major-General Lumsden, was wounded in an air raid and replaced temporarily by Major-General Messervy. Logistic shortages forced Godwin-Austen to deploy 4th Indian Division in much the same way as Morshead's 9th Australian Division the year before with one brigade in Benghazi, one at Barce and the third back at Tobruk where 7th Armoured Division and 22nd Armoured Brigade were refitting. Thus Rommel's opponents were again disposed like Neame's force in 1941 with similarly inexperienced and partially trained troops spread out over Western Cyrenaica on the assumption that the Afrika Korps would be in no fit state to counter-attack for many weeks.

Churchill and the British Chiefs of Staff were trying, as usual, to do too much with too little, accepting new commitments thrust upon them by the Japanese without reducing their ambitions in the Middle East. They had hoped to solve their Far Eastern problems by diverting troops and aircraft destined for the Middle East while avoiding taking away any which were already there. The 18th British and the 17th Indian Divisions, which were earmarked for the Middle East, went instead to Singapore and Burma. This policy was soon found to be inadequate, and Auchinleck was asked to despatch any troops not needed for 'Acrobat'. 7th Armoured Brigade left for Burma with two regiments of 'Honeys'. The 6th and 7th Australian Divisions followed, destined for New Guinea, and Auchinleck began to fear that he would lose the 9th Australian Division and 2nd New Zealand Division as well. Fortunately Roosevelt intervened with an offer of US Divisions for Australasian Defence. He also made enough US shipping available to move up to three divisions-worth of troops from the United Kingdom to the Middle or Far east – whichever the British Chiefs of Staff considered the most important at the time. The threat to Auchinleck's northern front had not diminished with the winter stalemate in Russia. The Germans might well choose to use the winter months for an attack on Turkey and a spring advance through Anatolia into Syria and Iraq. If that happened before fresh troops could reach the Middle East in the US shipping, Eighth Army might well be forced to withdraw to the Egyptian frontier to provide troops for the defence of Syria and Iraq.

On 19 January Ritchie and General Holmes, the Commander British Troops in Egypt, were given a precautionary directive. In this Auchinleck stated his aim: 'My present intention is to continue the offensive in Libya and the objective remains Tripoli.' He then went on to lay down his policy for withdrawal from Cyrenaica if this proved unavoidable, prescribing three major defensive positions on which Eighth Army would stand to defend Egypt: first, the frontier area, using the old Axis defences between Sidi Omar and Halfaya; then Mersa Matruh; and finally the El Alamein bottleneck between the Mediterranean coast and the Qattara Depression. Two paragraphs are important in the light of subsequent events:

  (6) It is not my intention to try to hold permanently Tobruk or any other locality west of the frontier . . .
 (10) Work will be continued in accordance with the original plans on the El Alamein position as opportunity offers until it is completed.

                                        (Despatches: Appendix 6, pages 377-8).

The Cs-in-C Middle East were jointly resolved not to risk another siege of Tobruk which had been so expensive in naval and air effort. Though this directive was sent back to London, it seems to have remained at staff level as a precautionary plan to meet a hypothetical situation. It is doubtful if Churchill ever saw it. As far as he was concerned Ritchie was getting ready to launch 'Acrobat', 'D' Day for which was to be about 15 February. This was too late. Rommel struck first.

   Rommel's second raid into Cyrenaica, for that was all he intended, started at dawn on 21 January and ended a fortnight later with almost but not quite as great a defeat

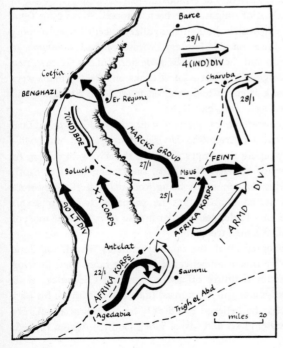

Fig 32 Rommel's Second Raid into Cyrenaica:
21st January to
6th February 1942

for British arms as his first raid in 1941 which had carried him to Tobruk and on to the Egyptian frontier. He advanced in three columns: Crüwell's Afrika Korps through the desert 20 miles south of the via Balbia; Gambarra's XX Italian Mobile Corps in the centre; and an *ad hoc* group of mobile infantry battalions and artillery from 21st Panzer and 90th Light Divisions under Colonel Marcks on and to the north of the via Balbia. Rommel accompanied the Marcks' Group.

During the first day the British withdrew as planned through a series of pre-planned delaying positions. The 1st Support Group lost more than it should have done through dive-bombing attacks, vehicles bogging in soft sand, and general inexperience. To be fair, 15th Panzer Division, leading the Afrika Korps, did little better but was able to recover its stranded vehicles later. That night General Messervy decided to move 2nd Armoured Brigade forward ready to assail the German's open flank, if Rommel broke through the 200th Guards Brigade and 1st Support Group screen.

On the second day the Marcks' Group set off early and did succeed in bursting through the Guards' column holding the via Balbia, reaching Agedabia by 11 am. Rommel's radio intercept service gave him a clear indication that the whole of 1st Armoured Division was still to his south-east and might be encircled if he moved quickly. He ordered Crüwell and Gambara to follow the Marcks' Group through Agedabia and then to turn eastwards to Saunnu to set a line of stops across 1st Armoured Division's withdrawal routes to Msus which he knew was its main supply base. His plan nearly succeeded. Had it not been for a serious lapse in the Afrika Korps' staff work and the practical difficulty of establishing an encircling stop-line in desert country, 1st Armoured Division might have been trapped. A running fight developed during the 23 January in which the British artillery excelled itself helping to extricate the division. By dawn on 24 January, Messervy had managed to concentrate 1st Armoured Division and the Guards Brigade north of the German net, covering Msus. 2nd Armoured Brigade had lost a lot of tanks but the Germans were not unscathed; 15th Panzer's tank strength had dropped from 80 to 61 tanks; and 21st Panzer, which had only 20 to start with, had 10 left.

As far as the Germans were concerned, 24 January was a wasted day at tactical level. Rommel did not realise that 1st Armoured Division had escaped and so his divisions spent a fruitless day sweeping the empty desert in the wrong direction. At strategic level there was a flurry of activity. Cavallero, the Italian Chief of Staff, arrived from Rome with Kesselring determined to bring Rommel to heel. They were singularly ineffective. Rommel stated bluntly that he proposed to continue his offensive as long as he could and only Hitler could order him to stop, because most of the fighting was being done by his German troops.

On the British side, Ritchie adopted much the same attitude as Wavell had done the year before. He did not believe that Rommel could be doing more than fighting for elbow room in which to mount a future offensive to regain Cyrenaica. With laudable robustness but faulty judgment Ritchie refused to be deflected from his own preparations for 'Acrobat' by what he believed could only be a spoiling attack. He ordered Godwin-Austen to cover Benghazi and Msus. When Godwin-Austen replied, saying that he though Messervy's division might be too weak to hold Msus, Ritchie gave him discretion to withdraw to to Mechili if it became necessary to do so. Prudently Ritchie ordered the thinning out of logistic units from Benghazi and the preparation of the port for demolition. He also ordered Norrie's XXX Corps HQ to move forward from the Egyptian frontier to reconnoitre and prepare a defensive position running south from Gazala to Bir Hacheim, covering Tobruk.

25 January was a bad day for Godwin-Austen's XIII Corps. Rommel struck northwards with the Afrika Korps towards Msus with its two panzer divisions advancing abreast.

Von Mellenthin describes what happened:

> On the right flank 21st Panzer met little opposition, but 6 miles north-west of Saunnu 15th Panzer ran into very superior tank forces. These were overwhelmed by 8th Panzer Regiment, closely supported by anti-tank guns and artillery; it soon became apparent that the British tank units had no battle experience and they were completely demoralised by the onslaught of 15th Panzer. At times the pursuit attained a speed of 15 miles an hour, and the British columns fled madly over the desert in one of the most extraordinary routs of the war. After covering fifty miles in under four hours 15th Panzer reached Msus airfield at 1100, overwhelming numerous supply columns and capturing 12 aircraft ready to take off.
>
> (von Mellenthin: page 87).

Rommel stopped his pursuit at Msus primarily because he was out of fuel and so could not repeat his 1941 advance on Mechili and Tobruk. Instead he decided to feint with the Afrika Korps towards Mechili while advancing on Benghazi with the rest of his force on three thrust lines: 90th Light up the via Balbia; Gambarra's Corps from Soluch; and the Marcks' Group, led by 3rd and 33rd Reconnaissance Units and accompanied by Rommel, over a difficult cross-country route from Msus via Er Regima to surprise and cut off the Benghazi garrison by reaching the coast at Coefia, 10 miles north of the port. Rommel hoped to surprise Ritchie and succeeded in doing so.

Relations between the British commanders began to show signs of strain and gave the first clear indication that the British had not yet found a command team capable of withstanding reverses. Godwin-Austen used the discretion given him by Ritchie and ordered the evacuation of Benghazi and withdrawal to Mechili. Auchinleck, accompanied by Tedder, arrived at Ritchie's headquarters soon afterwards and took the view, which Wavell had done in similar circumstances the year before, and which Ritchie had taken a few hours earlier, that Rommel must be near the end of his logistic tether – as he was in fact – and that he should be resisted. Ritchie was in no position to argue because this was his own view; and so he committed Neame's error of countermanding Godwin-Austen's withdrawal after it had already begun. At about 8.30 pm he put a brake on the withdrawal, and then at midnight cancelled it altogether, ordering 4th Indian Division to send columns south to attack Rommel's communication and 1st Armoured Division to block any German advance northwards on Charuba, protecting the Indians' flank. Godwin-Austen, backed by his divisional commanders, objected. 1st Armoured Division was down to 40 tanks and in some disorganisation; and 4th Indian Division had only one brigade far enough forward to react as Ritchie wished. Ritchie, with Auchinleck at his headquarters, refused to listen and overruled his Corps Commander, taking 4th Indian Division directly under his own command.

Rommel's intercept service caught the flavour of these disagreements but he could not profit by them on 26 January because he had to pause to bring up fuel and to organise his force for his advance on Benghazi which he had ordered to begin on 28 January. The weather broke on 27 January and prevented British air reconnaissance from detecting his redeployment. The clouds parted for just long enough for the RAF to report the Afrikan Korps feint towards Mechili. The other Axis columns remained shrouded from the airmen's view. That evening Ritchie decided that the Germans were developing two thrusts: one towards Mechili which he judged wrongly to be the main effort; and one towards Benghazi along the via Balbia which seemed to have less power behind it and to be composed mainly of Italian units. He ordered Godwin-Austen to deal with the Mechili thrust, using 1st Armoured Division, while 4th Indian Division attacked the via Balbia force. He wrote rather fancifully at the time 'The enemy has divided his forces and is weaker than we are in both areas. The keyword is offensive action everywhere!' (*British Official History:* Vol III, page 149). He had been horribly deceived.

About mid-day on 28 January, Tuker, commanding 4th Indian Division, reported a major Axis column approaching Benghazi from the south-east with some 47 tanks. He asked for permission to withdraw unless 1st Armoured Division could intervene. Ritchie demurred, saying that 1st Armoured Division was operating against the Afrika Korps and could not help. Tuker then obtained identifications of 90th Light and 21st Panzer Divisions on his front (the latter from 3rd Reconnaissance Unit) showing that he was not just opposed by Italians as Ritchie had assumed. This evidence persuaded Ritchie that he had been mistaken and it was time to abandon Benghazi. The demolition plan was put into effect, but the 7th Indian Infantry Brigade garrisoning the town did not manage to withdraw before Rommel cut the coast road to the north with the Marcks' Group. Undaunted, Brigadier H. R. Briggs turned his brigade back into the town and broke out southwards after dark, cutting across the German communications and reaching Mechili with remarkably little loss. Von Wechmar's hard worked 3rd Reconnaissance Unit re-entered Benghazi for a second time in less than a year.

The British fell back unmolested through the Djebel Akhdar. Ritchie decided, on the advice of the two divisional commanders, that there was no advantage in stopping short of Gazala once Benghazi had been lost. The nearer they were to the port of Tobruk, within reason, the better from the logistic point of view. On 6 February, Eighth Army began to settle into and fortify the Gazala Line which was to be its home for the next four months. Rommel followed up slowly, knowing that he did not possess the power to go any further as yet.

Eighth Army's repulse from the gateway to Tripolitania was disturbing. Harsh things were said about the performance of the British Armoured Corps. Auchinleck had already been critical of 22nd Armoured Brigade's defeat at the hands of Crüwell just after Christmas. Writing to Ritchie he had said:

> I am not in a position to pass any judgment, still less a hasty judgment, on anyone. All the same, I have a most uncomfortable feeling that the Germans outwit and out-manoeuvre us as well as out-shooting us, and I must know as soon as possible if this is so.
>
> If it is, then we must find new leaders at once. No personal considerations, or the possession of such qualities as courage and popularity must be allowed to stand in the way. Commanders who consistently have their brigades shot away from under them, even against a numerically inferior enemy, are expensive luxuries, much too expensive in present circumstances . . .
>
> (J. Connell: page 421).

In England the blame was placed at other doors. General Sir Alan Brooke, the C-in-C Home Forces, had just succeeded General Sir John Dill as CIGS when the latter was appointed British Military Representative with American Chiefs of Staff. He was a harder and more critical man than Dill, and at once started rooting out men about whom he had doubts. In one of his earliest letters to Auchinleck he suggested that Major-General Shearer, the Director of Military Intelligence in Cairo, had been persistently over-optimistic and had in two successive years under-estimated German capabilities in his appreciations for both Wavell and Auchinleck.

Like Haig in the First World War, Auchinleck defended his D.M.I. stoutly, but pressure for his replacement grew and he was forced to bow to the storm generated in Whitehall. Shearer was replaced by Colonel Francis de Guingand, who later became Montgomery's Chief of Staff.

One of Auchinleck's senior commanders resigned of his own accord. Godwin-Austen felt he could serve no longer under Ritchie who had over-ruled him so blatantly on the evacuation of Benghazi. Gott took his place as Commander XIII Corps and Messervy was given 7th Armoured Division. Lumsden was fit enough to return to the remnants of 1st Armoured Division. Ritchie survived as Commander Eighth Army, but Brooke was far from happy about this. He had doubts as well about Arthur Smith, the long suffering Chief of Staff to Wavell and Auchinleck who had borne the pressures of so many crises and was getting tired: 'Would you consider taking Ritchie as CGS and replacing him with Beresford-Peirse? Alternatively would Galloway be really good enough?' (*Ibid:* page 476).

Auchinleck agreed that Arthur Smith should be given a change of appointment after his long and loyal service in Cairo. His choice of replacement was not a happy one. He appointed Lieutenant-General T. S. Corbett, an eminent Indian Cavalry Officer, whom he had known in India. Unfortunately Corbett was not known by and did not know the British Army Officers in Cairo or Whitehall. He would have been better placed commanding Tenth Army in Persia which was composed largely of Indian troops. As Chief of Staff he never managed to dominate the complex staff organisation of GHQ Middle East. It over-awed him, making policy indecisive and characterless as all bureaucracies are apt to do unless firmly led. Corbett's appointment is generally acknowledged to Auchinleck's third mistaken selection of senior officers: the first was Cunningham and the second was Ritchie, although this was not yet apparent. He was soon to compound his second mistake by refusing Brooke's suggestion that he should move Ritchie. Replying to Brooke's letter he said:

> I do not want to take Ritchie away from Eighth Army in present circumstances. He has gripped the situation, knows what to do and has the drive and ability to do it, I feel.

(Ibid: page 476).

Thus the British High Command in Cairo and the Western Desert remained a well-meaning military democracy in which senior commanders continued to treat orders as a basis for discussion. The management of the 250,000 fighting men engaged on the British side became disastrously irresolute. Auchinleck believed in reaching decisions by debate; Corbett was in the hands of the various sectional interests in the staff; and Ritchie became progressively more like a puppet, acting on the instructions passed to him by Auchinleck in a voluminous shower of letters and signals. The British were still a long way from finding a successful command team. Everyone from C-in-C downwards would do his best, but the troops at one end of the scale and the CIGS at the other were beginning to realise that it was not just equipment that was at fault.

The foundations of Churchill's 'Super Gymnast' plan had collapsed. Rommel's raid had destroyed 'Acrobat'. British and American disasters in the Far East multiplied in a bewildering progression as the Japanese offensives gathered momentum. Roosevelt and Churchill had agreed at 'Arcadia' that the war against Germany should be given priority over the struggle against Japan, but Japan's onslaught had to be checked before this policy could be implemented. Commanders, troops and shipping allotted to 'Super Gymnast' had to be sent to the Far East. Alexander and Stilwell found themselves in Burma instead of French North Africa. And French opinion swung back to cynical belief in German victory.

Pearl Harbour affected the North African Campaign in one other way. Wavell, as C-in-C India, could no longer pay close attention to the defence of Persia and the North-West Frontier of India. Much against his will Auchinleck was persuaded by the British Chiefs of Staff to take over this extra load of responsibility, compelling him to spend yet more time and energy upon the affairs of his northern front. Admittedly German failure to reach the Caucasus in 1941 had given him some temporary relief from these anxieties, but he knew the threat would be renewed in the spring. However much Churchill might wish him to go forward to command Eighth Army in person, it was quite impractical for him to do so when he had to balance, as Wavell had to do before him, resources spread thinly over his vast theatre of operations. Eighth Army and the Western Desert front was only one of his problems. Wilson's Ninth Army in Syria and Quinan's Tenth Army in Persia and Iraq (previously under C-in-C India) needed his attention as well. Moreover, his northern front had been seriously weakened by the withdrawal of so many of his troops for the Far East. His instincts told him that he must be ready at all times to go on to the defensive in the

Western Desert to meet attack from the north.

It was not, however, the great German summer offensive in Russia, but the plight of the small island of Malta, which acted as the spur to action in the Mediterranean in the spring of 1942. Malta embarrassed both High Commands, forcing them to adopt tactical policies which did not conform to their strategic aims. The Italians realised that Rommel could not be supplied adequately unless Malta was eliminated, and yet they could not seize the island without German help. The British knew that Malta was the windlass in their torniquet on Rommel's supply lines on which they could not keep their grip unless they could drive Rommel back from the airfields in the bulge of Cyrenaica; but they could not advance on Benghazi again before they had built up adequate armoured superiority in the Western Desert. If they attacked too soon and lost the armoured battle they might lose Egypt in trying to save Malta. The German General Staff was coldly disinterested. OKW wished to avoid sideshows to concentrate its resources for the 1942 offensive in Southern Russia. Had it not been for Grand Admiral Raeder and the arguments of the German Naval Staff, a stalemate might have ensued in the Mediterranean. Raeder persuaded Hitler that the moment was opportune to clear the British out before the Americans could intervene. The German Naval and Air Forces had restored Axis superiority in the Central Mediterranean. There was not a single British capital ship fit for action, and the new Egyptian Government under Nahas Pasha seemed favourably disposed towards Axis interests. Malta should be seized as a preliminary to Rommel taking Tobruk and advancing into Egypt.

For a time naval arguments held sway in the German High Command, but in April the German commanders in the Mediterranean began to exert their influence against the Malta operation, code-named 'Hercules'. Kesselring claimed, justifiably, that his 2nd German Air Force had already neutralised the island. There was no immediate need for an invasion which would be costly and could only be executed at the expense of Rommel's operations in Libya. Axis convoys were now sailing unscathed through the Central Mediterranean and had landed 150,000 tons of equipment, stores and supplies in North Africa in the last two months. Only one per cent of these cargoes had been lost. The British, on the other hand, had singularly failed to resupply Malta. Their February convoy of three ships had proved a disaster – two were sunk and one had to return damaged to Alexandria without unloading. The March convoy had fared no better. Only 7,500 tons out of the original 26,000 tons in the convoy reached the people and garrison of Malta. Admiral Cunningham was forced to accept the impossibility of running further convoys under these conditions, and the need to withdraw all submarines and surface vessels from the Island as well. On shore, April proved to be Malta's worst month. 6,700 tons of bombs, almost 10 times 1941's monthly maximum, fell on the Island; 11,450 buildings were destroyed; but mercifully and surprisingly less than 1,000 people were killed and wounded thanks to the deep cellars and air raid shelters available in the easily worked Malta rock. Morale was sustained by the exceptional leadership of General Dobbie, a great Christian gentleman, whose sincerity and integrity appealed to everyone on the Island.

Rommel reinforced Kesselring's objections to Raeder's plans, exposing the view that the capture of Tobruk would do more for the Axis cause than the risky 'Hercules' operation. Tobruk would become his advanced base for his invasion of Egypt to which Axis convoys could be sailed via Crete, thus by-passing Malta. His Intelligence Staff had received evidence that the British were preparing another offensive in the Western Desert which he must forestall. Hitler and Mussolini debated these arguments at the end of April. Hitler's memories of German losses taking Crete and his psychological suspicion of naval strategy led him to accept Kesselring's and Rommel's views in spite of German naval and Italian protests. 'Hercules' was postponed and Rommel was authorised to advance on Tobruk. His operations were to be completed by 20 June to allow the 2nd German Air Force to return to Russia for the summer offensive; and he was strictly forbidden to go beyond Tobruk without seeking further authority.

On the British side the divergence of view between London and Cairo was more difficult to resolve. The key factor was the moonless period in each month when it was practicable to run convoys to Malta. Churchill cabled Auchinleck at the end of February asking for his plans and adding that according to his calculations Eighth Army should have a substantial measure of armoured and air superiority with which to renew its offensive operations. Auchinleck replied with a long and detailed appreciation showing that he would not be ready to attack before June at the earliest. The shock waves of the consequential Churchillian explosion did not die away until Auchinleck had been dismissed by his exacting master six months later. Brooke managed to stop Churchill sending back a vitriolic reply containing phrases like 'soldiers are meant to fight' and 'Armies were not intended to stand around doing nothing'. The actual cable despatched asked the C-in-C to reconsider his views and on 2 March Churchill asked Auchinleck to come home for consultation. To the consternation of his many friends in London, Auchinleck declined to leave his hard-pressed theatre for the fortnight which such a visit would have taken. The operational situation on both his fronts was too delicate to risk leaving affairs in the hands of a deputy for so long. He proposed instead that Brooke and Portal, Chief of Air Staff, should visit Cairo and see for themselves the conditions under which his soldiers and Tedder's airmen were fighting, the weapons and aircraft with which they were equipped and the shortages from which they all were suffering. These eminent members of the British Chiefs of Staff Committee would be able to hear views at first hand and thereby reduce the misunderstanding which had been growing up over the months between London and Cairo. His suggestion was turned down. Churchill construed his refusal in the worst possible light and contemplated his immediate dismissal. In the end he decided that Sir Stafford Cripps, accompanied by the Vice-Chief of the General Staff, General Nye, who were on their way to India for political negotiations with the Congress Party and Moslem League, should break their journey at Cairo to present the Cabinet's views to the Cs-in-C Committee. The *British Official History* sums up the outcome:

To the Prime Minister's annoyance his two emissaries proved to be Balaams; sent out to curse they could only bless ... Cripps stated that at the present time our strength neither in tanks nor in the air was such as to give any reasonable chance of a successful offensive. He agreed with Auchinleck that to attempt an attack before mid-May would be to take an unwarrantable risk ...

(Grand Strategy: Vol III, page 453).

The British Chiefs of Staff were forced to acknowledge mid-May as the earliest date for Auchinleck's next desert offensive. Churchill was far from happy, castigating the unfortunate Cripps in a cable to Nye on 22 March:

I have heard from the Lord Privy Seal (Cripps). I do not wonder everything was so pleasant, considering you seem to have accepted everything they said, and all *we* have got to accept is the probable loss of Malta and the Army standing idle while the Russians are resisting the German counter-stroke desperately, and while the enemy is reinforcing himself in Libya faster than we are ...

(J. Connell: page 470).

Churchill's ire might have abated with Auchinleck's acceptance of mid-May for the next offensive enabling a Malta convoy to be sailed during the moonless period of that month. By chance, a Chiefs of Staff appreciation of the situation in the Far East reached Cairo, suggesting that India was gravely threatened and that there was a possibility that the Red Sea supply route to Suez might be cut by Japanese naval operations in the Indian Ocean. This prompted Auchinleck to suggest that he assume the defensive in the Western Desert to release more Army and Air Force reinforcements for India. At the same time, he despatched a further detailed appreciation agreeing that the arrival of the American 'General Grant' medium tanks and the British 6-pounder anti-tank guns would enable him to attack with only a 3 to 2 numerical superiority over German tanks and even odds for the Italians. Nevertheless the speed of re-equipment was such that he could not open his offensive before the June dark period, and if, as seemed possible, the Italians managed to bring their new Littorio Armoured Division into the forward area, he might have to wait until August.

Churchill's reaction to the Indian reinforcement suggestion and to the postponement of the offensive to 15 June was cool:

The Chiefs of Staff, Defence Committee and War Cabinet have all earnestly considered your telegram in relation to the whole war situation ... We are agreed that in spite of the risks you mention you would be right to attack the enemy and fight a major battle, if possible during May, and the sooner the better. We are prepared to take full responsibility for these general directions, leaving you the necessary latitude for their execution. In this you will no doubt have regard to the fact that the enemy may himself be planning to attack you early in June.

(J. Connell: page 495).

The Cs-in-C Middle East were not prepared to accept London's dictates without protest. They re-stated their view that Malta was not vital to the defence of Egypt and

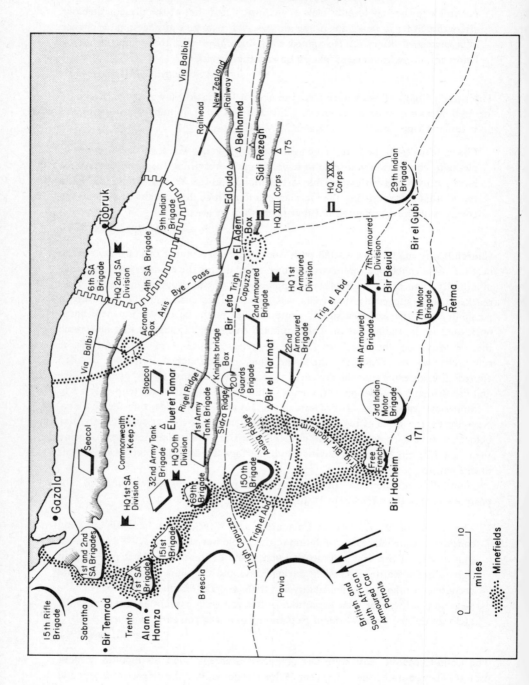

that it might be to their advantage if Rommel did attack first as this would give Eighth Army a chance to decimate his armour for well chosen defensive positions. The British Chiefs of Staff lost patience and replied with an ultimatum, insisting on an offensive to regain the airfields in Western Cyrenaica not later than the June moonless period. Churchill probably hoped this would force Auchinleck's resignation. Auchinleck resisted the temptation and acquiesced, pointing out that his margin of tank and air superiority would be too fine to guarantee success.

Before his reply reached London, it was already clear that the whole tiresome wrangle had been academic. The British Intelligence Staffs obtained hard evidence of Rommel's intention to launch an offensive to capture Tobruk towards the end of May. The British turned away from their own plans for an offensive and began to concentrate upon defensive preparations.

Ritchie had taken up the Gazala position originally as a temporary line designed to cover the construction of stronger defences on the Egyptian frontier, to which he would have retired, abandoning Tobruk, if Rommel had continued his offensive in February. Rommel's quiescence and Churchill's pressure for the resumption of the Eighth Army's offensive reversed the roles of the Gazala Line and Tobruk. The former became the screen behind which British preparations for an offensive could proceed and the spring-board from which it would be launched; and the latter became their advanced base at which some 36,000 tons of supplies were dumped to support Eighth Army's advance on Benghazi and Tripoli. The sudden need to reverse roles again was operationally and logistically embarrassing. The Gazala Line was far from ideal as a defensive position on which to fight a decisive desert battle; and the stocks built up around Tobruk particularly near Belhamed to which the railway had been extended by the prodigious efforts of the New Zealand Railway Engineers, were too far forward and a hostage to furtune if anything went wrong during the battle.

The Gazala Line was occupied according to the latest tactical fashion prevailing in the Middle East at that time. 'Crusader' had under-lined the need for closer integration of tanks, artillery and infantry. It had also shown that the armoured division with two armoured brigades and a support group was too unwieldly. Something more akin to the German panzer division with one tank and one infantry brigade was needed with the artillery closely associated with both brigades. Auchinleck decided to make two changes which had been advocated for some time in India, but found little favour in England. First, he made the brigade group the basic fighting formation instead of the division. There were to be three types of brigade group: 'armoured' with three tank regiments; 'motor' with three motorised infantry battalions; and 'infantry' with three infantry battalions which were only provided with transport when it was needed. Each brigade group was given its own organic field artillery, anti-tank and anti-aircraft artillery, engineers and logistic units. Divisional headquarters became the tactical co-ordinators of a variable number of brigade groups of different types. And the second change made by Auchinleck was the disbandment of the armoured divisional support groups to provide the artillery and infantry needed for the armoured brigade groups. Unfortunately, he was unable to provide a concentrated body of artillery like the Böttcher Group which could lay down an adequate weight of fire at decisive moments.

Changes had also been taking place in the critical balance between British and German tanks and anti-tank guns. On the British side the first American medium tank, the General Grant, was arriving in welcome quantities. It combined the merits of the German Pz III and IV, by mounting a 75mm field gun in a sponsen on the side of the hull, which was intended primarily for engagements with high explosive shell like the Pz IV's, and a 37mm gun, like the 'Honeys', in the turret with good capped anti-tank ammunition for the Pz III's anti-tank role. The Grant's armour was good and its reliability was excellent. It had, however, three less fortunate characteristics: first, its high silhouette; secondly, the position of the 75mm which was too low down in the hull; and thirdly, the limited traverse of the 75mm. The British were, however, so impressed with it that, in spite of the disadvantages of having two types of tank in a regiment, they decided to give every regiment one or two 'Grant' squadrons as the new tanks arrived.

In the anti-tank gun field, the new British Roberts' 6-pounder gun appeared in very limited numbers and was given to Royal Artillery anti-tank units whose 2-pounders were then handed over to the infantry battalions to strengthen their anti-tank defence. Only enough arrived in May to equip the 201st Guards Motor Brigade Group* and 7th Motor Brigade Group – the infantry brigades of 1st and 7th Armoured Divisions. 6-pounder ammunition was particularly scarce. The Germans received more 88mm guns and an issue of captured 76mm Russian anti-tank guns which had a better performance than their own 50mm guns. They also equipped a few Pz IIIs with a long barrelled, high-velocity, 50mm gun with improved anti-tank performance. Only 19 of these Pz III (Specials) were available in May.

The lay out of the Gazala Line† was based upon a series of infantry brigade group defensive 'boxes', sited in suitable areas of desert with some tactical significance. Each box was given a defensive perimeter of mines and wire, behind which the defending troops were dug in covered by their brigades' anti-tank guns and field artillery. In some boxes 'I' tanks were also positioned, but this was exceptional, as both 'I' tanks and Cruisers were normally held in reserve for counter-attack purposes. The boxes of the three brigade groups of Pienaar's 1st South African Division and of two brigade groups of Ramsden's 50th (Northumbrian) Division were well dug in, well mined and within supporting distance of each other defending the northern half of the front. The line then became more tenuous with a gap of 5 miles to the third brigade box of 50th Division, held by Brigadier Haydon's 150th Brigade Group, which blocked the area between the Trigh Capuzzo and Trigh el Abd. South of 150th Brigade there was nothing except minefields for the next 10 miles to Bir Hacheim where the Free French Brigade Group under General Koenig was well dug in. As the weeks passed more and more mines had been laid, many taken from Tobruk whose perimeter defences were not expected to be needed again. The term 'mine marsh' began to be heard. This referred to deep mine-fields laid principally in the 5 and 10 mile gaps either side of

* 200th Guards Brigade was renumbered again when it became a Motor Brigade.
† See Map VI.

150th Brigade Group's position. The term, though appropriate, was deceptive on operational maps because staffs tended to assume them to be impassable barriers, whereas, in fact, they had little delaying value unless they were covered by fire. They could be easily lifted, particularly by night as relatively few anti-personnel mines were available. Behind the main position there were a series of column bases and boxes, some occupied and others ready for occupation, with specific tactical purposes. On the coast 'Sea Col' had the task of watching for and opposing any amphibious landing. On the escarpment above was 'Commonwealth Keep' and 'Acroma Box' with supporting mine-fields designed to block routes inland. And on the desert plateau 'Stop Col' provided a mobile reserve behind the coastal positions. Further south the Trigh Capuzzo was blocked in depth by the 201st Guards Motor Brigade Group Box at Knightsbridge and the El Adem Box in which XIII Corps HQ was established. Still further south a box was just being completed at Retma for 7th Motor Brigade Group, and two further boxes were planned at Pt 171 and Bir el Gubi to strengthen the open desert flank of Eighth Army's position.

Within this pattern of fixed defences manned by infantry brigade groups, Ritchie had to dispose his armour. His two corps were still organised as they had been for 'Crusader'. Norrie's XXX Corps commanded the mobile armoured forces, consisting of 1st and 7th Armoured Divisions with brigades grouped as follows:

1st Armoured Division (Lumsden)
   2nd Armoured Brigade Group (Bir Lefa)
   22nd Armoured Brigade Group (Bir el Harmat)
   201st Guards Motor Brigade Group (Knightsbridge Box)

7th Armoured Division (Messervy)
   4th Armoured Brigade Group (Bir Beuid)
   7th Motor Brigade Group (Retima Box)
   3rd Indian Motor Brigade Group (Pt 171 Box)
   29th Indian Infantry Brigade Group (Bir el Gubi Box)
   1st Free French Brigade Group (Bir Hacheim Box)

Norrie had two tasks: he was responsible for manoeuvring the main armoured force; and was geographically in charge of the southern half of the front from the Trigh el Abd southwards. Lumsden's 1st Armoured Division was positioned to oppose any attempt by Rommel to thrust through the British centre along the Trigh Capuzzo or Trigh el Abd. He had also to be ready to move southwards to support Messervy's 7th Armoured Division if Rommel's attack came round the southern flank, which it was 7th Armoured's responsibility to delay and eventually destroy with 1st Armoured's help. Masservy's headquarters and 4th Armoured Brigade, which was the strongest in Eighth Army as its three regiments had two Grant squadrons each, were at Bir Beuid some 20 miles east of Bir Hacheim. His 7th Motor Brigade under Brigadier Renton was in 'Jock' columns supporting the British and South African armoured cars screening the British positions west of the Gazala Line. It was intended that it should fall back, fighting a delaying action into the Retma Box if Rommel came round the desert flank. Just before the battle, the 3rd Indian Motor Brigade arrived from Egypt to hold the embryonic box at Point 171 to the south-east of Bir Hacheim.

Gott's XIII Corps was still essentially an infantry corps, tasked to hold the northern half of the main line and the static posts in rear including Tobruk. For this task he had:

1st South African Division (Pienaar)
    1st, 2nd and 3rd South African Brigade Groups.
50th (Northumbrian) Division (Ramsden)
    69th, 150th, 151st Infantry Brigade Groups.
1st Army Tank Brigade (supporting 50th Division)
2nd Army Tank Brigade (supporting 1st South African Division)

2nd South African Division (Klopper) with 4th and 6th South African Brigades and 4th Indian Division's 9th Indian Brigade Group were holding Tobruk.

Ritchie himself held 11th Indian Division (Briggs) in reserve with only the 10th Indian and 2nd Free French Brigade Groups under command; but Auchinleck had advised him that 10th Indian Division (Rees) with three Indian Brigade Groups was on its way to him from Iraq, and one brigade of 4th Indian Division and 1st Armoured Brigade were moving up from Egypt.

On 16 May Ritchie issued his orders for the defensive battle he and Auchinleck expected to fight in the Gazala position. He was not a free agent. Auchinleck kept bombarding him with letters and cables giving well intentioned and usually very sound advice couched in permissive terms like:

> Do not think I am trying to dictate to you in any way, but this coming struggle is going to be so vital that I feel you must have the benefit of our combined consideration here, though I realise we cannot be so conversant with the details of the problem as are you and your staff . . .
>
> (J. Connell: quoting letter of 20 May, page 505).

The essence of Auchinleck's thinking was that Rommel had two alternatives: sweep round Ritchie's southern flank while mounting a holding attack on the centre of the main front in conjunction with a small amphibious landing between Tobruk and Gazala; or breach the centre with a concentrated attack on a narrow front, while demonstrating round the southern flank. Air reconnaissance had revealed some tank-carrying ferries on the coast, but Auchinleck rightly discounted the amphibious threat which could not be large unless the Germans shipped a force over from Europe and there were no signs of this. The key paragraphs in his letter dealing with operational policy dated 20 May were:

> 3. I feel myself that the second course is the one he will adopt, and that it is certainly the most dangerous to us, as if it succeeds, it will cut our forces in half and probably result in the destruction of the northern part of them. We must of course be ready to deal with the enemy should he adopt the first course, and in either event you must of course be most careful not to commit your armoured striking force until you know beyond reasonable doubt where the main body of his armour is thrusting . . .

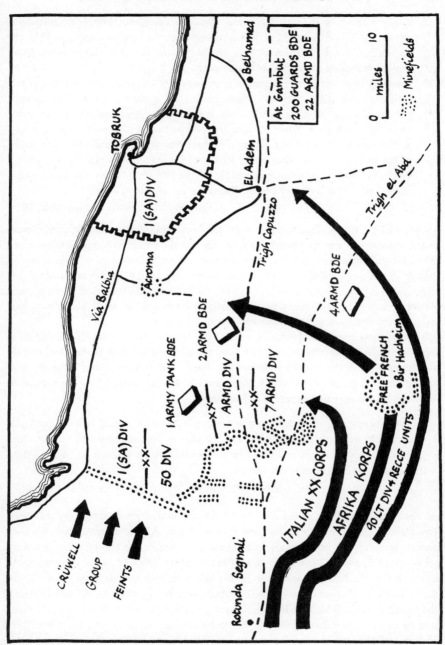

Fig 33 Rommel's Plan for Gazala
(showing British positions as the Germans thought them to be)

5. . . . I suggest both your armoured divisions complete should be positioned astride the Trigh Capuzzo. It does not look from the map as if this would be too far north to meet the main attack, should it come round to the southern flank instead of against the centre as I anticipate . . .

10. I suggest that you must reorganise your system of command for this battle. For a defensive battle I feel you must have your mobile reserve, that is your armoured force, freed from all static commitments and responsibilities. Your army falls, as I see it, into two parts, one whose task it is to hold the fort, which is the Gazala–Tobruk–El Gubi–Bir Hacheim quadrilateral, and the other whose task it is to hit the enemy wherever he may thrust and destroy him. I think Gott should be solely responsible for the first, and Norrie for the second. I would relieve the latter for responsibility for Bir Hacheim at once . . .

(J. Connell: letter dated 20 May, page 505).

Ritchie and his Corps Commanders were not so certain. Norrie thought there would be two thrusts – centre and south; and Ritchie felt the southern 'hook' was the more likely. He did not accept two important elements of Auchinleck's advice. He made no change in the responsibility of his Corps commanders, and he did not change the dispositions of his armoured divisions. Nevertheless he made sure that Lumsden and Messervy had well laid plans for the various contingencies with battle positions reconnoitred and routes to them worked out and rehearsed.

None of these command problems worried the British regimental officers and men. Life was uncomfortable in the summer heat, the flies and the dust storms, but morale was again high. A description written by Colonel 'Pip' Roberts (later General) who was commanding 3rd Royal Tank Regiment in 4th Armoured Brigade Group at Gazala gives the prevailing sense of enthusiasm:

There was much to to be done; a new tank to learn, HE shooting to learn, and new tactics to be evolved. But everyone now felt that he had an answer to the anti-tank gun and wouldn't the Hun in his Mark IIIs and IVs get a shock when the 75mm came in . . . so enthusiasm was terrific . . .

(Quoted by Liddell Hart: *The Tanks,* Vol II, page 158).

On the other side of the desert no-man's land personal relations were very different. The Panzer Group had been restyled Panzer Army, Africa. Rommel was his own master, brooking no interference from above and demanding complete loyalty from below. He did have problems, but of a different nature. Once he had won authority to attack at Gazala, he set about planning his offensive with his customary élan. There was a difference, however, between this operation and his previous offensives which had begun as raids. This time he was planning a major offensive *ab initio,* and showed himself to be a poor strategist. His approach was too cavalier and superficial. He made a bad plan based upon inaccurate intelligence and inadequate reconnaissance, which he made worse by insisting that it was never worth thinking more than 48 hours ahead in any battle. He decided to launch a series of holding attacks against the South Africans and to carry out minor amphibious landings in their rear to draw

British attention northwards. The Italian and German troops detailed for these operations were placed under Crüwell who had been on leave in Germany. Rommel with the Afrika Korps, now under General Nehring, and the Italian XX Mobile Corps would advance from Rotonda Segnali towards the British centre until dusk and would then swing southwards round the southern flank as Ritchie predicted. The Italians would pass north of the Bir Hacheim Box and the Afrika Korps would crash right through it as Rommel believed French resistance would not last more than an hour. The two panzer divisions would then head northwards towards Acroma, destroying the British armoured forces piecemeal, while 90th Light, simulating a panzer division by using aero-engines mounted on trucks to create dust clouds, surprised the British logistic units around El Adem and Belhamed. As soon as the British armour had been destroyed in about 24 hours, 1st South African and 50th Divisions would be attacked from the rear. The capture of Tobruk was expected to follow within about four days of the start of the offensive, and so Rommel's mobile force was to carry only four days' supplies and ammunition, expecting to replenish from the British dumps which would fall into their hands.

Rommel's actual plan was captured during the fighting and so it is possible to see how wrong his pre-battle estimates were. His Intelligence Staff had an accurate assessment of the total British order of battle in the Middle East, but were wildly astray in their ideas of the troops actually under Eighth Army's command forward of the Egyptian frontier. They missed out one armoured brigade group, one army tank brigade and three infantry brigade groups. They were also working on a map of British dispositions as they had been in March. They thought the mine-fields ended near the Trigh el Abd. They had no idea that 150th Brigade Group was in position between the two Trighs, providing some connection between the main 50th Division positions and the French Box which they knew existed at Bir Hacheim. And they were unaware of the mine marshes in the two large gaps either side of 150th Brigade Group's Box. Credit for this state of affairs must go to the British and South African armoured car regiments which had made close reconnaissance of the British positions difficult throughout the whole period of their occupation.

Rommel's plan had two other faults. Firstly, he belittled the British commanders and their troops. Events proved him right as regards the former, but quite wrong about the latter whom he acknowledged later fought with their usual bravery and determination. And secondly, he failed to achieve surprise. The British knew almost to the day when the offensive would open. All they did not know was which thrust would be his main and which his feint attack.

On 25 May, the day before Rommel attacked the numerical balance of armoured and air forces was:

	BRITISH		AXIS	
Medium Tanks	Grants	167	Pz III	223
	Crusaders	257	Pz III	
			(special)	19
			Pz IV	40
	Total with Armoured			
	Divisions	424		282
			Italian	
	'I' Tanks	276	Mediums	228
Light Tanks	Stuarts	149	Pz II	50
	Grand Total	849		560
Aircraft	Serviceable aircraft in			
	forward area	190		497
	Elsewhere within			
	reinforcing range	749		1000
		929		1497

(*British Official History:* Vol III, page 220).

Thus, Ritchie did possess the 2 to 1 superiority over the Germans and equality with the Italians which Auchinleck thought necessary for offensive operations. As he would be on the defensive, this should have been more than adequate. The air situation was not so satisfactory. On the other hand the weakness of the German plan and Rommel's failure to gain surprise should have given Auchinleck and Ritchie a real chance to win the North African Campaign in June 1942.

11

The High Water of German Professionalism
(May to July 1942)

'The fact that within three weeks of the launching of our offensive this magnificent British Army was reduced to a state of complete rout, must be regarded as one of the greatest achievements in German Military Annals.

(von Mellenthin: page 90).

If the Battles of Gazala had been fought by the British as they should have been, there would be no place in history for the Battle of El Alamein. Auchinleck and Ritchie would be remembered as the men who turned the tide of British fortunes in the Second World War. Instead both were to lose their commands as defeated generals before the summer was out – and rightly so. The British had at last achieved something approaching equipment equality, a valid, though not necessarily a battle-winning, tactical doctrine and enough battle experience, but they had failed to find a command team which could develop the full power of their growing resources. The lost battles of Gazala mark the high-water of German professionalism and the nadir of British military management in the North African Campaign.

The story of the sorry months of June and July 1942 in the Western Desert has none of the complexity and two-sidedness of 'Crusader'. It flows in a cumulative progression of avoidable disasters. No amount of tactical skill, courage or endurance at regimental level could make up for the weaknesses of the British higher command. The ultimate success of the same British regimental officers and men four months later under Alexander and Montgomery emphasises the inadequacy of the Auchinleck/Ritchie combination. The South African Official historians comment justifiably:

> . . . the Afrika Korps was a tightly woven fighting force, whose commanders had a common tactical doctrine and a high sense of discipline. In contrast it is no secret that personal relations between the British commanders – particularly in the armoured divisions – could not have been worse . . .
>
> *(South African Official History:* page 13).

The hard fact of the matter is that, unless a democracy can throw up a military genius early in a war, the creation of a successful command team takes longer than building and equipping an army. Britain's men of military genius were still standing unrecognised in the wings when Rommel attacked at Gazala. Each of the seven distinct phases of Rommel's operations exemplify the principles he laid down for desert warfare. They also illustrate the weakness of the British high command which Alexander and Montgomery were to correct when they arrived.

PHASE I — ROMMEL ATTACKS
(26 to 29 May 1942)

Rommel's 1st Principle
The main endeavour should be to concentrate one's own forces in space and time, while at the same time seeking to split the enemy forces and destroying them at different times.

(Rommel: page 199).

A hot, disagreeable 'Khamsin' blew most of 26 May as Rommel's troops carried out their preliminary moves for Operation 'Venezia'. Crüwell's group of Italian divisions closed up noisily to the British positions in the northern half of the Gazala Line, using heavy dive-bombing and artillery bombardments to impress the earnestness of their intentions. This alerted the British whose air reconnaissance did detect, as Rommel intended, the concentration of Afrika Korps vehicles moving due eastwards from Rotonda Segnali as if intent on attacking astride the Trigh Capuzzo, as Auchinleck predicted. After dark, the South African armoured car patrols, well west of the Gazala Line, reported major Axis columns moving south-eastwards towards Bir Hacheim. The 7th Motor Brigade Group columns, supporting the armoured cars, fell back, relaying a stream of similar reports to HQ 7th Armoured Division and HQ XXX Corps. Messervy and Norrie were both sceptical about these messages which could be exaggerated so easily by units withdrawing in the dark. Moreover, there was no evidence, as yet, that similar concentrations of Axis troops were not developing along the Trigh Capuzzo and Trigh el Abd. They saw no reason to jump to premature conclusions and decided to await the results of RAF reconnaissance at dawn. 4th and 22nd Armoured Brigade Groups were alerted, but were not told which battle positions they were to take up. Time slipped by and no positive British counter-measures were taken.

On the Axis side, the Afrika Korps night march was an exhilarating affair. Rommel's own description of it is worth recording:

At 2030 I ordered Operation 'Venezia' and the 10,000 vehicles of the striking force began to move. My staff and I, in our places in the Afrika Korps column, drove through the moonlight night towards the great armoured battle . . . I was tense and keyed-up, impatiently waiting the coming day . . . Shortly before daybreak we took an hour's rest some 10 or 12 miles south-east of Bir Hacheim; then the great force started to move again, and in a swirling cloud of dust and sand, thrust into the British rear.

(Rommel: page 206).

The RAF was the first to discover Rommel's striking force south-east of Bir Hacheim at dawn on 27 May. By the time that effective air strike could be launched, British and German forces had become closely engaged, making air intervention difficult. The first British Army units to see Rommel's formidable array belonged to the 3rd Indian Motor Brigade Group which had just arrived from Egypt to establish the new brigade box at Point 171, not far from the Afrika Korps' wheeling point. The last time that this brigade had been in action was when it tried in vain to stop Rommel at Mechili in the spring of 1941. It had only reached Point 171 the day before and many of its anti-tank gunners and other supporting units were still making their way from Egypt. It is not surprising that the Brigade Commander reported in some alarm to HQ 7th Armoured Division that 'they had the whole bloody Afrika Korps in front of them' as dawn spread over the desert. This was no exaggeration. Rommel had made a last minute change of plan. Instead of attacking the French in Bir Hacheim, he had taken his striking force further south and was wheeling north in a fan-like formation which brought the Ariete and part of the 21st Panzer opposite the Indians' scantily prepared Box; the rest of 21st Panzer and 15th Panzer were in the centre; and 90th Light with the reconnaissance units was on the extreme outer edge heading for the Retma Box and 7th Armoured Division's headquarters at Bir Beuid. The Trieste had lost its way and had run into British minefields north of Bir Hacheim.

The Indians, unready as they were, put up as stout a defence as they had done at Mechili, destroying some 50 Axis tanks before giving way. The Brigade was scattered, losing 400 officers and men, and eventually re-formed with the help of 29th Indian Brigade at Bir el Gubi. 15th Panzer Division, meanwhile, had met 4th Armoured Brigade Group which was moving south-westwards to take up battle positions belatedly assigned to it between the Indian and Retma Boxes. The commander of the leading British armoured regiment (Colonel 'Pip' Roberts) described the beginning of the first clash of armour:

> . . . the phone from Brigade rang again. 'Enemy movement is reported towards Bir Hacheim; the Brigade will take up position "Skylark" . . . What sort of enemy movement do you think it is?' asked the Adjutant – 'Sort of "Sinbad?"' 'Yes' said Brigade 'Something of that sort. We don't think it's anything very serious'.
>
> (Carver: *Tobruk*, page 177).

4th Armoured Brigade Group were soon disillusioned. A 'Sinbad' was the code-word for a reconnaissance in force. In the encounter battle which followed, 4th Armoured Brigade Group was caught before it could reach and shake out into its battle positions. The two leading regiments – 3rd Royal Tanks and 8th Hussars – came into action separately, both losing heavily but inflicting severe losses on their opponents. Brigadier Richards, who had taken over when Gatehouse was promoted to 10th Armoured Division, decided that he must disengage and withdraw to reorganise before he could do anything effective. Accordingly he fell back towards El Adem.

On the outer edge of the German wheel, 90th Light Division scattered the columns of 7th Motor Brigade Group before they could settle down in the defences of the

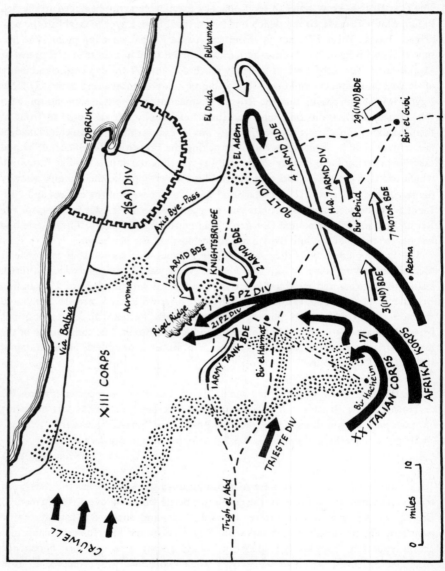

Fig. 24 The First Day at Gazala – 27th May 1942

22. The bombing of the Carrier "Illustrious" undergoing repairs in the Grand Harbour of Valetta, Malta.

23. The crippled American tanker "Ohio" towed into Valetta, low in the water and supported by a destroyer and a tug.

24. General Sir Harold Alexander, GOC-in-C Middle East and then Commander 18th Army Group; Prime Minister Winston Churchill; Lieutenant-General Montgomery, Commander Eighth Army.

25. Lieutenant-General Kenneth Anderson, Commander First Army and Lieutenant-General Omar Bradley, Commander II (US) Corps.

Retma Box, forcing them to withdraw on Bir el Gubi; and one of the German reconnaissance units found and dispersed the tactical headquarters of 7th Armoured Division, capturing Messervy and his senior General Staff Officer. Both men escaped later, having hidden their badges of rank, and some of their headquarter's vehicles reached El Adem safely. Nevertheless, 7th Armoured Division had been as effectively decapitated as Gatehouse's brigade during 'Crusader', and its three brigade groups had been driven off the battlefield within the first few hours of Rommel opening his offensive.

Not knowing what had happened to his southern division because communications had been disrupted, Norrie ordered Lumsden to move southwards to support Messervy. Lumsden objected on the grounds that an attack might still come in the centre along the Trigh Capuzzo. After some delay, 22nd Armoured Brigade Group did move south and, like 4th Armoured Brigade Group, ran into the two German panzer divisions before it could reach its pre-planned battle positions. It, too, fought hard and, after losing about 30 tanks, was pulled back by Lumsden to the Knightsbridge Box area from which he planned to mount a counter-attack.

By midday Rommel was congratulating his commanders on their success and urging them on to take risks to reach Acroma by nightfall thus cutting off Gott's XIII Corps in the main Gazala Line. He had fulfilled his first principle of concentration of force and had summarily dealt with four British brigade groups in turn. The ambitious objectives which he had set for Operation 'Venezia' did not seem so far-fetched after all. Basing his calculations on von Mellenthin's faulty appreciation of British dispositions, Rommel concluded that he had dispersed the available British armour and could safely set about ploughing into the rear of their infantry divisions. This was to prove a costly error. His divisional commanders obeyed, throwing caution to the wind and attacking without waiting to co-ordinate anti-tank gun and artillery support. 22nd Armoured Brigade Group halted and turned about near Knightsbridge, inflicting heavy losses on the leading panzer battalions with their new Grant tanks whose crews were shooting well. 2nd Armoured Brigade Group and the 1st Army Tank Brigade then began to attack both flanks of the German striking force. German tactical cohesion broke down as the afternoon wore on. The desert south of Knightsbridge became the scene of multiple armoured actions by small groups of British and German tanks brought on by random encounter. Rommel's description of the scene is significant:

> The British armour, under heavy artillery cover, poured their fire into the columns and panzer units of the Afrika Korps, which were visible for miles. Fire and black smoke welled up from lorries and tanks, and our attack came to a standstill. Again my divisions suffered extremely serious losses. Many of our columns broke into confusion and fled away to the south-west, out of the British artillery fire.
>
> (Rommel: page 207).

By nightfall Rommel's position was precarious. 2nd Armoured Brigade Group had cut through 15th Panzer Division's unsupported infantry regiment, and 1st Army

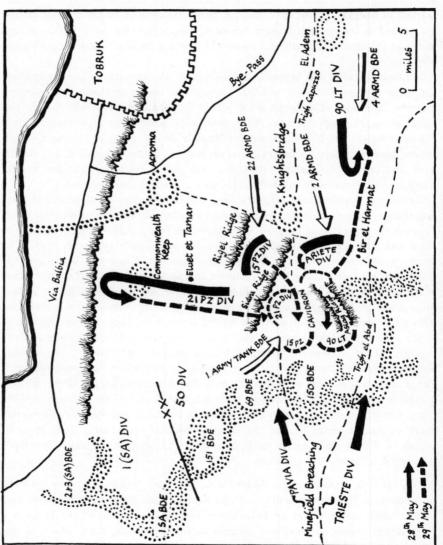

Fig 35   The Second and Third Days at Gazala: 28th and 29th May 1942

Tank Brigade had done the same to 21st Panzer Division's infantry. And 90th Light's career of destruction had come to an end near El Adem where 4th Armoured Brigade Group had come back into action to drive it away from the British supply dumps. The two German panzer divisions had lost one-third of their tanks. 15th Panzer was out of fuel north-west of Knightsbridge, and 21st Panzer was only slightly better off, though stronger in tanks, a few miles further to the west. Rommel himself was cut off from them at Bir el Harmat by the 1st Army Tank and 2nd Armoured Brigades' thrusts, and with him were most of the Afrika Korps' supply vehicles.

During the night, both sides acted upon 'hunches' as to how things had gone. The British organised a containing line to seal off Rommel's penetration while they tried to discover what had happened. Rommel confessed to his staff that he was worried but determined to pursue his 'Venezia' plan next day. His two panzer divisions were to continue their thrust northwards to cut the coast road, while he concentrated the rest of his striking force to protect their rear. He ordered 90th Light to give up its operations at El Adem and the Ariete to leave Bir Hacheim, and both to concentrate at Bir el Harmat to form a firm base protecting the supply columns. The Pavia and Trieste Divisions were to clear routes through the mine marshes blocking the Trigh Capuzzo and Trigh el Abd so as to shorten Rommel's supply route around Bir Hacheim.

28 May was another poor day for Rommel. 21st Panzer advanced northwards, taking Commonwealth Keep and bringing fire to bear on the coast-road from the top of the escarpment. 15th Panzer lay stranded most of the day out of fuel, harassed by 22nd Armoured Brigade Group. And 90th Light was caught by 4th Armoured Brigade Group as it tried to withdraw to Bir el Harmat and was forced to 'hedgehog' behind its anti-tank guns and artillery eight miles short of its objective. Meanwhile Rommel worked feverishly to find a way northwards through the British positions to re-supply 15th Panzer. In doing so he had several lucky escapes when he came under British artillery fire, and his headquarters was scattered during one of his absences. Only a man of great personal courage and iron determination could have persevered without thought of withdrawal.

The main Axis success of the day came surprisingly from the Italians. About midday Norrie decided that he could discern the shape of the battle clearly enough to order a repetition of the concentric attacks of 1st Army Tank and 2nd Armoured Brigades to isolate the Afrika Korps. These attacks did not start until late in the afternoon. By then the Ariete had reached Bir El Harmat and had established, under Rommel's personal supervision, an effective anti-tank screen covering the Axis supply columns. 2nd Armoured Brigade Group suffered severe tank casualties from 88mm fire before darkness ended the day's fighting. More significantly the Trieste and Pavia Divisions succeeded in making passable, though not easily used, gaps through the mine marshes where they crossed the Trigh el Abd and Trigh Capuzzo. Had it not been for the 150th Brigade Group Box between the two Trighs, Rommel would have been able to re-supply his striking force at will. As yet, he was unaware that this Box existed in his rear.

The next day, 29 May, ended Operation 'Venezia'. Rommel spent all his energies leading supply columns up to the stranded Afrika Korps. His faithful Westphal realised the supply situation was precarious and asked Crüwell to try to break through the South African and 50th Division positions to rescue Rommel, showing how grossly the German intelligence staffs had underestimated the strength of the main Gazala Line. The Sabratha Division did attack, but lost heavily, making scarcely a dent in the South African boxes. Crüwell was personally unfortunate. Trying to contact Rommel in a Feisler Storch liaison aircraft, he was shot down and captured by 150th Brigade Group. Efforts to help Rommel from the west came to nothing.

The armoured actions fought around Knightsbridge that day were some of the fiercest of the whole of the North African Campaign. Lumsden reopened his attacks on the eastern face of Rommel's penetration early in the morning. The Grants of 2nd and 22nd Armoured Brigade Groups did considerable damage to the two German panzer divisions, but they themselves suffered at the hands of the German anti-tank gunners, particularly on the Aslagh Ridge where 90th Light had joined the Ariete. The fighting took place in intense heat and blinding dust storms. When dusk came, both sides fell back into their night leaguers exhausted. Rommel accepted defeat and, realising his supplies were nearing exhaustion, ordered his striking force to fall back into a close defensive formation in the area which became known as the 'Cauldron'. 21st Panzer Division faced north on the Sidra Ridge; the Ariete faced east on the Aslagh Ridge and 15th Panzer and 90th Light Divisions faced south-west and west respectively to contain 150th Brigade Group's Box which the Germans had at last discovered.

Operation 'Venezia' had failed from the German point of view because of their faulty intelligence and Rommel's under-estimate of his opponent's fighting qualities. He should have been made to pay dearly for his temerity. He himself ascribes his escape to Ritchie's failure to concentrate his armour effectively. Writing after the event he says:

> Ritchie had thrown his armour into battle piecemeal and had thus given us the chance of engaging them on each separate occasion with just enough of our own tanks. This dispersal of the British armoured brigades was incomprehensible.
>
> (Rommel: page 208)

But the fault did not lie entirely with failure to concentrate and to co-ordinate the actions of British armour. Field Marshal Carver, who was a GSO II in XXX Corps at the time, has ascribed the British armoured brigades' failure to ill-conceived tactics:

> ... if, instead of a series of unco-ordinated advances at the enemy on a wide front ... a concentrated attack on a limited front, supported by the concentrated artillery available to an Armoured Division, had been delivered after a systematic attempt to locate and destroy by HE fire all the anti-tank guns within range, better results would have been obtained ... There was too much 'motoring'. What was needed was a deliberate attack, not just one more charge.
>
> (*South African Official History*: page 37, footnote 2).

Lumsden diagnosed a further fault. He believed that he had co-ordinated his tanks and artillery, but had not been successful because he had not used the third component of the 'all arms' team, the infantry. He began to advocate using infantry by night to deal with the anti-tank screens so as to open a way for his tanks when daylight came. The first British attempts to use infantry in this way was to prove disastrous.

PHASE II — ROMMEL SECURES HIMSELF IN THE CAULDRON
(30 May to 4 June)

Rommel's 2nd Principle
Supply lines are particularly sensitive, since all petrol and ammunition, indispensable requirements for battle, must pass along them. Hence everything possible must be done to protect one's own supply lines and to upset, or better still, cut the enemy's.

(Rommel: page 200).

Rommel's withdrawal into the Cauldron was construed by Ritchie and Auchinleck as the first stage of a disengagement and possible withdrawal by the German striking force. They agreed that their policy must be to hammer the German armour to bits with artillery fire while a counter-offensive was organised to enable the British to sweep forward to Benghazi and on to Tripoli. Ritchie's concept for his counter-offensive — Plan 'Limerick' — envisaged Gott breaking out south-westwards from the South African sector of the main Gazala Line, while Norrie sent his mobile troops round Bir Hacheim to join Gott astride Rommel's supply lines. The bulk of the British armour, however, would have to stay containing Rommel in the Cauldron in case he lunged for Tobruk. Concepts are one thing; operations are another. There was a lot of planning at HQ Eighth Army but it was rarely matched by action until it was too late. Plan after plan was overtaken by events.

On the German side, things were different. After deciding to abandon 'Venezia', Rommel set about re-building his striking force in the Cauldron. To do this he had to break through the Gazala Line in reverse. He decided, first to destroy 150th Brigade Group's Box to give himself a usable supply route through the minefields; and secondly, to wipe out the French garrison of Bir Hacheim so as to clear the whole of his southern flank before he drove north again to deal with Gott's XIII Corps and Tobruk. While he was doing all this he had to secure the northern and eastern faces of the Cauldron to prevent British interference with his operations. He ordered 21st Panzer on the Sidra Ridge and the Ariete on the Aslagh feature to dig in as quickly as they could and await the British attack which he knew must come.

Lumsden did attack again with 2nd and 22nd Armoured Brigade Groups on 30 May, but could find no way of penetrating the German anti-tank defences without further heavy loss of tanks. His continued failure to achieve anything decisive enabled him to convince Norrie and Ritchie that infantry should be used. This would take time to organise. Ritchie was less concerned with liquidating Rommel's force in the Cauldron than with mounting 'Limerick' which he hoped would be ready by 31 May. He was to be disappointed. Both Gott and Norrie protested that they could not be ready before 1 June. Rommel was thus left free to deal with 150th Brigade Group in his rear.

150th Brigade Group consisted of three battalions of Territorial soldiers from the mining and ship-building towns of the Tees and the Tyne who were accustomed to hardship and unaccustomed to giving in easily. They were supported by three squadrons of 'I' tanks from 1st Army Tank Brigade. Throughout 30 and 31 May they resisted all attacks and withstood the rain of shell and bomb thrown at them. When night fell on 31 May their defences were still intact, but there were no infantry reserves left; the artillery ammunition was down to 100 rounds; and only 13 'I' tanks remained serviceable. Somehow HQ Eighth Army and XIII Corps failed to appreciate what was happening until it was almost too late. A tardy realisation grew that Rommel was not withdrawing from the Cauldron and would have to be defeated there before it would be safe to mount 'Limerick'. Ritchie ordered Gott to establish an infantry brigade on the Sidra Ridge while Norrie did the same on the Aslagh Ridge to form a framework for Rommel's annihilation in the Cauldron and to draw Axis attention away from 150th Brigade Group. These operations started late on 1 June and were a miserable fiasco. Gott's attack was reduced for various reasons to battalion strength and achieved nothing; and Norrie's attack, which had been given to Messervy's re-formed 7th Armoured Divisional HQ, was cancelled through lack of time for reconnaissance. In the meanwhile 150th Brigade Group was over-run by 15th Panzer and 90th Light Divisions. The British Official Historians comment regretfully:

> It is sad that General Rommel had felt able to withdraw so many troops from the northern and eastern sides of the area beginning to be known as 'the Cauldron', with which to overwhelm the single brigade, so stoutly defending more than five miles of front and facing attack from every direction at once.
>
> (Vol III: page 228).

It was not just sad; it was inexcusable. British ignorance of the true situation and the inability to handle large forces with speed and determination enabled Rommel to eat up another British brigade group with the concentrated power of the Afrika Korps. 150th Brigade Group did not sell their lives cheaply. It took Rommel's personal leadership to defeat and overcome it. In the fighting Rommel led one of the assaults personally and lost General Gause and Colonel Westphal, who were both wounded, in addition to General von Vearst who had been hit the day before. But it was worth it. He had cut a route through to the west and could resupply his striking force.

The loss of 150th Brigade Group turned Rommel's position in the Cauldron from a near fatal encirclement into an advantageous wedge thrust deep into the British positions in the Gazala Line. And yet cheerful optimism continued to reign at HQ Eighth Army. The British attitude at the time is epitomised by Ritchie's signal to

Auchinleck reporting the loss; 'I am distressed over the loss of 150 Brigade after so gallant a fight, but still consider the situation favourable to us and getting better daily.' (J. Connell: page 532).

The British were beginning to reap the fruits of Auchinleck's unhappy selection of his command team. Ritchie might be able to direct a successful offensive when all was going well, but, in defeat, he was unable to dominate his subordinates who were senior to him in service and operational experience. His position was made more difficult by Gott and Norrie being close friends and tending, perhaps subconsciously, to resent his continued command of Eighth Army, which they had originally accepted as a temporary expedient. Their confidence in him was further undermined by their feeling that he was merely relaying Auchinleck's views to them and that these views were based on GHQ Cairo's incorrect assessments of what was really happening on the battlefield. Ritchie himself seems to have appreciated something of the unrealness of Cairo's advice. As the days went by he found that he had to pay less attention to Auchinleck and more to his Corps Commanders. Of the two, Gott was the stronger personality and in effect became the 'eminence grise', whose advice he began to prize as hopes of victory faded and were replaced with a growing realisation of defeat. Rommel had demonstrated the validity of his second principle of desert warfare by winning the tactical battle of supply which Ritchie should never have allowed him to do.

PHASE III - ROMMEL'S VICTORY IN THE BATTLE OF THE CAULDRON
(2 to 10 June 1942)

Rommel's 3rd Principle
The armour is the core of a motorised army. Everything turns on it, and other formations are mere auxiliaries. The war of attrition against the enemy armour must therefore be waged as far as possible by the anti-tank units. One's own armour should only be used to deal the final blow.

(Rommel: page 200)

How Ritchie could believe the situation was improving after the loss of 150th Brigade Group is hard to understand except in terms of the denseness of the fog of war. Under pressure from Auchinleck, he reverted momentarily to Plan 'Limerick', placing the 5th Indian Division under Gott for the south-westerly thrust from the South African positions. Norrie would continue to mask the Cauldron until Gott was through the crust and would then start his sweep round Bir Hacheim. This plan found no favour at all with the men who had to carry it out. Writing to Auchinleck to report his negotiations with his commanders Ritchie said:

I was as you are, most keen to carry out the offensive with the right shoulder forward, but the enemy in his present position makes it extremely difficult to form up a division behind our present frontage between Gazala and Alam Hamza without fear of its preparations being interrrupted. For this reason I had to discard that plan.

My next idea was to make a very wide turning movement with 5th Indian Division south of Bir Hacheim directed to Afrag*, but after the information I have had from the Corps Commanders today respecting the strength of our armour I cannot risk this.

It is absolutely essential that we should wrest from the enemy the initiative, which he is now starting to exercise and this must be done at the soonest possible moment. In the circumstances I have decided that I must crush him in the Cauldron. . . .

(J. Connell: page 535)

This letter disguised the acute differences of opinion amongst his subordinates. Gott asked Briggs, who had been promoted to command 5th Indian Division after his successful break-out from Benghazi in February, whether it was practicable to attack through the South African positions at 36 hours' notice. Pienaar had been coldly cynical about the whole operation. Briggs was doubtful and suggested the sweep round Bir Hacheim to join hands with the columns of 7th Motor Brigade Group and the South African Armoured Car Squadrons which were again operating west of the Gazala Line in Rommel's rear. Gott and Ritchie seem to have accepted this plan when Messervy counter-suggested a repetition of the direct attack on the Cauldron which he had cancelled on 1/2 June through lack of time for reconnaissance. This proposal had the advantage of not uncovering Tobruk and so won the day. Gott would have nothing to do with Messervy's ideas because he felt a direct attack by infantry into the Cauldron would be as costly as a First World War attack. Ritchie therefore gave the task to Norrie who decentralised responsibility for planning and execution of Operation 'Aberdeen' to Briggs and Messervy whose divisions were to provide the troops. Ritchie returned to Eighth Army HQ at Gambut with a glow of optimism to write another appreciation for Auchinleck on how he would conduct his operations after the Cauldron had been eliminated. It began by stating the 'immediate objective' as: 'To deny the use of Benghazi to the enemy and to secure for our own use the important air bases in Cyrenaica'. (J. Connell: page 540)

Six long pages of argument brought him back to the plan which he had just been forced by his subordinates to discard: "To break through the enemy defences in the coastal sector, to seize and hold the line Timimi – Mechili and so isolate the enemy force in the desert away from his water and forward dumps in the eastern Jebel, as the first step in the advance to secure Cyrenaica". (J. Connell: page 539)

John Connell rightly comments: 'Had Auchinleck had any inkling of what was really afoot in Eighth Army, it is inconceivable that he would not have gone up to restore order . . . In November, Galloway had acted. In June there was no Galloway'. (Page 540)

The British had no master plan, and without one, large armies of the size operating

---

* West of Bir el Temrad.

in the desert in 1942 could not be controlled. There has to be a unifying force to steer all the many strong-willed men in an agreed direction. That force is the commander's will, but it cannot make any impact without a policy and plan which all can understand.

While Briggs and Messervy made their preparations to destroy the Axis wedge in the British positions, Rommel was setting about eliminating all opposition south of the Cauldron to secure his rear. He despatched 90th Light southwards with the Trieste Division to clear Koenig out of the Bir Hacheim Box. He did not expect the operation to take more than 24 hours. In the meantime he ordered 21st Panzer to demonstrate northwards from Sidra Ridge to keep the British quiet.

21st Panzer's demonstration inflicted more tank casualties on the British, but 90th Light was not so successful against the French. Dust storms and minefields delayed Axis operations around Bir Hacheim until 4 June. Then the stubbornness of French resistance proved Rommel's 24 hours to be another under-estimate. 90th Light was momentarily defeated and needed reinforcement.

'Aberdeen' suffered the fate of all Ritchie's plans. It was whittled down and modified at each successive level of command as good and apparently valid reasons were found for troops not being available. The plan which Messervy and Briggs finally agreed was for the main attack to be made due eastwards from the Trigh Bir Hacheim onto the Aslagh Ridge and then through the heart of the Cauldron to the old 150th Brigade position on the far side with the aim of reblocking the minefield gaps. The attack would be in two phases. Briggs with his HQ 5th Indian Division

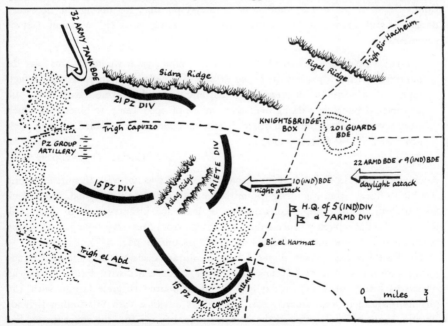

Fig 36 The Battle of the Cauldron: 5th to 6th June 1942

would command the first, which was to be a night attack by 10th Indian Brigade Group carried out behind a heavy artillery bombardment to capture and clear the Ariete's anti-tank gun screen off the Aslagh Ridge. Messervy with his HQ 7th Armoured Division would take over at daylight and thrust with 22nd Armoured Brigade Group and 9th Indian Brigade Group into the centre of the Cauldron. A diversionary attack by 32nd Army Tank Brigade was to be made on the western end of the Sidra Ridge to prevent 21st Panzer from interfering.

There were four interesting features in the 'Aberdeen' Plan. First of all the British were at last trying to use not only the close combination of tanks, infantry and artillery but darkness as well to defeat the German anti-tank screen. Laudable though this was they marred the concept by telling the tanks that their primary targets were the Axis tanks and that support of the infantry was secondary: 'In case of armoured action, infantry are self-supporting. They will not hamper the movement of 22nd Armoured Brigade.' (*British Official History*: Vol III, page 232).

The second point of interest lay in the assessment of troops required. One Armoured and two Indian Infantry Brigade Groups were to advance into an area strongly defended by the battered but virile 15th, 21st and Ariete Panzer Divisions, plus the strong Afrika Korps artillery, all firmly under Rommel's personal control. And thirdly, Norrie's XXX Corps HQ abrogated control of what was, in fact, a corps battle. Admittedly the two divisional HQs were located close together at Bir el Harmat and the two divisional commanders knew each other well, but such a command organisation was hardly a formula for success. If all went well it would work; but, if things began to go wrong, there was no-one responsible for taking the necessary decisions and renewing the battle with fresh reserves. Field Marshal Carver comments:

> ... the whole area occupied by the D.A.K. and Ariete would in this way be quartered with troops; but the broad arrows of the planners' maps would, in fact, represent a series of inexperienced battalions, weakly armed with anti-tank weapons, driving or walking over many miles of open desert to objectives which were several miles from each other. If ever an operation resembled sticking one's arm into a wasps' nest, this did ...

(Carver: *Tobruk*, page 195).

Auchinleck, back in Cairo, had his suspicions that all was not well. In spite of urging Ritchie to hurry up in regaining the initiative before he lost it for good, Auchinleck warned him not to skimp reconnaissance or leave the infantry without close tank support. Ritchie replied by forwarding a message from Messervy saying 'Everything ready for tonight and plenty of time for recce.' (J. Connell: page 542).

The Battle of the Cauldron was a British military disaster. 10th Indian Brigade Group's attack went in at 2.50 am on 5 June and succeeded with deceptive ease, all objectives being taken before daylight. 22nd Armoured Brigade Group with 156 Grants, Crusaders and Stuarts, then started its advance with 9th Indian Brigade Group. About two miles west of the Aslagh Ridge they ran into the concentrated fire of the Afrika Korps artillery and a formidable anti-tank screen. The British tanks were drawn into an armoured battle and left the infantry to fend for themselves. It transpired later that British intelligence of the Axis position and their reconnaissance of it had been grossly inaccurate. Their artillery bombardment and night attacks had fallen on a thin line of Axis outposts in an otherwise empty desert. The main Axis defensive front was further west. To make matters worse 32nd Army Tank Brigade's attack on the Sidra Ridge was an equally disastrous failure, leaving Rommel free to use both panzer divisions and the Ariete for counter-attack. This started in the afternoon with 21st Panzer and the Ariete attacking due east with limited success, driving some of the unsupported infantry out of the Cauldron. The real disaster occurred when 15th Panzer Division, accompanied by Rommel, slipped through a gap in the minefields south-west of Bir el Harmat, which it had cleared the previous day to recover some of its tanks knocked out in earlier fighting, and overran the two divisional headquarters, the two Indian brigade group headquarters and part of the 9th Indian Brigade Group which had not been committed, plus those elements of 10th Indian Brigade Group which had been forced out of the Cauldron by 21st Panzer's counter-attack. Control broke down, Messervy re-establishing his headquarters in Knightsbridge Box and Briggs in El Adem. Left in the Cauldron completely unsupported and without hope of relief were three Indian battalions, one reconnaissance battalion and four artillery regiments. Throughout the following day these units fought on with resolution always expecting reinforcements. The *British Official History* comments sadly:

> No help reached the doomed units in the Cauldron, for although the 2nd and 4th Armoured Brigades had been placed under General Messervy, who was now in sole command, he was unable in the prevailing confusion to bring them into action,
>
> (Vol III: page 234).

This was indeed a tragic and bitter end to the first British attempt to master the German defensive tactics using what was to prove to be the right formula in the end — the close co-operation of the three combat arms, using darkness and daylight to take advantage of their complementary characteristics.

The full extent of the Cauldron defeat was never really appreciated by the British higher commanders at the time because other disasters followed in bewildering succession, submerging the losses in the Cauldron which were: 10th Indian Brigade Group destroyed; two battalions of 9th Indian Brigade Group and one battalion and all anti-tank guns of 21st Indian Brigade Group lost; four regiments of artillery overrun; and Eighth Army's medium tanks reduced to 132. These losses, particularly of tanks and guns, started a cumulative decline in Eighth Army's strength from which it never recovered while under Ritchie's command. Early on 7 June he signalled Auchinleck 'Yesterday was a day of hard fighting in which we suffered considerably, but I am confident that enemy suffered no less.' (J. Connell: page 549).

Rommel had not suffered at all. He had repulsed and destroyed the expected British counter-attack on the Cauldron and was free to turn his attention on Bir Hacheim. He set 8 June as the target date for Koenig's destruction and set off personally to supervise its execution. Ritchie was in two minds as to whether Koenig should evacute Bir Hacheim, but Auchinleck advised against this because it would release German army and air resources at a time when Eighth Army needed as much time as possible to reorganise after the Cauldron failure.

8 June was a grim but triumphant day for the Free French. The Luftwaffe reopened its attacks using over 100 aircraft, and the German artillery provided 90th Light's infantry with effective support. French resistance did not falter, but by dusk Koenig was forced to report his men were nearing exhaustion and eating their reserve rations. Ritchie issued a warning order to prepare for evacuation. Rommel, on his side, summoned 15th Panzer Division less its panzer regiment to reinforce 90th Light and ordered a new assault for 10 June. The air and artillery preparation for this assault went on during 9 June. 7th Motor and 29th Indian Brigade Groups forced 90th Light to turn and face them, relieving some of the pressure, but the German assault on 10 June, which was supported by Axis aircraft dropping about 130 tons of bombs, resulted in one German assault group gaining a foothold in the French positions. Ritchie authorised the evacuation that night. 7th Motor Brigade Group ran a large convoy of trucks to within five miles of the western perimeter of Koenig's Box ready for the break out. 2,700 out of 3,000 Frenchmen reached safety, having created an epic which did much to re-establish the tarnished reputation of French soldiers. Koenig had bought precious time for Ritchie to regain the initiative, which he and Auchinleck talked about so much in their letters to each other, but proved so singularly incapable of achieving.

Headquarters Eighth Army was living in a 'fool's paradise'. It was superbly calm and unruffled, which is laudable in times of disaster, provided the consequences of those disasters are being squarely faced and not glossed over as temporary misfortunes. It seems doubtful whether Ritchie knew the true severity of his losses since Rommel's offensive began. If he did know them, he deceived Auchinleck as to their magnitude. On 11 June, the morning after the evacuation of Bir Hacheim, he dictated notes to his Brigadier General Staff in which he assessed the two sides as still being evenly matched stating that his plan was to:

Attack his (Rommel's) L of C . . .
(a) from the north on 50th Div front. Valentine tanks will be used to support these attacks;
(b) from the south with a motor brigade group and with such armour as I can spare from the Arena (Cauldron) area, without endangering security. At the moment I estimate this to be approximately thirty Stuart type tanks. In this way I hope to force the enemy to conform either by attacking me or by withdrawing troops from the Cauldron area to protect his L of C.

(Ibid: page 558).

He suggested also that Auchinleck was 'not in touch quite with our picture' (*Ibid:* page 556) and might like to send up a senior staff officer to gain a clearer idea of Eighth Army's problems. Auchinleck's unease increased and he decided to fly up to Gambut himself next day, 12 June.

Rommel's anti-tank units had fulfilled his third principle. The British had almost lost their tank superiority. The rival tank states at the end of the Battle of the Cauldron showed the British with 248 tanks opposing 219 tanks on the Axis side. Rommel was poised to reopen his offensive northwards to cut off Gott's XIII Corps and capture Tobruk.

PHASE IV — THE BATTLE OF KNIGHTSBRIDGE
(12 and 13 June)

Rommel's 4th Principle
Reconnaissance reports must reach the commander in the shortest possible time; he must take his decisions immediately and put them into effect as fast as he can. Speed of reaction decides the battle. Commanders of motorised forces must therefore operate as near as possible to their troops, and must have the closest possible signal communications with them.

(Rommel: page 200)

Gott had not been idle since Rommel broke off his offensive and retired into the Cauldron. He had organised and constructed a new line of posts, running east and west through Eluet et Tamar, linking the Acroma Box to 69th Brigade Group's Box in the main Gazala Line. Considerable quantities of mines had been laid to defend these posts and to create obstacles between them. They were garrisoned by detachments from the 1st South African and 50th Divisions. Relations between Gott and Pienaar, which had never been cordial since the latter's tardy performance during 'Crusader', grew worse during this period. During the 'Limerick' phase Gott had pressed Pienaar to attack south-westwards. Pienaar had objected on the grounds that his division could not take on the equivalent of one German and two Italian divisions opposing him. Ritchie had accepted his objections and Pienaar's operation was reduced to a brigade group raid. This was further whittled down, on grounds of lack of time for preparation, to a number of company sized raids across the width of the South African front on 7 June which achieved nothing for 280 casualties. Gott was openly critical of the South African performance and Pienaar's grudging half-heartedness in everything that XIII Corps asked of him. Gott's distrust of the South Africans grew apace and was reciprocated by Pienaar.

On 11 June, the day after the fall of Bir Hacheim, Rommel ordered his striking force to resume the offensive with a 'Venezia' type north-easterly wheel. 21st Panzer and the Ariete were at the pivot demonstrating northwards to pin the British armour in the Knightsbridge area; 15th Panzer and the Trieste were in the centre; and 90th Light was on the outer edge advancing on its old objective of El Adem. Another batch of eight PzIII (Specials) had reached the Afrika Korps with six even newer PzIV (Specials) mounting a formidable long barrelled 75mm gun. Rommel was, however, desperately short of infantry. 90th Light was down to 1,000 bayonets and the two panzer divisions' infantry regiments were about a third of their established strength. Ritchie, on the other hand, was strong in motorised infantry; and in the air both sides

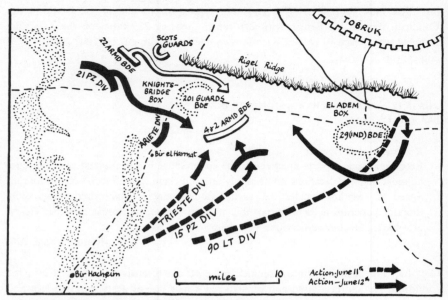

Fig 37 The Battle of Knightsbridge: 12th and 13th June 1942

were evenly matched and able to mount effective strikes at critical moments, provided the soldiers could give their airmen suitable targets, which was remarkably infrequent.

The British watched the German advance closely when it began about 3 pm on 11 June. By dusk it had not progressed very far. 15th Panzer Division skirmished with 4th Armoured Brigade Group which had moved south-east from Knightsbridge to intercept. Both leaguered for the night half-way between the Trigh Capuzzo and the Trigh el Abd. 90th Light leaguered with the reconnaissance units south of El Adem. Norrie appreciated that Rommel had split his armoured force. 15th Panzer lay temptingly exposed to an attack by the British armoured brigades in the Knightsbridge area with 21st Panzer Division some 20 miles further west on the Sidra Ridge. Norrie placed 2nd and 4th Armoured Brigades under Messervy's 7th Armoured Division to deal with 15th Panzer next day, leaving Lumsden's 1st Armoured Division to look after 21st Panzer with 22nd Armoured and 32nd Army Tank Brigades. The German radio intercept unit warned Rommel of what was afoot. He ordered 15th Panzer to 'hedgehog' and await attack, hoping that the British would continue to emasculate themselves attacking his anti-tank guns and 'Specials' in defensive positions.

Operations on 12 June started slowly and did not develop as either side expected. Messervy was unhappy about Norrie's plan and decided he must drive to Corps HQ to confer with him before setting 2nd and 4th Armoured Brigades in motion. On the way he ran into a column from 90th Light and had to seek refuge in a dry water cistern to avoid capture. His division had neither orders nor a commander. 15th

Panzer waited patiently for attack until midday and then was ordered by Nehring to attack 4th Armoured Brigade. The day was hot and hazy with poor visibility in which it was difficult to identify targets and to be sure what was happening. 15th Panzer's attack was sluggish and indecisive, reflecting the fatigue of German tank crews, but the anti-tank gunners took full advantage of the haze to close with the British tanks and inflict quite unnecessary losses on them while they awaited orders. In the early afternoon both Rommel and Norrie decided to act almost simultaneously on the scanty information in their possession. Rommel ordered 21st Panzer to move east and to attack 2nd and 4th Armoured Brigades' flank and rear, while 15th Panzer kept them engaged frontally. Norrie, realising something had happened to Messervy, ordered Lumsden to take tactical control of the battle. 21st Panzer moved quickly and attacked the rear of Messervy's commanderless brigades as they were beating off 15th Panzer's attack. Surprise was complete and devastating. Lumsden moved south with 22nd Armoured Brigade Group to turn the tables on 21st Panzer but was too late and lost heavily trying to do so. 4th Armoured Brigade was so badly mauled that it pulled back clear of the battle area well north of the southern escarpment. 2nd and 22nd Armoured Brigade Groups withdrew to positions just east of the Knightsbridge Box where they managed to halt the German pursuit as darkness fell. No exact figures are given for British tank losses on 12 June but they were probably not far short of 100. The balance of armoured advantage had swung decisively in Rommel's favour.

Auchinleck had been with Ritchie all day. No scent of disaster seems to have reached him before he flew back to Cairo that evening. His signal to London that night illustrates the detached atmosphere at Eighth Army Headquarters: 'Atmosphere here good. No undue optimism and realities of situation are being faced calmly and resolutely. Morale of troops appears excellent.' (J. Connell: page 562)

Rommel was with his troops; neither Norrie nor Ritchie were close enough to theirs to know what was happening. Orders should have been given that night for the evacuation of Gott's XIII Corps from the Gazala Line which was now a dangerous salient so that a new front could be established running due south from the Acroma Box before it was too late. Neither Auchinleck nor Ritchie felt the time was ripe. Both hoped that Rommel was nearing the end of his logistic, if not operational, endurance. XIII Corps might still be able to launch a decisive counter-attack to cut Rommel's communications if and when the Axis offensive faltered. Churchill applauded: 'Your decision to fight it out to the end is most cordially endorsed. We shall sustain you whatever the result. Retreat would be fatal. This is a business not only of armour but of will-power. God bless you all.' (Churchill: Vol IV, page 331)

But will-power was not enough to counter-balance the serious British tank losses of 12 June. Rommel had the upper hand, and despite the fatigue of his tank crews, reopened his offensive next day with an encircling attack on the remnants of the British armoured brigades clustered around the Knightsbridge Box. 21st Panzer attacked from the west along the Rigel escarpment eventually overcoming the 2nd Battalion Scots Guards who were holding its western end; and 15th Panzer and 90th Light cut in behind the Knightsbridge Box from the east. Gott, who had been placed in command of all operations around Knightsbridge, realised the Box had become

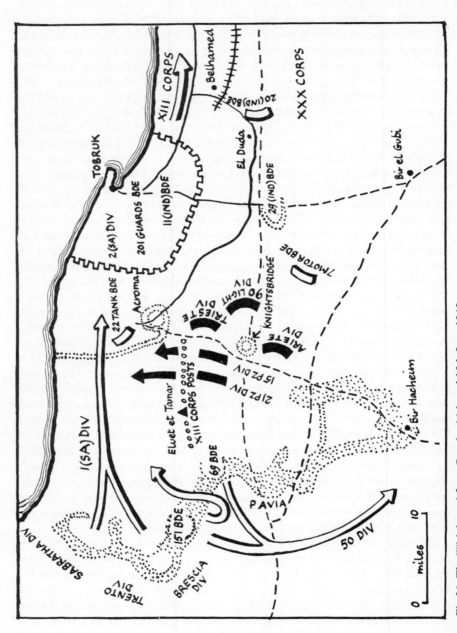

Fig 38 The Withdrawal from Gazala: 14th and 15th June 1942

untenable although it had not been directly attacked. He ordered its evacuation that night, reforming his front on his line of defended posts running east and west through Eluet et Tamar. The withdrawal of the South Africans and 50th Division from main Gazala Line could be delayed no longer. The British loss of the Battle of Knightsbridge spelt the end of the battles of Gazala and the beginning of the retreat to El Alamein.

PHASE V — ROMMEL INVESTS TOBRUK
(14 to 17 June 1942)

Rommel's 5th Principle
Speed of movement and the organisational cohesion of one's own forces are decisive factors and require particular attention. Any sign of dislocation must be dealt with as quickly as possible by reorganisation.

(Rommel: page 200).

By the evening of 13 June, Ritchie had been forced to acknowledge that the Gazala Line was untenable. The tank states showed only 50 cruisers and 20 'I' tanks left with which to cover the withdrawal of Pienaar's South Africans and 50th Division. Speed was vital if these two divisions were to slip through the narrowing gap between Knightsbridge and the sea. In the early hours of the morning of 14 June, Ritchie warned Gott and his own staff to prepare the withdrawal. There was no proper plan for this contingency but there was an old plan called 'Freeborn' which had been written after the withdrawal from Benghazi earlier in the year. This plan was seized upon by the staffs and used as the basis for extricating the two divisions. The routes and timings were designed to take them right back to the Egyptian frontier.

By 1020 am Ritchie had a fuller picture of the situation and ordered Gott to put 'Freeborn' into operation that night. By then Gott's staff had advised him that it would be impossible to pass both divisions through Tobruk in a single night and so he proposed that 50th Division should break-out through the Italian lines and fight its way back to the frontier moving south of Bir Hacheim. The South Africans were not to start their withdrawal until 50th Division was clear so as not to alert the Italians too soon and make 50th Division's task more hazardous. Pienaar, difficult as ever when asked to do something by Gott, complained that this would mean part of his division withdrawing in daylight. Gott gave way and authorised both operations to begin at dusk. All would depend on how successful he was in blocking the Afrika Korps if it reopened its thrust towards the coast.

Ritchie reported his intentions to Auchinleck as soon as he had given Gott his orders and in so doing started the first of a series of signals which led in the end to the loss of Tobruk with a garrison of 32,000 men instead of its abandonment without a fight as the Cs-in-C Middle East had intended.

In circumstances there is in my opinion no alternative but to draw out 1st SA and

50th Divs ... I have, therefore, ordered General Gott to withdraw these formations into Army Reserve while, at the same time, I will

(a) occupy frontier positions while

(b) building up as strong an armoured and infantry force as possible in the desert west of the frontier.

... I hope initially to be able to stand on position western perimeter Tobruk – El Adem – Belhamed with mobile forces operating from desert to south ...

Tobruk has a month's supplies and I believe we can restore the situation within that period and thereby save all the installations there. Alternatives therefore are

(a) To accept risk of temporary investment in Tobruk

or (b) to go the whole hog, give up Tobruk and withdraw to the frontier.

I am at any rate clearing all non-essentials out of Tobruk and making preparations for demolition. Do you agree to me accepting the risk of investment in Tobruk?

(J. Connell: page 566).

During the next few hours signals between Ritchie and Auchinleck crossed each other, weaving a pattern of cross-purposes which were further tangled by events taking place in the desert. At 1115 am Auchinleck replied with a short signal telling him to stabilize his front on the line of the minefield running south from the coast to Acroma and then along the escarpment via El Adem to Bir el Gubi. This would give some depth in front of Tobruk, whereas Ritchie proposed to use the western perimeter of Tobruk, manned by 2nd South African Division as the northern sector of his new front. What Auchinleck did not know, and Ritchie did not reveal to him, was that 1st South African and 50th Divisions had been ordered back to the frontier instead of to this new line.

Fifteen minutes later Auchinleck despatched a fuller signal the crucial sentences of which were:

... While I realise that our armoured forces have been defeated and are now weaker in quantity as well as quality than those of the enemy, I must stress my opinion that the enemy, who so far has won all his successes with two German armoured and one German motor divs, helped to some extent by one Italian motor div, cannot really be in position to carry out large scale offensive operations for indefinite period at pace he has been doing. He must I feel have lost heavily, and we know his ammunition is short. Moreover we are definitely superior to him in the air.

3. This being so Tobruk must be held and the enemy must not be allowed to invest it. This means that Eighth Army must hold the line Acroma – El Adem and southwards and resist all attempts to pass it. Having reduced your front by evacuating Gazala and reorganised your forces, this should be feasible and I order you to do it.

4. If you feel you cannot accept the responsibility of holding this position you must say so.

(*Ibid*: page 566).

Auchinleck's intentions were clear and, as far as he could see in Cairo, quite practical. Gott would have his two divisions – 1st South African and 50th Division – backed by 2nd South African in Tobruk to hold the Acroma – El Adem sector, and Norrie would have the scattered remnants of 1st and 7th Armoured Divisions and 5th and 10th Indian Divisions to re-form a mobile defensive force covering the desert flank down to Bir el Gubi. Somehow Ritchie found himself unable to tell Auchinleck what was really happening or to instruct his staff to conform to Auchinleck's orders. He allowed it to appear to Cairo that he was doing his best to meet Auchinleck's wishes while agreeing with Gott and Norrie to moves more in keeping with their own views of the need to withdraw to the frontier. Ritchie's Brigadier General Staff, Brigadier (later General) Whiteley explained later:

> There was no question of a Gazala Line, a Tobruk Line and then another Gambut Line. If the battle was lost, the withdrawal would be right back to the frontier. It was all one position with considerable depth and Tobruk and El Adem were part of that depth.
>
> *(South African Official History*: page 73).

This was the policy being pursued by Ritchie's staff and Corps Commanders. Gott became the dominant personality and busied himself with the preparation of Tobruk for 'temporary investment' while the rest of XIII Corps pulled back to the frontier. The garrison was to consist of Klopper's untried 2nd South African Division, 201st Guards Brigade, 11th Indian Brigade, 32nd Army Tank Brigade with 50 tanks, and two regiments of British medium and one regiment of British field artillery in addition to the South African divisional artillery. This was about the same size of garrison as Morshead's the year before. Gott volunteered to stay in Tobruk to conduct its second defence and is recorded as saying that Klopper's dispositions were 'a nice tidy show' compared with the state of affairs when Australians fell back into the fortress. (*South African Official History*: page 128). Ritchie, however, decided that HQ XIII Corps should not stay and must go back to organise the forces assembling on the frontier.

Gott was lucky on 14 June. Rommel ordered a resumption of the advance northwards by the two panzer divisions closely supported by the Panzer Army artillery, but his units were too exhausted to attack with their accustomed vigour. Conversely the British and South African garrisons of the line of posts and the remnants of 1st Armoured Division, protecting XIII Corps' withdrawal routes, fought with renewed determination knowing that they held the key to the Corps' survival. The day was again hot and dusty, and the German efforts to break through had an half-heartedness about them which is hardly surprising. About midday both Panzer divisions found themselves struggling to make breaches in the minefields connecting the British posts. Delays ensued while Sappers were brought up. The hours of daylight slipped away all too slowly for the British as they fought to prevent the Germans reaching the coastal escarpment; but they galloped for the weary Germans. 21st Panzer came nearest the via Balbia, but not near enough to endanger XIII Corps' withdrawal. As darkness fell the Germans pulled back into leaguer too exhausted to do more. Rommel, whose air reconnaissance reported the tell-tale increase of eastward traffic on the via Balbia, demanded a continuation of the advance during the night but to no avail. There were few Germans ears listening to his orders. The Afrika Korps had reached the end of its tether. Its men slept wherever darkness overtook them.

During the night Ramsden's 50th Division burst through the Brescia and Pavia Divisions successfully. Ramsden had formed a number of columns of all arms which broke out independently. Only one failed to get through. It turned back and withdrew with the South Africans via Tobruk. The others made their way across the desert to the frontier. The ease with which 50th Division broke out suggests that far more could have been done to help 150th Brigade Group during the battle in the Cauldron, and that a counter-offensive from the Gazala salient was much more practicable than Gott and Pienaar thought.

The South African withdrawal went tolerably well. Rommel arrived at 15th Panzer's HQ at 8 am to find nothing stirring. He ordered them northwards where they cut off the South African rear-guard before it could escape through the Acroma minefields. He sent the rest of his striking force eastwards towards El Adem and Gambut to start the second investment of Tobruk and to prevent Ritchie stabilizing a new front south of the fortress.

While Rommel acted the British commanders continued to make impractical plans to hold lines which had been undermined by German action. As 21st Panzer thrust eastwards past Acroma, Ritchie was reading a directive from Auchinleck which ran:

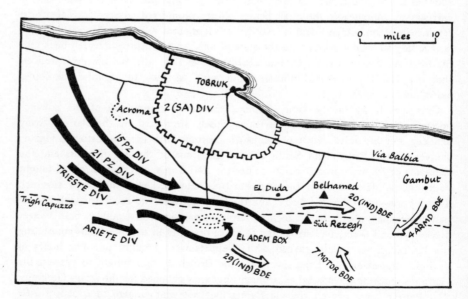

Fig 39 The Investment of Tobruk: 16th to 18th June 1942

Intention: To destroy the enemy forces in Cyrenaica . . .

Method: To deny the general line Acroma – El Adem – El Gubi . . . The defences of Tobruk and other strong places will be used as pivots of manoeuvre, but on NO account will any part of Eighth Army be allowed to be surrounded in Tobruk and invested there . . .

I am creating for you a strong and mobile reserve in the area Sollum – Maddalena for a powerful counter-offensive at the earliest moment.

(J. Connell: pages 567-568).

This directive had crossed a signal from Ritchie reporting his intentions for 15 June which concluded:

The policy which I recommend, therefore, with all my conviction is:
  (a) To fight alongside Tobruk and to prevent it being invested.
  (b) If I fail, to allow Tobruk to be invested rather than to order the garrison to fight its way out in difficult circumstances . . .

(*Ibid*: page 569).

The Prime Minister entered the arena that evening with a disturbing signal, showing that he was unaware or had forgotten that it had been decided as long ago as January not to accept another siege of Tobruk. Moreover, he was beginning to invest Tobruk with a symbolic significance which the commanders on the spot wished to avoid:

To what position does Ritchie want to withdraw the Gazala troops? Presume there is no question in any case of giving up Tobruk. As long as Tobruk is held no serious enemy advance into Egypt is possible. We went through all this in April 1941. Do not understand what you mean by withdrawing to 'old frontier'.

(Churchill: Vol IV, page 331).

Auchinleck replied in all honesty that his orders to Ritchie were:

  (a) To deny general line Acroma – El Adem – El Gubi to the enemy.
  (b) NOT to allow his forces to be invested in Tobruk.
  (c) To attack and harass the enemy whenever occasion offers . . .

(*Ibid*: page 331).

He did not know that his instructions were not being obeyed because Rommel had already taken affairs out of Ritchie's hands. The Prime Minister decided to make quite sure that Auchinleck's signal did mean what it said. He replied:

We are glad to have your assurance that you have no intention of giving up Tobruk. War Cabinet interpret your telegram to mean that, if need arises, General Ritchie would leave as many troops in Tobruk as are necessary to hold the place for certain.

(*Ibid*: page 331).

The carefully thought-out policy of the Commanders-in-Chief had been overturned. There could be no going back. Tobruk had to be held, but Auchinleck began to have doubts about Ritchie's real intentions. He decided to send Corbett, his Chief of Staff, up to Eighth Army Headquarters to ensure that his instructions were being complied with. Corbett, at last, found out the truth. 1st South African and 50th Divisions were heading for the frontier. No line was being built up from Tobruk to El Adem and Bir el Gubi, let alone from Acroma which had been abandoned before he reached Ritchie's headquarters. The meeting between the two men was stormy, but there was little Corbett could do. The bulk of Eighth Army was on its way back, leaving just 29th Indian Brigade Group in El Adem Box and 20th Indian Brigade Group in the Ed Duda – Belhamed area. The only mobile force left near Tobruk was Messervy's 7th Armoured Division with 4th Armoured Brigade, which was refitting at Gambut with tanks coming out of workshops, and 7th Motor Brigade Group in the open desert to the south. Corbett flew back to Cairo to report to Auchinleck that he must either accept the investment of Tobruk or order its evacuation. It could not be held as part of a defensive line as the chances of holding anything south of Tobruk had already gone. Auchinleck could not order Tobruk's evacuation after Churchill's intervention so he had to accept its investment, hoping it might only be temporary as Corbett suggested He sent off two signals on 16 June. One went to Churchill:

> The War Cabinet interpretation is correct. General Ritchie is putting into Tobruk what he considers an adequate force to hold it even should it become temporarily isolated by enemy . . . Basis for immediate future action by Eighth Army is to hold El Adem fortified area as pivot of manoeuvre and to use all available mobile forces to prevent enemy establishing himself east of El Adem or Tobruk. Very definite orders to this effect have been issued to General Ritchie and I trust he will be able to give effect to them . . .

> (J. Connell: page 578).

The other went to Ritchie:

> Although I have made it clear to you that Tobruk must not be invested, I realise that its garrison may be isolated for short periods until our counter-offensive can be launched. With this possibility in mind you are free to organise the garrison as you think best . . .

> (*Ibid*: page 578).

The second signal unintentionally destroyed the validity of the first. It breached the psychological dam which Auchinleck had been trying to build up in the minds of Ritchie and the Eighth Army staff by insisting on the defence of El Adem – Bir el Gubi Line. Instinct rather than logical thought controls tired men who are experiencing the effects of military defeat. Auchinleck's acceptance of the temporary isolation of Tobruk enabled Ritchie to bow to pressure from Norrie to extricate the Indian Brigades before it was too late. In so doing he destroyed any chance there might have been in forming a pivot of manoeuvre in the El Adem area. After resisting 21st Panzer Division's attacks for 36 hours 29th Indian Brigade slipped away from El Adem during the night 16/17 June and made its way to the frontier. 20th Indian Brigade was not so successful when it broke out from Belhamed the following night.

It ran into German columns across its path and lost heavily in its attempts to reach the frontier. And so did 4th Armoured Brigade in its last action west of the frontier. Messervy ordered it to manoeuvre into a position south of the Trigh Capuzzo to attack the flank of the German columns moving eastwards. The brigade had about 90 miscellaneous tanks manned by the remnants of seven regiments. Its artillery and infantry were not available as they had been sent off in harassing columns to help 20th Indian Brigade. Before the brigade could reach the position Messervy had selected, it clashed with 15th and 21st Panzer which had been ordered by Rommel to sweep south-eastwards from El Adem before turning north to cut the British withdrawal routes near Gambut. A fierce slogging match ensued in which 4th Armoured Brigade fought with the sun in its eyes and was badly handicapped by the absence of its artillery. After two hours hard fighting and with darkness falling it withdrew southwards to the Trigh el Abd and thence to the frontier. Rommel, who was present, stopped the pursuit and led the Afrika Korps northwards to cut the via Balbia north of Gambut. At 3 am 18 June, 21st Panzer reported: 'Via Balbia is reached and cut'. Tobruk was invested for the second time, just two days before the deadline set by the Axis High Command for the diversion of resources to 'Hercules'. Speed of movement and organisational cohesion – Rommel's fifth principle – had been amply demonstrated.

After 4th Armoured Brigade's defeat Ritchie felt it was time to replace Messervy who had had 'three divisional headquarters shot from under him'. Corelli Barnett records how Ritchie, polite and as calm as ever, said to him: 'Well, Frank, I'm afraid I've lost confidence in you – you seem to be out of luck. Nothing seems to be going right with you.' (C. Barnett– page 158). The British were beginning to realise that there *was* something wrong with their command team. Similar words were to be uttered at different levels with increasing frequency in the next few months.

PHASE VI – THE CAPTURE OF TOBRUK
(18 to 21 June 1942)

Rommel's 6th Principle
Concealment of intentions is of the utmost importance in order to provide surprise for one's own operations and thus make it possible to exploit the time taken by the enemy command to react. Deception measures of all kinds should be encouraged, if only to make the enemy commander uncertain and cause him to hesitate and hold back.

(Rommel: page 200).

Eighth Army's morale remained curiously high and quite unbroken as it fell back to the frontier. It had become a hardened army accustomed to ride the troughs of defeat almost as confidently as the peaks of victory. Men felt that the tide would turn again as Axis communications lengthened and became more vulnerable to RAF attack. These beliefs had more substance than the men in the desert realised. All Rommel's brilliant tactical victories were being jeopardised by Hitler's decision not to take Malta before Rommel attacked and, more important, before the 2nd German Air Force had to return to the Ukraine. While the Battle of Knightsbridge was being fought two supply convoys set out for Malta. The 'Harpoon' convoy from Gibraltar was fought through to Malta on 14 and 15 June with the loss of four out of the six supply ships and two destroyers, but 15,000 tons of supplies were landed in Malta. The 'Vigorous' convoy from Alexandria was forced to turn back by the intervention of the Italian Battlefleet and attacks by Axis aircraft and motor torpedo boats between Crete and Cyrenaica. Unfortunate though this was, Malta was stocked until September. Provided there was a good harvest and British submarines managed to run in sufficient aviation fuel, the island would become a threat to Rommel's supply lines again when the Luftwaffe departed for Hitler's summer campaign in Russia.

Churchill was able to give Auchinleck other heartening news. The British 8th Armoured Division and 44th Infantry Division who had been released from Home Defence by the arrival of US Divisions in the United Kingdom would reach Suez at the end of June and the middle of July respectively, together with large drafts of individual reinforcements including 11 anti-aircraft regiments. Auchinleck himself had ordered the New Zealand Division back from Syria to the Western Desert and it would arrive on the frontier shortly. No comparable reinforcements were reaching Rommel, because Hitler's drive towards Stalingrad and the Caucasian oil would absorb all German resources.

On the 18 June Auchinleck flew to Eighth Army Headquarters, which was at Sollum, to decide future tactical policy. He agreed that Tobruk should remain directly under Eighth Army's command; Gott's HQ XIII Corps should be responsible for the frontier defences and all harassing operations forward of it; and Norrie should go back with his HQ XXX Corps to Egypt where he was to set about forming a new mobile striking force as resources became available.

Back in Cairo the Cs-in-C despatched their considered views of the situation to London on 20 June. After reviewing the relative strengths of the two sides, the adequacy of the Tobruk Garrison and the level of its supplies for three months, they concluded: 'We hope, therefore, that Tobruk should be able to hold out until operations for relief are successfully completed after resumption of our offensive'.

They went on to point out that unless Hitler diverted substantial reinforcement to North Africa, the British would regain numerical and logistic superiority. Moreover, the Axis supply position would prevent further intensive operations. Their final conclusion is interesting in the light of subsequent events:

> There is no natural position east of Halfaya which the enemy could hold successfully against superior forces. Therefore, should both Tobruk and the frontier positions fall, enemy would be unlikely to attempt advance deep into Egypt unless our forces be decisively routed in the field or he has received considerable reinforcements.
>
> (*British Official History*: Vol III, page 260).

As the Cs-in-Cs' appreciation was being despatched to London it was being

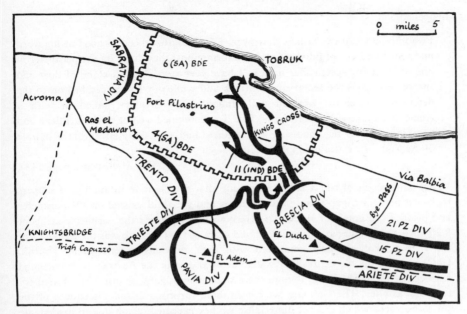

Fig 40 The Capture of Tobruk: 20th to 21st June 1942

discredited by events in the desert. Rommel lost no time in launching his attack on Tobruk. He used the plan which had been elaborated over so many frustrating weeks in 1941 before it was forestalled by 'Crusader'. He issued his orders on 18 June; used the 19 for assembly and final reconnaissance; and opened his attack at first light on the 20th. The operation, which was supported by every aircraft that Kesselring could assemble in time, was a masterpiece of rapid improvisation and ruthless determination to succeed. It also showed what good soldiers can do when buoyed up by success, however tired they may be.

The sector chosen for the assault was on the south-east corner of the perimeter, held by 11th Indian Brigade. To ensure surprise, the Afrika Korps assembled with the Ariete around Gambut as if getting ready to advance to the Frontier. 90th Light had already occupied Bardia, which tended to confirm this impression, but it was not the direction of the attack which deceived the British but its speed. On 20 June Ritchie and Auchinleck exchanged signals as the German blow was falling:

Ritchie (20 June 0100 hours)
There have been no signs today of any effort except with small recce detachments to press eastwards towards the frontier. I feel that having removed our air threat from Gambut group of aerodromes he is likely to turn his main attention on Tobruk . . .

Only four and a half hours after Ritchie despatched his signal Rommel was standing with von Mellenthin on the escarpment near El Adem. Von Mellenthin describes what happened:

> Promptly at 0520 the Stukas flew over. Kesselring had been as good as his word and sent hundreds of bombers in dense formations; they dived on the perimeter in one of the most spectacular attacks I have ever seen. A great cloud of dust and smoke rose from the sector under attack and while our bombs crashed on to the defences, the entire German and Italian Army artillery joined in with a tremendous and well co-ordinated fire. The combined weight of the artillery and bombing was terrific, and as we soon realised had a crushing effect on the morale of the Mahratta battalion in that sector.

> (Von Mellenthin: page 113).

Under this weight of fire it is not surprising that the German infantry and sappers managed to clear a gap through what mines and wire still existed on the perimeter and bridged the anti-tank ditch. The German tanks entered the perimeter at about 8.20 am – three hours after zero. What did surprise the Germans was the weakness of the British artillery reply compared with their previous experience at Tobruk. Unfortunately the old centralised system evolved during the Australian defence had not been re-established and, though there were enough guns, South African artillery control was poor. The Germans were even more surprised at the inadequacy of the counter-attacks which did not materialise as they expected, again due to inadequate co-ordination. Muddled and ill-conceived orders resulted in 32nd Army Tank Brigade and 201st Guards Brigade being frittered away. By midday both panzer divisions had fought their way to King's Cross – 21st Panzer to the east and 15th Panzer to the west. The Ariete had crossed the anti-tank ditch in its own sector but failed to make progress and was ordered to follow the Afrika Korps.

During the afternoon 21st Panzer Division fought its way relentlessly northwards towards Tobruk itself and by 5 pm was calling for the Axis artillery fire to be lifted off the port so that it could advance down the last escarpment into the town. 15th Panzer protected 21st Panzer's flank by pushing westwards along the Pilastrino Ridge. An hour earlier General Klopper had believed his HQ was about to be over-run and ordered the destruction of all equipment, radios, and papers, retiring himself to the 6th South African Brigade HQ in the north-western sector. 15th Panzer did not press any further westwards, and so Klopper had needlessly divested himself of effective means of controlling the battle.

When darkness fell the Germans went into close leaguers for the night in the heart of Tobruk. The South African Division's sector was still intact in the west; 201st Guards Brigade was still a cohesive force in the centre; and part of 11th Indian Brigade were still resisting in the eastern sector. The demolition plan had been put into effect around the port and chaos reigned in the rear areas where the logistic units were being rounded up by the Germans. Klopper realised the situation was hopeless and sent out a warning order for all units to prepare to break out that night. A series of radio messages to and from Eighth Army HQ about 9 pm ended with Ritchie telling Klopper 'Come out tomorrow night preferably, if not tonight. Centre line Medauar – Knightsbridge – Maddalena. I will keep open gap Harmat – El Adem. Inform me time selected and route. Tomorrow night preferred. Destruction of petrol vital.'* Then it transpired that most of the troops carrying transport had been lost when 21st Panzer captured the rear areas. After a series of discussions with subordinate commanders some of whom advocated breaking out with as large a force as could be mounted in the remaining transport while the rest fought on as long as possible, Klopper signalled Ritchie at 2 am 'Am sending mobile troops out tonight. Not possible to hold tomorrow. Mobile troops nearly nought. Enemy captured vehicles. Will resist to last man and last round.'* Three hours later when dawn was breaking, Klopper changed his mind realising that further resistance would not help Eighth Army and would lead to useless sacrifice of South African manhood. As dawn broke a white flag was raised above 6th South African Brigade HQ. 32,000 men: 19,000 British, 10,500 South Africans and 2,500 Indians – fell into Rommel's hands together with large quantities of supplies which could not be destroyed in time.

The fall of Tobruk shook the Allied cause as severely as the loss of Singapore earlier in the year. Churchill heard the news in Washington and on his return to London had to face a motion of censure in the House of Commons expressing no confidence in his conduct of the war. The reasons for the débâcle are many and complex but can be reduced to four. First of all, Tobruk was no longer a fortress. Most of its mines had been removed for use in the Gazala Line after the decision was taken not to defend the port again. The wire had fallen into disrepair; the anti-tank ditch was broken down in many places; and the field defences were silted up. There was not enough time between 12 June, when it became obvious that Tobruk might be invested and 20 June when it was attacked, to make good these deficiencies. Secondly, the German force, which attacked Tobruk, was very different from the scratch team which Rommel threw against it in the Spring of 1941. It was a highly professional panzer group with the experience of 'Crusader' and the victories of 'Gazala' behind it. In contrast, Klopper's 2nd South African Division was relatively new and inexperienced. Its morale was good, but it had not been tempered by battle like the Afrika Korps. Thirdly, Klopper and his staff were given a task beyond their capabilities. At the beginning of the first siege of Tobruk, HQ Western Desert Force had stayed in the fortress to organise the artillery support system, the counter-attack plans and rehearsals, and the logistic backing. It did not leave by sea until Morshead was satisfied that all was well and that the command system had settled down into a properly co-ordinated machine capable of handling the defence. But fourthly, the real blame must rest with Churchill, Auchinleck and Ritchie, who, through the interaction of opinion and the combination of circumstance, allowed Tobruk to be invested again. It could not stand in isolation after it had ceased to be part of the main Eighth Army front unless its garrison had the spirit and cohesion which Morshead's Australians acquired as the siege progressed. Klopper's South Africans, Indians and British troops were never given the time to settle down and develop a corporate morale. Rommel deserved his Field Marshal's baton which the grateful Führer bestowed upon him for the capture of Tobruk – the greatest victory of his brilliant military career.

* *British Official History*: Vol III, page 272.

PHASE VII — ROMMEL'S ADVANCE TO EL ALAMEIN
(22 to 30 June 1942)

Rommel's 7th Principle

Once the enemy has been thoroughly beaten up success can be exploited by attempting to over-run and destroy major parts of his disorganised formations. Here again, speed is everything. The enemy must never be allowed time to reorganise. Lightning regrouping for the pursuit and reorganisation of supplies for the pursuing force are essential.

(Rommel: page 200).

Rommel was not slow in putting his 7th Principle into effect. He regrouped quickly and using the large stocks of supplies which had fallen into his hands, despatched the Afrika Korps and the Italian Mobile Corps towards the frontier with only one day for reorganisation. He could not, however, cross the wire until he had received Mussolini's authority to do so as this was one of the strict conditions imposed on him when his offensive was given priority over 'Hercules'. Kesselring flew to Africa to confer with Rommel on 21 June. Von Mellenthin was present in Rommel's Command Vehicle when the two discussed the future:

> Rommel insisted that he must follow up his victory without waiting for the attack on Malta, but Kesselring pointed out that an advance into Egypt could not succeed without full support from the Luftwaffe. If this was given, the Luftwaffe would not be available for operations against Malta, and should the island recover, Rommel's communications would be in serious jeopardy. Kesselring maintained that the only sound course was to stick to the original plan, and postpone an invasion of Egypt until Malta had fallen.
>
> Rommel disagreed emphatically and the discussions became exceedingly lively. He admitted the Panzer Army had suffered heavily in the Gazala battles, but maintained that Eighth Army was in a far worse plight and we now had a unique opportunity for a thrust to the Suez Canal. A delay of even a few weeks would give the enemy time to move up new forces and prevent any further advance. The two commanders failed to reach agreement, and before leaving Kesselring made no secret of his intention to withdraw his air units to Sicily.

(Von Mellenthin: page 118).

Kesselring did not possess the political influence of Germany's newest Field Marshal who was being lionized by Nazi propaganda. Rommel appealed to Hitler and Mussolini. Hitler was quick to support him despite contrary advice from the German Naval and Italian General Staffs. Mussolini found little difficulty in agreeing with the Führer; the chance of entering Cairo in triumph and avenging the loss of his Ethiopian Empire dazzled him. And so the fatal decision, which was to lose the North African Campaign for the Axis, was taken. Malta was spared, and Rommel was authorised to advance into Egypt. His order of the day issued on 21 June ended: 'Now for the complete destruction of the enemy. We will not rest until we have shattered the last remnants of the British Eighth Army. During the days to come, I shall call on you for one more great effort to bring us to this final goal'. (Rommel: page 232).

The fall of Tobruk five days after El Adem threw all Auchinleck's and Ritchie's plans out of gear. They had hoped to gain enough time in which to rebuild a striking force with which to relieve Tobruk. Now they had insufficient time to prepare the frontier for successful defence against the Panzer Army which would not have to leave an investing force behind to watch Tobruk. Gott persuaded Ritchie, quite rightly, that the only thing to do was to place the 120 miles of virtually waterless desert between the frontier and Eighth Army, as Wavell had done in 1940, by retiring to Mersa Matruh. This would present Rommel with a critical logistic problem and expose him to the attacks of the RAF which still held the upper hand. Auchinleck flew up to make a new plan with Ritchie on 22 June and, although he felt the Matruh position could be turned just as easily by an armoured force as the frontier defences, he accepted Ritchie's reasoning and authorised him to fight a major battle in the defence of Egypt at Mersa Matruh. He arranged for General Holmes' X Corps from Syria to take over the Matruh area and to prepare it for defence with Freyberg's New Zealand Division and Briggs' 5th Indian Division. Gott's XIII Corps would hold the frontier as long as possible with 1st South African, 7th Armoured, 50th Northumbrian and 10th Indian Divisions. When they abandoned the frontier, the South Africans would go back to the El Alamein Line, which was being prepared by Norrie's XXX Corps, while the rest fell back into the Matruh position to give battle. When he returned to Cairo, Auchinleck wrote to the CIGS offering to resign:

> The unfavourable course of the recent battle in Cyrenaica culminating in the disastrous fall of Tobruk impels me to ask you seriously to consider the advisability of retaining me in my command ... For this theatre originality is essential and a change is quite probably desirable on this account alone ... It occurred to me that you might want to use Alexander* who is due here in a day or two ...

> (J. Connell: page 609).

In the desert Gott handled the British withdrawal to Matruh with his characteristic good humour and quiet efficiency. The Panzer Army deployed against the frontier positions on 23 June. The Italian Infantry divisions contained the Sollum – Sidi Omar positions, while the Afrika Korps, 90th Light Division and the Italian Mobile Corps (which had recently been reinforced by the new Littorio Armoured Division from Italy) plunged round the southern end of the line and crossed the frontier near Fort Maddalena. The British rearguards fell back when demolition of petrol, water and ammunition stocks had been completed. No major actions occurred. Rommel pushed on through the desert all night and the following day. Towards evening he turned northwards to cut the coast road well east of Sidi Barrani. His reconnaissance units drove on eastwards and by the evening of 25 June were in contact with the main British positions at Mersa Matruh. Brigadier Kippenberger of the New Zealand

---

* on his way back from Burma.

Division watched Eighth Army withdraw through Matruh:

> Eighth Army poured back through us, not looking at all demoralised except for the
> black South African drivers, but thoroughly mixed up and disorganised. I did not
> see a single formed fighting unit, infantry, armour or artillery.
>
> (Kippenberger: page 126).

The RAF, with its advantage of falling back on its base airfields like the compressing of
a spring, retained mastery in the air as the Luftwaffe suffered the debilitating effects
working at maximum extension. It was the RAF which was the real British fighting
force at this time. Its morale was very high as it rose to the occasion of saving Eighth
Army. The Afrika Korps war diaries contain constant references to the damage done
by British airmen and the failure of the Luftwaffe to intervene effectively.

The perimeter defences of Mersa Matruh had been constructed fitfully in 1940 and
1941 whenever Egypt seemed to be in danger of invasion. There were extensive
minefields along the western and southern face but none on the eastern side. Inland
there were two escarpments: the northern seven miles from the coast, and the
southern 15 miles further south. Two thin belts of mines stretched across the desert
between the two escarpments. When Rommel arrived, Holmes' X Corps was holding
the 7 miles between the coast and the northern escarpment with 10th Indian
Division (three brigades strong) in the Matruh defences and the remnants of 50th
Division (two brigades only) deployed in depth east of Matruh at Gerawla. Gott's
XIII Corps had fallen back into positions on top of the southern escarpment to protect
the open desert flank. He deployed 5th Indian Division, which commanded only 29th

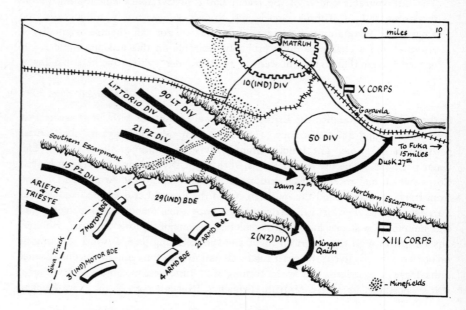

Fig 41 The Battle of Mersa Matruh: 27th to 29th June

Indian Brigade, on the southern escarpment itself and positioned two small columns to patrol the minefields between the two escarpments. Freyberg's New Zealanders (two brigades) took up positions in depth on the southern escarpment at Minqar Qaim with enough transport leaguered on the eastern side of their position to ensure the mobility of their infantry. 1st Armoured Divison with 4th and 22nd Armoured Brigade Groups under command, which had a scratch collection of about 160 tanks, was withdrawing in front of the Afrika Korps through the desert south of the southern escarpment, covered by 7th Motor and 3rd Indian Motor Brigades. HQ 7th Armoured Division had already withdrawn to El Alamein.

Rommel's plan for the Battle of Matruh was a replica of his operations against Tobruk and was to be the blueprint for the First Battle of El Alamein a few days later. The Afrika Korps was to attack astride the southern escarpment, followed by the Italian Mobile Corps, in order to drive the British Armour away from Matruh. 90th Light was take advantage of the Afrika Korps attack, advancing along the top of the northern escarpment and aiming to cut the coast road east of Matruh near Gerawla. Matruh would subsequently be stormed on its unmined south-eastern side. Whether this plan would have succeeded, if Ritchie had fought the battle as he planned it, is a matter of conjecture. He was relieved of his command before the issue could be tested.

The situation in the Western Desert was clearly ripe for some form of 'palace revolution'. More and more voices were heard in Cairo proclaiming different panacea for Eighth Army's lack of success. Much of this was idle gossip which always feeds on failure. The further from the battlefield the more virulent it becomes. Higher commanders are rightly reluctant to act in such circumstances because they know that the men fighting the battle are bearing enormous burdens of responsibility and must be supported and not criticised. Reports, however, were flowing back from RAF staff officers, and indeed through Army channels, which made Air Marshal Tedder act. He and Auchinleck saw eye to eye on most things. Auchinleck had saved him from Churchill's wrath before 'Crusader'. Tedder now set out to save Auchinleck from himself. After a long discussion the two men agreed that Ritchie must be relieved. At first Auchinleck wanted to put Corbett in his place. Then he realised that this would be an unfair burden to place upon him. The fate of the British position in the Middle East depended upon the fortunes of battle in the next few days. Auchinleck decided only one man could bear the responsibility – the C-in-C himself. On 25 June, as Rommel approached Matruh, Auchinleck took over personal command of Eighth Army. Churchill was delighted, commenting: 'He should have done this when I asked him to in May'. (Churchill: Vol IV, page 381).

The stolidly dominating authority which Auchinleck brought to Eighth Army in this hour of crisis could not show much return for some time. He could not change the detailed operational plans overnight but he could and did change operational policy. He imposed three changes straight away. First, he defined his new strategy in words he was to use several times in the next few weeks:

... to keep all troops fluid and mobile, and strike at enemy from all sides. Armour not to be committed unless very favourable opportunity presents itself. At all costs and even if ground has to be given up, *I intend to keep 8th Army in being* and to give no hostage to fortune in the shape of immobile troops holding localities which can easily be isolated.

(*British Official History*: Vol III, page 286).

The italics are the author's. These words were the key note of Auchinleck's policy for the rest of his command in the Middle East.

Secondly, he ordered a logical but organisationally questionable extension of the brigade group system to give Eighth Army greater mobility. Up to this time the British infantry battalions had not been entirely mobile and depended upon a pool of troop-carrying transport to lift their infantry platoons. This was a major cause of immobility. Auchinleck ordered the creation of mobile battle groups within each brigade based on the available artillery and transport. No more infantry than was needed to protect the guns and could be kept mobile was to be retained in the forward area. All surplus infantry was to be sent back either to El Alamein to help prepare defences there, or right back to Delta to start the construction of defences along the canals and tributaries of the Nile. Only mobile troops were to remain. This meant splitting formations and upsetting them with organisational changes at a time when a major battle was imminent. Freyberg refused to obey and took refuge in his right to appeal to his government.

And thirdly, he accelerated the development of the British Army's ultimate battle-winning technique of centralization of artillery at the highest practical level. Battle groups might be mobile; nevertheless their movements were to be far more closely co-ordinated with a centralised artillery plan than hitherto. Poor communications made this difficult at first, but it soon became established practice and was to win the first battle of El Alamein.

The German advance on Matruh began late on 26 June after a delay caused by shortage of petrol and air attacks which had inflicted considerable losses. 90th Light and 21st Panzer Divisions, advancing between the two escarpments, breached the thinly observed minefields and scattered the 5th Indian Division's columns before leaguering for the night. At daylight the Germans resumed their advance. 90th Light came under heavy artillery fire from 50th Division, and, although it managed to scatter one isolated British battalion, it was forced to withdraw and lie low for the rest of the day. 10th Indian Division tried to counter-attack southwards along the line of the minefields, but failed to close the gaps which the Axis forces were using. In the desert south of the escarpments, 15th Panzer had attacked and had been checked by 1st Armoured Division, and between the escarpments 21st Panzer was beginning to realise that it was overlooked by a substantial force – the New Zealanders at Minqar Qaim.

Just before midday Auchinleck signalled Holmes and Gott telling them that, if withdrawal became necessary, the two Corps would fall back in concert to Fuka. The code word for the withdrawal was to be 'Pike'. Communications were extremely bad. Neither Corps Commander had a clear picture of what the other was doing. During the afternoon 21st Panzer managed to work round to the rear of the New

Zealand position, scattering its transport. Gott may have seen this while roving the battlefield, as he was wont to do, and concluded that the New Zealanders had been over-run. They were, in fact, easily holding their own, though Freyberg had been wounded in the neck by a shell splinter. Gott seems to have decided that with the dispersal of the New Zealanders the battle was lost and withdrawal had become imperative. At 7.20 pm he ordered his Corps to disengage, giving 1st Armoured and 5th Indian Divisions destinations near Fuka. The New Zealanders were given no destination, presumably because they were thought to have been scattered beyond recall. In consequence, they were forced to fight their way out after dark, which they did with singular success, driving straight through 21st Panzer's night leaguer. The division reached the El Alamein Line instead of Fuka, having suffered 800 casualties in three days.

Gott had reported his decision to withdraw to Auchinleck, who had issued the code word 'Pike' at once. X Corps' communications were not working properly and Holmes did not receive it until early next morning, while he was in the process of mounting attacks southwards to take the pressure off Gott, whom he did not know had already withdrawn. He had little success, but 90th Light resumed its advance and cut the coast road behind Matruh during the night. Holmes had no alternative but to make plans to break out southwards as Ramsden had done at Gazala. Fortunately Rommel had plunged on eastwards with the Afrika Korps, leaving only 90th Light and the Italians to invest Matruh. Nightfall witnessed a spirited rough and tumble as Holmes' columns smashed their way through the Axis leaguers. Holmes estimated 60 per cent of his men reached El Alamein.

During 29 June the desert between Matruh and El Alamein was covered with small columns of British and Axis vehicles all moving eastwards, trying to avoid each other. Rommel turned the Afrika Korps off the coast road again at Fuka and advanced across the desert with little more than 40 tanks and 600 infantry, heading for the centre of the El Alamein Line. 90th Light was hustled forward unmercifully from Matruh to head the Axis advance on the coast road. At midday on 30 June it reported coming under heavy artillery fire near Tel el Eisa, a prominent hill on the south side of the coast road five miles west of El Alamein Station. The preliminaries of the First Battle of El Alamein had begun.

In Cairo one of the more regrettable incidents of the North African Campaign was taking place. 'The Flap' was on. The British Fleet left Alexandria; rumours multipled; and many of those, who should have known better, decided it was time to be elsewhere. Alan Moorehead, the journalist wrote:

In Cairo there was another curfew. The streets were jammed with cars that had evacuated from Alexandria and the country districts, and military traffic that had come from the front. The British Consulate was besieged with people seeking visas to Palestine. The east-bound Palestine trains were jammed. A thin mist of smoke hung over the British Embassy by the Nile and over the sprawling blocks of GHQ — huge quantities of secret documents were being burnt.

(Moorehead: page 168).

Rommel had reached the zenith of his career. Writing to his wife he said: 'Mersa Matruh fell yesterday, after which the Army moved on until late in the night. We are already 60 miles to the east. Less than 100 miles to Alexandria!' (Rommel: page 241).

The Nile Delta seemed within easy reach of the Panzer Army, Africa. Rommel's arrival at El Alamein, however, was barely commented on by OKW. Hitler was far too deeply immersed in what he hoped would be his decisive offensive in Russia which began the day Mersa Matruh fell. In Washington, the head of the US Army's Intelligence Division reported:

> ... it would be matter of a week or less before the final military decision and warned that the probability of the British catastrophe must now be counted upon. He therefore recommended that no more planes be sent to the Middle East and that all supplies at sea be stopped at Massawa until the military situation in Egypt becomes clarified.
>
> *(Strategic Planning for Coalition Warfare*: Vol I, page 251).

Amongst Rommel's principles of desert warfare there is, significantly, no reference to the need to win the strategic, as well as the tactical, battle of supply.

Part 3

AMERICAN MATERIALISM

The first essential of an army to be able to stand the strain of battle is an adequate stock of weapons, petrol and ammunition. In fact, the battle is fought and decided by the Quartermasters before the shooting begins.

Rommel on El Alamein in Retrospect
(*Papers;* page 328)

12

The Rising American Tide
(July and August 1942)

The *PRESIDENT* stated very definitely that he, as Commander-in-Chief, had made the decision that 'Torch' should be undertaken at the earliest possible date. He considered that this operation was now our principal objective and the assembly of means to carry it out should take precedence over other operations . . .

(Memorandum for U.S. Joint Chiefs of Staff dated 1 Aug 42).

As the German tide of military professionalism swept Rommel towards Suez, von Paulus towards Stalingrad and von Kleist towards the Caucasian oilfields, another tide was rising in the west. The mobilization of American resources was beginning to weigh in the military balance of power, bringing with it inter-Allied debate on how the growing numbers of new US Army divisions, air groups and naval forces should be used. The American Chiefs of Staff were firmly wedded to Plan 'Bolero' which concentrated upon shipping American forces to the United Kingdom in anticipation of a cross-Channel invasion of Europe in the fall of 1942 or early 1943 at the latest. Churchill arrived in Washington in the middle of June with an alternative strategy. He agreed that a cross-Channel operation was highly desirable, but none of his military planners had been able to devise a way of carrying it out with reasonable chance of success. If the US planners had a workable plan he would be delighted to co-operate, but, if not, it seemed to him that the old 'Super Gymnast' Plan for the invasion of French North Africa offered the best way of bringing US Forces into action against Germany at the earliest opportunity.

In the midst of the debate on future Anglo-American strategy, news of the fall of Tobruk was broken to Churchill by Roosevelt. Churchill recorded later:

This was one of the heaviest blows I can recall during the war . . . If this was typical of the morale of the Desert Army, no measure could be put upon the disasters which impended in North-East Africa . . . Nothing could exceed the sympathy and chivalry of my two friends. There were no reproaches; not an unkind word was spoken. 'What can we do to help?' said Roosevelt.

(Churchill; Vol IV; page 343-344).

The despatch of American ground forces to the Middle East had been considered by the American Chiefs of Staff after Ritchie's failure to hold Benghazi in February, but had been discarded because Mr Kirk, the American Minister in Cairo and his military

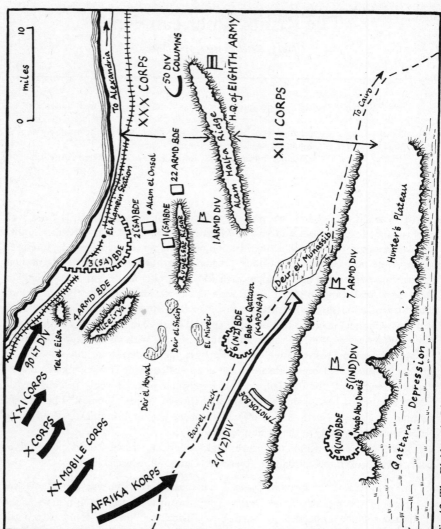

Fig 42 The El Alamein Line: 1st July 1942

attache, Colonel Fellers, were highly critical of the competence and tactical doctrine of the British Commanders in the Western Desert; and because it was felt undesirable to send American ground forces in action where they could become embroiled in controversial issues of British Imperial policy. Roosevelt waved these considerations aside and offered Churchill the 2nd (US) Armoured Division, which was just beginning its training with the latest American medium tank, the General Sherman, mounting a 75mm gun in its turret instead of in the unsatisfactory side sponson of the Grant. Major General George S. Patton was appointed Task Force Commander to take the division and its supporting troops to Egypt – Patton's first very short debut in British military affairs. The practical difficulties of operating a US Force within a British Theatre at short notice, and shortage of suitable shipping to carry the whole division to Suez, persuaded General Marshall to propose instead the shipment of 300 Sherman tanks and 100 self propelled guns to the British in Egypt. The offer was even more unselfish than it appears at first sight because these tanks and guns had to be withdrawn from American troops who had already started to train with them.

This generous gift of tanks and guns was only one of several actions taken by the President on hearing of the fall of Tobruk. There had been tentative proposals to send US air squadrons to the Middle East. These were finalised and authority given for the establishment of HQ US Army Air Forces, Middle East, with one heavy bomber, two medium bomber and three fighter groups. As these groups could not reach Egypt before August, the President agreed to divert aircraft from the Far East as a temporary measure. In addition, General Maxwell, head of the US Lend-Lease Mission in Cairo, was given military status as Commander US Army Forces, Middle East Theatre of operations, and was sent military engineer and logistic units to speed up the flow of Lend-Lease to the British and Russians via the Red Sea ports and Persian Gulf.

The El Alamein Line which Rommel reached on 30 June hardly existed. The South African Official Historians make the point:

> When the Riflemen heard the suave voice of the BBC announcer reporting that Eighth Army had reached the Alamein 'Line', they looked round at the empty desert, indistinguishable from the miles of sand to east and west, and commented as only Riflemen can . . . (page 272)

Successive Commanders of British Troops Egypt had set troops working on defensive positions in the 40-mile-wide gap between the Mediterranean and the Qattara Depression whenever Egypt had been threatened with invasion. The latest had been Lt-Gen Sir James Marshall-Cornwall who had sited and prepared three fortified positions in the gap. In the north he had completed a box for a division of three infantry brigades and a Corps headquarters, blocking the main coast road and railway. In the centre of the gap, he had laid out and partially dug, but not mined and wired, a brigade box at Bab et Qattara – nicknamed 'Kaponga' by the New Zealanders who had helped to dig it, giving good observation along the 'Barrel Track' leading from Fuka towards Cairo. And in the south, he had laid out but done no work on a brigade box on the escarpment overlooking the Qattara Depression at Naqb Abu

Dweis. Digging was brutally difficult over most of the area and required power tools and explosive.

Norrie had reached El Alamein with his XXX Corps HQ on 26 June. He made his own corps responsible for the northern half of the front. Apart from the prominent mound of Tel el Eisa, a few miles west of the El Alamein Box, his sector was flat and featureless, although closer acquaintance gave tactical significance to the Miteirya and Ruweisat ridges and the shallow depressions of Deir el Shein and Deir el Abyad. Norrie appreciated that Rommel would probably try to repeat his Tobruk and Mersa Matruh manoeuvres by thrusting around the southern face of the El Alamein Box to cut the coast road behind it. He gave Pienaar's 1st South African Division the task of holding the El Alamein Box and of blocking Rommel's way round between El Alamein and Ruweisat Ridge. He decided to defend Ruweisat Ridge itself with a new box constructed in Deir el Shein and manned by 18th Indian Infantry Brigade Group from Syria. Pienaar's method of carrying out his task was to organise his division into three brigade artillery columns as Auchinleck had ordered. He made his 3rd South African Brigade responsible for holding the El Alamein Box, while he disposed his other two brigade columns to block Rommel's potential out-flanking route: 2nd South African Brigade with his own divisional HQ at Alam Onsol, and 1st South African Brigade on the northern side of Ruweisat Ridge forming an artillery trap. When 1st Armoured Division finally disengaged on its way back from Matruh it was to withdraw with 4th and 22nd Armoured Brigades into the South African sector to give tank support.

The southern sector, south of Ruweisat, was to be the responsibility of Gott's XIII Corps when it arrived back from Matruh. His sector was much more broken with escarpments, depressions and more distinct hill features which grew higher – to some 700 feet – as they approached the lip of the Qattara Depression. The first troops to arrive in his sector came from the Delta. The New Zealand 6th Brigade, which had been reforming at the New Zealand Base Camps, was rushed forward to hold 'Kaponga' and to receive the rest of the division as it fell back from Minqar Qaim. It had only its three battalions, few anti-tank guns and practically no transport, but its Brigadier, George Clifton, purloined straggling anti-tank and artillery detachments from all sources as they appeared out of the haze along the 'Barrel Track', retreating from Matruh. The New Zealand Division itself reassembled in the Deir el Munassib some miles south east of 'Kaponga'. 5th Indian Division occupied the most southerly Box overlooking the Qattara Depression with its sole surviving brigade; and 7th Armoured Division, reduced to 7th Motor Brigade, withdrew into the gap between the New Zealanders and the Indians. The bulk of Holme's X Corps was to have gone straight back to the Delta when it broke out from Matruh, but its 50th Division was stopped and formed into three artillery columns alongside Auchinleck's Eighth Army HQ on the eastern end of Alam Halfa Ridge fifteen miles behind the front.

The final withdrawal of the two British armoured divisions was far from uneventful as they found themselves travelling parallel to and often amongst Axis columns. They inflicted significant damage on their opponents including destroying the Littorio Armoured Division's artillery and most of its remaining tanks. These actions delayed 1st Armoured Division's withdrawal. Only 22nd Armoured Brigade Group reached its battle position on the eastern end of Ruweisat Ridge near the 1st South African Brigade column by dark on 30 June. Lumsden's HQ lost its way and leaguered in the El Mreir depression south west of Ruweisat, and 4th Armoured Brigade Group at Tel el Eisa, just south of the coast road, next to 90th Light and actually in the assembly area chosen by Rommel for the forward concentration of the Afrika Korps! Lumsden reached his position on Ruweisat early next morning, but 4th Armoured Brigade had trouble with soft sand and was bogged twice before it reached its battle position near 2nd South African Brigade column, tired and far from fit for battle. 7th Motor Brigade mauled the Italian XX Mobile Corps on its way back and withdrew successfully in the southern sector.

Auchinleck has been criticised for not issuing a 'backs to the wall' order of the day on 1 July. He could not do so because it would have been inconsistent with his policy of mobile defence and 'keeping Eighth Army in being'. On 28 June he had sent a detailed appreciation of his intentions to the CIGS:

6. *Intention*
My intention, with which AOC-in-C is in full agreement, is to keep Eighth Army in being as a mobile field force and resist by every possible means any further attempt by the enemy to advance eastwards.

7. *Method*
(i) Utmost delay possible without entailing encirclement or destruction of Eighth Army will be imposed on enemy . . . on El Alamein position.
(ii) Should withdrawal from El Alamein position be forced on us: Eighth Army (less 1st S.A. Div) will withdraw along 'Barrel Track' leading from Deir el Qattara to Cairo and continue to oppose enemy, should he try to advance on Cairo direct. 1st S.A Div, now holding El Alamein defenced area, will withdraw on Alexandria.
                                                    (J. Connell; page 662).

As soon as Holme's X Corps HQ arrived from Matruh it was given the job of supervising these rearward preparations for defence of the Nile Delta – improvement of communications, building extra bridges over the Nile waterways, drawing up demolition and inundation plans, constructing fresh defence lines covering Cairo and Alexandria, and evacuation of non-essential personnel, women and children to Palestine and East Africa. None of this could be kept secret; nor could the arrival of the surplus infantry and other non-mobile troops sent back by Eighth Army. All these sensible precautions increased 'the Flap' in Cairo which reached its height in the first week of July. The message Auchinleck sent to his Army was prosaic:

General Auchinleck to All Ranks of Eighth Army: 30 June 1942
The enemy is stretched to the limit and thinks we are a broken army. His tactics against the New Zealanders were poor in the extreme. He hopes to take Egypt by bluff. Show him where he gets off.   (*Ibid*: page 628).

His subordinate commanders were far from sanguine about the outcome. Fortunately Norrie, on whom Rommel's main blow was to fall, had made up his mind and had told his subordinates that this *was* the last ditch. XXX Corps would fight and die where it stood. Pienaar was as obtuse as ever. He was saying quite openly that he believed Eighth Army should fight on the Suez Canal, while at the same time doing his utmost to see that his division fought its best at El Alamein to avenge Klopper's disaster in Tobruk. Gott was frankly defeatist, believing that the total loss of the Middle East was not far off. He shook his New Zealand subordinates by showing them a letter from Corbett detailing plans for the evacuation of Egypt. Brigadier Inglis, temporarily commanding the New Zealand Division, and Brigadier Kippenberger were shocked. Their division was full of fight and so, in their view, were most of the other troops. They were less concerned with Rommel's prowess than with British, and in particular, Gott's mood of depression. In Inglis's view: 'All Eighth Army needed to do was to face westwards and fight. (N.Z. Official History; page 144).

Rommel took greater care with his preparations for the assault on the El Alamein position than he had done at Matruh, possibly because he too had been impressed by BBC propaganda about the strength of the El Alamein 'Line'. Air photography showed the El Alamein Box and 'Kaponga' but not much else. His reconnaissance troops reported that an Indian Division was holding Deir el Abyad, possibly through mistaken map reading for 18th Indian Brigade Group's Box seven miles further east in Deir el Shein. His radio intercept service correctly gave the northern half of the position to Norrie and the south to Gott. It put 50th Division in the El Alamein 'box'

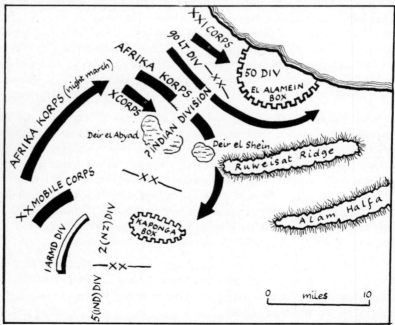

Fig 43 Rommel's plan for his first assault on the El Alamein Line showing the German view of British dispositions: 1st July 1942

instead of the South Africans; placed the New Zealanders correctly in 'Kaponga'; and 5th Indian Division in the extreme south. But they made two important errors which were to affect the battle of 1 July. They did not detect the two South African Brigade columns and 4th Armoured Brigade Group blocking the way round the El Alamein Box, and they placed 1st Armoured Division in front of Gott's southern sector.

Rommel's first idea seems to have been to attack through the southern sector as he directed the Afrika Korps in that direction from Fuka. He changed his mind and decided to attack, as Norrie expected, between the El Alamein Box and Ruweisat Ridge. Once he was through the British front he hoped to fan outwards, sweeping north to cut the coast road behind El Alamein and south to attack Gott's XIII Corps from the rear. 90th Light and the Afrika Korps would make the breach. The former would drive on as it had done at Matruh to cut the coast road, and the latter would carry out the drive southward. The three Italian Corps would hold the shoulders of the breach and follow up the German thrust. The Afrika Korps would start moving to its assembly area opposite the northern sector at dusk, and the advance would start at 0300 hours on 1 July.

First July was not a good day for Rommel. Little went right at a time when speed and smooth staff work were vital. All his worries about supplies and the tiredness of his men would vanish if he could hustle the British out of their positions and be able to use their stocks of petrol and food. He had 55 German medium tanks available including 15 Pz III (Specials) and another 30 Italian tanks. His greatest weakness lay in German motorised infantry of which 90th Light had barely 1,000 and the Afrika Korps 500. The Italians could bring a further 5,000 into action. He was strongest in artillery, having 330 guns of all types including 29 88mm guns. The Italians could produce another 200 guns. His assembly arrangements were over-ambitious, and the combined effects of RAF attacks and shortage of petrol led to the Afrika Korps being three and a half hours late. In consequence the initial advance had to start in daylight with the sun behind the British observation posts, giving the British artillery an unusual advantage.

90th Light did cross their start-lines on time but veered too much to the north and ran into, instead of avoiding, the El Alamein Box. When daylight came it was pinned down by the fire of 3rd South African Brigade and could not extricate itself until a dust storm rose around midday. The columns of the two panzer divisions had become intermixed during their night march to the assembly area, and at first light were further disorganised by a heavy RAF strike. They set off at 0645 hours, found nothing in Deir el Abyad; but were checked by the Indian Gunners near Deir el Shein. Heavy artillery fire from the direction of the 1st South African Brigade column as well showed Nehring that the Afrika Korps' proposed route was strongly held. He decided that Deir el Shein would have to be taken before the panzer divisions could start their southward wheel.

Rommel seems to have been in a jubilant mood on 1 July. He did not expect Deir el Shein to hold the Afrika Korps up for long and so he sent warning orders to the Italians to be ready to pursue the British by evening. He then set off to put new life in to 90th Light which had managed to advance about four miles during the dust storm.

The weather cleared just too soon and the division was caught in the open in full view of the Artillery observers of all three South African Brigades and 1st Armoured Division. 90th Light's war diary describes the result:

> A panic breaks out in the Division (1530 hours), which is stopped by the energetic action of the Divisional Commander and Chief of Staff. Supply columns and even parts of the fighting units rush back under ever-increasing enemy artillery fire. The Commanders of the Battle Groups, however, succeed in keeping the majority of their units facing the enemy and bring back the troops which have taken to flight. It is, however, impossible to resume the advance . . .
>
> (Quoted by *South African Official History*, page 296).

The South African and British Artillery commanders, who did the damage, had no idea how successful they had been. Visibility was poor. They could see some vehicles had been hit, but were quite unaware that 90th Light had panicked. Rommel came forward in an armoured car and tried to re-start the division's attack, but had to give up under the weight of British fire.

Nehring's attack on Deir el Shein was also launched in swirling clouds of dust, which helped rather than hindered his infantry and sappers as they tried to breach the mines and wire around the Indians' perimeter. It was 18th Indian Brigade's first battle, but it withstood the Afrika Korps' attacks all day. Unfortunately, like 150th Brigade Group at Gazala, no-one realised that it was in serious trouble until too late. Misunderstanding and plain muddle led to the brigade being over-run by the Afrika Korps as darkness fell. Nevertheless, the Indians' defence of Deir el Shein and the action of the South African and 1st Armoured Division artillery on 1 July was an unnoticed turning point in the North African Campaign. The British retreat from Gazala was over; the battles of El Alamein had begun.

Rommel did not give up straight away. He ordered a continuation of his plan on 2 July. 90th Light set off at 0400 am to cut the coast road but was stopped again by South African fire. By 10 am Rommel realised that he did not have enough German troops to continue attacking in two directions at once, so he ordered Nehring to support 90th Light with the Afrika Korps, leaving the Italians to push on southwards from Deir el Shein towards 'Kaponga'. At about the same time Auchinleck thought he saw a chance of seizing the initiative. He ordered Norrie to bring forward the reserve columns of 50th Division to reinforce the South Africans, and he transferred 1st Armoured Division to Gott's XIII Corps. Norrie was to hold the main German easterly thrust, while Gott tried to cut into their rear from the south, using 1st Armoured Division and the New Zealanders. For two days the opposing army commanders struggled for a decision, but neither had the resources to beat down the other's defences. In the north the South African and 50th Division columns neutralised the efforts of 90th Light; in the centre 1st Armoured Division blocked the Afrika Korps astride Ruweisat Ridge; and in the south the New Zealanders trapped and destroyed the Ariete Division's artillery. The New Zealanders made further progress towards Rommel's rear by reaching the El Mreir depression; and one column of 7th Motor Brigade actually reached Fuka, causing momentary alarm amongst the

Luftwaffe units on the airfield. Gott's advances from the south, however, could not be sustained because he had no reserves to maintain momentum.

By the end of 3 July Rommel was prepared to accept temporary defeat. He reported to OKW that further large-scale operations would have to be discontinued for the time being. Kesselring must have smiled wryly when he recieved a signal from Rommel saying:

> With the present fighting strength and supply situation an attack on large scale is not possible for the time being. It is hardly possible to supply the Army by night as the roads are almost completely denied by enemy air activity.
>
> (Quoted by *South African Official History*: page 314).

Rommel started regrouping so that he could withdraw his German units into reserve behind a static front line of Italian divisions, which were to dig-in, and wire and mine their positions so that they needed less German support. Rommel's eyes were fixed on the relative isolation of the New Zealanders. He told Kesselring in his signal:

> The intention is first of all to hold the front and regroup in such a manner that 2nd New Zealand Division can be encircled and destroyed ... It is urgently requested that 88mm A/A batteries be sent.
>
> (Quoted by *N.Z. Official History*: page 176).

The struggle for the rest of July developed into an evenly matched tug-of-war, in which the two teams grew in size as new units arrived on each end of the rope. The

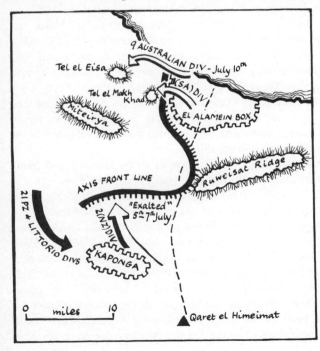

Fig 44 Operations from 5th to 14th July at El Alamein

German reinforcements began to appear on 5 July. Kessselring flew the 164th Light Africa Division over from Crete to Tobruk, followed by the Ramcke Parachute Brigade. The Italians shipped over their Folgore Parachute Division and the Pistoia and Friouli Infantry Divisions. Auchinleck brought Morshead's 9th Australian Division from Syria; 5th Indian Division was built up again to three brigades; and British artillery and tank units were steadily reinforced from the Delta as re-equipment of units progressed. 8th Armoured Division was landing at Suez and was expected to be available by the middle of the month.

In all, Auchinleck tried five 'heaves' in the tug-of-war to Rommel's one, but at no stage did the white mark in the middle of the rope favour one side or the other. Before each 'heave' Auchinleck's orders were couched in terms that assumed a breakthrough and a pursuit of the Panzer Army to Fuka. More attention seemed to be paid to the problems of pursuit than to the break-in. Between 5 and 7 July Auchinleck persisted in his first 'heave' – trying to break a way round Rommel's southern flank with Gott's XIII Corps. Though he was optimistic about his chances, no one else in Eighth Army thought it was really practical with the forces available. The New Zealand Official Historians comment aptly:

> Eighth Army had halted the Panzer Army's advance only by the most strenuous efforts in spite of the enemy's exhaustion. It was as nearly exhausted itself, and still an army of shreds and patches.
> (*New Zealand Official History*: page 177).

Rommel had no difficulty in fending off the New Zealand attacks, but they did draw his armour southwards. Auchinleck decided on 7 July that Gott had failed, and so he turned to the other end of his front and instructed Ramsden, who had taken over XXX Corps from Norrie, to attack south-westwards from the El Alamein Box with the fresh 9th Australian Division which had just arrived, and 1st South African Division. Their objectives were Tel el Eisa and Tel el Makh Khad respectively. They would exploit towards the Panzer Army's rear and attempt to disrupt its defence. The chances seemed good because the attack would fall on the Sabratha and Trento Divisions while the Afrika Korps tanks were engaged with the New Zealanders in the south. The operation was timed for 0330 am 10 July.

While these plans were being made, evidence began to accumulate at Eighth Army HQ that Rommel was about to attack through the New Zealand sector – which was quite correct. Gott was told to give up his gains in the south and to withdraw his exposed troops back to more secure positions on the general line of the El Alamein – Qarat el Himeimat track, abandoning the 'Kaponga' and Naqb Abu Dweis Boxes. Rommel detected and follow up Gott's withdrawal, and mounted a full-blooded assault with 21st Panzer and the Littorio Divisions on the empty 'Kaponga' Box on 9 July. Thinking that he had found a weak spot in the British defences, he pushed 90th Light Division and the Reconnaissance units eastwards to look for a way round Eighth Army's southern flank. No sooner had they set off than Rommel heard the rumble of heavy gunfire away to the north, heralding the Australian and South African attack. German accounts call it the heaviest artillery fire since the First

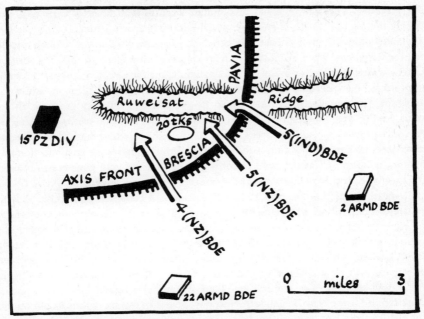

Fig 45 The First Battle of Ruweisat: 14th to 16th July 1942

World War. Losing no time, Rommel broke off his one and only 'heave' and rushed back to the coastal sector with his German mobile troops. It was as well that he did so. The Sabratha Division had collapsed. It was only the intervention of von Mellenthin with a scratch force from the Panzer Army HQ and the 164th Light Africa Division, which was just arriving, that stopped his whole northern front disintegrating. The Australians cleared Tel el Eisa and the South Africans took Tel el Makh Khad, and both had to repel continuous German counter-attacks until 14 July when German attention was diverted by Auchinleck's third 'heave'.

Realising that the Afrika Korps was now back in the north and very short of supplies and ammunition, Auchinleck decided to strike quickly at the Italians in the centre of Rommel's line where he hoped to catch the Pavia and Brescia Divisions unsupported. Gott's XIII Corps was to launch the main attack, using 5th Indian Division and 2nd New Zealand Division in a night attack to secure the western end of Ruweisat Ridge and then exploit north-westwards. Ramsden's XXX Corps would support the attack by pressing south-westwards from Tel el Eisa to take Miteirya Ridge. Although this would be a silent night attack of the type favoured by the New Zealanders, the artillery was to be on call with carefully prepared programmes co-ordinated by the Brigadier, Royal Artillery, of HQ Eighth Army. Progress was being made. This was the first healthy sign of the British artillery being used properly under centralised control. 1st Armoured Division was to protect the New Zealanders' open southern flank and was to carry out the exploitation north-westwards.

The first Battle of Ruweisat started on 14 July with brilliant success, but ended in bitter failure. The New Zealand and Indian infantry won most of their objectives during the night. The Pavia and Brescia Divisions collapsed. Unfortunately the New Zealanders unwittingly bye-passed in the dark a leaguer of 20 tanks belonging to 8th Panzer Regiment. They also failed to mop up some other German infantry positions nearby which they had over-run. When daylight came the German tanks attacked the unprotected New Zealand infantry who had found it impossible to dig-in and whose anti-tank weapons had been intercepted by the German infantry posts which had come to life behind them. 350 New Zealanders were taken prisoner before 1st Armoured Division could intervene. 22nd Armoured Brigade should have moved up onto the New Zealand position before daylight but, through some misunderstanding, had not done so. It was not until about 4 pm that vehicles and guns began to reach the surviving New Zealanders on the far side of the German salient.

Rommel heard that the two Italian Divisions had collapsed and feared that the centre of his position was about to be torn open. With his usual vigour he scraped together detachments from his three German mobile divisions and told Nehring to counter-attack. Nehring started off at 5pm with the sun behind him and over-ran 4th New Zealand Brigade. The British tanks again arrived too late to intervene effectively. 4th New Zealand Brigade lost another 380 prisoners and was forced off the ridge. Nehring was stopped by 22nd Armoured Brigade but this was little consolation for the New Zealanders. Next day, he put in two more attacks but by then the British front had been consolidated. The complimentary Australian attacks in the north achieved little and were stopped. The First Battle of Ruweisat died away by the evening of 16 July. The New Zealanders, who came out of battle with 1,400 casualties, were understandably critical of the British tank regiments.

While the infantry and tank units were failing to support each other as closely as either would have liked, Auchinleck was grappling with the larger problems of the Middle East as a whole. The Cs-in-C, Middle East cabled London for policy direction on priorities for dealing with the northern front which had been denuded of troops in spite of the threat generated by the German successes in Southern Russia. The Germans could be in Northern Persia by mid-October or, if they chose to invade Turkey, be in Syria by mid-September. Which, the Cs-in-C asked, was the more important: to transfer troops from Egypt to the northern front, securing the Persian oilfields but risking Egypt; or putting everything into the defence of Egypt and depending on the Russians to hold the Caucasus and thereby protect the oil? The reply from Churchill was cold, carping and critical. It was addressed to Auchinleck personally:

> The only way in which a sufficient army can be gathered in the Northern theatre is by your defeating or destroying General Rommel and driving him at least a safe distance . . .

> (Quoted by Arthur Bryant in *Turn of the Tide:* page 420).

Auchinleck decided he must 'heave' once more, not just to obey Churchill, but to take advantage of Axis weakness which British Intelligence sources were reporting quite accurately. On 21 July, Rommel had made a long and depressing report to the

German High Command. His German troops had been fighting for eight weeks and had lost heavily. He had been forced to disperse them amongst the Italians who were causing him great anxiety. He thought the El Alamein position could be held but his German divisions were emaciated and his loss of experienced men was critical. He rated the New Zealand and Australian troops highly, praised the British artillery and envied the British ammunition supply. The RAF had the upper hand and were attacking everything. His own supply situation was precarious. He had enough fuel for defensive purposes but not for a large-scale offensive. Captured transport was plentiful, but was a wasting asset because of lack of spares. The RAF was destroying about 30 vehicles a day. He demanded more shipping space for German as opposed to Italian equipment, particularly for 'Special' tanks and 88mm guns.

For his fourth 'heave' Auchinleck chose to attack German strength rather than Italian weakness, hoping thereby to destroy the backbone of Rommel's Panzer Army. He selected the Ruweisat sector again with the aim of breaking through between Deir el Shein and El Mreir and pursuing the defeated Axis forces to Fuka. As the battle never went beyond the first phase, Auchinleck's plans for subsequent exploitation are immaterial other than to show that a decisive battle was intended as Churchill required.

Gott's XIII Corps was made responsible for the offensive. The first phase of his attack was to be by night, using heavy artillery support, to enable 161st Indian Motor Brigade of 5th Indian Division and 6th New Zealand Brigade to break through the crust of the Axis defences across Ruweisat Ridge. The newly arrived 23rd Armoured

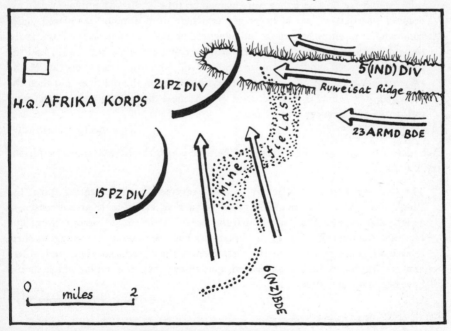

Fig 46 The Second Battle of Ruweisat: 21st to 22nd July

Brigade of 8th Armoured Division would exploit through a wide gap, which was to be cleared during the night in the Axis minefields. It was thought that these minefields could be detected and cleared quite quickly. Care was taken to ensure close tank support for the New Zealanders, but the tank commanders were not prepared to move their tanks by night amongst minefields and so reliance had to be placed on moving them up at first light.

The Second Battle of Ruweisat turned out to be worse than the First. The Indian and New Zealand infantry reached their objectives during the night, but were scattered and over-run at dawn because tanks and anti-tank guns did not reach them in time. Undetected and uncleared minefields; the presence of German tanks within the objectives taken by the infantry; and continued weaknesses in tank/infantry co-operation led to this second disaster. The 23rd Armoured Brigade made a charge reminiscent of 'Balaclava' in a vain effort to break through, losing 87 of its tanks to the Afrika Korps' guns and mines. It was later found that the Afrika Korps Headquarters was holding the sector with both Panzer divisions. Fighting went on until 23 July. When it was over New Zealand bitterness welled over. They had lost another 900 men to no avail. Kippenberger, whose brigade was engaged in the Ruweisat battles records:

> At this time there was throughout the Eighth Army, not only in the New Zealand Division, a most intense distrust, almost hatred, of our armour. Everywhere one heard tales of the other arms being let down; it was regarded as axiomatic that tanks would not be where they were wanted on time . . . For what it was worth my opinion was that we would never get anywhere until armour was placed under command of infantry brigadiers and advanced on the same axis as the infantry. In some operations I conceded that the armour commander should control and the infantry employed should be under him and still both arms should operate on the same axis. We fought one more unsuccessful battle on the old lines and then the principle, for which I argued, and which must have had very much more influential protagonists, was adopted.
>
> (Kippenberger: page 180).

But there was something else wrong at the time which the New Zealand Historians try to define:

> The successes had been offset by so many reverses that the fighting spirit, the 'elan' of the Army, had not been raised to such an extent as to give it reason to believe that with another hard punch the Panzer Army could be sent reeling. The fact that Auchinleck's advisers and planners had the opposite idea suggests their remoteness from realities. In their remoteness they produced plans and orders more fitting for a tactical exercise without troops than a situation which should have been known to them.
>
> (*New Zealand Official History*: page 325).

The malaise in Eighth Army's planning began to be felt in XXX Corps as well. Each time XIII Corps had attacked Auchinleck had rightly insisted that XXX Corps should create a diversion and be ready to exploit if Gott was successful. This had resulted in a series of wearing battles around Tel el Eisa and Miteirya Ridge which had placed great strain on the Australian and South African brigades with little to show for their losses. As Second Ruweisat failed, Auchinleck hoped to renew his 'heaves' with another blow by XXX Corps in the North. Neither Morshead nor Pienaar were prepared to go on frittering their men away in this sort of ill-co-ordinated fighting. Ramsden found the two of them unco-operative and Auchinleck had to intervene. In the end it was decided to re-open offensive operations on the night 26/27 July. The South Africans were to make and mark a large gap in the Axis minefields south-east of Miteirya Ridge and an Australian brigade was to seize the eastern end of the ridge. 69th Brigade from 50th Division would pass through and gap any further minefields so that 1st Armoured Division could break through into the Axis rear at daylight. Another failure in co-ordination ensued. The tanks did not find the right gaps and some of the gaps were not made. In consequence two Northumbrian battalions and one Australian battalion were over-run by Axis tanks before the British tanks could reach them. Over 1,000 more men were lost, 400 Australian and 600 British. Auchinleck's fifth and last 'heave' had failed to shift his adversary. Rommel had come within measurable distances of defeat on several occasions, but the defensive qualities of his experienced Germans was just too good for the less professional British.

Both sides settled down in acute discomfort plagued by flies, heat, desert sores and all-pervading sand as they dug, wired and mined their respective front lines, giving the El Alamein position the frustrating strength of the trench systems of the Western Front in the First World War. There was no way round. As the fighting died away Auchinleck's Chief of Staff at HQ Eighth Army, Major General 'Chink' Dorman-Smith, presented him with a very full appreciation of the situation. This is sometimes said to have been the 'blue print' for Montgomery's first successful battle a month later, but close examination does not bear this out. It did, however, make several very important points. First, Eighth Army could not be ready to resume the offensive until mid-September. Secondly, Rommel could be expected to attack again, probably in the southern sector, about the middle of August. Thirdly, when Eighth Army was ready, it should try to break through in the north near El Alamein and the newly arriving divisions should be trained for this purpose. But within this appreciation there was also a ring of defeatism or of realism, depending on the point of view of the reader. One long paragraph goes into the defences of Cairo and Alexandria, reporting that these would be 'well forward by 14 August and should be completed, in so far as defences are ever complete, by the end of August' (For whole appreciation see Appendix I of J. Connell; page 937-43). It was this conflict between repeated orders to attack and precautionary orders for withdrawal which undermined confidence in the British high command at this time. Kippenberger noted:

> The whole attitude of Eighth Army was that of having one foot in the stirrup, and it was evident that for the time being, the initiative had passed to the enemy.
>
> (page 191).

The unhappy truth is that Auchinleck had managed to pull the British troops together just sufficiently to stop Rommel, who had miscalculated his logistic reserves, but he was unable to give Eighth Army the leadership it needed to profit by Rommel's embarrassment. Only a change at the top could restore British morale. Fortunately, the one man who could recommend change sensed that it was not just Ritchie who had failed. As early as 17 July, the CIGS, General Sir Alan Brooke, made up his mind that he must go out to Cairo to find out for himself what was wrong with Eighth Army. He could not go at once because an important American Mission, sent by the President, was about to arrive in London. He had to deal with its business first.

General Marshall, Admiral King and Mr Hopkins arrived in London on 18 July to persuade the British that a cross-Channel operation was still possible in 1942. Realising this was a forlorn hope, the President had armed them with instructions to agree to any one of a number of alternative plans for bringing US ground forces into action against the Germans in 1942. Marshall and King met with the expected rebuff but appreciated that a revival of 'Super Gymnast' would win the loyalties of both President and Prime Minister more surely than any other operation. On 30 July, the President gave his approval to 'Super Gymnast' – the Allied invasion of French North Africa, and at Churchill's suggestion renamed it 'Torch'.

The President's acceptance of Churchill's favourite plan, though welcome, did not clear the path for 'Torch' entirely, because the British and American military planners were not in sympathy over aims, scope or timings of the operation. The British planners had their eyes fixed on Tunisia as the back door to Rommel's position in Libya. They argued that Tunisia must be occupied quickly to pre-empt the Axis seizure of the French bases at Tunis and Bizerta, and to enable the Allies to secure their own position there before the onset of the Russian winter released German troops and aircraft from the Eastern Front for use in the Mediterranean. They envisaged landing as far inside the Mediterranean as air cover would allow – certainly as far east as Algiers or perhaps Bone. Landings in Morocco could take place if shipping would allow, but they doubted if they would serve any useful purpose because port facilities were poor and communications between Morocco and Algeria were very limited indeed. Moreover, they warned their American colleagues that the surf on the Atlantic beaches in the autumn would make landing operations hazardous. The American Staffs agreed with most of the British reasoning but were less optimistic about the risks which the British were prepared to run in mounting a major operation through the Straits of Gibraltar which could be closed so easily behind them. They wished to hedge their bets with a Moroccan landing; and they did not think their 2nd Armoured Division would be able to absorb its new tanks and reach an adequate state of training before 7 November. This was too late for the British who wanted to land by mid-October to forestall the Germans in Tunisia and to synchronise with the major offensive in the Western Desert which London hoped would be mounted in September.

The man responsible for resolving these differences was General Eisenhower, who had been appointed Commander of the European Theatre of Operations, US Army, in London, and who was subsequently appointed Allied Commander for 'Torch', He completed his first draft plan on 9 August with two concurrent landings, one inside and the other outside the Mediterranean, timed for early November. If surf conditions prevented the landing on the Atlantic coast, then the task force concerned would be brought inside the Mediterranean. This plan did not please the British Chiefs of Staff. In their view it was too late. The success of the enterprise would depend more upon German unpreparedness than upon the training of the Allied troops. Training should be sacrificed to speed. The American staffs could not refrain from pointing out the penalties which the British had paid for putting speed before training and preparation in their amphibious operations in Norway in 1940 and Greece in 1941.

On 25 August Eisenhower presented a second draft plan to meet the main British objections but in so doing alienated the US Chiefs of Staff in Washington. The new plan called for landings at Oran on 15 October by an American Task Force, sailed direct from the United States, and at Algiers and Bône by a British Task Force from the United Kingdom. The US War Department considered this wholly unacceptable because the US Force at Oran could not secure its lines of communication back to the United States if the Germans seized the Straits of Gibraltar with or without Spanish help. The impasse was complete and could only be resolved by the provision of more shipping at the expense of other Allied operations – probably US operations in the Pacific, or by a political decision to reduce the scale of 'Torch' to something more in keeping with the resources available. The political decisions could not be taken at once because the Prime Minister was elsewhere.

General Brooke was about to leave for Cairo after saying farewell to the American team when to his consternation, Churchill decided to accompany him and then to fly on to Moscow to acquaint Stalin with the decision to mount 'Torch' instead of the cross-Channel operation in 1942, and to assess whether the Russians meant to defend the Caucasus in earnest or not. On 3 August all the great men controlling Britain's strategic affairs converged on Cairo. Brooke's first business was to discuss operational policy with the Cs-in-C. Part of their conclusions ran:

> A spreading of Middle East base installations by judicious thinning out from Egypt may well be advisable, and this is for you (Cs-in-C Middle East) to judge; much will depend on whether you are able to defeat Rommel. Should the worst arise i.e. if we were unable to send you adequate forces and the Russian southern front broke, you must hold on to the Abadan area in the last resort – even at the risk of losing the Egyptian Delta . . .
>
> (*British Official History*; Vol III: page 365).

Churchill did not agree with his military advisers. He told them that they were not to divert anything from Egypt until a decision was reached in the Western Desert. Auchinleck was not satisfied that this policy was practical. He feared that the northern threat would develop during his advance into Libya. Churchill temporised and said that final decisions would be taken on his return from Moscow.

Formal business over, Churchill and Brooke began a whirlwind tour of Eighth Army units, visiting and talking to as many people as possible to discover what was wrong with the Middle East Command. The views they heard were many and varied, and did not flatter the senior commanders. Both concluded that:

A drastic and immediate change should be made to impart a new and vigorous impulse to the Army and to restore confidence in the High Command. A new start and vehement action were needed to animate the vast but baffled and somewhat unhinged organisation.   (*British Official History*: Vol III: page 367).

The changes they proposed were of two types: organisational and personal. Churchill decided, and Brooke reluctantly agreed, that the Command should be divided to reduce the load on the C-in-C. The northern front with Persia and Iraq should be hived off, retaining the title 'Middle East Command'; and the rest of the old Middle East – Egypt, Libya, East Africa, Palestine and Syria should become the 'Near East Command'. Churchill proposed that Auchinleck should take over the former with his communications running back to India; and General Sir Harold Alexander (British Task Force Commander designate for 'Torch') should take over the latter with his GHQ in Cairo. Alexander's place in 'Torch' would be taken by Lt. Gen. B. L. Montgomery. After some hesitation Gott was chosen as Eighth Army Commander because everyone had confidence in him though he himself confessed to being tired and lacking in new ideas which he felt were needed in the desert. Three men, who had come in for considerable criticism – Corbett, Dorman-Smith and Ramsden – were to go elsewhere. Within a day of these decisions being taken Gott was killed returning to Cairo by air. Two German fighters forced down the transport aircraft carrying him and many other passengers. He got out but went back to rescue others and was killed when the fighters attacked the crashed aircraft again on the ground. It was a sad passing of a legendary Western Desert warrior. By this chance encounter, two unknown German Luftwaffe pilots brought together what was to be the winning British Command team. Montgomery was appointed Commander Eighth Army in Gott's stead under the overall command of General Alexander. Eisenhower was given Lt-General Kenneth Anderson to take Montgomery's place in 'Torch'.

Auchinleck accepted his dismissal with dignity. He refused Churchill's offer of the Middle East Command as he believed it an unworkable solution – and so it might have been if the Russian front had collapsed. The fact that it did not collapse changed the whole atmosphere under which his successors in Cairo were to work. Alexander and Montgomery did not need to look over their shoulders as Auchinleck had been forced to do throughout his tour in command. Some months later he returned to India to take over as C-in-C again when Wavell became Viceroy.

On 10 August, before flying off to Moscow, Churchill wrote out his famous directive on a sheet of British Embassy notepaper and handed it to General Alexander who had just arrived in Cairo:

1. Your prime and main duty will be to take and destroy at the earliest opportunity the German-Italian Army commanded by Field Marshal Rommel together with all its supplies and establishments in Egypt and Libya.

2. You will discharge or cause to be discharged such other duties as pertain to your Command without prejudice to the task described in paragraph 1 which must be considered paramount in His Majesty's interests.

(*British Official History;* Vol III: page 369).

Montgomery arrived two days later. Both men set about taking over their new Commands in their own distinctive ways. Alexander, charming, polite, always immaculately dressed and as easily at home in palaces as slit-trenches, was ideally suited for the politico-military atmosphere of Cairo. He was one of the most battle-experienced soldiers. His views on strategy may not have been original, but his great strength lay in his military judgment born of fighting in most of the great battles of the First World War and in the many minor operations from the Baltic to the North West Frontier which gave military experience to British officers between the wars. He had seen too much life lost to allow battles to go to extremes, and he had a deep appreciation of the qualities of British and Indian soldiers which enabled him to avoid psychological mistakes in dealing with them. But above all he was a man who knew how to decentralise; how much rein to give a subordinate; and when to step in if things were going wrong. He was an ideal master for the strong, demanding and abrasive Montgomery.

Montgomery, too, was ideally cast. He had more staff than battle experience because he had been badly wounded in 1914 and had served on brigade and divisional staffs during the First World War. Unlike Alexander, who could not tolerate useless sacrifice of life, Montgomery detested the poor organisation which led to such loss of life. It was the organisational challenge that drove him rather than feelings of humanity. And yet paradoxical ly, he was more at home talking to officers and men in public than Alexander. He had a sharp, rasping voice and a malicious wit, which could hold an audience spellbound. He had a flair for contrived publicity and a streak of showmanship within his great military capacity. His prime characteristic, however was his far-sighted professionalism which enabled him to visualise an operation through to its conclusion before it had begun. He could give his men a plan which they understood and they knew would work. He was just the man to give Eighth Army back its confidence and raise it to the level of enthusiasm which it had shown before 'Crusader'.

The stories of Alexander's and Montgomery's arrival in Egypt are apocryphal; all the usual things that happen when new brooms take over happened. Faces changed. Alexander chose Major-General Richard McCreery as his Chief of Staff. McCreery had been Auchinleck's armoured adviser and had fallen out with him over the performance of the British armour in July. He was about to return to England when Alexander stopped him. Montgomery accepted de Guingand, Auchinleck's Brigadier General Staff of HQ Eighth Army and made him his Chief of Staff, empowering him to act on his behalf within Eighth Army. Lt-Gen. Brian Horrocks, one of Montgomery's former subordinates in England, arrived out to take Gott's place in XIII Corps. Ramsden remained temporarily in command of XXX Corps until another of Montgomery's nominees – Lt-Gen. Oliver Leese – arrived out from England as well.

The new team agreed that they had three immediate tasks to perform: revive Eighth Army's confidence in itself; defeat Rommel's next attack which British Intelligence predicted would come on about 26 August during the full moon; and prepare their own offensive, which was code named 'Lightfoot', and was to be co-ordinated with Eisenhower's 'Torch'.

There was a 'chicken and egg' situation about the first task. Eighth Army's morale could not be fully restored until Rommel had been demonstratively beaten; and yet he would not be beaten unless morale was restored. Montgomery knew that he had to show himself; show that he knew what had to be done; and show that he knew how to do it. In any society action depends on communication, but communication between the large numbers of human beings composing an army is extraordinarily difficult to achieve in spite of all the military aids of discipline, ordered staff work and radio communication. There has to be a plan which is known to everyone so that the thousands of individuals, upon whom corporate action depends, not only know what they have to do but have the incentive to do it. No battle ever goes according to plan as it is a three-sided affair – the two opponents and random chance. The genius of a great military commander lies in his ability to give his army a plan which withstands the first clash of battle and remains valid however events may turn out. Montgomery showed himself to his Army as he visited all units; heard their commanders' views; talked to the soldiers; and made sure that he left an impression in their minds. His acceptance of the Australian slouch hat with its adornment of all 9th Australian Division's badges; his wearing a Tank Corps beret with two badges – theirs and his General's badge; and his studied informality of dress, were all contrived to make him part of their world as quickly as possible and to demonstrate that he was concerned with the substance and not the formality of military life. Nevertheless, all this would have been wasted effort unless what he said to the officers and men made sense to them and coincided with what they believed instinctively was the right answer. They were too disillusioned by all they had been through to accept at face value the views of some unknown general out from England with 'his knees still pink'. What they heard they liked. It did make sound sense to them. They were prepared 'to give him a try'.

Montgomery studied the dispositions of Eighth Army and the plans left by Auchinleck and Dorman-Smith and concluded that they had three basic weaknesses which he must rectify at once. The first stemmed from the dispositions of XXX Corps, defending the northern half of the front from the coast to Ruweisat Ridge. Its three divisions – 9th Australian, 1st South African and 5th Indian – were deployed in contiguous boxes, blocking the front, but their dispositions were too shallow and over-influenced by the possible need for quick withdrawal. More troops were required to give the northern sector adequate depth and a new sense of resolution was needed amongst its defenders. The second and third weaknesses lay in XIII Corp's dispositions and plans to meet a Gazala-type offensive by Rommel. XIII Corps was deployed to cover the southern half of the front with the New Zealand Division in a box between Ruweisat and Alam Nayil Ridge, and the remainder of the front down to the Qattara Depression was covered by 7th Armoured Division's two mobile brigades – 7th Motor and 4th Light Armoured – watching two belts of minefields which filled the gap. If Rommel swept through these minefields and turned northwards to attack the British boxes from the rear, he was to be stopped on the Alam Halfa Ridge which ran eastwards from the New Zealand positions on Alam Nayil Ridge. The faults which Montgomery detected in these dispositions were that the important Alam Halfa

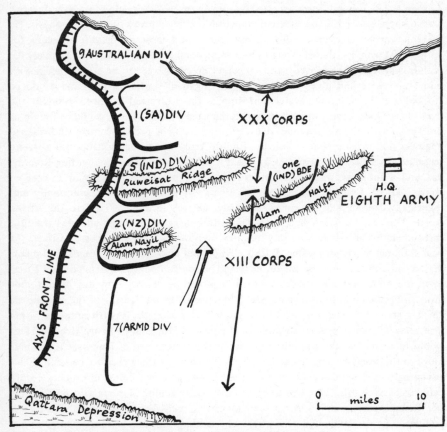

Fig 47 Dispositions taken over by Montgomery on 13th August

Ridge was garrisoned by only one Indian Brigade and there was a large gap between the New Zealanders and this brigade. 7th Armoured Division was expected to withdraw into this gap, but this would have left Rommel free to advance due eastwards without opposition.

Before Auchinleck had handed over to Alexander, Montgomery was already demanding the despatch of reserve troops from the Delta to reinforce XXX Corps' front, and the whole of the newly arrived 44th Division to man Alam Halfa properly. As soon as his demands were accepted by GHQ Cairo, he was ready to say exactly what was to happen with his characteristic repetition of key phrases to create emphasis. He told his various audiences eight things. First, and most important, all plans for withdrawal from El Alamein were to be scrapped; all transport held forward ready for withdrawal was to be moved to the rear; all defences were to be strengthened with mines and wire and given as much depth as possible; and all positions would be stocked with ammunition, water and supplies for protracted defence. Secondly, the days of the 'Jock' or any other type of column were over. Divisions would be fought as divisions, with Corps HQS and Army HQ exercising a proper control of artillery, engineer and logistic policy. Thirdly, Eighth Army was to be built up into a strong balanced force disposed in such a way that it could not be upset by anything Rommel did, and could go on with preparations for its own offensive which would, in his own words, 'knock Rommel for six out of Africa'. It would remain operationally and logistically balanced at all times. Fourthly, he was forming a rival to the Afrika Korps. General Lumsden had been placed in charge of X Corps and was training three armoured divisions and one infantry division to form a 'Corps de Chasse' to beat Rommel at his own game. Fifthly, if Rommel attacked in the August full moon period through the southern sector, he would be confronted with a firm position based upon the Alam Halfa Ridge from which he would be destroyed by dug-in anti-tank guns and tanks in hull-down positions. There would be no 'loosing of the armour' in cavalry style. Rommel would destroy himself attacking the British anti-tank guns vice-versa as had happened so often in the past. Sixth, Eighth Army Headquarters would move out of its uncomfortable site at the eastern end of Ruweisat Ridge and move to the seashore next to the Desert Air Force HQ at Burg el Arab, combining the advantages of closer co-operation with the RAF and greater comfort in which the staff could work. Seventh, there was to be no more 'Belly-aching'. Orders were orders, and not the basis for discussion. Any Commander who 'belly-ached' would go. The eighth and final point dominated the whole of his thinking and is fundamental to an understanding of his policies, actions and reactions. There was to be no more failure. Risks were to be minimised. There were no short cuts to victory.

The effect of these talks was electric, though not necessarily popular at all levels at this stage. He was given the benefit of the doubt by most people, because they were delighted to have a firm line; the more cynical awaited practical proof of his policies. Meanwhile an action was taking place at sea which was to have a profound effect upon his eventual offensive.

The Battle of Malta had raged throughout July as Kesselring tried to keep the island subdued with the small force of bombers left under his command in the

Mediterranean. While Churchill was initiating the changes in command in Cairo, a powerful British fleet was being assembled to escort a 16-ship convoy to Malta which included the American tanker *Ohio*. The 'Pedestal' convoy was to be given priority over all other naval operations, and an attempt was to be made to give the convoy really effective fighter cover as well as surface ship support. Fighter reinforcements were flown off HMS *Furious* to raise Malta's serviceable aircraft to 120 fighters and 55 bombers and reconnaissance planes. Three carriers – *Victorious, Indomitable* and *Eagle* — were to accompany the convoy which was to be escorted by the battleships *Nelson* and *Rodney*, seven cruisers and 24 destroyers.

'Pedestal' sailed through the straits of Gibraltar on 10 August. Its passage has become an epic in naval history. *Eagle* was sunk; *Victorious* and *Indomitable* were severely damaged; and two cruisers were lost with two others damaged. Only five out of the 16 merchant ships, one very low in the water and the *Ohio* lashed up between two destroyers, reached Malta and discharged their 47,000 tons of cargoes safely. Malta was thus restocked until December on subsistence rations. The master of the *Ohio* won a very well-deserved George Cross. The people of Malta still had several months of hardship ahead of them, but British air and naval forces, using the island as a base, became a growing threat to Rommel's tenure in Africa. Ranges of aircraft, improvement in reconnaissance devices and in weapon efficiency, and the developing skills of both British airmen and submarine crews caused a rising toll of Axis shipping. The figures were: 6 Axis ships sunk in June; 7 in July; and 12 in August. 'Pedestal' was as important as the coming battle of Alam Halfa in turning the tide in the North African Campaign.

Rommel complained bitterly to OKW that supplies reaching the front barely matched daily consumption and allowed no margin to stockpile reserves for an offensive. Moreover, the Italians were taking an unfair proportion of the cargo space available. Axis Intelligence reported to him the successive arrival of Allied convoys in the Gulf of Suez, underlining the need to strike hard and soon if he was ever to reach the Suez Canal. 26 August was tactically the right date for his next offensive, provided fuel stocks would allow. The Italians promised him seven ships in the last week of August and a further five in the first week of September. Kesselring also promised to fly over fuel from Crete, and to transfer some of his Luftwaffe stocks to the Army. On these assurances Rommel decided that although 26 August was too early, he would have enough fuel by 30/31 August to make an offensive practicable. Four of the seven August ships were sunk by the British. In spite of this he decided to gamble on capturing British fuel stocks and reported to OKW that his offensive would start on the evening of 30 August. He also reported that he was a sick man and would need a deputy, suggesting that General Guderian should be sent to North Africa. Guderian was not available and Rommel went ahead with his preparations for the offensive, lacking some of his old fire.

In the first fortnight of Montgomery's command, Eighth Army set about hardening its defences with renewed confidence and sense of purpose. XXX Corps was reinforced to give each division three brigades and greater depth. Horrocks' XIII Corps sector was transformed. The New Zealanders were given a brigade of 44th Division to

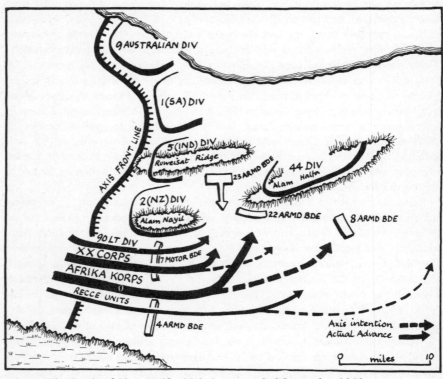

Fig 48 The Battle of Alam Halfa: 30th August to 3rd September 1942

replace their 4th NZ Brigade, which had been decimated at Ruweisat in July; and the rest of 44th Division dug itself in on Alam Halfa behind extensive minefields. In the gap between the New Zealanders and 44th Division, 22nd Armoured Brigade was dug-in with its tanks and anti-tank guns carefully concealed on the south-western spurs of Alam Halfa. This did not quite fill the gap. The remaining four miles was prepared for occupation by 23rd Armoured Brigade whose primary task was to support XXX Corps in the Ruweisat area. The minefields running south from the New Zealand positions were still covered by the two light mobile brigades of 7th Armoured Division which would withdraw eastwards if attacked, but they would be falling back onto the newly arrived 8th Armoured Brigade which Montgomery placed as a long stop south-east of Alam Halfa. A new 'cauldron' had been devised for Rommel if he did attack through the southern minefields. If he swung north he would be blocked by Alam Halfa; and if he continued eastwards he would be blocked by 8th Armoured Brigade and 7th Armoured Division with the whole of the Alam Halfa garrison and artillery on his northern flank and the impassable Qattara Depression to the south.

When Churchill arrived back from his visit to Moscow and visited HQ Eighth Army in its new location by the sea, he was delighted, as was Brooke, with the change of atmosphere. The briefing which Montgomery gave him was a masterpiece, showing how firmly he had grasped the situation in a very short time. As Churchill left he wrote in Montgomery's visitors book: 'May the anniversary of Blenheim, which marks the opening of the Command, bring to the Commander-in-Chief of the Eighth Army and his troops the fame and fortune they will surely deserve. (Churchill Vol IV; page 465).

Rommel appreciated that the northern half of the British front had become too strong to breach. Priding himself on the German superiority in a mobile battle, he decided to do what everyone predicted. He proposed to assemble his mobile striking force between the old New Zealand Box at 'Kaponga' and the Qattara Depression with 90th Light Division in the north, the Italian XX Mobile Corps with the Ariete and Littorio Armoured Divisions in the centre, and the Afrika Korps with its stalwart 15th and 21st Panzer Divisions in the south. Further south, on what was to be the extreme outer edge of the Afrika Korps' wheel, the German reconnaissance units were grouped together. The Afrika Korps, still under Nehring, had just 200 medium tanks of which 97 were 'Specials'. Major General von Vaerst was in command of 15th Panzer and Major General von Bismark commanded 21st Panzer. Rommel's Chief of Staff for the battle was Colonel Bayerlein. On the British side, Gatehouse was commanding 8th and 22nd Armoured Brigades with his HQ 10th Armoured Division alongside HQ 44th Division on Alam Halfa where Horrocks' XIII Corps tactical HQ was established as well. He had 210 medium tanks of which 164 were Grants and 46 Crusaders. 23rd Armoured Brigade was not under his command initially and was equipped with obsolescent Valentine 'I' tanks.

Rommel once again gave his Striking Force an over-ambitious time-table. It was to advance an hour before midnight, plough through the British minefields covered by 7th Armoured Division, and fan out into battle array facing northwards by 6 am. The

Afrika Korps had the furthest to go and had to travel over 30 miles in the dark through rough and uncertain going to reach its forming-up area due south of Alam Halfa's highest point and, incidentally, within 8th Armoured Brigade's defensive area. It was a plan which could only succeed if the British reacted in their usual piecemeal fashion, using their armour in penny packets and being eaten up brigade by brigade as they ran into German anti-tank guns.

Rommel made elaborate plans to achieve surprise, which deceived no one. Under Montgomery's guidance, the RAF flew heavily escorted reconnaissance sorties over the southern sector as soon as a southward drift of German troops was detected not long after he assumed command of Eighth Army. German fighters reacted angrily to these probes, confirming there was something to hide. Eight RAF reconnaissance and 15 other aircraft were lost penetrating the German fighter screen, but the results were worthwhile. On 21 August, 'round the clock bombing' of the Panzer Army's concentration area was started in earnest, reducing Axis morale significantly and destroying valuable equipment.

At dusk on 30 August, the RAF detected the final assembly of the Axis Striking Force and launched exceptionally heavy bombing raids with the help of flares dropped by Royal Naval aircraft. Diversionary Axis attacks came in on XXX Corps' front, but these too deceived no-one. The Axis striking forces reached the first British minefields about 2 am and found themselves actively opposed by 7th Motor and 4th Light Armoured Brigades, both of which fought well-controlled delaying actions. It was not until dawn that the Afrika Korps, which by then should have been facing Alam Halfa, managed to force its way through the first belt of minefields. Nehring had been wounded and von Bismark killed. Rommel seriously considered calling the offensive off at 8 am but was dissuaded from doing so by Bayerlein who had taken temporary command of the Afrika Korps. Instead, he cut down the distance to be travelled eastwards before wheeling north, contenting himself with what amounted to a frontal attack on 22nd Armoured Brigade's position.

Dust storms blew up as the Axis columns thrust their way through the remaining minefields, harried by 7th Armoured Division's brigades, but protected from the RAF by the low visibility. 15th Panzer was the first to advance northwards, followed by 21st Panzer an hour later on 15th Panzer's left flank. 22nd Armoured Brigade tried to decoy the Germans on to their hidden positions with some Crusaders, but they sheered off and seemed to be heading for 44th Division's positions. 22nd Armoured Brigade had to show themselves deliberately before the Germans would turn towards them. The engagement did not start until dusk was falling. In the hour's daylight that was left both sides hammered each other at close range. Brigadier 'Pip' Roberts, now commanding 22nd Armoured Brigade has described his view of the action:

At about 15.30 hours reports from the right of the two squadrons begin to come in – 'Strong force of enemy tanks moving north-east!'

Now I can see the enemy myself through my glasses. They are coming up the line of the telegraph poles which lead in front of our position . . . It is fascinating to watch them, as one might watch a snake curl up ready to strike . . .

And now they all turn left and face us and begin to advance slowly. The greatest concentration seems to be opposite the CLY (County of London Yeomanry) and the anti-tank guns of the Rifle Brigade. (Eighty-seven German tanks were counted at this time opposite this part of the front). I warn all units over the air not to fire until the enemy are within 1,000 yards. It can't be long now and then in a few seconds the tanks of the CLY open fire and the battle is on. Once one is in the middle of a battle time is difficult to judge, but it seems only a few minutes before nearly all the tanks of the Grant squadron of the CLY were on fire. The new German (Long) 75mm is taking a heavy toll. The enemy tanks have halted and they have had their own casualties, but the situation is serious; there is a complete hole in our defence. I hurriedly warn the Greys (in Brigade reserve) that they must move at all speed from their defensive positions and plug the gap. Meanwhile the enemy tanks are edging forward again and they have got close to the Rifle Brigade's anti-tank guns, who have held their fire marvellously to a few hundred yards. When they open up they inflict heavy casualties on the enemy, but through sheer weight of numbers some guns are over-run. The SOS artillery fire is called for; it comes down almost at once right on top of the enemy tanks. This together with the casualties they have received, checks them . . .

(Liddell Hart; The Tanks; Vol II; pages 221-222).

One British tank squadron had been destroyed, but it was the Germans who had been forced to give up this time and retire into leaguer for the night in the lower ground south of Alam Halfa, leaving the battlefield to the British.

That night, as the dust settled, the RAF came out in force and created new storms of their own.

A night of continuous bombing left a pall of smoke from countless petrol fires and burning vehicles. Of this and the next few nights the DAK recorded that not only was the damage very great but officers and men were badly shaken and their fighting capacity considerably reduced by the enforced dispersal, lack of sleep, and the strain of waiting for the next bomb.

(British Official History, Vol III; page 387).

A far cry from the days of the Gazala 'cauldron' when the RAF complained 'Once more it seems to have been impossible for the Army to lay down a satisfactory bomb line . . .' (*Ibid*; page 235).

As soon as Montgomery was certain that the whole of the German striking force was committed at Alam Halfa, he released 23rd Armoured Brigade to Horrocks. He then gave instructions to Ramsden to thin out his XXX Corps front to form a new reserve; and to Horrocks to develop his battle so that the New Zealanders could work down from the north to close the minefield gaps behind Rommel, while 7th Armoured Division worked its way along the edge of the Qattara Depression to close them from the south. Lumsden's X Corps HQ was brought up hastily into the rear of the Army area to take charge of all reserves and be ready to push through to Fuka if an Axis collapse occurred. First September opened with 15th Panzer trying to feel its way round 22nd Armoured Brigade's eastern flank. 21st Panzer could not operate because it was short of fuel. Gatehouse had ordered 8th Armoured Brigade to join 22nd on Alam Halfa. In trying to do so it clashed with 15th Panzer, which threw out its usual anti-tank screen, and taught this new British armoured brigade the usual lesson. The main weapons being used by the British, however, were artillery and air forces. The Headquarters of the Afrika Korps lost seven officers during the day, and Rommel had a lucky escape when a bomb splinter pierced a shovel above a slit trench in which he was taking cover. By evening he was again on the point of giving up.

The night 1/2 September was the worst the Afrika Korps had ever experienced. Bombing and shelling was continuous and by dawn everyone, including Rommel, had had enough. He ordered his striking force to go over to the defensive, while he organised a carefully planned withdrawal to take place over the next three days. Montgomery was tempted to launch a counter-offensive as soon as German intentions became apparent, but he stuck to his principle of avoiding all risk of failure, only allowing Horrocks to continue operations to close the minefield gaps.

Freyberg did attack southwards on 3 September, using 132nd Brigade from 44th Division and his own 5th New Zealand Brigade under Kippenberger. The attack was not a success and was stopped after the loss of about 275 New Zealanders and 700 British troops. 7th Armoured Division did do some damage in the south, but the main source of Rommel's discomfiture remained artillery and air bombardment. In the four days' battle 500 RAF aircraft flew 2,500 sorties in direct support of the land battle. And for the first time the US Army Air Force intervened in a British Army battle, flying 180 sorties with Liberators, Mitchells and Kittyhawks.

Losses on both sides were evenly matched. The British lost 1,750 men to the German 1,859 and Italian 1,051; British tank losses totalled 67 against the Axis 49; and in the air 68 British aircraft were lost against 41 by the Axis. Alam Halfa, however, was a far-reaching psychological victory for the British; not so much over the Axis as over themselves. Montgomery had shown that he knew what he was about and how to do it. The whole of Eighth Army redoubled its efforts to be ready for its real offensive which he had promised was to come after Rommel had been decisively stopped.

13

Command and Material Superiority at Last

(September to November 1942)

It will be a decisive battle, a hard and bloody battle and there must be only one result. Success will mean the end of the war in Africa and an end to this running backward and forward between here and Benghazi . . .

General Morshead briefing his officers
before the Battle of El Alamein
(*Australian Official History*; page 662).

Three years after the outbreak of war the Western Allies, at last, achieved material superiority and the British found a successful command team; and yet, it was to take another three years' fighting before the Axis forces finally disintegrated. It is right to ask whether there was not a quicker and less costly way of winning the war. Those, who are ardent supporters of General Marshall's American strategy of the direct approach across the English Channel to the heart of Germany, think that there was; while others, who prefer Churchill's British peripheral strategy, have valid reasons for doubting the practicability of the American plans. The crux of the matter lies in whether an Anglo-American force could have crossed the Channel in late 1942 or early 1943 and stayed there. 'Sledgehammer' and 'Round-up' – the proposed cross-Channel operations for 1942/43 – were never carried out, so the question can only be answered by extrapolating what happened in the last six months of the North African Campaign. Would the Allies' performance during the 'Torch' landings have been good enough for successful landings in France? And would the standard of their subsequent operations, which led eventually to the destruction of all Axis forces in Tunis and Bizerta have enabled them to sustain a foothold on the European Continent in 1943? Put another way the question is were the final months of the North African Campaign an essential first rehearsal for the cross-Channel operation or an expensive waste of time?

Churchill returned from Moscow and Cairo on 24 August and breathed new life into the preparations for 'Torch'. He reopened his personal correspondence with Roosevelt and soon broke the deadlock which had paralysed military planning. Having won the President's agreement to mount 'Torch', he gave way on all lesser issues to avoid giving Marshall any chance to plead, as he himself had done in killing the cross-Channel operation, that no acceptable military plan could be devised. He agreed to the postponement of 'Torch' until 7 November; he tolerated the cautious American insistence on securing Morocco rather than using all resources inside the

Mediterranean; he did not object to the elimination of landings east of Algiers; and he accepted the need for Americans to land first on all beaches to minimise probable French hostility to the British.

The final 'Torch' concept, which Churchill and Roosevelt endorsed in September, was for landings by three Task Forces – Western, Centre and Eastern – at Casablanca, Oran and Algiers respectively. The Western Task Force was entirely American. It was trained, organised and mounted by Major-General Patton in the United States, and would be escorted and covered during its passage across the Atlantic by the us Naval Forces under Admiral Hewitt. The Centre and Eastern Task Forces were Anglo-American and mounted from the United Kingdom. The Royal Navy would escort and cover the convoys into and within the Mediterranean. The

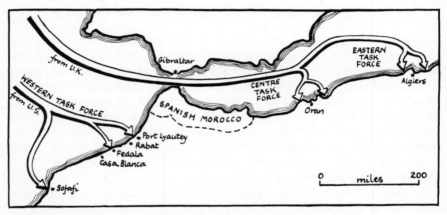

Fig 49 The Final 'Torch' Concept accepted on 5th September 1942

army element of the Centre Task Force was American under command of Major-General Fredendall. The Eastern Task Force was more mixed. Its Army element consisted of a predominantly American assault force under Major-General Ryder while its 'follow-up' echelons were British. The intention was to turn the Eastern Task Force into the British First Army under Lieutenant-General Anderson as soon as it was practical to do so for the eastward drive into Tunisia.

The commanders of the 'Torch' operation were far from confident about its outcome. It was the first amphibious operation of this magnitude ever mounted over such long distances. The 'Battle of the Atlantic' was far from won; and yet the Allies were about to sail 112 ships with 75 naval escorts from the United States; and 240 ships with 94 naval escorts from the United Kingdom, through U-boat concentrations in the 'Western Approaches' to the British Isles and off Gibraltar. Admiral Cunningham, who was appointed Naval C-in-C under Eisenhower, appreciated that he might, by achieving surprise, minimise losses in the assault convoys, but he would be hard pressed to protect the 'follow up' convoys once their destination had become obvious to the Axis High Commands.

Lack of precedent upon which to base planning estimates was another worry. Both countries had run small amphibious warfare establishments in peace. Their work, though useful, was no substitution for large-scale practical experience which did not exist anywhere in the world. After the evacuation of Dunkirk Churchill had given priority to the establishment of the British Combined Operations Headquarters, first under Admiral Sir Roger Keyes and then under Admiral Lord Louis Mountbatten. Extensive trials of amphibious techniques were undertaken and limited numbers of assault ships and craft were designed and built, but in 1942 the British still lacked an adequate amphibious force with a proven tactical doctrine. The same was true of the United States where assault ships and craft were under construction but would not start coming from the shipyards in quantity until 1943.

The difficulty of assessing probable French reaction to the landings was another cause for concern and divided council. Optimists could not bring themselves to believe that the French would not welcome the Americans with open arms as Liberators. Middle-roaders, who had a knowledge of the terms of the Franco-German Armistice Agreement, agreed that the French would fight because they were pledged to defend French overseas territory against all comers. What degree of resistance they were capable of offering was another matter. Their Navy would fight hard, but their Army and Air Force were not well-enough equipped. The pessimists thought that French resistance would be resolute and effective. They foresaw the arrival of German troops in Tunis by air from Sicily and Sardinia and their advance with French help into Algeria and Morocco. They were also convinced that Franco would use 'Torch' as an opportunity to bring Spain into the war on the Axis side, closing the Straits of Gibraltar and seizing his share of the spoils in French North Africa.

There was one man in a position to judge French reactions with some accuracy. Mr Robert Murphy had been US Consul General in Algiers since the fall of France, and had been responsible for the supervision of US aid to French North African Territories which the British had allowed to pass through their naval blockade on the strict understanding that no supplies were channelled to the Axis. His network of aid supervisors enabled him to keep his finger on the French pulse and to maintain contact with those elements who were prepared to accept General Giraud as their leader when the time was ripe. Giraud had an untarnished reputation in French North Africa, where he had served with distinction, and in the French Army as a whole. He had escaped from a prisoner of war camp in Germany and was living in unoccupied France under house 'surveillance'. His principal supporter in Algeria was General Mast, the commander of the Algiers Division – a key position as far as the 'Torch' planners were concerned. Mast suggested to Murphy that he should meet Allied military representatives to concert plans. On 21 October Major-General Mark Clark, Eisenhower's Deputy, was landed with a small negotiating team from the

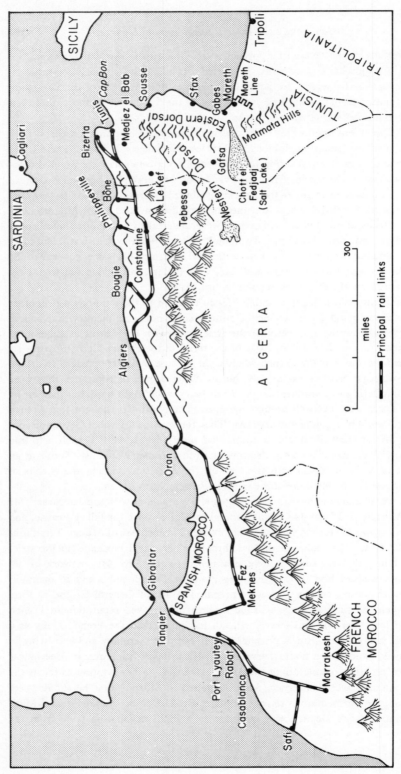

Map VII: French North Africa

British submarine *Seraph* for a clandestine meeting with Mast at Chercel, 90 miles east of Algiers. In spite of the alarms and excursions associated with such meetings, a useful exchange of views took place. Mast said that given four days warning, he could guarantee that there would be little resistance from the French Army and Air Force in the Algiers area. Blida airfield near Algiers and the port and airfield at Bone were in the hands of pro-Giraud sympathizers. He could not speak for the French Navy which would probably resist. Before the meeting broke up for Clark and his party to return to the *Seraph* and Mast to elude the French police, a document was drawn up which, subject to Eisenhower's approval, invited Giraud back to North Africa on three conditions: the Allies would restore France to her 1939 boundaries; France would be accepted as an ally; and the French would assume supreme command in North Africa 'at an appropriate time,' following the landings, establishment of bases and the rearming of French troops. These terms would have been entirely satisfactory to Giraud whose attitude was: 'We do not want the Americans to free us; we want them to help us free ourselves, which is not quite the same.' (*U.S. Official History*; page 82). But the third proviso was to prove embarrassing and impractical. After landing General Clark's party back at Gibraltar, *Seraph* headed north to pick up Giraud at a rendezvous on the French coast and to convey him to Gibraltar where he met Eisenhower on 7 November – too late to influence events.

Working on Murphy's estimate of the likely severity of French resistance, the three task force commanders had to be prepared for a hostile reception, while hoping for the reverse. This was not easy and created a conflict of thought, planning and action which led eventually to the Axis winning the race for Tunis. The crux of the problem lay in the loading of the limited number of ships available. If stiff resistance was met, fighting troops, weapons and ammunition would be needed; but, if the French co-operated, logistic troops, transport and fuel would be required for the 500-mile advance from Algiers to Tunis. As it could not be assumed that French resistance would be light, the assault convoys had to be loaded for fighting and units needed for the eastward thrust into Tunisia had to be relegated to later convoys which would arrive at about fortnightly intervals.

On the German side there was a surprising lack of appreciation of the probable Allied plans. Hitler did start to show some concern about events in the West during September. He withdrew a number of panzer formations from Russia to strengthen the German garrisons in Western Europe, weakening his drive towards the Caucasus in so doing. He admitted the possibility of an invasion of French North Africa but was inclined to think that Dakar was the most likely Allied target. He was also concerned about the British developing a threat to Crete to outflank Rommel's strong defensive position at El Alamein, and he showed more sensitivity to potential threats to Rommel's supply lines than to the French position in North Africa. The Italians were nearer the mark in their estimates of Allied plans and repeated their demand for an Axis occupation of Tunisia to secure Rommel's rear. Hitler would not agree. He believed that, if the Allies were foolish enough to enter French North Africa, Marshal Pétain would welcome the opportunity to ask for Axis help to protect French interests, and might voluntarily join the Axis to win a 'place in the sun' for France in

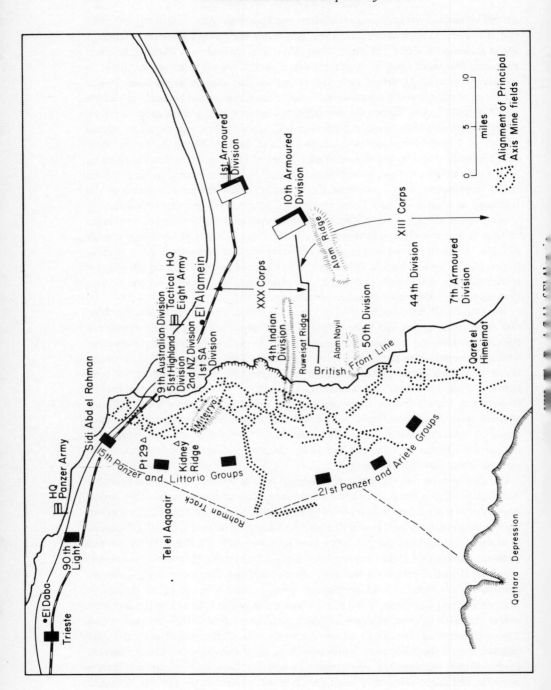

post-war Europe. Though taking precautions, Hitler did not believe that a major Allied landing was likely anywhere in the West before the Spring of 1943. The growing naval activity reported around Gibraltar was thought to be in preparation for another Malta convoy on a larger scale than 'Pedestal'.

One unique feature of 'Torch' was the integrated nature of Eisenhower's staff. Under his extraordinarily magnetic personality the Allied Force Headquarters was a genuinely Anglo-American staff with British and American officers intermingled and inter-changeable at every level. There were only two exceptions to this rule – one deliberate and the other regrettable. The former was in the logistic field where differences in sources of supply, logistic systems and types of equipment made separate staffs inevitable. The unfortunate exception was in the air. There were two separate Air Commands; General Doolittle's XII (US) Air Force acting as the Western Air Command, supporting the American Western and Centre Task Forces; and Air Marshal Welsh's Eastern Air Command, consisting of the RAF's 333 Group, covering the Eastern Task Force and First Army's subsequent advance eastwards into Tunisia. Both reported independently to Eisenhower who had no Air Deputy. Failure to centralise control of air power at the highest level had unfortunate results.

Integration of staffs, and the positive determination of everyone in the 'Torch' team to make this great international enterprise successful, could not overcome three special and inter-related weaknesses of the venture. First, there was not enough time for the complex and detailed planning needed for a major international amphibious operation. Subsequent experience showed that a minimum of four to five months' preparation was required for an operation of the size of 'Torch'. Secondly, there was not enough time for training and none for proper rehearsal. Assembly of the large number of merchantmen needed for 'Torch' had to be left as late as possible to reduce the adverse effect on feeding the British Islands and sustaining Allied forces in the Middle and Far East. The Western Task Force was to have had rehearsals on the American Atlantic coast, but the U-boat threat forced their cancellation and substitution of more limited exercises inside Chesapeake Bay. The Centre and Eastern Task Forces carried out small-scale exercises off Scotland. None of the task force commanders felt that their men were more than partially trained in landing techniques or in co-operation between sea, land and air forces in an amphibious environment. And thirdly, there were no professionals; all commanders, staffs and troops were amateurs groping into the unknown beyond the frontiers of known operational techniques. It was to be hoped that the sea would be kind, and French resistance light.

At the other end of the Mediterranean equally vigorous but more experienced planning, training and rehearsal had been going ahead under the new and dynamic leadership of the Alexander/Montgomery team. As soon as the last echoes of Alam Halfa died away, Montgomery began his preparation for Operation 'Lightfoot'. Churchill, as was his custom, tried to insist upon the mid-September D-day which had been suggested tentatively by Auchinleck before he was superseded by Alexander. Alexander refused to be hustled. His very extensive battle experience had taught him the need for careful planning, patient training and full rehearsal before major

operations of the magnitude and importance of 'Lightfoot'. He supported
Montgomery who, in his dogmatic way, said: '. . . our preparations could not be
completed in time for a September offensive, and an attack then would fail: if we
waited until October, *I guaranteed complete success*. In my view it would be madness
to attack in September.' (*Memoirs*, page 117).

Churchill gave way with his equally characteristic reluctance, insisting as he did so
that the Middle East Command must win a decisive victory over Rommel before
'Torch' was launched on 8 November to encourage Frenchmen in North Africa to side
with the Allies and to discourage Franco's Spain from joining the Axis and closing the
Straits of Gibraltar.

Montgomery's first idea was to punch two major breaches in the Axis defences with
his infantry divisions – one in the north and the other in the south – through which
he would pass his armour which would position itself on good defensive ground
astride the German lateral communications and there let the German panzer
divisions exhaust themselves trying to prize the British tanks off their supply lines.
Alam Halfa was to be fought again in the rear of the German defences. The two
breaches would not be equal in size or importance. The main breach would be made
in the northern sector by XXX Corps, which was now under Lieutenant-General
Oliver Leese's command. He would use four infantry divisions – 9th Australian in the
north, 51st Highland and 2nd New Zealand in the centre, and 1st South African in
the south – attacking on a 10-mile front and aiming to reach objective 'Oxalic' drawn

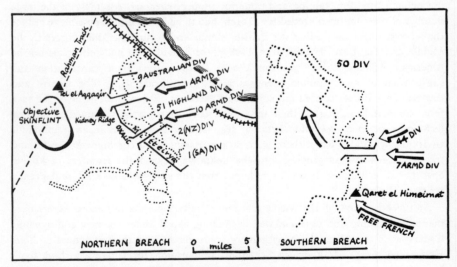

Fig 50 Montgomery's First Plan for 'Lightfoot'

along the rear of the known Axis defences some three to five miles from the British front line. Within this breach the Sappers were to clear two wide mine-free corridors for the passage of the armoured divisions of Lumsden's X Corps, which were to break out and establish themselves on defensable ground astride the Rahamn Track near Tel el Aqqaqir in an area code-named 'Skinflint'. The northern of the two corridors, which would be used by Major-General Briggs' 1st Armoured Division, ran due west through the Highland Division sector to 'Kidney Ridge'; and the southern corridor, which was for Major-General Gatehouse's 10th Armoured Division, struck south-westwards over Miteirya Ridge in the New Zealand sector. The second breach would be made by Horrocks's XIII Corps in the southern sector for divisionary purposes. Major-General Harding's 7th Armoured Division, suitably reinforced, would clear two lanes through the two old British minefields, which Rommel had held since his withdrawal from Alam Halfa, and would then pass 4th Light Armoured and 22nd Armoured Brigades through to engage the Axis armour in the southern sector. Montgomery stressed that Horrocks was not to allow 7th Armoured Division to suffer heavy losses. Its task was to simulate a major attack and no more.

There were two novel aspects in Montgomery's earliest concept for 'Lightfoot'. First, he was attacking through the strong northern sector. All his predecessors and Rommel had gone round the open southern flank or through the weaker southern sector. There was thus an element of surprise in his plan. And secondly, he was proposing to win the armoured battle with essentially defensive tactics. In other respects Montgomery was following orthodox desert philosophy. He was aiming to defeat Rommel's armour on the assumption that the Panzer Army would fall apart once the Afrika Korps had been beaten.

Rommel was faced with several intractable problems. He knew that the British offensive was coming. He could not pull back to, say, Fuka to evade the blow because he did not have enough transport to lift the large numbers of Italian infantry which had been brought forward to secure his front line. He had no alternative but to dig-in and make his position as impregnable as he could. Early in September he had been told that he could return to Germany for medical treatment, followed by sick leave. He would be replaced temporarily by Panzer General Georg Stumme from the Russia front. Before he left on 22 September he put a number of measures in hand to make his position as unattractive as possible. About 500,000 mines were laid in two major fields running north and south across the whole front about two miles apart and interconnected by lateral mine belts giving the position a 'honeycomb' effect. The easterly field was covered by out-posts and the westerly field by the main infantry and anti-tank positions. Within the cells of the honeycomb, Rommel instructed his Sappers to sow what he called 'Devil's Gardens', consisting of random patches of anti-tank and anti-personnel mines and as many booby traps as the local defenders could devise. Fortunately for the British he was short of wire and so entanglements, where they existed, were not as dense as he would have liked. Axis battalions were given sectors averaging about a mile wide by two to three miles deep, and German and Italian units were alternated along the front to prevent the British concentrating upon the weaker and less well armed Italians as they had done during the July fighting. Rommel's greatest difficulty, however, lay in the deployment of his armour. Shortage of fuel and the vulnerability of his tanks to RAF attack when on the move forced him to break his cardinal principle of concentration and to deploy his armour in six mixed Italo-German groups close behind the front ready to counter-attack any British penetration before it could become a breach. 15th Panzer and the Littorio Divisions formed three mixed groups in the north, and 21st Panzer and Ariete Divisions did the same in the south. 90th Light and the Trieste Divisions, his only reserve, were grouped further back guarding the coast at El Daba against a threat of amphibious landings.

On leaving Libya Rommel called on the Commando Supremo in Rome and then went on to see Hitler and OKW in Berlin. At every leave he stressed the inadequacy of the logistic support and reinforcements which 'His Africans' were receiving. His complaints could do little good. No-one could reverse the effects of his own fatal decision to advance into Egypt instead of waiting for the capture of Malta. The figures of relative strengths given by the British Official History speak for themselves:

Eighth Army		*Panzer Armee*	
Men	195,000	104,000	Including 50,000 German
Infantry battalions	85	71	Including 31 German
Medium Tanks	1,029	496	
Anti-tank guns	1,451	800	Including 88 of the 88 mm guns
Field and Medium Artillery	908	500	

Moreover, the British had been able to build up unlimited supplies of ammunition, fuel and other stores. The Germans were short of everything. Malta had played its full part in creating this unhappy situation for the Axis.

But numerical and material superiority alone was not necessarily enough to ensure victory, as Gazala had shown. Alexander and Montgomery knew that the key to success lay in thorough training and careful rehearsal – not only to train the troops but also to perfect techniques, establish timings and uncover organisational weaknesses. Dummy positions were created in the desert well away from the battle area where brigades went in turn to practise their part in the coming battle and to work out for themselves the solutions to the tactical problems of their own particular sectors. The only division that could be withdrawn from the line complete was Freyberg's 2nd New Zealand Division, which carried out a full scale rehearsal with live ammunition, the artillery firing a token barrage ahead of the advancing infantry, and the tanks being given realistically placed dummies to engage during the consolidation phase. The data generated by the New Zealand exercises was used in assembling and dove tailing the complex timings of the 'Lightfoot' plan.

As preparations went ahead during September doubts began to grow in many minds. By the end of the month Montgomery was beginning to have misgivings himself about the standard of training and his own ability to put things right in time:

> I was watching the training carefully and it was becoming apparent to me that the Eighth Army was very untrained ... By the end of September there were serious

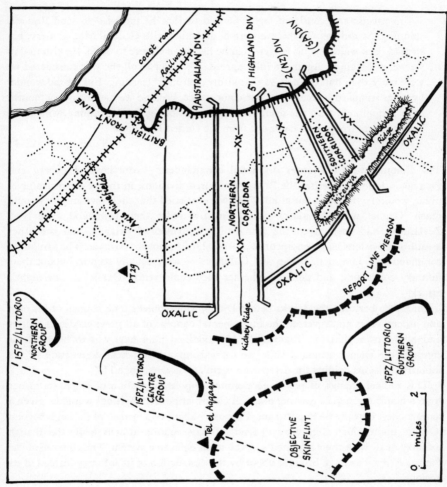

Fig 51 The Final Plan for 'Lightfoot': 6th October 1942

doubts in my mind whether the troops would be able to do what was being demanded; the plan was simple but it was too ambitious.

(Montgomery; *Memoirs*: page 119).

There were many contrary views. Major-General Tuker, commanding 4th Indian Division objected to Montgomery's analysis of where the faults lay:

> ... in precise and confident terms he told us that he intended to send Rommel spinning. So did we. On this we were of one mind with General Montgomery, but we had been waiting a bit longer than he had for a chance to do so. He also told us we were ill-trained. Again we fully agreed. We never in all the war considered we were more than half trained, so thankfully continued learning. But we did wonder by what standard he measured our competence, because we had for many months been acquainted, with the disappointing results of the battle-training, which had been given to troops who came out from the United Kingdom!

(Tuker: page 223-4).

The Commonwealth infantry divisional commanders – Morshead, Freyberg and Pienaar – doubted whether the British armoured divisions, in their current frame of mind, would try to break out at all. They were satisfied that their own infantry could reach 'Oxalic' with the tanks placed directly under their command. The New Zealanders had been given the whole of 9th Armoured Brigade, and the other assaulting divisions had a regiment each from 23rd Armoured Brigade. The armoured commanders – Lumsden, Briggs and Gatehouse – were equally sceptical about their infantry colleagues, and doubted whether they could reach 'Oxalic' in one night's attack.

On 6 October, just two weeks before D-day, Montgomery took council of his own and others' fears and reversed the fundamental concept of all previous desert battles and of his own plan for 'Lightfoot': 'My modified plan now was to hold off, or contain, the enemy armour, while we carried out a methodical destruction of the infantry divisions holding the defensive system'. (*Memoirs*: page 119).

This radical change of policy necessitated only an alteration of emphasis rather than a major revision of existing plans. X Corps' armoured divisions would be given a more modest objective – Report Line 'Pierson' – about two instead of six miles beyond 'Oxalic' upon which they were to fend off Axis counter-attacks while the British infantry dealt with their opponents in the main defensive system. The collapse of the Panzer Army was to be brought about by the destruction of its infantry instead of its armour.

Great thought was given to the problems of mine clearance which had contributed so much to the British failures in July on Ruweisat and Miteirya Ridges. Electronic mine detectors had been developed but were far from reliable; and 'Scorpion' flail tanks were in their infancy and equally unreliable. The only sure way of clearing mines was slow and laborious prodding by hand using steel probes or bayonets. Each assaulting infantry division was to use its own Sappers to clear paths forward for its supporting tanks and anti-tank guns. The northern and southern mine-free corridors for X Corps were to be cleared by special minefield task forces. These would follow close behind the assaulting infantry to clear a way for 1st Armoured Division to Kidney Ridge and 10th Armoured Division up to and over Mitierya Ridge. If the infantry divisions and minefield task forces had not reached 'Oxalic' by dawn, the armoured divisions, using their own Sappers, were to fight their way out to 'Pierson'.

The air plan followed the pattern which had become routine. In the first phase priority was given to disrupting the Axis supply lines at sea and on land. As D-day approached the emphasis switched to counter-air action with attacks on the Axis air bases designed to suppress the enemy air forces. Just before the Army started to move towards its assembly areas a major effort was to be mounted to eliminate Axis air reconnaissance. Thereafter equal priority was given to keeping the Axis air forces subdued and helping the Army by attacks on ground targets in the battle area. Tedder had 104 squadrons at his disposal with about 530 serviceable aircraft to oppose 350 serviceable Axis aircraft in North Africa and about another 130 on call from elsewhere in the Mediterranean. British air superioritity was thus far from a foregone conclusion, and Tedder was grateful for support from General Bereton's small force of American fighters and bombers which reached Egypt just in time for the preliminary air operations.

In all great set-piece battles the attacker tries to deceive the defender about the exact point and time of the assault. Montgomery's deception plan was worked out and executed with meticulous attention to detail. Its aim was to suggest to the Axis High Command that the southern sector was under greatest threat; and that the full moon at the end of November was the most likely time for the next British offensive. Vehicle densities were adjusted constantly by the prolific use of dummy vehicles and tanks to create the illusion of a southerly concentration; bogus radio traffic was propagated to corroborate visual evidence; and a dummy pipe line was laid at a rate of construction which would confirm the end of November as the probable British D-day. Some of these measures did affect Axis thinking. Entries in the Panzer Army's war diaries and its reports to OKQ show that Stumme and his staff were convinced that the real danger lay south of Ruweisat Ridge. They were nearer the mark on timing and do not seem to have been deceived by the bogus radio traffic or the pipe line. On 20 October Stumme warned his commanders that a British offensive was imminent in the northern half of the southern sector. On the same day he heard the depressing news that one more important tanker had been sunk by the RAF. Reporting to OKW, Stumme estimated that he had just enough fuel for eleven days, fresh bread for 21 days, and practically no fresh vegetables or fruit. Sickness was rising through under-nourishment, and serviceability of weapons, transport and equipment was dropping alarmingly due to shortages of spares. Furthermore, the water-supply system, on which a great deal of effort had been lavished, was not working properly. OKW was disinclined to help. One of its visiting staff officers stated on 23 October that in OKW's view there was no danger of a British offensive in the near future. (Quoted by NZ Official Historians: page 202).

On the British side Montgomery's change of plan did not entirely relieve the disquiet about his leadership. The senior commanders were not convinced that his military policies, though an improvement on Ritchie's, would lead to success. Lumsden, in particular, was far from happy about the apparently illogical order that his armoured divisions must fight their way out to 'Pierson' if the infantry assault fell short of 'Oxalic'. His experiences during the battles of the 'Cauldron' and later at Ruweisat did not encourage him to believe that his tanks would be any more successful during 'Lightfoot' trying to fight their way through anti-tank gun screens and minefields in broad daylight. He was particularly worried that they would find themselves pinned down in the open in full view of German 88mm guns brought up to seal the breach when daylight came on the first morning of the battle. He warned his brigade and regimental commanders that they were not to rush Axis anti-tank guns and that they were to make sure that the exits from defiles like minefield gaps were not under anti-tank fire before trying to advance through them. The three Commonwealth infantry divisional commanders remained equally disinclined to accept Montgomery's ebullient confidence. In their view, his habit of wearing a black Tank Corps beret with two badges in it did not make him an expert in armoured warfare. Moreover, as planning progressed intelligence reports began to suggest that the Axis position was such deeper than had been first thought. General Leese reported this growing disquiet to Montgomery's Chief of Staff, de Guingand, who brought it to his Army Commander's attention. He received an inflexible refusal to make any further changes of plan. There was to be no more 'belly-aching'. General McCreery, Alexander's Chief of Staff, commenting later said:

> In my opinion Monty made a big tactical mistake over the conduct of the battle . When it was clear well before D-day that Rommel would have too much depth to his defences for our infantry attack to reach beyond the minefields, it would have been far sounder to make two bites at the cherry. In other words, XXX Corps should have had a second set piece attack either on the following night or if it was necessary to move many guns, then the next night.
>
> (McCreery; *XIII Royal Lancers' Journal*, page 38).

Disquiet at command level was not reflected amongst the majority of Eighth Army's officers and men. There were three great differences between a Montgomery battle and the previous British battles of the Second World War. In the first place, he made his plan crystal clear to every level by his system of personal addresses which he gave during his pre-battle tours of units. The Australian Official Historian catches the feeling of the time:

> As these men (9th Australian Division) sat before Montgomery – these down-to-earth commanders to most of whom he had been perforce a distant and somewhat enigmatic figure – as they listened to his precise and clipped but confident speech and perceived his mastery of his subject they developed instantly a strong confidence in the Army Commander himself and his plan.
>
> (*Australian Official History*; page 662).

In his talks to officers and men he foretold the course of the battle in a language they understood and could grasp. There would be three distinct phases: the 'Break in', the

'Dogfight', and the 'Break out'. He envisaged a quick 'Break-in' by XXX and XIII Corps; then a week's 'dogfight', in which the infantry would 'crumble' the enemy's defences behind the protection of the British armour while it broke up the Afrika Korps' counter-attacks; and finally a decisive 'Break-out' by X Corps, his 'Corps-de-Chasse'. The flavour of his addresses comes through in the last five paragraphs of the notes which he used for these addresses:

8. *General conduct of the battle*
Methodical progress; destroy enemy part by part,
slowly and surely.
Shoot tanks and shoot Germans.
He cannot last a long battle: we can.
We must therefore keep at it hard; no unit commander must release the pressure;
organise ahead for a 'dog fight' of a week.
Whole affair about 10 days (12).
– Don't expect spectacular results too soon.

(*Memoirs*; pages 126-127).

The second great difference is explained by Field Marshal Carver:

What course would events have taken if Gott had not been killed? It is probable that it would have made little difference to the result of Alam Halfa, but it is difficult to imagine Gott facing the prolonged attrition of El Alamein or even planning for it. Like Montgomery he was greatly influenced by his experiences of the First World War, but his reaction took a different form. Montgomery was appalled at the inefficiency and lack of professional skill which led to failures and heavy casualties. It was not so much the casualties themselves which horrified him as the waste, because nothing was achieved by them. He did not shrink from the direct approach, if it were efficiently done. Gott on the other hand was determined to avoid a repetition of anything that even resembled First World War operations. He sought an alternative in the mobile battle and the indirect approach as Rommel did.

(Carver, *El Alamein*, page 196).

Under Montgomery's leadership Eighth Army was to face up to the fact that there was no short cut to victory. The Germans had to be fought to the limits of human endurance. An attritional battle of the type which Montgomery knew he had to fight could not be won without determined leadership at every level. His orders about leadership issued on 6 October expressed this aspect of his thinking:

Orders about Leadership:
This battle will involve hard and prolonged fighting. Our troops must not think that, because we have a good tank and very powerful artillery support, the enemy will all surrender. The enemy will NOT surrender, and there will be bitter fighting.
  The Infantry must be prepared to fight and kill, and to continue doing so over a prolonged period . . .

(*Memoirs*: page 124)

These orders would have made little difference to men's attitudes if there had not been a ground-swell of opinion in their favour. The dreary story of the fall of Malaya and Singapore and of the disastrous summer campaign in the Western Desert made men sick of vacillating leadership.

The amateurism of the British Army was on the wane. Professionalism of the German order was ready to take its place. Montgomery, the supreme professional, hastened the process, and exorcised the ghosts of the Somme and Passchendaele which had so weakened British military determination in the first half of the Second World War.

The third difference was Montgomery's handling of reserves which had begun to show at Alam Halfa. He always had a large reserve, which, as soon as it was committed, was reconstituted by drawing in formations and units from quiet or uncommitted sectors. This technique gave him the 'balance' for which he always craved. It requires great willpower to build up adequate reserves. None of the other commanders in the desert had been able to do so.

On 23 October, Montgomery issued his order of the day which reflected his personality and supreme confidence in himself:

1. When I assumed command of the Eighth Army I said that the mandate was to destroy Rommel and his Army, and that it would be done as soon as we were ready.

2. We are ready now.

The battle which is now about to begin will be one of the decisive battles of history. It will be the turning point of the war. The eyes of the whole world will be on us, watching anxiously which way the battle will swing.

We can give them their answer at once 'It will swing our way' . . . Let us all pray that 'the Lord mighty in battle' will give us the victory.

(*Memoirs*; pages 127-128)

THE 'BREAK-IN'
(24 – 26 October 1942)

At 9.40 pm on 24 October the opening artillery and air bombardment on the German and Italian gun positions heralded the onset of the final Battle of El Alamein. Its muted rumble heartened the British troops as they moved up to their start-lines after lying cramped and uncomfortable all day in slit trenches in their forward assembly areas; and it warned the Panzer Army that its supreme test had come – the 'Battle without hope' as Rommel called it. Possibly there might have been some hope if Rommel had been in command at the very beginning because there were several occasions in the long struggle when the decision was finely balanced and might have gone in Rommel's favour had he not been on sick leave when D-day came.

The four assault divisions of XXX Corps made rapid initial progress through the eastern minefield belts where the Axis outpost line offered little resistance as Rommel had intended. Difficulties began to accumulate and delays to snowball as they forced

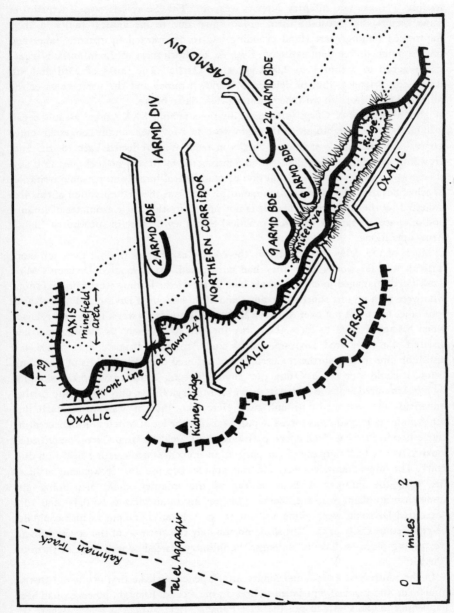

Fig 52 The Position at Dawn on 24th October 1942

their way through the 'Devil's Gardens' where random mining slowed down the leading 'I' tanks and infantry support weapons. The 'Scorpions' were successful in some sectors, but most of them broke down due to mechanical faults in their improvised flailing gear. Hand prodding had to be resorted to in many lanes and proved much slower than expected. Even so, by dawn most of the infantry brigades had reached to within 1 to 2,000 yards of 'Oxalic'. The tanks of 23rd and 9th Armoured Brigades, though delayed by random mines and the narrowness of the minefield gaps, were up with the infantry before dawn broke.

The advance of X Corps' armoured divisions behind XXX Corps' assault began well but became a nightmare as the night wore on. Movement on the congested routes grew slower and more erratic as checks in front were reflected back to the units crowding up behind. The night will be remembered by those who took part in it as a slow crawl through a colloidal solution of sand, petrol fumes and personal irritation as schedules slipped and frustration mounted. This was the first operation of this size mounted by the staffs concerned. It is not surprising that their estimates of timings and of space allocations were less practical than they became in subsequent Eighth Army operations.

Much of the delay was caused by the Mine Task Forces finding their job more difficult and far slower than they had anticipated. 1st Armoured Division's Mine Task Force managed to clear a single lane as far as the leading Australian infantry, who were held up just short of 'Oxalic'; and 10th Armoured Division's Force cleared four lanes up to but not over Miteirya Ridge. All Lumsden's worst fears were realised when his tanks tried to force their way forward to 'Pierson' as Montgomery had ordered. 1st Armoured Division, led by 2nd Armoured Brigade, met mines and anti-tank fire in the Northern Corridor and suffered considerable loss of Shermans before it could even reach 'Oxalic', let alone 'Pierson'. 10th Armoured Division, led by 8th Armoured Brigade, nosed its way over Miteirya Ridge, only to run into further minefields and well-sited anti-tank guns. Here, too, 'Pierson' was out of reach, and 8th Armoured Brigade was forced to pull back into the lee of Miteirya Ridge, creating congestion in the New Zealanders' positions which Field Marshal Carver described as looking like 'a badly organised car park at an immense race meeting held in a dust bowl'. The tanks themselves were far from popular because they drew enemy artillery fire onto the infantry without as far as the infantry could see, doing any commensurate damage to the enemy. This was an unfair view as both 1st and 10th Armoured Divisions were taking a steady toll of Axis tanks and guns which could not be replaced as easily as the British. Unfortunately the attrition of the enemy armour was taking place on 'Oxalic' amongst the infantry instead of well clear of them on 'Pierson'.

In the south XIII Corps' divisionary attack penetrated the first of the old British minefields and reached, but failed to breach, the second. Enough, however, had been happening in the south to pin the 21st Panzer/Ariete armoured groups where the Germans believed the decisive British thrust might still be launched.

After reviewing the situation during the morning of 24 October, Montgomery decided to press on for a further 24 hours with the 'break-in' phase before turning to the 'crumbling' process. X Corps was to continue its attempt to break out from both corridors to reach 'Pierson'; 1st Armoured Division attacking with 51st Highland Division towards Kidney Ridge during the afternoon; and 10th Armoured advancing over Miteirya Ridge and through the minefields on the far side after dark that night. The day would belong principally to the RAF which was to hammer the areas in which the 15th Panzer/Littorio Groups were thought to be operating. In all, over 1000 RAF sorties were flown that day with another 170 flown by the US Army Air Force. 15th Panzer and the Littorio Divisions had an uncomfortable time.

On the Axis side the command structure was temporarily upset by the loss of General Stumme who was reported missing after going forward to see what was happening. His body was not found until next day. His vehicle had been fired on by the Australians. The Colonel with him was killed. Stumme had been trying to jump out when the driver turned and drove off at full speed unaware that his General was hanging on outside. Stumme had had a heart attack and had fallen off without the driver realising it. The Commander of the Afrika Korps – Major-General Ritter von Thoma – assumed command and decided that the British penetrations could be contained without any major change in dispositions . The 15th Panzer/Littorio Groups had reacted as intended and had established a containing line approximately on 'Pierson' and were responsible for checking X Corps' attempted advance westwards. Von Thoma's confidence confirmed what Montgomery had refused to accept – that the Axis positions were too deep for a single night's attack. Further proof of this came from the remarkably few prisoners taken and practically no guns, suggesting that the main anti-tank gun positions were west of 'Oxalic'.

The second attempt by X Corps to fight its way into the open began in the afternoon of 24 October with 51st Highland Division helping 1st Armoured Division to open the Northern Corridor to Kidney Ridge. Hard fighting brought 2nd Armoured Brigade to within 1000 yards of its objective when darkness stopped further progress. 31 Shermans had been lost but the brigade could claim 30 German tanks destroyed in its sector. 10th Armoured Division's attempt to clear the Southern Corridor did not start until after dark, and produced, not unexpectedly, a clash between Montgomery and his armoured commanders.

Lumsden was far from optimistic about the chances of Gatehouse's 10th Armoured Division breaking out during the night. Gatehouse was to advance with his two armoured brigades abreast, organising his own minefield gapping with his divisional engineers. Congestion in the Miteirya Ridge area did not ease his problems. Shortly before zero hour at 10 pm, a Luftwaffe aircraft unloaded its bombs by chance on 8th Armoured Brigade as it was trying to form up, setting several vehicles on fire whose blaze attracted all German guns within range. When the Sappers did get forward to start breaching, they found more mines than expected. This delayed the gapping and further delays were caused by units dispersing to avoid presenting another air target. The brigade commanders suggested to Gatehouse that the attack was so far behind schedule that it should be called off, otherwise they would be caught out in the open again on a forward slope when daylight came. Gatehouse went back to his main headquarters to report this conclusion to Lumsden who put the position forcibly to de

Guingand. The latter realised a critical decision had to be made and that only Montgomery could make it. Summoning both Lumsden and Leese to Eighth Army's Tactical HQ, de Guingand took the unusual step of waking Montgomery who, under normal circumstances, objected to be woken with reports during the night. Montgomery listened to what his Corps Commanders had to say. Both believed that the battle had gone so wrong that it should be broken off to avoid further profitless expenditure of life and resources. Their plea fell on determinedly deaf ears. Montgomery reaffirmed his earlier orders that the armour was to fight its way out to 'Pierson'. If the armoured commanders were not prepared to do so, he would find others who would. This was probably the psychological turning point not only of the Battle of El Alamein, but of the North African Campaign as well. Previous Eighth Army Commanders would have flinched from giving such an order for fear of repeating the unreasoning obstinacy of First World War commanders. Montgomery did not hesitate. His corps and divisional commanders now knew where they stood. 'Lightfoot' would be fought to the limits of British as well as German endurance.

While Montgomery was winning this personal battle, events on the battlefield were making his decisions tactically irrelevant. The tanks of 10th Armoured Division had been slowly working their way through two very narrow gaps which the Sappers had managed to clear through the minefields. There were reports that some tanks had reached 'Pierson' but this proved to be incorrect as neither armoured brigade was much more than 1000 yards west of the ridge when dawn began to break. They could find few hull-down positions from which to engage the German armour and so they withdrew once more east of the ridge rather than be destroyed lying out in full view of 88mm guns. In the south, Horrocks had been no more successful, and had given up trying to breach the second of the old British minefields. The 'Break-in' had not gone according to plan as Montgomery has so often claimed. The 'Dog-fight' would have to start with the armoured divisions amongst, instead of in front of, the Infantry.

THE DOG-FIGHT
(25 to 31 October 1942)

Montgomery had intended to start the 'crumbling' process with an attack south-westwards from Miteirya Ridge, using Freyberg's New Zealanders, while Briggs' 1st Armoured Division probed forward from the Northern Corridor to engage Axis tanks around Kidney Ridge. During the morning a sense of frustration and stalemate settled over the congested Miteirya area. Tank crews, dog-tired, were engaging enemy targets at long range; equally tired New Zealand infantry huddled down in their slit trenches cursing the British tanks for drawing retaliatory fire; and behind the ridge a jumble of artillery and logistic transport clogged the narrow tracks through the uncleared minefields. Montgomery conferred with his principal commanders at about midday and concluded that it would be costly and difficult to renew the battle in the Mitierya area. Reports from the north were more encouraging. Morshead was well ahead with his own plans for 'crumbling' northwards from his

Australian sector to take the Point 29 spur, which had been recognised during 'Lightfoot' planning as the key feature in the coastal sector. Australian patrols had found it lightly held and apparently free of mines. Montgomery accepted Morshead's proposal to 'crumble' northwards and cancelled any further effort by Freyberg and Gatehouse. The Highlanders and 1st Armoured Division would continue operations around Kidney Ridge, and all divisions in contact with the enemy would push out patrols to detect signs of an Axis withdrawal – an optimistic gesture which paid no dividends for 10 more long and hard-fought days.

Morshead's preparations were so well advanced that he agreed to attack that night. During the day the Australian patrols captured the German regimental commander and one of the battalion commanders responsible for the defence of the Point 29 area. They confirmed the absence of mines, enabling the Australians to risk mounting their infantry in armoured carriers to rush the position at speed after dark. Their attack was simple, well planned with close artillery and tank co-operation, and was completely successful. Meeting no mines made all the difference. The Point 29 spur was taken and consolidated by first light. By contrast the 1st Armoured Division/51st Highland Division effort around Kidney Ridge was less successful with mines, misunderstanding and muddle making progress disappointing.

26 October – the third day of the battle – was a day for second thoughts on both sides. Rommel had arrived back at his HQ late in the evening of 25 October. He was far from well and the picture given him by von Thoma was not reassuring. Losses had been heavy, primarily from British artillery and air bombardment, the former being more concentrated and better co-ordinated than in the past. The Trento Division had been decimated; 164th Division had been severely mauled; and, although the 15th Panzer/Littorio Groups had successfully contained the British breach in the northern sector, they had lost heavily in doing so. Before deciding how to handle the battle, Rommel decided that he must regain Point 29 as its occupation by the Australians threatened the security of the important coastal sector. He also gave instructions that tanks were to be husbanded and 88mm guns used to deal with British tanks wherever they tried to break through. During the 26 October his immediate counter-attacks on Point 29 were broken up by Australian artillery and RAF bombing. By evening he decided that he must risk moving the 21st Panzer Division northwards to give himself enough armour to mount an effective counter-offensive. He decided also to bring forward the 90th Light and the Trieste Divisions from El Daba to reinforce his coastal sector. As he issued these orders he heard that two more Axis tankers had been lost.

Montgomery, for his part, began to look ahead to the 'break-out' and started to withdraw troops into reserve to re-create a force with which to renew the battle and so prevent a stalemate. 'Crumbling' would go on in a lower key while Eighth Army was reorganised for the decisive phase. The Australians would develop their operations towards the coast road on the night 28/29 October; 1st Armoured Division would make ground westwards around Kidney Ridge; and the rest of the Army would readjust its sectors to release the New Zealanders, 9th Armoured Brigade and 10th Armoured Division into reserve. 7th Armoured Division would be withdrawn from

XIII Corps' southern sector and moved north into reserve as well.

Rommel managed to collect a striking force quicker than Montgomery and decided that he would launch his counter-stroke directly at the 'Oxalic' penetration. 90th Light supported by those units of 15th Panzer which could be extricated from the line, was to attack the Australian salient from the north-west; and 21st Panzer with as many mobile troops as possible would attack the 1st Armoured Division/51st Highland Division sector just south of Kidney Ridge through an area code-named 'Snipe', held by 7th Motor Brigade. The attack was to be launched out of the sun late on 27 October with the customary violence which in the past had won so many of Rommel's engagements. Kesselring's Luftwaffe squadrons were to support the attack with every aircraft they could muster.

This time Rommel misjudged British determination to resist and the ability of his own men to launch such an attack. A 'sea change' had come over the Eighth Army under Montgomery. It was prepared to absorb and not to evade a panzer assault. And the panzer divisions themselves, hard and keen though they still were, no longer had the equipment superiority to fan their enthusiasm. Rommel's description of the battle ran:

> At 1500 hrs our dive bombers swooped on the British lines. Every artillery and anti-aircraft gun which we had in the northern sector concentrated a violent fire on the point of the intended attack. Then the armour moved forward. A murderous British fire struck into our ranks and our attack was soon brought to a

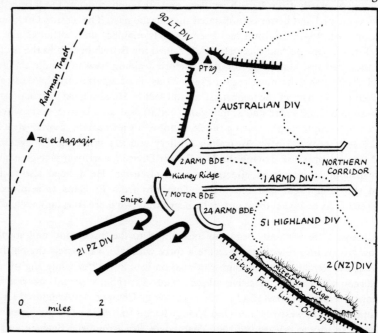

Fig 53 Rommel's counter-offensive – 27th October 1942

halt by immensely powerful anti-tank defence, mainly from dug-in anti-tank guns and a large number of tanks. We suffered considerable losses and were obliged to withdraw . . .

(Rommel: page 310).

This was a far cry from 'Tottensontag' a year earlier! The brunt of the panzer assault had fallen on 7th Motor Brigade who were better equipped and far more experienced than 5th South African Brigade had been. Colonel Turner's 2nd Battalion, The Rifle Brigade, fought its finest action of the war, standing its ground with its supporting Royal Artillery anti-tank battery and inflicting crippling losses on 8th Panzer Regiment. Turner was awarded the VC which reflected the courage and endurance of the whole battalion that day – a day which spelt the end of Rommel's ability to snatch victory out of defeat by the violence of his attack. The British stayed balanced as their Commander was determined that they should do at all times. There had been no British failure, but, as yet, there was no sign of British success.

Rommel ordered the Panzer Army to go over on to the defensive again hoping to enforce a stalemate. He moved more units northwards from opposite XIII Corps and strengthened his hold on the coastal sector, appreciating that this was the most likely area in which the British would make their decisive effort. If he could beat Montgomery's renewed offensive he had every chance of maintaining his position at El Alamein.

When Morshead reopened his Australian attack northwards from Point 29 on the night 28/29 October, hoping to cut the coast road and to encircle the German units still holding out in the coastal sector, he met much stiffer resistance. Progress was made but the attack fell short of its objectives in the face of opposition from 90th Light Division which had reinforced the Axis line. Nevertheless Rommel was becoming a worried man. Montgomery's crumbling process was succeeding. The attrition caused by British artillery and air bombardment and the loss of more tankers off Benghazi and Tobruk persuaded him to take the prudent precaution of reconnoitring a new defensive position at Fuka to which he could withdraw if all else failed. He knew that retreat to Fuka would mean abandoning the bulk of his infantry and so he decided:

. . . to make one more attempt, by tenacity and stubbornness of our defence, to persuade the enemy to call off his attack. It was a slim hope, but the petrol situation alone made a retreat, which would inevitably lead to mobile warfare, out of the question.

(Rommel; page 312).

Rommel might well have succeeded against a less forceful and less professional British Commander. A number of British voices, even in the forward area, were beginning to suggest that Eighth Army had shot its bolt. Confidence drains quickly when poured on the sands of repeated failure. Churchill became restive as he noted the withdrawal of divisions from the line. Brooke recorded in his diary how he ran into a storm of reproach from the Prime Minister:

What was my Monty doing now, allowing the battle to peter out . . . He had done nothing for the last three days, and now he was withdrawing troops from the front. Why had he told us he would be through in seven days if all he intended to do was to fight a half-hearted battle? Had we not a single general who could even win a single battle?

(Arthur Bryant; *Turn of the Tide*; page 512).

Brooke managed to stop Churchill sending Alexander one of those goading cables from which Wavell and Auchinleck had suffered. His faith in the new commander which he had appointed to Eighth Army was repaid. Montgomery was already organising his 'Break-out' which he had decided would begin as soon after Morshead's second northward attack as possible. It was to be a replica of the original 'Lightfoot' assault on a smaller scale and was code-named 'Supercharge'. XXX Corps would 'break in', using Freyberg's New Zealand Division, reinforced by 151st Brigade from 50th Division and 152nd Brigade from the Highland Division, and supported by 23rd Armoured Brigade's 'I' tanks. The breach in the Axis containing line was to be about 4,000 yards wide and the infantry would advance some 5,000 yards in the dark to enable 9th Armoured Brigade to pass through and cut the Rahman track 2,000 yards further on before dawn. At first light, Lumsden's X Corps, led by Briggs' 1st Armoured Division would break-out into Rommel's rear to defeat the remnants of the Afrika Korps. Great care was to be taken to ensure better co-ordination this time in passing 9th Armoured Brigade and then 1st Armoured Division through in successive stages. The only thing in doubt on 29 October was the exact axis for 'Supercharge'.

Montgomery's original intention was to launch 'Supercharge' near the coast road. During 29 October, Alexander visited Eighth Army with Mr Casey, the Minister of State, and McCreery, Chief of Staff, to reassure themselves before replying to the Defence Committee's cables that Montgomery was not allowing the offensive to lose momentum. They all showed some disquiet about the proposed axis for 'Supercharge' because it seemed to strike, like Auchinleck's 2nd Ruweisat, one of the strongest sections of the Axis line. Alexander was rightly not prepared to interfere with his Army Commander's tactical handling of the battle and so left things as they were. Later, intelligence began to accumulate showing that Rommel had concentrated 90th Light Division as well as 15th Panzer and the Littorio Divisions in the path proposed for 'Supercharge'. Montgomery accepted his staff's conclusions and switched the 'Supercharge' axis further south to a line just north of the original Northern Corridor to bring his armour out onto the Rahman track near Tel el Aqqaqir.

THE BREAK-OUT
(1 to 8 November)

Montgomery had planned to launch 'Supercharge' on the night 31 October/ 1 November, but Freyberg found that he did not have enough time to move the necessary artillery, to regroup units for specific tasks and to assemble them in the

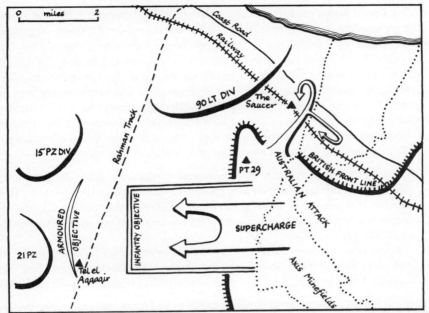

Fig 54 Australian Attack of 30th/31st October, and 'Supercharge' of 1st/2nd
      November 1942

congested area behind the point of 'break-out'. Montgomery had great faith in
Freyberg's judgment and postponed the attack 24 hours without demur. In order to
keep up the pressure on Rommel's troops, Morshead agreed to attack for a third time
in the north with the aim of cutting the coast road and railway, and isolating the Axis
garrisons of the coastal sector which were still holding out. The final touches to
'Supercharge' were added at Montgomery's co-ordinating conference when he
demanded 'determined leadership, faith in the success of the plan, and no
"belly-aching".' (Carver; page 158).

While Freyberg pressed ahead with his preparations, Morshead did keep Rommel
occupied. The Australian attack on the night 30/31 October, though opposed by
additional Axis troops, was more successful than their second attack had been. They
cut road and railway and attempted to exploit to the coast, and in doing so drew
Rommel's personal attention to the problems of stopping them. Fighting became
severe. Throughout 31 October and 1 November the Australians matched Turner's
riflemen on 'Snipe' with their defence of the 'Saucer'. Rommel played a personal part
in the determined efforts made by 21st Panzer and the 90th Light to extricate the
Axis coastal garrisons. Morshead's men suffered heavy casualties but held their
positions drawing more and more German strength northwards away from the
'Supercharge' axis.

'Supercharge' started well. Preliminary air attacks mounted early in the evening by
87 RAF bombers caused major explosions in the Axis rear. It transpired later that the

Afrika Korps' communications were disrupted by this bombing. When the British infantry attacked just after midnight behind a well co-ordinated artillery programme success came more easily than in 'Lightfoot' because there were fewer mines. 9th Armoured Brigade was not so lucky when it moved forward to pass through the infantry. Its regiments had difficulty in making their way through in the dust-laden darkness, and marrying-up with artillery observers, who had been working with the infantry in the first phase, went wrong. The artillery programme had to be postponed half an hour to 6.15 am — just half an hour before dawn — leaving too little time for the brigade to reach its objectives in the dark. The Australian Official historians pay the British armoured regiments a well-deserved tribute:

> The battles fought that day by the armoured regiments debouching from the 'Supercharge' bridgehead were not great field victories, but they were the final decisive engagements of the Eighth Army's offensive. Not for two days did the enemy front break; but that it would eventually break was rendered certain by the end of the day . . .
>
> If the British armour owed any battle debts to the New Zealand infantry, 9th Armoured Brigade paid them dearly and liberally that morning . . . At first they carried all before them.   *(Australian Official History;* page 731).

They did not do so for long. As daylight increased and longer range shooting became possible, they found themselves opposed by the bulk of Rommel's remaining 88mm guns. Most of the squadron commanders became casualties early in the day, reducing the action to individual tank engagements. 70 out of the 94 tanks, which crossed the start line, were knocked out, but they had destroyed some 35 Axis tanks and guns. Events later in the day showed that they had fractured Rommel's containing screen, though they did not break it.

Briggs' 1st Armoured Division was slow in emerging from the congested minefield gaps and chaotic conditions which were prevailing in the rear of New Zealand attack. Freyberg became anxious about 9th Armoured Brigade and asked Lumsden to hurry Briggs on, but this was easier said than done. By the time 1st Armoured Division had shaken itself out amongst and on the flanks of the remnants of 9th Armoured Brigade, Headquarters XXX Corps had detected signs of the expected Axis counter-attack and ordered all units to be ready to meet it. Briggs' tanks continued to press forward cautiously with decreasing success as Axis opposition stiffened. His circumspection helped to win the battle, which could well have been lost if he had pushed on blindly as Freyberg was demanding. He stayed 'on balance', as Montgomery required, and successfully rode out the coming crisis.

During the night Rommel had jumped to the conclusion that 'Supercharge' was being delivered from the Australian sector around Point 29, and had ordered von Thoma to counter-attack there with every available tank as he judged this was the decisive British attack. When dawn came, he realised that the breach was further south. Von Thoma was stopped in time, but it took until 11 am before the Panzer divisions could be redeployed and set in motion against the real British breach. Von Thoma delivered two major assaults — at 11 am and 2 pm — without success. 1st

Armoured Division won both contests, using artillery, air and hull-down tanks and anti-tank guns in unison. 117 Axis tanks (70 German) were lost in this last desperate attempt to force a stalemate. During the melée round the breach, two armoured car regiments tried to nose their way through the cracks made by 9th Armoured Brigade. The South Africans tried north-west and failed; the Royal Dragoons probed south-west and broke through into the rear of the Panzer Army, causing what annoyance they could in the Axis rear areas.

Sensing that Rommel must be near the end of his resources and feeling that the south-west offered the greatest opportunities, Montgomery directed Lumsden to go on making ground due west with X Corps, while Leese's XXX Corps attacked with Highland Division south-westwards. The Highlanders mounted a successful attack that evening wresting the 'Skinflint' area from the tiring Trieste Division, which gave up 160 dispirited prisoners. Lumsden was not so successful against the tougher opposition of the Afrika Korps. 7th Motor Brigade tried to open a breach during the night through the Rahman Track defences near Tel el Aqqaqir. Shortage of time for preparation led to faulty arrangements and to failure. There were no signs of German resistance slackening as yet.

The resolution of the German defence was deceptive. During the evening von Thoma reported to Rommel that he had held the British, but he was down to 35 fit tanks. He was out-numbered and out-gunned, and he had less than a third of his establishment of men left. The only way to save the Afrika Korps was to withdraw quickly before the British realised what was afoot. Their methods were usually so

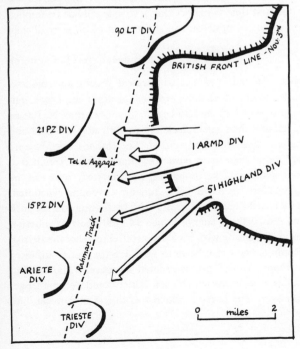

Fig 55 The Final Break Through: 3rd to 4th November 1942

deliberate that there was a fair chance of saving at least the valuable mobile troops on which to rebuild the Panzer Army back in Tripolitania. Rommel agreed and wasted no time in ordering preliminary steps to be taken for a withdrawal to Fuka, reporting his action with reasons to OKW as he did so. The Italian infantry in the south were to be drawn back straight away to the old German front line and then be lifted to Fuka on whatever transport could be mustered. The Africa Korps and the Italian and German mobile troops in the north would hold on until as many infantry units as possible had been got away. They would then withdraw by stages to Fuka as well.

Third November started slowly. Von Thoma and Rommel could detect no sign of the British renewing their offensive and so decided to take full advantage of the lull to send away as many 'useless mouths' as possible. Some of the Axis withdrawal moves were detected and Montgomery began to make preparations to exploit success. The Highland Division, reinforced with one of 4th Indian Division's Brigades, would develop its attack south-westwards, while 1st Armoured continued its pressure due westwards. The rest of the Eighth Army was alerted for a probable Axis withdrawal.

The Highland Division's attack should have met little resistance if Rommel had been able to carry out his withdrawal plans as he had intended. He was astonished to receive during the afternoon of 3 November a personal signal from Hitler countermanding his decision:

> In the situation in which you find yourself there can no other thought but to stand fast, yield not a yard of ground and throw every gun and every man into battle . . . Your enemy, despite his superiority, must also be at the end of his strength. It would not be the first time in history that a strong will has triumphed over bigger battalions. As to your troops, you can show them no other road than that to victory or death.

(Rommel; page 321 footnote).

Rommel hesitated but obeyed. He cancelled his withdrawal orders and made a genuine attempt to re-establish his line some miles west of the Rahman Track, but even he could not reverse the process which he had begun, any more than Neame or Ritchie could when, first, Wavell and then Auchinleck had tried to stop the 1941 and 1942 withdrawals from Benghazi after they had started. The Italians were beyond caring, and the German troops found their great powers of improvisation stretched to the limit. The Highland Division's attack, though ill-co-ordinated, over-ran its objectives successfully during the night. At dawn Tel el Aqqaqir was found evacuated. The British Armoured Brigades nosed their way forward with increasing success until midday when the overstrained Axis defence snapped open and fell apart as cohesion was lost. Von Thoma was captured fighting with his Kampfstaffel to delay the British advance. By late afternoon Rommel knew that he must abandon the Italian infantry if he was to save his mobile troops. At 5.30 pm he ordered a general withdrawal to Fuka, reporting his reasons to OKW in terms which even Hitler could not challenge. The Battle of El Alamein was over. The pursuit, which was to end in Tunisia, had begun.

*　　*　　*

A successful pursuit after a great battle of attrition is seldom possibly. Montgomery had made all his arrangements to exploit his victory which he saw was coming 48 hours earlier, but Eighth Army found itself nearer exhaustion than it realised when the final Axis collapse came. Its staff work was not up to the moment due to the cumulative fatigue and mental stress of the last 12 days. Field Marshal Carver paints the confusion of the first night of the break out:

> Little, if any, attempt seems to have been made on a higher level to co-ordinate the confusion that was bound to arise from so many divisions struggling to push out through the bottle-neck of the salient area. It would have been hard enough if all had been under command of the same corps; with two different corps, who were not on the best of terms anyway, both trying to carry out the same task in the same area, it was chaotic.
>
> (Carver; page 184).

Rommel had one advantage. The unbroken coast road lay behind him along which his mobile troops could make better progress, covered by rearguards, than the British pursuers who had to hook southwards into the desert to outflank his successive delaying positions. The British columns were also held up by petrol shortages; by infuriating checks to deal with old mine-fields of previous battles, some of which turned out to be British dummies; and by the skill of the German rearguards. The execution done by the RAF, who had undisputed command of the air, was disappointing. The airmen claimed many successes, but there was less evidence of these in the form of burnt out transport on the road-side as Eighth Army advanced than their claims suggested. The root cause of Army and Air Force disappointment lay in psychological fatigue. The Australian official historians remark: 'Some of the pursuing formations were delayed by real difficulties, some by imaginary ones, some by their own lack of impetus. None evinced the initiative and drive needed to snatch the prize.' (*Australian Official History*; page 742).

Rommel stood momentarily at Fuka on 5/6 November, and at Mersa Matruh on 7 November. Then the heavens opened, rain deluged down, and the 'bottom fell out of the desert', bringing all cross-country movement to a halt. These storms have often been credited with allowing Rommel to escape. It did bring the immediate pursuit to a decisive halt, but Rommel had already effectively escaped. Thereafter, Montgomery advanced with circumspection, making sure that he was always well balanced, operationally and logistically, so that he would not suffer the fate of the other British commanders who had reached El Agheila before him.

At the other end of the Mediterranean the darkened hulls of the 'Torch' assault convoys were passing Gibraltar as Eighth Army lay immobilised in the mud. And back at El Alamein the process of rounding up the stranded Italians and collecting the booty was going on. The profit and loss account cannot be calculated precisely. Out of an Army of about 100,000 Rommel left 40,000 as prisoners in British hands, all but 20 of his tanks, and over 1,000 Axis guns of all types. What his battle casualties were can only be guessed at about 20,000 killed and wounded. The most telling statistic is the strength of his principal German formations on 10 November.

Afrika Korps 2,200 men, 10 anti-tank guns, 11 tanks.
90th Light Division 1,000 men, 10 anti-tank guns.
164th Afrika Division 800 men.
Ramke Parachute Brigade 700 men, 5 anti-tank guns.
British losses are put at 13,000 men and 500 tanks, of which only 150 were a total loss.

(*British Official History;* Vol IV; page 95 (footnote)).

The Battle of El Alamein was far from perfect. Few battles ever are; Montgomery's triumph was no exception. It has been and will be criticised on many scores, but all are irrelevant in the light of what it achieved. The British, and indirectly, the Western Allies had found the missing link in their great military effort. They had had material superiority twice before during 'Crusader' and at Gazela; and, yet they had let victory slip through their fingers. None of the ingredients of Montgomery's military policy is outstandingly impressive on its own, but when they were all melted, like the constituent metals of an alloy, in the crucible of his egocentric determination always to succeed, and never to allow failure, they became a battle-winning formula which inspired his Army. They did more than this. They gave the British what they had been seeking since 1940 – a successful command team. Success breeds success and emulation is the sincerest form of flattery. There grew up a large number of commanders and staff officers who modelled themselves and shaped their policies on his example.

*   *   *

After dark on 7 November the 'Torch' assault convoys reached their craft-lowering positions and dropped anchor off the Moroccan coast either side of Casablanca, and in the Mediterranean either side of Oran and Algiers. The first dress rehearsal for the cross-Channel operation, which, in the end, would not take place until the Spring of 1944, had begun in an atmosphere of uncertainty and anxiety associated with such occasions. No-one knew what would happen; how long anything would take; whether units, equipment and stores had been loaded in the right order; what the hazards of tide, wind and weather would do to precise navigational calculations; how difficult the run-in and off-loading upon the beaches would be; whether the command and control mechanisms would work; and, above all, what the French would do.

Much to Admiral Cunningham's surprise, and indeed everyone else's, the assault convoys lost no ships on passage from the USA and the UK. Two factors contributed to this welcome beginning: tight security measures which successfully prevented Axis agents from penetrating the 'Torch' secret; and fortuitous circumstances. German intelligence sources and their air surveillance over the Atlantic failed to detect what was afoot, and so the U-boat packs were left deployed for routine attrition of Allied convoys across the Atlantic. One pack was stationed to watch the Western Approaches to English and Scottish ports, while another watched the Straits of Gibraltar. The former did not react in time to catch the south-bound convoys from the United Kingdom, and the latter was diverted at the crucial moment to attack a merchant convoy reported sailing northwards from Sierra Leone. This convoy lost 12 valuable ships, but their sinking temporarily cleared the path of the Western Task Force from the United States to Morocco, and of the Central and Eastern Task Forces on their way into the Mediterranean.

The fortunes and misfortunes of the three Task Forces varied but they had one thing in common: staff estimates, particularly of timings, went sadly awry through lack of experience. Admiral Hewitt's Western Task Force was divided into three sub-Task Forces, each assigned to a separate landing. General Patton, commanding the land forces, had decided to put his main sub-Task Force ashore on the beaches around the small port of Fedalla, just north of Casablanca, while two flanking sub-Task Forces were to be landed near Port Lyautey to the north to take its airfield, and at Safi to the south because it was the only port other than Casablanca, where the Seatrain *Lakehurst* could discharge medium tanks. The Fedalla sub-Task Force was based on the 3rd (US) Infantry Division under Major-General Jonathan W. Anderson, reinforced by armoured and other specialised units; Port Lyautey was to be mastered by Major-General Lucien K. Truscott with the 9th (US) Infantry Division; and Safi was to be dealt with by Major-General Ernest N. Harmon with troops from 2nd (US) Armoured Division.

Weather reports during the approach passage had been unfavourable, but Admiral Hewitt judged that the risks of going ahead outweighed the disadvantages of sailing his force into the Mediterranean and landing it west of Oran. He was to be proved

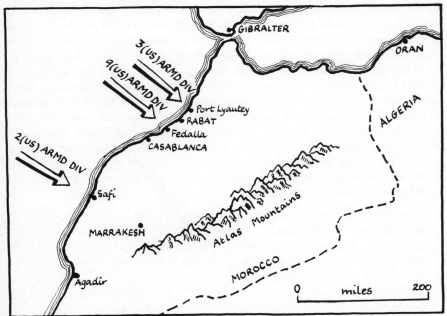

Fig 56 The Landings of the Western Task Force: 7th to 8th November 1942

right, but only just. The landings came close to disaster, in critical sea conditions which worsened as time went by. Fortunately the small ports of Fedalla and Safi were captured before beach working became impossible. All three sub-Task Forces found that lowering their assault craft and embarking the assault troops in them took much longer and proved more difficult in the Atlantic swell than they had anticipated. Most landings were behind schedule and in chaotic order, pointing to the impracticability of the theoretical timings of the planners and the inadequacy of training of the troops. Losses in landing craft were heavy due to the high surf, and had it not been' for the sporadic nature of French resistance, the landings could well have failed.

The first success came at Safi where two old American destroyers – the *Bernadon* and the *Cole* – were used to land troops inside the harbour, while assault craft touched down on beaches north and south of the port. The French garrison resisted and at daybreak their shore batteries opened fire, only to be subdued by US naval gunfire. By 2 pm Safi was in American hands and the *Lakehurst* was berthed and started unloading her tanks. Harmon was able to begin his 150-mile advance on Casablanca on the morning of 10 November after dispersing French forces from Marrakesh which attempted to interfere.

At Fedalla unloading was critically slow and nearly half the landing craft used in the initial assault were wrecked in the surf. Others lost their way on the run-in, and fetched up on the rocky coast several miles away. As at Safi there was little resistance until daylight; then the French shore batteries opened effective fire, forcing the American shipping to pull back out of range, thus lengthening the run to the shore. A French cruiser, seven destroyers and eight submarines put to sea from Casablanca. It was a forlorn gesture for they were successively overwhelmed by the US naval covering force. The other French warships, like the uncompleted battleship *Jean Bart,* fared little better though they stayed in harbour. The 16-inch shells of the US battleship *Massachusetts* put the *Jean Bart* out of action, and US carrier-borne aircraft helped the surface ships to deal with the remaining French warships. There was momentary anxiety that the powerful French squadron at Dakar might attempt to intervene, but it did not appear. The position ashore, however, remained precarious until Fedalla harbour was captured during the afternoon, giving some shelter for off-loading. By this time only one-third of the landing craft remained serviceable, but Anderson had secured a beach-head and hoped to advance on Casablanca from the north next day. General Patton was far from happy about the performance of Anderson's troops:

> General Patton, up before daylight on 9 November, went almost at once to check the situation at the beach. He considered it 'a mess' with leadership negligent ... In a state of exasperated frustration over the slackness which he observed and over some cases of fright during a French air attack at 0800, he remained on the beach until afternoon.

> *(US Official History;* page 137).

Anderson's advance on Casablanca was slow and exhausting for the troops on 9 November because too few vehicles and support weapons had been landed. For a time the advance was stopped, not by French resistance, but by lack of equipment and transport. Unloading improved during the day and enabled Anderson to reach the outskirts of Casablanca at dusk on 10 November where the French garrison of some 4,000 men with 90 guns showed every sign of resistance. Plans were laid to assault the city on 11 November.

At Port Lyautey, everything went wrong from the start. Navigation was inaccurate; a chance encounter with a French coastal convoy alerted the French garrison; slow disembarkation caused cumulative delays; and French batteries, which should have been captured before daylight, were able to interfere at dawn with the shipping lying off the beaches. Poor co-ordination of naval gunfire support did not help, and the French Airforce showed themselves particularly unfriendly. Stubborn resistance by the local French garrison, supported by antiquated French tanks, went on throughout the 9th and 10th without any sign of a French capitulation.

Similarly unflattering events were taking place off and on the beaches of the Central and Eastern Task Forces inside the Mediterranean. Sea conditions, with no rise and fall of tide, should have made landings easier, but this advantage was offset by two quite different considerations. First, the task forces were inter-Allied with British and American soldiers and sailors trying to work together for the first time, neither realising fully the differing meanings of the same English words. The British treated the Americans as 'British' in US uniforms and with British thought-processes and instincts. Neither really appreciated that the different uniforms did contain different types of men, with wholly different backgrounds. Co-operation would have been easier had the superficial differences been greater and more obvious.

Secondly, the Mediterranean landings were nearer to the Axis air and submarine forces based in the central Mediterranean. The combined Task Forces, which sailed through the Straits of Gibraltar during the nights of 5 and 6 November in a carefully co-ordinated and intricate pattern of fast and slow convoys with escorts and naval covering forces, were programmed to arrive off Oran and Algiers after dusk on 7 November. The course assigned to each convoy was designed to maintain the illusion of a major operation to re-supply Malta. The deception lasted just long enough to catch the German and Italian maritime commanders in the Mediterranean 'off balance'.

The first information that something big was afoot in the Mediterranean is recorded in OKW's war diary on 4 November when a battleship, two carriers, five cruisers and 20 destroyers were reported at Gibraltar by the Luftwaffe. The conclusion drawn was: 'The concentration of such important naval forces in the Western Mediterranean seems to indicate an imminent operation, perhaps another convoy to Malta.' (Quoted by *US Official History;* page 186).

It was not until the 'Torch' convoys actually entered the Mediterranean on 5/6 November that the Germans began to suspect a landing might be possible. Their fixation with Rommel's L of C led them to assess the probability of landings in the order Tripoli and Benghazi, Sicily, Sardinia, Italian mainland and, lastly, French North Africa. Kesselring appreciated the strengths and the limitations of air power and predicted correctly that the landings, if they came, would be outside the range of

Axis air bases in Sardinia and Sicily and thus in Western Algeria. He was supported in his view by Mussolini, who prided himself on his own skill as a pilot, but Hitler would not be shifted from his Tripoli – Benghazi theory. The wish was probably father to the thought. He hoped to repeat the 'Pedestal' slaughter as Allied convoys passed through the Sicilian Narrows. 9 German and 26 Italian submarines set off for patrol lines in the supposed path of the Allied convoys, and 76 German aircraft were airborne, searching for them on 7 November. They had little success as both Task Forces wheeled southwards to Oran and Algiers well to the west of the Axis search area.

As darkness fell on the Western Mediterranean on 7 November, the two Task Forces successfully picked up their marker submarines positioned to ensure correct navigation, and started the final run-in towards their craft-lowering positions. It was a nostalgic moment for many of the British officers in the force. The author, standing on the deck of the Dutch East-Indiaman, *Tegelberg*, recalls the uncanny feeling of following in the path of so many British military expeditions of long ago – some successful like Nelson's, and some tragic like Bing's. No-one knew what lay ahead at Oran or Algiers.

Oran proved the toughest of the two objectives for two reasons: the French Navy at Tel el Kebir were in no mood to join the Americans and were still bitterly hostile to the British; and secondly, General Mast's pro-Allied underground organisation was less well developed and not so ably led as in Algiers. Two disasters occurred at Oran on the first day. A gallant attempt was made to run two old American destroyers, the

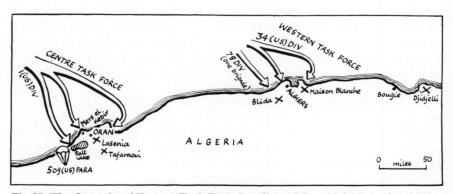

Fig 57 The Central and Eastern Task Force Landings: 7th to 10th November 1942

Walney and *Hartland,* manned by the Royal Navy and carrying nearly 400 US Infantry, through the harbour entrance to prevent the sabotage of the port installations. *Walney* broke through the boom, followed by her consort, and both came under an intense fire from French shore batteries and French warships in the port. Neither survived.

The other disaster at Oran was the complete mismanagement of the parachute assault on the La Senia and Tafaraoui airfields. There were the two plans: 'War' and 'Peace', depending upon French reactions. An estimate had to be made before the parachute aircraft left Cornish airfields as to which was the more likely. 'Peace' was chosen, though a last minute change to 'War' could be made, provided communications worked properly. The *US Official History* records what happened:

> Rain, fog, faulty radio intercommunication, and defective running (navigation) lights interfered with the maintenance of formation. When the planes climbed through clouds to 10,000 feet above sea level to surmount the crests of Spain's northern mountains, they became completely dispersed. The beacon signal from the ship off Oran, being sent on a frequency other than that expected by the transport planes, was never received. The widely separated aircraft, unaware that 'War' plan had been reinstated while they were in flight, were heading for a hostile reception.

> *(US Official History;* page 212).

Out of the 39 aircraft which set out, 7 failed to reach Algeria at all – one landed at Gibraltar, two in French Morocco and four in Spanish Morocco; 12 dropped their men over a day's march from their objectives; 16 landed on the great salt lake south-west of Oran, enabling their paratroopers to join up with the seaborne forces landing on the beaches; and the last four, including the Force Commander's plane, landed on the salt too far away and were captured by the French. French Air Force fighters and anti-aircraft artillery forced down and destroyed a number of the US aircraft. Only 14 of the Parachute Force aircraft survived and a week later a bare 300 out of the 556 parachute troops, who had set out, could be re-assembled for future operations.

The seaborne landings at Oran went more smoothly than those on the Atlantic coast, but delays and misjudgments were just as prevalent. Some unexpected and awkward sand bars were discovered just offshore, which stopped landing craft reaching the beaches. Vehicles which tried to drive through the intervening water gap were often 'drowned'. There was practically no resistance until daylight when French batteries opened fire, scoring several damaging hits on ships offshore. The battleship *Rodney* subdued but could not destroy the French guns; and naval aircraft set about crippling the French Air Force, destroying 70 aircraft on La Senia, which were later found to have been fully armed and ready to attack the invasion fleets. Throughout 8 November sporadic fighting went on on land while the American assault troops were building up in their three beach-heads. Tafaraoui was taken by midday and La Senia late in the afternoon. By the end of the day the three US Regimental Combat Teams of Major-General Terry Allen's 1st US Infantry Division, reinforced by

Colonel Paul D. Robinett's tanks from 1st (us) Armoured Division, were converging on Oran and meeting growing French resistance. Major-General Lloyd R. Fredendall, Commander II (us) Corps in overall charge of Central Task Force land operations, decided to use 9 November to build up his forces and to draw an encircling noose around the city, hoping that the French would see reason and give in rather than face an assault. His hopes were not fulfilled. The French did their best to delay his advance, and forced him to open his attack early on 10 November. His tanks were the decisive factor in disrupting the French resistance, and by noon Oran was in his hands. His victory was real and substantial, but unfortunately deceptively simple. There was just enough French opposition to make the American soldiers feel that this was war, but too little to give them battle experience.

The Algiers landings were different again and more highly charged with political overtones because Algiers was the capital and administrative centre of French North Africa in which the most important political and military personalities resided. It was the place where major political decisions could be taken, and where General Mast had managed to organise significant support for General Giraud and a loosening of the straight-jacket of loyalty to Marshal Pétain as the legitimate ruler of France. The degree to which Mast could sway the loyalties of the majority of French officials in Algiers would determine the length of French resistance in the whole of French North Africa; and, conversely, the chances of successful German intervention if French resistance was prolonged.

The Naval 'coup de main' operation to seize the port of Algiers was just as unsuccessful as at Oran. Two old British destroyers, *Brooke* and *Malcolm,* with us Rangers on board failed to find the harbour entrance on first approach. *Malcolm* was badly damaged by coastal batteries and had to retire. *Brooke* broke through the boom and managed to land her Rangers. It was another forlorn hope. Changing her position several times to avoid gunfire, *Brooke* was eventually forced to leave, foundering next day. On the beaches either side of Algiers, unloading went relatively smoothly with little or no French resistance because Mast's pro-Allied movement had managed to gain temporary control of many of the key French military installations. The Allies took considerable risks in flying off fighters from Gibraltar to land at Maison Blanche and Blida airfields. They did not have enough fuel to return to Gibraltar, if a hostile reception awaited them. The risk paid off. Maison Blanche was occupied without resistance before the Gibraltar aircraft arrived. At Blida, Lieutenant B. H. C. Nation, flying a naval aircraft overhead, saw a white handkerchief being waved. He landed and accepted the French Air Commander's invitation to Allied aircraft to use the field.

Inside Algiers an exciting political drama was enacted. Mast had taken advantage of a provision in the French Emergency Defence Plan for Algiers which authorised civilian agencies to take over key installations like communication centres to release the military personnel for more active defence tasks. Early in the night of the landings young men of the patriot movement loyal to Mast and Giraud took over Algiers, locking up any recalcitrant officials and placing a guard on the residence of the French C-in-C in North Africa, General Juin. Mast was relying on the rapid advance of American troops into Algiers to relieve his supporters, and for the immediate appearance of Giraud to provide a political focus. Both arrived too late; and, although the action of Mast's supporters enabled the Allies to land safely, the coup miscarried in Algiers itself because the Allies realised how successful Mast had been and did not move quickly enough. As the hours ticked by more and more of the orthodox officials regained control and began to honour their oath to Petain.

In the early hours of the morning of 8 November, while Juin's house was still guarded by French resistance supporters, Mr Murphy called upon him and told him of the overwhelming strength of the Allied landings, asking him to co-operate. Juin insisted that Murphy's request must be referred to the C-in-C of the French Armed Forces, Admiral Darlan, who happened to be in Algiers visiting his son who was dangerously ill. Darlan was brought to Juin's villa where Murphy reminded him of his previously expressed willingness to turn against the Axis as soon as 500,000 American soldiers, fully armed and equipped, were ready to intervene. These troops were now landing. He must decide which way the French North African forces should react. Darlan, who had only Murphy's word for the scale of the Allied landings, played for time and was rewarded for his prevarication. The pro-Allied guards on the villa were driven off by French Gardes Mobile, and the tables were turned, Darlan and Juin going off to the military headquarters at Fort L'Empereur, leaving Murphy under arrest. Juin, however, soon discovered that the Allies were as strong as Murphy claimed and too firmly established ashore for him to restore the situation. The forts that had not surrendered voluntarily at Mast's instigation, were being shelled by the Royal Navy and bombed by carrier-borne aircraft; the main airfields were in Allied hands; and Allied troops were on the high ground overlooking the city. At 4 pm Juin advised Darlan to negotiate. Major-General Charles W. Ryder of the 34th (US) Division arrived at Juin's headquarters and concluded a cease-fire agreement by 6 pm. By 8 pm Algiers was securely in Allied hands and all French troops were confined to barracks. Next day Giraud reached Algiers, hoping to rally French support to the Allied cause, but found he could make little impact. General Mark Clark also arrived and took over negotiations with Darlan, which after many tense moments ended in the issue of a cease-fire order to all French troops in North Africa. This saved Casablanca from assault and ended the French resistance at Port Lyautey. It was the first of two major steps which were to bring the French North African forces over to the Allied side.

At the Eastern end of the Mediterranean, the Royal Navy seized the opportunity of German and Italian preoccupation with French North Africa to run a convoy of four large merchant ships to Malta. The 'Stoneage' convoy reached the island unscathed. Times had changed in the Mediterranean. They had also changed in Russia where von Paulus' Sixth Army was being surrounded by Russian forces, which broke through the German defences on the River Volga on 19 November.

In England the church bells, which had been silent since Dunkirk, because they were to be used as part of the invasion warning system, rang out in celebration of Montgomery's victory at El Alamein and Eisenhower's successful 'Torch' landing. Churchill wrote: 'Before Alamein we never had a victory. After Alamein we never had a defeat.' (Churchill: Vol IV, page 541).

General Truscott referring to the 'Torch' landings remarked: 'A hit and miss affair that would have spelled disaster against a well-armed enemy intent on resistance.' (*US Naval History:* Vol II, page 123).

14

Unequal Battle Experience
(November 1942 to February 1943)

American soldiers who survived the bitter months of January and February 1943 in
Tunisia will never forget them – or forget Tunisia. For it was during this period in
the deserts and mountains . . . that American forces first crossed swords with veteran
German legions and learned war from them in the hard way. These American
soldiers, suffering from faults in leadership, from their own ignorance, from inferior
equipment, reeled in defeat and yet rose to victory.

(General Lucian K. Truscott: page 124).

When Darlan's cease-fire order became effective in Morocco and Algeria late on
10 November it looked as if Rommel's forces were trapped between the two Allied
Armies advancing from either end of the Mediterranean. The general consensus of
opinion at the time was that the jaws of the Allied pincer would meet somewhere
near Tripoli. The military commentators of the world press misjudged the German
reaction and failed to appreciate the effects of the marked inequality in training and
experience which differentiated Alexander's and Eisenhower's forces. While Eighth
Army drove inexorably westwards, the Allied forces in French North Africa struggled
from one crisis to another. Had it not been for the gratuitous internal friction which
grew up amongst the Axis commanders in North Africa, Eisenhower's forces would
have been in a much sorrier state when Mongomery reached Tunisia in March 1943.

The story of the 'blooding' of Eisenhower's Anglo-American forces in French
North Africa instead of in Normandy falls into two phases: the inital race for Tunis
which Eisenhower lost in teeming rain and squelching Tunisian mud; and his army's
subsequent fight for survival against experienced German troops flown and shipped
in from Hitler's central reserves and from Russia.

THE RACE FOR TUNIS

The gamble was great but the prize was such a glittering one that we abandoned
caution in an effort to bring to General Anderson every available fighting man in
the theatre. There still existed the fear that the Germans might thrust air forces
down across the Pyrenees into Spain, to attack us from the rear.

(Eisenhower: page 135)

Hitler's first reaction to the news of the landings was one of delight that the Allies had

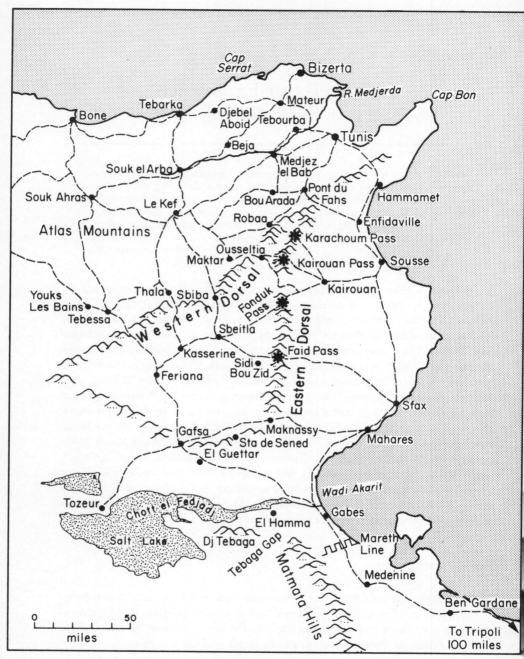

Map IX: Tunisia

committed a strategic and political blunder of the first magnitude. It seemed that Franco-German collaboration could, at last, be consummated by a German offer of military help for the defence of French North African territories against the Allies. Kesselring received instructions to send plenipotentiaries at once to North Africa to arrange the reception of Axis forces. The officer sent to Algiers was turned back at Setif by pro-Allied French authorities, but two others reached Tunis and were well received by the French Resident, Admiral Esteva, and by the French Naval Commander, Admiral Derrien. Hitler was further encouraged by a Vichy announcement that Luftwaffe aircraft would be welcome to use French air bases in Tunisia.

News of the sporadic nature of French resistance to the Allied landings soon dampened Hitler's enthusiasm and made him suspicious of French motives. Summoning Pierre Laval to München, ostensibly to discuss collaboration, Hitler alerted all troops earmarked for the German contingency Plan 'Anton' (the occupation of Vichy France), and instructed Kesselring to take full advantage of the French offer of air bases in Tunisia by occupying them as soon as possible with whatever troops and aircraft he could despatch at short notice. By the evening of 9 November German fighters and bombers had been flown into Tunis's El Aouina air base with a German parachute battalion and Kesselring's personal guard unit.

Laval's talks with Hitler and Ciano on 10 November could not have come at a worse time for the French. Pétain had been inclined to accept Darlan's announcement of the cease-fire in French North Africa as a 'fait accompli', but Laval persuaded him to repudiate the Admiral in the longer term interests of Franco-German collaboration. Darlan was bitterly upset by Pétain's 'volte face' and attempted to rescind his cease-fire order, but was arrested by the Allies before he could do so. Hitler placed the worst possible construction on these events and demanded access to the ports of Tunis and Bizerta and all Tunisian air bases for Axis forces. Laval hesitated, saying only Petain could decide; and added that, in his view, France could never agree to Italian participation in a German 'occupation' of Tunisia. Hitler lost patience and that night, 10/11 November, ordered Plan 'Anton'. Ten German divisions marched into Vichy France, breaking the Franco-German Armistice of 1940 and toppling the facade of Pétain's independent French State. The second and final act in the drama of bringing French North Africa on to the Allied side had been played out. Darlan and most of the senior officers and officials in Morocco and Algeria, who had genuine reasons of conscience for preserving their oath of allegiance to Pétain up to that moment, felt free to co-operate with the Allies as the Germans had unilaterally broken the 1940 Armistice.

This pro-Allied political tide did not flow as far as Tunisia where the Vichy authorities were in a more precarious position with the Germans in their midst and Allied help too far away. They were receiving conflicting instructions from the two French factions in Algiers and Vichy. The Germans trod warily until they had enough troops in Tunis and Bizerta to act. Admirals Esteva and Derrien also played for time by adopting an attitude of strict neutrality, but General Barré, commanding the French Tunisian Division, took a more robust view and decided that it was safer to deal with the Germans from the comparative safety of the Tunisian hills. He withdrew all his troops westwards to Beja and Medjez el Bab, and from there continued to parley while he waited to see whether the Allies would arrive in sufficient strength to support him.

Hitler's political decision to occupy Vichy France was accompanied by a complementary military decision to form an Axis bridgehead around Tunis and Bizerta within which a major force could be assembled to oppose the Allied advance from Algeria and to protect the rear of Rommel's Panzer Army. The first Axis troops came tumbling in by sea and air on no pre-arranged programme. They were scraped together from reinforcement holding units in Italy, from troops waiting shipment to Rommel, and from German central reserves in France and Germany. On 16 November, General Nehring, the former Afrika Korps Commander wounded at Alam Halfa, arrived to take over the bridgehead with an 'ad hoc' headquarters called the XC Corps. By the end of November he expected to have about 15,000 German troops with 50 medium tanks and 20 of the new and formidable heavy 'Tiger' tanks, mounting 88mm guns, in the bridgehead. In the north, covering Bizerta, he formed an 'ad hoc' division under Colonel von Broich based upon the 11th Parachute Engineer Battalion and the Barenthin Glider Regiment with miscellaneous supporting artillery and tank units. Covering Tunis, he had the leading elements of 10th Panzer Division and the 5th Parachute Regiment. And the Italians provided their Superga Division from Italy and the 50th Special Brigade from Tripoli, containing remnants of such experienced units as the Ariete Division which had been

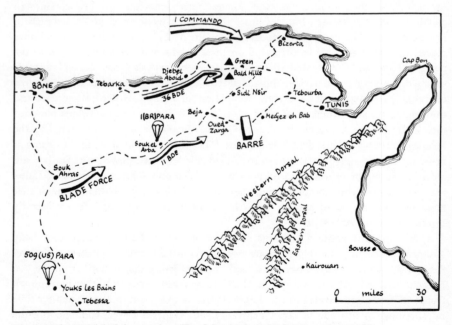

Fig 58 The British Advance into Tunisia: 11th to 17th November 1942

decimated at El Alamein, to garrison the coastal towns of Sousse, Sfax and Gabes.

On the Allied side, the strategic decisions taken when mounting Torch began to hamstring their efforts to compete with the German build up. Two thirds of the Allied assault forces had landed at Casablanca and Oran, and where thus too far away to support a quick advance on Tunis. No logistic units to operate the long lines of communication from Algiers to Tunis would be available until the follow-up convoys started to arrive with additional equipment and transport. Moreover, American attention was still focused on a possible German descent through Spain, and this fear anchored most of the XII (us) Army Air Force in Morocco and Western Algeria.

Algiers is 500 miles as the crow flies from Tunis which could be reached either by sea or by two tortuous mountain roads running through the length of the Atlas mountains. There was a French railway as well, but the chances of it working effectively for some weeks were not high. General Anderson, whose task it was to seize Tunis with his embryonic First British Army, started his advance eastwards before the cease-fire. The only forces at his disposal were Major-General Evelegh's 78th (Br)* Division with the 11th and 36th (Br) Brigades on light assault scales, and Colonel R. A. Hull's 'Blade Force' consisting of the 17/21st Lancers' Regimental Group from 6th (Br) Armoured Division reinforced with a squadron of armoured cars, a battery each of field artillery, anti-tank and anti-aircraft guns, a company of motor infantry and a troop of sappers. The 17/21st Lancers themselves were equipped with a mixture of obsolescent 'Crusaders' and 'Valentines'. He could also call on certain British Commando and us Ranger units, and one British and one American parachute battalion.

Anderson planned to work his way eastwards along the coast with amphibious landings until he reached Bône, and then to advance overland, using whatever transport he could acquire from the local French authorities to turn the Germans out of Tunis and Bizerta. Brigadier Kent-Lemon's 36th (Br) Brigade landed at Bougie unopposed on 11 November, but a heavy surf on the beaches prevented the occupation of the airfield near Djidjelli and stopped any fuel being brought ashore although the local French Air Force Commander was ready to welcome Allied fighter aircraft. In the interval between landings at Bougie and the eventual establishment of fighters on Djidjelli on 13 November, there was no proper fighter cover over the port. Axis torpedo aircraft sunk three valuable assault ships – the *Cathay*, *Awatea* and *Karanga* and damaged the monitor *Roberts*. It was a costly lesson in failure to ensure adequate air cover – a lesson which was repeated all too often in the next few weeks. And, at sea, Axis submarines began to take a mounting toll of Allied shipping, sinking the liners *Viceroy of India* and *Nieuw Zeeland* off the Algerian coast.

Bone was occupied like Bougie without French opposition, and Anderson started to push Evelegh's two brigades and 'Blade Force' eastwards; Kent Lemon's 36 Brigade advancing along the north coast road through Tebarka to Djebel Aboid, aiming for Bizerta; Cass's 11th Brigade taking the inland route to Souk-el-Arba, Medjez el Bab and Tebourba, aiming for Tunis; and 'Blade Force' following up part by rail and

---

* (Br) and (us) will be used to distinguish between British and American units when necessary.

part by road to support Cass. The 1st British Parachute Battalion landed unopposed at Souk el Arba airfield on 16 November, and Colonel Raff's 509 (US) Parachute Infantry, which had suffered so heavily at Oran, was dropped at Youks-les-Bains in Central Tunisia to help the local French forces secure the southern flank of Anderson's drive on Tunis.

Realising how slender Anderson's forces were, Eisenhower ordered as many US troops as possible forward from Oran. He met with considerable frustration from the keen but inexperienced American staff officers. He recalls:

> In the office when I arrived was Brigadier General Lunsford E. Oliver, commander of Combat Command 'B', a portion of the US 1st Armoured Division. He had made a reconnaissance of the front, had determined that railway communications were inadequate to get him to the battle area promptly, and was seeking permission to march a part of his command in half-tracks over the 700 miles between Oran and Souk-el-Arba. The Staff Officer to whom he was appealing was well informed as to the characteristics of the half-track and refused. permission on the ground that the march would consume half the useful life of the vehicle.
>
> The young Staff Officer was not to blame for this extraordinary attitude. He had been trained assiduously, through the years of peace, in the eternal need for economy, for avoiding waste . . . He had not yet accepted the essential harshness of war; he did not yet realise that the word is synonymous with waste, nor did he understand that every positive action requires expenditure . . .
>
> (Eisenhower; page 132).

Oliver was given his authority at once on Eisenhower's orders, but the incident was symptomatic of the twilight atmosphere between the habits of peace and the ruthlessness of war which reigned amongst the American Staffs at this time. No-one expected much to happen in French North Africa for three months, by which time all the paraphernalia of a great base area would have been established and the force would be ready to advance eastwards. Even Oliver's Combat Command 'B', as it rattled forward through the Atlas mountains on its way to Souk-el-Arba, had a holiday spirit about it. The British war correspondent, David Divine, who was travelling with it, could not help admiring their supreme confidence in themselves and their equipment. The strip cartoon notion of the heroics of war had been confirmed in their minds by their success at Oran.

The first actions on land occurred on 17 November when German battlegroups probing westwards clashed with the British advance-guards. Kent Lemon's 36th Brigade fought a sharp engagement with 11th Parachute Engineer Regiment on the north coast road in which both sides suffered substantial losses. Next day the 1st (Br) Parachute Battalion destroyed a German armoured reconnaissance force near Sidi Nsir. The main fighting, however, occurred at Medjez-el-Bab on 19 November when Nehring attempted to force Barré out of his neutrality by issuing him an ultimatum at 4 am which had to be complied within three hours. At 7 am dive bombers attacked Medjez and the 5th German Parachute Regiment tried to storm Barré's positions but

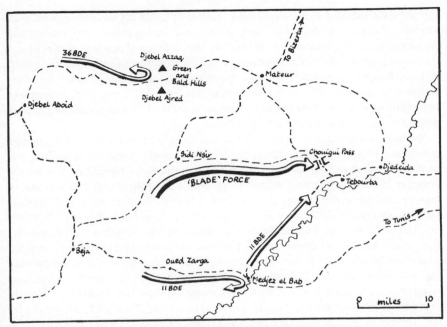

Fig 59 First Army's advance on Tunis: 24th to 30th November 1942

was beaten off. The French stood their ground all day and in the evening withdrew to Oued Zarga covered by 1st (Br) Parachute Battalion and an American battery equipped with British 25-pounder guns.

Evelegh's plan for his advance on Tunis was not a happy one. It committed all the old British faults of advancing on too wide a front with forces out of supporting distance of each other, and of tanks being used in unsuitable country with too few infantry in support. He envisaged a two-phase advance: first, the occupation of the line Mateur–Tebourba; and then the advance on Tunis and Bizerta. Kent Lemon would continue on the north coast road aiming for Mateur; Cass would retake Medjez and then advance on Tebourba; and Hull's 'Blade Force', reinforced by 1st Battalion 1st (US) Armoured Regiment in 'Honeys' would push through the hills in between. All three columns would be supported by detachments of American artillery and tanks.

Little went right with Evelegh's advance. Kent Lemon was badly ambushed between Djebels Azag and Adjred – later known as 'Green' and 'Bald' Hills. After three days hard fighting he was forced to give up, and 'Green' and 'Bald' hills became the front line of the northern sector for most of the campaign. Cass was just as unsuccessful. His attack on Medjez was repulsed with loss. 'Blade Force', however, had an unexpected success. Major Barlow's company of Honey Tanks from 1st (US) Armoured Regiment reconnoitring ahead crushed several German outposts, by-passed others, and he found himself overlooking Djedeida airfield on which the Luftwaffe were bombing up flights of Stukas which had just returned from attacking 'Blade

Forces' main columns. Barlow's 17 light tanks swept onto the airfield destroying 20 aircraft, shooting up buildings, fuel dumps and ammunition, and successfully withdrawing at dusk with the loss of only two men killed, and one tank destroyed and its crew captured. News of this encounter had an immediate and unexpected effect. Nehring became unjustifiably alarmed, believing that strong Allied tank forces were within nine miles of Tunis with little to stop them reaching the city. He ordered the immediate evacuation of Medjez and the concentration of all Axis troops for the close defence of the Tunis and Bizerta bridgeheads.

Nehring's uncharacteristic loss of nerve was short-lived, but it lasted long enough to enable Cass's 11th Brigade to occupy Medjez, and, after handing its defence over to Barre's Frenchmen, to advance and seize Tebourba on 27 November. Subsequent attempts by British infantry, supported by American artillery and Grant tanks, to capture Djedeida and its bridge over the Medjerda River failed in the teeth of resolute German opposition which came not only from the ground but increasingly from the air. Luftwaffe aircraft from airfields in Sicily as well as Tunisia began round-the-clock dive-bombing and ground straffing to save the German bridgehead. Air attacks, which had been persistent throughout Evelegh's advance, rose to a crescendo during the last three days of November. Evelegh was forced to concede defeat and recommended to Anderson that he should pause to allow the Allied Air Forces to improve his air cover and to await the arrival of the rest of Oliver's CC 'B' and the 1st (Br) Guards Brigade, which were on their way eastwards from Oran and Algiers. The first British attempt to reach Tunis had been stopped by the combined efforts of Nehring's troops and Kesselring's aircraft.

The weakness of Allied air cover stemmed from four planning mistakes. Firstly, like the Army, the Air Force units had been despatched on 'Torch' with the lightest possible scales of men and equipment. They did not have the servicing capacity to support the sortie rate demanded by the naval and army commanders. Serviceability of aircraft dropped alarmingly, leaving some fighter squadrons with less than half their aircraft. Secondly, the Allies lacked airfields from which to support Anderson's forces in Tunisia. The only all-weather field was at Bône, 120 miles from the front. The other fair-weather strips were at Souk-el-Arba, 60 miles fron Tebourba; at Youks-les-Bains, 140 miles away; and at Canrobert, 165 miles away. In contrast the Axis were operating off all-weather fields at Tunis and Bizerta, only 20 miles away, with some forward strips less than 5 miles from the front. Thirdly, and most regrettably, few of the lessons in Army/Air co-operation, learnt in the Western Desert, were really appreciated in the Eastern Air Command which had been set up by men more familiar with the Battle of Britain and the night bombing of Germany than operating in close conjunction with land forces. Moreover, RAF communications, radars and fighter direction systems brought in with the assault convoys were inadequate for the distances involved, and the rudimentary nature of local French communications made matters worse. Command and control in the Eastern Air Command can only be described as chaotic. Army/Air Headquarters were not co-located, and there were far too few Forward Air Controllers. And fourthly, lack of an overall air command for 'Torch' began to be felt. Although the Eastern and

Western Air Commands were not dissimilar in strength, the sorties flown during the period 22–30 November speak for themselves. The RAF flew 1,710 sorties, losing 45 aircraft; while the XII (US) Air Force flew 180, losing 7 aircraft. The Luftwaffe flew 1,084 sorties, losing 63 aircraft. The Italians probably flew about half the German total. But whereas the bulk of the Luftwaffe's effort was against the Allied troops advancing towards Tunis and Bizerta, the RAF's effort was absorbed flying fighter cover over the ports of Algiers, Bougie and Bône, and over Allied shipping off the Algerian coast, and in bombing Axis shipping and airfields around Tunis and Bizerta to slow down the flow of Axis reinforcements. There was little effort left over to support of Anderson's soldiers who saw nothing but ground-straffing Axis aircraft. When Allied planes did appear, there was no certainty that they would strike Axis targets. There were several regrettable incidents of British and American aircraft attacking friendly columns, in spite of the display of large white stars on Allied vehicles.

Anderson accepted Evelegh's plea for a pause at Tebourba, but he did not hold the initiative. Kesselring had arrived in Tunis with orders from Hitler to drive the Allies back into Algeria. He was highly critical of Nehring's withdrawal from Medjez, and ordered him to mount an immediate counter-offensive with Fischer's 10th Panzer Division to retake Tebourba and to drive the British out of Medjez and back into the hills.

11th Brigade and 'Blade Force' held tolerably good defensive positions around Tebourba. 2nd Hampshires were dug in on a low ridge overlooking Djedeida, backed up by 1st Surreys which had companies on the dominating feature of Djebel Maiana and at El Bathan Bridge over the Medjerda south of the town. 'Blade Force' less the 17th/21st Lancers was on the Chuigi Pass to the north. Cass's reserve consisted of 17th/21st Lancers and 5th Northamptons at the Tebourba Gap west of the town where the road to Medjez squeezes between the river and the mountain spurs. 2nd Battalion 13th (US) Armoured Regiment with Grants was in support of the Surreys.

Fischer's plan was a typical German encircling operation. He organised four groups. Group 'Koch', consisting of 10 companies of parachute and regular infantry with artillery and anti-tank detachments, was to mount a holding attack along the south bank of the Medjerda to the El Bathan Bridge and later to the Tebourba Gap. The main attack would come from the direction of Mateur in the north and would aim at destroying 'Blade Force' – the main armoured threat to Tunis. This attack would be carried out by two armoured groups: Group Lüder with 20 tanks from due north; and Group Hudel with 40 tanks from the north east. Once these groups were engaged, the fourth group, called Group 'Djedeida', made up of scratch reinforcement battalions and supported by a few 'Tigers' would attack the Hampshires to clear them away from the airfield.

Fischer's plan went remarkably smoothly despite the improvised nature of his force and the poor communications available to him. Most of the success was due to his own personal drive. Group Lüder attacked at 0745 on 1 December and drew 'Blade Force's' attention northwards. The supply echelons were being got away when Group Hudel, led by Fischer himself, struck 'Blade Force' from the east, dispersing it and

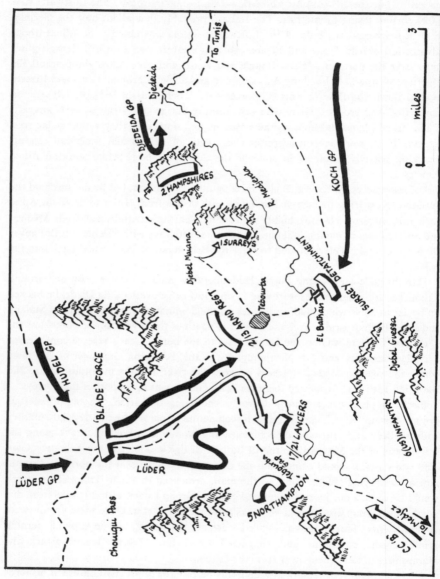

Fig 60 The Battle of Djedeida: 1st to 3rd December 1942

sending it reeling back to the Tebourba Gap. The 17th/21st Lancers moved north to cover the withdrawal, but lost five Crusaders in the process. They fell back to a covering position just north west of Tebourba to protect the supply route through the Tebourba Gap. Concentrated British and American artillery fire brought Lüder and Hudel to a halt before they could reach this vital road link to Medjez.

As soon as the German armoured thrust was spent, Fischer moved to Group 'Djedeida' and started its attack on the Hampshires. Group 'Djedeida' exasperated him with its incompetence. Even with the support of the 'Tigers', he could make little impression on the Hampshires' defence. By nightfall, 11th Brigade's positions were still intact, but 'Blade Force' had suffered heavily. During the night attempts were made to co-ordinate the actions of British and American tank units to oppose Lüder and Hudel when daylight came. Lack of compatible communications made these efforts largely abortive. The main body of Combat Command 'B' under General Oliver was, however, approaching from Medjez and it was Evelegh's intention that it should relieve 'Blade Force' at the Tebourba Gap on 2 December while Cass held onto Tebourba.

2 December was a disappointing day for both sides. Fischer had the greatest difficulty in forcing Group 'Djedeida' to face the Hampshires, but continual dive-bombing and steady losses from shell fire so weakened the battalion that Cass had to withdraw it to Djebel Maiana. Several ill co-ordinated attempts were made by allied tank units to attack the Lüder and Hudel Groups. Attacks were made without properly co-ordinated artillery support and in piece-meal fashion because close liaison proved difficult in such a mixed force. Instead of letting the Germans run onto concealed tanks and anti-tank guns, the Allies threw away their numerical advantage by attacking the Germans who were waiting for them. The arrival of Brigadier General Robinett, Commander of 13th (US) Armoured Regiment helped to stem the pointless loss of tanks. Cass and he agreed to act defensively until better co-ordination could be achieved. Nevertheless, the second day of the Battle of Djedeida ended ominously for the Allies. Even if the Germans did give up and withdraw, Allied tank and infantry losses had been so heavy that they would not be able to resume their drive on Tunis immediately. The Luftwaffe's attacks showed no signs of slackening and were beginning to affect morale. The Allies would have been even more worried had they known that part of 10th Panzer Division's 86th Panzer Grenadier Regiment had landed in Tunis that day and was being rushed forward to join Group 'Djedeida' during the night of 2/3 December.

Fighting on 3 December resulted in an unmistakable German victory. The Lüder/Hudel Group managed to narrow, though not actually cut, the Allied supply route through the Tebourba Gap. Group Koch was stopped from interfering with this route from south of the river by the arrival of the 6th (US) Armoured Infantry on the Djebel El Guissa on the south bank. Fischer's main effort came from the 'Djedeida' Group, reinforced by his own Panzer Grenadiers and heavily supported by Luftwaffe dive-bombing. He attacked Djebel Maiana about 10 am and eventually wrested it from the Hampshires and Surreys. Repeated British counter attacks came tantalizingly near regaining the feature. Towards evening the Germans made a decisive break through along the river on the south side of the position. Almost out of ammunition and in danger of being cut off the British infantry withdrew, evacuating Tebourba and trying to save their heavier equipment by using an unmade track near the river. This broke up and forced them to abandon most of their vehicles and guns, the men making their way back on foot in small groups to the Tebourba Gap. The Hampshires arrived at little over 200 strong and the Surreys about 340. Had it not been for the timely arrival of Oliver's Combat Command 'B', Fischer would have been able to take Medjez-el-Bab, as Kesselring had ordered, without further ado.

Eisenhower, reporting the Allied rebuff at Djedeida to the Combined Chiefs of Staff, placed responsibility for the failure to reach Tunis on inadequacy in the air:

> We have gone beyond the sustainable limit of air capabilities in support of ground forces in a pell-mell race for Tunisia . . . the scale of possible support is insufficient to keep down the hostile straffing and dive-bombing which is largely responsible for breaking up all attempted advances by ground forces.
>
> (Mediterranean Theatre: page 320).

But Eisenhower knew that the Combined Chiefs of Staff would not accept the defeat at Djedeida, nor the inadequacy of Allied air-cover as reasons for giving up. After discussions with Anderson he set 9 December as the target date for resuming the Allied offensive. Hitler had no intention of giving up either. Exploitation of his Tunisian bridgehead would give him a three-fold advantage: an alternative supply route for Rommel; a means of holding the Allies at arm's length from the 'soft underbelly' of Europe; and, by keeping the central Mediterranean closed, a way of forcing the Allies to go on squandering shipping on the long Cape route to Suez. He too needed shipping if he was to continue reaping the advantages of the Tunisian bridgehead which could not be held without a secure sea and air bridge from Sicily to Tunisia. Temptation lay close at hand in the form of the French Fleet at Toulon and the French merchant shipping lying in Mediterranean ports. On 27 November he ordered the seizure of all French warships not already under German control. His plan misfired. The French Admirals, who had refused repeated requests by Darlan to sail their ships from Toulon to North Africa, scuttled them before the German tanks could break into French naval dockyards. In Tunis, Hitler was more successful. General Gause, Rommel's Chief of Staff during 'Crusader', arrived with an ultimatum from Hitler, demanding the demilitarisation of French ships, shore batteries and installations, and the disarmament of all Frenchmen who had thrown in their lot with the Axis. Admirals Estera and Derrien were given no opportunity to resist. Gause carried out his orders with brutal efficiency. All French influence in Tunisia was removed, and Hitler ordered the German garrison of the Tunisian bridgehead to be raised to the equivalent of six to seven divisions, including three panzer divisions. And, early in December he dispatched the dour uncooperative and unsmiling Colonel General Jurgen von Arnim, who had been commanding a corps in Russia, to take over from Nehring whose XC Corps was to be renamed the Fifth Panzer Army. Von Arnim brought with him the able General Heinz Ziegler as his

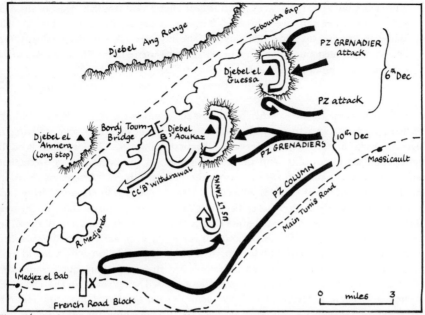

Fig 61 10th Panzer Division's offensive towards Medjez-el-Bab: 6th to 11th December 1942

Chief of Staff and set about expanding the Axis bridgehead by ordering Fischer to continue his offensive to retake Medjez-el-Bab.

After withdrawing from Tebourba, Cass's 11th Brigade took over the defence of the Tebourba Gap, and Oliver became responsible for the defence of the Djebel El Guessa on the south bank of the Medjerda with part of his CC 'B'. The Americans were naturally delighted to be re-united as a command team because they felt rightly that most of their troubles at Tebourba had stemmed from trying to fight under British command, using methods and tactics alien to their own training and instincts. Now they had their own sector and could do things in their own way.

Fischer decided not to force the Tebourba Gap, but to approach Medjez by the Tunis – Massicault – Medjez Road, south of the Medjerda River. Before he could do this, he had to clear CC 'B' off Djebel El Guessa and Djebel Bou Aoukaz, which gave the American artillery observers a splendid view across his proposed axis of advance. Fischer attacked early on 6 December after a dive-bomber strike, and succeeded in hustling the Americans off Djebel El Guessa with an encircling attack. Oliver reinforced Djebel Bou Aoukaz and sent two weakened tank battalions – one of medium and the other of light tanks – to counter-attack Fischer's force threatening Bou Aoukaz. Arrangements were too hurried and co-ordination of tanks and artillery was skimped. 1st US Armoured Division's History paints the picture:

> Those who watched the battle saw an appalling defeat instead of the triumph for which they had hoped. Cooke's column ... attacked, using three separate

approaches onto the rocky area just north of Djebel Bou Aoukaz. Most of the M3s and all the Shermans were hit and burning in about fifteen minutes . . . The enemy anti-tank guns had a field day . . . The day's lessons were deeply disturbing. The enemy's armament and tactics had been extremely effective. American armament and tactics had failed.

(*Battle History of 1st Armoured Division;* page 86 – 97)

Worse was to come as the weather began to add its adverse affects to Allied military inexperience and German tactical efficiency. Allied convoys had been arriving in Algerian ports at fortnightly intervals. The first group on 22 November brought logistic and air force units, and the second group, at the beginning of December, carried the balance of 78th (Br) Division, the bulk of 6th (Br) Armoured Division, and Lieutenant-General Charles Allfrey's V (Br) Corps Headquarters. Allfrey took over the Tunisian front on 6 December three days before the target date for the next Allied offensive and recommended quite rightly that it must be delayed until the Allies could reap the benefits of the third group of convoys due to arrive in mid-December. In the meantime he advised withdrawing to a more defensible line which would have meant abandoning Medjez. French protests killed this suggestion, but Eisenhower, who was brought in to adjudicate, agreed to a limited withdrawal to the Djebel El Almara, north-east of Medjez, which was soon to earn fame as 'Long Stop' Hill. He also fixed 24 December as the new target date for reopening the offensive to take Tunis.

Allfrey's limited withdrawal towards 'Long Stop' was to be carried out on the nights 10/11 and 11/12 December. All positions south of the Medjerda were to be abandoned except for a small bridgehead held by the French covering the Medjez bridge. CC 'B' was to withdraw from Djebel Bou Aoukaz via the bridge at Borj Toum which was to be held by British rear-guards until Oliver's men were clear. On 7 December the Tunisian winter rains broke, turning the valleys and plains into quagmires of thick yellowish-gray mud of a glutinous consistency which bogged vehicles, beat the power of tank engines, and made men's lives a constant battle with the all-pervading clay of the Tunisian countryside in winter. Those who lived through the next three months in Tunisia will never forget the clawing, clogging ooze that surrounded them day and night.

Fischer chose to open the second phase of his offensive towards Medjez on 10 December, the day CC 'B' was due to start its withdrawal. He thrust his Panzer Grenadiers at Djebel Bou Aoukaz, but was repulsed successfully by 6th (US) Armoured Infantry. His 7th Panzer Regiment made the main attack down the Massicault-Medjez road, and was checked three miles short of Medjez by a French artillery battery. When the German tanks tried to deploy off the road they were bogged and were forced to withdraw after winching out their tanks. Oliver had seen their predicament and sent a force of light tanks and tank destroyers to intercept and destroy them with a flank attack. The American detachment was no match for 7th Panzer Regiment, who outgunned and destroyed the American tanks as they, in their turn, tried to manoeuvre off the road and were bogged as well. Nineteen Stuarts and most of the tank destroyers were lost, the crews escaping after dark on foot back to their old leaguer behind Djebel Bou Aoukaz.

Worried by Fischer's continued aggressiveness, Oliver decided to disengage and to fall back over Bordj Toum bridge in one instead of two nights. What exactly went wrong is difficult to analyse from the various accounts. It appears that Oliver sent a light tank force ahead to make sure that the bridge was securely held. Finding no British troops actually on the bridge the American tanks turned north-east and ran into German outposts. Sporadic firing and some random shelling started. Rumour spread back to the leading unit of the main body of CC 'B' that the bridge was held by the enemy. Without checking the report, the column commander turned the whole force south along an earth track on the south bank of the Medjerda. The Division's History records:

This error of judgment prevailed over all advice against it. Soon scores of vehicles which had been brought thousands of miles to Africa and across north-west Africa to Tunisia from Oran were digging their own graves. As they bogged down and wore themselves out, the order was issued to abandon them and walk to Medjez El Bab.

(History of 1st Armoured Division; page 92)

For a few days the rains stopped; Allied hopes rose of reaching Tunis by the New Year; and plans were pushed ahead for the Christmas offensive. Allfrey intended to advance astride the Medjez'– Massicault – Tunis road with 6th (Br) Armoured and 78th (Br) Divisions. Before he could do this he had to be sure that the Germans could not use the excellent artillery observation from the top of 'Long Stop'. A preliminary operation was to be mounted on the night 22/23 December by the 2nd Battalion Coldstream Guards, who were to secure the feature and hand it over before dawn to the 18th Regimental Combat Team of Allen's 1st (US) Division, which was arriving to protect the northern flank of Allfrey's drive on Tunis. Heavy rain began again as the Guards advanced on 'Long Stop'. They took the hill but various delays resulted in their having to start their withdrawal before the US infantry had taken over completely. The Guards were convinced that there were no Germans left on 'Long Stop'. Daylight proved them wrong and troops of the 18th RCT were soon heavily counter-attacked and driven off the hill. 2nd Coldstream returned the following night and in drenching rain re-took, as they thought, the whole of 'Long Stop'. When daylight came they found that the knoll which they had assumed to be the summit was dominated by yet another mound of rock – the Djebel Rhaa – on the far side of a low col which was strongly held by the Germans. During the evening of 24 December the Guards attacked again and took the further knoll but found they could not hold it against German counter-attacks and heavy mortar and machine-gun fire when daylight came. On Christmas Day the Germans regained most of 'Long Stop' in the type of fighting which was to characterise the struggle at Cassino in Italy a year later. 'Long Stop' to the British became 'Christmas Hill' to the Germans, who held it as their front line above Medjez el Bab until the end of the campaign.

Meanwhile Eisenhower had driven from Algiers to Tunisia to decide what should be done:

> Rain fell constantly. We went out personally to inspect the countryside over which the troops would have to advance and while doing so I observed an incident which, as much as anything else, I think convinced me of the hopelessness of an attack. About thirty feet off the road, in a field that appeared to be covered with winter wheat, a motor-cycle had become stuck in the mud. Four soldiers were struggling to extricate it but in spite of their most strenuous efforts succeeded only in getting themselves mired in the sticky clay ... We went back to headquarters and I directed the attack to be indefinitely postponed. It was a bitter decision.
>
> (Eisenhower; page 127)

THE WINTER FIGHT FOR SURVIVAL

> ... Due to continual rain there will be no hope of immediate attack on Tunis ... Am attempting to organise and maintain a force to operate agressively on the southern flank."
>
> (Eisenhower to Combined Chiefs of Staff on 24 December)

The disappointments of December were not all on the Allied side. The Germans had their failures too. In Tunisia, they were facing an enthusiastic but amateur force which, though well equipped, had not shown itself capable of using its weapons effectively. In Libya, Rommel was falling back before a highly professional force, equipped with the same weapons as the Allies in Tunisia, but knowing how to use them. The principal Axis commanders had met near El Agheila on 24 November. Rommel was blunt and uncompromising. His German units did not amount to much more than one weak division and his three Italian divisions could not be allowed to cross swords with the British. Tripolitania must be evacuated and the Panzer Army united with the German forces in Tunisia. Once united they could destroy the Anglo-American forces before turning on Eighth Army which would, by then, be over-stretched, operating 1,500 miles from its base in Egypt. Kesselring and the Italian Chief of Staff, Cavallero, did not agree. Mersa Brega must be held as it had been after 'Crusader'. There must be no withdrawal without the authority of the Commando Supremo.

Rommel gave up arguing and flew back to Germany to put his case to Hitler. He could not have arrived at a worse time. Hitler's attention was focused on von Paulus' operations at Stalingrad. Rommel recorded his own impressions of his stormy interview with the Führer:

> At about 1700 hours I was ordered to the Führer. There was a noticeable chill in the atmosphere from the outset. I described all the difficulties ... Unfortunately, I then came too abruptly to the point and said that, since experience indicated that no improvement in the shipping situation could now be expected, the

abandonment of the African theatre of war should be accepted as long term policy
... The Führer flew into a fury and directed a stream of completely unfounded
attacks on us ... He said it was a political necessity to hold a major bridgehead in
Africa and there would, therefore, be no withdrawal from the Mersa Brega line.
He would do everything possible to get supplies to me.

(Rommel; page 365–366)

Rommel returned to Africa in a cynically fatalistic mood. He had lost the Führer's
support and he was out of sympathy with Kesselring, who bore him a grudge over his
rudeness during the El Alamein disaster. Strangely he achieved some understanding
with Mussolini and Cavallero. Both accepted the loss of Tripolitania as inevitable.
Mussolini was mollified by the thought of gaining Tunisia and possibly Algeria
instead; and Cavallero was concerned that Rommel should withdraw the Italian
infantry divisions in time to prevent their capture by the British.

Montgomery's immediate pursuits of Rommel after the Panzer Army's collapse at
El Alamein may have been disappointing operationally, but his 1,500 mile advance
from Egypt to Tunisia in little over two months was a logistic triumph. Operationally
he was very cautious, being determined not to suffer a setback at Mersa Brega as
Neame and Ritchie had done in the two previous years. He remained determined to
stay operationally and logistically 'on balance' at all times and never to risk failure.

Rommel withdrew into the Mersa Brega position on 23 November and proceeded to
mine his front as heavily as he could. Montgomery followed with light forces and on
the advice of his logistic staff set 15 December as the target date for his attack. He
planned to pin Rommel with a frontal assault by two divisions while Freyberg's New
Zealanders carried out a wide 200 mile out-flanking march through desert to the
south in order to block Rommel's withdrawal along the coast road. Rommel's air
reconnaissance spotted Freyberg's out-flanking column and this was enough for him
to convince the Commando Supremo that it was time to leave, if the Italian infantry
divisions were not to be lost. He would dearly have loved to launch the Afrika Korps
at Freyberg, who was out of supporting distance of Montgomery. Shortage of petrol
made the idea impractical. Freyberg approached the coast road on the night 15/16
December, but he was not strong enough to bar the withdrawal of the Axis rearguards
which broke through his cordon on 16 December, moving at high speed in small
groups. The British catch was quite small – 18 tanks, 25 guns and 450 prisoners. But
Eighth Army had, at last, rounded the corner into Tripolitania at its third attempt.

Rommel's next stand was at Buerat, 200 miles east of Tripoli. Another conference
of Axis commanders at Hitler's HQ in East Prussia from 18 to 20 December reiterated
the demand that Rommel should fight to the last at Buerat. Saner councils prevailed
in the following weeks and the Commando Supremo authorised his withdrawal into
Tunisia, provided he delayed Eighth Army for at least two months before falling back
to the old French fortifications of the 'Mareth Line' just over the frontier. Rommel
had little faith in the Mareth Defences, which he considered antiquated and too easily
turned. He would have preferred to retire 15 miles further west to the 'Gabes Gap'
where he could have held the line of the Wadi Akarit between the sea and the

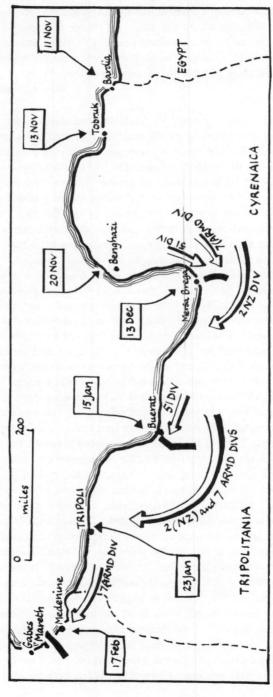

Fig 62 Eighth Army's Advance from El Alamein, 12th November 1942 to 23rd January 1943

extensive salt marshes of the Chott-el-Fedjadj* which made out-flanking as impossible as the Qartara Depression had done at El Alamein. He gave no guarantee that he could hold Montgomery for two months, but he did agree to send 21st Panzer Division back to Tunisia to help von Arnim check any attempt the Allies might make to cut the Axis communication along the Tunisian coast with a thrust to Sfax or Gabes.

This was exactly what Eisenhower and the American members of AFHQ in Algiers had in mind. Anderson's First Army had shot its bolt in the north. It was time to see what the American and French troops could do in Central Tunisia. An advance from the Tebessa area to Sfax or Gabes would be the classic armchair strategist's solution to the defeat of the Axis in Northern Africa. Eisenhower gave the task of planning this operation, codenamed 'SATIN', to General Fredendall's HQ II (US) Corps, which moved from Oran to Tebessa to establish the logistic infrastructure for the 'SATIN' force which was to include Major-General Orlando Ward's 1st (US) Armoured Division and Major-General Welvet's French 'Constantine' Division. Fredendall's staff worked laboriously on their preparations for 'SATIN' but their efforts were frustrated by British objections and German reactions.

The British objections came at the Casablanca conference when Roosevelt, Churchill and their Combined Chiefs of Staff met to decide future Allied strategy. Eisenhower took the opportunity to seek Brooke's and Alexander's advice on the advisability of 'SATIN'. Both were totally opposed to risking the inexperienced 1st (US) Armoured Division by interposing it between the two veteran Panzer Armies. They foresaw it being crushed by a concentration of the three panzer divisions available to Rommel and Von Arnim. Eisenhower accepted these arguments and had the invidious task of cancelling the operation on which his American staffs had lavished so much effort. He directed Fredendall to adopt an 'aggressive defence' in southern Tunisia from his Tebessa base, keeping Ward's Division concentrated so that it could deal rapidly with any Axis attempt to gain elbow room in Central Tunisia. This was a wise precaution, but one which events prevented Fredendall obeying.

The topography of Tunisia is shown on Map VII. The key features which influenced operations at this stage of the Tunisia campaign were the coastal plain in which lay the ports of Sousse, Sfax and Gabes; and the two mountain ranges, called the Eastern and Western Dorsals which ran due south and south-west respectively from the Cap Bon Peninsula. The Eastern Dorsal formed a protective screen for Axis communications through the coastal plain and had five militarily significant passes through it: the Karachoum Pass in the north; the Kairouan and the Fonduk Passes in the centre; and the Faid and Maknassy Passes in the south. The Western Dorsal formed the forward glacis of the Atlas Mountains protecting north-western Tunisia and Algeria.

As rain stopped operations in the north, General Juin, now French C-in-C under Giraud, brought forward as many French divisions as he could release from internal security duties in Algeria and Morocco to occupy the passes in the Eastern Dorsal,

* See map VII.

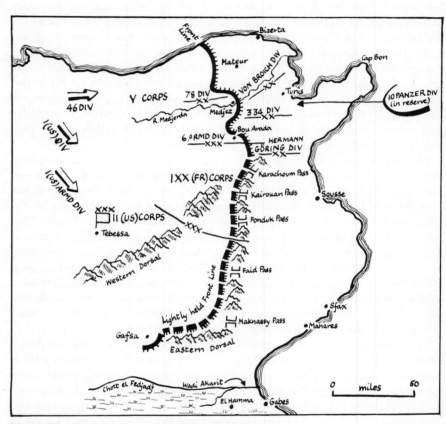

Fig 63 The Tunisian Front in mid-January 1943

while the majority of the American troops, as they arrived, were held in reserve along the Western Dorsal or in the plain between the two. The command system was complicated by the refusal of the French to serve under the British. This forced Eisenhower to assume tactical control of the front with Anderson's First Army in Northern Tunisia, General Koeltz's XIX Corps holding the passes of the Eastern Dorsal down to Fonduk, and Fredendall's II (US) Corps at Tebessa with Welvet's French Division forward on the Eastern Dorsal at the Faid Pass and at Gafsa. He tried to exercise this command through an Advanced Command Post at Constantine, manned by Major-General Lucian Truscott as his Deputy Chief of Staff. Nothing could have been more unsatisfactory. Eisenhower was too enmeshed in the politico-military affairs of Algiers; and Truscott lacked the authority to impose a tactical plan. The obvious choice for tactical commander was Anderson but he was debarred by French objections. Moreover, it is doubtful whether he had the creative ability or warmth of personality to inspire such a multi-national force. And Fredendall was totally untried and, as the weeks passed, showed himself unfitted to command an American Corps let alone an Allied Army. In short, the tactical command structure of the Allied armies in Tunisia lacked a dominant personality to create and impose a dynamic master plan. The Germans soon had the Allies dancing to their tune and would have defeated them ignominiously had it not been for command problems of their own.

The German difficulties stemmed from personal jealousy amongst their senior commanders and the inefficient Italo-German chain of command. Kesselring was a great optimist, who fell out with Rommel on several occasions because the latter was so demanding and gratuitously rude to himself and to the Italian General Staff through whom he, Kesselring, had to work. Von Arnim was a difficult, secretive type of man, who bore grudges easily and was self-centredly unco-operative. He could see no further than the interests of his Fifth Panzer Army and always felt that Rommel was trying to over-shadow him. And Rommel himself was far from well and knew that intrigues were afoot in Rome and Berlin to have him recalled. At times he showed flashes of his old genius, but most of the time he was realistically depressed by the deterioration of the German position in North Africa caused by the inability of the Axis to supply the two Panzer Armies.

Von Arnim never received the six to seven divisions promised by Hitler. Von Paulus' surrender at Stalingrad prevented more than the equivalent of four divisions reaching Tunisia: Division Von Broich (later Manteuffel) in the Bizerta sector; Weber's 334th Division opposite Medjez-el-Bab; the Hermann Göring Division opposite the British 6th Armoured Division in the Bou Arada sector; and Fischer's 10th Panzer Division which acted as Von Arnim's main striking force. The passes in Eastern Dorsal, which were to become the key tactical features in the Allies' struggle for survival, were held by French units and watched by Italian units with German artillery and tank detachments in support. Soon after taking over in Tunisia, von Arnim was directed by Kesselring to seize them all and thus give the Axis control of all sally-ports into the Tunisian plain. He planned to carry these instructions out with Operation 'Eilböte' which was designed to roll up the Allied positions in the

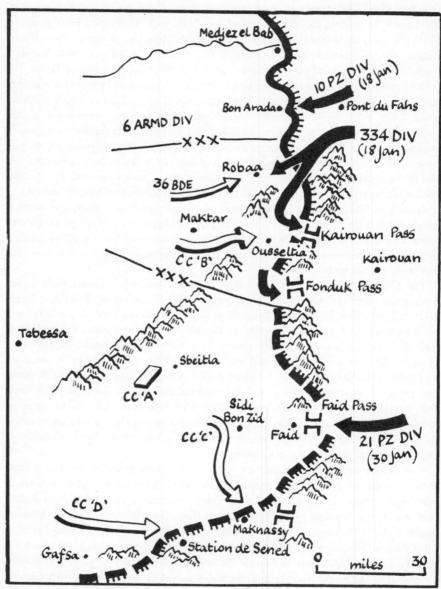

Fig 64 Operation/Eilböte'; 18th to 25th January 1943

Eastern Dorsal from north to south.

'Eilböte' started on 18 January with a diversionary attack by Fischer's 10th Panzer Division on 6th (Br) Armoured Division at Bou Arada. Fischer did not get far. His tanks were quickly stopped by artillery fire, mines and Tunisian mud. Many of the German tanks were found later that evening by British sappers,* who went out to blow them up, with their engines still ticking over as they had been abandoned by their crews, their tractive power having failed to beat the glutiny of the Bou Arada clay.

Behind 10th Panzer, battle groups from Weber's 334th Division, reinforced by mountain troops, struck southwards along the Eastern Dorsal cutting off and destroying the French garrisons as they advanced. The French divisions, lacking anti-tank weapons, fell back demoralised. The rot was only stopped by the despatch of elements of Kent Lemon's 36th (Br) Brigade to Robaa and the CC 'B' to Ousseltia. Oliver had been promoted Major-General and had handed over CC 'B' to Robinett, Commander of the 13th (US) Armoured Regiment. Robinett led CC 'B' with the unusual combination of élan and sagacity. Although outnumbered by the Germans, he managed to hold Ousseltia long enough to put an end to 'Eilböte'. The Fonduk Pass was lost but the Faid Pass to the south remained in Allied hands.

'Eilböte' thoroughly alarmed the Allied High Command. The French divisions of Koeltz's XIX (Fr) Corps had collapsed with the loss of 3,500 men; and the Allied command structure had proved halting and unresponsive during the crisis. It had been thought that the French troops, though badly equipped, would give a good account of themselves in the mountains where German tanks would be at a disadvantage. Their failure forced Eisenhower to withdraw Koeltz's divisions in succession to re-equip and train them with American weapons. In the meantime they had to be replaced in Koeltz's sector by British and American units thus weakening other sectors of the already precarious front and adding to the inter-mixture of units. The command problem was no less intractable. Eisenhower tried to solve it by asking Anderson to 'coordinate' the front, using his First Army Headquarters, without giving him actual powers of command. Anderson did his best to make this work, travelling many hundreds of miles over the atrocious Tunisian roads in an attempt to sort out, by persuasion, the tangled deployment of units caused by constant improvisation since the campaign began. This did not work, but its obvious failure enabled Eisenhower to persuade Juin, and through him Giraud, to accept orders from Anderson. The change came too late. Anderson was no Montgomery, and could not impose his personality or a master plan on his subordinates before the two Panzer Armies joined hands.

Four days after Anderson assumed full command of the front von Arnim launched an attack to complete 'Eilböte' with the seizure of the Faid Pass, using 21st Panzer Division from Rommel's Panzer Army. As it happened Fredendall was in the midst of an operation of his own devising to give his Corps the 'aggressive defence' posture which Eisenhower had asked for after the cancellation of 'SATIN'. His target was

---

* Including the author who was commanding a squadron of 6th Armoured Divisional Engineers.

Maknassy at the southern end of the Eastern Dorsal which was in Italian hands. On assuming command Anderson had ordered him to dispose Ward's 1st (US) Armoured Division with Brigadier General McQuillan's CC 'A' at Sbeitla to support Welvet at the Faid Pass, and Robinett's CC 'B' at Muktar in case von Arnim should continue operations via the Fonduk Pass. Determined to carry on with his Maknassy operation, Fredendall ordered Ward to organise two improvised combat commands: CC 'C' under Colonel Stack, using his 6th Armoured Infantry; and CC 'D' under Colonel Maraist, the divisional artillery commander. Unwisely Fredendall decided to give his troops a preliminary 'blooding' by raiding Italian-held positions at Station de Sened,* half way to Maknassy. Stack's CC 'C' enjoyed the raid in which it took 100 Italians prisoner and killed as many more, but the raid alerted the Axis Command to US interest in the Maknassy area.

Intelligence of Axis movements towards Faid made Juin and Welvet nervous about the pass. They recommended to Fredendall that the main Maknassy attack should be postponed so that Ward's division could be concentrated to support the French troops at Faid. Fredendall refused on the plausible grounds that his capture of Maknassy would draw the Germans away from Faid. He ordered Stack's CC 'C' to approach Maknassy from the north-west via Sidi Bou Zid, while Maraist's CC 'D' was to retake Station de Sened and advance on Maknassy from the west. The operation was timed to start early on 31 January.

Von Arnim beat Fredendall by 24 hours. During the early hours of 30 January the 21st Panzer Division, re-equipped and rejuvenated after its long march from El Alamein, slid through the main Faid Pass and surrounded the French garrison, taking the village of Faid in their rear. Juin appealed for help, but Fredendall continued to misjudge the situation. Instead of stopping the Maknassy operation and concentrating Ward's division to deal with 21st Panzer, he let CC 'D' and CC 'C' go on with their irrelevant action, while McQuillan's CC 'A' tried to extricate the French. McQuillan took all day to send two weak battalion groups, reinforced by tanks and artillery, to retake Faid village on 31 January. Both groups ran into 21st Panzer's well placed covering screen and were repulsed with the loss of nine tanks and over 1,000 Frenchmen were forced to surrender. All the passes in the Eastern Dorsal were now in von Arnim's hands.

The loss of Faid would have been bearable if the Maknassy Operation had been successful. Stack's CC 'C' never came into action at all because Fredendall hesitated in deciding whether to divert it to Faid or let it continue to Maknassy; and Maraist's CC 'D' met with disaster trying to retake Station de Sened which had been reinforced by a mixed German and Italian force. German air attacks caused heavy casualties in CC 'D' and panicked one of Maraist's battalions. After dark another battalion was led past the American outposts by mistake and had most of its men captured. In the end Maraist did take Station de Sened but was checked four miles beyond. German air attacks continued. 1st (US) Armoured Division's History describes what happened: '... some of the troops, jittery from air attacks and other causes, may have

---

* See Map IX.

interpreted a shift of position by the self-propelled 105s as a retreat. Whatever the cause, the road to the rear was soon boiling with vehicles hurrying westward in the dusk . . .' (*History of 1st US Armoured Division:* page 132).

Maraist's CC 'D' had been 'blooded' in an unfortunate way. But events at strategic level soon made Maraist's misfortunes insignificant.

Allied Intelligence sources, including radio intercept, started giving warnings of a major Axis offensive in Central Tunisia timed for mid-February. Indications were that the main thrust would probably come through the Fonduk Pass with subsidiary thrusts at Gafsa and Faid. Anderson ordered the Maknassy Operation to be stopped and Wards' 1st Armoured Division to be disposed behind the Eastern Dorsal ready to meet the German threat wherever it developed. Robinett's CC 'B' was to remain in Army Reserve at Maktar ready to deal with the thrust through Fonduk; Stack's CC 'C' was to move to Hadjeb el Aioun, half-way between Fonduk and Faid; and McQuillan's CC 'A' was to hold Sidi Bou Zid and the surrounding hills to block any further Axis advance from Faid. Ward would establish his headquarters at Sbeitla with units of Maraist's CC 'D' in Divisional Reserve.

Allied Intelligence was not far wrong. Rommel had been hustled out of the Buerat position by Montgomery on 15 January and had started his withdrawal to the Mareth Line. On 19 January he had ordered the demolition of Tripoli's port installations and the blocking of the harbour; and on 23 January Montgomery had taken the formal surrender of the city as Rommel retired over the Tunisian frontier. The Commando Supremo began issuing directives for the defence of Tunisia by the combined Panzer

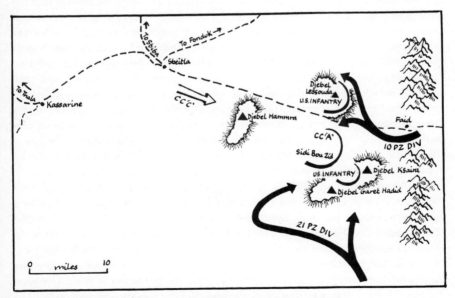

Fig 65 The Battle of Sidi Bou Zid; 14th to 15th February 1943

Armies. The first idea was for von Arnim to exploit his success at Faid with a thrust to Tebessa by 10th and 21st Panzer Divisions. Von Arnim protested that this plan was over-ambitious and proposed to launch an operation of his own, called 'Frühlingswind', in which he would use the two panzer divisions to roll up the Allied front with a north-westerly thrust from Faid to Fonduk. Rommel then made a counter-proposal, demanding that he should be allowed to mount a spoiling attack against Fredendall's Corps, using all three Panzer Divisions – 10th, 15th and 21st – together with the Italian Centauro Armoured Division, before he had to deal with Montgomery when he attacked the Mareth Line. Von Arnim opposed this plan, and Kesselring flew to Tunisia to adjudicate between his two uncooperative Panzer Army commanders. The outcome was an unhappy compromise. Von Arnim was allowed to go ahead with his 'Frühlingswind', but was to release 21st Panzer Division as soon as he had taken Sidi Bou Zid to help Rommel clear his own rear with an attack on Gafsa, called 'Morgenluft'. The objectives of both 'Frühlingswind' and 'Morgenluft' were strictly limited and much more modest than originally intended. The Germans were over-estimating the abilities of their opponents, and mutual antagonism within their own High Command did not augur well for the future.

On the Allied side there was a different type of friction. No-one really trusted anyone else to do the right thing. Anderson gave Fredendall detailed instructions about the defence of II (us) Corps area; and Fredendall, in his turn, over-supervised Ward's 1st (us) Armoured Division. On the strength of Anderson telling him how important it was to hold Sidi Bou Zid and Sbeitla strongly, Fredendall gave Ward detailed tactical orders on how Sidi Bou Zid was to be defended. He insisted that the three major hill features around Sidi Bou Zid, Djebel Lessouda in the north and Djebels Ksaira and Garet Hadid to the south, which stood out prominently on his war room maps, were to be held by two battalions of 168th (us) Infantry from Ryders 34th (us) Division. McQuillan's CC 'A' was to be disposed between them in Sidi Bou Zid, having provided the battalions on the djebels with tank, artillery and tank destroyer detachments. On the maps in II (us) Corps HQ these dispositions may have seemed ideal but on the ground they were out of scale. The djebels were too big for their garrisons, too far apart and too far from Sidi Bou Zid for McQuillan to support them adequately. McQuillan and his officers were worried about this dispersion of effort, but the dispositions were laid down in an order signed personally by Fredendall, whose relationship with Ward was beginning to show signs of strain.

Von Arnim placed his Chief of Staff, Ziegler, in charge of 'Frühlingswind'. 10th Panzer, now commanded by von Broich in place of Fischer who had been killed by a mine, was to make the main attack westwards from Faid to Sidi Bou Zid, whilst Hildebrandt's 21st Panzer made a long detour southwards on the seaward side of the Dorsal range to approach the American positions from Maknassy. McQuillan's CC 'A' was in danger of being encircled by the two Panzer Divisions, and would either have to fall back before it was trapped, or be reinforced by the rest of Ward's Division if it was to have a chance against Ziegler's force. Neither remedy was contemplated by Fredendall, Anderson or Eisenhower who were unaware of the scale of the German operation.

26. British tanks bogged in the Wadi Zigzaou during the Battle of Mareth.

27. Debris of destroyed Axis equipment in the path of 1st British Armoured Division in the Tebaga Gap.

28.   US tanks advancing on El Guettar.

29.   US Infantry dug in at El Guettar.

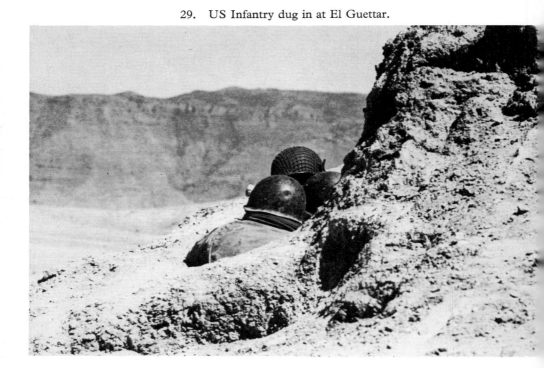

Eisenhower visited the central Tunisian front on 13 and 14 February with Truscott. When they reached Fredendall's HQ in a canyon east of Tebessa, Eisenhower was upset to find that the II (US) Corps engineers had tunnelled a large underground shelter for Fredendall and his staff. Fredendall had been impressed with reports of German efforts to 'Take out' enemy headquarters during the Blitzkreigs of 1939 and 1940, and was determined that he would not be taken out. The atmosphere at II (US) Corps HQ, in consequence, had become remote and divorced from the realities of life on the Eastern Dorsal. Later that evening Eisenhower's party went forward to the CC 'A' HQ at Sidi Bou Zid where he discussed the situation with Ward and McQuillan. Eisenhower was left in no doubt about the 1st (US) Armoured Division's treatment by Fredendall and the unsoundness of CC 'A's dispositions in its precariously isolated position at Sidi Bou Zid. When he left at about 2 am a high wind was blowing, masking German movements around Faid. Anderson's HQ had, however, issued an alert to all troops to meet a German offensive the following morning.

Towards dawn noises of tanks moving in the Faid Pass were occasionally heard between the gusts of wind. Stand-to was brought forward an hour, and the ususal defensive screen consisting of Major Norman Parson's Company G of medium tanks from Hightowers 3rd Battalion, 1st (US) Armoured Regiment moved out towards Faid, supported by reconnaissance, artillery and tank destroyer detachments, to give warning of any German advance. Visibility was poor; the strong wind was blowing up the dust of the arid plain; and little could be seen in the half light of dawn. Some shooting was heard towards Faid but nothing was heard from Parsons. He had run into the leading elements of 7th Panzer Regiment. His tank was knocked out within seconds of the German tanks looming out of the murk in front of him, and with it went the rear-link radio communications back to Djebel Lessouda six miles away. Most of the other tanks, guns and half tracks of the screen were overwhelmed. The first indications that US observers had of the disaster was the appearance of German tanks churning their way round the north side of Lessouda. McQuillan ordered Hightower to 'clear up the situation', but his tank battalion ran into 88mm guns supporting the 69 Panzer Grenadier Regiment, and only a handful of his tanks survived. Fortunately for McQuillan, 21st Panzer Division was delayed by soft sand in its approach from Maknassy, and so 10th Panzer continued its attack unsupported. CC 'A' resisted a series of dive-bomber and tank attacks until early afternoon. Then the appearance of 21st Panzer to the south forced McQuillan to make a fighting withdrawal with his mobile troops to the next suitable defensive position on a low ridge called Djebel Hamra 10 miles west of Sidi Bou Zid to avoid encirclement. When dusk fell the Germans occupied Sidi Bou Zid but did not attempt the pursue the CC 'A'. McQuillan's losses had been heavy. Hightower's battalion had lost 44 tanks; two artillery battalions had been destroyed, one by dive-bombing and the other over-run by tanks; all but two of CC 'A's tank destroyers had been lost; and, worst of all, the two battalions of 168th Infantry had been left behind isolated on their djebels at the mercy of the two Panzer Grenadier regiments and artillery of the Panzer Divisions.

General Zeigler reported to von Arnim that he considered his mission complete. He ordered 10th Panzer to start reconnoitring northwards towards Fondouk; 21st Panzer to get ready to move to Gafsa to join Rommel; and the less mobile elements of both divisions to start mopping up the American infantry on the djebels. Suspecting that the Americans would counter-attack next day, he warned the divisional commanders to have defensive positions reconnoitred to defend Sidi Bou Zid and to prevent any rescue of the trapped US infantry. 10th Panzer was to cover Lessouda while 21st covered Ksaira and Garet Hadid.

During the evening of 14 February the Allied Command was far from sure what had happened. The 10th Panzer Division had not been identified at Sidi Bou Zid, and so it was assumed that only 21st Panzer Division was involved. 10th Panzer was thought to be near Kairouan ready to advance through the Fondouk Pass as suggested by the Allied Intelligence assessments. There were indications of an Afrika Korps advance on Gafsa, but Anderson saw no reason to change his original view that the main Axis threat would still come through Fondouk. He, therefore, refused Fredendall's request for the release of Robinett's CC 'B' from First Army reserve, though he did allow Lieutenant-Colonel Alger's 2nd Medium Tank Battalion of 1st (US) Armoured Regiment to be transferred from Robinett to Ward's direct command to help him mount a counter-attack to rescue the trapped battalions. He also insisted on Fredendall pulling in his horns by evacuating Gafsa, which was done during the night 14/15 February to the consternation of the local inhabitants. The garrison was withdrawn to Feriana.

Ward decided to use Stack's CC 'C' from Hadjeb el Aioun, supported by Alger's medium tanks, for his counter-attack on Sidi Bou Zid. The force could not be ready before mid-day. It was to consist of little more than one tank battalion reinforced with an extra tank company, a battalion of armoured infantry, a battalion of armoured field artillery and a company of tank destroyers. If ever there was a repetition of the charge of the Light Brigade at Balaclava this was it. How it was thought that this small force could rescue two infantry battalions over 13 miles away with even one, let alone two panzer divisions ready to dispute its passage is hard to imagine.

Colonel Stack set up his Command Post on Djebel Hamra from which he could see the whole battlefield. The *American Official History* describes the start of the advance:

> ... Even through field glasses Sidi Bou Zid, about 13 miles distant, was a tiny spot of dark hued evergreens and white horses behind which rose the hazy slopes of Djebel Ksaira ... There was a considerable mirage. The dips and folds of the plain were for the most part gradual but several steep-sided deeper wadis creased it in general from' north to south ...
>
> At 1240 the attacking formation started over this expanse with great precision until its vehicles were reduced by distance to the size of insects and obscured by heavy dust. In the lead were the tanks ... Tank destroyers were grouped on each wing. The artillery and then the infantry in half tracks followed ...

> (Mediterranean Theatre, page 420)

The tragedy was slow to unfold. The Germans allowed Alger's tanks to cross the first deep wadi unopposed; at the second they suffered some anti-tank fire and were encouraged by successfully over-running a German anti-tank battery; but at the third wadi frontal opposition became intense and a Stuka attack threw the artillery and armoured infantry into confusion. The Americans gradually became aware of tanks appearing on their northern flank (those of 10th Panzer) but they were, as yet, unaware that the tanks of 21st Panzer were emerging on their southern flank. They were being sucked into a well laid trap. Turning to face 10th Panzer, Alger's own tank was hit and he was captured. Then the pressure from 21st Panzer on the southern side started to have its effect. The armoured infantry had to pull back precipitately to avoid being cut off. The tanks and artillery tried to fight their way out. Few of the tanks escaped. Most were trapped astride the Wadi Oued Rouana where they were destroyed. Forty rusting hulks were found there two months later. The artillery succeeded in fighting off their attackers and managed to get back to Djebel Hamra after dark. Realising that the battalions on the djebels could not be relieved, Fredendall had orders dropped to them to break out during the following night. About 200 of the men on Lessouda escaped but most of those on Ksaira and Garet Hadid, who had further to march were caught in the open by German mechanised troops and forced to surrender. In three days Ziegler had destroyed two tank, two artillery and two infantry battalions of Fredendall's II (us) Corps. He now awaited orders for his next move.

The opposing high commands made radical changes in their plans during the next 48 hours. Anderson came to accept the Sidi Bou Zid operation as the main enemy effort. He released CC 'B' to Ward, and ordered a general withdrawal to the Western Dorsal from Ousseltia southwards. He also reduced Fredendall's sector by moving Koeltz's XIX Corps boundary southwards, and despatched units of the British 6th Armoured Division and 1st Guards Brigade to take over the defence of the Western Dorsal passes at Sbiba and Thala. Fredendall was to concentrate initially on the defence of Sbeitla and Feriana, and then upon holding the passes in the Western Dorsal leading to Tebessa, including the Kasserine Pass.

On the German side Rommel entered Gafsa on 15 February unopposed and pushed his reconnaissance units on towards Feriana. Von Arnim refused to release 21st Panzer Division on the grounds that Rommel no longer needed it to take Gafsa, and proceeded with his own Fifth Panzer Army plan to strike northwards. Ziegler was ordered to take Sbeitla with 21st Panzer Division and to despatch 10th Panzer north to Fondouk. Rommel hesitated at first and actually ordered the Italian Centauro Division to start its return march to Mareth. Then his old aggressiveness came back and he proposed to Kesselring:

> On the basis of the enemy situation, as of today, I propose an immediate enveloping thrust from south-west on Tebessa and the area north of it, provided Fifth Panzer Army's supply situation is adequate. This offensive must be executed with strong forces. I therefore request that the 10th Panzer and 21st Panzer Divisions be assigned to me and move immediately to the assembly area Thelepte – Feriana.
>
> (Quoted in Mediterranean Theatre; page 438).

Kesslering gave Rommel his full support but it took time to obtain agreement from OKW, the Commando Supremo and Mussolini to such a major change of plan. Rommel was forced to kick his heels while von Arnim pressed on with his own operations.

Ziegler did not start his advance upon Djebel Hamra and Sbeitla until the afternoon of 16 February, after he had received information through the Axis radio intercept unit that the Allies proposed to abandon Sbeitla as part of their general withdrawal into the Western Dorsal. By this time Robinett's CC 'B' had arrived in Sbeitla and was covering the southern half of the town, and McQuillan had gone back personally to reconnoitre the northern half for its occupation by CC 'A' and CC 'C' that night. As dusk fell McQuillan abandoned Djebel Hamra and fell back to join Robinett's CC 'B' in the Sbeitla defence line. 21st Panzer Division's reconnaissance troops, supported by a few tanks, followed the American rear guards closely, and hoping to find that the Americans were withdrawing through Sbeitla rather than holding it, opened fire in the dark as they reached the outskirts of the town. Their rounds fell amongst some of CC 'A''s units which were refuelling from dumps and others landed near McQuillan's Command Post. Unwisely McQuillan withdrew his headquarter vehicles to the west of the town and in so doing triggered another spontaneous withdrawal of the Maknassy type. Most of the men in CC 'A' units were nervy after their recent experiences and had never been involved in a night action before. Vehicle after vehicle pulled out of leaguer and flooded onto the road, heading west without orders. Most of the tanks and artillery stood firm, and the German advance guard reported back to Zeigler that the Americans were still showing fight in Sbeitla and were not retiring as had been thought. Ziegler ordered them to stand fast until daylight. By then some order had been restored in CC 'A'.

Anderson authorised the abandonment of Sbeitla and Fériana during 17 February while insisting they should be held as long as possible. When Hildebrandt reconnoitred Sbeitla in daylight he concluded that the approach to CC 'A's sector was too difficult and unattractive for 21st Panzer, and selected Robinett's sector instead for his assault. Robinett fought a well judged defensive battle all day and did not abandon the town until 5.30 pm. The CC 'A' and CC 'C' were not hard pressed and disengaged successfully but were heavily bombed as they made their way by various routes to Tebessa, where they were joined by the CC 'B' next day. Fériana and Thélepté were also abandoned. Thirty-four unserviceable Allied aircraft had to be destroyed on Thélepté airfield before it was evacuated.

In the early hours of 19 February Rommel and von Arnim received the anxiously awaited directive from the Commando Supremo. It pleased neither of them. Rommel was directed to advance on Le Kef on the grounds that this would force the British V Corps to withdraw more effectively than the defeat of II (US) Corps at Tebessa; and von Arnim was to send back 10th Panzer from Fondouk and place it and 21st Panzer under Rommel's command. Von Arnim protested but was over-ruled by Kesselring. Unknown to either Kesselring or Rommel, he did not send back all 10th Panzer Division; nor did he send its supporting 'Tiger' tanks which Rommel badly wanted as he had never had any under his command before. Von Arnim suffered a blistering

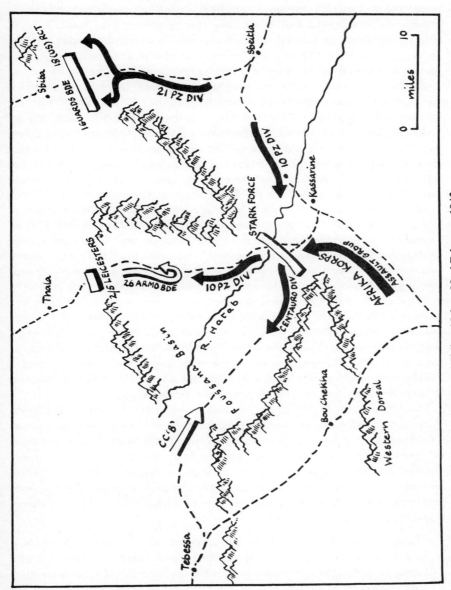

Fig 66   The Battles of Kassarine, Thala and Sbiba: 19th to 22nd February 1943

rebuke from Kesselring a few days later for this deliberate omission, but by then it was too late. At 0450 on 19 February Rommel ordered the Afrika Korps Assault Group and the Centauro Division to seize the Kasserine Pass through which he would advance via Thala to Le Kef. At the same time he ordered 21st Panzer to break through the Sbiba Pass and make for Le Kef as well. As 10th Panzer could not return to Sbeitla in much less than 48 hours, Rommel decided to await its return before committing it in support of 21st Panzer at Sbiba or of the Afrika Korps at Kasserine.

21st Panzer found the Sbiba Pass more heavily defended than expected. Anderson had managed to concentrate the 1st Guards Brigade, the 18th RCT of Allen's 1st (US) Division, three battalions of Ryder's 34th (US) Division, the 16th/5th Lancers and the 2nd Hampshire to hold the pass and the djebels either side. Hildebrandt's first attack was driven off in pouring rain by the Guards. His subsequent efforts to work round the northern flank, where the American units were holding the hills, were equally unsuccessful. Rommel concluded that there was no easy way through at Sbiba and ordered 10th Panzer to reinforce the Afrika Korps at Kasserine instead.

The only Allied troops available to hold the Kasserine Pass were one battalion of Colonel Stark's 26th (US) Infantry and Colonel Anderson Moore's 19th Combat Engineer Regiment which lacked heavy infantry weapons and the tactical training needed for a major defensive battle. Fredendall summoned Stark and ordered him to take over the defence of the pass, promising him reinforcements and saying: 'I want you to go to Kasserine right away and pull a Stonewall Jackson!' (*Ibid;* page 447).

The Kasserine Pass is an opening in the southern face of the Western Dorsal which is about a mile wide and leads into the 20 mile wide Foussana Basin. The road and railway run through the pass alongside the Hatab River. At the top of the pass the railway and river run through the centre of the basin, but the road divides with the main road to Thala hugging the eastern side of the basin and the secondary road to Tebessa running along the western side. Stark laid out his defence with his own men holding the Thala road and the Engineers the Tebessa road.

The Afrika Korps Assault Group was being commanded temporarily by General Buelowius, its senior gunner. Buelowius decided to try to rush the pass at day-light on 19 February, using the 33rd Reconnaissance Unit. Stark's men were alert and drove off the attempt with well directed artillery fire. Buelowius then tried to force a way through using two battalions of the Panzer Grenadier Regiment, 'Afrika', supported by tanks of 8th Panzer Regiment. Progress was slow in pouring rain, but Buelowius assured Rommel that he would have the pass by nightfall. He was proved wrong. Rommel commented bitterly:

> The trouble was that they had gone the wrong way about it. After fighting for so long in the desert, the officers had suddenly found themselves confronted with terrain not unlike the European Alps. The hills on either side of the pass ran up to some 5,000 feet and were held by American troops accompanied by artillery observers. Menton (Commander of Panzer Grenadier Regiment, Afrika) had unfortunately confined his attack to the valley, probably having under-estimated the Americans.
>
> (Rommel; page 403).

Rommel left Buelowius with instructions to seize the pass by dawn on 20 February when 10th Panzer would arrive in his support. 10th Panzer was to head for Thala, while the Centauro Division made for Tebessa. During the night Buelowius's infantry infiltrated amongst the American positions on both sides of the pass. The 19th Combat Engineers had a rough time and were largely dispersed by dawn; and the Germans had gained dangerous footholds amongst Stark's infantry on the other side of the pass. Both Anderson and Fredendall had been sending forward reinforcements. Brigadier Dunphie's 26th Armoured Brigade of 6th (Br) Armoured Division had reached Thala and had sent its motor battalion – Lieutenant-Colonel Gore's 10th Rifle Brigade – with a squadron of tanks and a battery of field guns to support Stark on the Thala road. Robinett's CC 'B' was on its way to provide similar support on the Tebessa road. It was not until mid-afternoon that Rommel's men broke through the pass into the Foussana Basin. The Centauro Division advanced a short distance down the Tebessa road and then leaguered for the night. 10th Panzer Division ran into Gore's battalion group, covering Stark's withdrawal on Thala. Gore fought a classic withdrawal action back to Dunphie's main blocking position which was established half way to Thala. The American official history pays Gore a well deserved tribute.

> The valiant stands of Colonel Gore's detachment forced General Buelowius to commit his 1st Battalion 8th Panzer Regiment to force the breakthrough. The British fought until their last tank was destroyed. Casualties were severe.
>
> (*Ibid;* page 455).

The Kasserine Pass had been lost but the Battle of Kasserine was far from over. Stark had held his ground just long enough to change the whole course of the battle though the Allied Command did not know it at the time. In times of defeat there are always personal failures, but there are also men who make their name in adversity. When an Allied force is faced with defeat these problems are magnified. The Allied chain of command during Kasserine became a tangled skein of misunderstanding, duplication of effort, over-lapping responsibility and consequential muddle. Anderson suspected, with some justification, that Fredendall had lost control of his Corps. Fredendall, for his part, doubted Ward's ability and had not been on speaking terms with him for some days. He had asked Eisenhower to relieve Ward; and Eisenhower had rather too hastily sent for Major-General Harmon who was commanding 2nd (US) Armoured Division in Morocco. At the last moment Eisenhower realised it might be Fredendall who was at fault not Ward, and so he sent Harmond forward to Fredendall as 'a useful assistant to have around in time of crisis'.

The Command crisis reached its peak on the evening of 20 February. Anderson despatched Brigadier Nicholson, deputy commander of 6th (Br) Armoured Division to Thala to co-ordinate its defence. Fredendall had already told Robinett, without reference to Ward, to cover the Tebessa road; and had further told Dunphie to hold Thala and co-ordinate his own and Robinett's defence of the Foussana Basin. Then Harmon arrived and was told by Fredendall to take over the tactical control of the whole of the II (US) Corps front, using Ward's staff! And to cap everything, Brigadier McNabb, Anderson's Chief of Staff, reached Thala ahead of Nicholson, and drew up a plan with Robinett and Dunphie for the defence of the Foussana Basin. McNabb agreed that they should disregard Fredendall's instructions to mount a counter-attack to regain Kasserine. Instead CC 'B' and 26th Armoured Brigade would adopt a defensive posture until the Axis offensive had been halted and would then advance along the hills either side of the basin to regain the pass. Nicholson arrived later and agreed the plan; and next day these three sensible men – Robinett, Dunphie and Nicholson – set about their task of stopping Rommel in spite of the chaos around them.

Rommel had been impressed with Stark's defence on the 19th and 20th, but was astonished with the amount of undamaged equipment he found abandoned when he drove through the Kasserine Pass that evening. His comments are interesting:

> The Americans were fantastically well-equipped and we had a lot to learn from them organisationally. One particularly striking feature was the standardisation of their vehicles and spare parts. British experience had been put to good use in the American equipment.

> (Rommel; page 404).

21 February was a day for strong nerves. Robinett's CC 'B' successfully blocked the Centauro Division's advance on Tebessa. 10th Panzer, with Rommel goading it on, forced Dunphie to retire slowly on Thala where a newly arrived battalion – the 2nd/5th Leicesters of 46 (Br) Division – was digging in on the ridge south of the town awaiting the arrival of the artillery of the 9th (US) Division which Eisenhower had hastened forward by road from Oran.

Dunphie held 10th Panzer at bay all day but a disaster occurred as his tanks fell back through the Leicesters' position at dusk. The Germans used a captured British Valentine tank to head their advance. The Leicesters had not been in action before and thought the column led by this Valentine was part of Dunphie's brigade. Once inside the Leicesters' position the German tanks following the Valentine opened fire, taking the Leicesters from the rear. Dunphie's tanks returned to rescue the infantry and the Germans withdrew taking many prisoners with them. During the night Nicholson launched a series of tank counter-attacks in the dark which gave the Germans the impression that Thala was strongly held. Reports from Arabs of large Allied reinforcements entering Thala from the north during the night – probably 9th (US) Division's guns – convinced von Broich that he should go over on to the defensive to absorb the probable Allied counter-attack before resuming his advance on Le Kef. Heavy rain was falling as von Broich made his recommendation to Rommel who accepted it and then drove back to meet Kesselring at the Kasserine Pass.

The Rommel/Kesselring meeting on 22 February was decisive. Rommel confessed that he had misjudged the nature of the country. It was quite unsuitable for wide ranging mobile operations and the four days' torrential rain, through which his men had fought the Battle of Kasserine, had confined his tanks to the few roads that existed in the mountains. Von Arnim's failure to send him the whole of 10th Panzer and the Tigers had not helped, but it was no use crying over spilt milk; he must get back to Mareth to deal with Montgomery before Eighth Army grew strong enough to open its next offensive. Kesselring agreed; and before he left he offered Rommel command of Army Group, Africa, which he had been proposing should be set up to command the two Panzer Armies in Tunisia. Hitler had already said that he favoured von Arnim as its commander, but Kesselring had found von Arnim's behaviour so obstructive that he was prepared to recommend Rommel instead. Rommel was back in one of his moods of depression and refused the offer, but his refusal was construed by Kesselring as diplomatic rather than actual. Next day a directive arrived from the Commando Supremo appointing Rommel to command the Army Group, Africa, and Italian General Messe to Panzer Army, Africa, which was to be renamed the First Italian Army, though the Afrika Korps was to remain a substantial part of Messe's Army for the defence of the Mareth Line. The directive further stated that, although 'Frühlingswind' and 'Morgenluft' had been successful, they were to be broken off to enable Messe to deal with Eighth Army. 10th and 21st Panzer Divisions were to withdraw to the coastal plain to refit before joining Messe. The Afrika Korps Assault Group was to go direct to Mareth. The Axis defence line in Tunisia would be re-established on the Eastern Dorsal. As the Allies must have denuded their northern front to help Fredendall, von Arnim was to take full advantage of this by mounting major raids to improve his Army's positions.

It took the Allies 48 hours to realise that the Germans had gone. Advancing gingerly over mined roads, blown culverts and demolished bridges, the British and American troops reoccupied the Kasserine Pass on 24 February and closed up to the Axis positions in the Eastern Dorsal from which they had been driven 10 days before. They were then faced with the painful business of analysing what had gone wrong; who had failed; and what should be done to eradicate the deficiencies which the German offensive had revealed. The Americans were themselves far more critical of their own short-comings than the Germans. Rommel had been impressed by their performance:

> Although it is true that the American troops could not yet be compared with the veteran troops of the Eighth Army, yet they made up for their lack of experience by their far better and more plentiful equipment and their tactically more flexible command ... The tactical conduct of the enemy's defence had been first class. They had recovered very quickly after the first shock ...
>
> (Rommel; page 407).

What would have happened, if the Axis Army Commanders had been united and Rommel had not been a sick man, must remain a matter of conjecture. The Allied command structure had been thrown into disarray. If the German pressure had been maintained an Allied collapse could have occurred. This would have been more likely if von Arnim had collaborated with an offensive in the north, pinning 6th (Br) Armoured Division in the V (Br) Corps sector. The fact that no collapse occurred must be credited to the many individual commanders and men who stood their ground when panic swirled around them. Faid, Sidi Bou Zid, Sbeitla and Kasserine were costly lessons for II (us) Corps.

As if to underline his contrariness, von Arnim refused to accept the Commando Supremo directive to send the panzer divisions to Messe and proposed a new offensive

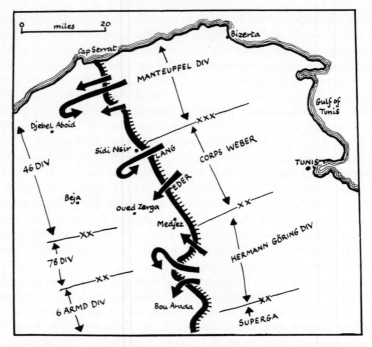

Fig 67 von Arnim's 'Ochsenkopf' offensive: 26th February to 19th March 1943

of his own in the north. He flew back to Rome, without informing Rommel, his new
Army Group Commander, and persuaded Kesselring to allow him to mount this
offensive, code-named 'Ochsenkopf', which had three principal objectives: Division
Manteuffel in the north, should drive the British back from 'Green' and 'Bald' Hills
to Djebel Abiod, capturing their radar installation on Cap Serrat; Weber's 334th
Division, now titled Corps Weber, in the centre, should mount a special armoured
force under Colonel Lang with 14 Tigers and 63 medium tanks to seize Sidi Nsir and
advance to Beja, while an infantry force under Colonel Eder would cross the mountains to attack Oued Zarga and Medjez from the rear; and in the south, the Hermann
Göring Division would attack Medjez from the Bou Arada direction. It was an ambitious plan which made Rommel furious when he heard about it. Why hadn't von
Arnim mounted this offensive concurrently with the Battle of Kasserine?

'Ochsenkopf', which started on 26 February, gained a great deal of ground, but
failed in its principal purpose of pushing Fifth Panzer Army's front beyond the important lateral road from Djebel Abiod through Beja to Medjez. Its weight fell upon
the newly arrived and inexperienced 46th (Br) Division, which was forced to give
ground, but it failed against Evelegh's mature 78th (Br) Division. Manteuffel drove
46th Division to within four miles of Djebel Abiod but he was pushed back to 'Green'
and 'Bald' Hills again by 1 April. Lang's drive on Beja was a disaster. He over-ran an
isolated British battalion and battery of guns at Sidi Nsir, and was then then caught
in a well laid British anti-tank gun trap at 'Hunt's Gap', a defile ten miles north-east

of Beja. When he withdrew, he had to admit the loss of 22 tanks with a further 49 disabled but recovered. Eder was also stopped before he could threaten the Oued Zarga – Medjez road, and the Hermann Göring Division was uniformly unsuccessful in the three thrusts which it mounted. The unsatisfactory nature of the 'Ochsenkopf' offensive did not escape Rommel's critical and antagonistic eye.

> It made me particularly angry to see how the few Tigers we had in Africa, which had been denied us for our offensive in the south, were thrown in to attack through a marshy valley where their principal advantage – the long range of their heavy guns – was completely ineffective ... Of the 19 Tigers, which went into action, 15 were lost ... I very soon gave orders to Fifth Army to put a stop to the fruitless affair ...   (Rommel; page 410).

But Rommel was gloating over von Arnim's discomforture just too soon. He, himself, was about to suffer an even worse defeat at the hands of the British, illustrating, if illustration was needed, what experienced troops could do with about half the equipment which the Americans possessed in Tunisia.

On 28 February, Rommel in his capacity as Army Group Commander, discussed with Messe and the panzer divisional commanders the spoiling attack which they were to mount against the Eighth Army. During the Kasserine Battle, Montgomery had been asked to attack the outposts of the Mareth Line to relieve the pressure on Eisenhower's forces. Against his better judgment, he had moved Leese's XXX Corps

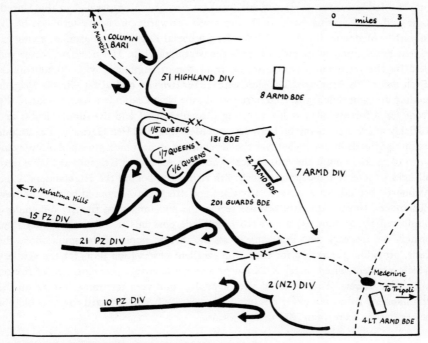

Fig 68   The Battle of Medenine: 6th March 1943

with the 51st Highland and 7th Armoured Divisions up to Medenine* to drive in Rommel's screening troops, although he knew he was running logistic risks by so do- ing before the flow of supplies through Tripoli matched his needs. The nearest sup- porting division was the 2nd New Zealand Division back in Tripoli. Rommel was thus presented with the opportunity of hitting these two isolated divisions while Montgomery was temporarily 'off balance'. The plan which Messe presented to Rommel was for the Afrika Korps with 10th, 15th and 21st Panzer Divisions, now commanded by General Cramer, to move southwards through the Matmata Hills* and to attack Medenine from the west and south-west, while a mixed German and Italian Group, called Column Bari, launched a holding attack due southwards from the Mareth Line. Rommel did not like Messe's plan very much but was persuaded by the panzer commanders that it was the best that could be devised.

Unfortunately for the Axis, British radio intercepts and air reconnaissance gave Montgomery early warning of what was afoot. There were clear indications on 27 and 28 February of the panzer divisions moving from Kasserine towards Mareth. Montgomery took immediate steps to regain balance, sending forward the New Zealanders, 8th Armoured Brigade and 201st Guards Brigade to reinforce XXX Corps, and instructing Leese to prepare for attack. The reinforcing formations could not reach Medenine until 4 March. In the meantime Leese must do his best to strengthen his positions as quickly as he could.

Leese disposed his Corps in a great arc around Medenine with the northern flank on the Mediterranean coast and his front, at first, running parallel to the Mareth Line and then curving back south and south-eastwards on the western side of the Mareth – Medenine Road which ran along a useful ridge of high ground, giving ex- cellent observation westwards towards the Matmata Hills. His northern sector was held by the Highland Division whose front was strengthened with 70,000 mines. Then came 7th Armoured Division with 131st Brigade and 201st Guards Brigade holding an eight-mile front. And in the south, the New Zealanders were to extend the front for a further eight miles, covering Medenine itself and the supply depots and airfields which were being built up between Medenine and Ben Gardane. The unique feature of the defensive layout was the dependence on anti-tank guns and infantry in- stead of tanks to blunt the Axis attack. The three Armoured Brigades available were all held in reserve for counter-attack: 8th Armoured behind the Highlanders; 22nd Armoured behind 7th Armoured Division; and 4th Light Armoured behind the New Zealanders. In each infantry brigade sector, the anti-tank guns (mostly 6-pounders, reinforced by 2-pounders) were sited in enfilade positions to kill tanks rather than protect the infantry who were dug in on the reverse slopes of the spurs above the guns, providing protection for them and excellent observation posts for the artillery which was centralised under XXX Corps' control to ensure concentration of fire on important targets. There was no wire available, and very few mines except on the Highlanders' front, but every position was so carefully camouflaged that it could not be seen from more than 200 to 300 yards.

---

* See Map IX.

Eighth Army's intelligence staff managed to intercept the date of Messe's offensive as 6 March, but they could not be certain about the direction of the assault. They guessed wrongly that it would come from the north out of the Mareth Line, which had, in fact, been Rommel's preferred solution.

6 March dawned cold with a low mist covering the plain between the Matmata Hills and the British positions. Patrols from the Guards Brigade, probing the Matmata Hills gave the first warning of the approach of panzer columns. The 51st and 7th Armoured Divisional sectors came under long range artillery fire soon after daylight. Then tanks and infantry were seen approaching cautiously in a number of columns from the west. The German tank commanders stopped frequently, viewing the front with their glasses as if uncertain where their objectives lay and quite unconscious how near they were to the hidden British positions. 10th Panzer Division, on the most southerly axis, came within 400 yards of the New Zealand position before the anti-tank guns opened up, knocking out five tanks at once and throwing the attack off balance. 21st Panzer struck 201st Guards and lost its three leading tanks and 12 more shortly afterwards. Only 15th Panzer really pressed home its attack against the three Queens battalions of 131st Brigade. Brilliant shooting by the anti-tank guns of 1st/7th Queens accounted for 27 tanks by the end of the day. At one time the Brigade HQ thought it might have to move back and asked for tank support. A squadron of Shermans was moved up into hull-down positions and thickened the Queens' defence. They were to be the only British tanks engaged that day. All other attacks, including a number launched by Column Bari against the Highlanders were broken by concentrated artillery fire, the anti-tank guns and the infantry from their concealed reverse slope positions. When darkness fell on what, to the British, was a very long hot 6 March, their three divisions pushed out patrols and prepared to repel further attacks. The Germans made several attempts to recover their tank casualties during the night but artillery concentrations brought down whenever noises were heard soon stopped their efforts. At dawn next day the dust of the withdrawing German columns was seen disappearing into the Matmata Hills. Rommel had ordered Messe to disengage. In his memoirs he records:

> . . . the attack had been launched a week too late. The operation had lost all point the moment it became obvious that the British were prepared for us. We had suffered tremendous losses, including 40 tanks totally destroyed.
>
> But the cruellest blow was the knowledge that we had been unable to interfere with Montgomery's preparations. A great gloom settled over us all.
>
> (Rommel; page 415).

Montgomery sums up the Battle of Medenine in his characteristic way:

> It had been a model defensive engagement and a great triumph for the infantry and anti-tank guns. Only one squadron of our tanks was actually engaged in the fighting, and we lost no tanks. Fifty-two knocked out enemy tanks were left on the battlefield, and all but seven (dealt with by the tank squadron) had fallen to our anti-tank guns. Without wire or mines our infantry with strong artillery support,

had repulsed an attack by three panzer divisions and incurred only minor losses in the process. Very great care had been taken in positioning our anti-tank guns, and it should be noted that they were sited to kill tanks at point blank range: and not to defend the infantry.

(Montgomery; *El Alamein to the Sangro;* page 46).

Eisenhower's 'Torch' forces had survived the winter months in Tunisia, but there seems little doubt that they would not have done so in France where the full weight of the Wehrmacht could have been brought to bear upon them. Montgomery's battle of Medenine high-lighted just how short of battle experience they were from Commander-in-Chief downwards. They all lacked practical judgment of what was possible and what was not. The Allied losses during the Axis offensive in central Tunisia were: 7,000 prisoners, 200 tanks, 110 guns and 300 trucks were taken or destroyed by the equivalent of two panzer divisions in 10 days. But although Eisenhower's Anglo-American forces were inexperienced at every level, they did not lack courage, endurance, and, above all, the willingness to learn. As the next and last chapter will show, they took their lessons to heart and learned their trade very quickly.

15

The Sword is Forged
(March to May 1943)

1 ... You are appointed Deputy Commander-in-Chief of the Allied Forces in French North Africa. Further you are appointed Commander of the Group of Armies operating in Tunisia.

2 This appointment takes effect on 20 February 1943 on which date you will take command of all Allied forward forces engaged in operations in Tunisia ...

3 Your mission is the early destruction of all Axis forces in Tunisia ...

(Eisenhower's Directive to Alexander)

One of the decisions taken at the Casablanca Conference was that General Alexander and Air Marshal Tedder would become Eisenhower's Army and Air Force Deputy Commanders as soon as Eighth Army crossed the Tunisian frontier. Alexander's principal task would be to establish 18th Army Group Headquarters from which he would exercise tactical command of the land battle in Tunisia on Eisenhower's behalf. Alexander and his Chief of Staff, General Richard McCreery, reached Algiers on 15 February as Ziegler opened the 'Frühlingswind' offensive at Sidi Bou Zid.

It was the first time that a British Commander had taken over operational command of such a large body of American troops as II (us) Corps with its one armoured and three infantry divisions. Wasting no time in Algiers, Alexander went forward to Anderson's First Army HQ and from there toured the front for four days. He could not have arrived at a more critical time. As he drove southward into II (us) Corps' sector, memories came flooding back of his days as a junior officer in the Irish Guards in the Retreat from Mons; as an acting brigade commander trying to stem the German onslaught in Flanders in March 1918; as the British rearguard commander at Dunkirk in 1940; and, most recently, as the British commander sent out from England by Churchill to extricate British forces from Burma after the Japanese invasion.

Alexander was thus no stranger to defeat and withdrawal. He recognised all the tell-tale signs of loss of control in the higher levels of command in II (us) Corps, and of demoralisation amongst its soldiers. Eisenhower had told him to take over on 20 February. Like Montgomery at El Alamein, he took charge at once, taking some of the burden off Anderson's shoulders and establishing the sense of calm balanced judgment for which he had become famous. Writing to General Alan Brooke in London that night he minced no words:

The general situation is far from satisfactory. British, American and French units are all mixed up on the front, especially in the south. Formations have been split up. There is no policy and no plan of campaign. The air is much the same. This is the result of no firm direction or centralised control from above ... My main anxiety is the poor fighting value of the Americans.

(*British Official History*, Vol IV, page 304).

It was an unfortunate introduction to American troops which was to make an indelible impression on his mind. The American official historians comment justifiably: 'General Alexander's unfavourable estimate (of American troops) was destined to linger, encouraging him to depend more heavily on British units than later circumstances warranted.' (Mediterranean Theatre; page 475).

As the previous chapter showed, it would be wrong to credit Alexander with a share in forcing the German withdrawal from Thala. Rommel withdrew of his own accord with some persuasion from Robinett, Dunphie and Nicholson. It would be equally wrong *not* to credit him with the success of the rest of the Tunisian campaign. It was his concept, carried out under his direction, and in his way. He earned his title, Lord Alexander of Tunis. His was a fervent believer in what he described as his two-handed strategy, using the analogy of a boxing match. He would feint with one fist and strike with the other; or strike several times with one before loosing the other and so on. There were innumerable permutations, but in Tunisia he suffered an important limitation. He two fists were unequal in striking power. Eighth Army – his right – could be relied on to find its mark and inflict serious damage; First Army was less experienced, lacked confidence, and its thumb – II (US) Corps – was badly bruised. He planned, therefore, to do most of the attacking with his right, using his left for feints and short carefully controlled jabs until it was fit and ready to launch a full scale offensive in its own right.

As early as 21 February, two days after assuming command of 18th Army Group, Alexander announced his outline plan for destroying the Axis forces in Africa. He envisaged operations in two distinct phases: first, to unite his Army Group by passing Eighth Army through the narrow 'Gabes Gap'; and second, to tighten a land, sea and air noose around the Axis forces in Northern Tunisia and so weaken them by naval and air blockade that a 'coup de grace' could be delivered by Anderson's First Army without excessive loss of life. The key to the second phase would be the capture of Axis airfields in the central Tunisian plain to help Tedder establish complete Allied air supremacy, thus making the blockade of Tunis and Bizerta total.

Passing Eighth Army through the Gabes Gap would not be easy. The Gap itself between the salt lakes of the Chott el Fedjadj and the sea was narrow and it was protected in depth by the Mareth Line some 15 miles to the east. In Alexander's view the combination of the Mareth Line and the Gabes Gap gave Messe a stronger position than Rommel had defended at El Alamein. It was to be Eighth Army's task to breach these two positions, while First Army and II (US) Corps mounted strictly limited operations to gain favourable tactical positions for the second phase of operations and to prevent von Arnim sending troops to help Messe. On no account was II (us) Corps to launch a 'SATIN' type offensive to cut the Axis lines of communication in the central Tunisian plain. It must stay within the comparative safety of the Eastern Dorsal and not risk another confrontation with the Afrika Korps.

The establishment of HQ 18th Army Group in Tunisia was not universally welcome. Its appearance at the moment of American discomfiture at Sidi Bou Zid, Sbeitla and Kasserine did not endear it to HQ II (us) Corps; and Anderson's First Army HQ could hardly be expected to applaud its own loss of status. Furthermore, it was the antithesis of Eisenhower's multi-national AFHQ. It was a British HQ, organised on British lines, and staffed by hand-picked British staff officers from Cairo with a few American and French officers added principally for liaison purposes. With the best will in the world it could hardly escape giving the impression of professionals arriving to teach amateurs their job. Its first instructions to its three subordinate formations – First Army, II (us) Corps and Eighth Army – did nothing to increase its popularity. Alexander decided rightly that he must sort out the muddled state of the Tunisian front and improve the training of the British, French and American troops before Montgomery started his offensive against the Gabes Gap during the next full moon period around 19 March. Alexander's formula resembled Montgomery's before El Alamein. In a series of instructions he made seven points:

1. All troops were to be grouped into national sectors under their own commanders.
2. Divisions were to live, train and fight as divisions.
3. There was to be no more withdrawal.
4. A general reserve was to be created.
5. Battle schools were to be established, manned by experienced British officers.

The sixth and seventh points will be quoted verbatim from one of his instructions to First Army because they give the flavour of his policy:

Training must be carried out intensively by all troops. The fighting spirit of all must be raised to the highest possible pitch. Training with a definite 'aim' is a great help in this.

Battle experience for those without it must be gained, starting with small raids and leading up to bigger operations. Such operations must be successful; this is important.

(Alexander to Anderson, 20 February; quoted by Truscott, page 168).

These paragraphs reflect Alexander's own experience as a regimental officer in the First World War in which he learned the importance of hard training, painstaking rehearsal and the gradual commitment of new troops to battle, always ensuring that they are successful in their first engagements which invariably have a traumatic effect upon them and which must, therefore, be kept well within their capabilities.

These instructions seemed so ordinary to Truscott that he commented in his memoirs:

I have often wondered what General Anderson's reaction was to this operations instruction. In view of the crucial situation of the front at the time it was issued, and the strenuous efforts both General Eisenhower and General Anderson had been making for weeks to accomplish its specific intent, it has always seemed to me to have been most untimely – rather like telling a man who has a bear by the tail to 'hold on'.

(Truscott; page 169).

But the difference lay in Alexander and McCreery's ability to put these simple concepts into effect. Eisenhower and Anderson had been buffetted by events and had conspicuously failed to do so.

While Alexander was establishing himself on the Allied side, Rommel was trying to do the same thing with his new Army Group, Africa. Early in March he called for appreciations from von Arnim and Messe on which to base his Army Group strategy. Von Arnim stated with his usual bluntness that if he were in Eisenhower's shoes he would concentrate upon cutting the Axis sea/air bridge from Sicily by naval and air action. The Axis bridgehead would not last much beyond July if this happened. He estimated that there were 350,000 Axis servicemen in Tunisia, two thirds of them being German. The Army Group would need about 120,000 tons of supplies a month if it were to undertake offensive operations. As only about half this tonnage was being supplied at the very most, the front must be shortened to save men, ammunition and fuel. Messe was equally depressed and tended to agree with von Arnim. He did not believe he could hold the Mareth Line and wished to withdraw before he became inextricably engaged with Eighth Army.

With these two appreciations in his hands Rommel presented his views to Kesselring who forwarded them to OKW and Hitler with his own covering note. Rommel recommended that Messe should be allowed to retire to Northern Tunisia where he and von Arnim would hold a defensive perimeter from Cap Serrat in the north through Sidi Nsir to Oued Zargo and Medjez (which must be taken from the Allies), and then eastwards from Djebel Mansour to Enfidaville on the coast due north of Sousse.* Kesselring dissented from this view in his covering note, stressing that the loss of Central Tunisian airfields would make the Axis air stiuation intolerable, and recommending that the present Axis positions should be held. Shortening the front might save soldiers, but it would lead to the destruction of the Axis bridgehead by Allied air action. Hitler was in no mood to give up ground. He supported Kesselring's view, pointing out that Rommel had claimed, as a reason for abandoning Tripolitania, the increased chances of success in Tunisia. Further efforts were to be made to raise supplies to 120,000 tons per month by installing German naval staff officers in Italian naval headquarters.

On 9 March Rommel left Africa for the rest of his interrupted sick leave, handing over the Army Group, Africa, to von Arnim, as he thought, temporarily. On reaching Rome, he realised that the Commando Supremo did not expect to see him back in Africa. He went on to Hitler's forward HQ in Russia, where he was cordially received by the Führer His account of his interview is interesting:

* See map IX.

He (Hitler) seemed very upset and depressed about the Stalingrad disaster . . . He was unreceptive to my arguments and seemed to pass them all off with the idea that I had become a pessimist. I emphasised as strongly as I could that the 'African' troops must be re-equipped in Italy to enable them to defend our Southern Europe Flank. I even went so far as to give him a guarantee . . . that with these troops I would beat off any Allied invasion in Southern Europe. But it was all hopeless. He instructed me to take some sick leave and get myself right so that I could take command again later for operations against Casablanca! It simply never occurred to him that things could go wrong in Tunisia.

(Rommel; page 409).

With Rommel's compulsory retirement from North Africa, the Axis command team became von Arnim, Army Group Commander; von Vaerst (another wounded Afrika Korps Commander), Fifth Panzer Army in Northern Tunisia; and Messe, First Italian Army in Southern Tunisia. The boundary between the two Axis Armies was the line Maknassy – Mahares on the coast.

On the Allied side there were changes too. Alexander was highly critical of Anderson and wrote to Montgomery asking if Leese could be spared from XXX Corps to replace him. Leese, however, was already engaged in the preparations to breach the Mareth Line with his XXX Corps, and so Alexander agreed to keep Anderson for the time being. He thought even less of Fredendall, but was not prepared to meddle in American domestic affairs. Fortunately Eisenhower had his suspicions of Fredendall's competence as well. After consulting other American generals, he concluded that a change must be made in the II (US) Corps' Command which had lost the confidence of its troops. When Eisenhower sought Alexander's views, the latter commented that he was sure that the American Army had better men. This was enough for Eisenhower, who summoned Patton from Morocco to take over II (US) Corps temporarily, giving him Major-General Omar Bradley as his deputy. Bradley would probably take over II (US) Corps when Patton had to return to Morocco to start detailed planning and preparation for the invasion of Sicily for which he was US Task Force Commander designate.

Patton did for II (US) Corps what Montgomery had done for Eighth Army. Whirlwind tours in his command car, stars burnished, horns blaring and outriders roaring behind him, impressed his presence on every officer and enlisted man in the Corps area. Tightened discipline of martinet standards, including the compulsory wearing of steel helmets and regulation uniform, brought back some of the Corps' lost self-respect, and his flamboyant use of language created enthusiasm and pride in everything American. But like Montgomery, he had his detractors. The Historians of 1st (US) Armoured Division wrote sourly:– 'But it is hard today to find anyone who was in the 1st Armoured Division who remembers any substantial boost in spirit as a result of Patton's short exercise of the Corps command.' (page 204).

PASSING EIGHTH ARMY THROUGH THE GABES GAP

> During these preliminaries, the Eighth Army proceeded to the crucial battle
> (Mareth) with the majestic deliberation of a pachyderm.
>
> (Mediterranean Theatre; page 521).

The imbalance of Alexander's two fists meant that the pace of operations would be
dictated by the successes and failures of Eighth Army as it fought its way through the
Gabes Gap. The operations of Patton's Corps did not figure very highly in
Alexander's or Montgomery's calculations. Montgomery, however, found the passage
through the Gap more difficult than he expected and this forced him to ask for
Patton's help, first grudgingly and then with growing anxiety. He made five such
requests and on each occasion Alexander varied his directions to Patton, sometimes
giving Patton the freedom he craved to show what his Corps could do, but more often
to curb his enthusiasm and prevent him jeopardising the overall plan. The British
attitude to Patton is illustrated by a letter which Montgomery sent to Alexander on
8 March:

> I suggest that II (us) Corps should limit the scope of its operations to:
> 1. Securing Gafsa.
> 2. Holding it very firmly.
> 3. Building up and maintaining there petrol for me. Having got Gafsa they could
>   demonstrate down the Gabes road. If I can count on a dump of petrol at Gafsa, I
>   could drive on towards Sousse without a pause at Sfax. *Don't let them be too
>   ambitious and ruin the show.*
>
> (Nigel Nicholson; page 180).

These ideas of Montgomery's coincided with Alexander's own views of American
capabilities at that time. 18th Army Group instructions to Patton were to hold the
Western Dorsal strongly; retake the Thélepté airfield complex, and then Gafsa where
the supply dump for Eighth Army was to be established; and, if all went well,
demonstrate to Maknassy and El Guettar. The American Official History comments:

> The forthcoming operations were therefore designed to permit small successes and
> the application of training lessons taught in battle schools instituted by 18th Army
> Group during the preceding fortnight. A few such victories, it was hoped, would
> bring the performance of American units up to the required level by developing
> their capabilities and justifying their self respect. But the Americans, particularly
> the more aggressive like the new Corps Commander, General Patton, tugged
> against the restraining leash from the start.
>
> (Mediterranean Theatre; page 544).

Montgomery had been planning his assault on the Mareth Line since early January
when he was still east of Buerat. He had despatched patrols of the Long Range Desert
Group to find a way round Mareth's open desert flank. These patrols confirmed that
there was a practicable route through the desert west of the Matmata Hills leading to

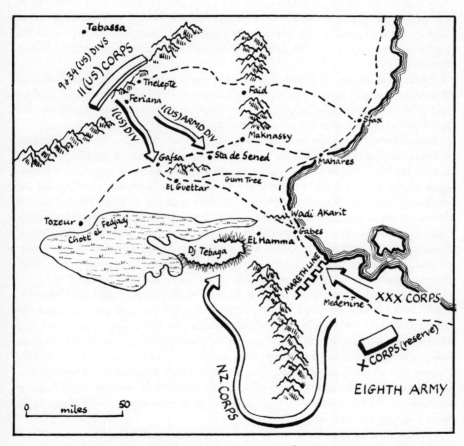

Fig 69 Montgomery's plan for the Battle of Mareth and Patton's for Operation 'Wop'.

El Hamma in the Gabes Gap via a narrow pass between the northern end of the Matmata Hills and the Chott El Fedjad, called the Tebaga Gap. Montgomery decided to use this route as a threat to Messe's rear.

Montgomery issued his orders for the assault on the Mareth Line on 26 February — over a week before his successful defeat of Rommel's spoiling attack at Medenine. Leese's XXX Corps with 50th and 51st Divisions would breach the Mareth Defences in the coastal sector between the main road and the sea. Freyberg would organise his New Zealand Divisional HQ into a temporary Corps HQ, and take a force consisting of his own division, 8th Armoured Brigade and General Leclerc's Free French Force 'L',* on the long out-flanking march to the Tebaga Gap. Horrocks' X Corps would be held in reserve with 1st and 7th Armoured Divisions ready to reinforce either Leese or Freyberg.

Freyberg set off on 10 March in a series of night marches through the Matmata Hills to an assembly area in the desert beyond, covered by Leclerc's Force 'L'. Leclerc had a brush with German reconnaissance troops, but Freyberg's concentration was not detected until it was complete on 12 March.

Leese's problem was how to close up the main Mareth defences. Meese was holding a strong outpost line on the Wadi Zeuss, covering the old French fortifications built behind the Wadi Zigzaou. The Young Fascist Division held the coastal sector; then came the Trieste, flanking the 90th Light which held the main road; and beyond the main road stood the Spezia and Pistoia Divisions with the German 164th Division anchoring the line in the Matmata Hills. 15th Panzer Division and Panzer Grenadier Regiment, Africa, were in First Italian Army reserve, and 10th and 21st Panzer Divisions were north of the Gabes Gap under the Afrika Korps in Army Group reserve. A special Italian force called the Sahariano Group of some seven desert-trained frontier battalions held the desert flank and the Tebaga Gap.

Leese planned his operations in three phases: 'Walk', on the night 16/17 March, would be an attack by 201st Guards Brigade to clear the high ground called the 'Horseshoe' held by 90th Light Division astride the main road from which the Germans enjoyed artillery observation over the coastal sector; 'Canter', on the same night, would be a general advance by 50th and 51st Divisions to throw back the Axis outpost line to the Wadi Zigzaou, enabling the assault brigades to reconnoitre the enemy main position; and 'Gallop' would be the main attack over the Wadi Zigzaou launched by 50th Division with 51st Division's flanking support on the night 20/21 March during the full moon.

Patton called his plan for II (US) Corps' operation against Gafsa Operation 'Wop'. He was far from happy about the restrictions placed upon him by Alexander and about the care with which 18th Army Group staff officers supervised his planning. Ryder's 34th and Eddy's 9th Divisions were to hold the Western Dorsal through which Allen's 1st Infantry and Ward's 1st Armoured Divisions would debouch to over-run Thélepté and Fériana. Allen would then advance to attack Gafsa early on 17 March while Ward covered his northern flank with an advance across the plain

* Leclerc brought Force 'L' across the Sahara from French Equatorial Africa and joined Eighth Army at Tripoli.

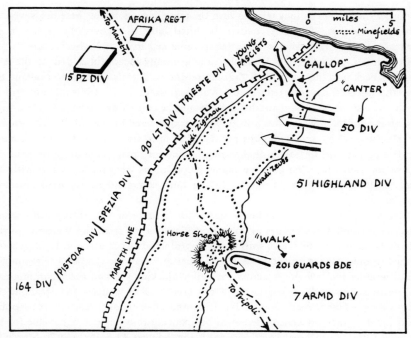

Fig 70 XXX Corps Attack at Mareth – 19th March

between the two Dorsals to threaten Station de Sened from the north west and west. If all went well, 18th Army Group would authorise a further advance to El Guettar and Station de Sened but no further.

There were thus three preliminary operations timed for 16/17 March – 'Walk', 'Canter', and 'Wop'. The second two were successful, but the first, which was expected to cause least trouble, proved a costly failure. British Intelligence reported the 'Horseshoe' feature, which 201st Guards Brigade were to attack in 'Walk', was lightly held, and so only two Guards battalions were committed. Time for reconnaissance was short and the few patrols, which could be sent out in the time available, reported no mines. The artillery programme was more than adequate, Montgomery jokingly saying, 'It is going to be a party, and when I give a party it is always a good one!' The trouble was that there were a number of uninvited and undesirable guests present. The position was far from lightly held. On it were three of 90th Light Division's Panzer Grenadier battalions which had had plenty of time to prepare the commanding ground of the 'Horseshoe'. Their positions were heavily mined by anti-personnel as well as anti-tank mines. And at the last moment a British gunner officer was captured with his map marked with the supporting fire plan and exact timings. No amount of courage, tactical skill and discipline could outweigh these disadvantages. It is to the great credit of the two Guards battalions – 3rd Coldstream and 6th Grenadiers – that they took most of their objectives. They were too weak by then to hold them. Over 38 officers and 500 men were lost, many to anti-personnel mines as they tried to rush the minefields. Some of these fields were so densely sown that 700 mines had to be lifted later to recover the bodies of 69 Grenadiers. The 'Horseshoe's' observation remained in 90th Lights' hands.

In 'Canter', 50th and 51st Divisions were generally successful in driving the Axis outposts back into the main Wadi Zigzaou positions. Patrols sent out to examine the Mareth Line defences reported that the Wadi had water in it but it would not present much of an obstacle. The main difficulty would be caused by a deep anti-tank ditch dug on the far bank which was mined, wired and covered by the old French concrete blockhouses and by anti-tank guns positioned in open field works. Plans were made for dealing with the anti-tank ditch, using fascines of brush-wood dropped from the supporting tanks into the gap. No major preparations were made to deal with the Wadi itself across which patrols, including tank commanders, reported adequate crossing places.

Patton's 'Wop' was outstandingly successful in spite of the Spring rains which broke in torrential downpours as Allen and Ward set off from the Western Dorsal. Allen's 1st Division took Gafsa with a well co-ordinated attack early on 17 March and pushed reconnaissance units on towards El Guettar where the Centauro Division was found holding the low ridges across the valley blocking the two roads running east and south east towards the coast – the 'Gum Tree' road to Mahares and Sfax, and the main Gafsa – Gabes road. Ward's 1st Armoured Division also reached its assembly areas for its attack on Station de Sened but pouring rain made it impossible for his armoured units to manoeuvre off the roads for the next 48 hours. On 20 March he opened his attack on Station de Sened, feinting with McQuillan's CC 'A' along the Gafsa – Maknassy road, while Stack's CC 'C' and the 6th (US) Infantry Regiment from Eddy's 9th Division climbed Djebel Goussa and launched surprise attacks from the north west. The Italian 50th Special Brigade evacuated Station de Sened and fell back on Maknassy on 21 March. The American soldiers were regaining their confidence with the limited successes as Alexander had intended.

Freyberg started his advance on Tebaga from his assembly area on the far side of the Matmata Hills when darkness fell on 19 March. He hoped his movements were still unrecognised by the Axis High Command as a serious threat, but in this he was to be disappointed. German air reconnaissance had alerted Messe, who came to the conclusion that a major force was heading for El Hamma. On the evening of 20 March, when 50th Division opened the main attack, Freyberg was only 10 miles from the entrance of the Tebaga defile and was making his preparations to attack the Sahariano Group's positions the following evening.

Leese's XXX Corps was also out of luck. The Spring rains, which had deluged Patton, had also fallen in the Matmata Hills, though not on the coastal plain. When the attacking battalions reached the Wadi Zigzaou they found the water had risen, and, though it did not create an infantry obstacle, the bottom of the Wadi had lost its firmness and was becoming impassable to tanks and wheeled vehicles. The infantry seized their objectives with the Italians surrendering willingly. Four tanks crossed the Wadi and dropped their fascines into the anti-tank ditch, but the fifth broke through the thin crust of the Wadi floor and sank up to its turret, totally blocking the crossing.

Eighth Army Engineers worked with a will all 21 March collecting material to build a causeway over the Wadi during the second night of the battle. The infantry, with their four tanks, managed to hold their bridgehead during daylight and when dusk fell set about extending it. They over-ran the remaining Italian positions which could cover the crossing and found the occupants embarrassingly willing to surrender in large numbers. The sappers too were successful in establishing a causeway across the Wadi. Then a major error of judgment occurred which lost Leese the battle. Instead of sending the lighter infantry support vehicles towing 6-pounder anti-tank guns across first, the Valentine tanks of 50th Royal Tank Regiments equipped only with obsolete 2-pounder guns were given priority over the crossing. 42 tanks crossed, churning up the causeway and making it impassable even for other tanks. Repair work started but a downpour, this time in the battle area, put an end to crossings for that night. Dawn came with only a 2-pounder equipped tank regiment and no towed 6-pounders in the bridgehead.

21 March was also a critical and decisive day amongst the High Commands. Montgomery made his first request for Patton's help. Signalling Alexander he said:

> Enemy obviously intends to stand the fight, and I am preparing dog-fight battle in Mareth area which may last several days. Strong eastward thrust of the US armoured division through Maknassy to cut Sfax – Gabes road would have very good results.

(Nigel Nicholson; page 181).

Alexander had partially anticipated this request 48 hours earlier and had made his first change in Patton's directive. He ordered Patton to take Maknassy and to send a light armoured force through the pass beyond to raid the Axis airfield complex at Mezzouna, 10 miles east of the Eastern Dorsal. Patton was delighted with this welcome loosening of the rein and ordered Ward forward, only to find Maknassy empty, the Axis garrison having withdrawn to the hills to the east of the town. If Ward had attacked then and there he might have broken through the Eastern Dorsal, but, mindful of Alexander's warning to make sure all attacks were properly supported and co-ordinated, he paused to collect his division. When he attacked next day, 22 March, he found himself opposed by German mobile troops of high quality. The Axis reserves had begun to move.

The Axis High Command had reacted during the 21 March by dispatching a panzer division to meet each identified threat to their position. Messe ordered his immediate reserve, 15th Panzer, to deal with Leese's bridgehead over the Wadi Zigzaou; and then sent his 164th Divison, under Major-General von Liebenstein, to Tebaga, where it was to be joined by 21st Panzer from Army Group Reserve, to block Freyberg's outflanking force. Von Arnim dispatched Cramer's Afrika Korps HQ with 10th Panzer to reinforce the Centauro Division facing Patton at El Guettar; and he also sent an *ad hoc* force under Colonel Lang, containing Rommel's old personal guard unit, to check Ward east of Maknassy.

164th Division and 21st Panzer Division did not reach Tebaga in time to stop Freyberg seizing the entrance to the Tebaga Gap from the Sahariano Group during the night 21/22 March. If Freyberg had risked thrusting 8th Armoured Brigade through in the darkness he might have torn open the Axis blocking position, but, like Ward, he decided to wait for dawn. He was far from happy about his exposed position on the far side of the Matmata Hills and his uncertainty was increased by conflicting intelligence reports of the movements of the panzer divisions. He suspected that he might have to face two, if not all three because the Germans were unlikely to accept his threat to their rear without a violent reaction. When 8th Armoured Brigade advanced early on 22 March the fleeting opportunity had gone. Enough German troops and guns had reached the Tebaga Gap to block it effectively.

15th Panzer Divison's counter-attack on the XXX Corps bridgehead was grimly successful. In the early afternoon of 22 March the British units holding the bridgehead saw their worst fears confirmed. Out of the smoke and swirling dust haze, which hung over the battlefield, loomed the tanks of the 8th Panzer Regiment with their supporting Panzer Grenadiers as they nosed their way forward cautiously, using the folds in the ground for concealment. The British artillery slowed but could not break up their attacks. 50th Royal Tank Regiment, outgunned and under-armoured, sacrificed themselves to protect the infantry. By dusk the bridgehead was all but eliminated. The few surviving tanks were clustered round the churned-up crossing, and the infantry were clinging on in the anti-tank ditch. With heavy hearts the staff of XXX Corps started preparations for a further attempt to build a causeway for wheels during the early part of the night so that a fresh effort could be made to secure a viable bridgehead after midnight. HQ Eighth Army was, however, reacting to the afternoon's disaster. With commendable speed and decision Montgomery changed plan, and indirectly made Alexander do so as well. XXX Corps was told to stand fast and make no further attempt to cross the Wadi Zigzaou.

Montgomery's new plan was to switch his main effort to Freyberg's front. XXX Corps was to maintain frontal pressure on the Mareth Line to pin Messe's troops in their fortifications, while Horrocks took his X Corps HQ and 1st Armoured Division over Freyberg's desert route to reinforce the New Zealand Corps for a major assault on the Tebaga Gap. 4th Indian Division would make a shorter left hook through the Matmata Hills to outflank the Mareth Line through the positions abandoned by 164th Division when it moved to Tebaga. These moves would take some time – Horrocks would need at least three days – making it unlikely that Eighth Army's effort could be renewed before 25 or 26 March. Montgomery again asked Alexander if Patton could help in the meantime:

> If II (US) Corps could move south-east and sit tight in the gap about 15 miles north-west of Gabes none repeat none, of the enemy army facing us could get out of the net. It is worth making a great effort to achieve this desirable end. No, repeat no, enemy could possibly escape. What can you do about this?
>
> (*Ibid;* page 181)

Alexander felt this was asking too much of Patton's novice Corps. Although he made his second change in Patton's orders, he did not ask him to do as much as Montgomery suggested. Replying to Montgomery during the night of 22 March he

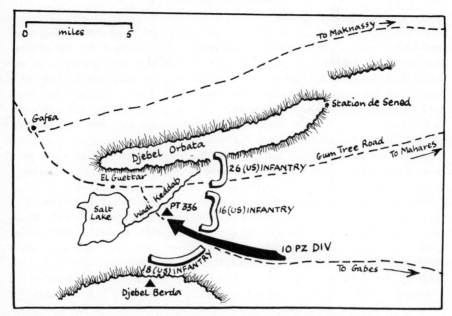

Fig 71 ´ 10th Panzer Division's attack at El Guettar – 23rd March 1943

said:

> The role you suggest for II (US) Corps is too ambitious at the moment. It is not
> sufficiently trained, and maintenance so close to Gabes would be difficult because
> 10th Panzer Division, believed now on the move, might attack their rear.
>
> (*Ibid;* page 181)

His instructions to Patton, issued at the same time, substituted a strong armoured
column for the light raiding force and, instead of the Mezzonna airfields, the
objective was changed to Axis supply dumps on the coast near Mahares. These
instructions had hardly been received in II (US) Corps HQ when Patton's Intelligence
staff warned him that 10th Panzer was heading for El Guettar. In the early hours of
23 March the noise of tanks was heard approaching Allen's positions.

Allen's three regiments were deployed in line to block the two roads leading east
from El Guettar where a series of ridges between Djebel Orbata on the northern side
of the El Guettar valley joins hands with the spurs of Djebel Berda on the south side.
26th Infantry held the 'Gum Tree' road under the shadow of Djebel Orbata; 16th
Infantry held the ridges between the roads; and 18th Infantry held the ground south
of the Gabes road with a Ranger battalion covering its flank on the lower slopes of
Djebel Berda. The Centauro Division's positions were, in general, on the higher
ridges and overlooked the Americans who were forced to dig in on the reverse slopes.
At the rear of the American position was a large salt lake into which ran the Wadi
Keddab. This Wadi had been strengthened with minefields as an emergency stop-line

in the rear of Allen's position.

10th Panzer, under the Afrika Korps' command, started its advance at 3 am along the Gabes – Gafsa road, intending to reach Allen's rear areas by dawn. The advance did not go as quickly as expected because the Germans were uncertain of the American positions. When daylight came, they had penetrated between 16th and 18th Infantry. At first, everything went in their favour. Two American artillery battalions were over-run and a number of their infantry positions were captured with heavy loss of American life. Hill 336 in the rear of Allen's positions was also taken. It looked as if another major Allied disaster was in the making. Then quite unexpectedly fortunes changed. The German tanks ran into the Wadi Keddab minefields which were covered by tank destroyers and artillery. Some 38 German tanks were knocked out – avenging Sidi Bou Zid – and the Germans pulled back to reorganise.

American radio intercept warned Allen to expect another attack at 4.30 pm. This attack started with a heavy Stuka raid, followed by a tank/infantry advance. Allen's men were ready. Using the magnificent artillery observation available, the American gunners 'crucified them with high explosive shell and they were falling like flies. Tanks seemed to be moving to the rear; those that could move'. (Report of 18th Infantry; Mediterranean Theatre; page 562). 10th Panzer withdrew back to the Centauro's positions which it helped to reinforce. Times had truly changed. An American infantry division had stopped a German panzer division in full cry. Patton was delighted. He felt his men deserved a larger role in Allied strategy.

Ward, unfortunately, was not so successful at Maknassy. He attacked Lang's positions throughout the 23rd, 24th and 25th. On Patton's orders, he personally led the final attacks on 25 March but with no more success. His infantry were exhausted. Lang came near to defeat as well, but Rommel's old veterans outlasted the Americans. Ward's days in command were numbered. Patton was losing faith in him as Fredendall had done.

Alexander reacted generously to Patton's success, releasing Major General Manton Eddy's 9th (US) Division to II (US) Corps for a full-blooded attack towards Gabes on 28 March, timed to synchronise with Horrocks's attempt to burst through the Tebaga Gap. Alexander had decided to hit instead of jab with his left. Informing Montgomery of this third change in his orders to Patton, Alexander wrote:

> Saw Patton today, and decided to employ 9th Infantry Division with 1st Infantry Division on axis Gafsa – Gabes. As soon as these divisions have firmly secured defile of El Guettar, I hope to pass 1st (US) Armoured Division through for strong thrust to Djebel Tebaga.
>
> (Nigel Nicholson; page 182).

Montgomery replied on 26 March:

> Enemy reinforcing El Hamma. I understand Patton attacks with three divisions tomorrow, and a vigorous and determined thrust by this Corps down to Gabes would enable us to round up all this party.
>
> (*Ibid;* page 182).

Both Alexander and Montgomery were now over-estimating Patton's abilities. It was one thing to stop a panzer division attacking; it was quite another to beat one in the defence when it was holding ground favourable to it. For the moment, however, all eyes – Allied and Axis – were focused on Tebaga.

When Horrocks reached Tebaga ahead of his Corps, he received a cool reception from Freyberg who naturally resented the imposition of a junior British Commander with a corps staff to handle what had been conceived as a New Zealand operation. Despite the awkwardness of the situation the two men did their best to make the diarchy work. They submitted a number of joint proposals to Montgomery, who rejected them all in favour of a novel plan by Air Marshal Broadhurst, who had taken over the Desert Air Force from Cunningham. It seemed to him that the situation at Tebaga was ideal for air intervention on a grand scale. The narrow Tebaga valley could be saturated with air and artillery bombardment, literally blasting a way through for 1st (Br) Armoured Division. The whole weight of the Desert Air Force would be used to stun 21st Panzer and 164th Divisions. Montgomery described his ideas in a signal to the two generals:

> I want to speed up your thrust as much as possible, and I think we can do a great
> deal to help you by heavy air bombing all night and day. To take full advantage of
> this you would have to do an afternoon attack with the sun behind you. The plan
> would be as follows;
>   (a) Continuous bombing by Wellingtons and night-bombers on night D–1/D.

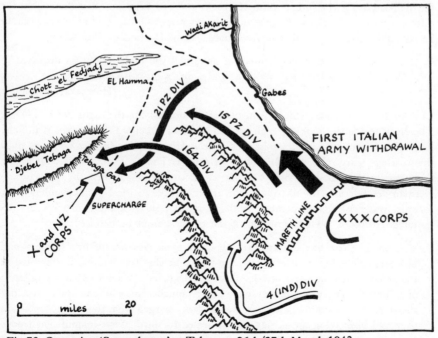

Fig 72 Operation 'Supercharge' at Tebaga – 26th/27th March 1943

(b) Intensive artillery shelling for say one hour before Zero. Smoke etc on high ground on flanks and/or to cover mine lifting.

(c) Air cover and attacks by fighters on any movement to and from battle area.

I do not believe that any enemy could stand up to such treatment . . .

(British Official History; Vol IV; page 346).

Freyberg and Horrocks accepted the concept, but could not meet Montgomery's request for 25 March as D-Day. The 26th was, therefore, fixed, but even so 1st (Br) Armoured Division only just arrived in time. The operation was christened 'Supercharge', after its predecessor at El Alamein.

The two generals elaborated Montgomery's and Broadhurst's ideas. The night before the attack the New Zealanders would seize the dominant feature on the south side of the gap so that their assaulting infantry could dig in unobserved behind the old Roman wall – little more than an earth rampart – which ran across the valley. They would lie there throughout the 26th ready to assault with 8th Armoured Brigade's tanks when the air and artillery lifted at 4 pm. Their objectives were some three miles inside the Axis position, which, it was calculated, should take them through the crust of the German defences. Once the New Zealand Infantry reached their positions 1st Armoured Division would pass through and continue a further two miles in the failing light. It would then leaguer until the moon rose at midnight, when it would crash on down the valley in close formation, making for El Hamma. It was a bold and ingenious plan – the first real blitzkrieg practised by the British Army, which was to set the pattern for the future. Both Horrocks and Freyberg had their doubts but for different reasons: Horrocks because of his heavy responsibility; and Freyberg because he still did not trust the British Armoured Corps. He said to Horrocks:

If we (the New Zealanders) punch a hole, will the tanks really go through?

Yes, they will, Horrocks replied, And I am going with them.

(Horrocks; page 152).

The Air Forces dropped 400 tons in the battle area during the night before D-Day. The New Zealanders took the high ground and dug in behind the Roman Wall. The 26 March broke gusty, and sandstorms developed preventing further bombing until the weather cleared half an hour before Zero hour. The Air Forces then made up for their earlier absence by flying 412 sorties in two hours against the unfortunate German defenders in the narrow sector under attack. As the New Zealanders went forward waves of fighter-bombers with 30 aircraft in each wave struck every 15 minutes. Horrocks' own description of the battle cannot be bettered:

The battle went like clockwork. My chief memories are of our fighters and bombers screaming in at zero feet, the first time that this had been attempted in the desert. Then the tanks of 8th Armoured Brigade . . . advanced up the valley in open order. They thought they were being launched on a second Balaclava, but there was no hesitation. The New Zealanders emerged from their trenches where they had been lying up all day and swarmed forward. What magnificent troops they were. Finally the really awesome sight of a whole armoured division moved steadily forward. It impressed me so what must it have looked like to the German defenders? Tanks and still more tanks moving continuously towards them ...

Then suddenly it was dark, and we halted. This was the most trying time of all: we could not even risk that Eighth Army panacea for all ills, a brew up. We just had to sit, deep in the enemy positions and wait ... At last, thank goodness, we were off again. It was just possible to make out the dim shape of the tanks in front ... at times the tanks were crunching over occupied enemy trenches, and we could see terrified parties of Germans and Italians running about with their hands up. ... Our progress was desperately slow. That was my chief worry. If we didn't succeed in getting through in the dark, the situation in the morning did not bear thinking about. We should be surrounded by the enemy and dominated by the hills either side of the valley ...

(Horrocks; 153–154).

Progress of 1st (Br) Armoured Division's night advance had been slowed by the large number of wadis which had to be crossed in the dark. The German defence of the valley collapsed, but von Liebenstein, commander of 164th Division, who had been put in charge of all Axis troops in the sector including 15th and 21st Panzer Divisions, scraped together enough 88mm and other guns to organise an anti-tank screen at the exit of the valley three miles south of El Hamma which stopped Horrocks' advance when daylight came. The weather deteriorated bringing dust storms and helping him to keep Horrocks and Freyberg at bay for just long enough for Messe to withdraw the bulk of his First Italian Army through the Gabes Gap. By 29 March the battles of Mareth and Tebaga were over, and Horrocks X Corps was nosing into the Gabes Gap, hoping to unseat Messe before his troops could settle down properly in its defences based upon the Wadi Akarit, which ran across the northern half of the Gap.

Patton's plan for the first phase of his offensive was for Allen's 1st (US) Division to clear the Gum Tree Road and the Axis positions between the two roads. Eddy's 9th (US) Division was to clear the Gabes road and the high ground dominating it from the south, in particular Point 369. The attack started on the night 28/29 March as von Liebenstein finally gave way and fell back into the Gabes Gap. Allen's experienced division drove back the Axis defenders of the Gum Tree Road and secured most of its objectives but could not take Point 482 which dominated Eddy's sector on the Gabes Road. Eddy's 9th (US) Division suffered the fate of all new divisions attacking for the first time with an over-ambitious plan. The officers and men had only just arrived: they did not know the area; and it was to be their first battle as a division. Too little time was allowed for reconnaissance and briefing at all levels, and the country was cruelly difficult for a night attack even by experienced troops. Maps were poor and did not give a true idea of the positions of the most important ridges, which were a jumble of bare rocky mounds devoid of vegetation and eroded by numerous unmarked wadis. Map reading in daylight was difficult enough; at night a compass and a keen sense of distance were the only guides. The two leading battalions mistook the silhouette of Point 290 on the main Gabes road for Point 369, their objective, and

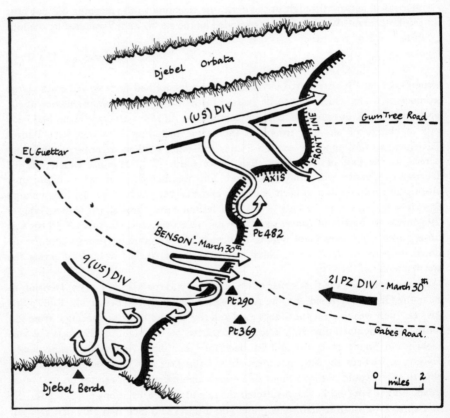

Fig 73 Patton's First offensive at El Guettar: 28th/29th March 1943

30. An artillery observation post in typical Djebel Ang country: shell bursts can be seen on the far peak.

31. A German "Tiger" knocked out near Tunis; a British Churchill tank and armoured scout car are just behind it.

32. The end of Panzer Army Group, Afrika: German troops after their surrender.

33. General von Arnim on his way to England.

veered north clearing the Axis defences in their path but failing to secure either Point 290 or 369. The third and fourth battalions to be committed lost their way completely in the valleys and gulches of Djebel Berda for 36 hours. Reinforcing battalions brought up in trucks drove too close to Point 290 and were dispersed by Axis artillery fire. Most of the men escaped back to their start point, thoroughly demoralised; the remainder were pinned down by fire and only managed to straggle back in small parties after dark next night.

Patton's failure was disappointing, because Messe's Army was 'off balance' and might easily have been hustled out of the Wadi Akarit position by the combination of a sharp frontal thrust from Horrocks' X Corps with a threat to his rear from Patton. Alexander revised Patton's orders for the fourth time. He knew it was a moment to take risks with his enemy so clearly in trouble. He told Patton in some over-detailed instructions to secure Maknassy, Sened and Gafsa with his infantry divisions and to launch a strong armoured force down the Gafsa–Gabes road next day to help Horrocks shake Messe into premature withdrawal.

Neither Horrocks nor Patton managed to shift Messe who knew he could not withdraw until reasonable arrangements had been made to evacuate his immobile Italian infantry from Wadi Akarit to Northern Tunisia. Horrocks quickly concluded on 30 March that, if Montgomery was prepared to accept heavy casualties amongst his mobile troops, it might be possible for X Corps to break through with another Tebaga type assault; otherwise Leese's XXX Corps would have to be brought up to batter a way through. Montgomery needed his mobile troops for the advance across the Tunisian plains beyond Wadi Akarit and so he decided to bring up XXX Corps, but decided not to wait, as was his usual practice, for the next full moon. He would attack on 6 April, the soonest that the necessary ammunition dumping, troop movement, reconnaissance and planning could be completed. He continued to hope that Patton would draw off another panzer division.

Patton chose to ignore Ward and the standard organisation of 1st (US) Armoured Division in setting up the armoured force to break through down the Gabes road. He selected an old friend, Colonel C. C. Benson, whose aggressiveness he admired, to lead the force which was to be composed of two armoured, one armoured infantry, one infantry, one reconnaissance, one tank destroyer, and two artillery battalions with supporting engineers and service troops. The artillery of 1st and 9th Divisions would be massed in his support, and their infantry regiments were to attack Points 482 and 369 again to cover his flanks as he tried to break through on an axis of advance just north of the Gabes road.

Patton's second offensive started at 6 am on 30 March. The artillery bombardment enabled Allen's men to take and hold most but not all of Point 482, and Eddy's men to reach but not hold Point 369. When Benson started to advance at noon his flanks were far from secure. Anti-tank fire started cutting into his column, particularly from Eddy's sector south of the road. His advance was brought to a halt by a minefield which could not be cleared until after dark when his engineers managed to open one lane for him before dawn.

Early next day, 31 March, Benson's own infantry helped to clear his southern flank by seizing Point 290 which had defied Eddy for so long. Patton was tempted to order Benson to blast his way through regardless of loss to enable II (US) Corps to share the possible fruits of Montgomery's coming attack on Wadi Akarit. On second thoughts, he decided to organise a full blooded assault with the support of the Allied Air Forces. He also ordered McQuillin's CC 'A' in Maknassy to attack Lang's blocking force to draw off German reserves. It was as well that he chose caution because the opposition at El Guettar had grown dramatically in the last 24 hours. First, Panzer Grenadier Regiment, Africa, had arrived to help block Benson's initial attack on 30 March; and then the whole of 21st Panzer Division came up in time to make sure that Benson did not break through on 31 March. To add to Benson's difficulties Kesselring ordered maximum air effort by the Luftwaffe to be devoted to the El Guettar front to quell the American threat to Messe's rear.

Patton had, however, achieved one of Alexander's principal requirements. He had succeeded in drawing and holding two German Panzer divisions away from Montgomery's front.

Tempers shortened on the Allied side. Alexander was clearly disappointed by Patton's failure to make more progress. And Patton for his part blamed Alexander's original caution which prevented him from sweeping forward from Gafsa to Gabes at the beginning of the offensive. He would have been able to push the Centauro Division aside without much trouble and would have been in possession of the El Guettar ridges before the Germans could intervene. Alexander was now asking him to clear those ridges with the Centauro and two panzer divisions holding them. Patton was also angered about the inadequacy of Allied air support. His troops were suffering severely from Luftwaffe dive-bombing; and his own headquarters had been 'plastered'. Some regrettably ill-considered signals passed between II (US) Corps and the Tactical Air Forces, and led to personal recriminations at the highest levels which could only be stilled by Eisenhower's and Alexander's tact and charm. Patton's irritation found another outlet in the failures of 1st (US) Armoured Division. Its history records:

> The Division was tired, frustrated and depressed. Its reputation in higher headquarters was suffering, and in response to Alexander's request and his own misgivings, Patton determined to give the Division a new commander to build it up again.
>
> (*Battle History of 1st Armoured Division*; page 216).

General Harmon was again summoned from Morocco and took over from Ward who returned to the United States and subsequently commanded another armoured division in North West Europe with distinction.

Benson's failure and the arrival of 21st Panzer Division at El Guettar made Alexander change Patton's orders for the fifth and last time. II (US) Corps was to revert to using its infantry in the El Alamein 'crumbling' style: careful reconnaissance and planning; limited objectives; plenty of artillery; and as near certainty of success in each bite as there ever can be in battle. For the next six days, while Eighth Army got ready to assault the Wadi Akarit, 1st and 9th (US) Divisions gnawed away at the Axis held djebels. Successes were sparse and casualties high. Both divisions became so short of infantry that they had to use their engineers in the line. On 5 April unusual movements were detected behind the Axis front. Patton concluded that they heralded another panzer counter-attack similar to 10th Panzers' attack which 1st (US) Division broke up on 25 March. Immediate steps were taken to meet this attack, including reinforcing the Wadi Keddab again as the final stop-line.

The irritation felt in the Allied High Command was relatively insignificant compared to the friction which was growing on the Axis side in the shadow of defeat. No positive policy could be agreed. Von Arnim was certain that the deteriorating supply position would force Messe's withdrawal, even if the Allies could not. Kesselring, as optimistic as ever and determined not to lose airfields, believed that Southern Tunisia could and must he held. With an unusual measure of realism, the Commando Supremo wished to issue an instruction ordering von Arnim to hold southern Tunisia as long as possible while authorising him to withdraw to the north if he could not contain II (US) Corps' threat. Kesselring objected that this was a psychologically bad order and would make commanders 'retreat minded'.

General Westphal, Kesselring's Chief of Staff, flew to Tunis on 30 March to explain Kesselring's policy to von Arnim and his staff. He received a rough reception in Tunis when he complained that Army Group, Africa, was 'always squinting over its shoulder.' Von Arnim replied acidly 'Yes, for ships; we are without bread and ammunition, as was Rommel's Army before. The consequences are inevitable' (*British Official History*; Vol; IV; page 360). In the end, Messe was left with the

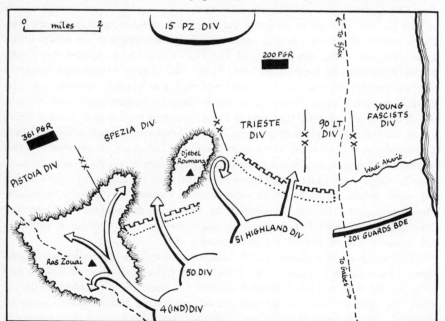

Fig 74 The Battle of Wadi Akarit: 6th to 7th April 1943

unhappy compromise of holding Southern Tunisia while preparing to retreat northwards without letting anyone but his most senior officers know what was afoot. Von Arnim, himself, put in hand limited and highly secret plans to thin out administrative units and staffs, sending them back to Italy on the grounds that they were 'useless mouths'. He did not suggest evacuating Tunis and Bizerta because he knew this would be politically unacceptable to Hitler and Mussolini. He was beginning to organise the defence of his final bridgehead round the two ports. conscious that he would have to withstand a long siege.

The strength of the Wadi Akarit position did not depend on the Wadi itself, which was not much of an obstacle, but upon an abrupt ridge of hills running eastwards from the coast and along the northern edge of the Chott-el Fedjadj. For most of its length the ridge was not more than a mile deep, but in the very centre, half way between the coast road and the road to Gafsa, there was a two mile deep jumble of djebels, rising to about 1000 feet called the Ras Zouai. A little nearer the coast road there was another though less prominent section called the Djebel Roumana which gave observation over the coastal area and Eighth Army's road to Tunis. Some work had been done by Axis engineers on this line to make it tank-proof. The Wadi itself was good enough as far as the main road. Then anti-tank ditches and minefields had been provided between the road and Djebel Roumana and between Djebel Roumana and Ras Zouai. Other obstacles had been placed in the various small passes further west, including a block on the Gafsa road.

Montgomery's first assessment of the problem of breaching Messe's position was that XXX Corps would need only one infantry division to make a large enough breach to pass X Corps through to exploit to the Mezzona airfield complex in Messe's rear. Patrol reports showed that he was under-estimating the strength of the Axis position. Leese proposed to use 4th Indian and 51st Highland Divisions against Ras Zouai, Djebel Roumana and the hills between. Tuker, 4th Indians' experienced mountain warfare commander, saw that Ras Zouai was too big to be held effectively against a silent night attack, using infiltration tactics at which his Indians were expert. Patrols, which he sent out, reported that most of Zouai's defences were sited in enfilade, firing across the fronts of neighbouring sectors. The Axis defenders seemed to think that the forward slopes were unscalable by a major force. The Indian patrols reported that this was not so. Using special patrol boots – stocks of which Tuker had purloined some months earlier – 4th Indian's battalions could neutralise the feature by stealth during the night before the main attack went in, thus clearing Ras Zouai's formidable observation off the Highland Division's front. After some debate, first Leese, and then Montgomery, accepted Tuker's proposals and substituted 50th Division to carry out 4th Indian's original part in the main assault.

Tuker's attack was a decisive success which the pachyderm-like qualities of Eighth Army almost failed to exploit. The Gurkha and Indian battalions of Tuker's two brigades (the third was lost in Tobruk) cleared Ras Zousi, using cold steel during the night 5/6 April and were on the high ground overlooking 50th Division's sector by daylight. They had also opened a route for tracks and wheels round the western end of the anti-tank ditch.

Meanwhile 50th and 51st Divisions' attacks went forward at dawn with heavy artillery support, described by Messe as an 'apocalyptic hurricane of steel and fire'. 51st Division took Roumana and cleared two passages through the minefield and over the ditch. 50th Division was not so successful and had difficulty with the anti-tank ditch, but not for long. By about 9.30 am the Italians were again showing willingness to surrender in embarrassing numbers.

The opposing Army Commanders reacted very differently to the morning reports. Messe ordered 15th Panzer to move up to block any breach which might occur between Roumana and Ras Zouai. Von Arnim had been anticipating events and had, on 5 April, ordered the Afrika Korps to withdraw its 80 available fit tanks into reserve at El Guettar. This was probably the movement detected by Patton and misconstrued as signs of a Panzer attack. During the early hours of 6 April von Arnim released the Afrika Korps tanks to Messe and by 10.30 am they were reported on their way from El Guettar to Wadi Akarit.

Montgomery did not react so quickly. What went wrong that morning is only known to the actors themselves. For unrecorded reasons X Corps did not start its advance with 8th Armoured Brigade leading the New Zealand Divison until 1.30 pm. As 8th Armoured Brigade advanced cautiously round the western end of Djebel Roumana, its leading tanks were hit by defilated 88mm guns tucked in behind the feature. 15th Panzer had got there first and was blocking the point of breakthrough. It was decided to halt exploitation until the following morning so that X Corps could burst through with the full support of the combined X and XXX Corps artilleries. The British were over-estimating their opponents. At about 5 pm Messe's German divisional commanders and his Chief of Staff reported that although they had stopped an immediate breakthrough they would not be able to for much longer. If First Italian Army was to be saved, they must fall back at once. Von Arnim accepted Messe's report and authorised him to start his withdrawal during the night towards the Northern Tunisian bridgehead. Cramer, at El Guettar, would conform.

Next day, 7 April, Eighth Army and II (us) Corps found their opponents had gone, leaving behind them a harvest of mines and demolitions, covered by light rearguards. Patton brought out his whip, ordering Benson to push towards the coast for a 'a fight or a bath'. That evening the extreme western patrol of Eighth Army's armour car screen met Benson's leading patrols on the Gafsa-Gabes road due south of Maknassy. Eighth Army had been passed successfully through the Gabes Gap, and the two great Allied Armies, one from the eastern end of the Mediterranean and the other from the Atlantic coast had met exactly five months to the day after the 'Torch' landings.

DRAWING THE NOOSE AROUND THE AXIS BRIDGEHEAD

Within the African theatre one of the greatest products of the victory was the progress achieved in the welding of Allied unity and the establishment of a command team that was already showing the effects of a growing confidence and trust among all its members.   (Eisenhower; page 174).

Historians have been rightly critical of Eighth Army's consistent failure to trap its opponent or to cut off any sizeable portion of his force. Rommel always slipped away. Now Messe had done the same thing, but, in this case, Montgomery could not be blamed. It was Alexander who had not trapped his opponent. His strategy had been designed to pass Montgomery through the Gabes Gap rather than encircle Messe. It was only the growing confidence of Patton's Corps and the demands of Montgomery that had led him to try to use his left fist at all. On the two occasions when he did start to use it he was too late. The first had been Patton's abortive offensive at El Guettar. The second was to occur at Fonduk as he started to draw the noose round von Arnim's forces.

When Alexander had made the third change in Patton's directive and had released Eddy's 9th (US) Division to II (US) Corps on 25 March, he had also placed Ryder's 34th (US) Division under Patton's command to open up the Fonduk Pass through which General Crocker's IX (Br) Corps would descend upon the flank of Messe's retreating army at the appropriate moment. Crocker's Corps was Alexander's Army Group Reserve, the principal formation of which was 6th (Br) Armoured Division. Ryder did not do as well as Alexander hoped. His division was still without real battle experience, having spent much of its time guarding communications and defending key points during the Kasserine period, and was sharply rebuffed by a mixed German and Italian force which contained units of a German penal division whose men were keen to 'rehabilitate' themselves and so fought hard in an effort to gain transfers back to their own units. Alexander decided to speed things up by sending Crocker to take charge. Anglo-American misunderstandings marred the operation from the start. Crocker's plan was faulty; and Ryder's method of carrying out his part of it was questionable. Suffice it to say that Ryder's Division was again beaten back on 8 April, and Crocker was ordered by Alexander to launch 6th Armoured Division at the Pass to break through to Kairouan regardless of tank losses. 6th Armoured Division did break through with great gallantry and heavy loss of tanks. Tragically its great effort was to no avail. As it emerged from the Eastern Dorsal, Messe's rearguards were already falling back through Kairouan. 6th Armoured Division trapped only a few stragglers, as the First and Eighth Armies met just south of Kairouan, squeezing Patton's II (US) Corps out of the line. The last chance of cutting off any of Messe's force before it entered von Arnim's bridgehead had gone.

While the soldiers had been driving the Axis forces back into the Tunisian 'corner' on land, the Allied Navies and Air Forces had been fighting to cut the Axis sea-air bridge from Sicily to Tunisia while at the same time protecting Allied shipping on the Algerian coast and their lines of communication through the Atlas Mountains. Irritating though the Christmas stalemate in the mud of Northern Tunisia had been to the Allied commanders, it had been a god-send to their logistic staffs, enabling them to develop the base ports, improve the rail, road and coastal shipping capacity to the front, and to build up adequate reserve stocks. While this was going on in Algeria, quite the opposite had been happening to the Axis quartermasters. Allied bombing, which had been fitfully ineffective in November, December and most of January due to lack of airfields and low serviceability, began to bite in February, Axis tonnages landed in Tunisian ports falling from 70,000 tons in January to 29,000 in April and 3,000 in May.

Von Arnim's logistic staff estimated that a minimum of 65,000 tons per month was needed to sustain the Axis force: and 120,000 tons per month would be required to build up for the advance on Casablanca which Hitler had in mind.

Failure to ship the minimum tonnages required forced the Axis to use German transport aircraft which were badly needed on the Russian front. Flights, which included the large Me323 transports lifting ten tons of freight, ferried reinforcements, high priority ammunition and latterly petrol into the Tunis airfields. The Allied Air Forces began to get the measure of this traffic towards the end of February. Early in March a special interception programme called Operation 'Flax' was mounted to deal with it. The climax came on 22 April when Kittyhawks and Spitfires of four South African Squadrons, a Polish flight and 79th (us) Fighter Group caught and shot down 16 out of 21 of the Giant Me 323s carrying petrol.

As far as the Armies were concerned the balance in the air over their heads changed as Messe withdrew northwards and allowed the Allied fighters and light bombers to settle on the numerous Axis airfields in the Central Tunisian plain. Kesselring's predictions came uncomfortably true for the Axis. It was now their soldiers rather than the British, American and French units that felt the weight of tactical air strikes; and it was their soldiers who, when looking up, saw only the silver shapes of Allied bombers heading east to drop their loads on Axis logistic installations. Aircraft carrying the black cross were rarely to be seen. Tedder had achieved complete air superiority over the battlefield as he had intended when he took over as Eisenhower's Air Deputy. The rough times suffered by II (us) Corps and First Army while he was winning the air battle seemed well worth it in retrospect.

It is against this background of logistic debilitation of the Axis forces and their loss of air superiority that Alexander's final offensive in Tunisia must be judged. It is remarkable that with such odds against them that the German and Italian forces fought so hard to hold their last bridgehead in Africa long after it was clear to everyone except Kesselring and Hitler that they should have been evacuated while there was yet time to save at least part of Panzer Army Group, Africa. Hitler allowed no plans to be made to do so, and thereby condemned some of his best soldiers to years in Allied prison camps. Von Arnim was left to defend his bridgehead short of ammunition of all kinds, without tank or gun replacements, and so short of fuel that he could only contemplate local counter-attacks.

In contrast, Alexander's forces were growing rapidly and wanted for nothing except experience in some of the more recently arrived units like the 1st and 4th (Br) Divisions which reached the front in early April and were seeing action for the first time since Dunkirk. American losses in February had been made good; and Koeltz's French divisions were returning to the line re-equipped with American weapons. Alexander would have a total of 19 Allied divisions, including three armoured divisions with which to crush von Arnim's 15 emaciated divisions; and he would have over 1,000 tanks in the forward area to deal with von Arnim's 150. The only question which arose was how quickly and with what economy of life could he meet the Chiefs of Staff deadline for the invasion of Sicily which required operations in Tunisia to be completed by the beginning of May.

The 18th Army Group Staff had been planning 'Vulcan', the final offensive, ever since they had been established in February. In its first draft, the 'Vulcan' plan excluded II (us) Corps on the grounds that it was not possible to support logistically more than the available British divisions over the poor roads of Northern Tunisia. Moreover, the American divisions needed further training before embarking for Sicily and this could be provided while First and Eighth Armies finished off von Arnim. This reasoning was as naive as it was insulting to the Americans. General Omar Bradley was the first to appreciate the significance of certain of 18th Army Group orders. After consulting Patton, he flew back to Algiers to protest to Eisenhower. The latter had little difficulty in persuading Alexander that the American public would never accept their men being shut out of the final climax of the campaign after all the sacrifices they had made to bring it to a successful conclusion. The only problem was how to deploy II (us) Corps on the extreme northern flank – the only logical place for it – without interrupting First Army's supply routes as it moved across them, and without over-straining the most northerly supply routes once it got there. These difficulties were, however, more than outweighed by the advantages of giving the Americans a self-contained sector and a major objective of their own – Bizerta. Patton returned to Morocco as soon as El Guettar was over to prepare for Sicily, and Omar Bradley took over the Corps, moving it successfully with great organisational skill to assembly areas at Djebel Abiod and Beja where he managed to supply it in spite of the forebodings of the British logistic experts.

Rivalry between American and British troops for the victory honours was matched by rivalry between the two British Armies. Montgomery was in a highly acquisitive mood and could not resist trying to influence events. In a signal verging on impertinence he said:

I suggest a decision is required as to who plays the major part in the final assaults on the enemy's last positions. There seem to be two alternatives:

A. Eighth Army does it. In this case I must move forward using all my divisions and face up to a real battle on the Enfidaville position. In this case I would have to ... have at my disposal all the resources in Northern Tunisia ...

B. First Army does it. In this case I would sit tight and merely exert pressure ... On no account must we split our effort and launch two or more thrusts none of which can be sustained. Presumably you will decide if it is to be A or B.

(quoted by Nigel Nicolson; page 387).

Alexander was short in his reply on 11 April:

Main effort in next phase will be by First Army. Preparations already well advanced for attack earliest date 22 April. Most suitable area for employment armour is in plain west of Tunis so require 1 Armoured Div and 1 Armoured C Regt to join IX Corps from you as early as can be arranged. Hope you can develop maximum pressure against Enfidaville position to fit in with First Army attack ...

(Ibid; page 397).

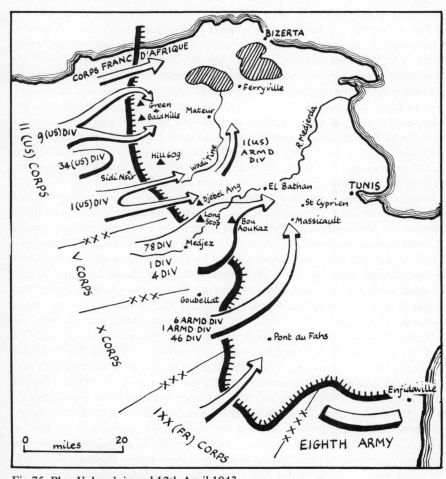

Fig 75 Plan Vulcan': issued 12th April 1943

On 12 April, as Eighth Army was advancing past Sousse on its way to Enfidaville, Alexander issued 'Vulcan' in its final form. He was very much master of his Army Group in spite of Montgomery's attempts to usurp his authority. The task which he gave to his three subordinate formations were: First Army to capture Tunis; II (US) Corps to protect First Army's flank and capture Bizerta; and Eighth Army to draw enemy reserves away from the fronts of the other two. The reputation of Eighth Army should make its task all the easier.

The tactical plans of his three subordinates can be briefly summarised. Anderson, whose First Army was the main striking force, chose an enveloping manoeuvre. Allfrey's V (Br) Corps with 1st, 4th and 78th (Br) Divisions was to attack along the Medjerda Valley north-eastwards on the old Christmas route to Tunis, clearing the hills either side of the river and aiming for the Bathan – St Cyprien area on the main road to Tunis. Crocker's IX (Br) Corps with 1st and 6th (Br) Armoured Division and 46th (Br) Division was to attack across the Goubellat plain, swinging north to meet V Corps at St Cyprien, thereby encircling the strongest part of the Axis line blocking the main Medjez – Tunis road. Koeltz's XIX (Fr) Corps with the Moroccan, Algiers and Oran Divisions was to clear the Axis salient between First and Eighth Armies and to open Pont-du-Fahs to approach Tunis from due south.

Bradley's II (US) Corps was faced with the exacting task of ousting Division Manteuffel and 334th Division from their mountain fastnesses: 'Green' and 'Bald' Hills of evil fame on the northern road to Bizerta; the brutal hill positions around Hill 609 blocking the Sidi Nsir – Mateur road in the centre; and the difficult positions on the Djebel Ang range on the boundary between the American and British sectors. Bradley decided upon the 'sweat saves blood' policy, and based his plans on hard climbing along the mountain ridges to outflank the German positions, rather than trying to blast his way up the valleys. In the north, Eddy's 9th (US) Division was to outflank 'Green' and 'Bald' Hills by wide turning movements through the inhospitable scrub-covered hills north and south of the main Bizerta road. His northern flank would be helped forward by the presence of French North African mountain troops of the Corps Franc d'Afrique which would be working their way through the coastal hills. In the centre, Bradley gave Allen's 1st (US) Division the task of clearing the hills astride the Sidi Nsir – Mateur road and those overlooking the Wadi Tine Valley from the north. Bradley appreciated that the Wadi Tine Valley, which he called the 'Mouse Trap', was the obvious tank approach to Mateur and Bizerta, which Harmon would eventually use, but it was so obvious that it would be (and was) heavily mined and covered by anti-tank guns. Before Harmon could use it, the northern face of the Djebel Ang range, which overlooked the valley from the south, would have to be cleared as well. Allen was made responsible for this too and was given Harmon's 6th Armoured Infantry to help him with the task. Harmon's 'tank heavy' combat commands would remain in reserve until the Tine's defences has been outflanked. Bradley also held Ryder's 34th (US) Division, which was last to arrive from Central Tunisia, in reserve for probable reinforcement of Allen's thrust in the centre.

Montgomery, on the extreme eastern flank of Alexander's cordon remained a law unto himself. He and his army hoped that some unforeseen turn of events might still enable them to capture Tunis first. There was a real chance that the morale of Messe's Army would be so weakened by its retreat from Wadi Akarit that it might collapse if hit quickly and hard. Montgomery expressed the feelings of his Army when writing to Alexander as Eighth Army reached Enfidaville: '. . . All my troops are in first class form and want to be in the final Dunkirk . . .' (*Ibid:* page 402).

The Enfidaville line resembled the Wadi Akarit position in that it was based upon a line of sharp hill features, but there the resemblance ended. Behind these hills lay not an open plain but the jumbled mass of the combined Dorsal ranges as they ran northwards into the Cap Bon Peninsula. There were three roads, which led to Tunis, through these hills. The coast road, running up the narrow coastal plain to Hammamet, was blocked by an anti-tank obstacle between the sea and another Djebel Tebaga, and was held by the faithful 90th Light Division. The central road ran through the main hill mass via the prominent feature upon which stood the village of Takrouna. And the western road ran diagonally into the French sector and on to Pont-du-Fahs. Tuker again noted that the western road was dominated by the Djebel Garci which was not unlike the Ras Zouai at Wadi Akarit and might be tackled in the same way.

Montgomery gave Horrocks the task of hustling Messe out of the Enfidaville position before First Army was ready to launch 'Vulcan'. He believed that there were only eight German battalions corsetting the Italians and that Italian morale was at a low ebb. Horrocks was not so sure. His plan of attack was for Freyberg's New

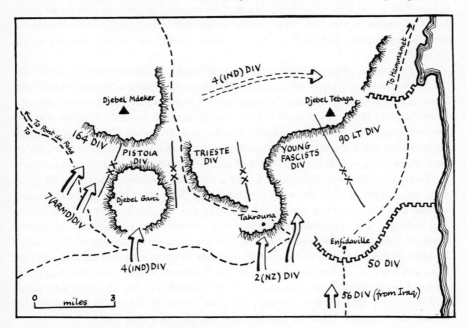

Fig 76 Montgomery's Attacks at Enfidaville

Zealanders to take Takrouna, while Tuker's Indians infiltrated Djebel Garcia, as they
had done at Ras Zouai, and then advanced through the hills in a right-handed sweep
to appear in the rear of the Axis defenders of the coast road. Leese's 50th Division
would be used to hold the coastal sector; and 7th Armoured Division would
demonstrate on the extreme western flank.

Horrocks's plan was over-optimistic. Freyberg's and Tuker's divisions had only two
brigades each. They were essentially mechanised divisions with no pack transport or
pack artillery for mountain warfare. They could only hope to succeed by frightening
their opponents into a premature withdrawal. It was worth the attempt, but it did not
succeed. The New Zealanders took, but could barely hold the Takrouna feature.
Tuker did little better. His Indians displayed great courage in taking a substantial
part of Djebel Garcia, but they were too few to hold their gains against German
counter-attacks. Axis morale had, if anything, hardened. Both the German and the
Italian soldiers knew they were holding the 'last ditch' with their backs to the sea,
across which there was no escape.

Eighth Army made one more effort on 28 April after 'Vulcan' had started, using
the newly arrived and inexperienced 56th (London) Division which had motored from
Iraq to Enfidaville, some 3,200 miles, in 32 days. Like the new American divisions in
their first battles, 56th Division did not do well. It seized its objectives, but was
thrown into disorder by counter-attacks. Montgomery, who was not well at the time
and had become involved in planning for his future role as British Task Force
Commander for the invasion of Sicily, realised that his hopes of reaching Tunis
before First Army were unrealistic. He gave up pressing his attacks and on 30 April
asked Alexander to visit him. The meeting turned out to be a decisive one, but this is
anticipating events. We must go back to look at 'Vulcan' which had begun on
22 April.

After a number of preliminary operations, including an abortive spoiling attack by
the Hermann Göring Division near Medjez, the main 'Vulcan' offensive opened and
lived up to its name in that the German reserves were knocked to pieces by multiple
Allied hammer blows on the anvil of their own bridgehead defences. Progress was not
spectacular; losses were heavy on both sides; but von Arnim could neither replace nor
replenish his spent ammunition and fuel, whereas Alexander could. The fortunes of
each Allied corps varied, as they developed their offensives in the last 10 days of April.

The first to strike was Crocker's IX Corps. 46th (Br) Division attacked on 22 April
with the support of over 200 guns to clear a way though the crust of the Hermann
Göring Division's defences for the 6th and then the 1st (Br) Armoured Divisions to
pass through. The operation took longer than expected and by dusk 6th Armoured
Division was only just beyond 46th Division's positions. Next day 1st (Br) Armoured
Division joined in and the two armoured divisions thrust northwards towards the low
hills dividing the Goubellat plain from the Medjerda Valley. German resistance
stiffened progressively and, although Crocker manoeuvred his divisions with some
skill, he could find no way through the Axis anti-tank screens surrounding the
12-mile-deep breach which he had made in von Arnim's defences.

Allfrey's three divisions came into action on successive days. Evelegh's veteran

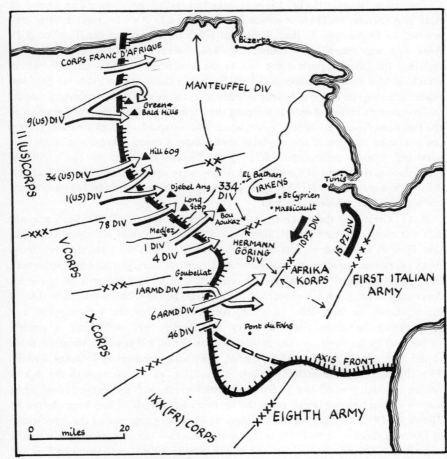

Fig 77 'Vulcan': 22nd to 28th April 1943

78th Division struck on 23 April along the crest of the Djebel Ang and at 'Long Stop'. In five days' fighting he secured the main Axis strong points and, at last, tore 'Long Stop' from German hands. The final seizure of 'Long Stop' was notable for the surprise feat of the North Irish Horse who managed to drive their Churchill tanks up on to the djebel to help the infantry take the last and most difficult peak, the Djebel Rhaa.

The newer 1st and 4th (Br) Divisions attacked east of the Medjerda on 23 and 24 April respectively. 1st Division struck northward to CC 'B's Christmas disaster area around the Djebel Bou Aoukaz. It did not reach the summit of the 'Bou' until 27 April and was immediately counter-attacked, losing the feature in very severe fighting. 4th Division pushed due east to the area where the first German panzer attack on Medjez in December had been bogged in the Tunisian mud. 4th Division made little progress and was heavily counter-attacked as well. Von Arnim had reacted to First Army's offensive by side-stepping the Afrika Korps into the southern half of the Hermann Göring Division's sector, which had collapsed, to check Crocker; and by concentrating the rest of the available tanks under Colonel Irkens, one of his best surviving panzer commanders from 15th Panzer Division, to block Allfrey. Nevertheless, the defeat of Crocker and Allfrey were costly victories from which the Axis did not recover. By 1st May there were only 69 German tanks including 4 Tigers operational in the whole bridgehead.

II (US) Corps had the toughest and most thankless task of all. Bradley's primary role was to protect First Army's flank, though his politico-military objective was to take Bizerta. His offensive was not closely connected with the main stream of First Army operations. Bradley was not under Anderson and so fought his own battles with little or no guidance from Alexander who left him to find his own glory for his Americans in the stark hill country of the northern sector. For the first three days of his offensive, he had little to show, like Crocker, for the grinding toil and demoralising casualties. He did worry von Arnim, who authorised a general withdrawal by his troops in the northern sectors to new hill positions some five miles to the rear. On 26 April Bradley decided to increase pressure by bringing Ryder's 34th (US) Division into action between 9th and 1st (US) Divisions with the task of seizing the high ground east of Sidi Nsir which overlooked and prevented his units using the Sidi Nsir – Mateur road, the southern side of which had been cleared by Allen's 1st Division. Looking at the maps, no-one really appreciated the significance of Djebel Tahent – or Hill 609 as it is better known – the capture of which was to cause heavy American casualties, and was to give Ryder's 34th Division its first and most lasting sense of achievement. The five day struggle for Hill 609 has become an American epic. 34th Division found that all the surrounding hills were mutually supporting and, though held by comparatively few Axis troops, had to be taken one by one before the core of the defence on Hill 609 could be quelled. In the end it was a combined infantry and tank attack on 30 April which finally secured Hill 609, the tanks having had the same surprise effect as they did at 'Long Stop' because they appeared where they were least expected. 34th Division's task at Hill 609 was not over. For two more days the Germans counter-attacked persistently, trying to regain the hill but its splendid observation enabled the American artillery to break up every attempt.

The loss of Hill 609 unhinged the Axis defences north of the Wadi Tine Valley. Similarly determined operations by 9th (US) Division led to the withdrawal of Manteuffel's men from 'Green' and 'Bald' Hills on 1 May; and to a decision by von Arnim to withdraw to a closer bridgehead around Bizerta which was carried out on the nights of 1/2 and 2/3 May. Harmon's 1st (US) Armoured Division suddenly found the 'Mousetrap' clear; and on 3 May its tanks were rumbling into Mateur which was found unoccupied, the German defenders having withdrawn to the hills to the east.

While Bradley's troops had been fighting their way stoically eastwards, Alexander had realised that his 'partridge drive', as Montgomery rudely referred to First Army's offensive, was losing momentum and would have to be revitalised. He would have to deliver a concentrated 'coup de grace' if he was to meet the Chiefs of Staff timings. His first idea had been to use 6th (Br) Armoured Division and 78th Division in the V Corps Sector, leaving 1st (Br) Armoured Division to keep the Afrika Korps pinned in the Goubellat area. Then on 28 April reports of Eighth Army's second failure at Enfidaville and Montgomery's request for a conference arrived. The solution was at hand.

Alexander drove to Eighth Army HQ on 30 April, keeping his own counsel. Montgomery fell into the trap of hinting that First Army had made a mess of its offensive and that it was time for Eighth Army to finish things off. Alexander did not accept his views, and asked him to provide his two best divisions – one infantry and

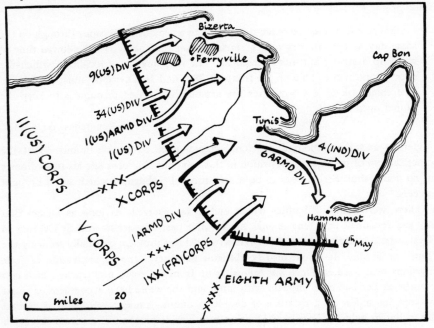

Fig 78 Operation 'Strike': 6th May 1943

one armoured – plus a brigade group for transfer to First Army for his decisive attack which was to be mounted by IX Corps, Tebaga fashion with massive air and artillery support, straight down the Medjaz – Tunis road. Montgomery nominated 4th Indian and 7th Armoured Divisions and 201st Guards Brigade. There could not have been a happier choice. Eighth Army might not be delivering the decisive blow, but three formations that had been fighting the North African Campaign since 1940 would take part. O'Connor's force at Sidi Barani in 1940 had contained 7th Armoured Division and 4th Indian Division. 22nd Guards Brigade, later to be re-numbered 201 Guards Brigade, joined the Western Desert Force only slightly later. Crocker, however, would not be commanding IX Corps because he had been accidently wounded at a demonstration of a new anti-tank weapon, so Horrocks was sent across to take command of Operation 'Strike', timed for 6 May. His experience at Tebaga was invaluable.

'Strike' was to be on twice the scale of Tebaga. The two infantry divisions – 4th British and 4th Indian – would attack side by side at 3 am on 6 May on a very narrow 3,000 yard front astride the main Medjez – Tunis road. They would be supported by 650 guns with about 350 rounds per gun and by every aircraft the Tactical air-forces could sensibly use. The 25th Army Tank Brigade in Churchills would give them close tank support and Scorpions would be available to help breach the minefields. As soon as adequate breaches had been made the two British armoured divisions – 6th and 7th – would pass through heading at speed for Tunis. Alexander was determined that von Arnim should be given no time to recover. His written instructions to Anderson said:

> . . . Every effort must be made to pass the two armoured divisions through on the same day as the infantry attack starts so that the enemy is not allowed time to build up a strong anti-tank screen . . . The mopping up of localities, which the enemy continues to hold on the fronts of 78th and 1st Divisions, must come later. The chief task of V Corps after the armour has passed through is to keep the funnel open . . .

(Despatches: page 882).

Anderson and the armoured divisional commanders had some doubts about the practicability of by-passing opposition in this way, but Horrocks left his subordinates in no doubt that 'Strike' was to be a repetition of Tebaga in which speed brought success.

There were some difficulties which had to be resolved. As long as Djebel Bou Aoukaz remained in I xens' hands, an advance past Massicault and St Cyprien to Tunis would be difficult. 1st (Br) Division solved this problem by finally securing the 'Bou' on 5 May. It would also be difficult to conceal the concentration of four divisions near Medjez. Dust was billowing up from the roads and tracks which two months earlier had been slippery with mud, and the white haze above Medjez could be seen for miles. As a measure of deception dummy tanks were deployed around Goubellat to help 1st Armoured Division create an impression of renewed threat on the old IX Corps axis. Alexander claimed that this did deceive the enemy, but contemporary records do not bear this out.

Von Arnim was well aware through radio intercept that Eighth Army divisions had moved to Medjez. He matched these moves by removing 15th Panzer Division from Messe and sending it to reinforce Irkens opposite Medjez. He also tried to move parts of 10th and 21st Panzer across from the Afrika Korps sector but shortage of fuel delayed these moves until it was too late. Von Arnim did, however, succeed in establishing a 'lay-back' position near Massicault, manned by anti-aircraft units with 88mm dual purpose guns. 15th Panzer absorbed Group Irkens and together managed to position about 60 operational tanks near Massicault. A useful windfall of 1,100 tons of ammunition and 100 tons of fuel was landed by small ships during 4 May and another 70 tons of fuel and 30 of ammunition arrived by air. This was the last re-supply von Arnim was to receive. All remaining Axis aircraft were withdrawn to Sicily. On the evening of 5 May, 15th Panzer stood ready to fight its last great battle, short of men, tanks, ammunition and fuel.

'Strike' began as darkness fell on 5 May with heavy night bomber attacks on the Axis rear areas in the path of IX Corps' coming attack. At 3 am the Infantry Divisions advanced behind a crippling artillery programme with 16,600 shells landing in two hours on 4th British Division's sector alone. The 115th Panzer Grenadier Regiment was almost annihilated in the holocaust. The armoured divisions moved forward at about 7.30 am and by 10.30 am they were passing through the minefield gaps. Horrocks describes the scene:

> By mid-day we were through the crust and the tanks were grinding their way forward down the valley towards Tunis. It was a most inspiring sight to see these two well-trained and experienced armoured divisions being used for the role for which armoured divisions were specifically designed – to exploit a break-through deep into the enemy's heart. They worked like efficient machines, aircraft, guns, tanks, infantry and vehicles each fitting into the jigsaw of battle in its proper place.
>
> (Horrocks; page 170).

During the afternoon the advance was checked as 15th Panzer fought its last action around Massicault and St Cyprien. Both British armoured divisional commanders began to worry about forming firm bases by bringing up their lorried infantry brigades before pushing their tanks on into what appeared to be growing tank and anti-tank gun opposition. This all took precious time and was in direct contradiction to Alexander's orders. When dusk fell both divisions settled into night leaguers either side of Massicault, convinced that they would face strong opposition next day. They felt isolated being about eight miles ahead of the infantry divisions.

They need not have worried. Von Arnim had lost control of the battle during 6 May due to the disruption of his communications by air bombing. His evening report to OKW acknowledged the coming loss of Tunis: 'The bulk of 15th Panzer Division must be deemed destroyed . . . there can be no doubt that on 7 May the road to Tunis will be open to the enemy and the fall of the city of Bizerta is only a question of time.' (Quoted by *British Official History*; Vol IV; page 451).

In the American and French sectors Axis resistance remained resolute as Bradley and Koeltz re-opened their offensives towards Bizerta and Pont-du-Fahs. 7 May was to bring a 'sea-change' to the whole front. The two British Armoured Divisions fought against rapidly failing resistance around St Cyprien during the morning, and then, as happened at El Alamein, Axis resistance snapped and the armoured car regiments of the two divisions were able to motor through into Tunis where they arrived almost together in the middle of the afternoon to a tremendous welcome from the inhabitants. Almost simultaneously Eddy's 9th (US) Division entered Bizerta; Harmon's 1st (US) Armoured Division took Ferryville; and Koeltz' French Corps took Pont-du-Fahs.

For the next four days sporadic Axis resistance continued in pockets all over the bridgehead as the better German commanders and soldiers obeyed Hitlers's orders to resist to the last man and last round. Most German units took this to mean the last round and had a splendid time firing off their remaining stocks of ammunition. Von Arnim withdrew his HQ to the mountains north of Eighth Army's front but could never re-establish control, because 6th (Br) Armoured Division, closely followed by 4th (Br) Division, swung rapidly eastwards and cut across the base of the Cap Bon Peninsula, preventing it being used as a final refuge. Army Group, Africa, dissolved into a pool of surrendering units, each making its own submission, according to its lights and making its own way on foot or in its own transport to the nearest Allied prisoner of war camps. Over 250,000 men fell into Allied hands. It was not until 12 May that von Arnim ordered the destruction of his radio sets when 4th Indian Division approached his headquarters. He surrendered to General Tuker. The most notable surrender, however, was that of the Afrika Korps. Just before midnight on 12/13 May Cramer sent out its last signal:

> Ammunition shot off. Arms and Equipment destroyed. In accordance with orders received Afrika Korps has fought itself to the condition where it can fight no more. The German Afrika Korps must rise again. Heil Safari! Cramer, General Commanding.
>
> (*British Official History*; Vol IV; page 457).

On the Allied side Alexander cabled to Churchill: 'Sir, it is my duty to report that the Tunisian Campaign is over. All enemy resistance has ceased. We are masters of the North African shores . . .' (*British Official History*; Vol IV; page 459).

The British had bought the time they needed to gather resources and allies; the Americans had gained battle experience; and the Allied Staffs had started to learn the techniques for handling the vast forces assembling for the invasion of Europe. Without the dress-rehearsal of the North African Campaign, the story of 'Overlord' might have been very different.

Bibliography

1. OFFICIAL PUBLICATIONS

a. *Despatches of Commanders published in the London Gazette*
Alexander of Tunis:
  The African Campaign from El Alamein to Tunis, 19th August 1942 to 13th May 1941 (Published 1948).
Anderson, Sir Kenneth:
  Operations in North West Africa from 8th November 1942 to 13th May 1943 (Published 1946).
Auchinleck, Sir Claude:
  Operations in the Middle East from 1st November 1941 to 15th August 1942 (Published 1948).
Cunningham of Hyndhope:
  The Battle of Matapan (Published 1947).
  The Control of the Sicilian Straits (Published 1948).
  The Fleet Air Operations against Taranto (Published 1947).
  The Landings in North Africa (Published 1949).
  The Mediterranean Convoy Operations (Published 1948).
Harwood, Sir Henry:
  The Battle of Sirte (Published 1947).
Longmore, Sir Arthur:
  Air Operations in the Middle East from 1st January 1941 to 3rd May 1941 (published 1946).
Platt, Sir William:
  Operations of East Africa Command, 12th July 1941 to 8th January 1943 (Published 1946).
Somerville, Sir James:
  Cape Spartevento (Published 1948).
Wavell:
  Operations in East Africa, November 1940 to July 1941 (Published 1946).
  Operations in the Middle East:
    from August 1939 to November 1940 (Published 1946).
    from 7th December 1940 to 7th February 1941 (Published 1946).
    from 7th February 1941 to 15th July 1941 (Published 1946).

Operations in the Somaliland Protectorate (Published 1946).

b. *Official Histories*

Australian:

Air War Against Germany and Italy: Tobruk to El Alamein.

British:

Air Battles for Malta, June 1940 to November 1942

Grand Strategy, Vols. III and IV.

Mediterranean and the Middle East, Vols. I to IV.

Mediterranean Fleet, April 1941 to January 1943.

Ministry of Information:

Battle of Egypt (Published 1943).

Destruction of an Army (Published 1941).

Eighth Army (Published 1944).

RAF: the Middle East (Published 1945).

Royal Air Force, 1939–45; Vols. I to III.

Royal Air Force, Middle East from February 1942 to January 1943.

Strategic Air Offensive; Vols I to IV.

War at Sea; Vols. I to III.

War Office, Notes from the Theatres of War, Nos. 1, 2, 4, 10 and 14.

Indian:

The East African Campaign, 1940–41.

The North African Campaign, 1940–43.

New Zealand:

Alam Halfa and El Alamein.

Bardia to Enfidaville.

Battle of Egypt: the Summer of 1942.

Episodes and Studies.

Relief of Tobruk.

Second New Zealand Expeditionary Force Surveys.

South African:

East African and Abyssinian Campaign.

Crisis in the Desert, May to July 1942.

The Sidi Rezegh Battles, 1941.

United States:

Army Air Force in World War II; Vols. I and II.

Mediterranean Theatres of Operations: North West Africa; Seizing the Initiative in the West.

Military Intelligence Division Studies:

No. 1 The Libyan Campaign.

No. 2 Artillery in the Desert.

No. 8 Development of German Tactics in the Desert.

No. 0 German Campaign in the Balkans.

Naval Operations in World War II; Vol. IX.

Strategic Planning for Coalition Warfare.
Twelfth (US) Air Force; History of.
White House Papers; Vol. I (Robert E. Sherbrook).

2. OTHER PUBLICATIONS OF INTEREST

Aglion, R: *War in the Desert; the Battle for Africa*
Alexander of Tunis: *The Alexander Memoirs 1940–45* (Edited by John North)
Alexander of Tunis: *The Battle of Tunis*
Badoglio, P: *Italy in the Second World War*
Barclay, C. N: *Against Great Odds; the Story of the First Offensive in Libya.*
Barnett, C: *The Battle of El Alamein; Decision in the Desert*
Barnett, C: *The Desert Generals*
Barré, G: *Tunisie 1942–43*
Bidwell, R. G. S: *The Development of British Field Artillery Tactics, 1940–42*
Blumensen, N: *Kasserine Pass*
Braddock, D. W: *The Campaigns in Egypt and Libya 1940–42*
Bradley, O. N: *A Soldier's Story*
Caccia-Dominioni, P: *Alamein; an Italian Story*
Carver, R. M. P: *El Alamein*
Carver, R. M. P: *History of 4th Armoured Brigade*
Carver, R. M. P: *A Short History of 7th Armoured Division*
Carver, R. M. P: *Tobruk*
Clark, M. W: *Calculated Risk*
Clay, E. W: *The Path of the 50th Division*
Clifford, A: *Three against Rommel: the Campaigns of Wavell, Auchinleck and Alexander*
Clifton, G: *The Happy Hunted*
Connell, J: *Auchinleck; a biography*
Connell, J: *Wavell; Scholar and Soldier*
Cowie, D: *The Campaigns of Wavell*
Crisp, R. J: *Brazen Chariots*
De Guingand, F: *Operation Victory*
De Guingand, F: *Generals at War*
Divine, A. D: *Road to Tunis*
Douglas, K: *Alamein to Zem Zem*
Dupuy, T. N: *Land Battles; North Africa, Sicily and Italy*
Eisenhower, D. D: *Crusade in Europe*
Evans, G. C: *The Desert and the Jungle*
Farran, R. A: *Winged Dagger*
Gallagher, W: *Backdoor to Berlin*
Giraud, H: *Un Seul But, la Victoire; Alger 1942–44*
Harding, J: *Mediterranean Strategy, 1939–45*

Hart, B. H. L: *A Battle Report; Alam Halfa*
Hart, B. H. L: *Rommel Papers* (Edited)
Hill, R: *Desert Conquest*
Hill, R: *Desert War*
Hingston, W. G: *The Tiger Strikes*   Indian Divisions
Hingston, W. G: *The Tiger Kills*   in Northern Africa
Horrocks, B. G: *A Full Life*
Houghton, G. W: *They flew through Sand*
Ingersoll, R: *The Battle is the Pay-Off*
James, A. Brett-: *The Fifth Indian Division in the Second World War*
Joly, C. B: *Take these Men*
Juin, A. P: *Memoires,* Vol. I
Kennedy, J: *The Business of War*
Kippenberger, H. K: *Infantry Brigadier*
Koeltz, L: *Une Campagne que nous avons gagnée; Tunisie 1942–43*
Langer, W. L: *Our Vichy Gamble*
Lewin, R: *Montgomery as Military Commander*
Lewin, R: *Rommel as Military Commander*
Longmore, A: *From Sea to Sky*
McCreery, R. L: *Recollections of a Chief of Staff*
Macmillan, H: *The Blast of War*
Majdalany, F: *The Battle of El Alamein*
Maule, H: *Out of the Sand: General Leclerc and the fighting Free French*
Montgomery, B. L: *El Alamein to the Sangro*
Montgomery, B. L: *Memoirs*
Moorehead, A: *African Trilogy*
Moorehead, A: *The Desert War*
Moorehead, A: *Montgomery*
Murphy, R: *Diplomat among Warriors*
Netherwood, G: *Desert Squadron; the RAF in Egypt and Libya, 1940–42*
Nicholson, N.
Owen, D. Lloyd-: *The Desert my Dwelling Place* (Long Range Desert Group)
Peniakoff, V: *Private Army*
Phillips, C. E. L: *Alamein*
Pollock, A. M: *Pioneer of Alamein*
Potts, C: *Soldiers in the Sand*
Robinson, H. Rowan-: *Auchinleck to Alexander*
Robinson, H. Rowan-: *Wavell in the Middle East*
Rommel, E: *Rommel Papers* (Edited by Liddell Hart)
Schmidt, H. W: *With Rommel in the Desert*
Slim, W. J: *Unofficial History*
Stevens, G. R: *Fourth Indian Division*
Sykes, C: *Orde Wingate*
Tedder, A. W: *With Prejudice*
Tuker, F: *Approach to Battle*

Wavell, A. P: *Speaking Generally*
Westphal, S: *Notes on the Campaign in North Africa, 1941–43*
Willison, A. C: *The Relief of Tobruk*
Wilmot, C: *Tobruk, 1941*
Wisdom, T. H: *Triumph over Tunisia*
Woolcombe, R. M: *The Campaigns of Wavell*
Young, D: *Rommel*

Index